THE CAMBRIDGE HISTORY OF CHINA

General editors

DENIS TWITCHETT and JOHN K. FAIRBANK

Volume 14
The People's Republic, Part 1:
The Emergence of Revolutionary China 1949–1965

THE CAMBRIDGE
HISTORY OF
CHINA

Volume 14

The People's Republic, Part 1:
The Emergence of Revolutionary China
1949–1965

edited by

RODERICK MacFARQUHAR
and
JOHN K. FAIRBANK

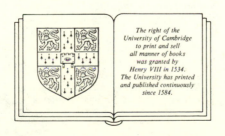

The right of the
University of Cambridge
to print and sell
all manner of books
was granted by
Henry VIII in 1534.
The University has printed
and published continuously
since 1584.

CAMBRIDGE UNIVERSITY PRESS

CAMBRIDGE
NEW YORK   PORT CHESTER
MELBOURNE   SYDNEY

Published by the Press Syndicate of the University of Cambridge
The Pitt Building, Trumpington Street, Cambridge CB2 1RP
32 East 57th Street, New York, NY 10022, USA
10 Stamford Road, Oakleigh, Melbourne 3166, Australia

First published 1987
Reprinted 1989

Printed in the United States of America

Library of Congress Cataloging-in-Publication Data
(Revised for volume 14)
The Cambridge history of China.
Bibliography: v. 10, pt. 1, p.
Includes indexes.
Contents: – v. 3. Sui and T'ang China, 589–
906, pt. 1 –   – v. 10. Late Ch'ing, 1800–1911.
pt. 1. –   – v. 14. The People's Republic.
pt. 1. The emergence of revolutionary China, 1949–1965.
1. China – History.   I. Twitchett, Denis Crispin.
II. Fairbank, John King, 1907–
DS735. C3145   951'.03   76–29852
ISBN 0 521 21447 5

British Library Cataloguing in Publication Data
The Cambridge history of China
Vol 14: The People's Republic
Pt. 1: The emergence of revolutionary
China, 1949–1965.
1. China – History
I. Twitchett, Denis   II. Fairbank, John
King   III. MacFarquhar, Roderick
951   DS735

ISBN 0 521 24336 X

GENERAL EDITORS' PREFACE

As the modern world grows more interconnected, historical understanding of it becomes ever more necessary and the historian's task ever more complex. Fact and theory affect each other even as sources proliferate and knowledge increases. Merely to summarize what is known becomes an awesome task, yet a factual basis of knowledge is increasingly essential for historical thinking.

Since the beginning of the century, the Cambridge histories have set a pattern in the English-reading world for multivolume series containing chapters written by specialists under the guidance of volume editors. *The Cambridge Modern History*, planned by Lord Acton, appeared in sixteen volumes between 1902 and 1912. It was followed by *The Cambridge Ancient History*, *The Cambridge Medieval History*, *The Cambridge History of English Literature*, and Cambridge histories of India, of Poland, and of the British Empire. The original *Modern History* has now been replaced by *The New Cambridge Modern History* in twelve volumes, and *The Cambridge Economic History of Europe* is now being completed. Other Cambridge histories include histories of Islam, Arabic literature, Iran, Judaism, Africa, Japan, and Latin America.

In the case of China, Western historians face a special problem. The history of Chinese civilization is more extensive and complex than that of any single Western nation, and only slightly less ramified than the history of European civilization as a whole. The Chinese historical record is immensely detailed and extensive, and Chinese historical scholarship has been highly developed and sophisticated for many centuries. Yet until recent decades the study of China in the West, despite the important pioneer work of European sinologists, had hardly progressed beyond the translation of some few classical historical texts, and the outline history of the major dynasties and their institutions.

Recently Western scholars have drawn more fully upon the rich traditions of historical scholarship in China and also in Japan, and

greatly advanced both our detailed knowledge of past events and institutions and also our critical understanding of traditional historiography. In addition, the present generation of Western historians of
China can also draw upon the new outlooks and techniques of
modern Western historical scholarship, and upon recent developments in the social sciences, while continuing to build upon the solid
foundations of rapidly progressing European, Japanese, and Chinese
sinological studies. Recent historical events, too, have given prominence to new problems, while throwing into question many older
conceptions. Under these multiple impacts the Western revolution in
Chinese studies is steadily gathering momentum.

When *The Cambridge History of China* was first planned in 1966,
the aim was to provide a substantial account of the history of China
as a bench mark for the Western history-reading public: an account
of the current state of knowledge in six volumes. Since then the
outpouring of current research, the application of new methods, and
the extension of scholarship into new fields have further stimulated
Chinese historical studies. This growth is indicated by the fact that
the *History* has now become a planned fifteen volumes, but will still
leave out such topics as the history of art and of literature, many
aspects of economics and technology, and all the riches of local
history.

The striking advances in our knowledge of China's past over recent
decades will continue and accelerate. Western historians of this great
and complex subject are justified in their efforts by the needs of their
own peoples for greater and deeper understanding of China. Chinese
history belongs to the world, not only as a right and necessity but
also as a subject of compelling interest.

JOHN K. FAIRBANK
DENIS TWITCHETT

CONTENTS

MAPS

TABLES

PREFACE TO VOLUME 14

In 1949 a new stage was reached in the endeavors of successive Chinese elites to meet domestic problems inherited from the Late Imperial era and to respond to the century-old challenge posed by the industrialized West. A central government had now gained full control of the Chinese mainland, thus achieving the national unity so long desired. Moreover, it was committed for the first time to the overall modernization of the nation's polity, economy, and society. The history of the succeeding decades is of the most massive experiment in social engineering the world has ever witnessed. Volumes 14 and 15 of the *Cambridge History of China* attempt to chronicle and analyze that experiment.

The very power and purposefulness of the Chinese Communist regime have shaped the format of these volumes. Unlike in the imperial and republican periods, under the Chinese Communists no aspect of life, no region of the country has been immune from the determined efforts of the central authorities to revolutionize China. It is simply not meaningful to examine any part of Chinese society except in the context of the Communist Party's efforts to transform it. Perforce, one must start by looking at China from the viewpoint of the Party's Politburo and the government's State Council in Peking.

The division of this volume into two sections has been dictated by the major change in Party policy that took place in 1958 and affected all sectors of society. The division between this volume and the succeeding one reflects the watershed of the Cultural Revolution launched by Mao Tse-tung in 1966.

Of course, the ideas, objectives, strategies, policies, and actions of Chairman Mao, his colleagues, and his successors do not amount to a history of China. The greater part of these two volumes is concerned with assessing the impact they have had on the Chinese nation. Given the enormous quantity of new data released and the easier access to the mainland allowed by the People's Republic in recent years, it is possible now to delineate more clearly the outcomes of the experiment so far.

Nevertheless, we are conscious that ours must be an interim judgment – not so much because there remain vital data that have not been released, for it is very likely that some never will be; nor because the events we describe are so recent, for the assessments of historians are continually subject to revision no matter how great the advantage of distance; but because the experiment is far from over, and only near its completion – a century hence? – will a rounded perspective on these earliest decades be possible.

This is the fifth volume of *The Cambridge History of China* covering the nineteenth and twentieth centuries. From the beginning of this endeavor we have been conscious of our indebtedness to every significant contribution to the field. Only our footnotes can tell that story.

We can, however, express our gratitude to the experienced chief manager and processor of this volume, Joan Hill, who pursues precision with good humor, and a perseverance worthy of Chairman Mao's Foolish Old Man Who Removed the Mountains. Chiang Yung-chen has given us valuable assistance with the Chinese bibliography and calligraphy. Our thanks go also to Katherine Frost Bruner and Gwendolyn Stewart for highly skilled indexing.

In January 1983, we ran a working conference of contributors under the aegis of Harvard's Fairbank Center, which was excellently organized by Patrick Maddox, assisted by Debra Knosp and generously financed by the Rockefeller Foundation. We are delighted to acknowledge also with gratitude the support of the Ford and Mellon foundations, which has been critical to sustaining the production of these volumes, as well as the backing of the American Council of Learned Societies and the National Endowment for the Humanities. We are indebted to Harvard University and especially to Philip A. Kuhn for assistance in his capacity as Center director.

RLM
JKF

ON ROMANIZATION

For purely technical reasons we continue, as in preceding volumes, to use the Wade-Giles system for transcription of Chinese into alphabetic writing. The main reason is that, in order to avoid confusion, we have to use here the forms used in previous volumes – for example,

Chou En-lai, not Zhou Enlai. At the same time, we note that names and terms in publications today, both from the People's Republic and from around the world, are using the official *pinyin* romanization, based on the incontrovertible assumption that a nation has the right to decide how it wishes its writing system to be romanized abroad. To meet this situation we have inserted conversion tables at the back of the book, just before the Glossary-Index.

To avoid enslavement by the arbitrary nature of any romanization system, we have consciously tolerated deviations, especially in personal names. Thus the reader will sometimes find *chow* instead of *chou, yi* instead of *i, hwa* for *hua, teh* for *te*, Anhui for Anhwei, and almost always Peking for Beijing. (Such deviations need not be called to our attention.) We also take no responsibility for the name *Chen*, which should often be *Ch'en*.

ACRONYMS

Some of these abbreviations represent publications; others stand for names and titles in the text. Characters for publications will be found in the Bibliography; those for names and titles, in the Glossary-Index.

AAPSO	Afro-Asian Peoples' Solidarity Organization
APC	Agricultural Producers' Cooperative
BDRC	*Biographical dictionary of Republican China*
CASS	Chinese Academy of Social Sciences
CB	*Current Background*
CC	Central Committee
CCP	Chinese Communist Party
CFJP	*Chieh-fang jih-pao*
CHOC	*Cambridge History of China*
CI	Comintern
CPPCC	Chinese People's Political Consultative Conference
CPSU	Communist Party of the Soviet Union
CQ	*China Quarterly*
CSYB	*Chinese statistical yearbook*
ECMM	*Extracts from China Mainland Magazines*
FBIS	*Foreign Broadcast Information Service*
FYP	Five-Year Plan
GLF	Great Leap Forward
GPCR	Great Proletarian Cultural Revolution
HC	*Hung-ch'i*
HHPYK	*Hsin-hua pan-yueh k'an*
HHYP	*Hsin-hua yueh-pao*
IASP	International Arts and Sciences Press
ICC	International Control Commission
IMH	Institute of Modern History
JAS	*Journal of Asian Studies*
JMJP	*Jen-min jih-pao*

JPRS	Joint Publications Research Service
KMJP	*Kuang-ming jih-pao*
KMT	Kuomintang
KTTH	*Kung-tso t'ung-hsun*
LHCC	*Lu Hsun ch'üan-chi*
LSYC	*Li-shih yen-chiu*
MAC	Military Affairs Commission
Mao, *SW*	*Selected works of Mao Tse-tung* (English translation)
MC	*Modern China*
MTHC	*Mao Tse-tung hsuan-chi*
MTTC	*Mao Tse-tung chi*
NCNA	New China News Agency (Hsin-hua she)
NEFA	Northeast Frontier Agency
nei pu	"Internal use only"
NFJP	*Nan-fang jih-pao*
NPC	National People's Congress
NSC	National Security Council
OECD	Organization for Economic Cooperation and Development
PC	*People's China*
PKI	Communist Party of Indonesia
PLA	People's Liberation Army
PR	*Peking Review* (later *Beijing Review*)
PRC	People's Republic of China
SCMM	*Selections from China Mainland Magazines*
SCMP	*Survey of China Mainland Press*
SEATO	Southeast Asia Treaty Organization
SMR	South Manchurian Railway
SWB/FE	*Summary of World Broadcasts (Far East)*
TCNC	*T'ung-chi nien-chien*
URI	Union Research Institute
USC	Universities Service Centre
Wan-sui	*Mao Tse-tung ssu-hsiang wan-sui*
WFTU	World Federation of Trade Unions

CHAPTER 1

THE REUNIFICATION OF CHINA

PHASES OF HISTORICAL UNDERSTANDING

Our comprehension of the great Chinese revolution of modern times has developed through a series of well-marked phases. A brief review of these phases is the best introduction to this volume of *The Cambridge History of China*, which deals with the first sixteen years of the People's Republic, 1949–65. A brief look at the phases that preceded our present understanding may give the reader a useful perspective on the current state of the art represented in this volume.[1] These phases of understanding may be characterized as missionary, diplomatic, journalistic, and social-scientific.

The missionary phase, inaugurated by the Jesuits and other Catholic missionaries of the sixteenth, seventeenth, and eighteenth centuries, gave us mainly a view of the ancient Chinese classical teachings, the long series of dynasties, and what we may call the myth of the state – the official doctrines of morality and history that emanated from the ruling class and served to indoctrinate both the Chinese masses and people in the West as they gradually heard about China. It was, needless to say, a picture of benevolent government by scholars, in the service of maintaining the family system and the traditional Chinese social order, capped by the office of the emperor.[2]

The diplomatic phase was ushered in by British attempts, beginning in the late eighteenth century, to expand trade with China. The Macartney mission of 1793 and the Amherst embassy of 1816 led eventually to the Opium War of 1839–42, which opened China to foreign contact under the unequal treaty system. During the nineteenth century the treaty system of extraterritorial status for foreigners of the treaty powers and for their business activities in the

---

1 For helpful comments I am indebted to Allen S. Whiting, Roderick MacFarquhar, Philip A. Kuhn, and Benjamin I. Schwartz.
2 For a survey of early European images of China see Raymond Dawson, *The Chinese chameleon: An analysis of European conceptions of Chinese civilization*. For the early period, copious details and illustrations are provided in Donald F. Lach, *Asia in the making of Europe*, vol. 1, *The century of discovery*, ch. 9, "China," 730–835.

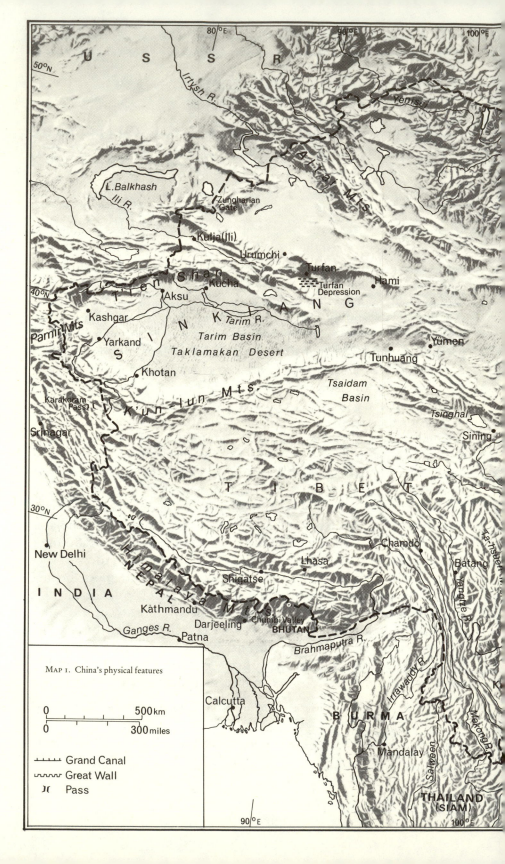

MAP 1. China's physical features

0	500 km
0	300 miles

+++++ Grand Canal
∿∿∿ Great Wall
)(Pass

treaty ports continued to expand and be refined.[3] By 1917 ninety-two ports were open for trade, and several generations of foreigners had dwelt in China and written home about it.

The phase of understanding to which they contributed was, on the whole, one of disillusion. The ideal features of government and humane society reported by the Jesuits were now visible at first hand to peoples who were in the early stages of the Industrial Revolution and believed in Western progress as well as Christianity and even democracy, Western-style. To them, China seemed like an ancient kingdom falling into a shambles.[4] The diplomatic phase of Western understanding came to its climax in 1898 with the attempted establishment of foreign spheres of influence and in 1900 with the Boxer Rebellion. In the latter year the decrepit Ch'ing dynasty hoped for a time to throw out the foreign invaders, and when this failed the settlement of 1901 ushered in a new twentieth-century era of reform and revolution.[5]

What I am calling the journalistic phase of the Western view of China arose in the 1890s with the modern journalism of mass-circulation newspapers and foreign correspondents. George Morrison, for example, who was correspondent of the London *Times*, became an informant to the Western world on the machinations of the Chinese political leaders until eventually some of them made him their adviser.[6] Journalism as the chief mode for understanding the Chinese revolution has had a steady and fruitful growth throughout the twentieth century. Television can bring the Chinese revolution into the home of every Westerner.

All these three phases had, of course, been an accumulation. The

3 The complex system of treaty rights was set forth in W. W. Willoughby, *Foreign rights and interests in China* (2nd ed., 1927).

4 For the most comprehensive disillusioned view, see S. Wells Williams, *The Middle Kingdom: A survey of the geography, government, education, social life, arts, religion etc. of the Chinese empire and its inhabitants*. This was only the most successful of a genre of books telling all about China. See Henry Charles Sirr, M.A., *China and the Chinese: Their religion, character, customs and manufactures; the evils arising from the opium trade; with a glance at our religious, moral, political and commercial intercourse with the country*. R. Montgomery Martin, *China: political, commercial and social*. The leading predecessor of these works was John Francis Davis, *The Chinese: A general description of the empire of China and its inhabitants*.

5 China's role as an object of international rivalry was put in context by William L. Langer, *The diplomacy of imperialism 1892–1902*. On Chinese-American relations the most balanced, multilingual study is by Michael H. Hunt, *The making of a special relationship*.

6 For Morrison's letters, see Lo Hui-min, ed., *The correspondence of G. E. Morrison*, vol. 1 (1895–1912), vol. 2 (1913–1920). The two British pundits, J. O. P. Bland and Putnam Weale (B. Lenox Simpson), between them published a dozen large, popular books.

Western missionaries continued to translate the classics and lecture to their home constituencies on the promise of Christianity for the Chinese heathen. The diplomats all continued to defend the unequal treaty privileges, especially extraterritoriality, and further entrench the foreign position in China until they were eventually thrown out. Through the revolution of 1911, then the revolution of the 1920s under the Nationalist Party (or the Kuomintang: KMT) in its first united front with the Chinese Communist Party (CCP), through the Japanese invasion of China from 1931 to 1945, and then throughout the Communist period, the reporting of the current scene in China has continued to progress in technique and expand in coverage.

These developments prepared the way for the period of social-scientific understanding of China that got started in the 1920s and 1930s with the rise of the social sciences in Western civilization. This broad development followed many institutional channels and went through minor phases of its own. In general, the social sciences were applied to China first in the fields of law and political science, studies that reflected the proliferation of treaty and trading privileges and the unequal status of China in an era of imperialist competition. The application of economics to China began with the study of the China trade, long a British specialty, and was then expanded by efforts to understand the Chinese farm economy. By this time the Japanese invasion of China had also triggered Japanese studies of Chinese resources, production, and marketing.[7] The 1920s saw not only the rise of the Social Science Research Council in New York but also mass education experiments in North China and the building up of the Peking Union Medical College by the Rockefeller Foundation. In short, after the end of the old dynasty in 1912, waves of foreign influence rolled over China through the channels of treaty-port trade, missionary education, and the training of a new Chinese intelligentsia in Western institutions.

A turning point in the social-scientific approach was inaugurated during World War II by the growth of area studies, which were an effort to focus the various disciplines on China in an integrated fashion and in the experience of each student. Language, history,

---

7 On law, see in addition to Willoughby, *Foreign rights*, C. Walter Young, *The international relations of Manchuria*. On foreign economic relations, C. F. Remer, *The foreign trade of China* and *Foreign investment in China*. On farm economy, J. Lossing Buck, *Land utilization in China*. On early Japanese work on the Chinese economy, see J. K. Fairbank, M. Banno, and S. Yamamoto, *Japanese studies of modern China*, part 7.

geography, economics, political science, sociology, anthropology, and eventually literature and the more detailed disciplines within disciplines – all began to produce trained specialists.[8] As concern about the "Communist menace" entered its heyday in America in response to the creation of the People's Republic of China, the Marxism-Leninism of the Chinese revolutionaries stimulated Western efforts at analysis.

Out of all this, after several generations, has emerged the present ideal of understanding China through both its history and its current reality, through both its own tradition and the techniques of social science.[9] This volume shows the emergence of the social scientist-historian who may function as a specialist in one or another discipline especially concerned with its subject matter but is at the same time aware of the other approaches in the context of which work must be done. Fluent reading and speaking of Chinese, traveling and interviewing in the country, and the amalgamation of fact and theory are the stuff of this new scholar's existence.

This growing capacity in Chinese studies has ushered in a new era. The long sinological tradition of scholarship, focused on the Chinese record, had so absorbed the attention and energy of pioneer students that it cultivated a "Chinese exceptionalism." Beginning with the writing system, Chinese history displayed many extraordinary, if not unique, features such as oracle bones, silk culture, early practice of bureaucratic government, the examination system, the gentry class, and above all the longevity of the state and its continuous records of administration.[10] Explication of such topics, and many more, still necessarily occupies much time in the teaching of Chinese history. But the context has changed.

Because the social sciences by definition concern principles and evidence of worldwide scope, they are essentially comparative. So it follows that the uniqueness of China has been diminished. "Chinese exceptionalism" in subjects like social structure, the family system, religious cults, administration, foreign trade, xenophobia, national-

---

8 The boom in American area studies of China is summarized in John M. H. Lindbeck, *Understanding China: A report to the Ford Foundation.*

9 See, among others, G. William Skinner, "Asian studies and the disciplines," in *Asian Studies Newsletter,* 29.4 (April 1984), 7–8. Fernand Braudel, *The perspective of the world,* vol. 3 of *Civilization and capitalism: 15th–18th century*: "And today now that it is in touch with the various social sciences, is history not also becoming a science of a kind ... ready to ask questions as much as to answer them, to be a measure of the present as well as of the past?" (see pp. 619–20).

10 Surveyed in Kenneth Scott Latourette, *The Chinese: Their history and culture through 3,000 years of cumulative development and recent radical change.*

ism, communism, and technology transfer has been reduced by the study of China to one case among an array of cases. This, of course, has produced new insights and broader perspectives.

Yet troubling questions arise. How far do the broadly competent social scientist-historians find in China mainly what, according to their categories, they seek? This perennial question, needless to say, haunts all observers and investigators of humankind, no matter what academic flags they fly. We shall not attempt an answer here. We may assume that if earlier generations of scholars were culture-bound creatures of their times, then we are too. We can claim only to be more conscious of this fact.

Chinese scholars, like us, are now studying China through the social sciences as members of a single world community of scholarship. Therefore, it is desirable here to trace the phases by which their Chinese predecessors have understood the history of China since the eighteenth century. In other words, the Chinese counterpart to the Western image of China, its history and its conditions, is essential to our picture of the modern revolution. The Chinese view is less well understood by outsiders, but the following phases may be briefly distinguished: the dynastic cycle phase, which led into the period of statecraft; the self-strengthening phase, which led into the reform movement; the Republican revolutionary phase, which led into party dictatorship; and finally the Communist phase of recent years, which has led into "modernization." Naturally, these phases blend into one another.

The dynastic cycle phase, in the Chinese understanding of modern history, was posited on one of the grand theories that underlay the Chinese state, which we must discuss at greater length farther on. Beginning in the late eighteenth century, Chinese scholars noted increasing difficulties in administration, the decline of morale, and the rise of rebellion. These phenomena, from the late eighteenth century to about the 1870s, were slotted into the traditional cubbyholes of the dynastic cycle theory.[11] So were the remedies attempted under the general name of statecraft (*ching-shih*), the techniques by which scholar-administrators could deal with the problems of government.

11 That much neglected but remarkably insightful scholar, Thomas Taylor Meadows in *The Chinese and their rebellions*, expounded to Western readers the Chinese myth of the state, including the theory of virtuous government, the Mandate of Heaven and the right of rebellion that underlay the dynastic cycle, all of which he had learned from his Chinese teachers. For a useful survey, see Frederic Wakeman, Jr., *The fall of imperial China*, ch. 4, "The dynastic cycle," 55–70.

These involved a revival of scholarly studies in order to revive the morale of the scholar-official class, ingenious administrative arrangements to meet the needs of governing the masses, efforts at economy and probity in government, and a series of other well-known means by which the Chinese imperial order had been from time to time resuscitated and kept going over the centuries. Imperial Confucianism had survived partly through a capacity for reform by a reassertion of its ideals.[12]

One of the objectives of statecraft was to pacify the rebellious barbarian traders on the frontier, both in Central Asia and in Canton in the 1830s. Finding the Europeans to be more powerful, statecraft scholars set about studying them and their technology. This was the modern beginning of the opening of the Chinese mind to the outer world.[13]

The phase of self-strengthening and Westernization grew out of the recognition that Western arms could be helpful in suppressing Chinese rebels and that treaty settlement with the invading British and French could get their support for the dynasty to preserve it against rebellion. In this way the treaty system appeared to Chinese statesmen in the first instance as a device for taming the barbarian with a "loose rein" (*chi-mi*) in the same way as one gets a powerful horse to carry its rider or pull loads. It was a concept derived from long experience in placating and sometimes collaborating with nomadic invaders of China.[14] The superior military technology of the

---

12 On Confucian reformism, see W. T. DeBary, *The unfolding of neo-Confucianism*; James T. C. Liu, "The variety of political reforms in Chinese history: a simplified typology," in Paul A. Cohen and John E. Schrecker, *Reform in nineteenth century China*, 9–13. For an early exposition of the control system maintained by statecraft, see Kung-ch'uan Hsiao, *Rural China*. For a recent conspectus, see the bilingual symposium volume, *Proceedings of the conference on the theory of statecraft of Modern China (Chin-shih Chung-kuo ching-shih ssu-hsiang yen-t'ao-hui lun-wen chi)*. On the rise of statecraft, see Judith Whitbeck, ibid., 323–40, "From k'ao-cheng to ching-shih: Kung Tzu-chen and the redirection of literati commitment in early nineteenth century China"; and Benjamin Elman, *From philosophy to philology*. Also Wang Erh-min, "Ching-shih ssu-hsiang chih i-chieh wen-t'i" (The problem of definition in statecraft thought), in *Bulletin of the Institute of Modern History, Academia Sinica*, 13 (June 1984), 27–38.

13 One leader was the versatile New Text scholar Wei Yuan, *Hai-kuo t'u-chih* (An illustrated treatise on the maritime kingdoms), several editions: 1844, 50 *chüan*; 1847, 60 *chüan*; 1852, 100 *chüan*. On Wei Yuan's career, see Wang Chia-chien, *Wei Yuan nien-p'u*. Jane Kate Leonard, *Wei Yuan and China's rediscovery of the maritime world*. A first systematic geography was by Hsu Chi-yü, *Ying-huan chih-lueh* (A short account of the maritime circuit). See Fred W. Drake, *China charts the world: Hsu Chi-yü and his geography of 1848*. On the parellel Ch'ing policies in Kashgar and Canton in the 1830s, see Joseph Fletcher in *CHOC*, 10. 375–85.

14 On the "loose rein" policy for temporizing with and making use of barbarians too powerful to coerce, see Lien-sheng Yang, "Historical notes ..." in J. K. Fairbank, ed., *The Chinese world order*, esp. 31–3.

West was therefore the first thing to be borrowed, in the form of firearms, cannon, and gunboats.

Military industry, of course, involved other kinds of heavy industry, and the Chinese went steadily farther into attempts at Westernization (*yang-wu*)[15] State mines, steamship lines, and eventually factories were adapted to Chinese use from foreign models and with foreign help. Meanwhile foreigners were taken into the Chinese administration as a means of controlling other foreigners, particularly through the Imperial Maritime Customs Service. The dictator of this service, Robert Hart, knew how to serve as a minor Chinese official while wielding influence greater than that of some foreign ambassadors.[16] Late nineteenth-century imperialism thus entailed synarchy, Chinese collaboration, and Sino-foreign cooperation in many fields. Missionaries found that evangelism could be helped and indeed supplanted by good works. Merchants found that the administration of the treaty ports by foreign consuls and merchants had to have Chinese cooperation and participation.[17]

In this phase, reform was induced by those scholars who saw the West and its products and recognized that China had fallen behind and must make great changes. The early reformers tended naturally to become Christian converts, at least for a time. But Chinese fear and dislike of the foreign invaders were so pervasive that efforts to start a daily press, build up industries, and modernize the military were delayed for a generation.[18] The lightning Japanese victory over China in 1894 was a stunning blow that opened the eyes of a whole generation. K'ang Yu-wei proclaimed that China must reform or perish. In the 1890s foreign teaching of Social Darwinism supported this conclusion.[19] After the fiasco of the Boxer Rising in 1900, even the moribund Ch'ing dynasty launched reforms. The turn of the century thus saw a great revolution in Chinese thought begin among the scholar class, who alone could lead revolution.

15 On early Westernization in general, see Albert Feuerwerker, *China's early industrialization*. On military industry, Thomas Kennedy, *Arms of Kiangnan: Modernization of the Chinese ordnance industry 1860–1895*. On the economic institutions and practices that grew up in Sino-foreign trade, see Yen-p'ing Hao, *The commercial revolution in nineteenth-century China: The rise of Sino-Western mercantile capitalism*.
16 Stanley F. Wright, *Hart and the Chinese Customs*; J. K. Fairbank, K. F. Bruner, and E. M. Matheson, *The I.G. in Peking: Letters of Robert Hart*; J. K. Fairbank, "Synarchy under the treaties," in *The Chinese world order*.
17 Albert Feuerwerker, "The foreign presence in China," *CHOC*, 12. 128–207, and Albert Feuerwerker, "Economic trends in the late Ch'ing empire 1870–1911," *CHOC*, 11. 1–69, esp. 38–39 citing Wang Ching-yü.
18 See Paul A. Cohen, *Between tradition and modernity: Wang T'ao and reform in Late Ch'ing China*.
19 James R. Pusey, *China and Charles Darwin*.

The subsequent phase of revolution seemed to bear out the theory of the dynastic cycle. The dynasty collapsed in 1911 and was soon followed by a period of chaos and warlordism.[20] From the Chinese point of view, one chief achievement of this period was the substitution after 1921 of a dictatorial party for the dynastic family. Acceptance (beginning within ten years after the end of the dynasty) of the Soviet model with the establishment of the CCP in 1921 and the reform of the KMT on Soviet lines in 1923 had several advantages: It created an ongoing and self-perpetuating powerholder but did so by mobilizing the most committed revolutionaries as patriots intent on saving China. The dynastic families had tried to provide capable power-holders (emperors) from a harem that might produce twenty or thirty sons in the palace, while providing bureaucrats from an examination system open to talent in all the provinces. Party dictatorship instead dispensed with the family lineage, opened the powerholding politburo to competing talent from within the Party, and had Party members supervise government at all levels. The era of party dictatorship thus launched an ongoing struggle between two parties, the KMT and the CCP.[21]

By the time the Chinese Communists came to power in 1949, Chinese patriots had spent two generations borrowing from Western models of government and theories of social order. British liberalism at the turn of the century was followed by the Japanese example of political reform early in the 1900s. Western theories of politics loomed largest in the conscious thought of Chinese revolutionaries. Around 1911, leaders ranging from Sun Yat-sen and Sung Chiao-jen to Liang Ch'i-ch'ao mainly had in mind the British and American (and also the Japanese) creations of parliamentary democracy in nation-states. During the 1920s Ch'en Tu-hsiu, Li Ta-chao, and other leaders of the Chinese Communist Party saw their precedents in the great French and Russian revolutions against feudalism and class oppression. Meanwhile both the CCP and Sun Yat-sen and his Kuomintang colleagues, including Chiang Kai-shek, were impressed with Leninist party dictatorship as a means to counter imperialism.

The foreign models of revolution and nation building fitted the Chinese situation sometimes only superficially, sometimes more fundamentally. In order to appraise the degree and form of their

20 Chūzō Ichiko, "The role of the gentry: An hypothesis," ch. 6 in Mary C. Wright, *China in revolution*.
21 On the first united front, see C. Martin Wilbur, *The Nationalist Revolution in China, 1923–1928*.

influence, we must look first at certain basic concepts in Chinese traditional thinking about politics, especially the nature of state authority.

THE CHINESE ACHIEVEMENT OF UNITY

Our best starting point is the theory and practice of the dynastic cycle, so prominent in Chinese political folklore and historical writings. Let us begin at the simplest level and view it as an explanation of events, before probing the assumptions underlying it. Without going into the extensive literature on the rise and fall of dynasties, we can note the historical circumstances that chroniclers have cited as typical of a period of dynastic change and reunification.[22] What I try to summarize here comes from concepts put forward by Chinese official historiography. First of all, it was preceded by *prolonged disorder* produced by a combination of factors: *unvirtuous conduct of the ruler* that would cost him the Mandate of Heaven; *fiscal bankruptcy of his regime* due partly to extravagance and partly to corrupt withdrawal of upper-class land from taxation, increasing the tax burden on the peasantry, whose defaults impoverished the government; *declining popular welfare* due inter alia to population pressure on resources and failure of the regime to maintain public works, especially dikes for flood prevention and granaries for famine prevention; *low public morale* due to an increase in corruption on a *sauve qui peut* basis, expressing the alienation of both officials and populace from the rulers; *military weakness*, evident in the inability to suppress invaders (foreign-based rebels) and domestic rebels.

This destructive syndrome was usually paralleled in retrospect by the constructive achievements of the new dynastic founder: *personal* – he was a charismatic leader who shrewdly induced able colleagues to accept his command; *strategic* – he built a territorial base of

22 Western students of the dynastic cycle may best begin with Lien-sheng Yang, "Toward a study of dynastic configurations in Chinese history," in his *Studies in Chinese institutional history*, 1–17 ("Dynasties rise and fall just as man is mortal," p. 17). For a useful analysis, see Wakeman, cited in note 11 above. See also Mary Clabaugh Wright, *The last stand of Chinese conservatism: The T'ung-chih restoration, 1862–1872*, ch. 4, "The idea of a restoration." Richard J. Smith, *China's cultural heritage: The Ch'ing dynasty, 1644–1912*, on pp. 104–5 notes the influence of the Buddhist concept of cycles. Burton Watson refers to "one of the most persistent patterns of Chinese historical writing: the rule of a new house set up by a man of extraordinary virtue and wisdom, and the gradual decline of the dynasty until its termination under a monarch completely incapable or evil," in *Ssu-ma Ch'ien: Grand historian of China*, ch. 1, "The world of Ssu-ma Ch'ien," 3–39, esp. 5. On the massive anatomy of the dynasties see Charles O. Hucker, "Introduction: Governmental organization era by era," in his *A dictionary of official titles in imperial China*, 1–96.

fighting men and food supply where his power could grow to dominant proportions before expanding; *ideological* – the rebel leader often asserted a popular faith that promised a new life for the people; *military* – the unifier inspired his troops with a superior will to win, so that they outmaneuvered and demoralized the enemy and won popular support by their exemplary conduct; *diplomatic* – his regime allied with other disaffected elements, domestic or foreign, secretly recruited turncoat literati and bought over or neutralized minor opponents; *managerial* – his team of loyal and talented assistants divided the tasks of warfare, administration, and ideology and so were prepared to take power.[23]

Finally, when this rise of the new regime intersected the decline of the old, a sudden and accelerating swing of opinion seemed to transfer the mandate to rule. Government efforts at repression became more desperate and severe but from a steadily shrinking base of loyalty. In this situation the folklore of the dynastic cycle – Heaven's mandate as the legitimizing myth of the state – became a self-fulfilling prophecy. Like the stock market speculator's expectation of an economic cycle of boom and depression, popular assumptions about Chinese politics contributed to the outcome. Once popular opinion shifted, the outgoing regime rapidly lost the power to govern. Its demise was settled by force of arms.[24]

Such cycles, of course, were not to be found only in the history of China. Foreign invaders, whose military and administrative resources might accumulate on the frontier during the decline of central power and allow them to break in and seize control, had figured in the history of most empires. In China, "barbarian" invasion and rule had been recurrent from earliest times. They were based on the geographic fact of Inner Asian aridity, which fostered animal husbandry and so the striking power of tribal cavalry. Nomadic incursions had become more and more frequent until the dynasties of the Mongols

---

23 On the participation of nomadic or semi-nomadic tribal regimes, see O. Lattimore, *Inner Asian frontiers of China*. Accounts of dynastic foundings are in Arthur F. Wright, *The Sui dynasty: the unification of China AD 581–617*; Howard J. Wechsler, "The founding of the T'ang Dynasty," ch. 3 in Denis Twitchett, ed., *CHOC*, 3. 150–241. Edmund H. Worthy, Jr., "The founding of Sung China, 950–1000: integrative changes in military and political institutions" (Ph.D. dissertation, Princeton, 1975); Edward L. Dreyer, *Early Ming China: A political history 1355–1435*; John W. Dardess, *Confucianism and autocracy: Professional elites in the founding of the Ming dynasty*; Joseph F. Fletcher, Jr., and Gertraude Roth Li, "The rise of the Manchus," *CHOC*, 9 (in press), and Frederic Wakeman, Jr., *The great enterprise*. On the Ch'ing decline, see Susan Mann Jones and Philip A. Kuhn, "Dynastic decline and the roots of rebellion," *CHOC*, 10. 107–62.
24 On the suddenness of shifts of loyalty see, for example, Edward J. M. Rhoads, *China's Republican revolution*, ch. 9.

(Yuan, 1279–1368) and the Manchus (Ch'ing, 1644–1912) became major eras of Chinese history. Indeed, the Manchus had so identified themselves with the imperial office that China's modern nationalists could not accept constitutional monarchy as a transitional form of government with which to enter the twentieth century.[25]

More important for historians of today are the assumptions that underlay and were implied by the dynastic cycle mode of explaining events. The major assumption was the unity of the whole Chinese realm, a polity coterminous with Chinese culture and society. To see this concept as a Chinese version of the Western idea of the nation-state would be nonsense. The nineteenth-century unification of Italy or Germany, for example, was a wholly different type of phenomenon, the creation of a national polity within the broad expanse of Western civilization. When Chinese patriots of the 1890s took to heart the Western examples of nation building by Peter the Great, Cavour and Garibaldi, or Bismarck, they were clutching at straws.[26]

To be sure, their effort to save China from invasion during the century and a half after the Opium War consciously stressed the necessity to fight fire with fire, to defend China by learning the secrets of Western power, and therefore to know and apply both foreign technology and in the end foreign ideas. Western theories of revolution and nation building thus appear to have dominated the conscious thought of revolutionary leaders all the way from Sun Yat-sen to Mao Tse-tung, from Social Darwinism at the turn of the century to Stalinism in the 1950s. Moreover, this evident concern with Western ideas made it all the easier for Western observers to take the Chinese at their word and assume that the Chinese revolution could be understood in Western terms such as feudalism, democracy, capitalism, liberalism, socialism, or communism.[27] Leaving aside the moot question whether such terms even in the West still have operational meaning, we can only conclude that the Chinese and we have deluded ourselves on a grand scale. Of course, one cannot deny that Western ideas and examples had increasing influence; yet a

25 Harold Z. Schiffrin, *Sun Yat-sen*, 293–99, notes how anti-Manchuism arose with anti-imperialism.
26 As early as 1861 the censor Wei Mu-t'ing pointed out that "Russia formerly did not have a navy. After . . . Peter came to the throne he personally went to Holland in disguise to . . . learn about naval affairs and firearms. . . . Now in Europe the Russian troops are the strongest." Ssu-yü Teng et al., *China's response to the West*, 68, translated from *I-wu shih-mo*, T'ung-chih, 2.36.
27 The prehensile ingestion of foreign political concepts by the generation of the early twentieth century is profusely illustrated by R. A. Scalapino and George Yu, *Modern China and its revolutionary process*.

moment's reflection will suggest that the revolutionary changes in China since 1840 have been inevitably superficial to the institutionalized structures of language and ethical values, family system, social norms, handicraft technology, agrarian-commercial economy, and imperial polity that had taken shape through countless vicissitudes over three thousand years of recorded and largely self-contained Chinese history. Behavioral science take note: The Chinese state and society in their contemporary guise are end products of a largely separate evolution, comparable but far from identical with that of the Greco-Roman, Judeo-Christian West.

The extent of our self-delusion is easily demonstrated. Who today, at first glance, will not subscribe to the thesis that the virtue of modern nationalism was demonstrated to Chinese reformers of the nineteenth century by the example of the imperialist powers encroaching on China, that Chinese nationalism thus inspired has been the great motive sentiment of China's twentieth-century politics, and that the People's Republic today is preeminently a nation-state proudly taking its place among the world's great powers?[28] All well and good, up to a point.

But a certain paradox has been overlooked: The peoples of Europe and North and South America all counted together have been generally no more numerous than the Chinese. There is even some question whether they have been ethnically more diverse. In numbers and even in ethnic variety, the Europeans and the Chinese have been rather comparable, of the same order of magnitude. Yet in their political life today, *a billion or so Europeans in Europe and the Americas live divided into some fifty separate and sovereign states, while more than a billion Chinese live in only one state.*[29] The disparity between one and fifty can hardly be overlooked, once one sees it.

The above as a simple statement of fact implies that our terms nationalism and nation-state, when applied to China, can only mislead us. China is not be understood by a mere transposition of Western terminology. It is a different animal. Its politics must be understood from within, genetically. Thus when the modern press facilitated the rise of mass nationalism in China a century ago, it

28 Nation-state nationalism is idealized in Chiang Kai-shek, *China's destiny*; see ch. 1, "Growth and development of the Chunghua (Chinese) nation."
29 See, for example, *Demographic yearbook 1982*, p. 132: total population of the Americas and Europe, 1,096 million; China, 995 million.

could be based on a strong sense of identity and one-time cultural superiority. We should call it cultural nationalism to distinguish it from the usual political nationalism we meet elsewhere.

As to how the gigantic Chinese state evolved, we can assert first that it grew by implosion, while the states of the West were the products of explosion. While the Europeans became seafaring traders, exploring and settling the New World, for example, the Chinese by the development of such things as rice culture in the well-watered hills of Central and South China could continue to pack their people more densely together. They expanded overseas only in modern times, mainly in foreign ships.[30]

Scholars have confronted this paradox for some centuries, but few have explored its implications. The first attempt at explanation has usually been geographical. In one way, of course, geography favored political unity in China and diversity in Europe: Ancient China's growth was not stimulated by rivalry with equal antagonists overseas like the Greeks versus the Persians or Rome versus Carthage. There was little occasion for China to develop sea power and receive the variety of stimulants that maritime trade and alien ships could offer. In the end, the multistate Europeans, being seafarers, spread overseas, the unistate Chinese stayed at home.

But does this fully explain the discrepancy? China and Europe began as political entities of similar size. The Han and Roman empires were of comparable scope in area and numbers. Europe's peninsulas and seas, to be sure, led outward. Yet geographically China is far from united. A mountain chain lines the southeastern coast, and other chains make a checkerboard between the coast and the western highlands. Three river systems – north, central, and south – drain the country from Central Asia toward the Pacific. But the Yellow River, being generally unnavigable, does not link Shensi and Shansi to the sea. Peripheral areas like Yunnan and especially Szechwan and Shansi have fertile cores ringed by mountains, ideal for independent bases. The Yangtze gorges, for example, strictly limit the eastern access to Szechwan. The Yellow River Plain in North China from Peking to the Huai River is no easier to traverse than the North European plain from the Urals to Hamburg. On balance, I think we must conclude that China's geographic terrain by itself did not

---

30 On expansion within China, see Herold J. Wiens, *China's march toward the tropics*. On foreign shipping, Robert L. Irick, *Ch'ing policy toward the coolie trade, 1847–1878*.

facilitate the rise of central power; on the contrary, its ancient unity
was a triumph of human institutions over geography.[31]

China's population growth, far from splitting up the state, seems to
have challenged it to greater feats of centralized though superficial
bureaucratic control. The Ch'ing record in the application of administrative methods under the general heading of statecraft bears this
out. The late imperial era saw a massive population spread over a vast
area who nevertheless had a propensity for order through political
unity. This consensus was buttressed by administrative arrangements
such as those for shared labor service (*li-chia*), mutual surveillance
and responsibility (*pao-chia*), official indoctrination of the populace
(*hsiang-yueh*), superior status of gentry degreeholders (*shen-shih*),
and the imperial cult.[32] Even more important were the cultural values
and assumptions that supported the state and social order through
deep-lying institutions: a single, theoretically all-powerful supreme
authority; the people's indoctrination in the classical teachings of
social order carried on through family lineages and encouraged by the
supreme authority; an examination system that sought out the most
talented for official service in the state bureaucracy; the function of
the local indoctrinated elite as the connecting stratum between
bureaucracy and populace – all these ingredients of the late imperial
Chinese polity, noted by pioneers like Max Weber three-quarters of a
century ago, are still evident today and still in need of analytic
integration by the exploration of China's sociopolitical institutions.[33]

The imperial Chinese state maintained its central power by all
manner of ingenious means. One was to monopolize or to license
large-scale economic activity. There is a vast literature on this
subject:[34] The result is that feudalism, capitalism, and socialism,
which play such protean roles in European history, have no strict
counterparts in China. European socialists see "socialism" as something to be striven for through the augmentation of state control over
the economy. To Chinese, however, this is what any central govern-

31 George B. Cressey, *Land of the 500 million*, describes China's terrain on the basis of 100,000
    miles of travel there. See also T. T. Meadows (*The Chinese*, 1856, p. 39): "The Chinese are
    one in spite of physical barriers – it is mind, O western materialistic observers, which has
    yonder produced homogeneity."
32 On these institutions, see Kung-chuan Hsiao, *Rural China*.
33 Two classic sources are Max Weber, *The religion of China*, and Etienne Balazs, *Chinese
    civilization and bureaucracy*. This task has been brilliantly pursued by Lucian W. Pye with
    Mary W. Pye in their *Asian power and politics: The cultural dimensions of authority*; see esp.
    ch. 7, "China: The illusion of omnipotence" (182–214).
34 See Karl A. Wittfogel, *Oriental despotism: A comparative study of total power*. A more
    up-to-date and multifaceted approach by leading European specialists is provided in S. R.
    Schram, ed., *The scope of state power in China*.

ment would naturally expect to do. The achievement of socialism in China would be very similar to the achievement of strong central government – that is, reunification.[35]

Comparable adjustments to Chinese traditional realities must be made in the case of the term "democracy." If we take its Western meaning to be the participation of the people in the processes of government or in the legitimation of the government's activities, then we find in the old China a bifurcation of function between literati and populace. When the literati degreeholders were allowed to memorialize or petition the authorities, they were participating in government; when the populace by violent rebellion destroyed a regime's mandate and accepted its successor, then the people had in the popular view legitimized it. The different meanings of democracy in the old China hinged on the difference in status between the literati ruling class and the largely agrarian masses.[36] This gap is not gone.

Thus we may posit that in addition to unity, one of the Chinese state's core perceptions was the idea of elitism as the natural order of things, of mind ruling over muscle. Another core feature flowed from this fact – the perception that the government's authority was normally to be maintained by its moral prestige, which had to be preserved by proper ritual acts, by propagation of orthodox beliefs, and by watchful suppression of heterodox ideas.[37] All these considerations led to one final core perception – that the task of the ruling elite was in moral terms paternal and in practical terms managerial. The one pervasive assumption of Chinese political life was the idea of the unity of the state as part of the order of nature. Let us take a moment to see whence this idea had come.

Origins of the ideal of unity

The claim to central power was first recorded by the rulers of the Shang kingdom in Honan early in the second millennium B.C. It was

35 Sun Yat-sen's rather vague idea of People's Livelihood (*Min-sheng chu-i*) used a phrase from the classics which was sometimes equated with socialism. Thus *min-sheng* was cited by Ku Yen-wu (1613–82) in an essay on centralized bureaucratic government (*Chün-hsien lun*): The latter's evils, he says, are already extreme and if no sage arises (to govern), it will be the old story: the people's livelihood will be daily poorer, China will become steadily weaker, and things will fall into disorder. Of Ku Yen-wu's nine essays called *Chün-hsien lun*, this is from Essay I. See T'ang Ching-kao, ed., *Ku Yen-wu wen*, p. 2 of text. (I am indebted to John Schrecker for this reference.)
36 See Balazs, "Tradition and revolution in China," 150–70 in his *Chinese civilization and bureaucracy*.
37 Richard J. Smith, *China's cultural heritage*, stresses the craving for social order. Pye, *Asian Power*, stresses the people's dependence on a single supreme authority.

repeated by their successors of the Chou dynasty (ca. 1122–256 B.C.) and then vigorously revived by the Ch'in dynasty reunification of 221 B.C. Again, after the decline of central power following the Earlier and Later Han dynasties (206 B.C.–A.D. 220), the Sui reunification of A.D. 589 reaffirmed the principle of unity in a fashion that lasted (with only brief interregnums like that of 907–60) down to 1912, when Mao Tse-tung was in school and Chiang-Kai-shek already a soldier.[38]

Archaeologists now tell us China's political style was formed in a rural scene where the authority of the ruler in his walled town was sanctioned by cosmic myth and ritual as part of this agricultural society's animistic belief in the unseen spirits of nature, particularly of the ancestors. In the early era of the Hsia, Shang, and Chou dynasties (ca. 2700–256 B.C.) the ruler was the head of a lineage and derived his authority from his genealogical descent from the ancestors and from his shamanistic capacity to communicate with the ancestors, aided partly by animal sacrifice. Indeed, it is now concluded that "the king himself was actually the head shaman." Since the earliest oracle bone writing recorded his ritual communications with the ancestors, writing was from the first an attribute of authority, used to buttress the ruler's moral claim to power: "The possessors of the oracular knowledge may thus be the first known members of the 'knowledge class.'" Religious belief, literacy, and political authority thus were closely linked from the beginning.[39] They created a long-lasting cultural orientation toward the primacy of the political order. The writing system began and was maintained as a pillar of state and culture. Not simply a monopoly of the scribes, it was a part of the political structure. Mastery of it was the hallmark of the ruling class.

In the Bronze Age the hundreds of lineage-based town-states that spread over North China were far less concerned with trade than their seafaring counterparts in the eastern Mediterranean. They remained rooted in an agrarian life in which historical myth and record agreed on the past unity of the state under the successive rulers of the Hsia, Shang, and Chou lineages. The China that was so characterized was essentially agrarian China, the heartland of intensive agriculture. Inner Asian regions of a largely pastoral economy, such as Mongolia

---

38 On the longevity of the ancient idea of universal kingship, see Benjamin Schwartz, "The Chinese perception of world order," in Fairbank, ed., *The Chinese world order*, 276–88.

39 K. C. Chang, *Art, myth and ritual: The path to political authority in ancient China*; see 45, 90. This development is put in a broad context in Benjamin I. Schwartz, *The world of thought in ancient China*, esp. ch. 1, "Early cultural orientations: issues and speculations."

and Tibet, were of strategic concern to be sure, but in social and cultural terms were only marginal to agrarian China.

Since China's terrain in many areas nurtured particularism, the late Chou saw the rise of more than a hundred separate states. The rivers, lakes, plains, and passes permitted the invasion of one state by another in tests of strength. Multistate diplomacy flourished among the aptly named Warring States of the late Chou era (463–221 B.C.). For the first several centuries of China's recorded history, geography facilitated interstate conflicts, negotiations, alliances, and mergers through fair means or foul.[40] If we suppose for a moment that the Yangtze River had been a Mediterranean Sea, then we can no doubt assume that there would have continued to be in China a counterpart to what became the Warring States of Europe – where, for example, Rome destroyed Carthage, and later the Iberian peninsula rivaled the British Isles. But the Chinese realm was after all finite, between Central Asia and the Pacific, and a long process set in of forming confederations and of larger states swallowing smaller ones up to the eventual Ch'in reunification of 221 B.C. In this turbulent and creative era, Confucius and the other philosophers entered history as political advisers on how to restore the presumed social order of earlier times.[41] Confucius taught that by his exemplary conduct a ruler could secure popular acquiescence in his rule which would constitute the Mandate of Heaven, for "Heaven sees as the people see." The goal of social order required the reunification of China.

It is highly significant that the Confucian classics used by the Han and later dynasties to indoctrinate both rulers and subjects were products of the era *before* the reunification of 221 B.C. They therefore enshrined the aspirations for peace that prolonged warfare had made dominant in the thought of Confucius and other advisors of the time. By expressing the poignant craving for order in an age of disorder, the classics perpetuated for all later ages the ideal of unity. In short, by its very absence before 221 B.C. unity became the summum bonum of Chinese politics thereafter. No doubt the founding myths that sanction most regimes preserve the rationale that supported their original

---

40 Richard L. Walker, *The multi-state system of ancient China*; Jacques Gernet, "The age of the principalities," ch. 2, 51–61, in *A history of Chinese civilization*, a translation of *Le Monde Chinois*.

41 "The different philosophers themselves were in actual fact 'creating antiquity.' ... Political thought ... never succeeded in wholly transcending the boundaries set in the pre-Ch'in age." Kung-chuan Hsiao, trans. F. W. Mote, *A history of Chinese political thought*, 1.12. For the Confucian teaching of government by benevolence, see 116–24. Herrlee G. Creel, *The origins of statecraft in China*, vol. I, *The Western Chou empire*, synthesizing the sources up to the late 1960s, asserts the vitality of the Chou imperial state of the era ca. 1122–771 B.C.

coming to power. In the Chinese case, the disorder of the centuries before 221 B.C. became the sanction for the ideal of unified order during the two thousand years that followed.

A second institutional development made the ideal of unity more feasible in China than in Europe. Chinese emperors who claimed the Mandate of Heaven to rule all-under-Heaven (*t'ien-hsia*) were no more grandiose than European kings who claimed to rule as incarnate deities or by divine right. The difference was that the Chinese ruling over a dense population had had to invent bureaucratic government. While the Roman state was still entrusting public duties to its equestrian class and other individuals, the Han emperors began to train and examine civil servants who were appointed for fixed terms on stipends at twenty levels of rank and strictly controlled by official correspondence, statutory inspections, and rewards and punishments. Second, the early invention of paper and printed books made possible by T'ang times the Chinese examination system, whose graduates formed a genuine civil service open to talent – one of the greatest political inventions of all time.[42] Behind it lay many factors – the esoteric nature of the Chinese writing system, the special concern of the ruler for the literati who preserved the rituals and compiled the records, the propensity of an agrarian society for regularity and routine undisturbed by the vicissitudes of sea trade and its foreign contacts. As a result, when the three and a half centuries of disunity that followed the decline of the Later Han after A.D. 220 were ended by the Sui reunification of 589, China avoided the breakup into separate regional states that followed the reign of Charlemagne in Europe.[43] A reunified China under the T'ang (618–906) became the most advanced part of the world, while medieval Europe fell behind.

---

42 On the earliest governmental structure, see Hans Bielenstein, *The bureaucracy of Han times*. See also Etienne Balazs, *Chinese civilization and bureaucracy*; on the examination system, Ping-ti Ho, *The ladder of success in imperial China: aspects of social mobility*; for a sophisticated approach to China's bureaucratic practice, see Thomas A. Metzger, *The internal organization of Ch'ing bureaucracy: Legal, normative and communication aspects.*

43 "Both Charlemagne and the Sui founder resorted to the old empire's tradition of codified law, Charlemagne first in the cumulative capitularies of old German law and later in an attempted revival of Roman codification. The Sui were able to draw on the codes of many of the successor states of the long-vanished Han.... Both Charlemagne and Sui Wen-ti faced, when they came to power, a great diffusion of central authority: Charlemagne the crazy quilt of claimants to local power – hereditary mayors of the palace, dukes, counts, and bishops – and Wen-ti the long-entrenched great families ... who regarded hereditary access to office as a right and the official appointment function as an inheritable privilege. Both took strong measures to reverse the centrifugal flow of power, but Sui Wen-ti strove to restore the administrative rationality of the ancient Han Empire while Charlemagne resorted mainly to the ties of sworn fealty and to gifts of land and serfs as means of insuring loyalty.... The legacy of trained officials which the Sui inherited was lacking in eighth-century Europe." Arthur F., Wright, *The Sui dynasty*, 9.

The Chinese ideal of unity was mightily reaffirmed and never came into question thereafter. Dynastic decline under the T'ang, Sung, Yuan, and Ming led only and always to reunification, and the same denouement was expected after 1911.

The big new fact in modern China from the 1880s had been the spread of mass nationalism of the modern type based on China's ancient culturalism, as we have already noted, and fed by a modern press in urban centers.[44] Unity as the legitimator of dynasties took on a new stature, bigger by a hundredfold, as the symbol of the Chinese people's existence not only as a culture but now as a nation, which through international contact gradually superseded the province as the identifying focus of loyalty for the Chinese elite. The menacing imperialism of the 1890s culminating in the eight-nation anti-Boxer invasion of Peking in 1900 injected a new and overriding necessity into political life, the preservation of "China."[45] Soon the 1911 Revolution led to the falling away of the outlying regions of the old Ch'ing empire. Outer Mongolia and Tibet were both autonomous by 1913. A unified Chinese nation became the great public ideal to struggle for. The common people's participation in politics, activated by the successive disorders of warlordism, revolution, Japanese invasion, and KMT-CCP civil war, revived the ideal of unity with a vengeance. By 1949, when people wanted peace at any price, China's tradition was such that only a unified central government could provide it

To create a central power over China's fissiparous terrain required leadership capable of reactivating bureaucratic administration. To achieve such leadership required the practice of coalition politics, the extension on an ever-wider basis of the network of personal relationships that began with the unifier's original faction. As this central faction spread its tentacles, active local leaders in outlying provinces and regions became attached to it, ever more firmly as the new cause neared its goal.[46] The lore of earlier dynastic foundings provided a full repertoire of situations and responses, requirements and strat-

44 Hao Chang, *Liang Ch'i-ch'ao and intellectual transition in China, 1890–1907*, 5–6.
45 See Mary Clabaugh Wright, "Introduction: the rising tide of change," pp. 1–6 in *China in revolution: The first phase 1900–1913*. Themes adumbrated in this pioneer volume are pursued in the *Cambridge History of China (CHOC)*, vol. 11.
46 Case studies of factionalism in China are still few. See Lucian Pye, *The dynamics of Chinese politics*; also his *The dynamics of factions and consensus in Chinese politics: A model and some propositions*, mainly post-Mao. Factions as personal power groupings were often animated by moral righteousness (*ch'ing-i*). For one famous instance, see Charles O. Hucker, "The Tung-lin movement of the late Ming period," pp. 132–62 in Fairbank, ed., *Chinese thought and institutions*. On *ch'ing-i* and the Ch'ing-liu faction, see Lloyd E. Eastman, *Throne and mandarins*, 16–29, and ch. 8. The "Gang of Four" in the Cultural Revolution provides a recent example.

agems for the new unifying faction to utilize. As its control spread, however, it soon reached a point where it could be consolidated and maintained only by the institution of bureaucratic government. Taken all together, the history of past dynastic foundings predisposed the Chinese people to expect and welcome a return of central power. The spawning of independent political offshoots, though it had often occurred, was not sanctioned by history. Since the unit of self-determination was now the entire society, this provided fertile soil for the rapid growth of modern mass nationalism in the twentieth century.

To simplify this situation, let us assert that at least two major features made China different: First was the strength of the Chinese tradition of comprehensive imperial rule. Second was the great size of the politically inert rural population – both its proportion relative to the urban and ruling elements of the society (say, 80 percent) and its absolute size (say, 325 million ca. 1900, 400 million ca. 1940). No other country had ever had so large and dense a rural population before the full onset of modern industrialization with its customary doubling or tripling of numbers.[47]

Thus from the very start in 1949 the Chinese Communist Party was saddled with a gargantuan task: Its legitimacy as a regime would rest, like that of its predecessors, on making good its claim to rule all China. Never mind that the population was rapidly doubling and by 1980 would total a billion people. Never mind that the rather new (since 1885) province of Taiwan was 100 miles overseas in rival hands protected by a hostile naval power. The precedents of history were compelling. Since "China has stood up!" it must again be a political unit under a central power. After all, the Ch'ing empire had broken up only thirty-seven years before. (After the Ch'ing came to power in Peking in 1644, Taiwan was not taken over until thirty-nine years later.) In 1949, reunification, feasible or not, was naturally first on the agenda.

Fortunately for the CCP, the modern development of transport and communications, of firepower and police networks, had given the new government of the People's Republic various means to control the Chinese state and, for a time, the society. Most important and equally necessary as means of control, these material facilities had grown up accompanied by a new view of the world, indeed of several

47 By the sixteenth century, most estimates suggest a Chinese population already double that of Europe proper; see Albert Feuerwerker, "The state and the economy in late imprial China," *Theory and Society*, 13 (1984), 297–326, esp. 300–1.

competing views of the world. Yet most patriots agreed that China should be a nation-state like the other major nation-states. This goal required that China's inherited culture be drastically revised and reshaped into a new orientation that would synthesize many elements of foreign as well as Chinese origin. Although in this chapter we are trying to look only at a restricted political sector of China's history, we cannot avoid looking also at the broader context subsumed under the term *modernization*.

THE ROLE OF MODERNIZATION

The term "modernization" is constantly on our tongues, but like "life," "time," or even "culture," it is a term with fuzzy edges. The fact that it is hard to define specifically does not seem to diminish the popular use of it. China's adoption in the early 1980s of the "four modernizations" as a national program (modernization of agriculture, industry, science and technology, and the military) requires that we try to sharpen our definition of this protean word.[48]

To begin outside China, the Industrial Revolution of the early nineteenth century had obviously outgrown the sphere of industry. After World War II the application of technology to national growth and international relations took the name of "development." In the 1950s, "modernization" was popularized as a term implying the overcoming of tradition, the substitution through technology of new ways for old. For a time it was felt that all industrializing societies were so in the grip of modern technological development that there would be a convergence of conditions worldwide, even though cultural residues would show superficial differences among the various peoples.[49] By the 1960s, however, it was becoming apparent that the peoples of different cultures coped with modernization and made use of modern technology in quite different ways under the influence of the deep-lying structures of their own cultural values and inherited institutions. These, of course, were not unchanging, but they appeared to change more slowly than the material gadgetry and processes associated with modernization.

48 The principal symposium, edited by Gilbert Rozman, is *The modernization of China*. The Institute of Modern History, Academia Sinica, Taipei, is publishing a series on modernization in various provinces.
49 The stages set forth in W. W. Rostow's *The stages of economic growth* were applied to China by him and others in *The prospects for Communist China*. Comparative development had been adumbrated by a journalist, Grover Clark, in his *A place in the sun*, based on his *The balance sheet of imperialism: Facts and figures on colonies*.

In recent years it has become plain that modernization, however defined, can be accepted only as a part of the forces of modern history. This is because the studies of modernization comparing different countries were obliged to center upon the most obvious changes that these countries had shared in the modern period. These changes were preeminently those that could be quantified, since numbers are most easily comparable. Consequently, population growth, urbanization, roads, rail traffic, factory production, and gross national product were parts of the economic and material complex of modernization.[50] When scholars looked from economic development to political development, they could no longer so easily quantify and compare the processes at work. Readership of newspapers, voting in elections, devotion to the nation-state, acceptance of science and technology, and the rise of individualism were subjects that became increasingly more difficult to quantify. Students confronted the aspects of society that changed more slowly and were more difficult to measure. Here it became evident that cultural configurations, like geographical terrain, have great persistence and indeed inertia, and thus there emerged a substratum above which the evidences of modernization were superficial. Motifs of religious belief, law and morality, as well as family systems and ideals of conduct, were parts of an underlying hard core of each culture. These core perceptions of the relationship of the individual to the state and the family were capable of change at only a slower rate.

In the modernization of China, we consequently confront an amalgam of old and new. Mule carts with ball-bearing wheels and auto tires were more efficient vehicles. Things foreign had to be adapted to native uses. At a more abstract level, the notions of "equality" and "participation" are likely to have different meanings when applied to China. The differential rate of change between elements of material modernization and elements of the cultural orientation thus sets the stage for students of the Chinese revolution. Scholars have theorized about the Chinese revolution from either a Western or a Chinese perspective, but neither approach has described it adequately.

From this brief sketch of Chinese experience in facing China's modern problem of adjustment to the outside world, we may draw certain tentative conclusions. The first is that the Chinese ruling class was able within a remarkably short time to give up the tenets of

50 See Cyril Black, *The modernization of Japan and Russia.*

traditional Confucianism and accept the tenets of outside nations as the new language to embody their patriotic purposes. Since 1900 the writings of Chinese reformers and revolutionaries have increasingly used Western ideas and subject matter.[51] The conscious thought of these patriots has coursed over the world seeking whatever ideas may help China. But while Chinese tradition in written form had been largely discredited as the guide to modern times, in fact the Chinese value system, the status of the individual vis-à-vis government, the dominance of the patrilineal family system in the villages, and a hundred other features of Chinese life have shown remarkable continuity. People sing different words to the same old tunes. The change has been greater in the realm of conscious thought than in that of daily conduct.

In the Chinese revolution, in short, we confront a problem where the use of customary categories like continuity versus discontinuity or indigenous versus exogenous do not help us. To be sure, at first glance the foreign and the innovative have seemed to confront the domestic and the traditional. Yet on closer inspection of late imperial times we may find innovations arising within native traditions, such as the entrance of the old gentry landlord-scholar-official class into commerce and local administration, while also finding foreign influences supporting ancient traditions, as when the gunboat, telegraph, and firearms are used to suppress peasant rebels. The resulting quandary may be exemplified by noting the Chinese application to modern history of the rubrics of inner (*nei*) and outer (*wai*). These two categories have, of course, been fundamental in Chinese thinking, which has been rather given to categories, since the most ancient times. In the nineteenth century *wai* easily encompassed things foreign, such as the opium trade, imperialism and wars, the treaty system, the Westernization (*yang-wu*) movement, Social Darwinism, liberalism, communism, and modernization.[52] The reader will note, however, that these phenomena display a tendency to move from a distinctly *wai* status to become eventually rather *nei*. The opium trade indeed moved into China, where native-grown opium made the Anglo-Indian import less in demand. *Nei* and *wai* proved to be

51 See Scalapino and Yu, *Modern China*.
52 The encyclopedia of government compiled by Chang Shou-yung and others published in 1902, *Huang-ch'ao chang-ku hui-pien* (Collected historical records of the imperial dynasty) is divided in two parts: inner (*nei-pien* in 60 *chüan*) and outer (*wai-pien* in 40 *chüan*). Everything new and even remotely concerned with foreign relations or foreign activities within China is in the *wai* part.

shifting sands. Western technology and then ideas were put to Chinese uses. Eventually, Mao Tse-tung in his application of Marxism to China was obliged to base his revolution not on the proletariat, as communism prescribed, but on the poor peasantry.

This problem can be met only by accepting a hybrid theory of modernization. In certain ways the world is obviously becoming one under the impact of modern technology, yet in other ways the world remains seriously divided among cultures and peoples. We are, I believe, forced to the structuralist position that Chinese society is based on ancient structures of social order and political values that are too deep for rapid change to transform them quickly. What Eisenstadt and others call the "core perceptions" change more slowly than material technology and the trappings of international modernity.[53]

This differential rate of change between core and superstructure is remarked upon by Marxist analysts, but with a reverse emphasis: that the material mode of production eventually determines the non-material class structure and values – legal, religious, political, and social. This difference in emphasis should not obscure the fact that Marxist and non-Marxist tend to deal with the same categories. Their understandings of the revolutionary process are not so far apart as to be mutually unintelligible or prohibit discussion.[54]

We can best illustrate the revolutionary process under conditions of hybrid modernization by singling out the changes in one typical aspect of China's deep-lying social structure, namely, the individual's subordination to the collectivity of family and state. While the rise of individualism is by no means an entire explanation of the revolutionary process, it can serve as a convenient example of it.

The litany of the individual's emancipation from the old society may well begin with the emancipation of women. Their degraded status was well symbolized by the custom of foot-binding which crippled them from childhood, made them less effective as manual workers, and yet was practiced so widely among the Han Chinese peasantry that its incidence has generally been estimated at 80 per

---

53 Prof. S. N. Eisenstadt's writings include *Modernization: Growth and diversity; Modernization: Protest and change;* and *Revolution and the transformation of societies: A comparative study of civilizations.* For an appreciation of his work, see Thomas A. Metzger, "Eisenstadt's analysis of the relations between modernization and tradition in China," in *Li-shih hsueh-pao,* no. 12 (June 1984), 348–418.

54 Within the Marxist camp, the relationship of Mao's thought to earlier socialist and Soviet ideas is analyzed in Brantly Womack, *The Foundations of Mao Zedong's political thought 1917–1935.* See also Stuart Schram, *The political thought of Mao Tse-tung,* and Arthur A. Cohen, *The communism of Mao Tse-tung.*

cent or more. Since the practice began at the capital in the court, its subsequent spread is presumed to have been first among the ruling class. Thus its prevalence among the peasantry in the nineteenth century seemed to confirm the idea that the ruling class set the style and the peasants followed it.

The anti-foot-binding movement which began in the 1880s and became vigorous in the twentieth century was fostered partly by missionaries, who saw the problem at first hand. The Western missionary brought into the Chinese scene a concern for the individual soul and fostered the rise of a Chinese Christian community that embraced Christian values. Meanwhile the feminist movement in the West was trying to get legal and electoral rights for women in the same early decades of the century when Chinese reformers were trying to stop the deforming of girls' feet.[55] Another step in female emancipation was the reform of marriage customs. By the time of the New Culture movement of 1917–21, this had become part of the rebellion of youth against family domination. Freedom of personal choice in marriage was still another innovation.

A degree of independent, even unorthodox, political thinking had raised its head first among the scholar class of the late eighteenth and early nineteenth centuries. Under the patronage of high officials, scholars of the Han learning in particular formed academic groups and contributed to a literati opinion that became somewhat independent of the imperial power.[56] This purely Chinese movement lay behind the later rise of the professions distinct from the public service. For example, in the late nineteenth century a noteworthy series of Chinese from Hong Kong became barristers with London law degrees. Surgeons received training at the early missionary hospitals. Journalists developed in the Treaty Ports. During the interregnum in central government between 1912 and 1949, the influx of foreign examples and the demands of modern life combined to nurture a new urban intelligentsia of writers, artists, and other professional people not in government service. As revolutionaries surfaced to become political leaders and military men received education as part of their training, China's old social structure was undermined on many fronts. In short, out of the stratum of the literati-official ruling class there emerged upper-class individuals of many types, some of whom in the 1900s embraced the ideas of Western

55 Howard S. Levy, *Chinese footbinding*.
56 Benjamin Elman, *From philosophy to philology*.

liberalism while studying abroad and returned to China with the ideal, for example, of using science for the salvation of China.[57]

A further step came with the concern of the new intellectuals for the emancipation of the peasantry. The movement of young revolutionary intellectuals into the villages began sporadically in the 1920s and became systematized under the Chinese Communist Party as one of its keys to mobilizing a new central power. Fostering this growth of contact was the major fact of modern means of communication. The railroad and then the bus line gave the urban intellectual access to the village communities. The telegraph and the press and then radio brought the villages into the network of news about the national and outside world, just as the growth of international trade had made farm production gradually and increasingly dependent on international prices for silk, tea, cotton, and other farm products. Even the conscripting of troops to serve in warlord armies broke the crust of village parochialism. The new world of the twentieth century, in brief, provided the means for peasant participation in a wider world.[58]

Nevertheless, the new roles for the Chinese individual that developed in this way remained, as suggested above, within a framework of great respect for Chinese cultural values and acceptance of familial claims and central authority. Social and political duties contrived to outweigh the appeal of Western doctrines of individual rights.

The mixture in practice: modern forms of old motifs

In order to give the past its due (as a guide for, or incubus upon the backs of, Chinese leaders), let us now look at a selection of problems that China's unifiers had often if not usually confronted as they came to supreme power. Examples can, of course, be selected from two millennia of history to illustrate almost any feature one fancies. Let us try, however, to characterize the major transition periods with an eye to three problem areas that also confronted the CCP: (1) the unifier's relations with his colleagues, (2) the degree of haste and excess in his efforts, and (3) his control of the military. The combination of these features differed in each dynastic case.

The first of these problems arose from the fact that no man ever

---

57 See Marianne Bastid, "Currents of social change," in *CHOC*, 11. 536–602. On saving China through science, see D. W. Y. Kwok, *Scientism*.
58 Lucien Bianco, *Origins of the Chinese revolution*.

took the empire singlehanded. Every unifier began as leader of a faction, primus inter pares. Yet once he assumed Heaven's mandate, the political system demanded that he be on another plane, suddenly above mankind and performing a superhuman role. For close associates who had known him when, this might be hard to take if the new emperor had not in fact already begun to act imperiously and set himself distinctly apart from his followers.[59] However, it was in the nature of factionalism to recognize this hierarchic distinction and join up as a follower, not as a junior partner. This loyal subservience was expected particularly from scholar-advisers who gave their military leader the capacity to become a lawgiver and initiate civil government.

The fact that a unifier came to power as head of a group of supporters and associates set the stage for his post-takeover relations with them. Chinese chroniclers make it clear that no Son of Heaven gained power without the help of sage counselors and able administrators. The First Emperor profited from the earlier Legalist reforms of Shang Yang, the leading Ch'in official (361–338 B.C.) who imposed upon the populace a system of strict rewards and punishments plus collective responsibility and hence spying and mutual informing upon one another. After Ch'in had conquered its last rival in 221 B.C., the First Emperor's adviser Li Ssu abolished all the old states (*kuo*) and their kings (*wang*) and divided China into 36 commanderies (*chün*) which were subdivided into *hsien* (translated later as counties), each typically a walled town and its surrounding countryside. Li Ssu also standardized the writing system, opposed private learning, instituted a literary inquisition that burned the books of non-Legalist thought, and is credited with burying dissident scholars alive. When the hyperactive and megalomaniac First Emperor died in 210 B.C., Li Ssu joined with the chief eunuch to engineer the succession, but the eunuch soon did away with him.[60]

After the Ch'in collapsed amidst widespread disaffection engendered by its excesses, the commoner, Liu Pang, who founded the Han in 206 B.C., at first backtracked. To satisfy his supporters, he "abandoned centralized control over the Empire and revived the political feudalism of the Chou dynasty." Almost two-thirds of the Han territory was divided into *wang-kuo* or "kingdoms," ruled over by the founder's brothers, sons, nephews, and assistants. Only later were

59 See Harold Kahn, *Monarchy in the emperor's eyes.*
60 On Li Ssu, see Kung-chuan Hsiao, tr F. W. Mote, *A history of Chinese political thought*, vol. 1, *From the beginnings to the sixth century A.D.*, 434–46.

these kingdoms reincorporated into the imperial administration. The Han rulers, though continuing to use Legalist practices, combined them with the Confucian teachings in the potent amalgam known as imperial Confucianism.[61]

The leader of the Sui reunification in 589, a general named Yang Chien, was, like the First Emperor of the Ch'in, unable to limit his ambitious demands upon the people. His rise was aided by a senior general of a preceding state named Kao Chiung who won crucial battles and guided the new emperor's regime at every step; also by a notably strict and ruthless commander named Yang Su, who set the custom of beheading all soldiers who retreated; and a more humane Confucian ideologist-administrator named Su Wei. In brutal haste the two Sui emperors (Sui Wen-ti, 589–604, and Sui Yang-ti, 605–18) drove their people unmercifully to complete their conquests and build the canals and capital city to sustain their central power. These ruthless exactions roused rebellion and gave the T'ang rulers who followed a memorable object lesson in how to try too much too fast. T'ang rule (618–906) could be longer lasting because it was more moderate, once Sui had again set up the structure of central government.[62]

After the T'ang collapse in 906, the Sung founder, Chao K'uang-yin, gave a sterling example of how to hamstring the power of the military so that centralized civilian control could be maintained in a time of peace. Chao had been commander of the palace guard. After it made him emperor (T'ai-tsu, 960–76) he pensioned off his generals, replaced the military governors with civil officials, and concentrated the troops in a new palace army while building up the civil service examinations and bureaucracy and centralizing the revenues.[63]

The Mongol and Manchu minorities who set up the alien dynasties of Yuan (1279–1368) and Ch'ing (1644–1912) were, of course, on their mettle to remain warlike and impervious to miscegenation. The Mongols collapsed after 89 years, but the Manchus succeeded in ruling for 268 years, in part because the Manchu military were kept under more strict control. Another part of the Manchu success lay in

---

61 Wang Yü-ch'üan, "An outline of the central government of the Former Han dynasty," *HJAS*, 12 (1949), 134–87.
62 Arthur F., Wright, *Sui dynasty.*
63 For Chao K'uang-yin's role in the triumph of civil over military power, see Edmund H. Worthy, Jr., "The founding of Sung China." Also Charles O. Hucker, *China's imperial past: An introduction to Chinese history and culture*, 267–71. On the Sung military, see "Introduction," 45–48, in Hucker, *A dictionary of official titles in Imperial China*; and Karl A. Wittfogel and Feng Chia-sheng, *History of Chinese society: Liao (907–1125)*, 535 and passim.

superior ability to recruit Chinese collaborators. Having done so in their territorial base outside the Wall, the Manchus' experience of administration had already prepared them to govern China.

Like every new regime, the Manchus faced the problem of what to do with the defeated elements of the old establishment and how to recruit, train, and ensure the loyalty of a new bureaucracy. After 1368, when Mongol rule collapsed in civil war, the Ming founder had revived the examination system that the Mongols had been unable to rely upon. When the Ming collapsed 276 years later, the Manchu conquerors of 1644 left the Ming gentry and bureaucracy largely in place, savagely destroyed the Ming holdouts in the lower Yangtze, and continued to recruit Chinese civil administrators through the examinations. When the K'ang-hsi Emperor came to power after 1667, he inserted his dynasty at the top of the Chinese society and culture with minimal disruption.[64]

Mao Tse-tung likened himself, rather impudently (perhaps to terrify the scholars), to the First Emperor, but his career resonates more clearly with that of the Ming founder, Chu Yuan-chang, a commoner whose life began in poverty when his family was largely wiped out by famine and pestilence. Chu got his meager education in a Buddhist monastery and had some contact with the secret sects of the Manicheans (Ming-chiao) and White Lotus (Pai-lien chiao). As disorder spread, in 1352 he joined a local leader, married this man's foster daughter, and succeeded to his command in 1355. The next year Chu seized Nanking and made it his capital; and in the next decade defeated rival warlords both up and down the Yangtze. Throughout his rise he added able scholars to his staff and after 1360 also created a ruthless secret service with police and judicial powers.

Once in power, Chu Yuan-chang denounced all secret sects. He intimidated Ming officialdom by having even high officials cere-monially beaten in open court. His suspicions grew to paranoid proportions. In 1380 he had his chancellor (Hu Wei-yung) and alleged accomplices executed and "more than thirty thousand people allegedly involved in Hu's case were ferreted out by the secret police over a period of fourteen years." In 1385 a vice-minister of revenue

64 See Wakeman, "Introduction: The evolution of local control in late imperial China," 1–25; Wakeman, "Localism and loyalism during the Ch'ing conquest of Kiangnan: The tragedy of Chiang-yin," 43–85; and Jerry Dennerline, "Fiscal reform and local control; The gentry-bureaucratic alliance survives the conquest," 86–120, all in Frederic Wakeman, Jr., and Carolyn Grant, eds., *Conflict and control in late imperial China*; also Jonathan D. Spence and John E. Wills, Jr., eds., *From Ming to Ch'ing: Conquest, region, and continuity in seventeenth-century China.*

and hundreds of others were executed on charges of embezzlement. In 1393 a veteran general (Lan Yü) who had repeatedly defeated Mongols and other rebels on several frontiers and been rewarded and ennobled accordingly, was executed along with more than fifteen thousand others, including several high commanders, on charges of plotting usurpation. Historians have concluded that the emperor used this case "as a pretext to destroy the last vestiges of the corporate independence of the military."[65]

Without adducing further details (which often spoil grand conclusions), let us suggest that Mao's achievements as a reunifier are in a special class along with those of the First Emperor after 221 B.C. and of the Sui founder after A.D. 589. Both were in a towering hurry to reorganize China, both pushed their people too far too fast, wore out their initial welcome, and left it to later rulers to mop up after them. Yet Mao's twenty-seven years in power, during which he turned against his comrades and all but destroyed the CCP for evils of "bureaucratism" and "revisionism," has also some striking resemblances to the Ming founder's thirty-year reign.

What we call "revolution" is of course usually identified by the striking discontinuities portrayed in events. Mao's decision in 1949 to "lean to one side" and set China to learning from a foreign land, the Soviet Union, seemed at the time to be a sharp break with the past. Yet preceding generations of Chinese leaders had accepted foreign models from Britain, France, Japan, America, and other sources. But in 1949 Mao and his colleagues of the CCP, as successful revolutionaries, were conscious of their creative capacities and the new needs of a new era. Their underlying problem in making history anew was how to break out of the parameters of China's past politics. China was far from being the "blank page" upon which, Mao boasted, new things could be written at will. On the contrary, even Mao's presumption of his power of innovation was characteristic of a new Son of Heaven. His repertoire of possible acts, though enormous, had its limits and, in the circumstances of the day, its

---

65 Article by Teng Ssu-yü in L. Carrington Goodrich and Chaoying Fang, eds., *Dictionary of Ming biography, 1368–1644*, 381–92. Edward L. Dreyer and Hok-lam Chan in *DMB*, 788–91. John W. Dardess, *Confucianism and autocracy: Professional elites in the founding of the Ming dynasty*, quotes at length the paranoid rationalizations by which Ming T'ai-tsu justified in Confucian terms his execution of innumerable subjects. On the other hand, Hung Wu was a developer; he sent Imperial Academy students out over the empire to encourage local public works. By 1395 completion was reported of work on 40,987 reservoirs and ponds, 4,162 projects on rivers and 5,048 on canals, dikes, and banks. See Lien-sheng Yang, "Economic aspects of public works in imperial China," 191–248 in his *Excursions in sinology*, esp. 199.

probabilities. For example, given the fact that one man had to be at the top, it was also a fact that most of Mao's predecessors had found it useful to be the objects of a religious cult.

Modern innovations must be viewed within the perspective of China's local scene. Despite the new ideas, terms, and even cosmology in the revolutionaries' minds, Chinese life has continued to show unusual continuity and historical consciousness. In self-image China differs profoundly from Europe and the Americas because its geographical base has been so constant. The westward course of empire from the ancient East to the modern West, from the Old World to the New, has no counterpart in China's experience. Chinese society suffered no geographical displacement of its center comparable to that from Athens to Rome or London to Washington. When Mao's Long March entered Shensi, thirty centuries looked down upon the loess canyons from which the Chou conquerers had once emerged. The historical precedents lying behind a Chinese reunification stretch back into the past with as much vital immediacy as if, in an American presidential election campaign, we knew that Caesar, Charlemagne, King John, and Henry VIII had all in their time sought central power by running for president across the rivers and plains and in the towns and cities of New York and Virginia, Ohio and Illinois. In China, the past is present in a way Westerners can hardly imagine.

If we now approach the CCP takeover of 1949 with these patterns in mind, we may well conclude not only that history was on the side of the takeover but that new modern factors arising in the twentieth century also aided it. First, in traditional terms, political conditions were ripe. The Chinese people had had little peace since 1911 and widely craved it. Meanwhile, the CCP after 1921 had become an integrated regime. It had known four years of revolutionary struggle under the first united front, 1923–27; a decade of warfare against the Nationalists, 1927–37; eight years of the second united front fighting Japan, 1937–45; and four years of civil war against the Nationalists, 1946–49. These twenty-six years of unremitting struggle and the experience of governing part of Kiangsi and later parts of North China had prepared the CCP to seize and wield power.[66]

Second, in modern social terms, Chinese nationalism had come of age, heightened by China's pervasive culturalism, the sense of cultural identity and former superiority. Profound changes in social structure had weakened the hold of the patrilineal extended family lineage

66 See L. Van Slyke, ch. 12 in *CHOC*, 13.

over women and youth. New professional roles had been acknowledged for the military, businessmen, teachers, literary and artistic intellectuals, publishers and journalists, even revolutionaries and party
members.

Meanwhile, in terms of foreign technology, innovations had moved
on from the use of steam power in industrial production and transportation by ship and rail to the use of the internal combustion engine
in buses and airplanes. Telegraphs and electric lighting had been
followed by the telephone and radio. Provision of urban services of
paving, street lighting, plumbing and sewage, public education, and
health care had been accompanied by modernized police and judicial
systems as well as a daily press, magazines, popular fiction, and a
cinema industry. Higher education and scientific research had paralleled the growth of extractive and manufacturing industries, banking
and investment, and government capacities to finance the extension of
military power and bureaucratic administration. All this growth and
change were fostered by population increase and by growing intercourse with the outside world. In the 1940s the political symptoms
of decline of central power dominated the public scene while the
potential for a new and more modern order of life and government
steadily accumulated, awaiting integration under a new regime.

Soldiers and students, it may be suggested, were to be building
blocks of the new regime. The twentieth century had seen a trend of
increasing militarism. When the Ch'ing empire was suddenly decapi-
tated by the removal of the Son of Heaven, Yuan Shih-k'ai became
China's strong man by virtue of his having trained the Peiyang Army.
Only he in 1912 could promise to maintain order and thwart foreign,
presumably Japanese, aggression. Warlordism after 1916 spawned
even larger armies. The Nationalist revolution achieved its Northern
Expedition from Canton to the Yangtze only after Soviet military aid
and the Whampoa Academy had produced a KMT party army to
be its spearhead. Indoctrinated in Dr. Sun's Three Principles of
Nationalism, Democracy, and the People's Livelihood, the Whampoa
cadets and Soviet aid formed the nucleus of Chiang's military power.
After China's nominal unification under the Nanking government in
1928, the effort at troop disbandment failed, and thereafter the armed
forces of Nanking, Manchuria, Kwangsi, and other sectors grew until
the War of Resistance to Japan finally militarized both the KMT and
the CCP regimes. In the end China's reunification came by force of
arms. After the CCP lost out in the first united front of the 1920s

because it had no army of its own, the lesson had been learned. In 1949, its armies reunified China.[67]

The production of modern students was far less simple. In the late imperial era the inherited edifice of the Chinese state began to fall apart most notably at the upper level, where the examination system had ordinarily produced scholars self-indoctrinated in the grand principles of social order and imperial Confucianism. The necessity to adopt Western learning and technology to strengthen China against the imperialist invaders ended the classical examinations in 1905. The subsequent attempt to set up a school system modeled on that of Japan was hampered by the weakness of central government under the late Ch'ing and early Republic. By that time, moreover, learning from Japan had begun to give way to learning directly from Western Europe and North America. To the Japanese-influenced educational reorganization of 1904 were added European academic ideals after 1911; and in 1922 Chinese higher education was reorganized again on the American model. Urbanization meanwhile was further differentiating modern city life from still traditional rural life. The top class of scholars who returned from abroad were often deracinated intellectuals trained to teach students for life abroad, rather than in China. They usually lacked the field experience, ideas, textbooks, and methods suited to China's rural needs. The result during the first two decades of the Republic was a buildup of higher education largely on foreign models that widened the gap between the highly selected and foreignized upperclass elite and the still largely illiterate rural masses.[68]

By the time the Nationalist government began in 1928 to revive a central power at Nanking, the modern universities had achieved a considerable degree of autonomy, either as Christian colleges financed partly from abroad, or as private Chinese institutions like Nankai University at Tientsin, or as national universities like Peita (Peking University) or Tsing-hua (financed by returned American

67 See P. A. Kuhn on the militarization of the orthodox elite, 105–64 in *Rebellion and its enemies in late imperial China: Militarization and social structure, 1796–1864*. On later developments, see Kwang-Ching Liu, "The military challenge: The North-west and the coast," ch. 4 in *CHOC*, 11, esp. 202–11 on "Ch'ing armies of the post-Taiping era." Militarism under the KMT was first analyzed by Ch'ien Tuan-sheng, *The government and politics of China*.
68 This theme of deracination, though perhaps overstressed by Y. C. Wang, *Chinese intellectuals and the West 1872–1949*, was a constant motif in the experience of returned students as well as revolutionaries. See Jerome Grieder, *Chinese intellectuals and the state*; Jonathan Spence, *The Gate of Heavenly Peace*.

Boxer indemnity funds), which enjoyed a special prestige in North China. The collapse of the KMT came partly from its inability to mobilize, inspire, and use China's intellectual talent.[69]

When the CCP in 1949 inherited the task of creating a new politically loyal managerial elite to staff a bureaucracy capable of governing China's masses, the old elite of the late imperial era, the literati self-indoctrinated in the Confucian classics, had long since disappeared, along with the Ch'ing empire. In their place modern times had produced an intelligentsia of varied loyalties and outlooks – journalists, writers, scientists, administrators, military, politicians – professional people nurtured in the learning and traditions not only of the old China but also variously of Japan, Western Europe, America, and Russia. Emperors had faced constant problems in the nurture and manipulation even of the Confucian-tinged literati. China's new intelligentsia were far less easy to control and utilize. Throughout the twentieth century, their ambivalent relations with government had been a central focus of strain between their roles as loyal servants of the state and as autonomous scholar-specialists. Republican China's multiform intelligentsia not only demonstrated how Chinese talent could catch up with modernity arising outside the country, but also could assume professional roles in a politically fragmented and therefore to some degree pluralistic new society. The Peking and Tientsin professors, even when they had migrated to form the Southwest Associated University (Lien-ta) at Kunming in war-time, continued to see themselves as exemplars both of modern Western academic freedom and of Chinese political morality.[70]

With its much tighter discipline, the CCP's claim to dominate the new intelligentsia had been asserted in Yenan. But after the CCP came to power in 1949 it would face a continuing dilemma: Intellectuals were needed for their skills in teaching, science, literature, and the arts, but they were not the most reliably loyal followers of the Party line. Systemically, they were not really successors to the self-indoctrinated examination graduates of the late imperial era, whose role as servants of the state had now been taken by the new class of cadres, activists in the CCP machine. While party dictatorship had taken the place of dynastic rule, the scholar class had

---

69 See E-tu Sun, "The rise of the academic community," ch. 13 in *CHOC*, 13.
70 John Israel, "An autonomous academy in a one-party state: The Lienta model," paper presented at the New England China Seminar workshop, "Chinese intellectuals and the CCP: The search for a new relationship," Harvard University, May 5, 1984. See also Merle Goldman, *China's intellectuals: Advise and dissent*, 3–9.

bifurcated into two groups – professional intellectuals and party cadres – who would now carry on the age-old struggle between the autonomy of the individual scholar and the state authority.

These considerations enable us to highlight the capacity for creative innovation that enabled China's leaders to meet both the traditional criteria of a dynastic reunification and the new requirements of social revolution and modernization coming in large part from abroad. These innovations began at least as early as the rise of the school of Han learning in the eighteenth and early nineteenth centuries, with its multifaceted reexamination of the hallowed classics and its questioning of the received consensus embodied in the Sung learning.[71] This growth of academies and their critics and iconoclasts was followed by the elite activism that had brought Chinese managerial talent into local administration in the late imperial era, especially after the beginning of the Taiping Rebellion in 1850.

In political discussion this trend was encouraged by the rise of a modern press in Hong Kong and the treaty ports, followed by the creation of patriotic study societies in the 1890s and of nascent political parties after 1898. The 1900s saw the rise of constitutionalism and the inauguration of local, provincial, and national assemblies. Although the open parties campaigning for parliament in the elections of 1912–13 were cut off, the Chinese Republic's early experiment in liberal representative government left precedents for posterity.[72] So also the flowering of liberal education during the warlord era, though decried by later power holders, was a seeming importation that nevertheless contained strong echoes of the Chinese past. The autonomy of scholarship was by no means a wholly foreign import, the remarkable Chinese talent for modern science and learning had ancient roots.

We have noted that the most spectacular of all twentieth-century innovations was the substitution of party dictatorship for rule by family dynasties. However, the first such powerholder, the KMT, remained riven by feuding factions almost as disastrously as the Mongol conquerors of the house of Chingis Khan. But the younger CCP until long after 1949 retained a notable cohesion of leadership. In short, a Chinese political tradition that had led the world in its early development of bureaucratic government proved quite capable

71 Elman, *From philosophy to philology*.
72 John H. Fincher, *Chinese democracy: The self-government movement in local, provincial and national politics 1905–1914*; Andrew J. Nathan, *Chinese democracy*; Mary H. Rankin et al., ch. 1, *CHOC*, 13.

in the twentieth century of creating a system of control suited to China's modern conditions. The proof lies in the fact that gargantuan China is still a single state.

This conclusion can, of course, be combined with the fact that China's revolutionary leaders chose the easiest path for creating a new China by keeping within the inherited framework of supreme authority, indoctrinated bureaucracy, and pervasive orthodoxy that could keep China in order. The Marxism that served as the modern form of this old motif, however, proved better at seizing and maintaining power than at economic modernization. Further innovation therefore ensued.

Because the chapters that follow in this volume focus mainly on the Chinese state and its policies under the rule of the CCP, let us look finally at the rural scene where the new central authority came into contact with the great mass of the Chinese people.

THE PROBLEM OF LOCAL CONTROL

China's size as a political entity suggests that our Western concentration upon the forms and vicissitudes of central government, so generally necessary and rewarding in the case of smaller countries, has brought us only part way to an understanding of Chinese political life. The fact is that the Chinese people, more than most, have therefore participated mainly in local, not central, government. There are few examples of the urban mob playing a political role in capital cities. The populace was, to be sure, the reservoir from which talent rose into the siphon of the examination system. But the world of the scholar-official entered by that route (as well as by purchase and nepotism) was a world apart, communicating in its own court dialect and official channels. The two strata of a myriad muscle workers and a selected few brain workers continued to bifurcate the society. For the modern revolution to escape from the trammels of history, it had to bring the rural masses into political life. This makes local government, the politics of the village and market center, a crucial topic, all the more so because it has been so relatively neglected.

Let us begin with the problem of the long-continued growth of the Chinese state, a phenomenon marked by a population total of roughly 200 million in 1750, 400 million in the 1840s, nearly 500 million in 1950, and a billion in 1982.

If we look first at the old local government structure, we find it focusing upon the *hsien* or county as the junction point where the lowest level of the imperial bureacracy met the local scene. In brief, as China's population had grown from the 60 million of Han times to the 400 million of the early twentieth century, the number of counties had not increased accordingly. Instead, it remained at a total of about 1,200 to 1,385, as though the imperial structure could not function with a greater number of bottom-level magistracies.[73] The result, at all events, was to inflate the population of the average county from roughly 40,000 people under the Han to a quarter of a million or so under the late Ch'ing. As the imperial authority embodied in the county (*hsien*) magistrate rose higher above the local scene, several devices had been used to induce among the people a degree of "self-control" (*tzu-chih*), an ambiguous term that is now usually translated "self-government." Actually, of course, for the people of their own accord to keep themselves in order may appear to some as self-government, while superior administrators may see the same situation as self-control. The most obvious Legalist devices were the collective responsibility systems created among the decimal hierarchies of families known as the *li-chia* for tax collection and labor services and the *pao-chia* for census registration and mutual surveillance. Meanwhile, in more Confucian terms, the family lineages were given legal responsibility for their members; and the local gentry degreeholders were accorded sociopolitical prestige to help them manage local matters of welfare, public works, defense, and order.

These devices, however, did not fill the widening gap between magistrate and populace. Being appointed usually for three-year terms and always outside their home provinces (by the so-called law of avoidance to reduce nepotism), magistrates commonly had neither kinship ties nor personal obligations in the local scene and all too easily might become purely career-oriented, not service-oriented, and often rapacious. Under such transient and alien masters, the local yamen underlings became self-serving and rapacious too. A magistrate who truly served the people thus became a paragon worthy of all praise. China's vaunted centralized bureaucracy (the *chün-hsien* system) suffered from endemic corruption and callousness.

To counter these evils, political philosophers like Ku Yen-wu of the early Ch'ing had urged a reversion to some aspects of the

---

73 G. William Skinner, ed., *The city in late imperial China*, 19. Skinner notes the "long-term secular trend beginning in the T'ang whereby the degree of official involvement in local affairs – not only in marketing and commerce but also in social regulation (e.g., dispute resolution) and administration itself – steadily declined, a retrenchment forced by the growing scale of empire"; ibid., 23.

feng-chien system ("feudal" decentralization of authority) of pre-Ch'in times. Ku advocated, for example, that magistracies be made hereditary so that the emperor's local agent would identify his interest with that of the local people. No one, however, succeeded in creating a new order at the village level.[74]

In this way certain residual features of the old polity would affect the new politics of revolutionary China. First of all, the continued need for unity in form and for the primacy of the center still required a fine-tuned balance between coercion and persuasion, between central domination and local acquiescence. A balance had been worked out during the millennia of the imperial era, which of course lay only one generation over the hill of history. As the imperial bureaucracy had been steadily thrust upward by growth of population, it had coopted as its local allies the composite degreeholding and landholding gentry class or local elite. This balance allowed the bureaucracy to be superficial so that the localities could be managed by gentry-level powerholders who had local roots and networks of influence, but who could not easily combine their small-scale local power with higher positions in the official ladder of administration. This isolation and confinement of the local ruling class to its locality was due partly, I suggest, to the frequently noted absence of midlevel institutions that could connect locality and center. In short, one secret strength of the late imperial regime was the gap it left between local-informal-commercial and central-formal-political institutions. There was no institutionalized political structure of market centers that could be stepping stones to the domination of a county. By having no formal structure below the county level, the imperial administration forestalled the domination of a county or a group of counties by rising local powerholders. In short, it may be suggested that the "backwardness" of political institutionalization below the county level was a defensive arrangement against the rise of particularism and the buildup under leading families of territorial bases of local control and potential aggrandizement.[75]

74 See a series of articles by Philip A. Kuhn: "Local self-government under the Republic: Problems of control, autonomy, and mobilization," in Wakeman, *Conflict and control*, 257–98; "Late Ch'ing views of the polity," in *Select papers . . . 4 (1979–80)*, 1–18; Philip A. Kuhn and Susan Mann Jones, "Introduction," *Select papers . . . 3 (1978–79)*, v–xix; and Philip A. Kuhn, "Local taxation and finance in Republican China," in ibid., 100–36. Ideas of Ku Yen-wu were taken up by the conservative reformer Feng Kuei-fen in the 1860s. See Kwang-ching Liu, "The Ch'ing Restoration," *CHOC*, 10. 487–88.

75 F. Mote, "Local power," in ch. 3, "Political structure," in Gilbert Rozman, ed., *The modernization of China*, 78–97. As to how the formal field administration was structured to contain informal commercial interests (as of 1893), see G. William Skinner, "Cities and the

This absence of local political institutionalization, so remarked upon by Western political scientists, went along with the Chinese lesser reliance on law and greater reliance on personal relations as the means for powerholding.[76] The importance of personal relations in turn meant that leadership could accrue to individuals who were moral exemplars of the official orthodoxy and so were tied in to the network of patron-client relationships and upward-looking loyalties that held together the bureaucracy and its hangers-on of the scholar-official or gentry class. In the final analysis, the organization of power by factions based on personal relations, rather than by law of a less personal nature, meant that the supreme powerholder must represent an absolute correctness of doctrine and conduct permitting of no imperfection (except what he himself acknowledged on the occasion of his ritual penance in the face of natural calamity). This amounted to saying that the ruler of the state embodied in himself the state power and claim to legitimacy of his regime. This made it impossible to admit the existence of a loyal opposition of the Western type that felt devoted to the state power but might oppose specific policies of the powerholder.

In this specifically Chinese situation, the CCP as a minority aspirant for supreme power was obliged either to join up in a united front in a subordinate position or else to turn to rebellion. The brief attempt in 1912–13 to set up representative party government had notably failed. Since dynasties were out of style, the only possible successor had to be a party dictatorship. The question for both KMT and CCP was whether they could raise up a new elite to substitute for the out-of-date gentry class at the local level.

Both parties had inherited from the late empire a trend toward gentry activism. By late Ch'ing times the glaring inadequacies of local government were being compensated for more and more by the

hierarchy of local systems," in Skinner, ed., *The city in late imperial China*, 275–351. One tactic was to divide each of 24 key cities between the jurisdictions of two counties. For another example, note how a thin leg of Chihli province extended southward between the commerical areas of Honan and Shantung (see 343–44). For a Japanese view of how the ruling class literati-elite became imbedded in local society, see Joshua A. Fogel, "A new direction in Japanese sinology," review of Tanigawa Michio, ed., *Chūgoku shitaifu kaikyū to chūki shakai to no kankei ni tsuite no sōgōteki kenkyū* (Studies on the relationship between the literati class and local society in China), in *HJAS*, 44.1 (June 1984), 225–47.

76 The intricate and sophisticated procedures of administrative laws within the imperial government are analyzed in Thomas A. Metzger, *The internal organization of Ch'ing bureaucracy: Legal, normative and communication aspects*. On the interpersonal networks, see James Polachek, *The inner Opium War*; Judith Whitbeck, "The historical vision of Kung Tzu-chen (1792–1841)," Ph.D. dissertation, U. of Calif. (Berkeley), 1980; and Elman, *From philosophy to philology*.

initiative of the local elite, outside strictly bureaucratic channels. Against the Taiping rebels, for example, local degreeholders had undertaken with the emperor's blessing to mobilize militia and create armies in which commanders at all levels felt personal bonds with their subordinates because they had themselves recruited them. In reconstruction after the suppression of midcentury rebellions, groups of gentry-managers took on tasks of local relief and rehabilitation, irrigation and flood control, and revival of agriculture and education. Indeed, the late Ch'ing saw a great efflorescence of local elite leadership in many aspects of modernization. In Volume 13 of this series it is argued that Chinese society by 1900 had begun to move out from under the confines of the old state domination of large-scale activity in economic, social, intellectual, and cultural matters. By the 1920s modern literature, higher education, commerce and industry, political discussion, and party recruitment were all advancing outside of central bureaucratic control.[77]

Republican China thus presented two faces to observers, who were predisposed to see one or the other. To the patriotic and plural-minded Westernizer, the small Chinese elite appeared heavily engaged in processes of modernization on a decentralized and pluralistic basis. In the early 1930s the Nanking government's efforts were still paralleled by those of foreign and Chinese business enterprise in the treaty ports and by missionary and other sino-foreign private efforts in medicine and education. All this growth, of course, seemed handicapped by the unreliability and malfeasance of local warlords and absence of central power, and so the other face the Republic presented to the patriotic observer of the 1910s and 1920s was the crying need for strong and enlightened central government.

This widespread demand fueled the Nationalist revolution of 1925–27 and conduced to China's nominal reunification under the Nanking government of 1928–37 and its leader, Chiang Kai-shek. The assumption that all public activity required official superintendence or leadership was thus reaffirmed. There had been many examples of this. In 1913 the frustrated first president of the Republic, Yuan Shih-k'ai, an old imperial official, had reasserted the tenets of centralized (*chün-hsien*) bureaucracy and so abolished the hundreds of small assemblies that had been set up by the gentry in the movement for constitutional government. After 1928 Chiang

---

77 On gentry activism, see P. A. Kuhn, *Rebellion*; and Mary Rankin, ch. 1 in *CHOC*, 13.

Kai-shek, a military man, once in power became fully engaged in the military politics of dealing first with rival warlords and then with Japanese militarist invaders. After he abandoned the first united front with the CCP, Chiang found no further use for the mass organizations that had helped his Northern Expedition, and let them wither away. Meanwhile, by having to absorb the armies and officials of the warlord era, the once revolutionary KMT became a catchall of opportunists and time servers, while Chiang sought to base himself on modern armies and personally loyal followers.

In this context local government received attention under the Nationalists mainly as an extension of central control downward, which greatly increased the burden of government without creating genuinely autonomous local organs capable of exercising initiative and inspiring support. The popular complaint throughout the modern era of reform from the 1890s to the 1940s was that upper-class and government reform programs constituted principally a further tax burden on the villagers, who saw little benefit to themselves from the roads, railroads, schools, clinics, and rural industries so admired by patriotic city people.[78] Amid wartime chaos Nationalist rule often deteriorated into cynical exploitation.[79]

The result was that the Chinese populace during the Japanese invasion and World War II became mobilized for political participation chiefly in the CCP areas. Yet here too the CCP's need to maintain its political control prevented genuinely autonomous self-government from ever taking root. Neither communist doctrine nor practice were inclined to depart from "officialism," the domination from the bureaucratic center, that had been the hallmark of Chinese political life since ancient times. The self-conscious tradition of governing the villages from the cities would continue to be the norm, even though the rural populace could take heart in a new doctrine of class struggle leading to peasant "liberation."

In the minds of CCP cadres at Yenan, however, there flourished the kind of enthusiasm for egalitarianism that had typified earlier popular movements. In some respects they were successors to the members of millennarian cults, individuals idealistically committed to a utopian vision and ready to share danger in pursuit of it. The novelty lay in their view of China's Marxist-Leninist revolution as

---

78 *CHOC*, 13, ch. 1 (Rankin), ch. 6 (Bianco).
79 Popular hatred of corrupt Nationalist powerholders was reported in detail. See Graham Peck, *Two kinds of time*; Theodore H. White and Annalee Jacoby, *Thunder out of China*.

a part of an international movement in the forefront of history. The new faith of these intellectuals in the revolution of the common man and the modern doctrine of liberation made them naturally concerned for the common people locally on whose support they were at the same time thoroughly dependent. Like previous rebels in Chinese history, they therefore cultivated a life style of egalitarian concern for the common man, and when they institutionalized measures for literacy, public health, military training, and food production, they made use of modern technology. Their ideas of scientific and social progress expressed a belief in human capacities for change. This essential ability to go among the common people and mobilize them in turn provided the basis for guerrilla warfare. The slogan of the New Culture of the World War I era, "science and democracy," seemed to some to be in process of realization under the CCP in North China during World War II.

Defeat of the KMT by Japan and the CCP

Basic to the fate of the rival party dictatorships was the fact of Japanese invasion of China. From 1931 this put the KMT government at Nanking under a heavy burden of defense through army-building and military industrialism. Most of all, the Japanese invasion required Chinese leadership by a military man. Chiang Kai-shek became the powerholder, and considerations of social revolution were shunted aside. Japan's attempt to conquer China was equally fateful for the CCP. Once the Communists had been dislodged from Kiangsi and had survived the Long March, their poverty-stricken habitat on the periphery of North China might have let them be starved out, had it not been for the Japanese invasion. In short, Japan supplied the major circumstance that led to KMT decline and to CCP survival, growth, and victory.

In comparison, the KMT fell behind in its competition as a party dictatorship to reunify and rule China for one principal reason: that it was an older organization, embedded in the outlooks and interests of an earlier time. The KMT dated from 1912 or before, the CCP from 1921 or later. Consequently, the KMT's failings were often mirror images of the Communist factors of success.

The KMT was a looser organization on which the structure of party dictatorship had been imposed only after the original party leaders of Sun Yat-sen's generation had spent twenty or thirty years in the chaotic, factional politics of the republican revolution and early Republic. Thus the KMT was a congeries of provincial groupings with a built-in factionalism almost impossible to eradicate. In ideology it was also transitory, combining the vaguely liberal Three Peoples Principles of Sun Yat-sen with a Leninist party structure and indoctrinated party army. The KMT thus was an amalgam of ingredients that could not stick together. The Soviet graft could not really take. While the Whampoa cadets staffed a party army, they found themselves intermingled with, and outnumbered by, nondescript warlord armies. Provided only with a vague Sun Yat-senism as ideology, they had to fall back on the ancient principle of loyalty to their commander. Similarly, KMT discipline in recruitment and indoctrination was woefully inadequate. The early KMT that came out of Canton was inundated, as noted above, by the taking in of local officials all across the land who simply could not be digested into the party structure and accept its discipline. Such promising new institutions as the mass organizations, once the Northern Expedition had succeeded, were allowed to disintegrate; patriotic youth were antagonized; and even the nascent capitalist class of the treaty ports were victimized rather than given opportunity under the Nanking government. The power structure soon became that of a warlord coalition subject to all the vicissitudes of armed factionalism.[80]

Imperialism also contributed to KMT weakness. The unequal treaty system, abolished only in 1943, impaired the Nanking government's sovereignty in a particularly insidious way by limiting its control of the preeminent economic center, Shanghai. The British-dominated Shanghai Municipal Council provided the modern public services, peace, and order to which foreigners pointed with pride. But the SMC was quite unable to organize and administer the social, economic, and political life of the tightly packed Chinese residents of Shanghai. At the same time, it prevented the warloads or the Nanking government from doing so. The result was the informal rule over the Chinese population of Shanghai by an underworld headed by the Green Gang (Ch'ing-pang). In the absence of a formal Chinese government able to pursue productive policies, the Shanghai underworld fed on crime, beginning with the illicit opium supply that was smuggled down the Yangtze from Szechwan and adjoining provinces. So lucrative was this traffic that it suborned not only Chinese, but

80 Parks M. Coble, *The Shanghai capitalists and the Nationalist Government, 1927–1937*; Marie-Claire Bergère, "The Chinese bourgeoisie 1911–37," in *CHOC*, 12. 722–825.

also some foreign authorities, especially in the French Concession
that lay between the old Chinese city and the International Settlement governed by the SMC. Battening on vice of all sorts, the
Green Gang, like the Mafia, existed for the sake of profit. In 1927 it
helped Chiang Kai-shek come to power and thereafter remained an
independent ally of the KMT regime.[81]

Nanking was also handicapped by having to take on the burden of
modernization at the same time that its resources went into the
attempt at military unification. Promising beginnings in the mid-
thirties like those of the military-industrial complex under the
National Resources Commission and German assistance were in any
case cut short by the Japanese war. The fate of the KMT was sealed
by the fact that it had become the government of a nominally unified
and nationalistic Chinese republic only a very few years before
Japanese militarism fell upon it as an obvious target for destruction.

Where the CCP had been reborn after 1927 in the ashes of defeat
and a bitter struggle for survival, and therefore had adopted a
stripped-down populist militarism as its only way forward, the KMT
lacked the motivation, the ideology, and the leadership that could
have enabled it to follow the CCP example. It was opposed to
people's war, opposed to class struggle and the mobilization of
villages on that basis, and not inspired by a doctrine of all-out
self-sacrifice for a common ideal. Being dependent already on foreign
trade for a substantial part of central government revenue, the
Nationalist regime could only enlarge its dependency on foreign
support, hoping for the Anglo-American defeat of the Japanese
invaders. American military aid as it swelled in volume made the
Nationalists increasingly dependent. This circumstance sapped their
innovative vitality, and moreover lost them credit in the eyes of
patriots.

Meanwhile the CCP in North China learned from experience. Its
cadres were young enough to follow new styles in thought and
practice. Because the CCP was isolated and Soviet aid indeed went
only to the Nationalist government, the Yenan regime learned to
modify Soviet doctrine to meet Chinese conditions. Through trial
and error it learned how to mobilize the villages by means of material
inducements, patriotic sentiment, egalitarian cooperation, military
control, and political manipulation.

81 For an early exposé, see Ernest O. Hauser, *Shanghai: City for sale*. Sterling Seagrave, from
    foreign sources only, has produced a sensationalized story of the Green Gang's pervasive
    influence: see his *The Soong dynasty*.

The creative performance of the CCP in the liberated areas and Border Region was like that of rebel movements of earlier times, but it occurred in new circumstances. The young intellectuals recruited as cadres at Yenan were separate from the city intelligentsia by choice, and they survived only by adapting themselves to local needs. From the first the CCP leadership maintained the domination of civil over military but attacked old custom in demanding that the leadership element cross class lines and work with their hands among the masses. Yenan democracy thus set a very practical and face-to-face style of social egalitarianism in support of a necessary party-military dictatorship. The CCP in practice survived by creating a new order at the village level. Abolition of private land ownership and state management of the labor force harked back to the "equal field system" of early T'ang in which equal allocation of land was primarily designed for the enhancement of government revenues through efficient allocation of labor. Previous rebels also had often been levelers. The Taipings had had the ideal of local groupings of 25 families each headed by a sergeant as the "building blocks of local society." But the Taipings were unable to apply their ideals and generally had to leave in place the local magnates who dominated the countryside. In contrast, the CCP through land reform wiped out the local land-based elite and established Party control.[82]

One great difference between China before and after 1949 would be that material means such as radio, other communications, and police firepower could be combined with ideological sanctions in the Soviet totalitarian form. This combination would now let the CCP state penetrate Chinese society as never before.

82 On the Taipings, see P. A. Kuhn in CHOC, 10. 278–79.

PART I

EMULATING THE SOVIET MODEL,
1949–1957

CHAPTER 2

ESTABLISHMENT AND CONSOLIDATION OF THE NEW REGIME

AN OVERVIEW

When the People's Republic of China (PRC) was formally established on October 1, 1949, the nation's new leaders faced daunting problems. Society and polity were fragmented, public order and morale had decayed, a war-torn economy suffered from severe inflation and unemployment, and China's fundamental economic and military backwardness created monumental impediments to the elite's goals of national wealth and power. Yet by 1957 the leaders of the Chinese Communist Party (CCP) could look back on the period since 1949 with considerable satisfaction. A strong centralized state had been established after decades of disunity, China's national pride and international prestige had grown significantly as a result of fighting the world's greatest power to a stalemate in Korea, the country had taken major steps on the road to industrialization and achieved an impressive rate of economic growth, the living standards of its people had made noticeable if modest progress, and the nation's social system had been transformed according to Marxist precepts in relatively smooth fashion.

Moreover, all this had been accomplished with only limited divisions within the Party elite. Thus Chairman Mao Tse-tung could convincingly claim at the Eighth CCP Congress in September 1956 that "we . . . have gained a decisive victory in the socialist revolution [and] our Party is now more united, more consolidated than at any time in the past."[1] A year later, intervening events and persistent problems set the stage for considerably enhanced elite conflict as the CCP began to evolve the bold new developmental strategy of the Great Leap Forward; yet Mao reaffirmed that the socialist revolution had been achieved,[2] while his leading colleague, Liu Shao-ch'i, plaus-

---

1 "Opening address at the Eighth National Congress of the Communist Party of China" (15 September 1956), in *Eighth National Congress of the Communist Party of China*, 1.7.
2 In his "Talk at a meeting with Chinese students and trainees in Moscow" (17 November 1957), in *CB*, 891. 26, Mao declared that the victory represented by the change of ownership

51

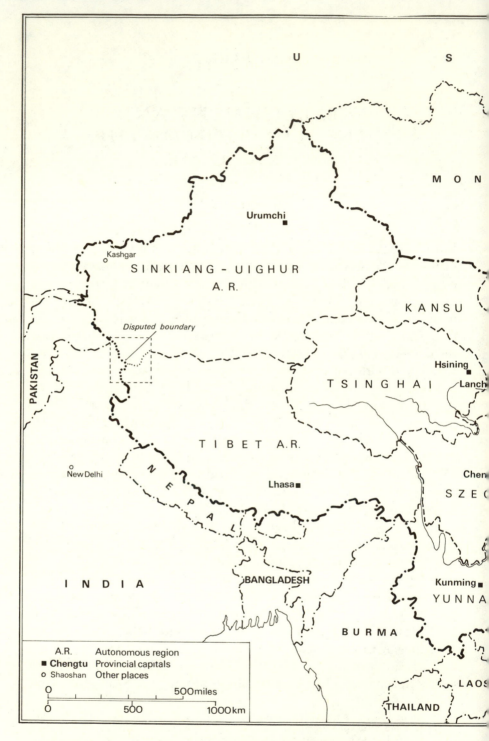

MAP 2. PRC: political (Wade-Giles romanization)

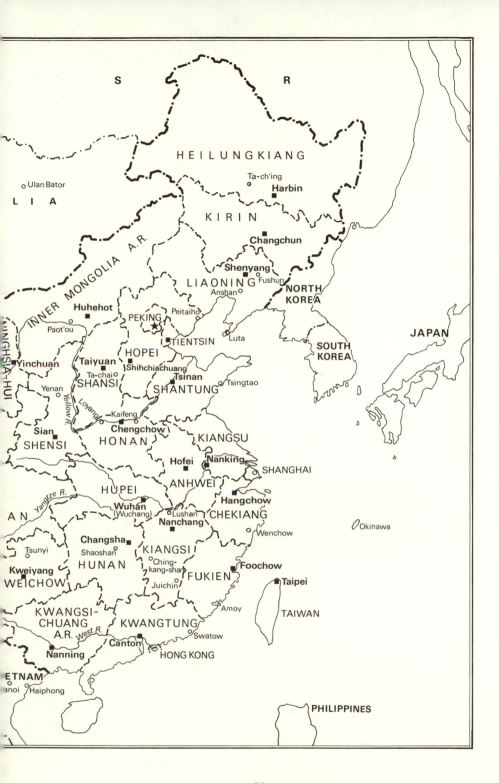

S   R

HEILUNGKIANG

Ulan Bator   Ta-ch'ing
L I A   Harbin

K I R I N

Changchun

Shenyang
LIAONING   Fushun
Anshan   NORTH
KOREA
Huhehot   Peitaiho
PEKING   JAPAN
Paot'ou   Luta
TIENTSIN
HOPEI   SOUTH
Yinchuan   Taiyuan   Shihchiachuang   KOREA
Ta-chai   Tsinan
Yenan   SHANSI   SHANTUNG   Tsingtao
Kaifeng
Lovang
Sian   Chengchow   KIANGSU
SHENSI   HONAN
Hofei   Nanking
HUPEI   ANHWEI   SHANGHAI
Wuhan   Hangchow
(Wuchang)   Lushan   CHEKIANG
Nanchang
Wenchow
Changsha   KIANGSI   Okinawa
Shaoshan
Ching-
Kweiyang   HUNAN   kang-shan   FUKIEN   Foochow
WEICHOW   Juichin   Taipei
Amoy
KWANGSI-   KWANGTUNG   TAIWAN
CHUANG
A.R.   West R.   Canton   Swatow
Nanning   HONG KONG
ETNAM
anoi   Haiphong   PHILIPPINES

KINGHAI-HUI

INNER MONGOLIA A.R.

Yellow R.

Yangtze R.

Tsunyi

AN

53

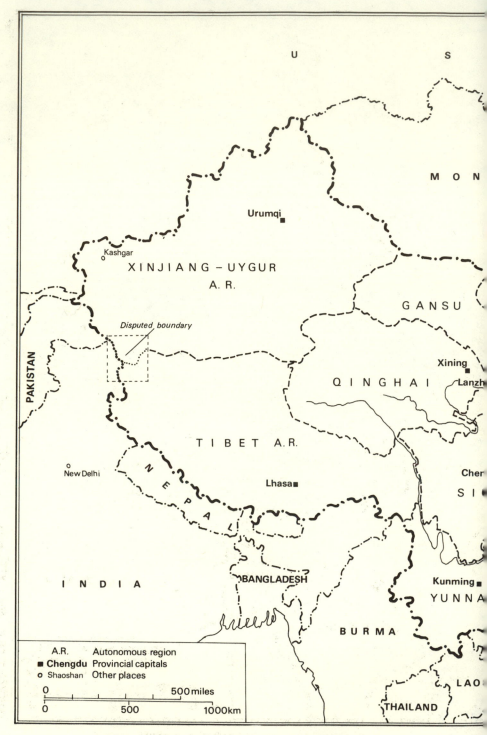

MAP 3. PRC: political (*pinyin* romanization)

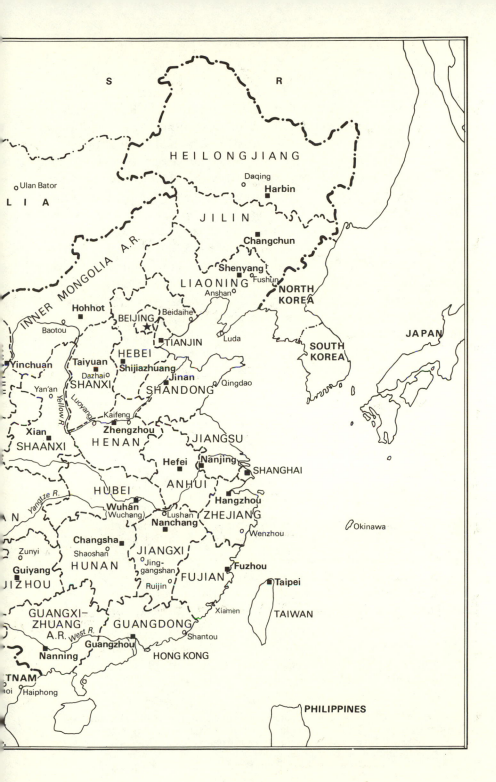

S   R

HEILONGJIANG

o Ulan Bator   Daqing
                               o   Harbin
L I A   JILIN

                          Changchun

                        Shenyang
                  LIAONING   Fushun
INNER MONGOLIA A.R.   Anshan   NORTH
Hohhot   KOREA
Baotou   BEIJING Beidaihe
                    TIANJIN   Luda   SOUTH
Yinchuan   HEBEI   KOREA
        Taiyuan Shijiazhuang
        Dazhaio   Jinan
Yan'an SHANXI   SHANDONG Qingdao
           Luoyang Kaifeng
        Zhengzhou
Xian   HENAN   JIANGSU
SHAANXI
                Hefei Nanjing
           HUBEI   ANHUI   SHANGHAI
Yangtze R.
        Wuhan   Hangzhou
        (Wuchang) Lushano ZHEJIANG
N   Nanchang
        Changsha   Wenzhou
Zunyi   Shaoshano JIANGXI
Guiyang   HUNAN Jing-
JIZHOU   gangshan FUJIAN Fuzhou
              Ruijin
GUANGXI-   Taipei
ZHUANG GUANGDONG
A.R. West R.   Shantou TAIWAN
Nanning Guangzhou
        HONG KONG
TNAM
oi o Haiphong

JAPAN

o Okinawa

Xiamen

PHILIPPINES

55

ibly argued that Party unity remained firm.[3] As China began to move in uncertain directions, the official judgment of the PRC's first eight years as a period of achievement and cohesion was still fully credible.

What explains the achievements of this initial period? To a considerable degree, the unity of leadership sustained throughout 1949–57 was the bedrock upon which other successes were built. The extent of this unity was remarkable in view of not only the drastic purges and bitter conflicts that marked the history of the Communist Party of the Soviet Union, but also the factional cleavages that had afflicted the inner Party life of the CCP in the 1920s and 1930s. Only one major purge – that of Kao Kang and Jao Shu-shih in 1954–55 – affected the top elite; as we shall see, even this conflict had a relatively limited impact on Party cohesion. Even more significantly, nearly all the surviving Central Committee members chosen at the Seventh Party Congress in 1945 were reelected in 1956. In addition, elite stability was reflected in the largely undisturbed pecking order within the higher reaches of the regime. While subtle shifts of rank and influence inevitably occurred, dramatic rises such as that of Teng Hsiao-p'ing who vaulted from the relatively low twenty-fifth position on the 1945 Central Committee to Politburo status in 1955 and then to the Party's General Secretaryship in 1956 were rare indeed. And apart from the very small number actually dropped from the Central Committee in this period, key figures who suffered losses of power and influence were generally restored to equal status after relatively short periods of penance.

Such leadership stability was an enormous political asset. With a strong elite commitment to maintaining both clearly defined power relations and the principle of Party unity, policy issues could be vigorously debated within official forums without danger to the regime. Since personal maneuvering for advantage was kept to a minimum under such circumstances – indeed, too blatant maneuvering would be counterproductive – relatively unfettered debate maximized the likelihood of balanced and flexible decisions. Once a decision was made, the commitment to unity as well as formal norms of Leninist discipline usually guaranteed prompt implementation by responsible leaders of the various hierarchies of the PRC.

systems in 1956 had not been conclusive but "genuine success in the socialist revolution" had been achieved as a result of political and ideological movements in 1957.
3 After various debates in 1957, Liu in December told visiting Indian Communists: "Our Party has guarded its unity at all times, there's been no split . . . ; no one has gone his own way." Cited in MacFarquhar, The origins of the Cultural Revolution, 1.311.

More broadly, the aura of authority and confidence generated by a united leadership served to impress ordinary officials and the populace and thus facilitate their enthusiasm for or acquiescence in Party programs.

The sources of leadership unity were varied. The victory of 1949 against considerable odds was obviously a crucial factor. This victory, which represented both the culmination of a protracted revolutionary struggle and an opportunity for national renewal, greatly enhanced the authority of the top leaders who had developed the Party's successful strategy. At a more prosaic level, revolutionary success provided the spoils of power which were widely shared within the elite. Individuals and groups from the many pre-1949 CCP civilian and military organizations, leaders whose revolutionary credentials were linked to particular episodes such as the Nanchang uprising of 1927, which marked the founding of the Red Army, or the December 9 movement of Peking students against Japan in 1935, and various personal networks within the leadership, all benefited from the parceling out of positions and influence. While the Long Marchers who were closest to Mao tended to predominate in the highest bodies overall, no major revolutionary group was discriminated against except those leaders who had challenged Mao before he achieved unquestioned preeminence, and even those figures received some symbolic positions and tangible power. Thus there were few groups with immediate grievances that threatened unity.

After 1949, moreover, shared ideological commitment to Marxism and a broad consensus on ambitious industrialization and social transformation further contributed to elite cohesion. While ideological movements are notorious for splits and infighting – phenomena the CCP would experience in later years – and broad agreement on goals does not necessarily prevent bitter conflict over means and priorities, circumstances operated to inhibit such developments in the early and mid-1950s. To a substantial degree, this resulted from the mutually reinforcing interplay of Party unity and policy success throughout the period. Unity contributed to effective solutions to problems; success in solving problems further deepened leadership solidarity. Success also served to mask or diminish any latent conflict over goals. As long as rapid rates of economic growth were attained, any unpalatable by-products of modernization would hardly give cause for a fundamental challenge to existing policy. Another vitally important element was the existence of a model that specified not only goals but means as well: the experience of the Soviet Union in building socialism. A wide consensus existed on following the Soviet model, which served to focus policy debate on incremental modifications rather than on fundamental approaches, and thus lower the stakes of any conflict.

The high level of unity from 1949 to 1957 did not mean an absence of leadership cleavages but simply that they remained latent in comparison with later periods. One potential source of division was the diversity of revolutionary careers among the Party elite. Although unified by the larger struggle, at the same time participants in different revolutionary events and organizations developed their own personal networks and group identities. During the Cultural Revolution after 1965, such groupings would become critically important: For example, those who had engaged in "white area" or underground work under the leadership of Liu Shao-ch'i generally shared the fate of their leader during the troubled 1966–67 period. From 1949 to 1957, however, contrasting pre-1949 experiences normally did not disrupt the larger leadership cohesion. The one major attempt to use such differences for political gain, the Kao Kang–Jao Shu-shih affair, was ultimately a failure.

Another source of tension carried over from revolutionary days was the inevitable friction among various personalities at the apex of the CCP elite. A clear example was the prickly relationship between Mao and one of his leading generals, P'eng Te-huai, which reportedly led P'eng to complain in 1953 that "The Chairman doesn't like me [nor] does he hold me in esteem."[4] Such personal conflict would arguably contribute to P'eng's dismissal as minister of defense in 1959, yet in the early years of the PRC it was basically submerged as P'eng's talents were utilized in key military roles and on the supreme policy-making body, the Party Politburo.

Other cleavages arose from the circumstances of the early years themselves. Inevitably the large agenda of policy issues facing the new elite produced different views and thus conflict among various advocates. One recurring cause of conflict was the question of how quickly to push economic development and social transformation. On any given question some voices would be heard for pressing ahead to achieve the desired goals, while others would be raised in warning against disruption due to too rapid a pace. Yet differences among various approaches were relatively narrow; furthermore, the

4 As quoted in a Red Guard publication, *Mass criticism and repudiation bulletin* (Canton), 5 October 1967, trans. in *The case of Peng Teh-huai 1959–1968*, 123.

positions of top leaders were not rigidly linked to one or another tendency but shifted according to the issue and circumstances. As a result, leadership polarization did not occur as it did in later periods, when conflicting policy views were much more fundamental.

A related source of limited, nonpolarized conflict was the increasing identification of individual leaders with institutions and departments they headed as the new system took shape and became increasingly bureaucratized by the mid-1950s. Thus, for example, Premier Chou En-lai undoubtedly had an interest in developing the roles and powers of the government apparatus as distinct from the Party organization, which was more the direct concern of Liu Shao-ch'i and Teng Hsiao-p'ing, while army leaders such as P'eng Te-huai had a natural concern with maximizing military resources. From 1949 to 1957, however, such conflicting bureaucratic interests were largely accommodated in the pursuit of larger goals, and direct institutional clashes such as that of Party and army during the Cultural Revolution were avoided. Despite an increasing tendency to approach issues from the perspectives of the departments they led, individual leaders still placed priority on the overall Party line and the consensus of the Politburo collective.

In sum, important cleavages and tensions existed within the CCP elite, including the Politburo, throughout the early and mid-1950s, but they did not seriously disrupt the predominantly consensual mode of leadership. Ultimately it was not the lack of tensions but the willingness of Mao and his colleagues to minimize the tensions that did exist which created the unusual unity of these early years. Such willingness, however, was inseparable from the circumstances examined in this chapter. When these circumstances no longer prevailed – when the Soviet model no longer commanded general agreement and official policies produced major disasters rather than a string of successes – latent cleavages became manifest and Party unity was eroded and then shattered. Throughout this drama the character of Mao Tse-tung's leadership was a central factor. We turn now to Mao's crucial role in sustaining the unity of 1949–57.

The role of Mao Tse-tung

Mao Tse-tung was clearly the unchallenged leader of the CCP throughout the 1949–57 period. Mao's preeminent position within the Party was already indisputable by the mid-1940s. Not only was Mao the subject of a major personality cult, but by 1943 his leading colleagues ceased voicing subtle doubts about his theoretical capabilities and in 1945 "the thought of Mao Tse-tung" was enshrined in the CCP's new constitution. Moreover, despite the emphasis of Party rules on collective leadership, Mao was granted formal powers to act unilaterally in certain instances.[5] The basis of Mao's burgeoning power was the success of Party strategies and policies after the onset of the Sino-Japanese War in 1937 which he had shaped more than any other leader; the conclusive success of these strategies and policies from 1945 to 1949 further bolstered his ultimate authority. Much as the victory of 1949 deepened Party unity generally, it also solidified Mao's authority. By virtue of that victory, Mao approximated the ideal charismatic leader whose exceptional abilities were acknowledged as the key to success, as well as the ideal founder of a new dynasty, with all the implications of obedience that role carried in traditional culture.

Mao's authority was further enhanced by his major initiatives in the 1949–57 period, instances where his individual judgment clashed with that of key colleagues and/or broader elite opinion. The Chairman apparently took such initiatives on only three occasions during these years. The first, in October 1950, concerned China's response to the northward march of American forces in Korea. On that occasion Mao seemingly overrode reservations of the great majority of his associates concerning costs and dangers, secured their acquiescence, and ordered the involvement of Chinese troops in the war.[6] While the costs of the PRC's Korean venture were indeed high, the benefits achieved in security and international prestige were widely perceived as outweighing these costs and thus reinforced Mao's reputation for political wisdom. The second instance, which will be examined in more detail later, was the Chairman's initiative to speed up the pace of agricultural cooperativization in mid-1955 despite an official decision a few months earlier to temper the rate of growth. The resultant basic achievement of collectivization by the end of 1956, far in advance of the most optimistic projections, once again seemed to demonstrate Mao's insight.

5 According to a recent inner Party report by Liao Kai-lung, "Historical experiences and our road of development" (25 October 1980), in Issues & Studies, November 1981, 92, in March 1943 a Politburo decision appointed a Secretariat of Mao, Liu Shao-ch'i, and Jen Pi-shih to handle day-to-day work, but granted Mao individually the power to make final decisions concerning matters before the Secretariat.
6 In addition to Cultural Revolution sources, this version of the Korea decision is supported by the excerpts from the recollections of P'eng Te-huai published in 1981. P'eng Te-huai tzu-shu (P'eng Te-huai's own account), 257–58.

The final initiative, Mao's efforts in the face of substantial reservations within the elite to promote intellectual criticism of the Party through the Hundred Flowers movement in 1956–57 (also analyzed later) was less successful. However, the damage to his prestige was minimized by his abrupt shift of position in mid-1957.

On balance, both the broader achievements of the initial period and the specific successes of Korea and collectivization left Mao's position at the end of 1957 as strong as ever despite the setback of the Hundred Flowers. The Chairman's strength was reflected in his moves, apparently dating from 1953, developed at the Eighth Party Congress, and reaffirmed in early 1958, to divide the leadership into two "fronts." Under these arrangements Mao would retreat to the "second front," where he could contemplate matters of theory and overall policy while divorced from daily operations. Such steps indicated not only great confidence that his ultimate authority was secure but considerable faith in his leading colleagues as well.

The fact of Mao's unchallenged authority was the linchpin of the entire edifice of elite stability. Apart from the decisive initiatives described above, Mao served as the final arbiter of policy disputes when his associates were unable to reach a consensus. Under these circumstances policy advocacy to a substantial degree was aimed at winning the Chairman's approval rather than functioning as a tool in the pursuit of supreme power as in the Soviet Union after the deaths of Lenin and Stalin. With all groups within the leadership owing loyalty to Mao, any latent tensions among them were largely kept in check.

While Mao's authority made leadership unity possible, it by no means guaranteed cohesion. Stalin had amply demonstrated how a supreme leader could consciously create disunity among his subordinates and in later years Mao's erratic behavior would exacerbate existing elite tensions. In the 1949–57 period, however, Mao sought to enhance elite solidarity by generally adhering to official Party norms of collective leadership and democratic discussion and more broadly by emphasizing ability and achievement as criteria for leadership. Unlike Stalin, Mao did not set his colleagues at each other's throats; nor did he demand that they have close factional links to himself. Instead, the ranking members of the ruling elite were men of talent and major figures in the history of the CCP in their own right. Liu Shao-ch'i had a quite distinct career involving work in the so-called white areas behind enemy lines, while Chou En-lai, the third-ranking figure and leading government administrator, had even opposed Mao in the early 1930s. Red Army leader Chu Te and economic specialist Ch'en Yun had been more closely associated with Mao but were still individuals of independent prestige, and only Teng Hsiao-p'ing of the inner core of the 1950s could be considered a member of Mao's longstanding personal faction. With his own power secure, Mao chose to utilize the considerable talents of such leaders and mold them into a cooperative team. Thus, in addition to there being no advantage in challenging the Chairman, there was little gain in exaggerating policy differences to outmaneuver potential rivals because of Mao's commitment to solidarity.

Closely linked to this commitment was Mao's willingness to observe, by and large, the formal rules of collective leadership. Although Mao obviously reserved the right to insist on his own way in matters of prime concern and collective leadership in fact did not mean simple majority rule,[7] his general practice in the early and mid-1950s was to arrive at policies through wide-ranging discussions where the opinions of all relevant officials were valued for the contributions they could make to informed decisions. Moreover, again with some lapses, Mao chose to observe the principle of minority rights, whereby dissenters within the leadership could retain their views and even reiterate them at a future date without fear of punishment. This relatively democratic style served Mao well by encouraging debate on key issues, deepening elite commitment to the relatively open policy process generally, and thus reinforcing the overall sense of leadership solidarity.

Mao's contributions to effective decision making and Party unity were further enhanced by the nature of his main political concerns during the 1949–57 period. In these years Mao tended to limit his interventions largely to those areas he knew best – agriculture and revolution above all else. The Chairman clearly considered himself an expert on the peasantry after years of leading a rural-based revolution, and in the 1950s he continued to spend considerable amounts of time in the countryside. By "revolution" Mao meant overall strategies for extending CCP power and furthering the process of socialist transformation, concerns well suited to his experience in the pre-1949 period.

7 Mao acknowledged this in 1962 when he defined his adherence to democratic centralism in the following terms: "[W]hen I say something, no matter whether it is correct or incorrect, *provided that everyone disagrees with me*, I will accede to their point of view because they are the majority" (emphasis added). "Talk at an enlarged central work conference" (30 January 1962), in Stuart Schram, ed., *Mao Tse-tung unrehearsed: Talks and letters: 1956–71*, 165.

In addition, together with Chou En-lai, Mao was the architect of China's foreign policy, as befitted someone who had dealt with major international actors during the anti-Japanese and civil wars. Finally, as the author of the CCP's basic policy on literature and the arts in 1942, Mao continued to take a keen if sometimes idiosyncratic interest in this sphere and the affairs of higher intellectuals generally. As a result, with the possible exception of the cultural sphere, in all these areas Mao possessed credentials his colleagues respected; his assertions of authority regarding them could not be regarded as arbitrary or ill-informed. Equally important was the fact that the Chairman generally restricted his role in areas he was not familiar with to the synthesis of and arbitration among the opinions of his more specialist colleagues. This was particularly the case in one of the most crucial policy areas of the period – economic construction. Thus both Mao's prestige and elite solidarity were reinforced by the hesitancy to impose his views in matters where, by his own admission, he lacked understanding. In contrast to later periods, Mao's *substantive* policy impact was relatively limited throughout 1949–57; his contribution to Party unity came from actively performing the role of ultimate arbiter while keeping dramatic personal initiatives to a minimum.

Finally, leadership unity was also bolstered by the fact that Mao's intellectual position in these years was on the whole orthodox and mainstream. In good Marxist fashion his notion of social change centered on the transformation of ownership patterns, and in good Stalinist manner he gave high priority to rapid industrialization. In most matters he shared with his colleagues a deep commitment to economic and technical advance, a keen awareness of objective limits to Party policies, and a determination to steer a course between "leftist" excesses and "rightist" timidity. Thus when debate did occur, generally Mao's relatively centrist position served to ameliorate conflict and build a consensus rather than polarize differences within the leadership. The Chairman's intellectual position, then, aided his pursuit of consensus politics. But both Mao's orientation and his consensual politics depended to a substantial degree on the existence of the Soviet experience of building socialism.

The Soviet model

In the 1949–57 period, broad agreement existed within the CCP leadership on adopting the Soviet model of socialism. This model

provided patterns of state organization, an urban-oriented developmental strategy, modern military techniques, and policies and
methods in a wide variety of specialized areas. As already suggested,
given the consensus on following the Soviet path, policy debate was
shifted from the fundamental to the incremental level. In contrast to
the bitter disputes of Bolshevik politics in the 1920s due to basic
differences over both the ultimate shape of and the means to achieve
socialism, with an established model of socialism already in existence
Chinese policy debates by and large dealt with matters of nuance and
degree.

The basic issues were these: Precisely what were the positive and
negative features of the Soviet model? How should the CCP adapt
the model to suit Chinese conditions? How fast should the Soviet
path be followed? While such questions did result in spirited debate,
they were hardly the type of issues to split the Party. In addition, the
presence of an existing and ostensibly successful socialist system in
the Soviet Union served to bolster the confidence of the Chinese elite
and society generally in official policies, since the broad outlines of
both process and outcome were presumed to be known.

Various aspects of the Soviet model and Chinese adaptations will
be analyzed in both this and later chapters. Here it suffices to say that
CCP leaders never adopted a position of uncritical borrowing from
the Soviet experience. The essence of Mao's program for revolution
before 1949 had been the need to address Chinese realities, and he
was not about to disown that principle during the stage of building
socialism. Moreover, Mao's strong nationalism had led in the early
1940s to a clear declaration of independence from any Soviet control
over CCP affairs, and this too militated against unthinking imitation.

Nevertheless, the willingness to alter the model varied considerably
from sphere to sphere and over time. Where the Party had its own
established competence, as in rural policy, distinctive Chinese
approaches were common – although even in such areas the Soviet
model remained relevant. In contrast, where the CCP was without
experience, its creativity was limited. As Mao put it after the fact: "In
the early stages of nationwide liberation we lacked the experience to
administer the economy of the entire country. Therefore, during the
First Five-Year Plan we could only imitate the methods of the Soviet
Union."[8] Yet CCP leaders gained confidence with time and by 1956

---

8 "Reading notes on the Soviet Union's *Political economics*" (1960–62?), in *Miscellany of Mao
Tse-tung Thought*, 2.310.

they began to modify Soviet experience regarding the economy and other key areas. It would only be with the Great Leap Forward of 1958, however, that a fundamental break with the Soviet model would take place.

Why was the Soviet model adopted so decisively by the Chinese leadership after 1949? To a certain extent this was a logical corollary of the decision to "lean to one side" in foreign policy. Whatever the possibilities might have been for a more balanced international posture had American diplomacy been less hostile to the CCP during the civil war, in 1949 the PRC found the Soviet Union the only available source of military and economic aid. Following the Soviet precedent was at least in part a price that had to be paid for securing that aid. More fundamental, however, was a long-term ideological orientation toward Soviet Russia. This not only involved a sense of being part of a common movement against international capitalism and imperialism but was also reflected in basic organizational principles and practices. Despite unique emphases and Mao's insistence on independence, in a fundamental sense the CCP had been following the Soviet model since its earliest days, when Leninist organizational principles and methods were infused into the fledgling Party by agents of the Communist International.

Moreover, even though Mao continued to insist on a degree of ideological distinctiveness in the immediate post-1949 period, there was still a sense in which the Soviet Union remained an authority on basic ideological questions. This was perhaps most graphically demonstrated by Mao's nocturnal visits to the residence of Soviet Ambassador Yudin to thrash out theoretical issues – sessions that may have contributed to doctrinal adjustments in the Chairman's *Selected works* when they appeared in 1951.[9] Given the acceptance of Soviet ideological authority in the broadest sense, Russian pronouncements on building socialism were sure to carry weight.

While international factors and general ideological orientation undoubtedly made CCP leaders receptive to the Soviet model, the crucial factor was their deep commitment to socialist modernization. The men who led the CCP to victory in 1949 were not mere agrarian revolutionaries; they were both Marxists seeking a socialist future and modernizers striving to realize the dream of a "rich and powerful" China. They were acutely aware of their own inexperience with

9 Khrushchev reported Mao's visits to Yudin in *Khrushchev remembers*, 464–65; see also *Khrushchev remembers: The last testament*, 242.

developmental problems. As Mao declared in mid-1949: "We shall soon put aside some of the things we know well and be compelled to do things we don't know well."[10] Given both the desire for development and the fact that the Soviet Union was the only existing example of a state which both was socialist and had achieved rapid growth on a backward economic base, the decision to follow the Soviet path was all but inevitable.

The decision was further facilitated by the fact that as good Marxists the CCP leaders accepted the transition to urban-oriented developmental strategies as a natural consequence of revolutionary success. Although CCP leaders were proud of their revolutionary traditions and concerned about the corrupting tendencies of the cities, there is little to indicate that Mao or anyone else initially saw any fundamental contradictions between the revolutionary experience of Yenan and the Soviet model. The predominant feeling, rather, was one of desirable progression to a higher stage. Mao had regarded guerrilla warfare never as an end in itself but rather as a necessary stage of struggle forced on the CCP by its relative weakness; when the time came for large-scale operations by massed troops, the more advanced military style was pressed enthusiastically.

Similarly, the whole rural phase of the revolution had been necessary but was always seen as a prelude to the capture of the cities. At the moment of victory Party leaders were eager to get on with the task of nation building and showed little awareness that the imported Soviet strategies might clash with CCP traditions. And even when that awareness developed in the mid-1950s they expected that any contradictions would be, in Mao's terms, "nonantagonistic" and thus safely handled by adjustments within the overall framework of the Soviet model.

In conclusion, a few general remarks about the Soviet "model" are in order. First, no single Soviet model in fact existed. While the basic institutional and economic pattern to be followed was that of the Stalinist system as it developed after the mid-1930s, CCP leaders had a whole range of periods and practices in Soviet history to choose from. During agricultural cooperativization, for example, the CCP looked for guidelines more to the principles articulated by Stalin in 1927-29 during his debate with Bukharin than to Stalinist collectivization practice after 1929. Second, even where a strong desire to institute Soviet methods on a broad scale may have existed, lack of

10 Mao, *SW*, 4.422.

requisite technical resources could severely inhibit their adoption. Another consideration is that in altering specific Soviet practices, the CCP was not necessarily rejecting Soviet advice. Throughout the 1949–57 period, Soviet leaders and specialists considered their mistakes as lessons the Chinese could and should benefit from. In particular, the Russians' own criticisms of Stalinist practice after the dictator's death often influenced CCP thinking on the need to alter existing approaches.

Finally, it is important to emphasize that Soviet influence had a wide impact beyond the attitudes of top policy makers. While key leaders were always, albeit in fluctuating degrees, aware of the need to adapt Soviet experiences to Chinese realities, ordinary officials and the general populace were often overwhelmed by the public emphasis on advanced Soviet experience. Propaganda treatment of the Soviet Union as a respected "elder brother" and such slogans as "The Soviet Union of today is our tomorrow" hardly encouraged critical emulation, with the result that mindless copying did occur in many fields. In still another sense, the positive image of the Soviet Union allowed elements of China's intelligentsia to pick up some less orthodox tendencies of Russian intellectuals despite the disapproval of both Soviet and Chinese officialdom. All in all, throughout the 1949–57 period Soviet influences affected both CCP policy and Chinese society in a variety of complex ways. In some senses the process was beyond the control of Party leaders, but more fundamentally it reflected their conscious choice. And when those leaders – or a dominant group of them – saw the need to break away from the Soviet path after 1957, it was well within their capabilities to do so, even though many Soviet influences inevitably remained.

CONSOLIDATION AND RECONSTRUCTION, 1949–1952

In 1949, victory came with startling suddenness. The traditional northern capital, Peking, fell by negotiated surrender in January. The People's Liberation Army (PLA) crossed the Yangtze and quickly seized Shanghai in April and the central China urban complex of Wuhan in May. Thereafter the PLA met little sustained military resistance. It took the southern commercial center of Canton in October shortly after the formal establishment of the PRC, and finally reached the southwest city of Chengtu in December. At the end of the year only Tibet and Taiwan were beyond the reach of the new leadership in Peking. The Tibetan situation would be rectified by 1951 through a combination of military action and negotiation with the local authorities, while the Taiwan question would remain a major item of unfinished national business over three decades later.

To a significant degree, the military victories of 1949 solved one of the major problems of the preceding forty years – the lack of national unity. This very fact was a substantial asset for CCP leaders as they grappled with still unresolved questions. The national unity which was necessary to restore China's greatness was a heartfelt goal for all patriotic Chinese. Mao expressed their sentiments in September 1949 by declaring, "Ours will no longer be a nation subject to insult and humiliation. We have stood up."[11]

But while the achievement of national unity considerably legitimized the new regime in the eyes of the educated elite, to secure the deeper political control required for both social transformation and modernization, it would have to confront the parochialism that had dominated Chinese society from time immemorial. While the CCP had attained some success in broadening horizons in the North China villages that the Party controlled during the revolutionary period, in most rural areas the awareness and interests of the peasants were limited to events in their villages and nearby areas. Even in China's cities, the lives of ordinary people were bound by small social groups and involved little consciousness of developments at either the municipal or national level.

An integrated national political system would, therefore, require the state's penetration of society in a way that had never been attempted by previous regimes, and such penetration in turn would necessitate both the careful development of organizational resources and intense mass mobilization to jar various sections of society out of their narrow frames of reference. By reaching deep into society, the CCP could tap new sources of support. At the same time, it ran the risk of alienating affected groups. The new leaders also faced tasks arising from the more immediate legacy of a dozen years of large-scale warfare – the need to overcome continued resistance by elements who had long struggled against the CCP, to rehabilitate a severely damaged economy, and to restore orderly governmental operations. All of this would tax CCP resources and ingenuity. But at the same time the situation created a substantial reservoir of backing from a war-weary populace longing for peace and order.

11 Mao, SW, 5.17.

In the early days of the PRC, Mao and his colleagues spoke of a three-year period to restore China's production to prewar levels and establish the political control and organizational capacity needed before socialist construction and transformation could be undertaken in earnest. The projection proved remarkably close to the mark.

This recovery period inevitably saw conflicting emphases. On the one hand, the initial needs of economic revival and political acceptance argued for reassuring key groups in society and making tangible concessions to their interests. The policy of reassurance, however, was in tension with the imperative of establishing firm organizational control as a prelude to planned development. While this contradiction was always present and the subject of debate within the leadership, a marked shift in emphasis occurred in late 1950. From that time, roughly corresponding with the Chinese entry into the Korean War, the CCP's social programs intensified, mass movements were launched, and the regime penetrated society in a much more thorough manner than initially. But in the first year or so of power, the stress was on reassurance in view of both the fragility of the situation and the limited resources the Party had at its disposal.

Initial problems and policies

The problems encountered in 1949 by the new leaders and the policies they designed for dealing with them varied enormously over the vast face of China. Differences in economic and cultural levels, agricultural patterns, local customs, and ethnic composition all required suitably varied responses. The crucial difference, however, was the degree of CCP presence in various areas before 1949. While the gradations in this regard are quite complex, in broad terms three types of areas manifested fundamental differences. First were the "old liberated areas" of North China, the Northeast, and parts of the Northwest and East China containing about one-quarter of the nation's population, where the CCP had basically established its power in the countryside by 1947–48 and often much earlier. These were the areas where the revolution was essentially won; as Mao put it in 1950: "It was the victory of the agrarian reform [in the old liberated areas] that made possible our victory in overthrowing Chiang Kai-shek."[12] Here the CCP had created an organizational presence down to the grass roots, drawn substantial numbers of

12 Ibid, 33.

peasants into the Party, basically eliminated organized resistance, and made substantial progress in social reform programs which generated considerable mass support among the poorer sections of rural society. As Mao indicated, it was from this base that the CCP launched its classic strategy of the "countryside surrounding the cities" as the conclusive battles of the civil war were fought in 1947–48. By 1949 the main tasks in these areas were to extend political control and begin land reform in those pockets where the Party had not ruled, and to check up on the results of land reform and develop low-level forms of cooperative agriculture elsewhere. By mid-1950 land reform was declared complete in the old liberated areas, and in that year something like one-third of peasant households in these areas had been organized into mutual aid teams, the first step on the road to collectivization.

In sharp contrast to the old liberated areas stood the "new liberated areas," consisting of much of East and Central China, the overwhelming portion of the Northwest, and the vast expanse of territory south of the Yangtze. Here, apart from some scattered revolutionary bases left over from the rural revolution of the 1920s and 1930s (plus some underground Communists in the cities), the Party lacked organizational resources or mass support. Unlike the protracted revolutionary struggle in the north, victory in the new areas came by military conquest from without by what were to a substantial extent alien armies. Rather than the countryside surrounding the cities, the pattern was the opposite one of first seizing cities and then extending control outward to the rural areas.

A corollary of the absence of a CCP presence was the strength of anti-Communist groups even after basic military victory. In its most extreme form, continued armed resistance was offered by remnant Kuomintang (KMT) military units and the forces of secret societies, ethnic minorities, and other locally organized self-defense groups. Even in mid-1950 Mao spoke of more than 400,000 "bandits" scattered in remote regions of the new liberated areas that had not yet been wiped out, and PLA mopping-up actions continued against such forces, especially in the Northwest, as late as 1954. Most areas, however, were reported clear by mid-1951. While such armed resistance obviously prolonged the process of establishing control, more significant was the political and social influence of local elites whose interest was in maintaining the status quo. To counter this influence, thorough land reform would be required, and it would have to start from scratch.

Finally, all the tasks that faced cities in the old liberated areas – establishing public order, restoring production, curbing inflation, and checking unemployment – also had to be dealt with in the urban centers of the new areas from a more precarious position, given the unsettled state of the surrounding countryside. While the more advantageous rural conditions in the old liberated areas allowed cities there to achieve the goals of urban reconstruction considerably more quickly than those in the new areas, China's urban centers, containing some 50 million people, can be considered a separate category from both the old and new areas.

With the exception of a few small and medium cities in North and Northeast China, the CCP had not held urban centers before late 1948, while its hold over those seized was often tenuous and short-lived. The vast majority of cities before 1949 were centers of anti-Communist power where CCP presence was limited to relatively weak underground forces, albeit much weaker in the south than the north. These forces could play only an auxiliary role in the takeover of the cities, and Party cadres from the liberated areas were often scornful of underground Communists who, in their eyes, had contributed so little to success. This attitude was further reflected in the new regimes established in the cities in which underground workers were given clearly secondary roles, while power gravitated into the hands of outsiders whose careers had been made in the PLA and rural areas.

As the CCP moved into China's major cities, it held substantial assets; but it also suffered from major inadequacies. Ironically, in some senses the problems encountered in 1949 were exacerbated by the very rapidity of a final victory that considerably exceeded the expectations of Party leaders. At the start of the civil war in 1946, many top leaders such as Chou En-lai anticipated a struggle of up to twenty years before the Communists could achieve ultimate success, and even in the spring of 1948, when the tide of battle in North China had turned in favor of the CCP, Mao predicted another three years would be required for victory.[13] The sudden and vast expansion of areas under Communist control left the Party acutely short of the personnel and skills needed for nationwide rule.

One solution was the rapid recruitment of new Party members as the CCP extended its geographical control; in the period from 1948

13 Chou's views are reported in *The New York Times*, 25 September 1946. Mao's prediction is in Mao, *SW*, 4.225.

to the end of 1950, CCP membership increased from about 2.8 million to 5.8 million. Such a vast influx at a time of revolutionary struggle and then the multiplying demands of rule could not be carefully regulated. At the 1956 CCP Congress, Teng Hsiao-p'ing criticized the "undue speed [of Party growth during] the two years just before and after liberation [where] in certain areas [the CCP] grew practically without guidance and without plan."[14] Given such uncontrolled growth and the lack of systematic training, the predominantly peasant new Party members often lacked even rudimentary knowledge of Marxist ideology or basic skills of literacy. An additional problem was that most new recruits had entered the fold under circumstances where eventual success was clear. As a result, Party leaders could not be sure whether such individuals joined out of genuine commitment or out of opportunism. Thus while the rapid Party expansion around the time of takeover was undoubtedly necessary, it was only a partial answer at best to personnel and skill shortages.

Inadequacies of manpower, skills, and experience affected the countryside of the new liberated areas but were most sharply felt in the cities. We have already noted the Party leadership's acute sense of inexperience when it came to the modern sector. In terms of personnel, the CCP had at its disposal some 720,000 qualified individuals to serve as civilian cadres in government administration where more than 2 million posts had been filled under the KMT.[15] But while the CCP's inadequacies and shortages were pronounced, it must be emphasized that the skills and experience the Communists brought with them from the rural base areas were considerable and relevant. Although the base areas were far less complex than the cities, the administration of more than 100 million people had obviously nurtured a whole range of governmental skills.

Similarly, despite the egalitarian ethos that marked the Yenan years, the CCP was already developing specialized career lines with cadres versed in finance, commerce, and education, as well as agriculture and military affairs. In addition, the CCP's control of cities as early as 1945–46, however restricted, had provided direct experience

14 Teng Hsiao-p'ing, "Report on the revision of the constitution of the Communist Party of China" (16 September 1956), in *Eighth National Congress*, 1.215.
15 The CCP figure is given by An Tzu-wen, "Training the people's civil servants," *People's China*, 1 January 1953. The KMT figure is estimated by Yi-maw Kau, "Governmental bureaucracy and cadres in urban China under communist rule, 1949–1965," 237, on the basis of data from the 1948 statistical yearbook of the Republic of China.

in consolidating urban control, dealing with the bourgeoisie, and actually running urban enterprises. Indeed, when the major cities fell in 1949, the CCP possessed sufficient cadres trained in economic management to take immediate control of the 2,700 large enterprises that dominated the modern sector. The radical excesses of the Party's earliest urban experience, moreover, facilitated the development of a more moderate policy in 1947–48 that became the basis of programs fully articulated in 1949.

But perhaps the most valuable asset the Party possessed was the attitude of its leaders that the urban phase of the revolution was to be eagerly welcomed. When Mao declared in early 1949 that "[t]he period 'from the city to the village' and of the city leading the village has now begun,"[16] he expressed not only a willingness to give priority to urban affairs but also a recognition that urban modes were most progressive and the only path to modernization. This was reflected in many ways, such as the 1950 decision to emphasize the recruitment of workers into the Party, a measure that had the bonus of bringing the CCP more into line with Soviet orthodoxy. The overriding effects of the leadership's orientation were to ensure that urban problems were dealt with on their own terms and to discredit the "charming but useless" notion of "urbanizing the countryside [while] ruralizing the towns."[17] The key to CCP success in the base areas of North China had been the insistence on focusing on the actual problems of the villages, and the achievements of the initial period of urban rule would similarly flow from a preoccupation with the tasks at hand there.

These assets notwithstanding, the shortage of skills and personnel clearly left the Party unable to assume total operational control of the cities in 1949. In these circumstances, two strategies were adopted. One was to limit Party involvement to critical areas while allowing other segments of society to carry on as before; the second was to tap additional sources of personnel to ensure the orderly functioning of government and public utilities. One of the earliest acts of the occupying authorities was to call on existing personnel to remain at their posts. Only a small number of people with close ties to the KMT were detained; the great bulk of officials continued to work in the same jobs and at the same salaries as before. Communist cadres were dispatched to the various administrative organs and key econo-

16 Mao, SW, 4.363.
17 From a 1949 CCP pamphlet cited in Suzanne Pepper, Civil war in China: The political struggle, 1945–1949, 379.

mic enterprises to assume political control and gain an understanding of operations, but actual administration and management to a substantial extent remained in the hands of the "retained personnel" from KMT days.

A second major source of personnel was the recruitment of "new cadres" (not necessarily new Party members) from the ranks of students and other literate urban youth. These intellectual youths possessed skills lacked by many "old cadres" from the base areas who had accompanied the PLA to the cities. While the inclusion of these additional groups was absolutely necessary, it led to considerable tensions within the hastily thrown together official class. Many old cadres considered themselves tested by years of revolutionary struggle and looked down upon new cadres and retained personnel as untrustworthy. In particular, they deeply resented the choice posts obtained by young intellectuals by virtue of their abilities and the fact that retained personnel continued to receive salaries while they received only daily necessities under the revolutionary supply system. New cadres and retained personnel, for their part, resented the domineering attitude of old cadres, who they felt received preferential treatment on the basis of past political services. In the short term Party leaders coped with the resultant problems by urging the various groups to lay aside their grievances and strive for amicable relations. In the longer term, from 1951 on, measures included transferring old cadres lacking the necessary skills for urban work back to the countryside, stepping up political and professional training of new cadres while at the same time weeding out those who were judged unreliable, and ousting retained personnel from official positions as newly recruited cadres became available.

While expanding its personnel resources, the Party initially limited its scope of activities. Given that many functions were beyond the new government's immediate capabilities, various private groups were allowed or even encouraged to provide services to the public. For example, the government mobilized traditional benefit societies to provide relief for the needy, while in 1950 private and religious bodies still controlled nearly 40 percent of China's higher educational institutions. This approach flowed from a decision taken early on not merely to limit but actually to contract the scope of Party activities. Despite warnings from the highest CCP authorities not to import the methods of rural class struggle to the cities, in late 1948 and early 1949 many of the cadres entering the newly liberated cities still clung to "leftist" notions of mobilizing the downtrodden and sought to do so on a broad basis. They spread their limited resources thinly and in uncoordinated fashion throughout residential areas and small-scale enterprises. This practice was reversed by measures initiated by Liu Shao-ch'i in Tientsin in April and May 1949 and subsequently adopted in other urban centers. Liu centralized political organization and reallocated cadres to the modern economic sector, the educational sphere, and government administration, while leaving the traditional sector to its own devices. The net effect was to enhance the CCP's capacity to shape the future course of events by giving it control of the institutions and forces that really mattered.

Liu's Tientsin interlude also enabled the Party to come to terms with the key economic problem which Mao had only shortly before singled out as the primary focus of urban work – the restoration of production, especially industrial production. Here again the enthusiasm of recently arrived cadres was proving an obstacle. Given both the Party's earlier official encouragment of worker demands under KMT rule and the continuing labor unrest, such cadres backed the workers against management, with the result that many factories did not function, owing to industrial strife. This, Liu argued, was a "leftist" deviation preventing economic recovery. He instituted policies calling for labor discipline, managerial authority to limit wages and fire excess personnel, and "reasonable" settlements of disputes. The interests of workers regarding wages and conditions were far from ignored, but the emphasis was to restrict their demands and appeal to them to make short-term sacrifices in the interest of long-term gains.

These policies succeeded in restoring production; on a national basis prewar peaks were achieved in many spheres by 1952. As a result, major inroads were made in alleviating serious urban unemployment. Moreover, the revival of industrial production, together with the opening of supply routes from the hinterland, helped bring under control the severe inflation that had discredited the KMT. These developments – together with such measures as removing money from circulation by taxes, bonds, and forced savings; curbing government expenditures; controlling key commodities through state trading companies; and severe punishment of speculation – succeeded in reducing the astronomical levels of KMT inflation to the manageable rate of about 15 percent by 1951.

Meanwhile, the CCP was able to combine economic recovery with an increasing capacity to control the private sector. While capitalists saw Communist-controlled trade unions as a useful device for securing labor concessions, the unions, together with labor laws, provided the CCP with potent devices for enforcing its demands as well as modestly improving the lot of urban workers. In addition, the leading economic role of the large nationalized enterprises, state trading companies, and banks provided potent external controls over capitalist enterprises through loans, contracts to purchase products and supply raw materials, designated selling agents, and officially determined prices. As a result, the process of economic recovery not only secured broad public support for the CCP, but further added to the Party's capabilities for determining subsequent developments.

United front and democratic dictatorship

One of the keys to the CCP's initial success in consolidating control was its ability to maximize support and minimize fears. A number of factors worked in the Party's favor. As previously indicated, the very fact of unification resulted in the patriotic support of educated elites and broader public relief that peace had been restored. This also had a traditional aspect, since the PRC was widely accepted as a new dynasty which had the right to establish its own orthodoxy. Another favorable circumstance was the near-total discrediting of the KMT, especially among urban middle classes. The Communists were welcomed even by groups such as the industrial bourgeoisie which had good reason to fear their ultimate aims. The hopes and receptiveness of the population, in the cities at least, was not simply a product of circumstances; it reflected sustained CCP efforts to reassure key groups and the public as a whole. As we have seen, civil servants were kept at their posts and capitalists were assisted in reviving their enterprises. Meanwhile, the populace as a whole was impressed by the generally impeccable behavior of the occupying troops – in sharp contrast to the performance of KMT forces when they returned to the cities in 1945.

These and other measures, it must be stressed, were not improvisations. Rather, they reflected one of the characteristic features of Mao's strategy – the united front. To a significant degree revolutionary success was built on the principle of gathering a wide collection of allies by setting relatively limited goals and defining enemies as narrowly as possible. It was this united front practice which was now applied to the postliberation situation.

The approach was reflected in the general program and institutional arrangements proclaimed at the founding of the PRC. A key element was the effort to seek the broadest base of legitimacy by linking the new regime to the past. In theory, the temporary supreme organ of state power pending the establishment of a system of people's congresses was designated as the Chinese People's Political Consultative Conference (CPPCC), a body which drew its lineage from the Political Consultative Conference convened by the KMT in early 1946 as a multiparty body ostensibly seeking to avoid civil war. Similarly, the united front itself was traced back to the founder of the KMT, Sun Yat-sen.

Into the united front and CPPCC were drawn the so-called democratic parties, the small, middle-class and intelligentsia-based groups which had futilely attempted to become a third force during the struggle between the KMT and CCP. Not only did delegates from these parties vastly outnumber those formally assigned the CCP, but more significantly eleven of the twenty-four ministers appointed in the new government were minor party representatives or unaffiliated "democratic personages." While political power clearly rested in the hands of the CCP, these positions were not mere formalities. More broadly, the advice of prestigious non-Communist figures was genuinely sought throughout the early years of the PRC.

Equally significant was the moderate, conciliatory nature of the CCP blueprint for the future: the Common Program. The hallmark of this document was gradualism. While longer-term objectives particularly in the economic sphere were included, the emphasis was on immediate tasks. In Chou En-lai's words, the ultimate goals of socialism and communism were "not put . . . in writing for the time being [although] we do not deny [them]."[18] Mao even more strongly emphasized the gradual nature of the Party's program in mid-1950 when he declared, "The view . . . that it is possible to eliminate capitalism and realize socialism at an early date is wrong [and] does not tally with our national conditions."[19]

In addition to gradualism, the Common Program adopted the classic united front tactic of narrowly defining enemies as "imperialism, feudalism and bureaucratic capitalism." Policies for reasserting China's national rights and squeezing out Western enterprises were genuinely popular, although this patriotic appeal was somewhat undercut by the decision to align with the Soviet Union. "Bureaucratic capital" – the limited number of large enterprises that had been run by figures closely connected with the KMT and were now

18 *Selected works of Zhou Enlai*, 1.406.   19 Mao, *SW*, 5.30.

confiscated by the new state – was also a popular target, particularly among private capitalists (the "national bourgeoisie") who had suffered grievously from KMT favoritism toward well-connected firms. Finally, feudal forces were defined as landlords, who made up only 3 to 5 percent of the rural population. Not only were rich peasants excluded from the list of enemies, but the need to maintain the "rich peasant economy" became a key aspect of CCP rural policies. This approach further served, as Mao elaborated in early 1950, to "isolate the landlords, protect the middle peasants [and] set at rest the minds of the national bourgeoisie," which was closely tied up with the land problem.[20]

The united front was also enshrined at the level of Marxist theory. A "new democratic state" was established that was not an orthodox dictatorship of the proletariat but, instead, a "people's democratic dictatorship" in which the peasantry, petty bourgeoisie, and national bourgeoisie joined the working class as ruling classes. In adopting this concept, the CCP broke with current Soviet orthodoxy on state forms. Although Soviet theoreticians had also accepted the bourgeoisie as part of the state apparatus in the East European "people's democracies" before 1948, that stand had been reversed in conjunction with the split with Tito, and the Russians now refused to acknowledge Chinese claims. By persisting in their position until 1953–54, when CCP writers began to acknowledge the fundamental similarity of the proletarian and people's democratic dictatorships, Party leaders indicated not only the importance they attached to the united front tactic but a determination to insist on ideological as well as political independence where circumstances warranted.

Such assertions of independence notwithstanding, the Soviet influence in the general theoretical as well as specific policy sense was considerable. Various Soviet theoretical texts were widely studied in China, and Lenin's New Economic Policy served as a reference for the gradualism of the new democratic economy. And in the larger political sense the state form was, of course, identical to that of the Soviet Union – the dictatorship was ultimately that of the Communist Party. For as the theory of the people's democratic dictatorship made clear, the classes making up the state were not an alliance of equals. The alliance was led by the working class – that is, its vanguard, the Party – and the other members were to be educated by the proletariat. In the case of the national bourgeoisie – a bone of

20 Ibid., 24–25.

contention with the Soviets – this education could be harsh indeed, since that class was described as vacillating and having an exploitative side. Initially the united front approach emphasized the role of the bourgeoisie and vast majority of the population in building the new China, but the democratic dictatorship could always quickly redefine the political status of any segment of the "people."

Military and regional rule

The situation in 1949 guaranteed that in the first instance Communist rule would be military and decentralized. Since the newly liberated areas fell to the PLA and the task of eliminating "bandit" opposition remained, Military Control Commissions were initially established as the supreme local authority. These, however, were explicitly temporary. According to the Common Program, the duration of military control would be determined strictly according to local conditions and it would give way to civilian authority as soon as feasible. Similarly, the great variations from area to area required decentralized administration because no uniform policy could apply to the whole nation. But this too was seen as transitional from the outset. For this function China was divided into six large regions (excluding Inner Mongolia and Tibet, which were administered separately). Reflecting the conditions of the period, four of these regions – the Central-South, East China, the Northwest, and the Southwest – were run by military-administrative committees, while North China and the Northeast were given people's governments to indicate the successful completion of the military tasks. These regional administrations, with some changes in nomenclature, remained in existence until 1954, but their powers were gradually transferred to the center as conditions allowed. Party regional bureaus and military regions existed on the same geographical bases, but these too were phased out in 1954–55.

The shift from military to civilian rule was remarkably smooth. While the Military Control Commissions initially exercised wide powers over governmental and Party organs, their personnel were soon absorbed into the units they were sent to control. Within a matter of months the commission became a coordinating and supervisory body whose offices were largely empty of staff as administrative functions were increasingly undertaken directly by the new governments. By 1951, its functions were largely reduced to security and garrison matters as local governments now issued decrees alone. The fact that close relations had been built up between political and

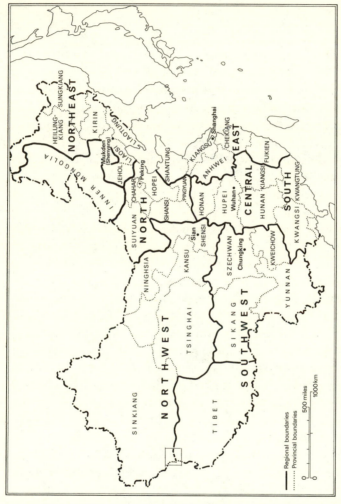

MAP 4. Administrative regions, 1949–54 (Note: By the end of 1952, Chahar had been divided between Inner Mongolia, Shansi, and Hopei, and Pingyuan between Honan and Shantung. In 1954, when the administrative regions were abolished, Sungkiang was incorporated into Heilungkiang; Liaotung and Liaohsi were combined to form Liaoning; Suiyuan was merged with Inner Mongolia, and Ninghsia became part of Kansu. In 1955, Sikang was divided between Szechwan and Tibet, and Jehol was divided between Inner Mongolia, Liaoning, and Hopei. Ninghsia reappeared as the Ninghsia-Hui Autonomous Region in 1958.)

military figures during the prolonged revolutionary struggle undoubtedly goes far to explain the smoothness of the shift to civilian rule. But at least equally important was the clear distinction between civilian and military authority that Mao articulated in 1938: "Our principle is that the Party commands the gun, and the gun must never be allowed to command the Party."[21] This principle was reflected in appointments to the large regions; the key position of Party first secretary was held by political figures in every region except the Central-South, where Lin Piao, one of the PLA's most successful commanders and a long standing favorite of Mao's, occupied the post. Moreover, the relatively limited degree of differentiation of political and military roles was to be significantly widened. The Common Program called for military modernization, including the formation of an air force and navy, and the Korean War provided the impetus for modernization in earnest with the help of substantial Soviet aid. While many PLA commanders adopted civilian roles, the great bulk found ample career opportunities in an increasingly professionalized military.

Meanwhile, the powers of the regional administrations remained considerable over the 1949–52 period. This was not apparent in the strict legal sense, since they were placed directly under the Government Administrative Council or cabinet in Peking, with no autonomous rights of their own. In fact, however, given that the fledgling governmental structure was finding its legs and had only rudimentary planning and statistical capabilities, much was necessarily left to the regions. In addition, given the vast differences in conditions and problems from area to area, central leaders remained uncertain as to exactly how much regional authority was required and allowed considerable local experimentation. The overall pattern was for the center to lay down policies in fairly general form and leave to the regions the issues of pace and means of implementation. For example, in mid-1950 the Peking authorities passed an agrarian reform law but apparently did not establish any central monitoring body; the process of implementation was placed in the hands of land reform committees set up in each regional administration.

The powers of the regions were also reflected in the fact that initially some of the CCP's most powerful figures headed military-administrative committees and people's governments. Looking at the top elite broadly, some two-thirds of the Central Committee served

21 Ibid., 2.224.

outside Peking in these years. One key sign of change was the gradual transfer of such leaders to the center as the period wore on. By 1952 the most powerful regional figures had assumed important duties in Peking, even if they generally still continued to exercise their local powers on a concurrent basis. Moreover, as the capacities of the central bureaucracies increased and conditions in the regions became more uniform, specific powers were transferred to Peking. Thus in March 1950 the Government Administrative Council enacted a decision unifying national financial and economic work, but in other cases, such as a November 1951 decision increasing the appointment powers of the regions, the continued need for decentralized administration was acknowledged.

Decentralized administration, of course, gave scope for the "localist" deviation of ignoring the spirit of central directives in order to further some parochial interest. Perhaps the clearest case of this in the 1949–52 period occurred with regard to land reform in the southern province of Kwangtung. There local cadres carried out a milder and slower process of reform than elsewhere, resulting in higher-level criticism and eventually the displacement of key figures by new leaders sent in from the outside. But what is significant about this episode is that the main antagonists of the local cadres were less the central authorities in Peking than the leaders of the Central-South military-administrative committee in Wuhan. Indeed, there is little evidence to suggest regional resistance to central authority in these years although the inevitable "errors" of the regions were criticized in Peking. The variations that did occur were accepted by the central leaders as not only necessary but desirable under the circumstances. Basically, this meant that programs were initiated first in North and Northeast China, where conditions were more stable and organizational resources more plentiful, and extended south only as the situation allowed. The Northwest and Southwest in particular lagged in the implementation of programs, but unlike the Kwangtung case this was accepted by Peking as logical given the strong resistance of "bandit" forces in these regions.

The outstanding case of regional particularity was the Northeast. This had little to do with later distorted charges that Kao Kang had established an "independent kingdom" there (to be discussed later). Rather it reflected the fact that the Northeast was the most advanced region and served as a bellwether for the rest of the country for a number of reasons. First, having benefited from industrialization under Japanese rule, the Northeast had the most developed economic base. It provided 34 percent of China's industrial output in 1949 and 52 percent in 1952. Second, by virtue of being the first region totally liberated, the Northeast could move more quickly toward comprehensive policies and was able to begin regional planning by 1950. And finally, proximity to the Soviet Union and Soviet holdings in the regional railroads and the port of Luta (Port Arthur–Dairen) combined to provide easy access to Soviet aid and influence. Thus the Northeast instituted Soviet methods of economic management, albeit with difficulty due to shortages of skilled personnel, and these methods were generally endorsed by the central leadership in Peking for extension to China as a whole.

The model role of the Northeast, whereby policies were tested and refined there before being popularized on a nationwide basis, was not limited to the advanced industrial sector. In youth work the region in general and Harbin in particular were held up for emulation, while one of the critical mass movements of the period, the Three Antis Campaign focusing on urban corruption, was first carried out on a trial basis in the Northeast. The attitude of the central leadership toward the Northeast was summed up in an article recording impressions of the region by Soong Ching-ling, Sun Yat-sen's widow and a leading united front figure in Peking. According to Soong, China had a bright future and "our Northeast is leading the way."[22] Peking encouraged the Northeast's trailblazing role while at the same time viewing the Northwest and Southwest as backward areas where far different policies were needed and proper.

Land reform

The crucial task for the new liberated areas generally was land reform. To this task the CCP brought experience and personnel that were often lacking for the more complex conditions of the cities. The Party, after all, had been engaging in rural revolution for over two decades by the time the PLA crossed the Yangtze. In that time Party leaders had attempted a variety of approaches and refined a set of methods for peasant mobilization. Yet in some senses the job facing the Communists in the vast rural areas was even more difficult than that undertaken in the cities. For one thing, it was not totally clear even to top Party leaders just how applicable past experience was to the new situation. Mao called attention to the altered circumstances in

22 *Jen-min jih-pao* (People's daily, hereafter *JMJP*), 1 May 1951.

early 1950: "[T]he agrarian reform in the north was carried out in wartime, with the atmosphere of war prevailing over that of agrarian reform, but now, with the fighting practically over, the agrarian reform stands out in sharp relief, and the shock to society will be particularly great!"[23]

Even more significant was the vastness of the territories now seized. Even if the CCP could have miraculously dispatched all its 4.5 million members in 1949 to these areas, the resultant cadre force would still have been inadequate for penetrating the widely dispersed peasant population. Moreover, the Communists came to the villages of the new liberated areas as outsiders with little knowledge of local conditions, carrying ideas based on quite different agricultural and ownership patterns, and often not even speaking the native dialect. Given both the sparseness of personnel and their alien status, the success of the CCP in completing land reform in areas occupied by over 90 percent of the rural population by fall 1952 is testimony to the relevance of its earlier experience and particularly to the determination of Party leaders.

The initial penetration of the countryside came in the form of PLA units that fanned out from the cities to the rural market towns and then to the villages. These troops, apart from "bandit suppression," generally limited themselves to disarming the local population, carrying out security functions, and organizing village militias. In the wake of the PLA, small groups or somewhat larger work teams of cadres came to the village. Only a small proportion, perhaps 10 percent at most, were old cadres with experience in the northern agrarian struggle. The bulk was made up of students and other urban intellectuals, young rural intellectuals with family ties to landlords and rich peasants, urban unemployed and, where available, local Communist underground workers. Extreme youth as well as questionable class backgrounds often characterized these political workers.

One of their earliest tasks was, with the aid of the PLA, to collect taxes to support the new regime. This undertaking was bound to create friction between cadres and peasants, as suggested by the fact that more than three thousand cadres were killed in the first year after takeover trying to collect the grain tax. As it became apparent that the new policies were shifting the burden away from the poor to the rich, however, support was generated for the new order. Other measures

23 Mao, SW, 5.24.

undertaken by the cadres in this initial period included the organization of peasant associations, carrying out a program of rent and interest reduction, and conducting struggles against "despots" or "local bullies," in other words, the most oppressive elements of the old elite. None of these efforts went without a hitch. "Despots" were sometimes arbitrarily designated; peasants frequently returned rent money to landlords in secret; and by the fall of 1950 in many areas only about 20 percent of the hastily organized peasant associations were judged reliable. Indeed, in these and later stages of land reform programs often had to be repeated two or three times before success was achieved. The limitations of the entire effort were further revealed by surveys at the end of land reform showing that only 40 percent of the peasants in some areas belonged to peasant associations.

All these measures were preparatory for the main work of agrarian reform – the confiscation and redistribution of landlord land. In June 1950 the central authorities promulgated the agrarian reform law to guide this work. Reflecting Mao's views on the differences of the current situation from the wartime land reform of North China and the policy of maintaining the "rich peasant economy," the new law and Liu Shao-ch'i's report on it advanced an explicitly economic rationale for the program. Thus the view that land reform's main function was to relieve the poor was rejected, while "freeing the rural productive forces" and "paving the way for industrialization" were emphasized. Moreover, the law was sanguine about the ease with which landlord opposition could be overcome under peacetime conditions and insisted on political order as a prerequisite for implementation.

This analysis was, however, already being undercut by difficulties encountered in preparations for land reform in the villages of the new liberated areas. One factor was peasant uncertainty as to how far the CCP program would go, especially the concern that redistribution would affect the land of rich peasants and even middle peasants. More ominous from the CCP's perspective was the traditional power and influence of the landlords over the peasantry generally. Ordinary peasants were simply afraid to oppose the forces that had been dominant on the local scene for so long, because they had little confidence that Communist rule was irreversible. A particularly difficult problem was the blurring of class lines in the traditional village. The distinction between various better off peasant strata and landlords was often clearer to work teams of outsiders than to local poor peasants. Also, social tensions were mitigated by traditional obligations of landlords toward peasants in hard times, as well as particularistic ties of family, local residence, and clan. All these links could be and were used by landlords to subvert the peasant associations, conceal land and other wealth, and maintain the existing power structure through secret societies and other devices.

As reports indicating the entrenched power of the existing rural social order came to the attention of responsible Party leaders in the late summer of 1950, policy began to be reconsidered. The shift to a more radical line came definitively in November and December – shortly after the Chinese intervention in Korea. Some official statements cited the Korean conflict as a justification, and certainly increased social tension and rumors of the return of the KMT were a factor. Nevertheless, the fundamental reason for the change was the great difficulties the relatively moderate program had already encountered.

As a result, the new land reform program of stepped-up implementation, an emphasis on class struggle, and mass mobilization even at the risk of some social disorder was in sharp contrast to the principles of the agrarian reform law. When Teng Tzu-hui, a leading Central-South official who would soon become the CCP's top agricultural specialist, attacked peaceful land reform and asserted that politics must come before economics, he was in effect criticizing the official line of six months earlier. It is important to note that even so substantial a policy shift had little political fallout, as Liu Shao-ch'i and others who had articulated the earlier line retained their prominence. Undoubtedly this was partially due to the fact that the milder policy had been Mao's own, but it also reflected the willingness of all concerned to treat program changes as necessary adjustments in the light of new evidence, rather than as issues for political advantage.

Under the new line, land reform proper was launched. The major steps were a class identification of all village inhabitants, followed by the confiscation and redistribution of landlord land and other productive property. A leading role in the process was played by work teams dispatched by county-level land reform committees, and one of their main functions was to purify the peasant associations and select activists from their midst for local leadership positions. This new leadership was predominantly drawn from the poor peasants, although official policy reserved one-third of the leading peasant association posts for middle peasants. In many areas, by virtue of their skills, middle peasants were able to dominate. In addition, the work teams sought to mobilize the entire village against the landlords through such devices as "speak bitterness" meetings and mass trials. These methods subjected the landlords to public humiliation, and the trials also resulted in the execution of members of this class on a significant scale, perhaps a million to 2 million individuals.[24] Moreover, under the new guideline of "not correcting excesses prematurely," the aroused masses frequently engaged in unchecked outbreaks of violence and brutality against landlords which resulted in additional deaths. While reports of peaceful land reform persisted throughout the movement, it appears that continued efforts to draw class lines and generate antagonism had a considerable cumulative effect.

As an economic reform program, land reform succeeded in redistributing about 43 percent of China's cultivated land to about 60 percent of the rural population. Poor peasants substantially increased their holdings, but middle peasants actually benefited most because of their stronger initial position. It remains debatable how much of a contribution land reform made to overall agricultural productivity. In any case, the main achievement of the movement was political. The old elite was stripped of its economic assets, some of its members were killed, and as a class it had been humiliated. The crucial fact was that the old order had proved powerless, and peasants could now confidently support the new system. The old village institutions of clan, temple, and secret society had been displaced by the new, which assumed their educational, mediatory and economic functions. And a new elite of village cadres emerged from the ranks of poor and middle peasants whose horizons had been broadened by the class-oriented perspective of the CCP.

In achieving this rural revolution, the Party had used both coercive and persuasive methods. Constant propaganda on the evils of the old system and benefits of the new was undoubtedly a significant factor in winning the peasants to the CCP program, but the force used against the landlords was crucial in convincing the entire rural population where power lay. Yet as important as coercion were the tangible rewards Party policies provided for the poorer elements in

24 In the absence of official statistics it is impossible to know the numbers involved, but it appears clear that early 1950s estimates by anti-Communist sources of 14 to 15 million deaths are far too high. For a careful review of the evidence and a cautious estimate of 200,000 to 800,000 executions, see Benedict Stavis, *The politics of agricultural mechanization in China*, 25–30. A larger number is suggested by reports based on refugee interviews of a "policy to choose at least one landlord, and usually several, in virtually every village for public execution." A. Doak Barnett with Ezra Vogel, *Cadres, bureaucracy and political power in Communist China*, 228.

the villages. A more equitable tax burden, reduced rents, and finally land – in addition to leading posts for the most active – did much to convince the peasant masses of the rightness of the Party's cause. By demonstrating its credibility during land reform as both a force to be feared and a provider of a better life, the CCP greatly enhanced its future persuasive capabilities among the peasants.

Urban mass movements

While land reform radically altered life in China's countryside, a series of urban mass movements left an indelible impact on the cities. The most important of these were the campaign to suppress counter-revolutionaries that was launched in February 1951 and lasted into 1953, and from fall 1951 to summer-fall 1952 the Three Antis Campaign against corrupt cadres, the Five Antis drive against the hitherto respected national bourgeoisie, and the thought reform campaign aimed at the intellectuals. All these movements were ex-tremely intense and generated considerable tension and apprehension in society. As in the countryside, official violence was used on a substantial scale, particularly in the counterrevolutionaries campaign and to a far lesser degree in the Three and Five Antis campaigns.[25] In addition, intense psychological pressure was brought to bear by various measures, including forced confessions in small groups and mass trials attended by tens of thousands (and broadcast to millions). This not only fostered a climate of distrust that broke down estab-lished personal relationships, it also resulted in large numbers of suicides – possibly on the order of several hundred thousand.[26] These campaigns indicated to broad sections of society the full extent of the Party's aims for social transformation. As the emphasis shifted from reassurance to tightening control, many groups that had hitherto been left basically alone were now drawn into the vortex of directed

25 Again, in the absence of precise official statistics, the number of executions cannot be known. But the primarily urban campaign against counterrevolutionaries may have resulted in as many as 500,000 to 800,000 deaths (see Stavis, *The politics of agricultural mechaniza-tion*, 29). The matter is obscure, since these figures are based on a 1957 reference by Mao to counterrevolutionaries who had been liquidated, but from the context it is impossible to tell whether the people in question were the targets of this particular campaign or a more general category including the victims of land reform and other movements.
26 The main sources on the scope of suicides are refugee accounts. Chow Ching-wen, *Ten years of storm: The true story of the communist regime in China*, 115, 133, estimates that more than half a million people committed suicide during the suppression of counterrevolu-tionaries and another 200,000 plus during the Three and Five Antis movements. While these estimates may be exaggerated, it is clear from official sources that suicides were a significant phenomenon.

struggle. By the end of 1952 the CCP had become, for the majority of China's urban population, a force to be reckoned with.

All these campaigns were launched after Chinese entry into the Korean War in late 1950, and their intensity was undoubtedly linked to Korea. Party leaders saw a genuine need for vigilance, given not only the danger of American attack but also the possibility of KMT efforts to return to the mainland. In any case, KMT sabotage operations were real, and dissident elements were encouraged by the potential opportunities created by the Korean involvement. The general level of social tension was further raised by a campaign directed at all groups to "resist America and aid Korea" launched in late fall 1950. The shift in leadership attitudes at the time of the Korean intervention is indicated in Mao's comments on counterrevolutionaries. In late September 1950, shortly before the decision to intervene, Mao declared, "It is imperative that we do not kill even a single agent"; by the start of 1951 he argued that "we must firmly kill all those reactionary elements who deserve to be killed."[27]

But while the Korean War undoubtedly contributed to the change in attitude and probably made the various campaigns harsher than they would have been otherwise, in another sense Party leaders used the Korean situation to press ahead on tasks which would have been undertaken anyway. Measures to deal with counterrevolutionaries had been drafted before Korea, and the "vacillating" bourgeoisie and Western-oriented intellectuals had clearly been targeted for ideological transformation. Indeed, the most significant campaigns started in the fall of 1951, a year after the Korean involvement, and Mao subsequently indicated that internal considerations were primary by observing that only "after the completion of agrarian reform [were we] able to launch the 'Three Antis' and 'Five Antis' campaigns."[28]

The suppression of counterrevolutionaries movement was aimed at spies and others engaged in active resistance to the new regime. High on the list of those under attack were former members of the KMT and KMT-linked organizations, as well as secret society leaders. The definition of "counterrevolutionary," however, was extremely broad, and in implementing the campaign it appears that not only active opponents but also genuinely popular local figures who had the potential to become alternative leaders were affected. In the conduct

27 "Comments on the work of suppressing and liquidating counterrevolutionaries" (1950–51), in *Miscellany*, 1.6.
28 "Summing-up speech at 6th expanded plenum of 7th CCP Central Committee" (September 1955), in *Miscellany*, 1.16.

of the movement, the CCP displayed a conscious effort to avoid
Soviet methods of public security work. While in many respects the
drive was a classic police effort marked by midnight arrests, Mao's
directives emphasized a uniquely Chinese approach. First, there was
an effort to secure mass participation in the process of uncovering
counterrevolutionaries and a sensitivity to the need to avoid offending public opinion by excesses; to this end non-Party personages
were invited to participate on committees overseeing the movement.
Even more important was Mao's insistence on Party committee
authority over all public security work. In direct contrast to Stalinist
practice, where the secret police were virtually an independent hierarchy capable of terrorizing the Party, Mao emphasized precise control
over counterrevolutionary matters by higher-level Party organs.

The general public seemingly found the counterrevolutionaries
campaign frightening but understandable, especially at a time of external threat. The three interrelated campaigns of 1951–52, however,
came as a rude awakening to groups who had up to then received mild
and even supportive treatment from the CCP. The key targets of the
Three Antis Campaign were urban cadres, especially those in financial and economic departments, who had become involved in corruption as a result of their dealings with the bourgeoisie. While these
individuals included some relatively high-ranking Communists
(although no one of Central Committee or ministerial rank), the vast
majority were either retained personnel or new cadres whose commitment to the Communist cause had always been suspect. The Five
Antis Campaign was directed explicitly at lawbreaking capitalists,
particularly large capitalists, who allegedly engaged in a whole range
of economic crimes and defrauded the state and public, but its larger
target was the national bourgeoisie as a class. And while thought
reform focused on higher-level intellectuals who assertedly aided
"American cultural imperialism," the more general objective was to
weaken the influence of all intellectual currents that strayed from the
CCP's version of Marxism-Leninism.

What was being attacked in the largest sense was a whole complex
of urban non-Communist values which had hitherto been tolerated.
Many cadres, taking their lead from official policy encouraging the
bourgeoisie, had come to regard capitalists as progressive and capable
members of society. Capitalists, for their part, hoped to continue
both their business practices and well-to-do style of life. Finally,
leading intellectuals valued independent thinking and resisted being
pushed into a Marxist straitjacket.

The overall effect of the three movements was to bring these elements to heel. This had several aspects. Direct punishment of the most serious offenders plus the enormous psychological pressures brought to bear destroyed the self-confidence of the concerned groups. Moreover, these pressures undermined existing patterns of social relations; *kuan-hsi* – that is, personal relations based on family, school or workplace ties – could no longer guarantee protection against the demands of the state. Related to this was the success of the Party in discrediting these groups in the eyes of others who traditionally had had submissive attitudes toward them. Thus workers in small enterprises who had previously accepted the paternalism of their employers now began to adopt official class struggle attitudes.

Organizationally, the control of the bourgeoisie over their enterprises was weakened by both the establishment of new trade union organs and the purging of existing unions which had often been run by friends and relations of the capitalists. Of critical importance was the recruitment of a new elite for lower-level positions in economic enterprises and government. As retained personnel and tainted new cadres were weeded out, their positions and others opened up by economic expansion were filled by worker activists who had emerged in the course of the Three and Five Antis or earlier. To a substantial degree, the attack on retained personnel was made possible by the availability of workers trained for administrative tasks in the preceding year who were now promoted to more responsible posts, and the campaign itself generated large numbers of new cadres ostensibly loyal to the CCP program. Given the continuing need for the managerial and intellectual skills of existing groups, the change was not as dramatic as in the countryside, but China's cities as well as villages saw the emergence of new elite elements in these years.

Finally, the Three and Five Antis campaigns had an important economic impact. Apart from generating substantial funds for investment and development through fines and back taxes, the movements greatly enhanced state control over private enterprises through new loans and government contracts which capitalists found necessary in their financially weakened state. Moreover, these toughened external controls were now accompanied by internal controls. A key measure was that businesses with heavy fines to pay would meet their obligations by selling stock to the state and creating joint public-private enterprises – a process that resulted in sending state cadres to assume leading positions in the concerned firms. Together with the strengthened trade unions, the setting up of Party branches in many large and medium enterprises, and especially the vast amounts of information gathered during the investigation of capitalists' "crimes," this now gave the authorities a much greater knowledge of the internal workings of the private economic sphere. As a result, CCP leaders had achieved a position where planned economic development was genuinely feasible.

SOCIALIST CONSTRUCTION AND TRANSFORMATION, 1953–1956

On the basis of the substantially increased political control resulting from the various mass campaigns in rural and urban areas, the PRC entered a new phase of socialist construction and transformation in 1953. In that year, nationwide economic planning began. At first, due to China's primitive planning and statistical capabilities, the demands of the Korean War, and apparent delays in negotiations with the Soviet Union for economic aid, only annual plans were possible. But with the Korean War and Soviet aid negotiations both concluded in mid-1953, more comprehensive planning could be started. Finally, in mid-1955 a 1st Five-Year Plan (FYP) for the entire 1953–57 period was approved.

With planned construction went socialist transformation – the change from private to state and collective ownership in agriculture, handicrafts, and capitalist industry and commerce. A new emphasis on transformation came with the formulation of the "general line for the transition to socialism" in mid-1953 and its public announcement in October. In some respects this general line reflected continuity with the preceding period. First, its hallmark was gradualism; both industrialization and transformation would take place over a fairly long period of about fifteen years in a step-by-step manner. Also, the practice of the general line was still within the framework of the united front. The national bourgeoisie in particular would continue to play a vital role. The initial stage of transition would be "state capitalism" where the private sector was increasingly linked to the state sector, but capitalists would still retain about one-quarter of the profits from their enterprises. Given the nature of the CCP's united front policies, however, the process of transformation naturally contained threatening aspects for the bourgeoisie, albeit in muted form. As Liu Shao-ch'i put it in September 1954, "The idea that there is no longer class struggle in our country is completely wrong

[but] the aim [of restricting capitalist exploitation] can be achieved by peaceful means."[29]

Despite its continuities, the general line meant a somewhat more radical policy, reflected in the concept of transition to socialism rather than New Democracy. The politics of its adoption in 1953, furthermore, indicated differences within the leadership going back several years over precisely how much emphasis to place on reassuring key groups in society and how much on controlling and transforming them. While Mao does not appear to have taken quite so individual an initiative as in the Korean War, agricultural cooperativization, and Hundred Flowers decisions, the Chairman now played a major role in shifting the emphasis more decisively to the side of transformation. At an important financial and economic work conference in summer 1953, Mao addressed a number of issues, including concessions to rich peasants and hesitations in developing socialized agriculture. But the sharpest issue, which became entangled in the Kao Kang affair (discussed later), was the new tax system introduced by Minister of Finance Po I-po in December 1952 that lightened the tax load on private capitalists. This, Mao declared, was based on "bourgeois ideas which are favourable to capitalism and harmful to socialism."[30]

The attack on Po served to warn others of like views of the need to step up the process of change. This warning was effective without being disruptive, since the policy shift called for was relatively moderate, and the Chairman emphasized the need to guard against "left" as well as "right" deviations. Moreover, the handling of Po's case was an instance of limiting elite conflict in the interests of Party unity. At the conference Mao declared that Po's error was not a mistake in line and appealed for unity. And although Po stepped down as minister of finance, in little more than a year he was again appointed to one of the PRC's leading economic posts.

By 1953 the CCP had amassed substantial resources on the basis of which socialist construction and transformation could begin. In economic terms, 70 to 80 percent of heavy industry and 40 percent of light industry were state owned in late 1952. State trading agencies and cooperatives handled more than 50 percent of total business turnover, while government leverage over the remaining sectors had

29 *Collected works of Liu Shao-ch'i 1945–1957*, 292–93.
30 Mao, *SW*, 5.104.

increased due to the development of joint firms and revamped trade unions. Organizationally, in addition to the large numbers of cadres and activists who had emerged from training programs and mass movements, the CCP had been strengthened as a result of a "Party rectification and Party building" movement begun in 1951 which would conclude in early 1954. This campaign for reform and recruitment weeded out about 10 percent of CCP members (some 580,000 individuals) who were either tainted by ties to enemy classes or simply lacked commitment to or understanding of Party programs, and at the same time in relatively cautious manner recruited about 1.28 million new members to bring total membership to 6.5 million at the end of 1953.

In another organizational move, by late 1952 the CCP had expanded its network to cover most elements of the urban population and part of the peasantry as well. In addition to the impact made by the campaigns of 1951–52, the Party extended its control to the urban grass roots by developing residents' committees on a street-by-street basis, a process which was finally formalized in 1954. At the same time, the articulation of bureaucratic "units" (tan-wei) further enhanced the CCP's organizational sway in the cities. The tan-wei became a potent force for political control both by providing the framework for work, residence, and social intercourse for most employees in official organizations, and by establishing regular political rituals involving all unit members in directed activities such as the study of documents and mutual criticism in small groups.

Moreover, "mass organizations" originally organized as national bodies in 1949 to educate and mobilize major population groups had taken on substantial proportions. By 1953, the New Democratic Youth League had grown to 9 million members, the trade unions numbered 12 million, and the women's federation at least formally enrolled 76 million. While these and other mass organizations were often passive in their actual activities, they nevertheless represented an impressive framework for providing contact with Party policies and some sense of popular participation. Such organizational scope with "the great majority . . . belong[ing] to some organization," Mao noted in 1955, had never happened in thousands of years. But as a result, he claimed, it had changed the oft-lamented Chinese condition of "being like loose sand" into national unity.[31]

In focusing these resources on economic development, the CCP

31 Ibid., 173–74.

won genuine support from a people attracted by the promise of both improved living conditions and national glory. Within leadership circles there was unanimity that *planned* construction was the only acceptable method – not only ideologically preferred but more efficient than "chaotic" capitalist development. One important consequence of the emphasis on planning was that it created a critical link between economic objectives and social transformation. The projected change in ownership patterns not only expropriated suspect classes, it gave the state the direct control over economic resources without which planning would be ineffective. Thus while arguments often raged over the precise nature of that link, there was fundamental consensus on socializing not only the modern sector but also agriculture, since, in the words of the Chairman of the State Planning Commission, Li Fu-ch'un: "Socialism cannot be built on the basis of a small peasant economy; it must have a foundation of large scale industry and large scale collective farming."[32] Clearly there was no basic contradiction between economic and political objectives for CCP leaders as the 1st FYP unfolded.

Another consequence of the planning ethos was the push for regularization in all spheres of life. At the overall institutional level this was manifested in the 1953–54 elections for a National People's Congress, and the adoption by that Congress when it met in September 1954 of a formal state constitution. Administratively, regularization meant centralization. As the State Planning Commission and new economic ministries were created in the latter half of 1952, various regional powers were reduced and others placed directly under central authority. Then, in 1954–55 the regional administrations and parallel Party and military bodies were abolished on the grounds of incompatibility with the needs of planned construction. Given the long buildup of increased central control, this explanation is convincing, although there are indications that the timing may have been influenced by the Kao Kang affair. More broadly, regularization affected a whole spate of efforts to codify administrative practice, organizational structures, and cadre recruitment, training, and wages. By 1955, new tables of organization appeared to standardize previously diverse administrative demarcations, staff offices were created to coordinate the work of related bureaus, new recordkeeping and accounting practices were introduced to provide a basis for compre-

---

32 "Report on the First Five-Year Plan for development of the national economy of the People's Republic of China in 1953–1957" (5–6 July 1955), in *Communist China 1955–1959: Policy documents with analysis*, 47.

hensive planning, cadre recruitment procedures completed the transition from ad hoc training classes and personal introductions to reliance on the regular school system and formalized assessments, and the previous uncoordinated mix of cash wages and supplies gave way to fixed, highly articulated salary scales for various categories of state employees. A particularly significant development was a series of military professionalization measures in 1955, including the introduction of insignia, ranks, and wage scales that significantly altered the informal and egalitarian traditions of the PLA. Clearly the new planned society contained elements at variance with the CCP's revolutionary history, but there is little evidence that in those days of high expectations Party leaders were particularly concerned about the discrepancies.

The start of planned economic construction also deepened the impact of the Soviet model; as Mao put it in early 1953: "There must be a great nationwide upsurge of learning from the Soviet Union to build our country."[33] The emulation of Soviet methods, study of Soviet theory, placing Soviet experts in key ministerial, enterprise, military, and scientific and educational advisory posts, dispatching Chinese students and specialists to Russia, and publication of large numbers of translated Soviet texts had been part of the Chinese scene since 1949–50 or earlier, but the arrival of even primitive central planning significantly enhanced the importance of these features. The crucial element, of course, was the Stalinist economic strategy of high rates of reinvestment, emphasis on capital-intensive high-technology projects, agriculture as a major source of funds for industrial growth, and priority investment in heavy industry. While there were continual debates over the details of the plan and allocation of resources within it, when the 1st FYP was belatedly formulated in 1955, it closely followed the Soviet model in principle. Also of great importance was Soviet financial and technical aid for the large-scale modern plants that were the core of the plan.

The great weight of the model and the assistance of the Soviet government, however, did not eliminate independent thinking in China. Some ministries discussed problems caused by too hastily adopting the Soviet model, and in areas where Chinese officials felt particularly competent they were known to reject Soviet advice. Nevertheless, the trend was the other way among many PRC admin-

---

33 "Closing speech of the fourth session of the [C]PPCC" (7 February 1953), in K. Fan, ed., *Mao Tse-tung and Lin Piao: Post-revolutionary writings*, 102.

istrators and specialists dealing with the modern sector. As Mao complained subsequently: "'Dogmatism' took hold in many fields: It didn't matter whether [a Soviet] article was correct or not, the Chinese listened all the same and respectfully obeyed."[34] In the 1953–55 period, however, there was little sign of effort from the top to correct this state of affairs.

The Kao Kang affair

Soon after socialist construction and transformation were launched, the CCP suffered its only major leadership purge of the 1949–57 period. The ousting of Kao Kang and Jao Shu-shih from key Party and state posts in early 1954, followed by their formal expulsion from the CCP a year later, marked not only the most serious high-level conflict of the period but one different in character from other instances of elite friction. The principals were among the most powerful in the regime: Kao was a Politburo member, head of the State Planning Commission, and the top Party, government, and military official of the Northeast region; Jao was director of the Central Committee's organization department, which controlled high-level appointments, a Planning Commission member, and the leading Party and government figure in East China. Seven lesser officials from the Northeast and East China were denounced with them, while Cultural Revolution sources linked about a dozen high-ranking central and local leaders to the affair with varying degrees of credibility.

The Kao–Jao affair has long been one of the most obscure chapters in CCP history. Contemporary sources were relatively limited in number and content, and the case received only minor attention during the Cultural Revolution. In the absence of extensive information, various analysts have advanced speculative interpretations emphasizing such factors as possible policy differences, regionalism, Kao's alleged ties to the Soviet Union, and Mao's health.[35] While all these explanations have some relevance, none is adequate. Fortu-

---

34 "Talks at the Chengtu conference" (March 1958), in Schram, *Mao unrehearsed*, 98.
35 The most comprehensive account of the Kao-Jao case is Frederick C. Teiwes, *Politics and purges in China: Rectification and the decline of Party norms 1950–1965*, ch. 5, which emphasizes Mao's deteriorating health as the key circumstantial factor influencing Kao Kang. Other interpretations include: Franz Schurmann, *Ideology and organization in Communist China*, ch. 4 (on policy differences); John W. Lewis, *Chinese Communist Party leadership and the succession to Mao Tse-tung: An appraisal of tensions* (on regionalism); and Mineo Nakajima, "The Kao Kang affair and Sino-Soviet relations," *Review*, March 1977 (on the Soviet connection).

nately, new data have become available in the post-Mao period that allow a more detailed and accurate understanding of the political maneuvering that briefly threatened the Party's hardwon unity.[36]

The essence of the Kao-Jao affair was their attempt to oust Liu Shao-ch'i and Chou En-lai from the number two and number three positions in the CCP. The primary target was Liu, who as the generally acknowledged successor to Mao, was the main obstacle to Kao's ambitions. Although there were maneuvers at formal Party meetings, Kao and Jao basically operated outside established bodies and conducted private negotiations with some of the regime's highest figures. As the 1955 official verdict on the case declared, their activities could fairly be described as "conspiratorial" and as an "unprincipled" effort to grasp enhanced personal power.

The immediate context for these activities, which were primarily carried out from June to December 1953, included both the process of centralization and regularization then under way and the debates surrounding the implementation of the new general line. The former consideration involved changes of institutional structure, and thus of personnel to staff new structures, to meet the needs of planned economic construction. In addition to a new state structure, consideration was also being given to holding an Eighth Party Congress, which would require electing a new Party leadership. The possibilities for reallocation of power inherent in this situation were intensified by the end of the year when Mao, who wished to lighten his responsibilities, raised the question of dividing the leadership into two fronts, with others taking over some of his duties. The second matter, debates relating to the general line, meant that policy discussions were taking place in a potentially divisive political climate. Although the policy issues were in fact comparatively narrow, the opportunity was there for ambitious politicians to attempt to enlarge differences into questions of line.

If these circumstances opened up the possibility of conflict, the key factor in Kao Kang's bid for power was his assessment of Mao's attitude. Although Kao was reportedly reluctant to leave his regional

---

36 The major post-Mao sources relied on in the following interpretation are: Ch'en Shih-hui, "Kuan-yü fan-tui Kao Kang, Jao Shu-shih fan-tang yin-mou huo-tung ti wen-t'i" (Questions concerning opposition to the anti-Party conspiratorial activities of Kao Kang and Jao Shu-shih); Cheng-chih hsueh-yuan Chung-kung tang-shih chiao-yen shih (Political academy CCP history teaching and research office), *Chung-kuo kung-ch'an-tang liu-shih-nien ta-shih chien-chieh* (Brief introduction to major events in the CCP's sixty years), 397–400, 405–9; *Teng Hsiao-p'ing wen-hsuan* (Selected works of Teng Hsiao-p'ing), 257–58; Liao Kai-lung, "Historical experiences," *Issues & Studies*, October 1981, 79; and discussions with Chinese officials and scholars.

power base,[37] when he arrived in Peking in late 1952 he both assumed impressive new powers as head of the Planning Commission and resumed his close personal relationship with Mao. Kao had been on friendly terms with the Chairman in Yenan. Mao respected Kao as a founder of the Northwest revolutionary base area and felt he was a local cadre with a good grasp of grassroots reality. The two also hit it off personally. After 1949, Mao was further impressed by Kao's achievements in the Northeast and considered him a capable leader who could strengthen the work of the Central Committee. This favorable disposition toward Kao coincided with a certain dissatisfaction toward the work of Liu and Chou – especially their advocacy of greater caution in both economic construction and the development of agricultural cooperatives than Mao desired. Mao expressed this dissatisfaction in several private talks with Kao in the first part of 1953. Whatever the Chairman's intentions, Kao took this as a sign of trust and an opportunity to move against Liu and Chou.

Another factor apparently feeding Kao's ambitions was the initial outcome of the post-Stalin succession in the Soviet Union, where the relatively youthful Malenkov assumed the reins of leadership despite the claims of the more senior Molotov and Kaganovich. By analogy, Kao seemingly reasoned, he could supersede Liu and Chou, who represented a slightly older generation of CCP leaders. By this point Kao had already gained the support of Jao Shu-shih, who became persuaded that Kao's rising status was a prelude to his supplanting Liu as successor. Jao did not want to back the wrong horse, despite his own historical links to Liu. In fact, historical connections enhanced Jao's receptiveness to Kao's blandishments, since Jao's deputy in the Central Committee organization department, An Tzu-wen, had much closer ties to Liu than he had. Jao apparently felt he was not in full control of his new post, and this facilitated his willingness to make common cause with Kao Kang against Liu Shao-ch'i.

Although the official verdict in both 1955 and the post-Mao period claimed that the Kao–Jao conspiracy lacked any policy content, this

37 The monopoly of regional power is the key to the official charge that Kao had set up an "independent kingdom" in the Northeast. Kao reportedly sought to place all power in the region in the hands of his close personal followers and deny real authority to other officials such as the second-ranking Party secretary, Lin Feng. This did not mean that the Northeast took an independent policy line from the center; in fact, the Northeast vigorously implemented central directives and was in turn repeatedly praised for its trailblazing efforts in carrying out new policies. The prompt implementation of central policy notwithstanding, Mao later cited Kao's exploitation of shortcomings in regional administration as one reason for subsequently abolishing the regions. Mao, SW, 5. 293–94. See Teiwes, Politics and purges, 184–91, for further analysis of the regionalism issue.

was not strictly the case. Kao and Jao did not present any comprehensive policy program of their own, but they did use the debates surrounding the new general line to attack the policies of others. The key instance was the attack on Po I-po's tax policies at the June–August 1953 finance and economic conference. Kao Kang initiated the attack by likening Po's policies to Bukharin's peaceful transformation. Mao seemingly was impressed with Kao's theoretical sophistication and joined the criticism. The Chairman, however, was unwilling to press the case to the extremes implied by Kao and by the end of the conference concluded that there was no mistake in line and that it was imperative to safeguard Party unity. It is unclear, however, whether Mao at this stage realized the full implications of Kao's activities. By attacking Po, much as was the case when Jao attacked An Tzu-wen at the subsequent September–October organization work conference, Kao was actually aiming at his patron, Liu Shao-ch'i. In any case, Mao seems to have contented himself with the appeal to unity and did not directly criticize Kao Kang.

Kao Kang also sought to bolster his position by cultivating good relations with the Soviet Union. As Party leader in the Northeast Kao naturally had close working relations with Soviet personnel, but these extended into gray areas. He apparently developed particularly close ties with Soviet consular personnel in the Northeast and with Kosygin, who was dispatched on business from Moscow. In discussions with these people, Kao pictured Liu and Chou as anti-Soviet in contrast to himself. Subsequently, once he had already been defeated politically, revelations of these links were used to build opinion against Kao. But while his relations were regarded as abnormal, they were not seen as equivalent to working for the Soviet Union. Contrary to some Western interpretations, which saw Kao as Stalin's agent in the Northeast, Kao apparently was attempting to bank on Soviet support in any fluid situation that might arise during his bid for enhanced power. Given the economic, political, and ideological ties with the Soviet Union in this period, a favorable attitude on Moscow's part could be a political plus. But it was a dubious game given the strong commitment to national independence among CCP leaders – a commitment none felt stronger than Mao. In the event, Kao's cultivation of the Soviets did not play a major part in his conspiratorial activities or his fall, but it was nevertheless part of the overall design.

More important than criticism of the performance of Liu, Chou, and their allies or the pursuit of Soviet support was Kao's effort to win backing for his cause by promising posts in a new Kao regime to high-level leaders, and by fanning resentment on the part of leaders whose revolutionary careers had centered in the Red Army or rural base areas against specialists in white area work behind enemy lines, such as Liu and Chou. The latter consideration seemingly had considerable force in the context of the forthcoming reallocation of posts. The opportunity was presented to Kao by a draft list for the new Politburo prepared by An Tzu-wen, supposedly without the knowledge of Liu Shao-ch'i, which shortchanged military leaders and gave disproportionate prominence to white area figures. The key distortion, from the point of view of military cadres, was that An's list included his white area colleague Po I-po but not the great military leader Lin Piao. Although such cadres could accept Liu Shao-ch'i's position as number two, given his many contributions to the revolutionary cause, they were disgruntled at the prominence given to P'eng Chen and Po at the expense of leading PLA figures.

Armed with this issue, Kao Kang headed south on summer holidays to recruit additional adherents to his cause. Already having secured East China through Jao Shu-shih, as well as his own Northeast, he calculated he could win over all of the six large administrative regions except North China, where P'eng Chen and Po I-po ruled. In his approaches Kao apparently claimed that he had Mao's blessing and this – together with the resentment generated by An's list – paid dividends. Both Lin Piao of the Central-South and P'eng Te-huai of the Northwest expressed agreement with Kao's views on reorganizing the Party and state and reallocating leading positions, although this apparently was the extent of their involvement. Kao was less successful in his dealings with two other key leaders, Teng Hsiao-p'ing and Ch'en Yun. Although Teng, the key figure in the Southwest, apparently found Kao's entreaties compelling enough to enter "formal negotiations" (*cheng-shih t'an-p'an*), he ultimately rejected them on the basis that Liu's role in the Party "was the outcome of historical development."[38] Ch'en Yun, the center's economic overlord who was offered a Party vice chairmanship upon Kao's return to Peking, seemingly was even less receptive than Teng.

The turning point came when Ch'en and Teng, apparently operating independently, brought Kao's actions to Mao's attention. Whatever the Chairman's intentions had been in his personal conversations

38 *Teng Hsiao-p'ing wen-hsuan*, 257.

with Kao at the start of the year, he now expressed anger at Kao's "underground activities." The culmination of the affair came at a December Politburo meeting when Mao proposed that he go on holiday and that, in accord with existing practice, Liu would take charge in his absence. Mao had been planning a holiday before Kao's maneuvers had been revealed to him, for several reasons – poor health, a desire to reflect on the new state constitution, and depression over the death of one of his sons in Korea. But at the Politburo meeting he drew out Kao, who now proposed leadership by rotation rather than entrusting power to Liu and indicated his own desire to be Party vice chairman or general secretary, or premier. Mao then did what he had failed to do at the finance and economic conference – he criticized Kao sharply. This, together with carrying out his holiday plans and entrusting Liu with the organization of the February 1954 plenum which would emphasize the theme of Party unity, effectively squashed the plans of Kao Kang and Jao Shu-shih.

Unity was indeed emphasized in the winding up of the affair. Mao apparently hoped Kao could be saved for important future duties, but Kao attempted suicide during the February plenum and eventually succeeded in August 1954. Lin Piao and P'eng Te-huai were not punished for their complicity; instead, their assertions that they had been deceived by Kao into believing he had Mao's support was deemed sufficient explanation.[39] Moreover, the need to repair the damage to unity which had been created by An Tzu-wen's list was recognized and Lin Piao, along with Teng Hsiao-p'ing, was raised to Politburo status in 1955.

Several lessons can be drawn from the Kao–Jao affair that at once indicate the importance and the fragility of Party unity. In political terms, Kao Kang could not expect to match the enormous strength of Liu and Chou. These leaders could not be easily categorized as white area figures; their careers intertwined with crucial experiences throughout the entire history of the CCP, including armed struggle in base areas. Indeed, Liu and particularly Chou had substantially broader contacts among PLA leaders than Kao Kang, who had played no role in the pre-1935 southern phase of the revolution. Yet this inherent weakness notwithstanding, Kao managed to win the support of four of China's six large administrative areas. Party unity started to fray at the possibility of the military being shortchanged in the new

39 Tensions continued to linger under the surface, however. A major reason for Liu Shao-ch'i's strong support of Mao against P'eng Te-huai at Lushan in 1959 was Liu's bitterness over P'eng's role in the Kao-Jao affair.

leadership structure. The commitment to Party unity on the part of Ch'en Yun and Teng Hsiao-p'ing, on the other hand, played a crucial role in derailing Kao's plans. These men valued the Party rules, which rejected secret factional activities of the type engaged in by Kao and Jao, and they feared the damage to the Party if those activities succeeded.

But undoubtedly the greatest lesson of the affair was the crucial role of Mao. The Chairman's private statements to Kao, whatever their intent, fueled Kao's ambitions and launched his activities. The claim that Mao supported his initiatives was enough to give pause to or gain support from those approached by Kao Kang. Finally, when Mao confronted Kao, the conspiracy collapsed with virtually no resistance. Mao emerged from the Kao Kang–Jao Shu-shih case as the crucial support of leadership stability. But the overall course of the affair also indicated his potential to threaten Party unity.

The constitutional and institutional pattern

In September 1954 the PRC replaced the temporary arrangements made in 1949 by adopting a state constitution. Strictly speaking, this was not a permanent constitution; it was designed to meet the needs of the period of transition to socialism. But given the long-term nature of that period, it was expected to last many years. Continuity with the past was explicitly asserted: "This constitution is based on the Common Program of the CPPCC of 1949, and this is an advance upon it."[40] In addition to the united front stance of the Common Program, there were some basic structural similiarities with the institutional arrangements laid down in 1949 by the Organic Law of the Central People's Government. Those arrangements, however, had been comparatively skimpy, and the constitution laid out a much more articulated state structure. The major changes reflected the difference between the unsettled conditions of 1949 and the new period of planned development. The system of people's congresses promised in 1949, theoretically the highest organs of state power, was now formally established.

Of greater political significance, the shift from military to civilian rule that had taken place in the first few years was also formalized. Thus under the Organic Law, the military, in the form of the People's

---

40 "Constitution of the People's Republic of China" (20 September 1954), in Harold C. Hinton, ed., *The People's Republic of China, 1949–1979: A documentary survey*, 1.99.

Revolutionary Military Council, had stood equal to the cabinet and directly under the Central People's Government Council. Now, however, a Ministry of Defense was established and placed under the new cabinet, the State Council, on a par with thirty-four other ministries and commissions.

Although Mao claimed in mid-1954 that the constitution was "based mainly on our own experience but has drawn upon what is good in the constitutions of the Soviet Union and the [East European] People's Democracies,"[41] in fact the document basically followed the pattern of the Stalin constitution of 1936. The basic structure consisted of "elected" congresses from the local to national levels, which theoretically appointed government administrative bodies at each level. These administrative organs were legally responsible both to the congresses that appointed them and to higher-level administrative organs. In addition, an ostensibly independent judicial system of courts and people's procurators was set up.

All of this, as well as a similar list of citizen's rights and duties, was found in the 1936 Soviet document. Of the differences that did exist, some – such as the Chinese failure to guarantee the universal, equal, and direct suffrage by secret ballot of the Soviet electoral system – were attributed to the fact that conditions lagged behind those in Russia and, indeed, often reflected provisions of the earlier 1924 Soviet constitution. In a few major instances, however, Chinese leaders clearly rejected Soviet practice as unsuitable. For example, a few state bodies and offices had no Soviet counterpart. The most significant was the creation of a clearly separate and highly visible state chairman – in the event Mao – rather than simply relying on top officials of the congress system (the Supreme Soviet in the USSR) to perform the functions of a head of state. In this CCP leaders were adopting imperial practice and, like the KMT before them, clearly felt that Chinese tradition required such an office.

Another area where the new constitution deliberately parted from Soviet precedent was in discarding the fiction that ethnic minority areas could secede. The PRC was declared a "unified multinational state" where "autonomous" minority regions were inalienable parts of the national territory. In the Soviet Union, the "right" to secede went back to the postrevolutionary civil war, when it was a useful weapon against White and foreign forces who temporarily held most minority areas. In addition, the fact that over the following decades

41 Mao, SW, 5.143.

minorities grew to half the Soviet population undoubtedly made any withdrawal of the "right" unseemly as well as unnecessary. In China, the problem is intrinsically less threatening, since minorities make up only 6 percent of the population. But it is a key issue, nevertheless, since minority areas occupy 60 percent of national territory, including most strategic borderlands, contain extensive mineral and pastoral resources, and had been a major preoccupation of successive pre-Communist regimes.

Historically, the Han (ethnic Chinese) had expanded their sphere of control outward from the North China plain by absorbing or pushing back the minority "barbarian" peoples that stood in their path. How to deal with these "barbarians" thus became an important question of imperial policy. The thrust of this policy was minimal control; it aimed at little more than nonaggression and securing a vague commitment of loyalty to the imperial court while interfering as little as possible in local ways of life. In contrast, the KMT regime, influenced by Western concepts of nationalism, followed a much more assimilationist approach denying minority autonomy, but the inherent weakness of that regime forced it to compromise or resulted in policies that alienated minorities without being able to impose domination.

When the CCP came to power, it had an incentive to avoid the counterproductive practices of the KMT, but its long-term goals required more than the minimal imperial policies. As in other matters, CCP leaders saw Soviet practice as the appropriate model. While the "right" to secede was not taken over (indeed it had been discarded as early as 1938, probably in response to the minority hostility that the Communists encountered on the Long March and the encouragement of independence movements by foreign powers), the basic Soviet institutional device of "autonomous" areas became the basis of Chinese policy. Administrative subdivisions from the provincial to autonomous village (*hsiang*) level were given "autonomous" status, often using traditional minority nomenclature; native languages and cultures were developed in these autonomous areas; and minority figures were placed in official positions, although ultimate power remained with the normally Han Party leaders.

While the autonomy principle has been a constant of the Soviet model, the content given it by the CCP reflected more the benign Soviet approach of the 1920s than the assimilationist approach of the Stalinist period after 1929. Thus the emphasis was on "nationalization" – a process that involved not only the adoption of national minority forms but also the recruitment of minority cadres, efforts to train Han cadres in local ways, and genuine cooperation with the "patriotic upper strata" – traditional leaders who had both local prestige and expertise and thus could guarantee smooth relations with the populace.

These policies were linked to others which sought gradually to deepen CCP control – the development of transport and communications links with Han areas, Han emigration to some but not all minority areas, modest efforts to improve economic conditions without disrupting local customs, the development of new administrative organs to replace traditional structures, political education emphasizing that minorities were part of the larger Chinese motherland, and social reforms in most nationality regions patterned on developments in Han areas but implemented more slowly in light of local conditions. Overall, CCP policies sought to draw the minorities gradually into the Chinese mainstream; they aimed at fundamental transformation but at a pace and in a manner sensitive to local customs and avoiding unnecessary disruption.

The CCP, using these policies, had considerable success in bringing the far-flung minority areas under central control and beginning the process of social transformation, but such efforts in areas traditionally hostile to the Han and possessing "backward" social structures inevitably produced tensions. Despite the relatively moderate approach, throughout the early 1950s reports surfaced of "Han chauvinism" as Han cadres alienated local populations by applying Chinese practices mechanically. During the relaxation begun in 1956 and extended during the Hundred Flowers movement in 1957 (see Chapter 5), official efforts to promote criticism of Party shortcomings led to a flood of attacks on Han cadre misbehavior and more fundamentally on the limitations of autonomy, and even resulted in separatist demands. The most extreme manifestation of minority alienation was a 1956 revolt in the Tibetan areas of Szechwan against the introduction of reforms. One consequence was the emigration of a significant number of refugees to Tibet proper who later became an important factor in the major 1959 Tibetan rebellion (see Chapter 7). Clearly, even the skillfully modulated policies of 1949–57 had not eliminated resistance to Chinese control; but on balance, the PRC had gained a much firmer foothold in minority areas than any previous regime.

As suggested by the minorities question, the actual institutional pattern in operation was more significant than the constitutional prescription, and here too there were similarities but also major differences from Soviet practice. Basically, this was a system of parallel Party and state hierarchies, with the Party, unmentioned in the constitution, the ultimate locus of authority. In this the Chinese system was patterned more on the formal relationships in the Soviet Union than on actual Stalinist practice. For Stalin the Party, although theoretically supreme, was merely one of several hierarchies including the virtually independent secret police which he could personally manipulate to guarantee his dominance. In China, true to Leninist principles, Party leadership had a more concrete reality. Ultimate policy-making power rested with central Party bodies, especially the Politburo and Secretariat, while at local levels Party committees were more powerful than people's governments. Party control was also ensured by the wearing of dual hats: Leading Party secretaries also held key administrative posts, a practice at variance with the more distinct Soviet hierarchies even after Stalin. Indeed, as the institutional pattern for planned construction was taking hold in China, the Soviet Party was only gradually reasserting its dominance in post-Stalin Russia.

In another regard, however, institutional relationships were fundamentally influenced by the Soviet pattern. The Soviet-style command economy required a set of centralized administrative practices that enhanced the relative position of the state structure. Although there was no question of ultimate Party authority over policy, a vast number of administrative decisions related to economic management fell to the State Council and its subordinate bodies. The dominant administrative pattern was that of vertical rule – units in the modern sector were placed directly under central ministries, thus bypassing local Party committees. Mao accurately captured the situation when he declared, "The major powers grasped by the Central Committee consist only of revolution and agriculture. The rest are in the hands of the State Council."[42] At the central level, operational decisions increasingly flowed to the specialists required by the capital- and technology-intensive Soviet model, and these administrators exercised direct control over skilled personnel at each subordinate level. This bolstered not only the position of Premier Chou En-lai but also those of such key economic officials as Ch'en Yun, Li Fu-ch'un, Li Hsien-nien, and Po I-po.

At the basic level in the modern sector, the industrial enterprise,

42 "Talks at the Nanning conference" (11–12 January 1958), in *Miscellany*, 1.84.

this often left the Party organization in a fairly peripheral role. After an initial period of considerable confusion and variation in the roles of factory Party committees, by 1953 the trend was toward restricting their functions to education and propaganda while the factory manager assumed control of overall operations. This situation, as we shall see, was changed by 1956, but in the early days of the 1st FYP, factory Party committees were often simply another functional organization within the enterprise. Overall the Party remained supreme, but throughout the 1953–57 period the state's powers frequently eclipsed those of specific Party organizations.

Another key part of the state apparatus, the "political and legal work system" of courts, procurators (public prosecutors), and police, was deeply influenced by the Soviet model, although it departed from Stalinist practice in crucial respects. As in the Soviet Union, not only were courts and procurators declared constitutionally independent, but by 1954 they adopted Soviet-style administrative practices that granted a substantial degree of functional autonomy. As part of the overall emphasis on regularization and professionalization in the mid-1950s, these bodies, as well as the police who theoretically were an integral part of the government under the Ministry of Public Security, increasingly handled individual cases without interference from local Party committees or government councils. Ultimately, of course, political and legal departments were subject to CCP authority in that basic policies were laid down by central Party bodies and closely coordinated with the overall goals of the official line. Moreover, local Party committees maintained general oversight over this sensitive area, which sometimes led to friction with the departments as they attempted to assert the autonomy sanctioned by state policy.

The police were clearly the most important of the political and legal departments. Although there are huge gaps in hard information about the public security apparatus, it obviously played a crucial role from the founding of the PRC as an instrument of public order and control. In addition to ordinary police functions and its obscure role as a political police, the public security force administers a large penal system, including labor camps whose inmates undoubtedly number in the millions and provide significant economic resources for the state.[43] With such resources at its disposal, the police have required

43 While remarkably little firm data are available on the PRC's labor reform system, useful descriptions are found in A. Doak Barnett, *Communist China: The early years, 1949–55*, 60–67; and the firsthand account in Bao Ruo-wang (Jean Pasqualini) and Rudolph Chelminski, *Prisoner of Mao*. Both sources speculatively estimate a labor camp population in the millions, with Bao and Chelminski (p. 10n) suggesting a likely number well in excess of 10 million.

firm Party control. As already indicated, Mao, unlike Stalin, moved to ensure that the police did not operate as an independent coercive apparatus capable of destroying the integrity of Party and state organizations. In the 1955 campaign against counterrevolutionaries, as in the earlier 1951–53 effort, strict oversight by Party bodies was again imposed. Day-to-day control over the police was exerted by Minister of Public Security Lo Jui-ch'ing, a Party official of high rank, but below Politburo status. Lo reported directly to Mao and also to P'eng Chen, the Politburo member most heavily involved in political and legal work.[44] While guidance of the public security apparatus undoubtedly provided individual figures with a potentially potent instrument for inner elite conflict, under the conditions of the 1950s it was a resource of strictly limited utility.

While the Party and state hierarchies were clearly crucial, an important auxiliary role was played by the various mass organizations. These bodies were designed according to Lenin's concept of "transmission belts." Although transmission belts performed the role of representing the views of their members to leading Party authorities, their primary function in both Leninist and Stalinist practice was as purveyors of Party policies to the masses they represented. In the initial period after liberation there was a significant debate as to the relative weight of these two roles in the most significant mass organization, the All-China Federation of Trade Unions, but the issue was settled by the end of 1951 in favor of orthodox Soviet practice.

In this debate many in the trade unions, apparently led by Li Li-san, argued that unions had become too subservient to management in both privately owned and state-run enterprises and as a result had alienated the workers. These cadres held that the basic task of the unions was to uphold workers' interests, and to accomplish this aim some degree of operational autonomy was necessary. At the end of 1951 Party leaders intervened to denounce these views as "economism" and "denying Party leadership of the trade unions," and in a top-level reshuffle of union personnel in 1952, Li Li-san was replaced as trade union chief. While Li's personal setback was limited – he

---

44 Foreign observers have speculated that K'ang Sheng, a Politburo member heavily involved in security work in the 1930s and early 1940s, continued to control the police after 1949, but this was not the case. K'ang was relieved of security duties after the Seventh Party Congress in 1945 and subsequently went on sick leave in 1949, allegedly out of pique that Jao Shu-shih was given the top regional post in East China. K'ang reemerged after the Kao–Jao affair but concentrated on theoretical work. It was only in the Cultural Revolution that he again became involved with coercive instruments of rule. See Chung K'an, *K'ang Sheng p'ing-chuan* (Critical biography of K'ang Sheng), 83, 96, 106–12, 114, 191, 284.

retained his posts as minister of labor and Central Committee member – and was perhaps related to the fact that he had been one of Mao's main opponents in the early 1930s, the net effect of the affair was firmly to subordinate the union structure to Party leadership. This standard Soviet role also applied to all other mass organizations, and it became even more pronounced in the 1st FYP period, when virtually all bodies centered their activities on plan fulfillment.

Agricultural cooperativization

The successful completion of agricultural cooperativization by the end of 1956 was one of the most significant developments of the entire 1st FYP period in a number of senses. First, it was an enormous achievement of social and institutional transformation to bring the great bulk of the Chinese people under socialist forms of organization – a task fundamentally more difficult than the socialization of the modern sector –.and one that on this ground alone demands detailed examination. Second, while Soviet collectivization more than twenty years earlier was relevant experience in a number of ways, CCP leaders developed their own approach and methods, which resulted in a far less disruptive process than had occurred in Russia. Moreover, as a policy issue, cooperativization was a hotly debated question within the leadership, although these debates did not fundamentally erode Party unity. Finally, the resolution of this issue came as a result of Mao's personal initiative in calling for a stepped-up pace of building agricultural cooperatives in mid-1955.

As Vice-Premier Ch'en I put it, Mao's intervention "settled the debate of the past three years."[45] Subsequently cooperativization was accomplished far more quickly than had been previously thought possible, although the pace also greatly exceeded Mao's expectations and the methods often violated his guidelines. In any case, the achievement of an almost totally socialized agricultural sector by late 1956 was widely seen as both a great success for the Party and a vindication of Mao personally. (For a more specifically economic analysis of this development, see Chapter 3.)

Moves toward socialized agriculture had begun even before nationwide liberation with the development of mutual aid teams (MATs) – arrangements for pooling peasant labor – in the base areas of North China. Mutual aid was developed after 1949 in both old and new

45 *JMJP*, 13 November 1955.

liberated areas so that by the end of 1952 about 40 percent of all peasant households were in MATs. Meanwhile, experimental Agricultural Producers' Cooperatives (APCs) were established, but it was only in 1952–53 that they appeared in substantial numbers. From 1952 until Mao's intervention in 1955, the rate of cooperativization intensified and relaxed several times. As Table 1 demonstrates, in the winters of 1952–53 and 1954–55 sharp increases were registered in the number of cooperatives, but in each following spring the rate of growth was reduced and some cooperatives disbanded. This pattern was clearly linked to the ongoing debate, but it also reflected the problems of disorganization and planning confusion, harsh cadre methods, and the alienation of better-off peasants that resulted from hasty implementation of the program. After Mao's intervention, in contrast, not only did the movement surge forward at a stepped-up tempo, but the following spring of 1956 saw the reorganization of the cooperatives into so-called higher-stage or fully collectivized bodies instead of a new period of consolidation.

Chinese policy contained several major modifications of the Soviet experience. First, cooperativization was designed as a gradual, stage-by-stage process, rather than the sudden and chaotic pattern of the Soviet Union. CCP policy envisioned a three-step process: first MATs, where labor was pooled but ownership rights over land and other productive factors were retained by individual peasants; then the lower-stage APC, where productive property was now controlled by the collective but each peasant received a dividend according to his relative contribution of land, tools, and animals; and finally the higher-stage APC (or full collective), where the dividend was abolished and payment was strictly according to labor.

Another important difference was the policy of restricting rather than liquidating rich peasants. In contrast to the forced deportation and killing of Russian *kulaks*, Chinese rich peasants saw their economic position eroded by various means and were used as a target for political mobilization until the latter stages of the movement, when they were allowed into the APCs. Thus while the rich peasants were still objects of class struggle, their comparatively mild treatment limited the disorder and destruction of economic resources that marked the Soviet campaign.

A third feature, which also ameliorated the rural situation, was CCP avoidance of Stalin's single-minded stress on extracting agricultural surplus to support industrialization. China's 1st FYP also relied heavily on agriculture supporting industry, but CCP leaders

TABLE I

Agricultural cooperatives: development and targets

	Existing APCs	1954–55 target	1956 target	1957–58 target
Fall 1952	3,644[a] (0.1%)[b]			
Spring 1953	5,800 reduced to 3,645 in Hopei province			
Mao 11/53	ca. 15,000 (0.2%)			700,000–1 million (ca. 15–22%) "by 1957"
Central Committee 12/53	14,900 (0.2%)	35,800 (ca. 0.5%) fall 1954		800,000 (ca. 18%) "by 1957"
Teng Tzu-hui 7/54 (Head of CCP Rural Work Department)	ca. 114,000 (2%)	600,000 (ca. 12–13%) spring 1955	1.5 million (ca. 33%) "by 1956"	3 million (ca. 66%) "by 1957"
Central Committee 10/54	ca. 230,000 (4.7%)	600,000 (ca. 12–13%) spring 1955		
February–March 1955	670,000 reduced to 633,000 (14.2%)			
Central Committee Rural Work Department spring (May ?) 1955	ca. 633,000 (14.2%)		1 million (ca. 22%) October	
June 1955	634,000 (14.2%)			
1st FYP 7/30/55	650,000 (ca. 14.3%)			33% "by 1957"
Mao 7/31/55	650,000 (ca. 14.3%)		1.3 million (ca. 29%) October	50% spring 1958
Average 17–20 provinces 9/55	?		37.7% spring	60.3% 1957
Central Committee 10/55	1.277 million (32%)			70–80% in advanced areas, spring 1957; 70–80% overall, spring 1958
21 provinces 11/55	1.583 million (41.4%)	70–80% in advanced areas, end 1955	70–80% overall, end 1956	
Mao 12/55	1.905 million (63.3%) (4% hi APCs)[c]		70–80% end 1956	

Table 1 *(cont.)*

	Existing APCs	1954–55 target	1956 target	1957–58 target
Agricultural draft program 1/56	1.53 million (80.3%) (30.7% hi APCs)		85% "in 1956"	"hi APCs practically complete by 1958"
March 1956	1.088 million (88.9%) (54.9% hi APCs)			
June 1956	994,000 (91.9%) (63.2% hi APCs)			
December 1956	756,000 (96.3%) (87.8% hi APCs)			

[a] Number of APCs; lower-stage APCs until December 1955, thereafter divided into lower- and higher-stage APCs as indicated. Number of APCs declines throughout 1956 owing to larger size of higher APCs.
[b] (%) = peasant households in APCs.
[c] hi = higher stage.
Sources: Shih Ching-t'ang et al., eds., *Chung-kuo nung-yeh ho-tso-hua yun-tung shih-liao* (Historical materials on China's agricultural cooperativization movement), 989–91; "Agricultural cooperativization in Communist China," *CB*, 373; Mao, *SW*, 5.139–40; and *Communist China 1955–1959*, 120.

realized that China's countryside had far less surplus to extract than Russia's. As a result, throughout the 1st FYP, official policy aimed at increasing agricultural production so that *both* the industrial development plans of the state would be met and peasant living standards would rise. While it remains uncertain just how consistently this objective was realized, the Party concern for peasant livelihood served to reduce resistance as well as build support. Finally, a more strictly economic and technical modification was the emergence by mid-1954 of a policy that in view of China's backward industrial base, collectivization should precede the mechanization of agriculture rather than be developed in tandem.

These substantial changes from the Soviet pattern did not mean total rejection of the Soviet experience, however. On the contrary, not only were various Soviet writings studied to bolster the official case for cooperatives, but the developed Soviet collective as laid down in the model *kolkhoz* (collective) rules of 1935 was the concrete form of higher-stage APC which the CCP basically adopted. In terms of process, moreover, the Soviet experience provided lessons and sources of support for all sides of the debate within the CCP. Those who argued against rapid expansion cited Stalin's warning against being "dizzy with success" when excesses threatened the Soviet program. But others, like Mao in July 1955, could argue that the Soviet experience showed it was possible to correct errors quickly and accomplish cooperativization according to a more optimistic schedule.

Some aspects of the crucial stage of the debate during the first seven months of 1955 are clear, including Mao's decisive role and the nature of the arguments, but the precise political contours are less certain.[46] As we have seen, there was undoubted consensus in early 1955 on the desirability of cooperativization for economic as well as social and political goals; promulgation of the 1st FYP in July reemphasized the importance of building APCs for planned economic growth. There was also the relatively recent agreement on collectivization before mechanization, although differences remained over precisely how far ahead of mechanization the socialization process should develop. Moreover, a shared awareness of the problems facing the CCP existed. Socially and politically, there was broad agreement that the continued existence of small peasant production engendered rural capitalism and thus threatened the consolidation of socialism. Economically, all participants believed the failure of agricultural growth to keep pace with the planned rate of industrialization threatened the entire 1st FYP, since agricultural production substantially determined industrial growth rates.

Since there is little indication of any key policy maker advocating a substantial scaling down of industrial targets, how to increase farm production became a key concern. The central issue was the pace of setting up APCs. Throughout these months a cautious approach was advanced primarily by the Central Committee's Rural Work Department and its head, Teng Tzu-hui, in conjunction with the Politburo's leading economic specialist, Ch'en Yun. This approach was initially endorsed not only by Liu Shao-ch'i but also by Mao himself. Teng

---

46 The following account differs somewhat from interpretations which, drawing on Cultural Revolution sources, emphasize differences between Mao on the one hand and a whole array of central officials on the other. See, e.g., Parris H. Chang, *Power and policy in China*, 9–17. The analysis offered here, in addition to documentary evidence from 1954–55, draws on "Agricultural cooperativization in communist China," *CB*, 373; Kenneth R. Walker, "Collectivisation in retrospect: The 'socialist high tide' of autumn 1955 – spring 1956," *CQ*, 26 (1966); and particularly documents in the post-Mao internal publication, *Tang-shih yen-chiu* (Research on Party history), 28 February 1981, viz. Teng Tzu-hui, "Tsai ch'üan-kuo ti-san-tz'u nung-ts'un kung-tso hui-i shang ti k'ai-mu tz'u" (Inaugural speech at the third national rural work conference) (21 April 1955) 1981.1, 2–9; and Ch'iang Yuan-kan and Lin Pang-kuang, "Shih-lun i-chiu-wu-wu-nien tang-nei kuan-yü nung-yeh ho-tso-hua wen-t'i ti cheng-lun" (A discussion of the debate within the Party in 1955 concerning the issue of agricultural cooperativization).

emphasized the overambitious planning, cadre excesses, and disillusionment of the more productive peasants which had accompanied the rapid expansion of APCs in 1954 and early 1955. In this view, a careful consolidation of existing APCs and a modest rate of future growth aiming for a million cooperatives by fall 1956 was called for if peasant hostility was not seriously to damage agricultural production. In pursuing this policy, Teng ordered the dissolution of 20,000 newly established but badly organized APCs. Against this approach were those advocating a more expansionary policy on the grounds that APCs had a demonstrated capacity for increasing production, could more easily obtain the agricultural surplus for the state, and would also check tendencies to rural class polarization that seemed to be growing with agriculture still overwhelmingly private.

As indicated earlier, Mao initially supported Teng's policies. In March the Chairman proposed the slogan "halt, shrink, develop," which reflected the importance of consolidation before new advances. In mid-May, however, Mao shifted his position to one of dissatisfaction with the pace of cooperativization, and a sharp debate with Teng ensued. While Teng upheld the rural work department's target of one million APCs by October 1956, Mao warned against a passive approach and argued for a goal of 1.3 million.[47] In retrospect, it appears Mao's initiative in the latter part of May, and not his 31 July speech on cooperativization normally cited by scholars,[48] was decisive in producing policy change. Not only were the number of APCs again expanding in June and July, but May also saw the decision to launch a new campaign against counterrevolutionaries – a major aim of which was to silence opposition to collectivization within society at large. Moreover, owing to conviction, conversion, or calculation, in the days before Mao's speech such leading officials as Minister of Agriculture Liao Lu-yen and Teng's erstwhile ally Ch'en Yun spoke out sharply in defense of collectivization.

Mao's intervention starting in May 1955 and culminating in his

47 Mao's target was laid down in his 31 July speech on cooperativization but was apparently argued during the May debate with Teng. See Mao, *SW*, 5.187; and Ch'iang Yuan-kan and Lin Pang-kuang, "Shih-lun tang-nei cheng-lun," 13.
48 Analysts writing without benefit of post-Mao information on the Chairman's May activities often stressed the suddenness and decisiveness of Mao's July speech because of its apparently more radical targets than those incorporated in the 1st FYP published the day before Mao spoke. See, e.g., Stuart R. Schram, "Introduction: The Cultural Revolution in historical perspective," in Schram, ed., *Authority, participation and cultural change in China*, 39. Such analyses, however, overlook the fact that the 1st FYP target of one-third of all peasant households in APCs "by 1957" was not necessarily more conservative than Mao's target of 50 percent by *spring 1958*, since the winter season of 1957–58 would surely be a period of significant growth.

July speech was less significant as policy innovation than as a decisive political act. In policy terms, although doubling the number of APCs to be established over the next fourteen months was a significant intensification of the campaign, Mao's program was not overly radical. It called for careful preparations for new APCs, allowed peasants to withdraw or even dissolve unsatisfactory cooperatives, and warned against rashness as well as timidity in cooperativization. Moreover, even though Mao's targets substantially raised those earlier decided on by the rural work department, the rate of increase was less than that achieved in the year from early 1954 to early 1955, and the absolute numbers involved were only slightly larger. Indeed, Mao's targets for 1956–57 were more conservative than the projection made by Teng Tzu-hui in mid-1954.

But if the Chairman's program was not excessively radical, its political impact was. Mao ended the hesitation of the previous months by indicating that expansion was the only ideologically correct course. He began his July speech with a criticism of "some of our comrades [who are] tottering like a woman with bound feet,"[49] and throughout this period applied the "right deviationist" label to Teng, who continued to express reservations. In the face of Mao's sharpened political definition of the issue, few officials held out; vigorous implementation of cooperativization unfolded.

Mao's success was undoubtedly due in the first instance to his unchallenged role as leader, but several other factors were working in his favor. One was the comparatively moderate nature of his program and the argumentation behind it. Although the political tone of the July speech was ultimately decisive, the marshalling of survey data and careful reasoning carried considerable weight. Also aiding Mao was the fact that his program at least came to grips with the serious problems facing the rural sector, while the more conservative approach held little promise of a breakthrough. Politically, the fact that Mao was not speaking alone but expressing the views of a significant segment of the elite gave his recommendations an important boost, as did the fact that even those opposed to rapid increases shared a belief in the desirability of APCs on both economic and social grounds. Although in later years objections would be voiced to using the "rightist" label against Teng Tzu-hui, at the time the traditional mild approach to inner elite dissent also contributed to closing ranks behind Mao. Teng was required only to make a self-

49 Mao, SW, 5.184.

criticism and temporarily suffered a reduction in power, but he never lost his posts. Finally, as the campaign picked up steam, the overfulfillment of the Chairman's targets seemed to discredit contrary views.

Indeed, the nearly complete establishment of fully collectivized APCs by the end of 1956 was due more to the zealous implementation of the campaign by the Party apparatus than to Mao's program. Cadres throughout rural China, reacting to the pressures created by Mao's speech and the campaign against counterrevolutionaries, concluded it was "better to err to the left than the right." From the time of the July speech until the end of 1955, China went through a cycle of Mao and the Party center setting goals, the provinces outstripping those goals, the center revising its targets upward, and the provinces once again overfulfilling central targets. Even at the end of the year, Mao estimated it would take another three to four years basically to complete the higher-stage APCs. But in 1956 the localities yet again greatly outstripped his targets. In the process, however, the policy of advance by stages which the Chairman had carefully advocated in 1955 was discarded. More than a quarter of all peasant families joined APCs without prior organization into MATs, and a widespread tendency to skip the lower-stage APCs altogether appeared. Although Mao continued to warn against leftist excesses in the fall and winter of 1955–56, he was fundamentally elated by the rapid progress. This breakneck speed would cause serious problems of adjustment in 1956–57, but the basic organizational breakthrough had been achieved.

In comparative terms, Chinese cooperativization was accomplished in a considerably smoother manner than its Soviet counterpart, but outright revolts apart, nearly all forms of peasant resistance that had occurred in Russia – withdrawing from cooperatives, reducing levels of productive investment and activity, slaughtering livestock, spreading rumors – appeared in China, albeit to a lesser degree.

Various factors explain the easier passage. The conscious adaptation of Soviet practice in the direction of gradualism and reduced social tensions were, of course, of major significance. Also crucial was the disciplined Party apparatus in the countryside, an organizational force which had been far weaker or even nonexistent in the Soviet case. Strong Party committees at the county level were able to organize large numbers of work teams and guide fundamental change in villages. Particularly important was the CCP's presence in the villages themselves. Seventy percent of all *hsiang* had Party branches by the start of 1955, and 90 percent had them by the end of the year.

The basis of this rural elite was the cadres who had emerged during land reform. Added to this base were new recruits drawn from activists during the cooperativization movement itself, a process which intensified and increasingly focused on poorer peasants in 1955, and demobilized soldiers who became available as the PLA stepped up modernization measures in 1954–55. Equally important were repeated training programs and indoctrination of this rural cadre force in socialist principles. Although there were pronounced tendencies of cadres seeking a life of independent farming at the end of land reform, such tendencies were checked by constant reinforcement which sought to relate all official tasks to the concept of socialist transformation. At no time did the rural leadership structure fall completely under the sway of small peasant production, as had happened in the Soviet Union in the 1920s.

Another major reason for the relative success of the Chinese program was the CCP's carefully constructed rural economic policies, which not only provided benefits for a majority of the peasants but also gave the peasantry as a whole little choice but to cooperate. Credit cooperatives, supply and marketing cooperatives, and the planned marketing of grain and other key commodities all increasingly restricted the private economic opportunities of rich peasants and channeled economic resources preferentially to the cooperative sector, thus increasing the attractiveness of joining the APCs.

Policies were explicitly framed with an eye to protecting the interests of the relatively well off and productive middle peasants who before mid-1955 often had a dominant role in APCs. Beyond this, the basic propaganda appeal emphasizing better living standards and the general ability of official policies to at least avoid a decline in standards despite fair to poor harvest conditions in 1953 and 1954 gave the peasants some reason to expect tangible results from the APCs. When the "high tide" of cooperativization was launched in the context of a bumper harvest in mid-1955, the regime's economic credibility, which had been established during land reform, was still working for it.

The potent combination of administrative pressures, normative appeals, coercion, and tangible results that had achieved remarkable success in land reform and the initial period of cooperativization now came into play during the "high tide." The situation differed markedly from the immediately preceding stage in that tangible benefits were now increasingly focused on the poorer peasants, to the detriment of better-off middle peasants. The cancellation of the land dividend in the higher-stage APCs represented a direct transfer of economic resources between the two groups, and given the numerical dominance of the poorer elements – estimated at 60 to 70 percent of the peasantry – a powerful interest group for the change was created. Normative appeals, which continued to be heavily laced with the promise of prosperity, as a result were especially potent for the poor, although even within this group those who hesitated were with some frequency forcefully herded into APCs. Pressure often bordering on coercion was applied to the better-off middle peasants, and outright coercion in the form of arrests and mass struggle was used against "counterrevolutionaries," including some rich peasants.

In all of this, the cadres continued to be a driving force that responded to a similar set of pressures. Increasingly drawn from the poor peasants by the recruiting measures of late 1955, village leaders were at once the prime target of educational efforts, the direct recipients of administrative pressures with coercive overtones, and the main beneficiaries of local transformation. The switch to higher-stage APCs not only benefited cadres as it did less well-off peasants, it also eased their administrative tasks because they no longer had to calculate the divisive land dividend. And it cemented their political dominance by weakening the middle peasants. With this key group highly motivated, the majority of peasants having reason to anticipate material gains, and disadvantaged groups under tight control but not threatened with liquidation, the momentum for rapid collectivization proved irresistible.

Transforming the modern sector and the first leap forward

By fall 1955 the mounting evidence of a breakthrough in cooperativization allowed Mao and his colleagues to turn some of their attention to the transformation of industry and commerce. The Three and Five Antis campaigns had been launched only after the basic success of land reform. Similarly, with the vast, difficult to control countryside now advancing rapidly toward socialism, Party leaders felt the time had come to use their great leverage in the modern sector. Earlier debates on the speed of the socialist transformation of industry and commerce had paralleled those over the rate of building APCs.

Some saw the need for pushing ahead in order to facilitate central planning, while others urged caution on the grounds that conditions were not yet ripe and overly hasty socialization would disrupt production and overwhelm the state's nascent planning capabilities. In the fall of 1955, however, there was general agreement that socialization of the modern sector would have to keep pace with cooperativization. Although socialized industry and commerce were well in advance of cooperativization in mid-1955, 1st FYP goals were modest in calling for only "the greater part" of privately owned businesses to adopt some form of state capitalism by the end of the Five-Year Plan period.

From the end of October through January, however, Mao and other leaders met with prominent capitalists to impress upon them the need for a stepped up pace of transformation while ostensibly soliciting their views. In these encounters Mao, as he had with agricultural cooperatives, warned against excessive rashness and even declared himself more cautious than Ch'en Yun, but the invited businessmen did not fail to pick up the essential message and quickly pledged support for an accelerated program. On the basis of these pledges, a new target of completing transformation into joint state-private enterprises by the end of 1957 was laid down.

What followed paralleled the overfulfillment of APC targets but in even more startling form. Ch'en Yun organized meetings of provincial leaders to press for the new target but was quickly overtaken by the actions of another Politburo member, Peking mayor P'eng Chen. In December P'eng set the end of 1956 as the target date for Peking, and in January the actual transformation was completed in the first ten days of the month. Other cities did not want to appear laggard, and by the end of January the process had been basically completed in all major urban centers. Obviously such an extremely rapid transformation was superficial. Instead of the prescribed process of careful preparatory work that allowed the state to take operational control, it amounted to a formal declaration of a change in ownership without any change in personnel or internal organization. To avoid disrupting production, the State Council in early February ordered that existing operations be unchanged for six months following transformation. The actual work of taking inventories and economic reorganization was done gradually and was heavily dependent on the private capitalists whose skills were still required in a modern sector where the shortage of cadres remained acute.

While the extension of rapid socialization from agriculture to industry and commerce was to be expected, a less predictable development occurred as Mao sought a "leap forward" in economic construction. In December Mao attacked "right conservative think-ing" in a wide range of work: "The problem today ... lies in agricultural production; industrial production; ... handicraft pro-duction; the scale and speed of capital construction in industry, communications and transport; the coordination of commerce with other branches of the economy; the coordination of the work in science, culture, education and health.... In all these fields there is an underestimation of the situation, a shortcoming which must be criticized and corrected."[50] In late 1955 and early 1956 Mao apparent-ly saw an opportunity to attack China's economic and cultural backwardness in much the same way as he had the socialist trans-formation. Despite continued warnings against "left adventurism" as well as "right conservatism," Mao's thought underwent a subtle shift in the direction of radicalism in the period between his July speech and the end of 1955.[51] This was particularly apparent in his com-mentary on a volume dealing with cooperativization where he claimed that "a raging tidal wave [is] sweeping away all demons and monsters" and if "600 million 'paupers' ... take their destiny into their own hands ... they can overcome any difficulty on earth."[52]

Mao would soon retreat from this highly optimistic view in the face of mounting problems, but at the time there was little to indicate significant opposition within top leadership circles. Whether because of genuine enthusiasm over the advances in socialization or an unwillingness to challenge a determined Chairman, other leaders joined in the effort to push China's first "leap forward."

In terms of concrete policies, in November 1955 Mao proposed a number of long-term measures to boost agricultural production which were expanded and approved in January as a twelve-year draft program for agricultural development over the 1956–67 period. This program laid down ambitious goals, including 100 to 140 percent increases in grain yields, something Mao had expressed doubts over as recently as the previous fall. To accomplish this, the mass mobi-lization of peasant labor and rural financial resources was assigned a central role. But the program also placed a heavy emphasis on scientific and technical inputs and material incentives. In im-

50 Ibid., 240.
51 See the 1980 report of Liao Kai-lung, "Historical experiences," *Issues and Studies*, Novem-ber 1981, 88, which traces the origins of Mao's "leftist" thinking to his late 1955 prefaces to *Socialist upsurge in China's countryside*.
52 Mao, *SW*, 5.244, 250.

plementing the program, the same phenomena occurred as with regard to socialist transformation – lower-level units significantly increased the targets of the draft program and began to implement its measures in a blind, disruptive manner. Similarly, spurred on by Mao's slogan demanding "more, faster, better, and more economical" results, officials at all levels raised short-term targets for both industrial and agricultural production in an effort to reach 1st FYP goals a year ahead of schedule. Various industrial ministries increased their 1956 targets by 25 percent or more; Chou En-lai set a 9 percent growth in grain output as a minimum goal for the year; and some *hsiang* leaders called for 40 percent increases in grain production. This too led to economic dislocations as the administrative system had again proved itself too responsive to pressures from above. These dislocations and the other problems arising from the "high tide" and "leap forward" soon forced their attention on the leadership, and dealing with them became a major feature of the period of adjustment which followed.

ADJUSTING THE NEW SOCIALIST SYSTEM, 1956–1957

The new course which emerged in early 1956 was built on a basic reassessment of conditions in China. According to Mao in January, the "high tide" of socialist transformation had resulted in a "fundamental change in the political situation."[53] This view, which would be modified by the latter part of 1957, reflected the orthodox Marxist concern with the relations of production – that is ownership. With the means of production now largely in the hands of the state or collective units, the victory of socialism over capitalism had been basically decided.

A number of related propositions flowed from this analysis. First, although class struggle was by no means eliminated, in the new situation where enemies of socialism no longer had significant economic means at their disposal, class conflict would markedly attenuate so that, as Mao would put it a year later: "The large scale, turbulent class struggles ... characteristic of ... revolution have in the main come to an end...."[54] Second, this situation called for a fundamental shift in Party priorities to economic development. Mao outlined this new direction while promoting the leap forward in January: "The

53 "Speech to Supreme State Conference" (January 1956), in Helene Carrère d'Encausse and
   Stuart R. Schram, comps., *Marxism and Asia*, 292.
54 Mao, *SW*, 5.395.

object of the socialist revolution [is] to set free the productive forces [and] wipe out China's economic, scientific and cultural backwardness within a few decades."[55] But the new priority was not simply a product of the economic push; later in the year, after the leap forward was discarded, the Eighth Party Congress identified economic backwardness as the heart of the "main contradiction."

A third proposition was that the broadest range of social forces could now be rallied behind the developmental effort in a new adaptation of the united front. Under the slogan of "mobilize all positive factors," the leadership sought not simply to win the backing of dubious sections of society but to encourage creative inputs by all groups, especially China's intellectuals, who had skills urgently required for modernization. Finally, the victory of socialism meant the establishment of a new system that inevitably had its shortcomings and conflicts – what Mao termed "contradictions among the people." In this view tensions in society were predominantly manifestations of legitimate divergences of interest, and the task of the Party became one of mediating the claims of different economic sectors and social groups while perfecting the new institutions of socialism.

A key innovation in these circumstances was a new policy toward intellectuals. In 1955, steps were taken to win intellectual support through forums addressing their problems and awards for top scientists, but these measures were compromised by attacks on such figures as the literary theorist Hu Feng in the context of the campaign against counterrevolutionaries. In 1956, however, the approach to the intellectuals was pursued in a more relaxed political atmosphere influenced in part by the thaw in Soviet treatment of its intelligentsia begun in late 1955, but more fundamentally by the assumption of the weakening of class struggle after socialist transformation.

A major statement of the new policy was made by Chou En-lai in January 1956 in the context of promoting the leap forward in the economy, and a further step came in a May speech by the head of the Central Committee's propaganda department, Lu Ting-i. Chou advocated improved salaries and living conditions, the provision of better working conditions and resources, and more rapid promotions and easier admission into the CCP, while Lu explained Mao's new slogan "Let a hundred flowers bloom, let a hundred schools contend." According to Lu, free discussion and independent thinking were necessary to avoid academic stagnation, and the imposition

55 "Speech to Supreme State Conference" (January 1956), 292–93.

of dogmatic restrictions on intellectual life was hostile to true Marxism-Leninism.

A further measure was an effort to bolster the status of the small democratic parties which had been drawn into the united front in 1949. Under the slogan of "long-term coexistence and mutual supervision," these parties of intellectuals, one-time KMT officials, and businessmen were urged to criticize the performance of the government and build up their own memberships and organizations. Despite the more relaxed atmosphere, all these measures were circumscribed by reassertions of the principle of Party leadership, calls for the continuing ideological remolding of intellectuals, and assertions that the handling of such dissidents as Hu Feng had been entirely correct. As a result, throughout 1956 most intellectuals responded cautiously, although there were enough sharp criticisms to cause a substantial number of cadres to adopt an obstructionist attitude despite efforts by the top leadership to push the new program.

While the new policies toward intellectuals continued to mid-1957, the economic leap forward, together with the rapid pace of socialist transformation, created a set of problems necessitating institutional adjustments and policy reversals by late spring 1956. By this time central officials were becoming aware of the imbalances and planning chaos in the overall economy plus peasant disillusion with both wasteful efforts to realize the draft agricultural program and the rigidities of the new APCs. Starting in April 1956 and continuing into the summer of 1957, measures to deal with these problems were undertaken under a program that became known as "opposing rash advance" – measures including insistence on realistic targets, emphasis on coordination in planning and quality in output, increasing the scope of peasants' private production within the APC framework, reestablishing a limited rural free market, reducing the size of APCs, and heavy criticism of coercive leadership methods by APC cadres. The major architects of this program were Chou En-lai and Ch'en Yun, and broad support by the Party's leading economic officials quickly formed.

Mao was far from enthusiastic. Although he surely agreed with some aspects of the program, particularly those increasing material incentives for the peasants, and initially accepted the need to curb excesses, by mid-1956 he was clearly distressed by retrenchment measures that had ended the leap forward in production. Nevertheless, Mao did not attempt to challenge the new program but, instead, accepted the views of his colleagues in an area where, by his own admission, he lacked competence. In so doing the Chairman adhered to the consensual style he normally followed in the 1949–57 period, but he also harbored doubts and regrets that would play a key role in the launching of the Great Leap Forward.

Adapting the Soviet model

As CCP leaders developed policies for the new situation, they began to examine the Soviet model in a more self-consciously critical manner. Previously Mao and his associates had made significant alterations in the Soviet pattern and called in a general way for adapting Soviet experiences to Chinese conditions, but they had not dwelled on Russian shortcomings or CCP innovations in public or internal statements. Indeed, as late as January 1956 Mao could still profess to believe that the CCP had merely elaborated on Soviet achievements and "since the October Revolution there have been no new things of note."[56] By this time, however, a systematic review of the Soviet model was already under way which would soon lead to explicit and sharp criticisms of defects in the Russian system.

All this would develop within the context of strains in Sino-Soviet relations following the Twentieth Soviet Party Congress in February 1956, but such strains were not a fundamental cause of the reexamination of the model. In any case, throughout 1956 and most of 1957, the emphasis was still on learning from the Soviet Union, but in a highly selective fashion that rejected backward aspects of Soviet practice.

A growing realization that the Soviet Union had begun from a much higher industrial base than the PRC, yet had only achieved a pace of growth that seemed somewhat slow, apparently set the stage for the reevaluation of the model. This involved Politburo discussions with leading personnel from thirty-four central economic departments and led to one of Mao's most significant speeches, the April 1956 "Ten great relationships." As Mao later observed, this talk, which drew general conclusions based upon the previous months' discussions and thus represented more than Mao's personal view, "made a start in proposing our own line for construction [which] was similar to that of the Soviet Union in principle, but had our own content."[57] While references to Soviet shortcomings covered a wide

---

56 "Tsai Chung-kung chung-yang chao-k'ai ti kuan-yü chih-shih fen-tzu wen-t'i hui-i shang ti chiang-hua" (Speech at the conference on the question of intellectuals convened by the CCP Central Committee) (20 January 1956), in *Wan-sui* (1969), 33.
57 "Talks at the Chengtu conference" (March 1958), in Schram, *Mao unrehearsed*, 101.

scope, in many areas such as agriculture Chinese practice had long been distinctive. Where Mao called for adjustments in existing practices, the changes suggested were modest and left the basic Soviet-style institutional structure and economic strategy in place.

A central question was the ratio of investment between heavy industry on the one hand and light industry and agriculture on the other. Mao attacked Soviet overemphasis on heavy industry but reaffirmed its primary claim for investment funds, asking only that "the proportion for agriculture and light industry must be somewhat increased."[58] This was indeed done in June 1956, when the ratio of heavy industry to light industry investment was marginally reduced from 8:1 to 7:1; and in September proposals for the 2nd FYP slightly increased agricultural investment from 7 to 10 percent in comparison to the 1st FYP.

Another key concern of the "Ten great relationships" was economic administration: "We must not follow the example of the Soviet Union in concentrating everything in the hands of the central authorities, shackling the local authorities and denying them the right to independent action."[59] Here too Mao was cautious, calling for greater consultation with the localities, the enlargement of their powers "to some extent" within the framework of unified central leadership, and further investigation of the problem. What was envisioned here was a move away from vertical ministerial control to a form of "dual rule" where powers were shared between the ministries and regional authorities, but there was no clarity as to method.

The State Council subsequently held a series of meetings on how to curb excessive centralization, and the proposals for the 2nd FYP assigned more construction projects to local authorities. Moreover, other approaches to combating overcentralization were advocated which emphasized indirect planning (norms for reference only) and the use of market mechanisms. Proposals in this regard were made by Ch'en Yun in September 1956 at the Eighth Party Congress, and in the following months experiments with methods of enhancing enterprise autonomy and selective purchasing on the market were carried out. In January 1957, however, the State Council decided that the basic pattern of planned allocation would continue for the year because of the complex administrative problems any change would require, and undoubtedly also because of the opposition of many economic planners. Similarly, despite intense debate in economic

58 Mao, SW, 5.286.   59 Ibid., 292.

journals over methods of decentralization throughout 1957, until the fall of the year no major decision had been taken.

Throughout this debate on how to modify Soviet-style administration, it is important to note, contemporary Soviet developments were a contributing factor. The Soviet Union had undertaken decentralization measures of its own in mid-1955, and views of Soviet economists on the need to overcome the rigidities of central planning had made a significant impact on leading participants in the Chinese debates. Indeed, even in areas where the CCP was far less beholden to the Soviet model than in economic planning, Soviet reforms played an influential role. Thus Party leaders had initially adopted the Soviet machine tractor station as the method for spreading the mechanization of agriculture. These stations, which were separate entities contracting their services to APCs, had many inefficiencies and often worked at cross-purposes with the cooperatives. Criticism of their faults in the Soviet Union and Eastern Europe and Soviet experiments with placing tractors under the direct control of collectives were already under way in spring 1956 when Politburo member K'ang Sheng represented the CCP at the East German Party Congress. The problem was discussed extensively at this Congress, and upon his return K'ang conducted an investigation in China. This resulted in a critical report in November, experiments with alternatives in 1957, and finally the decision to place agricultural machinery directly in the hands of the APCs in 1958, the same year the machine tractor station was abolished in the Soviet Union.

Additional aspects of modifying the Soviet model are illustrated by another issue raised in the spring 1956 Politburo discussions – the system of factory management. In the early 1950s the Soviet system of "one man management" which placed ultimate authority in the hands of the factory manager had been widely introduced in the Northeast. This system had been recommended, but not ordered, for the entire country in early 1953. Beginning in 1954, criticisms of the system were increasingly aired but defenses were also published, and during 1954–56 it continued to be allowed as one variant of enterprise management pending a Politburo decision. One of the factors at work in this case was that the PRC simply lacked sufficient numbers of competent personnel to make one man management work. The system not only never predominated in China as a whole but was only partially implemented even in the Northeast. In addition, there was significant resistance from Party cadres who objected to restrictions on their powers and resented the authority the system vested in managers from suspect class backgrounds.

Moreover, these cadres raised the potent charge that the system violated CCP traditions of Party control and collective decision making, that it was "only centralism and no democracy." Such arguments, in conjunction with the inadequate resources for one man management and the increasing number of Party cadres who had been recruited and trained in industry in the preceding years, were crucial when the leadership decided on a new system upgrading the powers of the factory Party committee above those of the factory manager. In announcing this decision to the Eighth Party Congress, the Party official responsible for industry, Li Hsueh-feng, emphasized the importance of Party traditions. This change, however, was far from a rejection of Soviet industrial methods. Indeed, in the same period Soviet-style piecework wage systems were being extended throughout most of China.

Another area where CCP traditions became a central issue in adapting the Soviet model was modernizing the PLA. By 1956, Party leaders clearly felt political traditions were being eroded by the Soviet-aided modernization effort and began a series of measures to check this trend. These included intensified political education for officers, a strengthening of the Party committee structure within the PLA, attacks on overspecialization and excessive emphasis on ranks and titles, increased PLA participation in production, salary cuts for higher-ranking officers, and an emphasis on democratic relations between officers and men. By such measures Party leaders sought, in the words of T'an Cheng, deputy director of the PLA's political department, to ensure that "no amount of modernization will change the fact that ours is a people's army."[60] This, however, in no way implied a downgrading of military modernization. Thus T'an criticized the "guerrilla" tendencies of those who refused to adjust to the needs of modern warfare; the need to assimilate Soviet military experiences albeit in an undogmatic manner continued to be emphasized; modernization measures continued unabated; and at the end of 1957 a program was unveiled for professionalizing all officers within five years. The basic aim of the 1956–57 adjustments was still to modernize, but within the context of PLA traditions. This would cause some strains within the officer corps, but Party and army leaders saw no inherent incompatibility in the effort.

60 "Speech by Comrade T'an Cheng" (18 September 1956), in *Eighth National Congress*, 2.265.

Other policy shifts in 1956–57 represented modifications of the Soviet model. Particularly in 1957, there was increasing attention to small- and medium-scale industry, in contrast to the Soviet emphasis on large, capital-intensive plants. Similarly, in education the expansion of elite specialized institutions which were the core of the Soviet approach slowed down, and a renewed emphasis on small community-run schools appeared (see Chapter 4). Thus a second low-technology leg was gaining increased prominence, but it would become a major feature of Chinese developmental strategies only under the "walk on two legs" slogan of the Great Leap Forward. For the time being, such programs were clearly auxiliary and did not challenge the continued predominance of the modern, large-scale sector. Finally, the reexamination of the Soviet model meant a new receptiveness to alternative foreign sources of ideas, including not only Communist Yugoslavia but also the advanced capitalist states of the West. But there was, in fact, little of such eclectic borrowing, and the Soviet-style structures and strategy remained fundamentally in place until late 1957.

The Eighth Party Congress

When the Party Congress convened in September 1956 for the first time in eleven years, the occasion was marked by an outpouring of both self-congratulation and self-criticism. There was indeed much reason for congratulation over both the victory of 1949 and the success of socialist transformation in 1955–56. Moreover, the Party had grown during the period of transformation into a mammoth organization of 10.7 million members which now penetrated most aspects of social, economic, and political life. But Party leaders also recognized that many tasks remained and many faults existed within the new system, and the Congress was marked by a remarkably frank yet ultimately self-confident analysis of the problems facing the regime.

The main task, as affirmed by the political resolution of the Congress, was getting on with the job of economic development. The policy line for this task elaborated the "opposing rash advance" theme, although (perhaps with a view to Mao's sensibilities) "right conservatism" received pride of place in the official listing of deviations to be avoided. The proposals for the 2nd FYP announced by Chou En-lai reflected balance, moderation, and realism, but they still called for a slight increase in the rate of reinvestment compared with the 1st FYP. Overall, the program of the Congress was not one of retreat, but the emphasis was decidedly on *steady* advance.

In many ways the 1956 Party Congress was less of a personal triumph for Mao than its predecessor in 1945, which had put the seal on his leadership of the Party. On the surface, several developments diminished Mao's role: The reference to his thought as part of the CCP's guiding ideology was deleted from the new Party constitution, and the Congress placed heavy stress on collective leadership. In 1956, however, there were a number of factors operating against any outpourings of adulation, although fundamentally Mao's position remained unchallenged.[61] One consideration arose from external events – Khrushchev's denunciation of Stalin's "personality cult" at the Soviet Party Congress in February. Under these circumstances, any lavish praise of the Chinese leader would have been unseemly, and Mao later stated that he fully concurred in the decision to delete his thought from the constitution.

A second consideration, one that suggests both Mao's self-assurance and his confidence in his associates, was the need to arrange for an orderly succession. Mao's subsequent statements indicate that he took several concrete steps at the Eighth Congress for his eventual retirement to the "second front" – removed from operational decisions – so that his colleagues could gain sufficient prestige to ensure a smooth transition after his death and thus avoid the strife that marked Soviet politics after Stalin. The post of honorary Party Chairman was created for Mao's eventual retirement; Liu Shao-ch'i's status as heir apparent was bolstered by entrusting him with the presentation of the political report (a role Mao filled in 1945); and strong collective organs were established in the Politburo Standing Committee and an enlarged Party Secretariat. None of this meant Mao was abdicating real power. As he put it in early 1958, when proposing new measures for his retreat to the "second front," "Whenever the nation is urgently in need ... I will shoulder this leadership task once again."[62]

Linked to Mao's continued dominance was a much broader pattern of leadership stability. This stability was reflected not only in the reelection of virtually all Central Committee members but in person-

61 This analysis (cf. Teiwes, *Politics and purges*, 226–30) differs from interpretations seeing "Mao in eclipse" at the Congress (e.g. Chang, *Power and policy*, 29ff.) and those emphasizing conflicts between Mao and other leaders (e.g. MacFarquhar, *Origins*, 1, part 2).
62 "Sixty points on working methods" (19 February 1958), in Jerome Ch'en, ed., *Mao papers: Anthology and bibliography*, 75.

nel arrangements at all levels. The new Politburo Standing Committee consisted of the same five men who had made up the old Secretariat, formerly the inner core of leadership, plus the rapidly promoted Teng Hsiao-p'ing. The size of the full Politburo was nearly doubled to take in all pre-Congress members plus most PLA marshals who were not already included and all vice-premiers except Teng Tzu-hui, who apparently was made to pay for his views on cooperativization. Within this top body there were some alterations in the pecking order, but apart from the significant rise of Teng Hsiao-p'ing and the dropping of Chang Wen-t'ien (an old opponent of Mao's in the 1930s) and K'ang Sheng to alternate status, these were relatively minor.

Similarly, the more than doubled ranks of full Central Committee members included not only nearly all former full members but also all but three alternates, who were promoted en masse. In addition, over 100 new individuals were added to the new Central Committee – roughly one-third as full members and the remainder as alternates – yet the background characteristics of the 170-person body were remarkably similar to the 1945 Central Committee.

The new central bodies also reflected the PRC's emerging institutional pattern. The expansion of the Politburo and Central Committee was essentially accomplished by coopting the key figures in the regime's various hierarchies. As a result, the broader elite tendency toward specialization was carried into the highest bodies, guaranteeing that the views and interests of each major sector would be represented. Particularly important at the Politburo level was the selection of three key officials responsible for the economy – Li Fu-ch'un, chairman of the State Planning Commission, Finance Minister Li Hsien-nien, and the chairman of the State Economic Commission, Po I-po (as an alternate) – who now joined Ch'en Yun on the vital policy-making organ. The appointments further demonstrated the centralized nature of the system under the 1st FYP, since nearly three times as many Central Committee members served in Peking as in the provinces. Finally, the composition of the new top elite also reflected the post-1949 shift to civilian rule and the central role of the Party in the system. Full-time civilian Party and government officials outnumbered PLA leaders by 2 to 1 on the Politburo and nearly 3 to 1 on the Central Committee, while the Central Committee ratio of full-time Party, government, and military leaders was something on the order of 6:5:4.

The institutional representation on the new Central Committee was a manifestation of the substantial degree to which Chinese politics had become bureaucratized. Party leaders had long been critical of various bureaucratic practices – red tape, organizational proliferation, decisions made in offices without firsthand knowledge of actual conditions – and by the mid-1950s were increasingly aware of the constraints placed on their options by the ever more specialized administrative machine they had created. Despite measures to reassert control, including transfers of Party cadres to key ministerial posts, strengthening the role of Party committees within government agencies, and attacks on excessive professionalization, leaders at all levels found their perspectives increasingly dominated by the organizations in which they served. Even the top decision-making generalists were entrapped; as Mao complained in early 1958: "The Politburo has become a voting machine, . . . you give it a perfect document and it has to be passed."[63] The qualms of Mao and others notwithstanding, in ways besides the composition of the new ruling bodies, the proceedings of the Eighth Party Congress represented a full flowering of bureaucratic politics.

With the period of revolutionary transformations ostensibly past and economic development the main task, the Congress heard a long series of speeches by leaders articulating their departments' opinions on how to accomplish the broader goal. Similarly, the need to adjust the institutions of the new socialist system generated proposals advancing the interests of specific organizations. In some cases a degree of restraint was required when decisions had already gone against the institution concerned, but even here bureaucratic interests were expressed. Thus Minister of Defense P'eng Te-huai could not explicitly call for more resources, since the decision had been made to cut defense spending from 32 to 20 percent of budgetary expenditure in the 2nd FYP, but he still emphasized the need to press ahead with military modernization and to strengthen defense.

Where policies were still undecided, however, appeals for organizational interests were often blatant. This was especially the case in speeches by provincial Party leaders who sought favorable consideration from the central authorities over resources and policy guidelines. For example, Shantung's T'an Ch'i-lung hoped that "the central Ministry of Water Conservancy . . . will give us support with regard to technology, investments, and similar problems," and also asked "the relevant central ministries when settling sowing plans . . . not to

63 "Talks at the Nanning conference" (11–12 January 1958), *Miscellany*, 1.80.

be too rigid [and] enable us to make a reasonable apportionment in accordance with ... actual conditions of the area."[64] Given the relaxed political atmosphere and the specialized nature of the job at hand, the Eighth Congress was a fitting occasion for articulating the views and interests of a vast array of bureaucratic organizations.

Party rectification and the Hundred Flowers

The criticisms of shortcomings in the system that had marked not only the Eighth Congress but much official commentary since spring 1956 foreshadowed a more systematic effort to overcome faults through a Party rectification movement. Initially, this campaign was to be patterned on the great Yenan rectification of 1942–44, an effort to combat by relatively persuasive means dangerous ideological and political tendencies within the Party so that it could more successfully pursue the struggle against the Japanese and KMT. Now, with new problems and opportunities arising in the socialist era, the Party would again be reformed in an even more low-key manner, like a "gentle breeze and mild rain," to make it a more effective force for economic construction.

A major target of the reform effort was "subjectivism," the backward ideological state where unfamiliarity with changing conditions caused Party officials to apply unsuited concepts and methods arbitrarily to current problems. A particularly significant manifestation criticized at this juncture was the dogmatic copying of foreign (Soviet) experiences, and the recommended cure was to raise the general level of Marxist-Leninist theory in the Party, develop knowledge of specialized fields, and carry out research into actual conditions.

Closely linked to "subjectivism" was the sin of "bureaucratism," the drifting away of officials from the masses and social reality and toward becoming a privileged elite. This was particularly dangerous because as a part of a ruling organization, Party members were in a position to seek their own advantage and ignore the interests of the people. Various forms of supervision were required to prevent such abuses.

The third main evil attacked was "sectarianism," the tendency of Party members to feel superior to non-Party people and discriminate against them in organizational life. This was a problem of critical

64 Cited in Roderick MacFarquhar, "Aspects of the CCP's Eighth Congress (first session)," paper presented to the University Seminar on Modern East Asia: China, Columbia University, 19 February 1969, 10, 13.

importance regarding the skilled intellectuals, and the Hundred Flowers and mutual supervision policies were aimed at overcoming it.

Concrete steps indicating a Party reform movement began in mid-1956 with a program for the study of rectification documents, but at the Eighth Congress rectification was still a relatively low-priority item despite frequent attacks on the three evils. External events – the Polish October and the abortive Hungarian revolt – forced a higher priority for rectification. Mao subsequently claimed the danger of letting problems fester revealed by Hungary and Poland convinced him of the need to handle "contradictions among the people" correctly, and at a November 1956 Central Committee plenary meeting the Chairman announced a mild rectification campaign for "next year."

The lessons of Eastern Europe, however, were ambiguous. On the one hand, restiveness of the population as a result of bureaucratic perversions – a situation manifested to a more limited degree in China by a significant number of industrial strikes in 1956 – argued for dealing with such deviations before matters got out of control and thus enhanced the significance of rectification. On the other hand, the situation in Eastern Europe exploded in large part because political controls had been eroded, and the official CCP analysis of these events cited "revisionism" – the challenge to orthodox Party rule – as the main danger. This position argued for caution regarding Party reform, and in January a decision for full-scale rectification was announced for 1958, not 1957.

Mao clearly contributed to this more cautious approach with warnings against an "antisocialist tide" that allegedly had appeared in the latter half of 1956, but it is equally clear that he did not want a total halt to reform efforts or a return to arbitrary methods of dealing with intellectuals. In winter 1956–57, however, many middle to upper-echelon officials and ordinary cadres attempted to do just that as a decidedly more restrictive atmosphere emerged.

By February Mao concluded that bold action was required if Party reform was not to be totally eroded, and he intervened with two major speeches. In them Mao reverted to the fundamentally confident view of 1956. Victory had been achieved, and the main task was attending to flaws in the system. The intellectuals were a basically loyal force which could make great contributions to economic and cultural development. Now the nation was united as never before, and shortcomings could be overcome in a nondisruptive fashion. The Chairman, however, when revealing that rectification was once again scheduled for 1957, also introduced some novel and unsettling ideas concerning reform methods. Not only would Marxism-Leninism not be stipulated as the guiding ideology for criticism, but intellectuals would be invited to play a key role in offering criticism of the Party. Thus the Hundred Flowers was converted from an encouragement of academic debate to a method of conducting rectification. Mao sought to reassure cadres that intellectuals' criticism would be of a helpful nature and that rectification would still be according to "gentle breeze and mild rain" methods. But the prospect of CCP members being directly criticized by bourgeois intellectuals was enough to send shudders of concern throughout the Party elite.

There was considerable resistance to Mao's innovative approach, although the precise contours of opposition remain unclear.[65] Mao himself claimed in April that 90 percent of "Party comrades" had a negative attitude toward the refurbished Hundred Flowers and added that "I have no mass base."[66] Indeed, there does appear to have been widespread opposition among lower- and middle-rank cadres charged with controlling intellectuals on a day-to-day basis. These officials, whose immediate powers and prerogatives were at stake, had a different perspective from the more removed top leadership. Fearing that the process would get out of hand, such cadres failed to encourage the "blooming and contending" of intellectuals, but instead indiscriminately attacked their critical opinions.

At higher levels, there is good reason to believe that some leaders in the Party propaganda apparatus responsible for both publicizing the Hundred Flowers and organizing many of the conferences of intellectuals where "blooming and contending" took place were less than enthusiastic about the new policy. Clearly the Central Committee's newspaper, the *People's Daily*, was laggard in responding to Mao's initiative and was sharply criticized by the Chairman as a result. This apparent resistance can be explained in essentially similar terms to the opposition of lower-ranking cadres – as officials responsible for the daily management of intellectuals, they probably felt the dangers of the new approach outweighed any possible benefits.

Conflict within the Politburo itself over rectification remains uncertain, despite some scholarly analysis that sees Mao seriously at

65 The following analysis and that for the subsequent section on the Anti-Rightist Campaign is drawn from Teiwes, *Politics and purges*, ch. 6–7. For contrasting interpretations, see the sources cited in note 67.
66 "Talk at the Hangchow conference of the Shanghai bureau" (April 1957), in *Miscellany*, 1.67.

loggerheads with his colleagues.[67] Certainly it is likely that such a novel policy, which exposed the Party of the proletariat to rebukes by intellectuals from bourgeois backgrounds, caused debate within the highest circles. Some information claims opposition to Mao on this issue by Liu Shao-ch'i and P'eng Chen, but the total pattern of evidence is inconclusive. P'eng in particular was a vigorous supporter of "blooming and contending" in his publicized statements, while Liu, although silent in public, nevertheless toured the provinces and advanced views consistent with Mao's to closed Party meetings. In any case, if reservations were expressed behind the closed doors of the Politburo, they did not sharply polarize the leadership. The combination of Mao's power and the general leadership commitment to free debate within Party councils but disciplined implementation outside undoubtedly were the crucial factors in dampening any divisions. Other factors were also at work – the broad consensus on the nature of the new situation; the fact that Mao had not over a long period consistently pushed radical rectification methods which might have crystallized opposition but instead had changed his position according to altered circumstances; and finally the fact that the initial response of the intellectuals to Mao's invitation was restrained and thus did not pose a dramatic threat to Party rule.

The at first tepid response of the intellectuals was understandable, given the ideological remolding they had been subjected to since the thought reform campaign of 1951–52. Despite anxiety that relaxation would be followed by renewed pressure, they finally reacted to repeated official prodding and to the fact that throughout May 1957 those who were bold enough to speak out were not punished with an outpouring of countercriticism. In one sense, the intellectuals' criticism by and large was not threatening to Party rule. The bulk of it dealt with problems and conflicts directly related to their roles and functions. Moreover, in the overwhelming number of cases, the criticisms advanced were similar to strictures directed at "subjectivism," "bureaucratism," and "sectarianism" in the official media since 1956. Even proposals for institutional change, such as the idea of turning the CPPCC into an upper house of the National People's Congress, reflected ideas which had been advanced by the highest Party leaders.

67 Major analyses holding that both the rectification and subsequent Anti-Rightist campaigns were occasions for major dissension within the top leadership are: MacFarquhar, *Origins*, 1, parts 3 and 4; and Richard H. Solomon, *Mao's revolution and the Chinese political culture*, ch. 17. This interpretation is also adopted in Chapter 7 of this volume.

In another sense, however, the attacks were deeply unsettling. This was due less to some suggestions that deviations might be somehow intrinsic to the system or even the few extreme sentiments calling for the Party's demise than to the cumulative vehemence of complaints concerning intellectuals' daily confrontations with Party authority and the depth of discontent they reflected. The strength of feeling was particularly apparent in the views and actions of students, who even took to the streets to articulate their grievances. By focusing on the shortcomings of Party cadres in the everyday affairs of their work units, intellectuals were in effect raising the issue of the Party's competence to guide China in the new period of socialist construction. Yet it must be emphasized that this did not amount to a rejection of the system. Even some of the most outspoken student critics still supported public ownership, hailed Mao as "the revolutionary leader who saved China," and expressed a loyal if ambivalent attitude toward the CCP: "We want Party leadership, but we are resolutely opposed to the Party alone making decisions."[68] The results of "blooming and contending" suggested continuing support for the broad outlines of the system and for the CCP program of building a new China, but at the same time a deep alienation among skilled groups from the concrete manifestations of Party rule. By mid-May the Party leadership was dismayed at what had unfolded. The extent of discontent among intellectuals who had been assigned such a key role in development and especially among students who had been raised in the PRC was deeply distressing. Moreover, cadre morale had suffered a severe jolt as a result of being required to endure the critical onslaught.

Why did the Hundred Flowers experiment fail? Essentially the failure was due to some fundamental misconceptions concerning the new situation in China. Assuming that the intellectuals essentially stood on the side of socialism and had no fundamental clashes of interest with the system, Mao concluded that they could make positive contributions even to so sensitive an affair as Party rectification. This did not take into account the facts that bourgeois intellectuals as a group had often been subjected to severe pressure since the early days of the PRC, that their interests as they conceived them had often been grievously violated, and that their relations with Party cadres were marked by mutual mistrust. When Mao thrust the intellectuals into the forefront of rectification, he in effect asked them

68 From a Peking student pamphlet translated in Dennis J. Doolin, *Communist China: The politics of student opposition*, 50, 55.

to perform an impossible task: to criticize boldly Party authorities they often feared and loathed, yet to do so in the spirit of a "gentle breeze and mild rain."

Party cadres too were placed in an unprecedented position. In effect, they were being asked to redefine Party leadership in ways which were never precisely stipulated to take into account the views and talents of non-Party intellectuals. Moreover, they were themselves subject to the criticism by these individuals of suspect class origins and backward ideology, something which seemed most unjust. Given the underlying tensions between cadres and intellectuals, any effort which exacerbated those tensions, however unwittingly, was bound to get out of control. (For further discussion, see Chapter 5.)

The Anti-Rightist Campaign

Although a direct counterattack was launched only in early June 1957, by mid-May top CCP leaders decided that unchecked "blooming and contending" was unacceptably weakening Party control over the intellectuals. Mao was in the forefront of this effort despite his earlier championing of the Hundred Flowers. Not only did the Chairman undertake the key initiatives that began the policy shift, but throughout the summer of 1957 Party policies toward "rightists," as the non-Party critics were dubbed, all bore his imprint. Mao, moreover, was not shy about reversing himself on a whole series of specific issues. For example, in April Mao hailed the non-Party Shanghai paper *Wen-hui pao* for publicizing critical opinions. In July he bitterly attacked the same newspaper as a "rightist" organ. In February he proposed a review of counterrevolutionary cases, but in October he denounced the democratic Party leader Lo Lung-chi for a similar proposal.

Whatever the reasons for so unscrupulous an about-face in these and other instances, the net effect was to remove any differences that may have existed between the Chairman and other leaders. With his illusions about the intellectuals shattered, Mao came down strongly on the side of firm Party control.

The counterattack on the critics took the form of an Anti-Rightist Campaign. This campaign was defensive in tone. It attempted to refute critical arguments advanced by intellectuals in the spring and restore Party dominance in the urban organizations where "blooming and contending" had been primarily conducted. Ironically, given the intellectuals' criticism of heavy-handed Party methods, organization-al measures taken in conjunction with the Anti-Rightist Campaign – particularly the transfer of reliable Party cadres to leadership posi-tions in educational and cultural units – resulted in a substantial increase in Party control compared with the situation before the Hundred Flowers. The main focus of the movement itself was initially on leading members of democratic parties who were singled out as the core of "rightist" groups. These individuals had quite accurately been disparaged by student critics as "cautious old men" for the moderate views they advanced in the spring, yet now they were charged with plotting the overthrow of the regime. They were subjected to violent press attacks and large-scale struggle meet-ings and forced into abject confessions; yet by late 1958–59 most were restored to posts in the democratic parties, indicating that the harshest accusations against them were not taken seriously.

Nevertheless, they served as useful symbols to set the tone for the campaign which spread to "rightists" generally within intellectual organizations from mid-July. While non-Party intellectuals were the key targets, Party intellectuals who had spoken out for their profes-sional rather than their Party interests in the spring also suffered on a smaller scale. The total impact on China's intellectuals was devastat-ing: Altogether some 550,000 were labeled "rightists," the psycho-logical pressures of struggle sessions resulted in a significant number of suicides, and reform through labor was apparently meted out on a large scale. In the post-Mao period the severity of the campaign has been regarded as a major mistake of "enlarging the scope of class struggle," with perhaps 98 percent of all "rightist" labels wrongly applied.[69] (For further discussion, see Chapter 5.)

The harshness of the movement should not obscure the fact that the leadership's attitude toward intellectuals did not become totally negative in mid-1957. In an effort to avoid complete alienation, official guidelines for the campaign held that only a small number of intellectuals were rightists and advocated a lenient overall approach. This reflected a continuing belief that intellectuals had an impor-tant role to play in China's modernization despite their ideological backwardness.

69 The 98 percent assessment, and also the 550,000 figure for rightists, appears in the 1980 report by Liao Kai-lung, "Historical experiences," *Issues and studies*, October 1981, 80–81. The 1981 official "Resolution on certain questions in the history of our Party since the founding of the People's Republic of China," *Beijing Review*, 27(1981), 19, more cautiously affirmed the correctness of counterattacking "rightists," but held that the scope of attack was too broad.

Mao expressed the leadership's ambivalence in July by attacking intellectuals as unwilling to submit to the Party but, nevertheless, citing the need to win over individual "great intellectuals [who are] useful to us."[70] The Hundred Flowers fiasco had demonstrated that intellectuals could not be relied on politically, but it did not settle the issue of their role in economic and cultural development. As the Anti-Rightist Campaign unfolded in the summer of 1957, overall economic policy initially remained on the same moderate course as 1956, an approach requiring a major role for professional expertise. Thus it was still quite possible that once Party control was reestablished, a policy of concessions to intellectuals short of a leading role in Party rectification could have been adopted. The severity of the Anti-Rightist Campaign, however, undoubtedly damaged the enthusiasm of intellectuals for the Party's developmental goals. The leadership, moreover, now had reason to doubt a strategy that placed wavering intellectuals in so central a role.

Other factors were also at work. The general attempt to deal with grievances in society by political relaxation had adverse social effects with important economic ramifications. Of particular significance was the situation in the countryside. The critical atmosphere toward APC abuses officially encouraged in 1956 led to what subsequently was called a "small typhoon" including substantial peasant withdrawals from the cooperatives in the winter of 1956–57. The Hundred Flowers led to further deterioration of the situation as disgruntled peasants, reportedly encouraged by press and radio reports of urban "blooming and contending," challenged the rural cadre structure and increasingly engaged in such "spontaneous capitalist" activities as decentralizing APC responsibility to individual peasant households, demanding more money and grain from the state while selling less surplus to it, and speculative activities.

Particularly disturbing was the fact that some cadres participated in "capitalist" behavior and conspired with peasants to conceal or underestimate grain output. This, together with another poor crop whereby food output lagged behind the rate of population increase, resulted in a severe grain supply crisis. Party leaders responded with a summer 1957 decision to clamp down on the rural free market and launch a rural socialist education movement. This movement conducted propaganda on the claimed superiority of socialism among the

70 "Tsai Shang-hai shih ko-chieh jen-shih hui-i shang ti chiang-hua" (Speech at the conference of all circles in Shanghai municipality), (8 July 1957) in *Wan-sui* (1969), 121.

peasants generally, arrested offending former landlords and rich peasants, carried out a limited purge of rural Party members who engaged in irregular practices, and as a result of bolstering the collective sector, restored overall cadre authority vis-à-vis the peasantry. Once again the combination of persuasive and coercive methods, together with a direct appeal to the interests of the new rural elite, was successful in achieving Party objectives.

Added to such social and political problems were related economic ones. The unsatisfactory performance of the agricultural sector was underlined by consecutive below-par years in 1956 and 1957. Not only had the new cooperative structure failed to provide a production spurt, but the subsequent emphasis on material incentives within the APC framework had also been unsuccessful. The lag in agriculture had its impact on industrial growth, and Chou En-lai announced a 20 percent cut in capital construction in June 1957. Following the logic of the "Ten great relationships," the leadership modestly increased total state investment in agriculture in 1957, but this promised no breakthrough. With the Soviet economic strategy called into question, one possible alternative was to focus on gradually increasing agricultural output while accepting a reduced rate of overall growth. But since Party leaders viewed a high rate of growth as a key goal, such as alternative was an unlikely long-term strategy.

Thus by fall 1957 a number of pressures were converging for change in developmental strategy: perceived deficiencies of the Soviet model, the questionable reliability of the intellectuals, the socially disruptive consequences of political relaxation, and a sluggish economy. Moreover, the cautious marginal adjustments which had been made to the Soviet model – greater awareness of the key economic role of agriculture, moves toward administrative decentralization, and more emphasis on smaller-scale industrial projects and locally supported education – provided outlooks and programs which could be developed into a grander innovative strategy. Finally, Mao and some of his leadership colleagues could look back from the latter part of 1957 over the events of the preceding two years and draw some dubious but nevertheless influential conclusions.

On the positive side, Mao decided that while his initial view on the decisive victory of socialist transformation in 1956 had been premature as success had been limited to the ownership front, the rectification and Anti-Rightist campaigns had achieved that fundamental victory on the political and ideological fronts. Therefore, the Chinese people were ready as never before to carry out an economic and technical revolution. From a more negative perspective, Mao declared that the "opposing rash advance" policies had been a serious mistake that not only caused economic losses by dampening the enthusiasm of the masses but also encouraged the "rightists" to launch their political assault. The lesson to be drawn was that the leap forward approach of early 1956 must be pushed without reservation in order to sustain the ardor of the workers and peasants. These ideas began to become dominant during the plenary meeting of the Central Committee in September–October 1957, and by the end of the year China was well on the road to the Great Leap Forward.

Conclusions

Although major problems faced Party leaders in late 1957, the overall performance of the PRC since 1949 had been remarkably successful. Despite resentment of particular features of CCP rule, the regime had obtained far-reaching popular support as a result of achievements in securing social order, launching economic development, improving living conditions, and restoring national pride. At the same time it had accomplished a basic social and institutional transformation so that by 1956 China had entered the socialist stage.

The reasons for these successes varied. As emphasized throughout this analysis, the Soviet model and leadership unity were critical factors, factors that would be removed or weakened with the Great Leap Forward. In particular, with the model providing clear goals and unity producing strong commitment to official programs, conditions were optimal for utilizing to full advantage the disciplined Party apparatus which had played such a central role in revolutionary victory. While hardly immune to organizational and political shortcomings, the Party organization generally proved responsive to major initiatives and policies – sometimes overzealously so. In the 1949–57 period, with the brief exception of the Hundred Flowers experiment, CCP programs reinforced the authority of this disciplined apparatus and thus enhanced the regime's capabilities for development and transformation.

Success was also due to CCP leaders' skilfully combining persuasive, coercive, and tangible appeals in securing compliance. Constant efforts to convince the populace of the Party's view persuaded many individuals and groups of the correctness of Communist policies and made even more people aware of acceptable modes of behavior. Coercion was used both to break the opposition of hostile groups and to impress the majority that the Party was a force that could not be resisted. And programs designed to further the tangible interests of key social groups – especially poorer peasants and the burgeoning cadre elite – provided crucial support for the CCP on the basis of perceived self-interest.

Another important factor was the applicability of strategies and methods which had served so well during the revolutionary period. The mass mobilization techniques developed in the rural base areas of North China proved adaptable to land reform and agricultural cooperativization throughout China after 1949. Also, notwithstanding the miscalculations of 1956–57, the united front tactic which had been effective against the Japanese and KMT generally succeeded in narrowing active resistance, neutralizing wavering elements, and maximizing support under conditions of CCP rule. Especially important was the fact that the pre-1949 realism and careful marshaling of resources largely prevailed between 1949 and 1957. While the ambitious programs of this initial period often stretched organizational resources, they rarely overextended them to the point where official hierarchies could no longer effectively guide social and economic change. And when this did occur in early 1956, it was corrected in a matter of months.

Finally, the accomplishments of the first eight years were due in large measure to the absence of any perceived incompatibility among the goals pursued or methods used by the CCP. Social goals and economic objectives were regarded as mutually reinforcing. Agricultural cooperatives were the accepted solution to production problems as well as ideologically desirable, while socialization of the modern sector both eliminated capitalism and facilitated planned economic growth. Similarly, institutionalization and mass campaigns were both accepted as appropriate means for socialist ends. Campaigns were suited to major efforts at social transformation, while strong institutions were needed to guide planned development and manage a socialist society. Even where tensions were acknowledged, as between military modernization and PLA traditions, it was assumed that contradictions could be resolved without damage to any important goal. In later years, as Mao and other Party leaders increasingly realized that economic objectives had major social costs, that strong institutions could threaten some values while safeguarding others, and that the very content of "socialism" was uncertain, the potential for conflict grew and the relatively smooth advances of the formative period became increasingly difficult to sustain.

CHAPTER 3

ECONOMIC RECOVERY AND
THE 1ST FIVE-YEAR PLAN

When the Chinese Communist Party (CCP) wrested control of China from the Nationalist party (the KMT) in 1949, the economy was near collapse. Long-term structural problems characteristic of premodern economies, such as low per capita income, short life expectancy, low rates of savings and investment, and the predominance of traditional methods of production, were compounded by the loss of both physical and human capital and the hyperinflation that had accompanied more than two decades of international and civil war. But by the mid-1950s the short-term problems had been largely resolved and the Chinese Communist Party was completing a five-year development program that successfully addressed the most persistent structural problems as well. The rate of savings and investment had increased dramatically, life expectancy had already begun to rise in response to public health programs that curtailed infectious and parasitic diseases, and modern technology was being adopted on a large scale in industry.

This chapter explores the magnitude of the development problems faced by the Chinese at mid-century, analyzes the policies adopted, and assesses the record of accomplishment through the 1st Five-Year Plan (FYP) (1953–57). It seeks also to illuminate why the relatively successful strategy of the 1st FYP was abandoned almost immediately and replaced by the Great Leap Forward, a program of massive and unprecedented failure, the subject of Chapter 8 of this volume.

THE ECONOMIC SETTING

Before the onset of the Sino-Japanese War in 1937, China's economy was largely premodern. Annual per capita national income in the 1930s ranked near the bottom of the world scale, about 58 yuan or 15 U.S. dollars per capita (1933 prices). The share of output allocated to additions to the capital stock was only about 5 percent, about one-third of the average savings rate in low-income countries. The premodern character of the economy is confirmed by the composition of output and the allocation of the labor force. Almost two-thirds of output originated in agriculture, less than one-fifth in industry. Moreover, since most industrial output was produced by traditional handicraft methods and most services were traditional as well, under 10 percent of aggregate output was produced by modern means. Similarly, more than 90 percent of the work force was dependent on traditional technology.[1]

The vast majority of the population was directly dependent on agriculture for its livelihood, but agricultural growth was constrained by the scarcity of arable land and the absence of modern agricultural technology. For centuries the expansion of the population had exceeded the increase in land under cultivation. By the 1930s, arable land per capita was less than one-fifth of a hectare, far less than in India at the time of independence, when arable land was about one-third of a hectare per capita. China's growing population had been sustained not through innovation in the mechanical technology of farming but through changes in the pattern of cropping. By adopting new crops such as corn, peanuts, potatoes, and tobacco, as well as improved varieties of cotton, average yields and value of output per unit of land under cultivation rose gradually from the sixteenth century onward.

This process was facilitated by increased specialization in production along lines of regional comparative advantage and rising rates of marketing. In regions with good access to transportation, it was common for more than three-fifths of all output to be sold off the farm, and for China as a whole the rate of marketing of agricultural products was about one-third, less than the rate in early Meiji Japan as modern economic growth began there but far higher than the marketing rates associated with subsistence agriculture. Thus by the 1930s yields per unit of land were remarkably high by international standards yet output per worker, and thus income, was low and despite short-term fluctuations, had evinced no change for several centuries.[2] Growth had been all demographic.[3]

---

1 The most comprehensive study of the Chinese economy in the 1930s is contained in Ta-chung Liu and Kung-chia Yeh, *The economy of the Chinese mainland*, and in subsequent revisions of this study by Kung-chia Yeh, for example, "China's national income, 1931–36," in Chi-ming Hou and Tzong-shian Yu, eds., *Modern Chinese economic history*, 95–128.
2 The best study of long-term agricultural growth in China is provided by Dwight H. Perkins, *Agricultural development in China, 1368–1968*.
3 E. L. Jones, *The European miracle*, 202–22.

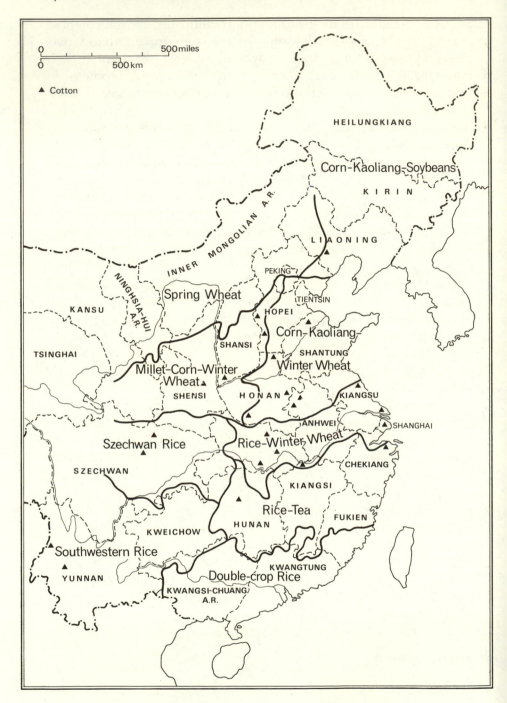

MAP 5. Agriculture: major cropping areas

The scarcity of arable land and the combination of high land but low labor productivity that prevailed in the 1930s posed a fundamental constraint. Economic growth could be sustained not through an expansion of the arable frontier, a source of growth exploited to varying degrees in all the earlier successful cases of modern economic growth, including to some extent even Japan, but through further improvements in what were already moderately high levels of yields per unit of land. That, in turn, implied the necessity of major investments in land infrastructure and in the chemical fertilizer industry.

The long-term structural problems of low income, low savings, and low labor productivity, particularly in agriculture, were compounded by unusually severe regional fragmentation. Although the best estimates show no evidence of sustained growth of average per capita national income in the decades preceding the outbreak of the Sino-Japanese War, significant growth was under way in Manchuria and in several treaty port cities in China proper.[4] Economic growth in Manchuria had been under way since 1860, when the Ch'ing emperor opened the region to settlement by Han Chinese. Rapid agricultural growth, stimulated in part by the development after 1895 of a railroad network (largely under foreign ownership) and by rising international demand for soybeans, gave way to rapid industrial growth under Japanese auspices after the late 1920s. By the mid-1930s per capita output in Manchuria was at least 50 percent greater than in China proper.[5]

Development of industry was not limited to Manchuria. Both Chinese and foreign-owned factories producing predominantly textiles, processed foods, and cigarettes developed rapidly after 1895 in Shanghai, Tientsin, Tsingtao, Hankow, and other coastal and riverine treaty port cities. The growth of industry (including Manchuria, excluding handicrafts) in the three decades prior to the Sino-Japanese War has been estimated as 7.5 to 9.4 percent per annum.[6] The rapid growth of the capital stock of modern industry and transportation depended initially in large measure on imported machinery and equipment, but domestic producer goods, especially in the engineer-

4 Dwight H. Perkins, "Growth and changing structure of China's twentieth century economy," in Perkins, ed., *China's modern economy in historical perspective*, 122.
5 Alexander Eckstein, Chao Kang, and John Chang, "The economic development of Manchuria: The rise of a frontier economy." *Journal of economic history*, 34.1 (March 1974), 239–64.
6 John K. Chang, *Industrial development in pre-Communist China*, 71.

ing sector, supplied a significant share of investment demand by the mid-1930s.[7]

Rapid industrial growth, however, was concentrated regionally and did not lead to sustained growth of national output. The size of the modern sector was too small and its linkages to other regions and sectors of the economy too weak to stimulate aggregate growth. Manchuria contributed only 10 to 15 percent of national output by the mid-1930s, so even its rapid development was not capable of directly propelling the entire national economy forward. Moreover, most industrialization in Manchuria was tied closely to Japan. Almost all the capital goods for Manchurian industrialization were imported from Japan, and a large share of the raw materials and intermediate goods produced in Manchuria were exported to Japan. Industrialization in Manchuria thus generated fewer backward linkages within the region than it would have had it been less closely tied to rising Japanese militarism. Moreover, the interregional trade in agricultural products and manufactured goods that had flourished in the 1910s and 1920s between the Northeast and China proper was drastically curtailed when the Japanese imposed an embargo on trade with China proper after they took over Manchuria completely in 1931. Thus the Northeast, during its most rapid growth in the 1930s, became an enclave with no significant economic linkages to China proper.

The spread effects of treaty port industrialization were also limited.[8] The modern sector was only a thin overlay on the traditional economy and a portion of it was also enclavelike, with raw materials imported from abroad and finished goods, such as cotton textiles, exported to international markets. In short, most of China was almost untouched by modern industry. An important objective of economic development policy after 1949 was to integrate the three separate economies inherited in 1949: Manchuria with its heavy industrial base; the coastal treaty ports, largely oriented toward textiles and light industry; and the vast hinterland, almost untouched by modern industry.

The Sino-Japanese War and the civil war exacerbated these long-term structural problems. Industrial output and the capital stock, largely because of rapid growth in Manchuria, continued to expand into the early 1940s, but fell thereafter. Wartime damage was signi-

---

7 Thomas G. Rawski, *China's transition to industrialism*, 6–28.
8 Rhoads Murphey, *The outsiders: The Western experience in India and China*.

ficant, and the Soviet Union removed over half of the industrial capital stock in Manchuria in 1945, the implicit price the Allies had accepted at the Yalta Conference to secure Soviet entry into the Pacific war.[9] The output of major industrial products in 1949 ranged from 15 to 80 percent of the peak levels of the 1930s. Agricultural production, since it was more dispersed, was less depressed than industry. The major cost of the war was substantial disinvestment, reflected in a marked decline in the amount of cultivated land under irrigation. Wartime disruption inhibited the extremely labor-intensive maintenance of irrigation systems built before the war. Moreover, the Nationalist government's deliberate breaching of the dikes on the Yellow River near Chengchow in 1938 in a vain attempt to stem the advance of Japanese troops devastated farmland and irrigation systems in parts of three provinces. By 1949 the area under irrigation was actually less than in the closing years of the Ch'ing dynasty and only about 60 percent of the average irrigated area in 1924–29. The prewar levels of irrigation were not reattained until the mid-1950s.[10]

The most burdensome legacy inherited by the Communist regime was hyperinflation. The Nationalist government had precipitated the inflation through its deficit financing of the war, only a minuscule portion of which was covered by the sale of bonds or other noninflationary means. The Nationalists were unwilling or unable to restructure the tax system to finance the war against Japan or against the Communists. Prices had begun rising as early as 1935 and accelerated after 1938 when the government lost control of the industrialized coastal areas to Japanese forces and moved the seat of government to Szechwan Province in the Southwest. As military expenditures increased in 1940, the share of government outlays financed through monetary expansion rose steadily. By 1945 in excess of 80 percent of outlays were financed through monetary expansion and, according to official government data of the period, the price level by the end of the year was 1,632 times the prewar level. No systematic effort was made to restructure the tax system after the conclusion of the Sino-Japanese War and, after a brief respite, the deficit rose to 70 and 80 percent of expenditures, respectively, in 1947 and 1948. Just prior to the collapse of the domestic currency in August 1948, the

9 Edwin W. Pauley, *Report on Japanese assets in Manchuria*, 36–37.
10 Perkins, *Agricultural development in China, 1368–1968*, 64.

wholesale price index in Shanghai reached a level 6,600,000 times that of 1937.[11]

Postwar recovery

The major objectives of the newly constituted government during the recovery period were to restore the war-damaged economy, to stop the inherited hyperinflation, and to lay the groundwork for the institutional transformations that would follow during the 1st Five-Year Plan. In the early years the regime relied primarily on indirect mechanisms, such as taxation and price and credit controls, rather than direct allocation of resources by bureaucratic means. But over time the scope of government control of production, marketing, and finance grew, and direct means increasingly replaced reliance on market levers.

After the proclamation of the establishment of the People's Republic on October 1, 1949, the civil war continued in the South and Southwest and government expenditures continued vastly to outstrip revenues, as they had for more than a decade under the Nationalists. Huge resulting deficits continued to be financed through expansion of the money supply, and inflation continued largely unabated for the first few months of the new regime. Between November 1949 and February 1950 the price level increased by more than one and a half times.

But within six months of coming to power, the new regime undertook an unprecedented centralization of finance and an expansion of the tax base that provided the critical preconditions for breaking the hyperinflation. The most important of the measures undertaken was the creation of a unified fiscal system in which the central government stripped local governments of the power to spend based on the tax revenues, such as the agricultural tax, that they administered. In 1928 the Nationalist government, largely because of inability to impose its control on local governments, had formally devolved the agricultural tax to provincial governments.[12] In 1950 the agricultural tax, as well as the commodity tax and a variety of

11 Comprehensive analyses of inflation can be found in Shun-hsin Chou, *The Chinese inflation, 1937–1949*; Kia-ngau Chang, *The inflationary spiral: The experience in China, 1939–1950*, and Arthur N. Young, *China's wartime finance and inflation, 1937–1945*.
12 Nominally central control of the land tax had been reasserted by the central government in 1941, primarily as a means of getting direct control of cereals. But the significance of this change, from a fiscal point of view, was nullified by the center's promise to compensate local governments for the loss of revenue. See Chang, *The inflationary spiral*, 140–41.

industrial and commercial taxes, came under the uniform allocation of the center, ending the system in which grain collected in kind and other tax revenues were spent by the localities. The state bank (known as the People's Bank) played a key role in the restoration of price stability. It was designated to serve as the government treasury and was the instrument through which the government exercised control of credit expansion.

The cumulative effect of increased administrative efficiency, a broadening of the tax base, and increasing production was a substantial increase in government revenues, from 6.5 billion yuan in 1950 to 13.3 billion in 1951. Although deficits in current revenue and expenditure were substantial in 1950 and 1951, a significant share of them was financed through bond issues. In 1950 more than 40 percent of the deficit was so financed, a sharp increase from the Nationalist era, when bonds rarely financed more than 5 percent of deficit spending.[13] In part the success of the bond drive appears to have been due to issuing the bonds not in terms of nominal currency units, but rather in "commodity equivalent units." Each bond, at the time of redemption, would carry a value equal to specified quantities of four basic commodities: rice, wheat flour, cotton cloth, and coal. Bank deposits were also issued in terms of commodity equivalent units, encouraging personal savings and reducing inflationary pressure.

Nothing captures quite so dramatically the contrast of the inherent weakness of the Nationalist government's fisc with the resource mobilization capacity of the Communist regime that replaced it than the share of national output allocated through the budgetary process under the two regimes. In the 1930s, prior to the outbreak of the Sino-Japanese War, government revenues (including central, provincial, and local authorities) comprised at most 5 to 7 percent of gross domestic product.[14] As early as 1952 the tax share of output was 24 percent and by 1957 it had risen to 30 percent, several times the prewar level and twice or more the average share in countries at comparable levels of economic development.[15]

By March 1950 the inflationary spiral was broken. Under the

13 The reported deficit was 289 million yuan, and bonds issued totaled 213.2 million yuan. But budgetary receipts include bond revenues, so the deficit based on current revenue (net of financing items such as bond sales) and expenditures was 502 million yuan. Thus slightly more than two-fifths of the deficit was financed by bond sales. Choh-ming Li, *Economic development of communist China: An appraisal of the first five years of industrialization*, 143, 152.
14 Thomas G. Rawski, *China's republican economy: An introduction*, 26.
15 Nicholas R. Lardy, *Economic growth and distribution in China*, 41, 165. Liu and Yeh, *The economy of the Chinese mainland*, 66.

pressure of increased government expenditures associated with the outbreak of the Korean War there was a renewal of inflationary pressure in the latter part of 1950. But overall inflation remained under control in 1951, with the price level rising only 20 percent, despite the burden of vastly increased military expenditures that followed Chinese entry into the war in the fall of 1950.

The reestablishment of price stability was due largely to the continued growth of tax revenues under the new fiscal system established in 1950 and the curtailment of investment and other nonmilitary outlays. Shortly after American entry into the Korean War, the policy of placing development in a tertiary priority, after war-related programs and the preservation of price stability, was proposed by Ch'en Yun, a high-ranking Party member who oversaw economic policy in the 1950s. It became known as the policy of "resistance, stabilization, and construction."[16]

Initially the program for restoring production was based on re-building war-damaged rail and other transport routes and factories, rather than a substantial program of new construction. Moreover, initially the state-owned sector was limited to the enterprises inherited from the Nationalist government. Government factories produced about a third of industrial output, but the state controlled directly far smaller shares of wholesale and retail trade. Because government ownership was limited and state policy promoted the coexistence of the public and private sectors, the economy remained largely market-oriented, as it had been in the 1930s.

The slackening of military expenditures in 1952 and the signing of the Korean armistice in 1953 set the stage for a more vigorous program of economic development. State investment outlays rose substantially and the share of industrial output produced by state-owned plants expanded, not through outright nationalization of private firms but by their gradual incorporation through economic inducements, such as discriminatory tax and credit policy, into the state sector. Between 1949 and 1952, the eve of the 1st Five-Year Plan, the share of modern industrial output produced by the private sector was squeezed down from more than half to less than a fifth, and the share of private wholesaling and retailing had shrunk substan-

16 Ch'en Yun, "K'ang-Mei yuan-Ch'ao k'ai-shih hou ts'ai-cheng kung-tso ti fang-chen" (The policy of finance and economic work after starting to resist America and aid Korea) in Ch'en Yun, *Ch'en Yun wen-kao hsuan-pien 1949–1956* (Selected manuscripts of Ch'en Yun, 1949–1956), 98–107.

tially as well. But the handicraft sector remained overwhelmingly private.

A gradualist approach to institutional transformation also prevailed in rural areas after 1949. The radical land-reform program adopted during the civil war in 1946 for application in so-called liberated areas was modified to ameliorate the class conflict that had inhibited the recovery of agricultural production. A complex scheme was adopted to classify the peasantry into five classes; landlords, rich peasants, middle peasants, poor peasants, and (landless) laborers. These classifications, in turn, served as the basis for the redistribution of landholdings. By the end of land reform in 1952, the ownership of between 40 and 50 percent of all cultivated land had changed hands.

The land reform improved the economic position of the poorest members of the peasantry decisively but was far from egalitarian in its final results. The share of income accruing to the poorest 20 percent of the farm population almost doubled between the 1930s and 1952. Since average per capita farm income was unchanged over the same period, the absolute incomes of the poorest members of rural society doubled as well. However, the share of income accruing to the richest 10 percent of the peasant population, corresponding roughly to the landlords and rich peasants in the categories of the Chinese Communist Party's land reform program, in proportional terms was reduced by only a modest amount, approximately 10 percent. Almost all of that reduction appears to have occurred in the incomes of the landlord class, which comprised a tiny minority of 2.6 percent of all rural households. Former landlords, according to one estimate, were left with about as much land as poor peasants held after the reform, while prosperous middle and rich peasants continued to own significantly larger amounts of land and to earn incomes well above average.[17]

While land reform was critical in consolidating the support of the peasant masses for the Party and was an effective means for emasculating the old rural elite, for several reasons it did not lead to a stable institutional equilibrium. Private ownership and the small holder system of production, the most salient characteristics of pre-1949 agriculture, were strengthened by the distribution of land to millions of former tenant farmers and landless laborers. This initially reduced

17 Charles R. Roll, "The distribution of rural income in China," 76.

substantially the proportion of land rented and labor hired. But since land could be bought and sold privately, these arrangements did not preclude the reemergence of a more concentrated pattern of land ownership. Despite a system of progressive rural taxation, there was almost immediate evidence of the reemergence in some localities of a politically dominant rich peasant class that controlled increasing quantities of land. Thus almost simultaneously with the conclusion of land reform, the Party promoted voluntary cooperativization that would lead ultimately to a system in which household incomes were linked primarily to their labor and in which land and other assets were owned collectively.

Not only was individual ownership ideologically suspect, but the initial preference of the Party leadership for collective production was enhanced by two other factors. First, there appears to have been a widespread belief that cooperative farming, which would consolidate small landholdings averaging less than a hectare per household, would capture considerable economies of scale in agricultural production. Retrospectively at least, it was claimed that cooperativization raised peasant income. But the evidence in favor of this proposition both for China and for Asia more generally is weak. Chinese claims were based on a survey of cooperatives that were not drawn at random but selected on the basis of other, nonspecified criteria. Moreover, the data do not distinguish between correlation and causation. For most developing countries, particularly in Asia, smaller farms invariably achieve higher levels of output per unit of land area and are usually more efficient in production as well.

Second, the ability of the state to extract resources from the countryside would be strengthened through the formation of cooperatives. As will be discussed later, by 1953 the ability of the state to channel agricultural goods, particularly grain, to nonrural uses preoccupied the planners in Peking.

Early forms of cooperative agriculture, called mutual aid teams (MATs), were an extension of traditional forms of peasant cooperation in which labor and the use of draft animals and farm implements were exchanged on a voluntary reciprocal basis, typically among fewer than ten households. Initially these were formed on a seasonal basis, but they were soon made permanent. Land, labor, tools, and draft animals were all pooled permanently, but ownership of the means of production, including land, was still individual, and individual income shares of members included returns on these privately owned assets. By the end of 1952, 40 percent of all peasant households were members of MATs.[18]

THE 1ST FIVE-YEAR PLAN

The 1st Five-Year Plan (1953–57), by conventional measures, was an unusually successful program of economic development. With limited resources and experience, the Chinese Communist Party was able to sustain the economic growth that began during the recovery period and to complete the institutional transformation that was initiated so cautiously between 1949 and the end of 1952. Thus China's experience during these years stands in contradistinction to that of the Soviet Union during its 1st FYP (1928–32), when institutional transformation in agriculture proved disastrous. What was the character of economic performance in China during its 1st FYP? What were the sources of growth? And why was the envisaged program of successive FYPs replaced by a far more radical and ultimately unsuccessful strategy known as the Great Leap Forward?

Measured in terms of economic growth, the 1st FYP was a stunning success. National income grew at an average annual rate of 8.9 percent (measured in constant prices), with agriculture and industrial output expanding annually by about 3.8 and 18.7 percent, respectively.[19] Since annual population growth was 2.4 percent, output grew at 6.5 percent per capita, a rate at which national income would double every eleven years. Compared to the pattern of growth in China during the first half of the twentieth century, in which output grew just barely as fast as population (each at about 1 percent per annum), the 1st FYP marked a decisive acceleration.[20] China's experience also compares favorably with most newly independent developing countries in which per capita growth averaged about 2.5

---

18 State Statistical Bureau, Ten great years, 35.

19 These are based on official value added data, which differ somewhat from the gross value data that were published in the 1950s. The growth rate for industry is subject to some upward bias, since it is based on a price structure that overweights the faster-growing producer goods sector and underweights the less rapidly growing consumer goods sector. Yang Chien-pai and Li Hsueh-tseng, "Nung, ch'ing, chung chieh-kou" (The structure of agriculture, light industry and heavy industry) in Ma Hung and Sun Shang-ch'ing, eds., Chung-kuo ching-chi chieh-kou wen-t'i yen-chiu (Research on problems in China's economic structure), 106.

20 Perkins, "Growth and changing structure of China's twentieth century economy," in Perkins, ed., China's modern economy in historical perspective, 122.

percent per annum during the 1950s.[21] For example, India, another continent-sized agrarian economy with initial economic conditions similar to those in China, achieved a per capita growth rate well under 2 percent during the 1950s.[22]

The limitations of national income as a measure of development, particularly in low-income countries, are well known, but the success of China's development program is borne out by other measures as well. Life expectancy, the single best indicator of a country's health status, rose from 36 years in 1950 to 57 years by 1957, fifteen years longer than the average life expectancy of low income countries at the time.[23] The share of the children of primary school age actually enrolled jumped from 25 to 50 percent over the same period and there were large increases in secondary and university enrollments as well. Urban housing standards rose as the state completed almost 100 million square meters of new housing for workers and staff. Private consumption expenditures, measured in terms of constant prices, also rose significantly. Nominal wages in the modern sector rose by more than 40 percent while the cost of living for those workers rose by only 10 percent. Thus wages rose by almost a third in real terms. Peasant income rose about a fifth as a result of rising production and a modest improvement in the terms of exchange of agricultural for manufactured goods.

Moreover, China's performance was achieved with only modest foreign financial assistance. While, as will be noted later, capital goods supplied by the Soviet Union were critical to the rapid buildup of several key branches of industry, most machinery and equipment acquired from the Soviets was paid for either on a current basis or on relatively short-term credit, rather than through unilateral transfers or long-term concessionary loans. Thus these imports did not significantly relieve the need to constrain the growth of current consumption.

Finally, by 1955–56 the CCP had completed, ahead of publicly announced schedules, a series of institutional transformations that eliminated the private sector as a significant source of output or employment. Individually owned farming and handicraft enterprises and factories were the source of about two-thirds of all output in 1953 but by 1957 were reduced to producing less than 3 percent. The

21 Organization for Economic Cooperation and Development, Development Center, *National accounts of less-developed countries, 1950–1966*, 22, 26.
22 Ibid., 21, 25.
23 *China: Socialist economic development*, vol. I, 98.

state consolidated its control of the economy by expanding the sphere of direct state ownership to encompass all of modern industry and by exerting indirect control of private handicrafts by reorganizing them into cooperatives. In agriculture, by the end of 1956 more than 95 percent of peasant households had been organized into Agricultural Producers' Cooperatives, effectively eliminating private ownership of land, draft animals, tools, and so forth.[24] Transformation of the system of property rights in agriculture was a remarkably smooth process compared to Soviet collectivization. Whereas agricultural output in the Soviet Union dropped by fully one-fifth in 1932 compared with the last year of private farming in 1928, output value rose by one-fifth in China between 1953 and 1957.[25]

The most striking difference, however, was in peasant investment behavior. Soviet collectivization was accompanied by massive disinvestment. The population of draft animals fell precipitously as peasants slaughtered them for their consumption value rather than turn them over without compensation to the newly created collectives. Similarly, private investment in farming collapsed. By contrast, in China in 1955–56 there was only a modest reduction in the stock of draft animals, and a 15 percent reduction in the number of hogs, since initially peasants received compensation for contributions of draft animals and other implements. Moreover, private and cooperative agricultural investment in the 1st FYP totaled 17 billion yuan, an average of 3.4 billion yuan per year, several times the state budgetary investment in agriculture.[26] Again, such investments were facilitated by the perception that a large share of the returns on them would accrue to those willing to forgo immediate consumption.

Strategy of the 1st FYP

The strategy of the 1st FYP rested squarely on the belief in the Marxist law of expanded reproduction that identifies the industries producing capital goods as the major source of growth. That strategy was reflected in a pattern of resource mobilization and allocation similar to the one prevailing in the Soviet Union from 1928 to 1937.

First, the rate of investment spurted from the prewar level of about 5 percent to an average well in excess of 20 percent. The rate at which current output was allocated to replace or expand the capital stock,

24 State Statistical Bureau, *Ten great years*, 35.
25 Paul R. Gregory and Robert C. Stuart, *Soviet economic structure and performance*, 108.
26 Lardy, *Agriculture in China's modern economic development*, 138.

rather than to increase current consumption, was almost twice that achieved in India during the 1950s and approached that prevailing during the peak of Stalin's forced-draft industrialization program, initiated in 1928. Even approaching the Soviet investment rate was remarkable, since deferring increased consumption must have been more difficult in China, where the level of per capita national income was only about one-fourth that in the Soviet Union in 1928.

The second parallel with the Soviet Union lay in the overwhelming allocation of investment resources to industry, particularly the branches of industry producing capital goods. Agricultural investment (not counting farmers' self-investment) was extremely modest, less than 8 percent of the total, given that it produced directly over half of national income and employed over four-fifths of the entire labor force. Over half of investment was channeled to industry, and of this almost 90 percent was allocated to producer goods branches such as the metallurgy, machine building, electric power, coal, petroleum, and chemical industries. The small share of industrial investment, 3 percent, alloted to expand the output of farm machinery and chemical fertilizer confirmed the low priority assigned to agriculture in the plan.[27]

Finally, China's industrialization strategy paralleled that of the Soviets in the 1930s in its preference for very large-scale, capital-intensive manufacturing. The core of the industrialization program consisted of 156 Soviet-aided projects, which collectively absorbed about half of total industrial investment. These plants were characterized by large scale and a high capital stock per employed worker.

The pattern of resource mobilization and allocation and preference for building very large-scale, capital-intensive manufacturing plants almost necessitated a centralized planning system similar to that of the Soviet Union. As early as 1949, economic planning was initiated in the Northeast under the chairman of the Northeast Administrative Area, Kao Kang. The Northeast, which came under CCP control in 1948, became an important testing ground for planning for several reasons. First, an unusually large share of the industrial plants in the region were government-controlled from the outset. The CCP took them over from the Nationalists, who previously had claimed them from the Japanese via the Russians. Thus, it was not necessary to expropriate or nationalize the major industries prior to initiating state

27 Ibid., 130.

planning. Moreover, the plants were predominantly in heavy industry, notably ferrous metallurgy, the highest priority sector for the
new government.

Finally, proximity to the Soviet Union may have been a contributing factor. The Soviets, since 1945, had controlled the Chinese
Manchurian Railroad (formerly Japan's South Manchurian Railway)
and ran plants associated with the railroad as well as the enterprises
associated with the Soviet-controlled naval base in Port Arthur. A
trade agreement between the Northeast People's Government and the
Soviet Union was signed by Kao Kang in Moscow three months
before Mao Tse-tung proclaimed the establishment of the People's
Republic of China. The Soviet role in the region increased as early as
1949–50, when Soviet experts began to arrive at major iron and steel
enterprises such as Anshan and Penchihu, the two largest steel
enterprises in pre-Communist China.[28]

The techniques of planning initially used in the Northeast were
soon adopted on a national basis. In October and November 1952 the
State Statistical Bureau and the State Planning Commission were
established under the chairmanships of Hsueh Mu-ch'iao and Kao
Kang, respectively.[29] At about the same time a panoply of vertically
organized industrial ministries was established to exercise control in
various specialized areas of production. Each of these ministries
exercised control of the most important enterprises in its sphere of
production, regardless of geographical location.[30]

The Chinese also adopted from the Soviets many of the systems of
resource allocation associated with this organizational structure.
Foremost among these was the system of material balance planning.
Under this system, the State Planning Commission and the central
government ministries drew up output and distribution plans for the
most important industrial products. That placed the distribution of
key commodities under the direct control of central planners, not the
market mechanism. Products were distributed in order to obtain plan
objectives. Between 1952 and 1956, the number of commodities
subjected to this form of allocation rose from 28 to more than 200.
Moreover, the share of output of these commodities subject to
material balances rose over time so that by 1956 the market allocation
of a portion of the output of these products was very sharply

28 M. Gardner Clark, *The development of China's steel industry and Soviet technical aid*, 4, 13.
29 Choh-ming Li, *The statistical system of Communist China*, 13; Audrey Donnithorne,
   China's economic system, 458.
30 The most exhaustive description of the evolution of the economic bureaucracy is contained
   in Donnithorne, *China's economic system*.

reduced.[31] Thus the role of relative prices in influencing the allocation of industrial goods was minimized.

Agricultural growth and transformation

Somewhat surprisingly, the adoption of a Soviet-style big push industrialization strategy involving massive resource mobilization for manufacturing and the neglect of agriculture does not appear to have been controversial within the CCP. There is no evidence that prior to the 1st FYP there was anything approaching the industrialization debate of the 1920s in the Soviet Union, which pitted E. A. Preobrazhensky's theory of a "big push" industrialization program against N. I. Bukharin's theory of balanced growth of industry and agriculture.[32] Rather, the Preobrazhensky view of rapid industrialization based on forced savings from agriculture was supported widely within the CCP, a remarkable occurrence for what at the time was the world's only major ruling Communist Party with a plausible claim to agrarian origins. But debate over the major resource allocation issues did emerge during the implementation of the 1st FYP, as critical underlying premises of the plan proved false.

A major assumption, unquestioned at least until 1954 or 1955, was that agriculture would not impose a significant constraint on industrialization. As planning work got under way in 1952, agricultural growth was unusually rapid. Output of China's two most important crops, grain and cotton, grew by an average annual rate of 11.5 and 37.3 percent during 1951 and 1952. Although it was recognized that this unusually rapid growth was partly a one-time recovery and could not be sustained, the target for the growth of cereal production for the 1st FYP, announced for the first time in July 1953, was a relatively high 5.3 percent per annum.[33] Moreover, it was envisaged that this rate could be achieved not through increased investment but largely through the more efficient utilization of labor, land, and other inputs, primarily through the spread of mutual aid teams. Cooperativization would proceed extremely slowly. The target set in 1953 by the Central Committee of the CCP envisaged that only 20 percent of households would be in cooperatives by the end of 1957.[34]

The planned rate of growth of agricultural output surpassed the

31 Lardy, *Economic growth and distribution in China*, 15, 206.
32 Stephen F. Cohen, *Bukharin and the Bolshevik revolution*.
33 Kenneth R. Walker, "Collectivisation in retrospect: The 'Socialist high tide' of autumn 1955-spring 1956," 24.
34 Ibid., 9.

anticipated growth of demand for cereals and other agricultural products, as determined by the rate of growth of population and per capita income, as well as by the income elasticity of demand for agricultural products. Consequently, planning for industrial development proceeded without careful examination of the linkages between industry and agriculture. The rate of growth of industrial output was presumed to be constrained only by the capacity of the producer goods sector. No serious consideration was given to the implicitly necessary rates of increase in the supplies of foodstuffs for the growing industrial labor force or of agricultural raw materials, such as fiber crops for the textile industry.

Yet agricultural growth slowed markedly in 1953 and 1954, precipitating a far-reaching debate over the character of the 1st FYP. In 1953 grain output rose by only 2.5 percent, well under the planned 9 percent increment, and raw cotton output fell by more than 9 percent, while the planned growth target was 16 percent. In 1954 grain output grew quite modestly, 1.6 percent, as opposed to a planned rate of more than 9 percent, while cotton production again fell by more than 9 percent, as opposed to a planned growth of 17.8 percent.[35]

Because of the predominantly agrarian character of the economy, these shortfalls had severe implications for the pace of economic development and for the 1st FYP, which was still in the formative stage although its first two years had passed. One of the reasons the plan could not be presented to the Central Committee of the Party by Ch'en Yun until March 1955 and made public by Li Fu-ch'un in a speech to the National People's Congress (NPC) in July was the issue of how to deal with the unexpectedly poor agricultural performance in 1953 and 1954.[36]

Declining agricultural growth forced planners to examine the fundamental premises of the 1st FYP. The linkages between agriculture and industry, which had been largely ignored in the early stages of plan formulation, became an especially salient part of this re-examination for at least two reasons. First, low agricultural growth impinged both directly and indirectly on industrial output. Agriculture supplied more than four-fifths of the raw materials for the manufacture of light industrial products, which comprised well over half of industrial output. Agriculture also influenced the pace of

35 Ibid., 23.
36 Ibid., 24. Kenneth Lieberthal, *A research guide to central Party and government meetings in China 1949–1975*, 68; Li Fu-ch'un, "Report on the First Five-Year Plan for development of the national economy," 42–91.

industrial growth indirectly. Government revenues were derived in
large part from the high indirect taxes that were included in the retail
prices of most manufactured consumer goods. The high prices meant
that factories producing light industrial goods were unusually profit-
able and, since these factories were government-owned, most of these
profits flowed directly to the government budget. A slowdown in
agricultural growth thus sharply reduced the growth of government
revenues, in turn reducing the flow of investment that could be
allocated to industry. Moreover, agricultural exports were the principal source of foreign exchange earnings used to pay for imports,
which in turn consisted predominantly of capital goods that formed
the core of the industrial investment program. During the 1st FYP as
a whole, farm and processed farm products (including cotton and silk
textiles) comprised fully three-quarters of all of China's exports,
whereas more than 90 percent of imports consisted of machinery and
equipment and other producer goods.[37]

Second, the slow pace of agricultural development led to a crisis in
food grain supplies throughout 1953. There were several symptoms
of that crisis, but they can be traced primarily to a single cause – state
intervention in grain marketing. In 1950 and 1951 the state had
encouraged the recovery of agricultural production by promoting
the revival of private rural marketing. The state sought to meet its
own needs (such as increasing the supply of grain to urban markets
to control the price level, supplying state-owned food processing
factories, and meeting export needs) through the agricultural tax in
kind and by purchases on rural markets. As state demands grew
while tax grain increased only modestly after 1951, state purchases
became an increasingly important source of supply. Because purchase
prices continued to rise, state procurement became increasingly
costly. To reduce the cost, the state sought to restrict private
marketing activity and establish a monopsonist position that it
could use as a lever to control the rise of or even force down market
prices.

But the strategy failed. Market prices of cereals and most other
agricultural products continued to rise in 1953, in part because
peasants were reluctant to sell grain to the state. In some areas private
merchants were paying peasants up to 40 percent more than the state,
and government procurement plans were substantially underfulfilled.

37 State Statistical Bureau, *Chung-kuo t'ung-chi nien-chien, 1981* (Chinese statistical yearbook,
      1981), 354.

Because demand for food in urban areas was continuing to rise and widespread floods in 1953 also increased the demand for cereals in rural areas, the state was forced to sell more grain than it was taking in. State controlled food stocks began to decline. In contrast with 1950 and 1951, when state inventories reached a low in June, just prior to the harvest of winter crops in central China, in 1953 state sales exceeded purchases throughout the summer. From July to the end of September, state stocks were reduced by 1.3 million metric tons, an alarming quantity since total reserves were only 8.7 million metric tons, of which a large portion represented irreducible demands for seed and normal working inventories.

Moreover, according to Ch'en Yun, the outlook for the remaining months prior to June 1954, when new grain would again come to the market, was bleak. Even if the procurement plan could be fulfilled, the estimated deficit was 4.35 million metric tons. But Ch'en revealed in October 1953 that it was unlikely the plan would be fulfilled, given the shortfalls in purchases through September and because severe flooding in the Northeast had reduced estimated production there from 22.0 million to 18.5 million metric tons, leading to a reduction of the procurement target from 5.0 million to 3.8 million metric tons.[38]

Finally, the grain crisis was evident in a sharp reduction in the ability of the state to move grain interregionally within China. Interregional grain transfers were essential to sustain the claim of the new government that it would deal more effectively with natural disasters than had the Nationalists. The key lay in the Northeast, the only region with reliable, relatively inexpensive rail transportation to most regions of China that was, in normal years, a surplus region. Because the Northeast was the first region to come under the control of Communist forces, when Lin Piao's Fourth Field Army decisively routed the Nationalists in 1948, it was able to supply, as early as 1949, 2.6 million metric tons of grain.[39] These supplies were transferred for consumption elsewhere, including most likely in large part to the military, which was increasingly swollen by the wholesale defection of Nationalist-led military units as CCP forces swept south in 1949. Northeast grain exports to the rest of China were reduced in 1951

---

38 Ch'en Yun, "Shih-hsing liang-shih t'ung-kou t'ung-hsiao" (Implementing planned purchase and planned sale of grain), in *Ch'en Yun wen-kao hsuan-pien (1949–1956)*, 189–203.

39 Allen S. Whiting, *China crosses the Yalu: The decision to enter the Korean War*, 19. On the decline in output and procurement in 1951 and the 1953 targets for production and procurement, see Ch'en Yun, "Shih-hsing liang-shih t'ung-kou t'ung-hsiao," in *Ch'en Yun wen-kao hsuan-pien (1949–1956)*, 190.

because of adverse weather but began to recover in 1952 and were planned to amount to 2.1 million metric tons in 1953. This would be almost half of the 4.8 million metric tons that the central authorities would have available to move interregionally to meet the consumption needs of concentrated urban populations such as those of Peking and Tientsin, and of peasants in regions suffering natural disasters of such a magnitude that regionally available surpluses were inadequate.[40] But the reduction in production and procurement in the Northeast reduced the surplus available for transfer out of the region to 1.3 million metric tons, cutting the total supply of grain in the grasp of the center to only 4.0 million metric tons, or about 2.4 percent of annual production.[41]

Thus, by the fall of 1953 a major crisis loomed. Grain prices had risen substantially in many rural markets; shortages were manifest in some cities – not just in regions of poor weather but in major cities such as Peking and Tientsin; state grain stocks were low and shrinking; and the supplies that could be moved interregionally by the central government to meet local shortages were astonishingly low.

One response to this crisis could have been to allow agricultural purchase prices to rise to at least the market level to provide incentives for increased sales to the government. But given the commitment to fixed prices for cereal products sold to the urban population, that course would have reduced the profits of the state-run grain distribution system and thus directly curtailed the growth of state revenues. Concomitantly, raising purchase prices would not only reduce the flow of funds available for investment but also necessitate a reallocation of this reduced investment in favor of the consumer goods sector, since ultimately the success of the incentive program would depend on increased supplies of consumer goods that would match the increase in peasant incomes. Thus raising procurement prices could not be envisaged as an isolated policy but was one that would leave fewer resources for investment in producer goods and thus a lower rate of investment in future years. Although there is

40 Ch'en Yun in a May 1951 speech bemoaned the absence of rail transport to move grain out of Szechwan Province, an area of substantial surplus. "Fa-chan nung-yeh shih t'ou-teng ta-shih" (Agricultural development is a matter of major importance), in Ch'en Yun, *Ch'en Yun wen-kao hsuan-pien (1949–1956)*, 129. This concern undoubtedly underlay the major effort to construct the Paochi-Chengtu rail line during the 1st FYP. The line, which provided the first rail link between the Szechwan basin and the rest of China, was opened to traffic in 1956.

41 Ch'en Yun, "Shih-hsing liang-shih t'ung-kou t'ung-hsiao" [Implementing planned purchase and planned sale of grain], in *Ch'en Yun wen-kao hsuan-pien (1949–1956)*, 190–91. Reiitsu Kojima, "Grain acquisition and supply in China," 66–68.

evidence that some individuals argued for a reduced scale of industrialization in the 1st FYP, that course of action was rejected: Rapid industrialization remained the highest priority.

The hoped-for solution was the implementation in the late fall of 1953 of a system of compulsory procurement of cereals at fixed prices and a modest increase in the pace of cooperativization. The planned level of procurement for the 1953 procurement year, which ended in June 1954, was stepped up by 5 million metric tons to a total of 22 million tons, compared with a 17 million ton target that had been approved in August for market purchases. To reach that higher target, the state restricted private grain marketing and forbade private millers to buy or sell grain on their own account. Rather, they became state agents, acting on behalf of the Ministry of Food, the state procurement agency. Traditional grain markets in cities and in market towns were converted to state grain markets, primarily to ensure that no transactions occurred until after stepped-up state procurement targets were fulfilled. Finally, the central government increased its ability to move grain interregionally by asserting its authority to make adjustments in these flows on an annual basis.[42]

In the short run the system of compulsory deliveries provided the resources to proceed with the forced draft industrialization program. Procurement rose 5 million tons to meet the 22 million ton target, providing the state with adequate grain to meet its multiple needs. In a sense, the CCP drew upon the reservoir of goodwill that had been created during land reform to step up procurement at lower prices so as to initiate the major industrialization drive. Because the procurement system provided the means for partially unrequited transfers out of the agricultural sector, the central authorities came to believe that the original high rates of growth planned for industry could be sustained with lower agricultural growth. Thus, after a year's experience with the compulsory delivery system, the planned rate of growth of cereal output for the 1st FYP was scaled back from 5.3 to 4.6 percent, but target industrial outputs were not reduced.[43]

Yet, as has already been indicated, agricultural growth in 1954 was quite disappointing, and it was not clear that the state would be assured of adequate supplies of grain at low prices through the system of compulsory deliveries. Thus the pace of cooperativization was gradually increased in order to strengthen CCP control in the coun-

42 Nicholas R. Lardy and Kenneth Lieberthal, *Chen Yun's strategy for China's development: A non-Maoist alternative*, xix.
43 Walker, "Collectivisation in retrospect," 24.

tryside and ensure the continued delivery of grain to the state. Yet by the winter of 1954–55 the cooperativization program was encountering considerable resistance from the peasantry. In order to meet targets for the number of Agricultural Producers' Cooperatives (APCs) formed, local cadres widely violated the principles of voluntarism and mutual benefit that underlay the program. Peasants were forced to join APCs, even against their will, via both economic and political discrimination. Cadres frequently withheld credit from private farmers and from MATs that were unwilling to form APCs, as well as labeling holdouts as capitalists. In some regions there was confiscation of private assets such as fish ponds, fruit trees, and livestock. The most serious problems arose in areas where cadres organized private farmers directly into APCs, bypassing the intermediate MAT stage. In these regions there was little basis for expecting cooperative agriculture to be successful, since there were no established rules for the allocation of output into labor and capital shares. For example, in Chekiang Province, in central China, land reform was completed late, and by 1953 only 3,300 APCs had been established. But in 1954 the number increased to 53,000.[44]

The most severe difficulties arose not because of problems of internal APC management and organization but because of the overprocurement of cereals by the state in 1954–55. Retrospectively, in 1956, both Chou En-lai, in his report to the NPC, and Mao Tse-tung, in his report on the "ten major relationships," alluded to the problems arising from what was described as procurement of 3.5 million metric tons in excess of the planned target.[45] While that amount is quite small relative to total cereal output, it was extracted primarily from those areas where APCs had already been formed. In short, the power of local cadres to increase grain extractions from the peasantry in response to political pressure, reflected in *People's Daily* editorials calling for increased procurement at all costs, was greatest in those regions that had already formed APCs. Party cadres in these regions could simply retain more of the APC output to deliver to the state, rather than having to negotiate with

44 Ch'iang Yuan-kan and Lin Pang-kuang, "Shih-lun i-chiu-wu-wu-nien tang-nei kuan-yü nung-yeh ho-tso-hua wen-t'i ti cheng-lun" (A discussion of the debate within the Party in 1955 concerning the issue of agricultural cooperativization), *Tang-shih yen-chiu*, 1981. 1, 11.
45 Chou En-lai, "Report on the proposals for the second five-year plan for development of the national economy," 286. Mao Tse-tung, "On the ten major relationships," in Mao, *SW*, 5.290–91.

individual peasant producers concerning the magnitude of deliveries that they would be asked to make.[46]

Thus, by the spring of 1955 there was a genuine supply crisis in the countryside, and many peasants who had been organized into APCs were experiencing extreme food shortages. One of the most severe cases occurred in P'ingyang County in Wenchou Prefecture in Chekiang. A joint investigation of the Central Finance Commission, the Discipline Inspection Commission, and the Chengfa Small Group subsequently reported that the severity of food shortages caused by excessive procurement had created "instability in Wenchou." By March, Teng Tzu-hui, the head of the Party's Rural Work Department, with the concurrence of the Party center, cabled the Chekiang Party Committee calling for a halt to the cooperativization program and an appropriate shrinkage in the number of APCs. Subsequently, the number of cooperatives shrank by 15,000 to total about 40,000.[47]

But the problems were not limited to Chekiang. In April, the State Council, the highest government organ, passed a resolution to apply to all of China calling for a halt to cooperativization. The hope was to restore incentives for producers prior to the onset of the spring planting season. At the end of April, Teng Tzu-hui's Rural Work Department convened the Third National Rural Work Conference to explain the retrenchment policy to provincial Party cadres. Teng, apparently following the suggestion of a critical meeting convened a few weeks earlier by Liu Shao-ch'i, called not for an across the board retrenchment but rather, for a regionally differentiated policy. Some provinces in the Central-South and Southwest regions, where the pace of cooperativization had been more moderate, could continue to organize APCs, although at a modest pace. Where APCs had been formed hastily during the winter of 1954–55, all organizational activities should cease until after the 1955 fall harvest had been completed. The APCs that had been formed without an adequate foundation, primarily in Chekiang and Hopei, but also in Shantung, Anhwei, and Honan, should be dissolved. The spirit of the policy was encapsulated in a three-character slogan: "halt, shrink, and develop."[48]

46 Ch'iang Yuan-kan and Lin Pang-kuang, "Shih-lun i-chiu-wu-wu-nien tang-nei kuan-yü nung-yeh ho-tso-hua wen-t'i ti cheng-lun," 11.
47 Ibid., 12.
48 Teng Tzu-hui, "Tsai ch'üan-kuo ti-san-tz'u nung-ts'un kung-tso hui-i shang ti k'ai-mu tz'u" (Inaugural speech at the third national rural work conference), ibid., 7.

The Third Rural Work Conference set off a divisive intra-Party struggle. Mao Tse-tung came to believe that the Rural Work Department was undermining the cooperativization program. Too many peasants had left APCs, and the scheduled pace of cooperativization in 1955–56 was too slow in his view. In a meeting on 17 May with provincial and municipal Party secretaries a few weeks after the conference, Mao sought to shift the emphasis of the policy that had been discussed at the Third Rural Work Conference to the third character, "develop."

Yet through the spring of 1955, Teng's views were widely supported. Most critically the Politburo, even before Mao's 17 May meeting, endorsed Teng's plan to use the following winter not to expand the number of APCs but to consolidate the remaining 650,000 APCs. During the last ten days of May, Teng and Mao had what was later characterized as a "violent dispute" over the planned pace of cooperativization in 1955–56.[49]

Because the Politburo had endorsed the policy and Teng refused to back down, Mao was temporarily isolated and had to seek an alternative approach to accelerate the pace of cooperativization. Mao's approach was to launch an attack on the rightism of Teng Tzu-hui and the Rural Work Department. The campaign was launched by Mao's famous 31 July 1955 speech to provincial Party leaders in which he argued that conditions were favorable for cooperativization, that the leadership of the Party was lagging behind the demands of the peasants, and that only APCs could prevent increased polarization along class lines in the countryside.[50] Apart from directly encouraging provincial party secretaries to accelerate the pace of collectivization, Mao appointed two of his most trusted associates, Ch'en Po-ta and Ch'en Cheng-jen, to serve as deputy directors of the Rural Work Department and began to lay the foundation for officially censuring Teng.

By the fall, when the Sixth Plenum of the Seventh Central Committee met in October, Mao had turned the tide. It was Ch'en Po-ta who delivered the upbeat report on agricultural cooperativization. Liu Shao-ch'i made a self-criticism of the conservative policy on the pace of cooperativization that he had endorsed the previous winter. Teng, apparently unrepentant, was isolated. He was personally

49 Ch'iang Yuan-kan and Lin Pang-kuang, "Shih-lun i-chiu-wu-wu-nien tang-nei kuan-yü nung-yeh ho-tso-hua wen-t'i ti cheng-lun," 13.
50 Mao Tse-tung, "On the cooperative transformation of agriculture," in Mao, SW, 5.184–207.

criticized by Mao and the resolution of the plenum denounced him as a "rightist empiricist." Shortly after the conclusion of the plenum, Mao's July speech, which had been circulating among Party members, was published by the *People's Daily*.[51]

The plenum laid the groundwork for a sweeping reorganization of agriculture. The high tide of socialist transformation predicted by Mao became self-fulfilling, for local party cadres perceived that their loyalty and political reliability would be judged by the pace of cooperativization. In the fall, less than 15 percent of all peasant households were members of APCs. By January 1956, three months after the plenum, 80.3 percent had joined.[52] The movement reached a fever pitch in 1956, when virtually the entire agricultural population was reorganized into APCs. At the beginning of that year almost all APCs were lower stage, averaging 30 to 50 households. By the end of the year, 88 percent of the peasantry was organized in some form of APC, but most were higher-stage APCs, which averaged 200 to 300 families.[53] The formation of higher-stage APCs was doubly attractive to Party cadres, because they demonstrated their own activism in persuading the peasantry to embrace a higher stage of socialism and they alleviated the frequently contentious process of dividing net farm income into rent and wage shares. Peasants who had made substantial contributions of land, draft animals, and tools preferred that a higher share of net output be allocated for rental payments as their reward for a contribution of assets to the APC. Poor peasants, who relied almost entirely on wage payments, preferred that a larger share of income be distributed in the form of wages. Advanced APCs obviated this conflict by eliminating all rental payments.

Although Mao appeared to have won a sweeping victory, the collectivization campaign of 1955–56 did not provide even a partial solution to China's agrarian problems. In the immediate aftermath, the policies accompanying collectivization were the source of a substantial short-run disruption of agriculture. Initially it was thought that the formation of higher-stage APCs would allow the institution of direct planning in agriculture, replacing the reliance on indirect or price planning that had prevailed since the early 1950s. Under price planning, central planners had sought to influence the allocation of land, labor, and current inputs on the basis of relative

51 Roderick MacFarquhar, *The origins of the Cultural Revolution, 1: Contradictions among the people*, 18–19.
52 Walker, "Collectivisation in retrospect," 35.
53 State Statistical Bureau, *Ten great years*, 35.

prices rather than direct commands dictating sown area targets. Thus when relatively more cotton than grain was thought desirable, as for example in 1950 and 1951, the cotton: grain procurement price ratio had been altered to encourage some substitution at the margin of cotton for grain, in respect of sown area, and the allocation of labor and current inputs (such as fertilizers). Such a policy, combined with rural markets in which sales of grain and other agricultural products were permitted after procurement targets had been filled, encouraged specialization along lines of local and regional comparative advantage. When higher-stage APCs were formed, an attempt was made to replace this system of indirect planning with a system of direct planning based on detailed national sown area and output targets drawn up at national level and then disaggregated and passed down the administrative hierarchy to provinces, counties, and ultimately APCs. Simultaneously with the introduction of direct planning, the state closed most of the tens of thousands of rural markets that facilitated comparative advantage cropping.

These extreme policies associated with the high tide of collectivization were quickly reversed. Rural markets were reopened in the summer of 1956, and in the fall the CCP Central Committee and the State Council implicitly admitted the shortcomings of direct planning in agriculture by endorsing a return to reliance on the manipulation of relative prices as the major tool to influence the pattern of cropping and the growth of various crops.

Although short-run excesses were reversed, cooperativization does not appear to have contributed to improved agricultural growth or productivity. The pace of growth in 1956 and 1957 remained far below the revised targets published in the Five-Year Plan. The worst excesses of Soviet collectivization were avoided, but this was not due simply to greater administrative finesse or the Party's familiarity with the rural scene. Rather, the relatively smooth transformation entailed significant short-run costs to the state that could not be sustained without major changes in development policy.

First, to persuade peasants that APCs were not simply a device for increasing the unrequited flow of resources into state hands, state procurement was scaled back from the level prevailing in 1954–55. Second, to reduce the previous reliance on coercion, the Party pledged in the fall of 1955 that 90 percent of the peasants who joined APCs would experience a rise in income.[54] Despite earlier claims, this

54 Vivienne Shue, *Peasant China in transition*, 293.

could not be assured through increased productivity, but was partially achieved in the short run through a vast infusion of credit from
the People's Bank to the APCs. Over several years the volume of
agricultural credit outstanding had increased annually by from 100
million to 200 million yuan, but at year-end 1956, loans outstanding
to APCs jumped by more than 2 billion yuan.[55] That allowed APCs
to increase their payout to members substantially. The infusion of
credit amounted to about 4 yuan for each member, a substantial
amount when peasant annual cash income was only about 15 yuan.[56]

Finally, collectivization was only partially successful in restricting
class polarization. Land reform had substantially redistributed land,
the most valuable rural asset, in favor of the poorest members of rural
society. The formation of lower-stage APCs presumably had little
effect on the distribution of income, since members were to receive
rent for their contributions of land and other assets such as draft
animals. Further equalization of income would not occur except to
the extent that the internal dynamics of the distributive process
within some APCs reduced the share of income paid as rent as
compared to the rental share of income prior to cooperativization.
Formation of higher-stage APCs marked an important step beyond
land reform toward more equal distribution both because it eliminated all payments for previous contributions of land and other
assets, and because labor payments were based on the collective
output of a larger number of families.

Yet when collectivization was completed in 1956, there were more
than three-quarters of a million separate producing and accounting
units, but only weak mechanisms for redistributing income or resources across these units. State expenditure and tax policies were
particularly weak redistributive instruments, since state expenditures
on agriculture were quite small and directed almost exclusively
toward a very small sector of state farms and large-scale water
conservancy projects. Moreover, agricultural taxation was predominantly indirect and not designed to achieve distributive goals. Thus
while there were one-time distributive gains from collectivization, it
did not establish any mechanisms to prevent increasing disparities in
income and wealth among higher-stage APCs.

Despite these difficulties, agricultural performance overall during
the 1st FYP was moderately good, given the low priority that the
sector enjoyed in the allocation of state investment resources and the

55 Lardy, *Agriculture in China's modern economic development*, 141.   56 Ibid., 243.

large unrequited outward transfers of resources generated within agriculture to support industrial development. Output in value terms rose by 4.5 percent annually, just above the published target rate. Grain crops rose 3.7 percent and cotton 4.7 percent annually, each just surpassing the final targets published in the plan in 1955.[57]

Yet in several respects agricultural growth must have been disappointing to China's political leaders. First, as suggested earlier, the growth targets for the sector had been scaled down on several occasions prior to the promulgation of the final plan. The 4.6 and 7.7 percent target rates of growth for cereals and cotton, respectively, that had been announced in 1954 were replaced by targets of 3.3 and 4.6 percent annual growth in the published 1st FYP.[58] Thus while performance met most of the targets, it was far below initial expectations. Moreover, contrary to expectations, the collectivization of agriculture did not lead to more rapid growth. On average, growth for 1956 and 1957 was below that of earlier years. Second, there were notable shortfalls below plan targets, as in the case of soybeans, the output of which grew at about one-third of the planned rate, and oil-bearing seeds (rapeseed, sesame, and peanuts) and meat, the output of which stagnated.

Third, the low rate of growth meant that consumption gains for most agricultural products on a per capita basis were modest to nonexistent. Per capita consumption of grain rose less than 3 percent between 1952 and 1957.[59] Consumption of cotton cloth was subject to more year-to-year fluctuation, but on average in 1956–57 was less than 10 percent greater than the average of 1952–53. Per capita consumption of edible vegetable oils declined significantly, while consumption of pork, beef, and mutton showed no increase.[60] For grain, cotton cloth, and vegetable oils, it was necessary to institute rationing to distribute limited supplies. Municipal administrations in some areas initiated rationing of cereals and vegetable oils as early as 1953, and in 1955 a standard coupon rationing system for all urban areas was instituted. Coupon rationing of cotton cloth for both urban

---

57 State Statistical Bureau, *Ten great years*, 118, 119. The growth of the value of output is measured in gross value terms. Measured in value added terms, the rate was only 3.8 percent. Yang Chien-pai and Li Hsueh-tseng, "Nung, ch'ing, chung chieh-kou," 106.
58 *First five-year plan for development of the national economy of the People's Republic of China in 1953–1957*, 115.
59 Lardy, *Agriculture in China's modern economic development*, 150.
60 Estimates of cotton cloth, vegetable oil, and meat consumption are based on official output and population data, the former adjusted for exports where appropriate. State Statistical Bureau, *Chung-kuo t'ung-chi nien-chien, 1981* (Chinese statistical yearbook, 1981), 144, 163, 221, 312.

and rural inhabitants was introduced in 1954 and was not discontinued until 1983. Slow growth of agricultural production also meant export performance was below expectations. By 1957 the export of peanuts, peanut oil, and hogs was up to 50 percent less than the export levels achieved in 1952, prior to the beginning of the plan.[61]

Finally, and in many respects most critically, deliveries of food grains into the hands of the state lagged behind the demand for cereals supplied through state distribution channels. On the one hand, the sum of taxes in kind and deliveries to the state at fixed prices reached a peak of 45 million tons in 1954 and then gradually declined. Initially, as discussed above, this was a result of a deliberate policy to reduce grain purchases below the level of 1954. But the drop continued in 1956 and 1957, in part because the state found it difficult to compel deliveries when prices peasants could attain on the private market were higher than those offered by the state. By the last year of the 1st FYP, procurement had fallen to 39.8 million tons, more than 10 percent below 1954.[62] Over the same period, grain production had risen 23 million tons. In effect, the share of the crop delivered to the state fell significantly.

As grain in the hands of the state declined in absolute terms, demand was rising inexorably. The nonagricultural population (primarily permanent urban residents, but including state employees resident in the countryside who were also eligible for rationed cereals and edible vegetable oils) rose from 83 million in 1952 to 98 million in 1954 and then to 106 million in 1957.[63] The introduction of comprehensive grain rationing in urban areas in the summer of 1955 was an attempt to reduce per capita grain consumption in the cities. But ration levels had to be increased in 1956, partly in response to the increased demand that followed a major reform which raised wages by as much as 30 percent. Moreover, the surge in urban population

---

61 Ibid., 368.
62 Lardy, *Agriculture in China's modern economic development*, 34.
63 The Chinese divide their population on the criteria of rural-urban and agricultural-nonagricultural. The former differentiation is based primarily on place of residence, although the minimum size a settlement must reach in order to qualify as urban and the treatment of peasants residing in the suburban areas of towns and cities has been changed with each census carried out since 1949. The differentiation agricultural-nonagricultural determines whether or not an individual is entitled to cereal sold by the state through the rationing system, an entitlement that became particularly important after the mid-1960s, when the price of grain was increasingly subsidized. The nonagricultural population simultaneously excludes some persons resident in urban areas, notably contract and temporary workers not entitled to permanent urban residence status, and includes some persons resident in rural areas, such as state workers involved in transportation, commerce, and government administration.

and in the industrial work force that occurred in 1956 placed further strains on the available supplies for feeding the nonagricultural population.[64] In addition, from the limited cereals at its disposal, the state had to supply the needs of the food processing industry (primarily for the production of distilled spirits), the animal feed industry, the consumption needs of the agricultural population engaged in animal husbandry and other nongrain crop production activities, and meet the demand for exports.

In short, while the growth of agricultural output exceeded that of population, it was low relative to the expectations at the beginning of the 1st FYP and stepped-up collectivization was not accompanied by more rapid growth, even with the encouragement of a twelve-year draft program for agriculture unveiled in January 1956. Moreover, some crops had not grown at all, and the state foresaw the demand for grain outstripping the quantities they could extract from the countryside, even under a system of compulsory deliveries. The potential magnitude of the conflict between rising urban demand on the one hand and rural needs on the other had already been foreshadowed by the rural grain crises of 1953 and the spring of 1955.[65]

Industrial growth

While agriculture lagged behind the targets envisioned at the outset of the 1st FYP, industry surged ahead of planned targets. Industrial output as a whole rose by 130 percent, substantially in excess of the 100 percent growth specified in the plan. Most of the above-plan growth was of producer goods, which topped the planned level of output by more than 40 percent. The largest share of increased output was accounted for by steel, machinery, and chemicals.[66]

While producer goods output more than tripled, consumer goods output grew only by 83 percent. Output of cotton yarn and cotton cloth, the most important inherited industry, grew by less than

64 Walker, *Food grain procurement and consumption in China*, 68. Ch'iang Yuan-kan and Ch'en Hsueh-wei, "Ch'ung-p'ing i-chiu-wu-liu-nien 'fan mao-chin'" (A fresh review of the 'anti-rash advance' of 1956), 35.

65 Kojima, "Grain acquisition and supply in China," 66–69. Thomas P. Bernstein, "Cadre and peasant behavior under conditions of insecurity and deprivation in the grain supply crisis of the spring of 1955," in A. Doak Barnett, ed., *Chinese Communist politics in action*, 365–99. Walker, "Collectivisation in retrospect," 14–15, 21, 26–27.

66 State Statistical Bureau, *Ten great years*, 88; *First five-year plan for the development of the national economy in 1953–57*, 47; Thomas G. Rawski, *China's transition to industrialism*, 34.

one-third.[67] The slow pace of development of light manufacturing reflected the slow growth of agricultural output. During the 1st FYP more than four-fifths of all consumer goods were dependent on raw materials supplied by agriculture. The growth of the cotton and silk textile industries, food processing industries such as flour milling and rice polishing, and the shoe industry were entirely dependent on raw cotton, cereals, and animal hides supplied by the farm sector. Many of these industries had substantial underutilized capacity due to shortages of raw materials throughout the 1st FYP. The relatively slow growth planned for these industries mirrored the low priority of agriculture in the allocation of state resources and the commitment to the priority development of producer goods, particularly steel and machinery.

The disparate growth rates of producer and consumer goods was reflected in the structural transformation of industry. On the eve of the 1st FYP, producer goods counted for only a third of all manufacturing output, whereas at the end of the plan the share had risen markedly to half.[68]

Industrial development during the 1st FYP also addressed the issue of regional fragmentation. Existing industrial centers, such as the Northeast and the former treaty port cities, had substantial advantages for future growth because of their considerable prior investment in social overhead capital and infrastructure, large numbers of highly skilled workers and experienced industrial managers, economies of scale, and so forth. On the other hand, these regions had few economic linkages with the hinterland, so it was likely that a strategy based on concentrated investment in regions of initial advantage would have few spillover effects and thus would lead to rapidly increasing regional disparities. During most of the 1st FYP the central leadership deliberately chose to redistribute human and investment resources from the advanced to the poorer regions. Investment projects in these areas included important infrastructure investments, particularly railroads and roads; natural resource-based extractive industries, notably coal, nonferrous metals, and petroleum; and manufacturing establishments producing goods for national markets.[69]

The development of transportation and other forms of infrastruc-

67 State Statistical Bureau, *Ten great years*, 88, 99.
68 Ibid., 90.
69 Lardy, "Regional growth and income distribution in China," in Dernberger, ed., *China's development experience in comparative perspective*, 176.

ture in the hinterland was a particularly important component of regional development policy. In 1950 less than a fifth of the Chinese rail system lay west of the Peking–Canton line, and the inland provinces of Sinkiang, Tsinghai, Ninghsia, and Szechwan had no rail lines at all. During the 1st FYP total railroad track more than doubled, with almost all of the new lines constructed in interior regions. By 1957 each of these inland provinces was linked by rail to the rest of China. These lines included, in addition to the Paochi-Chengtu line, lines linking Paotou in Inner Mongolia to Sinkiang; Chengtu to Chungking within Szechwan; and other major lines within Kansu, Inner Mongolia, and Kweichow.

In large measure these projects were feasible only because of large infusions of human and capital resources from more advanced regions. The unified fiscal system adopted in the early 1950s made it possible to transfer budgetary resources interregionally to a degree uncommon among either socialist or developing countries. Shanghai, which is the most visible example, produced a fifth of industrial output on the eve of the 1st FYP but was the site of only about 2.5 percent of national investment. Shanghai also supplied vast human resources to support industrialization elsewhere. By 1957 more than a quarter of a million workers, of whom 28,000 were specifically identified as technicians and 170,000 as skilled workers, had been permanently resettled away from Shanghai to industrial projects elsewhere.[70]

The consequences of these programs were notable both by comparison with Chinese historical experience and by comparison with development elsewhere, which generally reflects a pattern of increasing interregional inequality in the first several decades of modern economic growth. Overall, interprovincial variation in per capita output declined significantly as a result of notably slower than average growth in several of the most advanced regions – especially Shanghai and Tientsin – and substantially more rapid growth in poorer provinces, especially those targeted for industrial projects, notably Sinkiang, Inner Mongolia, Shensi, Tsinghai, and Kansu. While China's regional development program contained a number of obvious political white elephants, it did reverse the historic pattern of growth. Of course, a single FYP could not ameliorate the effects of the previous five decades of development. But a start was made.

70 Lardy, ibid., 176–77.

Magnitude and role of Soviet assistance

The rapid development of the producer goods sector and the geographic redistribution of industry during the 1st FYP depended critically on capital goods acquired from the Soviet Union. The core of the investment program consisted of 156 projects for which the Soviets supplied design and technical assistance, advice on construction and installation, as well as machinery and equipment. These projects absorbed almost half of all industrial investment in the 1st FYP.[71] Chinese dependence is also brought home by examining the import share of investment goods, including not only the complete plant projects but machinery and equipment imported for other projects as well. For the plan as a whole, imports were the equivalent of 30 percent of total investment.[72]

Almost all the Soviet-assisted plants were in the producer goods sector. They included 7 iron and steel plants, 24 electric power stations, and 63 machinery plants. Among these facilities were the largest and most important projects of the 1st FYP: two new steel mills built from the ground up at Wuhan, Hupei, and Paotou, Inner Mongolia; the rebuilding of the Anshan steel plant in the Northeast; the Changchun automobile plant; tractor and ball bearing plants in Loyang and Harbin; and the Lanchou oil refinery.

The regional distribution of the Soviet-assisted plants reflected the strong priority placed on ensuring the spread of industrial development away from coastal cities, built up before 1949, toward major new industrial centers in the North, the Northwest, and Central China, and the establishment of a foundation for future development in the Southwest. The great majority of the Soviet plants were in cities away from the coastal provinces, such as Wuhan, Hupei; Paotou, Inner Mongolia; Changchun, Kirin; and Chengtu, Szechwan.

Technical assistance provided by the Soviets equaled or surpassed in importance the machinery and equipment associated with these plants. About 10,000 Russian specialists worked in China during the decade, prospecting and surveying geological conditions, selecting

71 Lardy, *Economic growth and distribution in China*, 25.
72 Based on Chinese data on imports of producer goods and the share of national income alloted to "accumulation" (fixed investment and increased inventories), both measured in terms of Chinese currency. State Statistical Bureau, *Chung-kuo t'ung-chi nien-chien, 1981* (Chinese Statistical yearbook, 1981), 21, 354. This share is somewhat higher than estimates based on fragmentary information available before China published, in 1982, a complete time series of imports disaggregated into producer and consumer goods.

factory sites, supplying technical data, and training Chinese personnel. Moreover, project and design institutes within the Soviet Union were heavily involved in feasibility studies, project design, and the preparation of blueprints and working drawings.[73]

During the same years, 28,000 Chinese technicians and skilled workers went to the Soviet Union for training. The director, chief engineer, and a large number of workers for each of the 156 Soviet-aided plants received special training in Soviet factories: from the Changchun automobile factory, 500 went for training to the Moscow-Likhachev motor vehicle plant; 173 administrative staff and technicians from the Loyang tractor factory received training at the Khaikov tractor works in Moscow.[74]

The importance of Soviet technical assistance and capital goods would be difficult to overestimate. Its effort to transfer design capability has been characterized as unprecedented in the history of the transfer of technology. Moreover, China appears to have received the most advanced technology available within the Soviet Union, and in some cases this was the best in the world. In the iron and steel industry, the most important sector of Soviet assistance, the Soviets during the 1950s built and operated the world's best blast furnaces. Soviet designs for the Chinese plants at Wuhan and Paotou incorporated the latest in Soviet technology in blast and open hearth furnaces and in large-scale iron ore benefication.[75]

Moreover, although Western restrictions on trade with China left the Chinese with no visible alternative sources of supply, there is little evidence that the Soviets exploited China's dependence by manipulating the terms of exchange of this trade to their own advantage. Western studies suggest that the somewhat higher prices paid by the Chinese as compared to European countries for some Soviet goods appear to reflect higher transport costs rather than price discrimination, although Chinese accounts reflect a belief that the exchange rate established between the ruble and the yuan overvalued the Soviet currency, to the disadvantage of the Chinese.[76] Finally, China's treatment appears even more favorable when contrasted with the

73 Clark, *Development of China's steel industry*, 30.
74 Chu-yuan Cheng, *Scientific and engineering manpower in communist China, 1949–1963*, 200–201.
75 Clark, *Development of China's steel industry*, 36, 90–91.
76 Alexander Eckstein, *Communist China's economic growth and foreign trade, implications for U.S. policy*, 170–72; Wu Hsiu-ch'üan, "Sino-Soviet relations in the early 1950s," *Beijing Review*, 47 (1983), 20–21.

pattern of Soviet exploitation of the Eastern European states during those years.[77]

The Chinese, however, remained disappointed with the nature of their economic relationship with the Soviet Union because they had to pay for the goods and assistance they received. While Soviet-aided industrial plants were central to both the structural and regional transformation of China's industry, only a small share of these projects were made possible by credit, and the Soviets never provided aid in the form of grants. Mao in late 1949 journeyed to Moscow, his first trip abroad, where negotiation for Soviet support ensued for almost two months. The result was the first of two economic development loans. But the amount was only 300 million U.S. dollars, reportedly only a small fraction of the amount that had been sought by Mao. A second loan of 130 million U.S. dollars was announced when Nikolai A. Bulganin and Nikita S. Khrushchev led a delegation to Peking to celebrate the fifth anniversary of the People's Republic of China in the fall of 1954.[78]

These amounts pale when placed against the 25 billion yuan invested in industry during the 1st FYP. At the official exchange rate, the value of the credits was only 4 percent of total industrial investment. Moreover, the terms of the loans were relatively short. The 1950 loan, which consisted of trade credits dispersed at the rate of $60 million per year during 1951–55, was to be repaid in ten annual increments, beginning in 1954. As a consequence of the early repayment provisions, by 1957 China's net credit position with the Soviets was negative, meaning that China had to maintain a surplus in its balance of trade with the Soviet Union.[79]

Other aspects of the Chinese economic relations with the Soviet Union must have been equally disappointing. In the early 1950s the Chinese and the Soviets established a number of joint stock companies – for example, the Dairen shipbuilding company, companies for the exploitation of nonferrous and rare metals and for the extraction and refining of petroleum in Sinkiang, and an airline operating within northern and northwestern China and between the two countries. But by 1954 the Chinese requested that the companies

77 Eckstein, *Communist China's economic growth*, 170; William E. Griffith, *The Sino-Soviet rift*, 233.
78 O. Edmund Clubb, *China and Russia: The great game*, 402–3.
79 State Statistical Bureau, *Chung-kuo t'ung-chi nien-chien, 1981*, 350. Earlier Western estimates based on various Soviet sources showed the Chinese trade surplus emerging in 1956. Eckstein, *Communist China's economic growth and foreign trade*, 158.

be dissolved, although they had been established to run for thirty years. The Chinese, from the start, were sensitive to the Soviet use of similar joint stock companies as a mechanism of exploitation in Eastern Europe, and Mao by 1954 apparently felt it was no longer appropriate for another country to hold a privileged position within China.

Fortunately for the Sino-Soviet alliance, the post-Stalin leadership, notably Khrushchev, agreed, and the issue seems to have been settled without great rancor. The companies were formally dissolved in January 1955, but the Soviets insisted on payment for their capital contributions, valued at about 400 million U.S. dollars. The Soviets, in effect, extended a loan by allowing the Chinese to pay for these transferred assets over a ten-year period.

THE FORMULATION OF THE 2ND FIVE-YEAR PLAN

Discussion surrounding the formulation of the 2nd FYP foreshadowed a potentially significant evolution in China's development strategy. In part this evolution was an inevitable response to the successes and failures of the 1st FYP, but it also reflected an increasing independence and maturity of both the planning agencies at the center and leading non-Party economists such as Ma Yin-ch'u, the president of Peking University. Adherence to the Soviet model of economic development was criticized, and a systematic effort was made to shape a plan more congruent with China's low level of development, predominantly agrarian character, and immense population. (Ultimately this effort was to be thwarted by Mao Tse-tung's Great Leap Forward, the subject of Chapter 8.)

The impetus for the debate on the character of the 2nd FYP appears to stem from a series of unusual meetings in the late winter and early spring of 1956 when thirty-four central government ministries and the State Planning Commission presented detailed reports on industry, agriculture, transportation, commerce, and finance to Mao Tse-tung, Po I-po, and other high-ranking Party officials.[80] Although the CCP had always specified economic priorities that formed the basis of more detailed plans, this sequence of meetings provided planners and economists with an unprecedented opportunity to specify in

---

80 Po I-po, "Ch'ung-ching ho huai-nien – hsien-kei tang tan-sheng ti liu-shih chou-nien" (Respect and remembrance – marking the sixtieth anniversary of the founding of the Chinese Communist Party), *Hung-ch'i* (Red flag), 1981. 13, 64.

detail the economic costs and implications of specific policy choices. The context of these meetings was also unusual.

In late 1955 Mao had personally sought to increase the pace of economic development. That effort was not limited to the accelerated collectivization of agriculture discussed earlier, but included a stepped-up pace of transformation to state ownership of privately owned establishments in handicrafts and commerce, and an acceleration of industrial growth under the campaign slogan "more, faster, better, and more economically." Under mounting political pressure, the targets contained in the original annual economic plan for 1956, finalized by the State Planning Commission in November–December 1955, were raised in the second half of January 1956.[81] Although the texts of the survey and overview presentations of the planning agencies were never made public, they appear to have constituted a comprehensive refutation of excessive political intervention in plan formulation. In short, the reports highlighted the high economic costs of the political choices implicit in the mini-leap of 1956 that was then under way.

In the aftermath of the internal Party meetings, Mao Tse-tung prepared a summary report of the lessons learned entitled, "On the Ten Great Relationships." This report makes clear that the planners envisaged a strategy for the 2nd FYP that would diverge in several significant ways from its predecessor. Curiously, however, the report was not officially published until twenty years later.[82] Mao apparently had not yet fully accepted the approach of the planners and sought to reduce their independence by suppressing publication of his own report. Outwardly Mao's efforts seemed not to be successful. Work on the 2nd FYP appears at least initially to have gone forward on the basis of the reports Mao and other Politburo members received between February and April 1956. By June the production drive launched the previous winter was truncated, over the vigorous objection of Mao Tse-tung.[83]

But Mao's setback was apparently only temporary. Debate re-

---

81 MacFarquhar, *The origins of the Cultural Revolution, 1: Contradictions among the people,* 30. Even prior to the increases of late January, output targets for 1956 for specific agricultural crops were raised at least once between September 1955, when the report of the State Planning Commission set forth preliminary targets, and December, when the plan was finalized. Ch'iang Yuan-kan and Ch'en Hsueh-wei, "Ch'ung-p'ing i-chiu-wu-liu-nien ti 'fan mao-chin,'" 34.

82 First publication occurred in *JMJP*, 26 December 1976. The report was included two years later in vol. 5 of *Selected works of Mao Tse-tung*. A text had, however, become available to Western scholars during the Cultural Revolution.

83 MacFarquhar, *The origins of the Cultural Revolution, 1,* 86–91, 122–26.

emerged late in the year when the first in a pair of major articles by Ma Yin-ch'u appeared in *People's Daily*.[84] Ma supported the adoption of a more balanced growth strategy that had been endorsed by the State Planning Commission. The theme of his articles was "comprehensive balance and proportionate development," code phrases for planning based on a careful examination of the linkages and interdependencies among different sectors of the economy. Ma criticized the past neglect of agriculture, which had held down the growth of light industry; the emphasis on excessively large capital intensive enterprises; and the replacement of the price mechanism by bureaucratic planning in agriculture.

Nowhere was the divergence between the strategy implicit in the 1st FYP and that proposed by the planners and Ma Yin-ch'u for the 2nd FYP more clear than in the allocation of resources for agriculture. The State Planning Commission in April 1957 rejected the principle of "exclusive concentration on heavy industry and disregard or slight attention to agriculture and light industry" in favor of a plan that would achieve priority development of heavy industry "through the development of agriculture and light industry."[85] Both the commission's and Ma Yin-ch'u's writings recognized more fully than had the 1st FYP the importance of agriculture for raising the living standards of the population, both through its provision of foodstuffs and through its supply of raw materials to light industry. Thus the share of state investment resources earmarked for agriculture and light industry was to increase. At the same time there was increasing recognition because of the shortage of arable land that agricultural growth would become more dependent on increased yields, which in turn implied an increased need for chemical fertilizers and certain types of agricultural machinery. This marked a significant change from the 1st FYP, in which there was an emphasis on land reclamation and low priority for the development of chemical fertilizers and agricultural machinery.

84 Ma Yin-ch'u, "Lien-hsi Chung-kuo shih-chi lai t'an-t'an tsung-ho p'ing-heng li-lun ho an pi-li fa-chan kuei-lu" (A discussion of the theory of comprehensive balance and the law of planned proportionate development as it relates to Chinese reality), *JMJP*, 28, 29 December 1956. Reprinted in *Ma Yin-ch'u ching-chi lun-wen hsuan-chi* (Selected economic essays of Ma Yin-ch'u), 2.121–44. "Lien-hsi Chung-kuo shih-chi lai tsai t'an-t'an tsung-ho p'ing-heng li-lun ho an pi-li fa-chan kuei-lu" (A further discussion of the theory of comprehensive balance and the law of planned, proportionate development as it relates to Chinese reality), *JMJP*, 11, 12 May 1957, Reprinted in *Ma Yin-ch'u ching-chi lun-wen hsuan-chi*, 2.145–69.
85 State Planning Commission, "Ch'u-pu yen-chiu ti kuan-yü ti-erh-ko wu-nien chi-hua ti jo-kan wen-t'i" (Certain issues in preliminary studies on the 2nd Five-Year Plan), *Chi-hua ching-chi* (Economic planning), 1957. 4, 10–12.

Finally, with regard to agriculture, there was a recognition that compulsory procurement and excessive mobilization of investment funds within APCs had detrimental effects on peasants' incentives and that deductions from income for investment and other purposes should be limited to allow somewhat more rapid growth of personal consumption.

The State Planning Commission also sought to modify the 1st FYP's emphasis on very large-scale industrial enterprises and to reduce the emphasis on rapid industrial development in less developed regions. The change reflected a recognition that larger-scale plants and development of interior regions involved longer construction times and employed far fewer workers per unit of capital. The increased concern for employment reflected the slow growth of the labor force in modern sector industry during the 1st FYP and continuing high rates of urban unemployment. Industrial employment rose by only 2.6 million annually during the 1st FYP, a relatively slow pace given the preponderant share of investment resources industry absorbed and its relatively rapid growth.[86] Although total nonagricultural employment rose more rapidly, the rate of increase by all evidence was far less than the growth of the urban working-age population. Urban unemployment, a major problem inherited from the Nationalist government, actually increased during the 1st FYP. Aggregate male nonagricultural unemployment by the end of the plan is estimated to have been 10 million to 16 million.[87] In Shanghai, about which more accurate data are available, there were 670,000 unemployed at the end of the 1st FYP, which given the number employed, implies an unemployment rate of 22 percent.[88] Shanghai, in particular, would benefit from the reduction in the drain of its resources to promote industrialization in the interior.

Moreover, increased emphasis on smaller plants was related to a decision to reduce the heavy reliance of the 1st FYP on machinery and equipment imported from the Soviet Union. This decision may have been necessitated by the refusal of the Soviet Union to extend significant additional credits after 1954, credits that may have been requested by Mao on the occasion of his visit to the Soviet Union in late 1957 for the celebration of the fortieth anniversary of the

86 John Philip Emerson, *Nonagricultural employment in mainland China, 1949–1958*, 129.
87 Chi-ming Hou, "Manpower, employment, and unemployment," in Alexander Eckstein, Walter Galenson, and Ta-chung Liu, eds., *Economic trends in Communist China*, 369.
88 Christopher Howe, *Employment and economic growth in urban China, 1949–1957*, 39.

Bolshevik revolution. And it may also have reflected an internal assessment by the planners of the difficulty of sustaining agricultural exports sufficiently large to pay for continued large-scale machinery and equipment imports on a current basis. But the discussion surrounding the 2nd FYP clearly envisaged that a much smaller share of investment goods required by the plan would be imported.

Finally, the 2nd FYP foreshadowed a relaxation of the high degree of centralization of the control of resource allocation that had evolved during the 1st FYP. Mao's 1956 report signaled the need to reduce the planning and economic administrative bureaucracy at the center and to provide greater leeway for local decision-making power. This struck a responsive chord in many provinces, where local leaders had complained of excessively rigid centralized control from the very onset of the 1st FYP.

Although the planners appear to have had a vision of the 2nd FYP, it was never to be fully developed. Chou En-lai presented a report on proposals for the 2nd FYP to the CCP's Eighth Congress in September 1956 that reflected several of the principles discussed above. But more than a year later, Li Fu-ch'un's report on the plan to the All-China Federation of Trade Unions was restricted to a similar enunciation of principles and a few production goals, rather than setting forth more detailed targets.[89] The inability to set forth a fleshed out plan almost certainly reflected continuing debate over development strategy – a debate that was resolved decisively in the spring of 1958 when the Great Leap Forward was launched.

89 Li Fu-ch'un, "Kuan-yü wo-kuo ti-i-ko wu-nien chi-hua ti ch'eng-chiu ho chin-hou she-hui chu-i chien-she ti jen-wu fang-chen ti pao-kao" (Report on the achievements of the First Five-Year Plan and the tasks and directions in future socialist construction), *JMJP*, 8 December 1957.

CHAPTER 4

EDUCATION FOR THE NEW ORDER

Three diverse traditions came together in Chinese education during the 1950s, in an uncertain combination that has yet to be fully reconciled thirty years later. The tradition that the Chinese Communist Party inherited from the Republican era was itself an amalgam of modern Western-inspired learning grafted on an ancient Confucian base. The second tradition the Chinese Communists brought with them from their own recent experience as leaders of the rural Border Region governments in the 1930s and 1940s. The third tradition was introduced into China in the 1950s, when the new Communist government embarked on an ambitious attempt to learn from the Soviet Union. The influence of each of these three traditions can still be seen in Chinese education, their outlines now firmly etched in the public mind and in official discourse by the volatile combination they have produced.

THE HERITAGE FROM THE REPUBLICAN ERA

Table 2 shows, in statistical terms, the educational system inherited from the Kuomintang government in 1949,[1] and Table 3 presents estimates of the educational levels of the population as a whole in the same year.[2] These national statistics obscured the diversities that existed along every conceivable dimension. The most apparent were those that are most apparent everywhere: between urban and rural, between rich and poor, between economically developed coastal areas and the more isolated hinterlands, and between men and women.

In terms of basic literacy, the male-female dimension was the least ambiguous. Women in the early decades of this century probably comprised less than the 48.5 percent of the population revealed in the

---

1 *China: Socialist economic development*, Annex G, Education Sector, World Bank Document (1 June 1981), 1. The first part of this chapter deals with elementary education in the pre-1949 era which is dealt with, for higher education, in *CHOC* 13, ch. 8.
2 Ibid.

TABLE 2

Students in 1949

Institutions	Number of students	Percent of age group in school
Primary (grades 1–6)	24,000,000	25.0%
Secondary (grades 7–12)	1,300,000	3.0%
Tertiary	120,000	0.3%

TABLE 3

Graduates in 1949

College graduates	185,000
Secondary school graduates	4,000,000
Primary school graduates	70,000,000
Total number of illiterates (80% of the population)	432,000,000
Total working-age population	340,000,000
Total population	540,000,000

1982 census, and had an estimated literacy rate of 2 percent to 10 percent nationwide. Literacy rates among males are estimated to have ranged from 30 percent to 45 percent of their total number. These literacy rates are based on a definition which included those with knowledge of but a few hundred Chinese characters and who would today be classified as only semi-literate.[3]

For the rural areas alone, contemporary estimates of literacy varied widely. The lowest available is a 1939 estimate of 1 percent for the isolated districts that made up the Shensi-Kansu-Ninghsia Border Region, the Communists' main base area at that time.[4] Buck's frequently quoted survey of rural China in the early 1930s probably produced more reliable estimates, but did not concentrate exclusively on poor and backward border regions. His data, drawn from sample surveys conducted in 308 counties located in 22 provinces, revealed that only 30 percent of all males over 7 years of age, and 1 percent of all females over that age, had acquired a level of literacy sufficient to

3 Male-female population ratios for the present and past appear in: *Jen-min jih-pao (JMJP)*, 28 October 1982; *China Daily*, Peking, 9 November 1982; and John Lossing Buck, *Land utilization in China*, 375–77. For the most systematic attempt to estimate literacy rates in the past, see Evelyn Sakakida Rawski, *Education and popular literacy in Ch'ing China*, 23 and passim.
4 Cited in Peter J. Seybolt, "The Yenan revolution in mass education," *CQ*, 48 (October–December 1971), 642.

allow them to read a simple letter. Of the 87,000 persons surveyed on this question, 45.2 percent of the males and 2.2 percent of the females reported receiving some schooling. Of that number, the males had attended school on an average of four years and females an average of three years, which is sufficient to attain basic literacy but not necessarily to sustain it over time. Also, of the males who had been to school, 66 percent reported that the education they received was in the traditional style.[5]

The distinction between modern and traditional-style schooling was an important one, for it coincided with and thus reinforced the urban-rural dichotomy. In her recent study of education during the Ch'ing dynasty, Evelyn Sakakida Rawski has analyzed the extent and substance of the traditional schooling, and the reasons for its persistence in the rural areas long after the more urbanized elite had seen the future and enrolled its children in modern schools.

Traditional elementary schooling was diffused throughout the countryside and was not confined to towns and cities, although it was more prevalent there. Rural boys had access to basic literacy training through a number of channels, the most common being the private tutor and privately run classes. The children of the more affluent were usually taught within the home itself, either by a literate family member or a teacher engaged for that purpose. A variation of the household tutor was the village school teacher. The less well-to-do families in a neighborhood or village might jointly engage a tutor for their children. Expenditures for such instruction were not great, being confined largely to the teacher's salary toward which the parents of each child contributed an agreed-upon sum. Supplies and furnishings were provided by the parents themselves, who might also secure the use of a spare room in a village temple or some other building where their children could gather daily for instruction. Or pupils might go to the teacher's home for this purpose.

Such tutors were drawn from among the relatively large pool of advanced students and lower-level degree holders – numbering close to 3 million – that existed as an important by-product of the imperial examination system.[6] Only a small proportion of those who prepared for the examinations actually earned the higher degrees necessary to qualify for appointments within the imperial bureaucracy. For aspiring degreeholders and unemployed literati of modest means, the

5 Buck, *Land utilization in China*, 373–75.
6 See, for example, Ichisada Miyazaki, *China's examination hell: The civil service examinations of imperial China*; Ch'ien Mu, *Traditional government in imperial China*.

intellectual's prejudice against manual labor and other occupations held to be demeaning, such as those of clerk and bookkeeper, left few alternative means of earning a living other than teaching.

Literati also staffed two other institutions capable of providing elementary education. The first consisted of schools established by the extended family or clan organizations. The latter were financed not by individual households but from joint clan revenues. Some of these schools were established specifically for poor boys within the lineage whose parents could not otherwise afford to educate their children.

The second type of institution was the public elementary school inherited from the late imperial era, which was also intended to serve children from poor families. Some such schools were fully equipped and offered instruction entirely free of charge. Others required students to provide their own furniture and supplies. These public charitable schools, although established in accordance with imperial government directive, did not necessarily receive direct government financing and so had to rely on the interest and largesse of local benefactors. These included, in addition to local officials, wealthy families, guilds, merchants, and groups of ordinary villagers. Schools founded in this manner were endowed with land, money, or buildings, all of which were treated as investment capital and managed for the long-term support of the school through the return of rent and interest.

Such charitable schools, however, were able to accommodate only a fraction of the approximately 40.3 million boys that made up the 7 to 14-year-old age group in the mid-nineteenth century. Rawski estimated the proportion of that age group studying in such schools at less than 1 percent in all but two of the eighteen provinces for which information was available. In those two, Yunnan and Shensi, the proportion of the age group studying in such public charitable schools was calculated at 3.3 percent and 1 percent, respectively. The clan schools also probably served only a small proportion of the total school-age population. Thus the main channel for elementary education in the nineteenth century was the private tutor and privately established classes.[7]

Regardless of the means by which it was conveyed, however, the average boy who received it was exposed to such instruction for only two or three years, and its content was essentially the same every-

---

7 Rawski, *Education and popular literacy in Ch'ing China*, 95, 183–93.

where. Basic instruction at the elementary level was intended to teach children to recognize and write several hundred characters and to inculcate the fundamental Confucian values. These were conveyed through textbooks and teaching materials based on the classical works used in formal studies by the minority who went on to prepare for the imperial examinations. But at the elementary level which marked the beginning and the end for most of the boys who had access to such instruction, the objective was more modest. The end result for them was what might be called not so much functional as subsistence or survival literacy. The pupil would also have been introduced, through the primary textbooks, to the Confucian concepts of morality, filial piety, and correct conduct in interpersonal relations, as well as to basic information about China's past. Practical subjects including arithmetic and science were not normally included in the curriculum. Calculation, account keeping, and the use of the abacus appear to have been treated as specialized knowledge and reserved for apprentices in commerce. But the average student would probably have gained sufficient introduction to the skills of reading and writing to be able subsequently to teach himself, with the aid of popular illustrated character glossaries, enough practical vocabulary to master the simple written communications needed for daily life.[8]

The abolition of the imperial examinations in 1905 may have marked the abrupt end of traditional Confucian learning at the elite level. But contemporary edicts to establish a new school system with a modern Western inspired curriculum would take decades to be realized. In the interim, while new generations of teachers were themselves learning the new subjects of science, mathematics, history, geography, and technical training, traditional schooling persisted. By the 1930s, a network of modern schools, both government and privately funded, had been established from primary school through university.[9] Yet it was sufficient to serve but a small proportion of the nation's school-age population, while old-style teachers continued to offer instruction based on the classical Confucian texts to large numbers of students. Hence Buck's finding that of the rural males in his survey with some schooling, 66 percent had received only the traditional instruction.

Investigators found that rural people in particular actually preferred the old-style learning because it more closely matched the as yet unchanged patterns of their lives and work. The traditional-

8 Ibid., 44–53, 125–39.
9 See Theodore E. Hsiao, *The history of modern education in China*.

style teachers were older and therefore more respected than those in the modern schools; the new subjects were of no use, while the traditional curriculum was more appropriate to rural needs, still dominated as they were by the interpersonal relationships of village and family life; the style of instruction was more informal and there-fore more easily adapted to the dictates of farm work; and financial costs were lower.[10]

In this manner, education in Republican China became more sharply differentiated: The new Westernized learning was concen-trated at the national and elite levels and in the cities, while the rural areas remained to a much greater degree the preserve of traditional values and learning. A 1932 report sponsored by the League of Nations was highly critical of the disjointed nature of China's education system, which was by then clearly apparent.[11] The report referred to China's schools as "independent organisms modelled on the forms and ideology of private education instead of being included in an organised system of public education related to immediate social problems." The authors blamed first the Chinese educational tradi-tion of family, clan, and village schools which were confined by narrow private interests. Second, they blamed the new generation of Chinese intellectuals for equating modernization with the mechanical imitation of foreign educational institutions. Teaching plans, text-books, and teaching methods were all based on Western learning and example.

Especially alarming in this respect was the excessive influence of the American model. This was being introduced into China mainly at the secondary and tertiary levels via the American missionary schools and the enthusiasm of Chinese intellectuals themselves upon return-ing from their studies abroad:

The result is a favouring of schools of higher standard, generally rising far above the condition of the impoverished country whilst the primary and vocational instruction most indispensable for the people is neglected. There is also the lack of social ideals within the schools, an abstract kind of instruc-tion not directly connected with surrounding life and the necessities of the country's rebirth usually obtaining. This creates an enormous abyss between

10 Rawski, *Education and popular literacy in Ch'ing China*, 163–65.
11 The League of Nations' Mission of Educational Experts, *The reorganization of education in China*. The report was prepared at the request of the Chinese government and was based on data gathered during a three-month stay in China by the authors during the autumn of 1931. The authors of the report were European: Professor C. H. Becker, University of Berlin and former Prussian Minister of Education; M. Falski, Director of Primary Education at the Polish Ministry of Education; Professor P. Langevin, Collège de France, Paris; and Professor R. H. Tawney, University of London.

the masses of the Chinese people, plunged in illiteracy, and not understanding the needs of their country, and the intelligentsia educated in luxurious schools and indifferent to the wants of the masses.[12]

The report warned Chinese educators against superficial imitation of foreign models and suggested that they borrow instead that "spirit of originality with which Americans have succeeded in adapting the culture of Europe to American conditions."

The report was also critical of the deliberate elitist orientation apparent throughout the school system. For example, public kindergartens were frequently located in the wealthier neighborhoods. Enrollment was based on entrance examinations designed to select those already demonstrating mental and physical superiority. These were usually the children of the more affluent, thereby excluding the very children who most needed such schooling. Tuition fees were demanded from all alike, regardless of ability to pay. The same practices governed attendance at the public primary schools, so children from poorer families were denied access to them as well. At the same time, these schools were underutilized and attended by students whose parents could have arranged private tutoring for them if necessary. The pattern of preferential selection for the children of the more affluent and influential was duplicated at the secondary and tertiary levels. Public scholarships were used primarily to finance study abroad and were not awarded systematically on the basis of need. Among the report's recommendations for correcting these features of the education system were the abolition of entrance examinations and tuition fees in all public kindergartens and primary schools.[13]

Finally, the report found much to criticize in the system of higher education, which was then based on more than fifty institutions, all established within less than a quarter of a century. The points of criticism included: haphazard geographical distribution; the multiplicity of institutions concentrated in the same area and doing almost the same work without any rational division of labor between them; and the "hypertrophy of legal, political and literary studies" to the neglect of science and technology. Just over 59 percent of the students enrolled in full degree programs were studying law, politics, or the liberal arts, with another 6 percent in education. Just under 10 percent were studying in the natural sciences; 11.5 percent, in engineering; and only 3 percent, in agriculture. Without actually acknowledging

12 *The reorganization of education in China*, 21.   13 Ibid., 65–67, 92–95.

the ancient tradition that was reproducing itself in modern guise, the report noted regretfully that "the ambition of most Chinese university students is a career in the public service, central or local, and failing that, a post as a teacher."[14]

According to the statistics provided by the Chinese Ministry of Education, the number of pupils in primary school during the 1929–30 academic year was 8,839,434, or 21 percent of the 41.4 million children in the 6- to 9-year-old age group. This calculation was made with reference to the four-year junior primary system which the new Kuomintang government was then attempting to popularize. The authors of the League of Nation's report estimated that approximately 9 percent of the total 460 million population fell into that age group. The figures included students in the small single-classroom schools in towns and villages, which accounted for perhaps half the total number of existing primary schools. But it is unclear whether the statistics included students in private or traditional schools, as well as those in the new-style public ones.[15]

The Chinese Education Ministry provided two very different sets of statistics on secondary schooling which the authors were never able to reconcile. They concluded that the reality probably varied somewhere between the two, namely, 307,906 students attending 2,066 secondary schools, as opposed to 783,140 students in 13,596 schools.[16]

As of September 1931, the students in the nation's 59 national, provincial, and registered private universities numbered 33,847 of whom 5,170 were enrolled in less than full degree programs. An additional 8,635 students were attending short courses and preparatory programs at these same institutions. These figures did not include the 28 tertiary level technical schools with some 3,500 students.[17]

THE HERITAGE OF THE COMMUNIST BORDER REGIONS

It was of course the more traditional milieu which served as the base for the Chinese Communist Party's rise to power after it was driven from the cities in the late 1920s. Like others who concerned themselves with the problem, Mao Tse-tung discovered that the peasants preferred the old-fashioned schools, or "Chinese classes," as they called them, to the modern ones. They rejected the education pro-

14 Ibid., 151.   15 Ibid., 76–85.   16 Ibid., 99–100.   17 Ibid., 130–31, 141, 151.

vided by the new primary schools, referring to it as "foreign." They regarded it as inappropriate for the needs of village life.

In a hint of things to come, Mao recorded in his "Report on an investigation of the peasant movement in Hunan" in 1927 that a dispute had arisen between the county education boards and the developing peasant movement. The former demanded that education funds be used to establish modern foreign-style schools, while the latter wanted to use the money to support their own evening classes and "peasant schools." As a result, the funds were usually split between the two.[18]

But the larger conflict the dispute represented was not so easily resolved. Rather, it sounded the underlying theme that has reverberated in one variation or another throughout the history of Chinese education from that time to the present. The first major development of the theme occurred in the Shensi-Kansu-Ninghsia Border Region toward the end of the Anti-Japanese War. In the early 1940s, the education system of the Border Region had undergone a period of "regularization" aimed at raising quality and standardizing the content of what was taught. According to directives issued in 1942, this was to be achieved at the primary level by reducing the number of schools, eliminating the weakest and strengthening the more successful. The best of these were to be designated "central" schools, the forerunner of the controversial keypoint school system that would be developed in later years. The best teachers and facilities were to be concentrated in the central schools, which were given the responsibility of leading the less well-endowed institutions in their vicinity.

All six secondary schools in the Border Region were to be brought under the direct leadership of the Border Region Department of Education, and all were to adhere to uniform standards and regulations. Secondary school admission requirements became more restrictive, with fixed age limits and mandatory written entrance examinations. Teachers were required to limit extracurricular activities and increase the amount of time spent in the classroom.[19]

Criticism of the new system began within a year after the directives proclaiming it were officially issued. These were blamed on the Education Bureau, said to be staffed by former East Coast urban intellectuals who were trying to apply the standards of their own Western-inspired education to Border Region schooling. The subse-

18 Mao, SW, 5.53–54.
19 Seybolt, "The Yenan revolution in mass education," 650–52.

quent critique denounced their efforts as inappropriate to the war-time conditions of the rural Communist-led base areas. But the critique also pinpointed the dilemma of educational development generally when the goal is development as defined by the experience of the urbanized West and the target area is a predominantly rural, non-Western society. The critique, which appeared in the *Liberation Daily* on April 7, 1944, could have been a paraphrase from the League of Nations' report issued a decade earlier, and it would be reiterated countless times during later decades by administrators in many other countries besides China:

The old educational system (after the abolition of the imperial examinations) wanted to study foreign countries, so its soul was the returned students. Education in China was almost all of a kind to prepare students for abroad. Foreign countries were everywhere taken as a model. It was based not on its feet but on its head. The returned-student system has had its use. We should not, in general, deny this, like the pretended patriots who, the more they talk about restoring the classics, the more they cannot leave the foreign. But we should certainly see that the base of education is firmly rooted in the needs of the broadest mass of the people. The needs of the broadest mass of the people are some kind of mass education and education for the cadres working for the people. These two kinds of education are fundamentally different from the old system of education. They are not preparatory and are not concerned with passing to the next stage of education. They have their own independent and clear objective in actual life and work.

The problem more specifically was that the developing Border Region education system was of the formal kind which prepared students to move on from primary to secondary school, and on up the educational ladder. Yet only a minority could continue their studies past primary school, while the majority who had then to return home had nothing to show for their new-style modern education. They were dissatisfied, unwilling to work, and "actually worse off than if they had not gone to school."[20]

The correctives introduced in 1944 reversed the trend toward regularization in Border Region schools. The aim was to create forms of schooling more appropriate to the rural base areas, with their "backward" techniques of production and "undeveloped division of labor," where even the children had to participate in household and agricultural work. The *min-pan* school, or school run-by-the-people, was the answer to the problem of trying to encourage more peasants

---

20 *Chieh-fang jih-pao* (Liberation daily), 7 April 1944, trans. in Michael Lindsay, *Notes on educational problems in Communist China, 1941–47*, 56.

to send their children to primary school at the same time that these were being reduced in number to improve their quality.

The *min-pan* schools, financially supported and managed by the villages themselves, were not so much an innovation as an adaptation of a continuing tradition, the old-style privately run village school. The *min-pan* schools might receive some money from the local government. But the community which the school served was responsible for maintaining and supplying it and looking after the needs of its teachers, in much the same manner as the village had supported the traditional classes. Hence existing classes of this sort could be transformed with little difficulty into the new-style *min-pan* schools.[21] Education committees of local citizens were formed to manage the schools, which they did together with the local officials, obviating the need for the government's lowest-level district education offices, which were abolished.

School calendars and holidays were determined by the demands of farm work in the village, so that children could continue at the same time to help their parents and to study, as in the traditional village schools. The curriculum concentrated on the subjects the peasants were most willing to accept: basic literacy training and arithmetic, with the addition of practical knowledge wherever possible. Villages where the local people wanted to continue using the old Confucian textbooks as the basis of instruction in their schools presented something of a problem. Official guidelines directed that in such cases, the local authorities should persuade the village education committee that a Confucian classical education was no longer of any practical use.[22]

In fact, the full description of the new type of rural school was actually *min-pan kung-chu*, or "managed by the people with public help." Popular management cannot be separated from public help, cautioned one directive on such schools: "People's management still needs strong leadership, not laissez-faire." More to the point, public help meant "leadership in administration, system and methods of instruction; the introduction, cultivation and training of teachers; the printing of educational material; help in meeting expenses, etc."[23]

But the slogans for the development of the new schools were

21 Michael Lindsay reported on one such case in his *Notes on educational problems*, 38.
22 Ibid.
23 "Directive on Research and Experiment on 'People-Managed Public-Help' Primary Schools," 2 October 1944, from *Collected laws and regulations now in force* (Shansi-Chahar-Hopei Border Region Government, 15 December 1945), trans. in Lindsay, *Notes on educational problems*, 103–4.

"oppose the old-style uniformity" and "oppose regularity in education." The objective was to find a teaching medium for each locality that people there would accept. The *min-pan* schools were accordingly set up in many different ways and forms, based on the opinions of parents and students deliberately solicited for that purpose. In statistical terms, the result of this innovation was that the regular primary schools in the Border Region declined in number from a high of 1,341 in 1940 to 357 in 1946. Meanwhile, the *min-pan* schools had increased to 1,038.[24]

At the secondary level, the earlier goal of transforming the Border Region schools into college preparatory institutions was also abandoned as inappropriate for the time and place. The new standardized curriculum and enrollment procedures were revised to provide a terminal education for students who could then fill the personnel needs of the government, military, and production units within the Border Region. Age limits were dropped and local cadres were given preference in admission over recent primary school graduates.

The curriculum was redesigned with an eye to practical relevance, or courses more directly related to the war effort and production techniques. The nineteen courses in the standardized curriculum were reduced to eight. But flexibility was the hallmark of the new system:

The period of study in every level of school must differ according to the environment. It may at the shortest be less than one year and at the longest three or four years. The top two years in the old six-year system primary school can be joined to the first level of cadre school if the situation is considered to warrant this, and be made a preparatory course in the regular middle-school education, or it may be made into an independent training course.... Inequality of standards is unavoidable, and so an exact linking on of one stage of school to the next is almost impossible, but this is nothing to worry about.[25]

The authority of the education bureaucracy was bypassed at the central as well as the local levels with the demotion of the Border Region Education Department to an advisory capacity. Education policies were thereafter issued under the authority of the chairman of the Border Region government. Responsibility for administering secondary schools was sent down from the regional to the subregional level of government in an effort to associate the schools more

24 Seybolt, "The Yenan revolution in mass education," 663.
25 *CFJP*, 27 May 1944, trans. in Lindsay, *Notes on educational problems*, 60–61.

closely with the local government bureaus and work units, whose present and future cadres they would be training.[26]

LEARNING FROM THE SOVIET UNION

The objective of the 1944 movement to reorganize education was clearly stated: to create a system more appropriate to the immediate needs of life and work during wartime in the rural base areas. "To forget the future because of the present is incorrect," commented the *Liberation Daily* in announcing the reorganization measures, but "to forget the present because of the future is especially incorrect." It acknowledged, however, that the present was "not our ideal." In the future, the problems of passing from one grade of school to another or the need to regularize education would have to be confronted and new solutions found.[27]

Within little more than five years, the Party would find itself the leader not just of the backward border areas, but of the entire nation. New forms of education would have to be devised appropriate for a far more complex pattern of life and work. Undoubtedly, the ideological commitments of the CCP, plus the urgency of the task and their lack of preparedness for it, led Party leaders to embark upon the same course they had so recently criticized others for taking. But the net result was to imitate a foreign country – albeit a fraternal socialist one – with the same kind of enthusiasm their precedessors had shown in learning from the advanced countries of the West. The rationale was that since the best of Western (that is, British and American) science and technology had already been absorbed by the Russians, the "quickest and best way" was to take the distilled essence directly from the Soviet Union. And since education and industry are the main social institutions necessary for the application of science and technology, their organization and management were also reshaped in the Soviet mold.[28]

26 Seybolt, "The Yenan revolution in mass education," 658; also on these innovations and their larger context, see Mark Selden, *The Yenan way in revolutionary China*, 267–74 and ch. 6.
27 *CFJP*, 7 April 1944 and 27 May 1944, trans. in Lindsay, *Notes on educational problems*, 56–57, 61.
28 For early Chinese statements on acquiring the best of Western learning from the Soviet Union in the field of industrial management, see Suzanne Pepper, *Civil war in China: The political struggle, 1945–1949*, 364–66, 374–75; also Ch'en Po-ta, "Speech before the study group of research members of the Academia Sinica," July 1952, in Stewart Fraser, ed., *Chinese communist education*, 184–85.

One of the many difficulties with this approach, of course, was that Soviet education would itself soon be in a state of transition resulting from the general critique of the "Stalin model" that followed his death in 1953. Moreover, Stalin's model was a conservative reaction designed to accommodate the imperatives of industrialization. Toward that end, the revolutionary experiments introduced into Soviet education in the 1920s had been rejected and the regulations abolished which barred the children of bourgeois parents from higher education. Nevertheless, it was the more conservative Soviet model that the newly victorious Chinese revolutionaries sought to adopt, without giving any apparent thought to the incongruities it represented for them.[29]

The effort to learn from the Soviet Union was most evident in higher education, where Western influence had predominated in earlier decades. Nationalization was the first order of business. The exact number of tertiary-level institutions in China at this time varies according to the source. But according to Education Minister Ma Hsu-lun, there were, not including the new cadre schools, 227 institutions of higher learning in China as of mid-1950. Of these, 138 were state-run, 65 were private, and another 24 were run by foreign religious organizations. The system was also still characterized by an uneven geographic distribution, with schools concentrated in the coastal cities. In mid-1950, 37 percent of all institutions of higher learning were in the East China area, with 25 percent in Shanghai alone. Only about 15 percent were located in the predominantly rural old liberated areas.[30]

By the end of 1952, most of the foreign faculty and administrative staff had departed, and all private control had been eliminated. This paved the way for the reorganization of the entire system of higher education along Soviet lines, which was essentially completed during the following year. The objective was to create a more specialized division of labor appropriate for China's development needs. Marked for elimination were the American-style liberal arts college and the general undergraduate education characteristic of American and Brit-

29 Jan-Ingvar Lofstedt, *Chinese educational policy*, 50–58; Martin K. Whyte, "Educational reform: China in the 1970's and Russia in the 1920's," *Comparative Education Review* (February 1974), 112–28; on the general applicability of Soviet education to Third World countries, see Irene Blumenthal and Charles Benson, *Educational reform in the Soviet Union: Implications for developing countries*, World Bank Staff Working Paper, 288 (May 1978).

30 *JMJP*, 14 June 1950, trans. in Shi-ming Hu and Eli Seifman, eds., *Toward a new world outlook*, 12.

ish universities. Stated another way, the Soviet system was designed to produce fewer hard-to-employ liberal arts graduates and more of those trained to move directly into the specialized technical jobs necessary for economic construction.

The Chinese system of higher education was thus divided into several distinct kinds of institution, each with its own specialized function. This was accomplished by eliminating liberal arts colleges and also by splitting off arts and science departments from the larger universities to form the core of new-style comprehensive (*tsung-ho hsing*) universities. The remaining departments, schools, and colleges of the old universities were reorganized into separate technical institutes and/or merged with existing institutions of this kind. Twenty new polytechnic colleges were created in this manner by dividing up the old universities. Only thirteen comprehensive arts and science universities remained, distributed more or less evenly around the country with but one each in Peking (Peking University, Peita) and Shanghai (Fudan University). In addition, twenty-six new engineering institutes were established in specialized fields such as steelmaking, mining, and geology. Other specialized colleges and institutes that were either retained or reorganized at this time included those in the fields of agriculture and forestry, medicine, finance and economics, education, politics and law, and national minority training.[31]

As a result of this reorganization and the accompanying new national student enrollment and job assignment plans, students majoring in technical and engineering subjects rose from about 20 percent in the late 1940s to 35 percent of the total number of college students in 1952. By 1953, the percentage of students majoring in the fields of engineering, science, medicine, and agriculture had reached 63 percent of the total 212,000 college students enrolled at that time. Teacher training accounted for another 18.8 percent of that total. These percentages remained essentially the same thereafter.[32]

In this manner, the Soviet model finally transformed the generalist Chinese intellectual into a modern specialist. In 1931, the League of Nations' mission had found that a majority of college students were still preparing themselves for careers in government service. After

31 Tseng Chao-lun, "Higher education in new China," *People's China*, 12 (16 June 1953), 7.
32 Ibid., 8; "Communique of the State Statistical Bureau," New China News Agency (hereafter NCNA) – English, Peking, 13 September 1954, in *Current Background* (hereafter *CB*), 292 (1954), 9; Joseph C. Kun, "Higher education: Some problems of selection and enrolment," *CQ*, 8 (October–December 1961), 139–40.

1949, that career option was preempted by the Party, and as of June 1956, only 11.7 percent of its 10.7 million members were intellectuals.[33] Meanwhile, college students were being reoriented toward careers in the highly specialized fields for which the new Soviet-style system of higher education was preparing them. The traditional link between men of letters and public service was finally cut.

Intra-institutional organization was also further specialized in accordance with Soviet practice, through the subdivision of the academic departments into specialties. The new departments tended to be more broadly defined than their Western counterparts, and the specialties usually narrower than their Western equivalent, the undergraduate major. The net effect was to reduce the breadth of study in the average undergraduate course and to begin specializing earlier, with the specific aim of job training.

Further in accordance with Soviet practice was the institution of nationally unified teaching plans, materials, and textbooks for every specialty. An early account of the fixed teaching plan method described it in the following terms:

Each study-plan embodies a list of courses offered in the particular specialty, and each course has a carefully worked-out program of study which gives the concrete aim of the course and lists the various items to be taken up for study in the academic year or term. It also specifies the time allotted for each item and the exact material to be handled within each hour of instruction. Textbooks are written and compiled according to this program. In this way, standardization and uniformity have been brought about in methods and content of instruction throughout all institutions of higher education in the country.[34]

These teaching plans and outlines were in use in Chinese institutions of higher learning by 1952. The objective announced at that time was that all should eventually adopt uniform teaching plans as formulated by the Ministry of Education. In 1980, university administrators recalled in interviews that the fixed teaching plan of the 1950s was adhered to then "as though it was the law."[35] Similar national unified curriculums and teaching plans were also prepared for use in the regular primary and secondary schools throughout the country.

33 *Shih-shih shou-ts'e* (Current events), 18 (25 September 1956), trans. in *CB*, 428 (19 November 1956), 2.
34 Tseng Chao-lun, "Higher education in new China," 8.
35 Suzanne Pepper, "China's universities: New experiments in socialist democracy and administrative reform – a research report," *Modern China* (April 1982).

At the top of the administrative hierarchy, a separate Ministry of Higher Education was set up in November 1952, also following Soviet practice. At the bottom, the basic unit of this Soviet structure was the teaching-research group (*chiao-hsueh yen-chiu tsu*), one of the functions of which was to ensure that the teaching plan for each specialty was actually followed by every teacher. All were organized into these groups on the basis of the courses they taught, with one or more groups being formed within each specialty. This small group of teachers, usually comprising 10 to 20 persons, became the unit responsible for overseeing course work preparation for each of its members, training young teachers, exchanging experience and information, promoting new teaching methods, conducting mutual criticism and evaluation, directing research work, and training graduate students.

Complementing the forms and structures of Soviet learning were the people and knowledge necessary to set them in motion. According to one estimate, as many as 38,000 Chinese went to the Soviet Union during the 1950s for study and training, including scientists, technicians, teachers, students, and workers. Moving in the opposite direction, Soviet experts, advisors, and teachers entered as the Americans and Europeans withdrew. Some 10,000 Soviet citizens served in these various capacities in China during the 1950s, of whom close to 600 taught in China's institutions of higher learning. Among other things, the Soviet educators helped establish new courses and participated in compiling the new teaching materials.[36]

Soviet materials and teaching plans for new courses and old were translated for reference and for use as blueprints in devising Chinese equivalents, and sometimes simply copied therein. The Chinese Academy of Sciences organized the translation work and recruited some 2,700 Chinese educators to participate. The areas in which they were concentrated revealed those where Soviet learning would be most heavily relied upon: 58 percent of the translators worked in engineering and technology, including 14 percent in agriculture; 24 percent in pure science; and only 14 percent in the humanities and social sciences.

According to one study, books translated from the Russian

36 Lofstedt, *Chinese educational policy*, 62; Theodore Hsi-en Chen, *Chinese education since 1949: Academic and revolutionary models*, 35–40. Also, *Kuang-ming jih-pao*, 7 November 1958, trans. in *Survey of China Mainland Press* (hereafter *SCMP*), 1908 (5 December 1958), 1–2; Chang Chien, "Are the achievements in the study of Soviet experiences not essential?" *Jen-min chiao-yü* (People's education), 8 (9 August 1957), trans. in *Extracts from China Mainland Magazines* (hereafter *ECMM*), 105 (1957), 8–15.

accounted for 38 percent to 45 percent of all books published in China during the years 1954–57. Books translated from other foreign languages ranged from 3 percent to 6 percent. By 1956, approximately 1,400 textbooks had been translated from Russian into Chinese, including some for primary and secondary schools. Many of the new textbooks at these lower levels that were introduced in the early 1950s were essentially rewritten versions of Soviet originals, particularly in the fields of mathematics, physics, and chemistry. The content of history, politics, and economics at all levels was also naturally revised in conformity with the new socialist and pro-Soviet orientation. And the teaching of English as a foreign language at the secondary level and above gave way to the study of Russian.[37]

Soviet pedagogy and teaching methods were also widely studied and emulated. These created a fertile field for mechanical imitation, some efforts being more commendable than others, according to the recollections of former teachers and students. The Soviet five-point grading system, equivalent to the American grades A through F, replaced the more precise 100 points then in use. Also following Soviet practice, a plan to establish advanced academic degree programs was announced in 1955. The Chinese Academy of Sciences and Peking University were two institutions that began preparations for programs leading to the associate doctoral (*fu-po-shih*) degree, and some students were enrolled in them at this time.

The oral examination was another Soviet import, along with the props for conducting it. College students in cities as far distant as Kunming took their orals seated at cloth-covered tables on which were placed vases of flowers – "because that was the way the Russians did it." The extensive organization of extracurricular activities was also new to Chinese education. One such activity, for example, was that of the *Mi-chiu-lin* Small Group, named after the Soviet plant biologist Michurin. This group of students, organized in primary school classrooms, was responsible for tending the plants grown in each classroom's Green Corner. And young people were encouraged to emulate the spirit of Soviet heroes whose lives and exploits became for the 1950s generation as famous as those of Lei Feng and other Chinese model persons would be in the 1960s.

The danger of uncritical imitation is, however, best illustrated by

37 R. F. Price, *Education in modern China*, 102–6; Lofstedt, *Chinese educational policy*, 62; Chao Chung and Yang I-fan, *Students in mainland China*, 62–64.

an example outside the field of education. Chinese women were for a time actually rewarded as "heroine mothers" for giving birth to many children, following the measures being used to encourage population growth in the Soviet Union after World War II. Within the educational sphere itself, the consequences of such emulation were perhaps less bizarre but certainly no less dramatic. This was because the Soviet import was in too many respects the obverse both of the Western-influenced system it replaced at the elite level and also of the rural model devised in Yenan in the 1940s. Party leaders would soon learn that Westernized Chinese intellectuals could not easily be reprogrammed to accept the new system. And within the Party itself there remained a continuing commitment to the Yenan experience, inspired no doubt by the "objective" Chinese conditions from which it sprang. The Soviet model also required an accommodation with the "bourgeois" intellectual component of its population that the young Chinese Communist system was not yet ready to make.

THE 1950S IN PERSPECTIVE

According to a later report, the First National Work Conference on Education, held in December 1949, had anticipated a more balanced approach. It stated that: "The education of new China should use the new educational experiences of the old Liberated Areas as the basis, should absorb the useful experiences of the old education, and should make use of the experiences of the Soviet Union."[38] During the Cultural Revolution, Liu Shao-ch'i and others were accused of having violated Mao's intention to maintain this balance. They were accused of having done their utmost to uphold the old system and transplant the Soviet experience.

In fact, the three streams appeared to have been grafted one upon the other in the early 1950s, with little apparent attempt to anticipate or mitigate the contradictions that were bound to develop in the process. The exigencies of the moment would have made such careful deliberation difficult in any case. But the cavalier manner in which the three streams were thrown together appeared to preclude their development into a viable and integrated system. The experience actual-

---

38 Quoted in "Chronology of the two-road struggle on the educational front in the past seventeen years," *Chiao-yü ko-ming* (Education revolution), 6 May 1967, in Peter J. Seybolt, ed., *Revolutionary education in China*, 7. (An original report from this conference remains to be located.)

ly had a certain Maoist flare about it, as if underwritten by his mass movement dictum that any excesses occuring in the process could be corrected afterward.[39]

Rehabilitation and reorganization

By the end of the rehabilitation and reorganization period (1949–52), strains were already apparent and correctives being sought. The first problem to be overcome was dissent within the academic community. The reorganization of institutions of higher learning began in 1950, as did resistance from faculty and staff. As noted, the centers of higher learning in China were concentrated in the coastal cities, and virtually all of these institutions remained under Kuomintang control until the end of the civil war in 1948–49. Nevertheless, the majority of their faculty members remained at their posts after 1949. They did so for many reasons, not the least of which was dissatisfaction with the defeated Kuomintang government. But while those intellectuals were undoubtedly sympathetic to the socialist ideals of the CCP, there were probably few committed Communists among them. Educated primarily in the traditions of Western learning, Chinese university intellectuals in the 1940s seemed more inclined toward socialism of a liberal democratic variety. Certainly, there were few with more than a passing knowledge of the tenets of Marxism-Leninism or the writings of Mao Tse-tung.

In recognition of this fact, the CCP had long followed the practice of requiring all students, teachers, and other intellectuals in newly liberated areas to attend political education courses. This practice was written into the "minimum program" of the CCP, which outlined the basic principles of the New Democratic political system to be established following the Party's victory, and was carried out everywhere thereafter.[40] The subjects usually studied in the political training classes for intellectuals included the history of the development of society; political economy; the essentials of Marx, Engels, Lenin, Stalin, and Mao; and current events. The education aimed also at instilling an appreciation of the value of labor and destroying both

---

39 This thesis as it applied to the excesses in the movement for land reform and Mao's toleration of them is developed in Pepper, *Civil war in China*, 246, 250, 255–56, 258–60, 269–75, 325–27.
40 This was the "Common Program of the Chinese People's Political Consultative Conference," of which Article 47 read, "Revolutionary political education shall be accorded to young intellectuals and old style intellectuals in a planned and systematic manner." Reprinted in Lindsay, *Notes on educational problems*, 194.

illusions about the United States and ignorance of the Soviet Union.[41]

But sympathy for socialism and a basic introduction to Marxism-Leninism were not enough to overcome commitments to the existing structure and content of higher education, and reluctance to learn from the Soviet Union. Resistance was such that it inhibited the task of reorganization. This led to the decision, announced in October 1951, to launch an ideological reform movement as one of the current three main national tasks.[42] Political education escalated thereafter into a rectification-style campaign based on individual criticism and self-criticism and was developed among college and secondary school teachers throughout the country in 1951–52. This ideological reform movement, which followed a preliminary round against cultural aggression in American missionary colleges early in the year, then merged with the Three and Five Antis campaigns against cadres and capitalists. The result was an overall assault against corruption, bribery, waste, bureaucratism, and other adverse manifestations of the bourgeois mentality in enterprises and government offices, and also in schools and universities.

These campaigns, launched simultaneously with the Resist America, Aid Korea movement during the Korean War, produced the early literature of rectification, which inspired the term "brainwashing" in the West: confessions such as Chou P'ei-yuan's "Criticizing my decadent bourgeois ideology"; anti-American declarations such as that of Lu Chih-wei, president of Yenching University, against "U.S. imperialist cultural aggression"; and children criticizing their parents, as in his daughter's, "I denounce my father, Lu Chih-wei."[43]

According to Vice-Minister of Higher Education Tseng Chao-lun, the result in institutions of higher learning was that resistance dissipated and reorganization could proceed more smoothly. College teachers came to accept the movement to learn from the Soviet Union, or so it was claimed, together with the new focus on technology training, and even Russian language study. They also came to accept the job transfers that reorganization entailed. In some cases, the splitting off of a technical college from the main university meant no more than an administrative separation and perhaps the erection of

41 See, for example, Lu Ting-i, "Education and culture in new China," *People's China*, 8 (16 April 1950), reprinted in Fraser, ed., *Chinese communist education*, 90–91.
42 Tseng Chao-lun, "Improvements in higher education during the past three years," *Jen-min chiao-yü* (People's education) (January 1953), trans. in *CB*, 238 (25 March 1953), 2.
43 These statements are reprinted in Fraser, ed., *Chinese communist education*, 104–10, 136–58; for a fuller selection, see *CB* 107, 167, 169, 182, 185, and 213; also, Theodore H. E. Chen, *Thought reform of the Chinese intellectuals*, 30–79.

a wall to mark the new division of the campus. In other cases, an academic department from one school might be merged with another in a different city. Or as in the case of Shanghai's Chiaotung (Communications) University, virtually the entire campus was transplanted to Sian. The reorganization therefore entailed considerable uprooting and often to less desirable locations for college personnel, whose lives had already been disrupted a good deal in the preceding decade. Nevertheless, by the start of the 1953–54 academic year, reorganization had been accomplished in three-quarters of the nation's institutions of higher learning.[44]

The ideological reform campaign was thus used to ameliorate the strains created by trying to transform China's Western-influenced system of higher education in the image of the Soviet model. More difficult to contain were the tensions at the popular end of the educational spectrum. The hope expressed just after liberation was that within a decade, tens of thousands of workers and peasants would become "highly educated" and capable of standing together with intellectuals from other classes in service to their country.[45]

In pursuance of this aim, it was decided that all tertiary-level institutions should lower their admissions requirements for workers and peasants for the 1950–51 academic year. But only 400 students were actually enrolled under this ruling. In early 1952, when the ideological reform campaign was at its height, 10,000 cadres began six-month preparatory courses, after which they were admitted into institutions of higher learning.[46]

Also in pursuance of the same objective, the First National Education Work Conference of December 1949 directed that shortened three-year secondary schools for workers and peasants be set up. These were to be established by regular schools, factories, and military units, specifically for cadres of worker-peasant origin with three to eight years of work experience. Many students who enrolled in these schools in 1950 had no formal education and had acquired what knowledge they possessed through self-study. But it was claimed that they would be able to enter college after a three- to four-year course in the new accelerated schools.[47] "Under the new school system," declared Education Minister Ma Hsu-lun, "all roads

44 Tseng, "Improvements in higher education during the past three years," p. 3; *JMJP* (1 October 1953) in *CB*, 269 (1953), 30.
45 Lu Ting-i, "Education and culture in new China," 89.
46 Tseng, "Improvements in higher education during the past three years," 6.
47 NCNA–English, Peking, 27 September 1950, in NCNA, *Daily News Release*, Hong Kong, 29 September 1950.

lead to higher education." No longer would graduates from regular secondary schools constitute the only qualified candidates. All classes of people from all kinds of short-course and spare-time schools could now go on to college.[48]

At the primary level, the institution for expanding education among school-age children remained the *min-pan* school. These schools run by the people predominated in the rural areas at this time and continued to expand in number as land reform was carried out in newly liberated areas. Land reform also brought an expansion in winter schools and various kinds of short courses for adult peasants, as had been the custom in the old liberated areas before 1949. The purpose of this was partly political, in that the classes were supposed to be used to propagandize the peasants about land reform and other current events topics. But the primary objective was literacy training, and peasants were typically taught a few hundred characters during a single winter term. It was claimed that more than 42 million peasants attended winter schools during the 1951–52 season. Additional millions were said to be attending other kinds of spare-time schools for workers and peasants.[49]

Indeed, so enthusiastically was rural education work being pursued that during the first year after liberation a movement developed to turn the winter schools and study groups for adult peasants into regular *min-pan* schools for school-age children. The declared aim in 1950 was to establish a *min-pan* school in every village. One-third of the winter schools in Shansi were said to have successfully converted to regular studies by the autumn of that year. In the Northeast provinces, 6,000 of the 59,662 winter schools and 44,400 of the 59,300 study groups had also established themselves on a regular and permanent basis.[50]

The 1st Five-Year Plan

The approach of the 1st Five-Year Plan (FYP) in 1953, however, brought a sudden reappraisal. The State Statistical Bureau reported with reference to the 1949–52 period that many defects had occurred in education work. The words and phrases would become familiar in later years and already echoed those used during the 1942 reform in

48 NCNA–English, Peking, 26 September 1952, in *CB*, 220 (1952), 11.
49 Ibid.
50 NCNA–English, Peking, 27 September 1950, in NCNA, *Daily News Release*, Hong Kong, 29 September 1950, 8–9.

the Border Region a decade earlier: lack of planning and foresight; insufficient coordination with economic development; blind and rash advance; and giving importance to quantity and not quality in the anti-illiteracy work and primary school education.[51] Kuo Mo-jo wrote that leadership comrades in educational work had failed to coordinate needs with capacities correctly, sought quantitative achievements to the disregard of quality, striven for figures and speed, and tended to "look to the present to the disregard of the future." They did not understand that cultural construction was supposed to follow economic construction, not precede it.[52]

A meeting of the chairmen of the various administrative-region cultural and education committees was held in January 1953 to discuss these mistakes and the recommended solutions. The conference announced the new principles that would guide the education work plan drawn up to coordinate educational development with the first year of the 1st FYP: "adjustment and consolidation, keypoint development, raising of quality, and steady progress." The major tasks were: (1) to concentrate on the reorganization and administration of tertiary-level and intermediate technical institutions in order to produce the necessary personnel for economic construction; (2) to promote the appropriate development of secondary schools in order to guarantee the quality and numbers of students for the tertiary level; (3) to overcome the state of confusion in primary education and improve its quality.[53]

Suddenly, all roads no longer led to higher education. That same month, Vice-Minister Tseng Chao-lun wrote, "In view of the fact that the laboring masses of workers and peasants had been almost entirely deprived of the chance of education in the days of reactionary rule, our present attempt to have worker and peasant cadres of a certain cultural level admitted directly into institutions of higher education is bound to be an action of restricted scope."[54]

The new operative words were "systematic and planned." A national unified college entrance examination was given for the first time in 1952, and the fixed Soviet-style teaching plans began to be widely used during the autumn semester that same year. Their aim

51 NCNA–English, Peking, 29 September 1953, in *CB*, 262 (1953), 9.
52 *JMJP*, 1 October 1953, in *CB*, 269 (1953), 33; Kuo Mo-jo was then chairman of the Committee of Cultural and Educational Affairs, Government Administration Council.
53 Ibid., 34; these tasks were reiterated by Chou En-lai in his "Report on government work," NCNA–English, Peking, 24 September 1954, in *CB*, 296 (1954), 13.
54 Tseng, "Improvements in higher education during the past three years," 6.

was to bring "standardization and uniformity" into the methods and content of instruction throughout the country. Students without an adequate preparatory secondary education would have difficulty keeping up with the fixed teaching plans, as by other accounts did many of the cadre students of worker-peasant origin.

The new system being built along Soviet lines was in many respects, therefore, the antithesis of the Yenan model, which had served the needs of the Communist liberated areas from 1944 onward. That model had been launched under slogans to "oppose uniformity" and "oppose regularity." It stressed the needs of the present over those of the future and deliberately attacked the conventional use of secondary schools as college preparatory institutions. Within that system, "inequality of standards" was unavoidable and an "exact linking on of one stage of school to the next" impossible, but certainly nothing to worry about.

The attempt to purge the system of these rural antecedents began in earnest with the inauguration of the 1st FYP, but Vice-Minister Tseng summarized the insoluble contradictions that attempt contained:

In singling out the importance of education for the working people and the worker and peasant cadres in all grades of schools, and in stressing that proper connections and relations should be maintained between all grades and categories of schools, the new pedagogical system preserves harmony and unity within the educational system.[55]

The problem was that harmony and unity were not so easily achieved. Choices would have to be made, and in 1953 they began to come down on the side of quality and proper connections. Meanwhile, the number of primary schools was insufficient to cope with the total school-age population, yet there were still more primary school graduates than the existing secondary schools could accommodate. And the supply of secondary school graduates was insufficient to meet the demand for them at the tertiary level. But these were imbalances that now could "only be gradually solved and overcome over a considerably long period."

The new line for education remained unchanged for just half the 1st FYP period. During that time, primary school enrollments accordingly declined from 55 million as reported by the State Statistical Bureau for 1952, to 51.2 million in 1954 (see Table 4). The goal of a

55 Ibid., 5.

min-pan school in every village was dropped, enrollment quotas at secondary level normal schools (which train primary school teachers) were reduced, and some of the schools themselves were closed. At the college level, more than 80 percent of the 93,785 new students enrolled for the 1954–55 academic year came directly from senior secondary school, and only 3,700 were graduates from the accelerated middle schools for worker-peasant cadres.[56] These schools, the first of which was established in 1950, now numbered 87 and had altogether 51,000 students, indicating that their pass rates to college were not very high.[57]

That a stable equilibrium had not been achieved along the new line became apparent in 1955. During the latter half of the 1st FYP period, a sort of hybrid system began to develop in education which tried to combine the best from both worlds. This system sought to maintain the Soviet model at the elite level while drawing upon the CCP's past rural experience for popular use.

Li Fu-ch'un, chairman of the State Planning Commission, affirmed the principles of the former in his "Report on the 1st Five-Year Plan," in July 1955. The shortage of scientific and technical personnel had become a serious obstacle to economic development. But he called for balance and caution in the quantity-quality equation: "The tendency to go after numbers only and ignore quality is clearly not in the interests of the state plan of construction," he warned. Academic standards were not high enough, particularly in engineering institutes, where the number of students had increased too rapidly. These schools were therefore phasing out their two- to three-year special courses and lengthening their basic undergraduate course from four years to five. He also called for further steps to raise the qualifications of all college students. They should at least be "intellectually able to keep up with the class," he declared. "It is impossible or very difficult to turn students who do not meet these minimum requirements into useful construction personnel." The increases in college admissions were consequently revised for the latter half of the 1st FYP period.[58]

56 NCNA–English, Peking, 20 June 1956 in *CB* 400 (1956), 24; Chang Chien (Department of Financial Planning, Ministry of Higher Education), "More people go to college," *People's China*, 22 (16 November 1954), 23–24; "Directive Concerning Establishment, Development, and Reorganization of Normal Schools," NCNA, Peking, 19 June 1954, in *SCMP*, 844 (9 July 1954), 33–34.
57 "Short-term middle schools," *People's China*, 8 (16 April 1955), 39; "State Statistical Bureau Communiqué," *People's China*, 20 (16 October 1955), supplement, 8.
58 Reprinted in Robert R. Bowie and John K. Fairbank, eds., *Communist China: 1955–1959*, 76.

TABLE 4
Numbers of schools and students, 1949–1957

Year	Tertiary Schools	Tertiary Students	Secondary Schools		Secondary Students	Primary Schools	Primary Students
1949		116,000			1,268,000		24,390,000
1950	227	134,000	3,690		1,090,000	400,000	30,000,000
1951	195	128,000	4,015	general	1,290,000	440,000	37,000,000
			507	specialized	110,000		
			605	teacher training	165,000		
1952		203,000		general	2,982,000		55,000,000
				specialized	298,000		
1953		212,000		general	2,930,000		51,500,000
		4,200 (grads)		specialized	670,000		
1954	181	258,000		general	3,580,000		51,200,000
				specialized	608,000		
1955	194	288,000	6,120	general (senior)	580,000	504,077	53,130,000
		4,822 (grads)		(junior)	3,320,000		
			512	specialized	537,000		
			515	teacher training			
1956		380,000[a]			5,860,000[a]		57,700,000
		403,000[b] (including grads)		general	5,165,000[b]		63,464,000
				specialized	812,000		
1957		443,000[a] (planned)		general	5,566,000[a] (planned)		65,814,000 (planned)
				specialized	775,000 (planned)		
		440,000[b]			7,000,000[b]		64,000,000

Note: The figures should be treated as approximations only since it is often impossible to reconcile discrepancies in figures from different sources. For example, the two sets of primary school figures for 1956 *presumably* reflect the movement to set up rural schools that accompanied rural collectivization. Also, the figures here differ from those given in *Ten great years*. Sources: *1949:* Liu Shao-ch'i, "Political Report of the Central Committee of the CCP", 15 Sept. 1956, in Bowie and Fairbank, eds., *Communist China: 1955–1959*, 185. *1950:* NCNA–English, Peking, 27 Sept. 1950, in NCNA, *Daily News Release*, Hong Kong, 29 Sept. 1950. *1951:* NCNA, Peking, 4 Nov. 1951, trans. in *CB*, 140 (22 Nov. 1951), 4, 6. *1952:* State Statistical Bureau, "Communiqué on Rehabilitation and Development of National Economy, Culture and Education During 1952," 28 Sept. 1953, NCNA, Peking, 29 Sept. 1953, in *CB*, 262 (1 Oct. 1953), 8. *1953: Tertiary and Primary:* "Communiqué of the State Statistical Bureau on Results of 1953 State Plans," NCNA, Peking, 13 Sept. 1954, in *CB*, 292 (15 Sept. 1954) 9; *secondary:* Chou En-lai, "Report on Government Work," NCNA, Peking, 24 Sept. 1954, in *CB*, 296 (28 Sept. 1954), 13. *1954: Tertiary schools only:* Chang Chien, "More People Go to College" *People's China*, 22 (16 Nov. 1954) 23: State Statistical Bureau, "Communiqué on National Economic Development and Fulfilment of the State Plan in 1954," 21 Sept. 1955, in *People's China*, 20 (16 Oct. 1955), supplement, 8. *1955:* Shih-shih shou-ts'e (Current events), 23 (10 Dec. 1956), trans. in *ECMM*, 71 (1956), 27. *1956:* [a] Liu Shao-ch'i, "Political Report of the Central Committee of the CCP," 15 Sept. 1956, in Bowie and Fairbank, eds., *Communist China: 1955–1959*, 185. [b] State Statistical Bureau, "Communiqué on the Fulfillment of the National Economic Plan for 1956," 1 Aug. 1957, NCNA–English, Peking, 1 Aug. 1957, in *CB*, 474 (12 Aug. 1957), 9. *1957:* [a] Po I-po, "Working of the National Economic Plan for 1956 and Draft National Economic Plan for 1957," 1 July 1957, NCNA, Peking, 1 July 1957, trans. in *CB*, 465 (9 July 1957), 16. [b] Chou En-lai, "Report on Government Work," 18 April 1959, in Bowie and Fairbanks, eds., *Communist China: 1955–1959*, 516.

The inauguration of advanced degree programs was also announced at this time, and the undergraduate courses in a number of fields besides engineering were lengthened to five years in 1955–56. Reinforcing the demand for academic excellence, the Party proclaimed a new climate of intellectual liberalism in the spring of 1956. It acknowledged the need for trained personnel, and recognized that China could not rely solely on its Soviet advisers for expertise.[59] One result of this reappraisal was the policy "Let a hundred flowers bloom, let a hundred schools contend," inaugurated in May 1956.

Within the context of this new climate, Kuo Mo-jo articulated the grievances of the academic community when he called for free academic discussion together with an end to Marxist-Leninist dogmatism, the mechanical application of the Soviet experience, the neglect of research and theoretical study due to one-sided emphasis on solving technical problems, and the neglect of non-Soviet foreign learning.[60]

But 1955–56 also marked the upsurge of socialist transformation in the countryside. Commenting on the speed with which the Agricultural Producers Cooperatives (APCs) were being formed, Mao wrote at the end of 1955:

It tells us that the scale and speed of China's industrialization and the scale and speed of the development of science, culture, education, public health, and so on can no longer be carried out entirely as was first intended; these should all be appropriately expanded and accelerated.[61]

Balance and controlled growth may have continued to dominate the tertiary level, but speed and numbers had once again overtaken the country.

The new twelve-year program for agricultural development, adopted in January 1956, proclaimed the goal of universal compulsory primary schooling in the rural areas within seven to twelve years. The village min-pan schools were to make this possible, the "people" responsible for them now being the new collective unit in the village, the APC. Local people would have to be pressed into service as teachers. The Education Ministry criticized itself for having so recently reduced enrollment quotas for teachers' training schools;

59 See, for example, Chou En-lai, "On the question of intellectuals," 14 January 1956, reprinted in Bowie and Fairbank, eds., Communist China: 1955–1959, 128–44.
60 Kuo Mo-jo, "Long live the policy – 'Let diverse schools of thought contend!'" People's China, 17 (1 September 1956), 7–9.
61 From Mao Tse-tung's preface to Socialist upsurge in China's countryside; this preface was first published in JMJP, 12 January 1956, 1.

these would now be able to produce only a fraction of the 1 million teachers needed to fulfill the new plan for popularizing primary schooling. Primary school enrollments, nevertheless, resumed their rapid upward movement, rising from 51.2 million in 1954 to something between 57 million and 63 million in 1956, depending on the source consulted.

Also according to the new twelve-year program for agricultural development, illiteracy was to be eliminated within five to seven years after 1956. Mao complained that early postliberation efforts to eradicate it had fallen by the wayside, and a new campaign followed in the wake of the movement to collectivize agriculture. The standard for eradicating illiteracy was fixed at an ability to recognize and write 1,500 characters. The plan was to provide 240 hours of instruction per year in spare-time classes. These superseded the old winter schools as the preferred method of instruction, since the peasants tended to forget what they had learned from one winter to the next. Uniform teaching materials were found to be less effective than those compiled by and for each locality containing characters relevant to everyday life, such as the names of local people, places, animals, farm tools, and different kinds of work.[62] In keeping with the spirit of the times, it was announced that the accelerated middle schools for worker-peasant cadres, which had a combined enrollment of only 51,000 students during the 1954–55 academic year, were planning to admit 33,000 new students in 1955–56.[63]

Yet the enthusiasm generated in the course of the mass movement could not mask the tensions inherent in the system. Chou En-lai analyzed these in some detail in his "Report on the work of the Government" in June 1957. The report was a defense of his government's performance during the 1st FYP period. He acknowledged in the process the extent of the pressure its critics were mounting. He noted, for example, that "some people think that our 1st FYP has been completely bungled" and that "some people are against learning from the experience of the Soviet Union, and even say that the mistakes and shortcomings in our construction work are also the result of learning from the Soviet Union." Of education, he said:

62 "The draft program for agricultural development in the People's Republic of China, 1956–1967," 23 January 1956, reprinted in Bowie and Fairbank, eds., *Communist China: 1955–1959*, 125; "Decision concerning elimination of illiteracy," NCNA, Peking, 30 March 1956, in *SCMP*, 1266 (12 April 1956), 3–7; NCNA–English, Peking, 20 June 1956, in *CB*, 400 (1956), 19, 22, 24.
63 "Short-term middle schools," *People's China*, 8 (16 April 1955), 39.

In implementing educational reforms, the educational departments have in the past made certain blunders, mainly in rejecting certain factors that were rational in the old educational system, failing to systematically sum up and carry forward the experience of revolutionary education in the liberated areas, and in failing in the course of studying Soviet experience, to adapt it sufficiently to China's actual conditions. These shortcomings must be corrected. But if there are people who, because of these flaws, deny that the achievements in educational reforms are the main thing, or even deny that there was any need for such reforms at all and so attempt to turn the educational system of today back onto the old path of education in pre-liberation China, they will be all wrong.[64]

"Some people" were saying all these things and much more and had just done so during a month of concentrated criticism in May 1957.[65] In their criticism, the intelligentsia – teachers and students, managers and administrators including some Party members among them – sounded a discordant finale to the 1st FYP period. The new post-1949 order had failed to win the approval of China's educated elite. And they resented, among other things, the changes that had been imposed upon them within the education system.

Moreover, that system remained in one sense as bifurcated as it had been before 1949. The Soviet model was most evident at the higher level, where it was supposed to replace the influence of the West. But like that model before it, this new one also rested on a base of mass illiteracy which it could offer little hope of eliminating in the foreseeable future. According to Higher Education Minister Chang Hsi-jo, 78 percent of the total population was still illiterate in 1956, and only about 52 percent of the school-age children were attending primary school.[66]

The demands to improve quality through uniformity and standardization could be achieved only at the cost of reductions in the numbers of students and the rate at which teachers were trained to teach them. The goal of universal primary schooling would thus recede even further into the future under a rigorous application of the Soviet model, an unacceptable alternative for a party which had associated its interests so closely with those of workers and peasants. The only way there could be a school in every village was by reverting to the Yenan philosophy of not worrying too much about equalizing standards, since these could only be achieved in a state-

---

64 Reprinted in Bowie and Fairbank, eds., *Communist China: 1955–1959*, 310.
65 MacFarquhar, ed., *The Hundred Flowers Campaign and the Chinese intellectuals*, passim.
66 NCNA–English, Peking, 20 June 1956, in *CB*, 400 (1956), 21.

supported school system staffed by properly trained teachers. The answer in the short term was the traditional-style village school, albeit in its new updated version as a *min-pan* school run not by the state but by the organized effort of the rural collectives.

A second reason for reconsidering the Yenan experience was the changing structure of secondary schooling. As noted, the demand for tertiary-level students was greater than the supply of secondary school graduates, although by 1955 it had become apparent that college enrollments could not continue their rate of expansion indefinitely and maintain the desired standards. Nevertheless, through 1956 there were places in college for most of those graduating from senior secondary school, and most junior secondary graduates – except during 1954 and 1955 – were able to proceed to the senior level, or so it was claimed.

Chou En-lai announced in 1957, however, that this situation was "temporary and abnormal" and would not continue. Starting with the 1957–58 academic year, institutions of higher learning and senior secondary schools would be enrolling fewer students and would continue to do so thereafter in relation to the number of applicants. In other words, the pool of eligible candidates would be growing at a faster rate than enrollments at the next higher level. Hence increasing numbers of young people would have to curtail their studies and join productive labor, a fate that had already caused "tension" in 1954 and 1955 at the junior middle level.[67]

At the same time, the thwarted aspirations created by the rapid expansion of primary schooling, without a corresponding growth at the secondary level, were also making themselves felt. "The inability to send all the graduates from primary and middle schools to a higher school will be a general state of affairs not only for this year but also for a long time to come," warned the minister of education in early 1957. But even when primary and secondary schooling had become universal and everyone would by definition have "become an intellectual," they would still have to get used to the idea of engaging in

67 Ibid.; Chou En-lai, "Report on the work of the government," 26 June 1957, reprinted in Bowie and Fairbank, eds., *Communist China: 1955–1959*, 311. The numbers of senior middle graduates in comparison with college entrants are tabulated for each year from 1952 through 1959 in Joseph C. Kun, "Higher education: Some problems of selection and enrollment," 138. The contemporary claims that all junior middle graduates could go on to senior middle school is not borne out by the statistics available, although these do show a decline in pass rates during 1954 and 1955 (Bernstein, *Up to the mountains and down to the villages: The transfer of youth from urban to rural China*, 48). The claims should probably be interpreted to mean that any junior middle graduate who wanted to continue studying could do so.

productive labor afterward. Society could not exist with only intellectuals and no farmers or factory workers. For the structural problems of insufficient jobs and middle school places, the minister recommended that parents and local organizations help young people "to find some work in the family or take up private study at home." For the educational component of the problem, he recommended the intensification of labor training in the schools at all levels.[68]

The government therefore had to contemplate by 1957 another potentially disruptive problem symptomatic of educational development – that is, the necessity of devising equitable forms of secondary schooling that would be college preparatory for some but terminal and work-oriented for the majority. Here too the dividing lines would become more controversial, as it became apparent whose children could continue their studies and whose could not.

The education system at the end of the 1st FYP had clearly failed to adapt and merge the three strains of its heritage into a coherent whole. What existed instead was a contentious mix of Soviet and Western influences at the elite level where the new demands for specialization made quality increasingly imperative. This ensured that the existing educated elite would perpetuate itself into the indefinite future, because it was already clear by 1954 that the Party's early hopes for high worker-peasant college enrollments and innovative admissions policies could not be fulfilled if academic plans and standards were to be met.

Not surprisingly, then, the new generation of post-1949 college students shared the dissenting views and values of their elders, as was demonstrated in the outburst of May 1957. At that time, they had even criticized as unfair the moderate admissions policy which gave preference to five kinds of candidates (workers and peasants, certain army personnel, children of revolutionary martyrs, national minorities, and overseas Chinese), though only when their qualifications were otherwise competitive. The student critics were officially rebuffed during the Anti-Rightist Campaign, which followed, with statistics to show that the injustices left by the old society were still far from being eliminated. The majority of college students were still from bourgeois and landlord families. Only 34.29 percent of all undergraduate students in institutions of higher learning as of September 1956 were of worker-peasant origin. The figures for

68 NCNA–English, Peking, 16 March 1957, in *CB*, 446 (8 April 1957), 1–8.

graduate students in these institutions and at the national Academy of Sciences were 17.46 percent and 5.92 percent, respectively.[69]

Meanwhile, the only means of meeting the demand for even the most elementary education at the mass level was a system based on principles that were very different from those being promoted at the higher level. And in the middle there existed the growing pool of partially educated young people created by the campaigns to popularize primary schooling. Despite the rhetoric to the contrary, therefore, the gap between the elite and mass cultures that had widened with the abolition of the imperial examinations and the introduction of Western learning in the early years of the twentieth century changed little during the first decade of Communist rule. But the rhetoric remained, promoted by a ruling party within which peasants constituted 69 percent of the membership, and so did the pressures building within the system. The stage was set for a more radical attempt to merge the conflicting demands at both levels into a single integrated system.

69 Kuo Mo-jo, "In refutation of an anti-socialist scientific program," *JMJP*, 6 July 1957, trans. in *CB*, 467 (15 July 1957), 11. On the Anti-Rightist Campaign that was subsequently used to discredit the critics of May 1957, see also *CB*, 470 (26 July 1957), and 475 (28 August 1957); Theodore Chen, *Thought reform*, 171–201; and MacFarquhar, ed., *The Hundred Flowers Campaign and the Chinese intellectuals*, 261–91.

CHAPTER 5

THE PARTY AND
THE INTELLECTUALS

After 1949, the Party carried out a contradictory policy toward the intellectuals: On the one hand, it indoctrinated them in Marxism-Leninism-Maoism, which was imposed more comprehensively and intensively than Confucianism had been on the traditional literati. On the other hand, it tried to stimulate the intellectuals to be productive in their professions. This contradictory approach resulted in a policy that oscillated between periods of repression in which intellectuals were subjected to thought reform campaigns and periods of relative relaxation in which they were granted some responsibilities and privileges in order to win their cooperation in carrying out modernization.

These shifts were determined sometimes by internal economic and political factors and sometimes by international events. They also had a dynamic of their own. The Party pushed toward ideological conformity until the intellectuals appeared reluctant to produce; then it relaxed until its political control appeared threatened. In the intervals of relative relaxation, the Party fostered, or at least permitted, intellectual debate and discussion of Western ideas. It also allowed and at times encouraged criticism of the bureaucracy in order to root out abuses of the system.

THE HISTORICAL RELATIONSHIP BETWEEN THE INTELLECTUALS AND THE GOVERNMENT

Intellectuals in the PRC were heirs to the Confucian tradition of the literati's obligation to serve the state and to speak out when the government deviated from its principles. It was not so much their right, as in the West, but their responsibility, to criticize governmental misdeeds. They saw themselves as the court of moral judgment. They were to lead the way to what ought to be instead of what was and were to do so regardless of personal consequences, even at the risk of punishment and death. They had no institutional or legal sanctions, but they had a traditional ethic to speak out against misrule. Literati were to argue, protest, and criticize in order to correct mistakes and reform the government. There is a long tradition of using the written word both to bolster state policies and to exert political pressure. Like their predecessors, most of the intellectuals in the PRC were loyal to the system, but invariably a small number objected to official abuses that prevented the regime from achieving its goals. Unlike their predecessors, however, when they found that the leadership forced them to compromise their own principles, they could not withdraw to their study or to a hilltop to pursue the life of an honorable scholar or artist. In the PRC, they had to participate in the system.

As in traditional times, intellectuals expressed criticism primarily through official channels. As the emperor had opened the yen-lu, literally avenue of communication, which meant that literati were allowed to criticize on policy matters, so too did Mao Tse-tung at various times urge intellectuals to question and criticize official abuses in order to rectify the system. Intellectuals expressed themselves in Party-controlled newspapers, journals, and creative activities. Even when spontaneous, grassroots protests erupted as in the spring of 1957 and 1978–79, they were carried out with official sanction. When Mao suppressed criticism of his policies, as he did in the early 1960s, intellectuals resorted to a form of traditional dissent resembling that used by the literati when the ruler closed off the yen-lu. They camouflaged their dissent in indirect, figurative analogies used in discussions of history, literature, philosophy, art, and the theater. They also used the quintessential Chinese genre of dissent – tsa-wen, short, subtle, satirical essays, seemingly on innocuous subjects, but actually discussing political issues. This political device was used by the great Confucian thinkers Han Yü and Ou-yang Hsiu and by the great modern writer Lu Hsun. Intellectuals in the PRC were under even more pressure to mask their dissent because they were more tightly controlled than their predecessors.

The joining together of groups of intellectuals to reform Chinese society is not a phenomenon just of modern China. Such groups, engaging in ch'ing-i (pure discussion) emerged in traditional China at times of political crises and economic difficulties or when literati organized to address problems which they believed the government had not handled adequately. At these moments they sought to reinvigorate government and make it more responsive to social needs. Although some literati became martyrs, most criticized only when they had patrons and protectors in positions of power. Most often this occurred during periods of factional conflict when literati were used in political struggle. Similarly, in periods of factionalization in the PRC, as in the early 1960s, intellectuals in alliance with members of the top leadership were able to get a hearing for their views. Like the traditional literati, in the process of articulating their patrons' positions some inserted views and values that differed not only from the prevailing orthodoxy but also from the views of their patrons.

Intellectuals were also heirs to the May Fourth movement of 1919 and later which sought to create a new Westernized culture as a solution to China's social, political, and economic plight. Though the precise remedy was new, the method of cultural regeneration as the key to survival was traditional. The May Fourth writers of the 1920s and 1930s in particular regarded their writings as tools with which to fight social and political ills and shape political consciousness. They viewed themselves as a revolutionary elite whose mission was to mold public opinion and transform society. In the chaotic political situation of those decades and under the influence of Western liberalism, they conceived of their actions as free and independent of political control. Even those intellectuals committed to the Communist movement embraced the May Fourth spirit of pluralism, public debate, and intellectual autonomy.

Although intellectually independent, they were like the *ch'ing-i* groups in that they were politically involved. Though in despair over their nation, they were not alienated intellectuals. They did not withdraw from public affairs because of rootlessness or *Welt-schmerz*. On the contrary, they sought to tie themselves to their society and people. Thus the May Fourth tradition of intellectually independent yet politically committed intellectuals as well as the *ch'ing-i* precedent served as models for post-1949 intellectuals.

PRE-1949 CONFLICTS BETWEEN PARTY AND INTELLECTUALS

Shanghai in the mid-1930s

Even before it came to power, the Party, like the Confucian bureaucracy, regarded intellectual and creative endeavor as a handmaiden to its own political goals. Moreover, in emulation of the Soviet model, it expected intellectuals to assist it in transforming Chinese society. Like Stalin, the political leadership of the Chinese

Communist Party (CCP) looked to writers and artists to transform "the human soul" according to the Party's dictates. The Party's first effort to mobilize intellectuals to its cause began in Shanghai in the mid-1930s, primarily among the writers. Before the Party came to power and after the establishment of the PRC, virtually every turn in the political climate and often major political moves were signaled by vehement debates and polemics in the literary realm.

In the late 1920s and early 1930s, most of China's prominent writers lived in Shanghai. They had studied abroad or with Western-trained scholars. Most of them, having been frustrated in their desire for intellectual independence under Chiang Kai-shek's rule and alienated by the assassination of a number of their colleagues by the Kuomintang, turned to the CCP and left-wing organizations. They moved in a circle around Lu Hsun (1881–1936), whose stories of the ills, impotence, inhumanity, and darkness of traditional society, and the need for revolutionary change, set an example for a whole generation of Chinese writers. In March 1930 he established the League of Left-Wing Writers, which was actually a front organization for the Party, but because of its vigorous stance against imperialism and because of Lu Hsun's sponsorship, incorporated the majority of China's writers. Despite its left-wing orientation, its members represented a broad spectrum of political and artistic views. The league established a network of friendship, communication, and associations that provided a sense of intellectual community. Despite Kuomintang censorship and the increasing acceptance of Marxist and Soviet literary theories, there were wide-open debates on political and literary issues.

A number of controversies occurred in this community, but the one that was the most acrimonious with repercussions that reverberated into the Cultural Revolution after the founding of the PRC was the clash between Lu Hsun and the Party's cultural officials in Shanghai, who in 1935 under the direction of Wang Ming, on orders from Moscow, called for a united front. Chou Yang, the Party's chief cultural official, disbanded the league in 1935 without consulting Lu Hsun and replaced it with another organization, the United Association of Chinese Writers, which was to promote the united front in cultural circles. This organization brandished the slogan "literature for national defense" and welcomed writers with non-Marxist views. The only condition for participation was opposition to Japan.

While reluctantly accepting the united front policy, Lu Hsun and his disciples feared the dilution of the revolutionary spirit if nonleftist literary writers joined the association. He and his associates, the writers Hu Feng and Feng Hsueh-feng, set up their own organization, the Chinese Literary Workers, and adopted a more revolutionary slogan: "People's literature of the national revolutionary struggle." But the Party's cultural officials, Chou Yang and his colleagues the playwrights T'ien Han, Hsia Yen, and Yang Han-sheng, though ostensibly proclaiming a more liberal position, would not tolerate an alternative organization and slogan. In their counterattack they enticed Hsu Mou-yung, a disciple of Lu Hsun's, to write a letter insinuating that Hu Feng and his disciples were working against the Party. Lu Hsun replied by publishing Hsu's letter and attaching an angry retort in which he defended Hu Feng and accused Chou Yang and his associates of labeling people "traitors" merely to enhance their own positions. Lu Hsun's letters at the time reveal his disgust with the efforts of Party officials to control the works and activities of himself and his associates.[1]

The clash between Chou Yang and Lu Hsun in Shanghai foreshadowed the conflict between the Party's effort to control the intellectuals and the intellectuals' resistance in the PRC. Even though in this instance the writers took a more revolutionary stance than the Party, Lu Hsun and his followers sought to maintain an independent, nondoctrinaire attitude not only toward Marxism and literature but also toward the Party organization. Not only did they resist the Party's effort to push their work into a political straitjacket, they also resented having their intellectual leadership usurped by Chou Yang merely because of his Party authority. Although Chou had translated Tolstoy and the nineteenth-century Russian literary critic Chernyshevski, he had published nothing of distinction or of a creative nature. Yet because of his organizational skill and unquestioning obedience to the Party line, he quickly gained a position above others more famous and more talented than he. Henceforth, the Party's policies toward the intellectuals placed ideological and organizational considerations above individual and professional ones.

Yenan, 1942

After the Sino-Japanese War broke out around Shanghai and along the coast in 1937, many intellectuals and large numbers of students made their way to the Communist headquarters in Yenan, drawn

1 *Lu Hsun ch'üan-chi* (Complete works of Lu Hsun), 6.437–38.

there by the belief that the CCP was the only group capable of bringing China out of chaos. They arrived at a time when the leadership was concerned that the cadres were losing some of their revolutionary zeal and becoming more interested in finding and maintaining their niche in the bureaucracy. The leadership was also concerned that the influx of intellectuals and students, accustomed to the unregimented life of the large cities, would provoke undisciplined behavior within the community at large.

Threatened by both the Kuomintang and the Japanese, the Party in the early 1940s launched a campaign to mold a core of disciplined cadres and intellectuals, committed to the rightness of the Party's cause. Very much in the traditional Confucian spirit, it believed that before one could change society, one must rectify one's own thought. The movement to rectify thought, called *cheng-feng*, short for "rectification of style of work," came to be known as the thought reform campaign. Begun in Yenan and used periodically in the PRC, this kind of campaign was to develop into one of the most ambitious attempts at human manipulation in history.

The methods used in Yenan were the rudiments of techniques which were to become fully developed in the PRC. Although the harshness, thoroughness, and sophistication typical of later campaigns were not so apparent in the early 1940s, the procedures that would be used in the future were all present. In the first stage, small groups were formed within Party units in which members studied and discussed prescribed speeches and articles. Since there was no freedom of silence, each member had to express an opinion on these works. This was followed by a second stage of investigation of each member of the group. The ideas and attitudes that each one previously held were subjected to intense, prolonged criticism by the others. The incessant recitation of one's failings, persistent indoctrination, and increasing tension produced a profound emotional crisis that eventually broke the individual's inner will. One could find relief from these pressures and atonement for one's "sins" only by surrendering to the Party's authority and sense of values.

This led to the third stage, in which the individual presented a self-criticism to be approved by the group's leaders. Usually the initial confession was not accepted. Several self-criticisms were demanded, each one more corrosive than the last in its attack on one's personality. Repeating Communist doctrine or the official line was insufficient; the individual had to give convincing evidence that his past ideas and behavior were totally wrong and his surrender to the

Party's will was totally complete. The Party did not want merely passive acquiescence, but positive conversion to its beliefs. Consequently, when the individual's final confession was approved, he was released from his sense of guilt and felt rejuvenated. He regarded himself, at least for a while, as a "new" person, ready to carry out the Party's orders with zeal.[2]

Initially, the campaign was as critical of the bureaucratism and dogmatism of the cadres as of the liberalism of the intellectuals. At first the main targets were the Soviet-trained students and cadres around Mao's old adversary Wang Ming. Given encouragement by the top leadership, particularly Mao, to criticize the bureaucracy, a group of intellectuals from Shanghai, some of whom had been close to Lu Hsun, used the opportunity to condemn the growth of a privileged elite in Yenan and expose what they called the darkness in society as they and Lu Hsun had done in Shanghai. They continued the relatively free intellectual debates and associations they had had in Shanghai literary circles. The literary page of *Chieh-fang jih-pao* (Liberation Daily), under the editorship of the woman writer Ting Ling, became the vehicle for their ideas. Actually, even before the campaign began, Ting Ling wrote an article in the 23 October 1941 issue of *Liberation Daily* entitled "We need *tsa-wen*," in which she held up Lu Hsun as a model for her fellow intellectuals to emulate. She insisted that Lu Hsun's exposure of the dark side of society and his method of *tsa-wen* were needed at present because "this age of ours still needs the *tsa-wen*, a weapon that we should never lay down."[3]

A series of articles was published from March through April 1942 on the literary page of *Liberation Daily* in response to Mao's call for criticism. They represented a major current of thought in Yenan intellectual circles. Their authors, Ting Ling, Wang Shih-wei, Hsiao Chün, Lo Feng, and Ai Ch'ing, were Party members. Several of them, particularly Hsiao Chün and Lo Feng, had been part of Lu Hsun's inner circle. Not having hesitated in the past to criticize persons or situations with which they disagreed. they did the same in Yenan in the hope that their criticism would bring reform. Lo Feng stated their purpose: "I hope our literary page will henceforth be a

---

2 Robert Lifton, *Thought reform and the psychology of totalism*. This book describes the psychological techniques the Party used to remold the intellectuals.
3 *CFJP*, 23 October 1941, 4.

sword which will shock people and at the same time make them rejoice."[4]

Their *tsa-wen* depicted the apathy, hypocrisy, and bureaucratism of the cadres with the same sharp pens they had earlier used against Kuomintang officials. Though their essays were on different subjects, all of them expressed disillusion with finding that life in the revolutionary base did not measure up to the revolutionary ideal. As expressed by Lo Feng, "Clouds not only cover Chungking but frequently appear here."[5] Ting Ling, for example, complained that the equality for women which she had expected and which the Party propounded did not exist in fact.[6] Through their criticisms, they sought to halt what they considered to be the distortion of Communist ideals in practice and return the Party to its revolutionary goals.

Another theme running through their *tsa-wen* was disagreement with the leadership over the role of the writer in a Party-run society. Like their mentor, Lu Hsun, they believed that the writer's function was not to act as a publicist for each twist in the Party line, but to criticize and speak out against what he thought was wrong. They separated the intellectual's tasks from those of the Party. Whereas the Party was to concern itself with material and physical needs, the writers and other intellectuals were to care for spiritual needs. Ai Ch'ing, in virtually Neo-Confucian language, insisted that the writer's function was to compel his countrymen to scrutinize and criticize themselves. A writer was not "a Mongolian lark, nor a singer who sings only to please others." Writers were to look at questions for which Marxism or the Party had no answers. "Writers seek to answer questions men wonder about in isolated moments when they silently ask why they live."[7]

To fulfill this role, the *tsa-wen* writers insisted that creative freedom and a certain degree of independence of thought and action were necessary. Thus, although these writers were Marxists and Party members, they also were imbued with the Western idea of freedom as a prerequisite for creativity and reform. As Ai Ch'ing explained, writers had committed themselves to the government in Yenan "in the hope that this kind of government would guarantee the indepen-

---

4 Lo Feng, "Hai-shih tsa-wen ti shih-tai" (Still a period of *tsa-wen*), *CFJP*, 12 March 1942, 4.
5 Ibid.
6 Ting Ling, "San-pa-chieh yu kan" (Thoughts on March 8), *CFJP*, 9 March 1942, 4.
7 Ai Ch'ing, "Liao-chieh tso-chia, tsun-chung tso-chia" (Understand writers, respect writers), *CFJP*, 11 March 1942, 4.

dent spirit of literary creation. Only when artistic creation is given independence can art help advance social reform."[8]

The most daring and controversial of all the *tsa-wen* writers in 1942 was Wang Shih-wei, a Party member since 1926, a short-story writer, translator and interpreter of Marxist works. After studying in the Soviet Union from 1930 to 1935, he arrived in Yenan in 1936, where he became a member of the Academy of Marxist-Leninist Studies, later changed to the Central Research Institute. In 1941 he was in charge of the theoretical training for high-level cadres. Wang wrote two articles in early 1942 that went much further than his colleagues in demanding an independent role for writers and in criticizing the bureaucracy in Yenan. They combined the critical voice of the literati with the independent stance of the May Fourth intellectual.

On 17 February 1942 in *Ku Yü* (Grain Rain), the most popular literary journal in Yenan, Wang argued as Lu Hsun and his associates had in Shanghai that the artist provides spiritual inspiration for the revolution. Wang was the first to theorize on the need to separate certain spheres of activity from politics. The official was "the unifier, organizer, promoter, leader of revolutionary forces; his duty is primarily to reform the social system." The artist was "the 'engineer of the soul'; his duty primarily is to reform the souls of men (mind, spirit, thought, consciousness)."[9] Thus Wang gave the artist a task the Party had deemed should be performed only under its own direction. The artist "bravely but appropriately should expose all filth and darkness; and wash them out.... The work of exposure and cleansing is not just negative work; because as darkness decreases, light will naturally increase."[10] Wang acknowledged that some people think that if writers "expose our own defects this will provide the enemy with an opening for attack. This is a short-sighted view; our campaign today has already grown so strong, it is not afraid to expose its own defects."[11]

His next *tsa-wen*, "Wild Lily," published in two parts in *Liberation Daily* on 13 and 23 March, was one of the most controversial works ever written within the Chinese Communist camp and caused repercussions still felt in China today. Like Mao, he expressed concern about the increasing separation of the Party bureaucracy

---

8 Ibid.
9 Timothy Cheek translation of Wang Shih-wei's "Statesmen and artists" in unpublished article, "The fading of wild lilies," 61.
10 Ibid., 65.   11 Ibid.

from the masses. In answer to those who insisted that Yenan did not have a system of ranks, he replied that this "does not square with the facts since such a system palpably exists." Though he declared that he himself was not an egalitarian, he said "to divide clothing into three and food into five different grades is definitely neither necessary nor rational."[12] While "there is no noodle soup for sick comrades to eat and students only get two meals of thin congee a day," Wang complained that "relatively healthy 'big shots' get far more than they need or than is reasonable to eat and drink with the result that their subordinates look upon them as a different species."[13]

The one-time rebels against inequality had now become new bureaucrats in their own system of injustice. They suffered from the very same evils of corruption and indifference that they had tried to destroy. Unlike the Yugoslav Milovan Djilas, who would speak fifteen years later of a new class as an outgrowth of the Party itself, Wang considered this development a carryover from the old society: "Since our camp exists in the old, dark society, there is bound to be darkness here too."[14] By reminding Party leaders of their ideals, he believed he was upholding the orthodox view of Marxism. He was also acting in the Confucian tradition of criticizing the leadership in order to ensure the success of their rule.

The methods and approach of later campaigns against intellectuals were developed in the Party's response to the criticisms of these *tsa-wen* writers. It marked the start of suppression of independent and critical intellectuals and the extension of Party control to intellectual activity. By the spring of 1942, the rectification movement shifted from its somewhat equal criticism of bureaucratism and liberalism almost wholly to criticism of the liberalism of the intellectuals. These writers were singled out to dramatize particular patterns of thought which the Party regarded as inimical to its current policies. Their independence and critical stance, which had been helpful in Kuomintang territory, were no longer desirable now that they lived under Party rule. These writers were used as negative examples to remold the thinking of intellectuals and cadres. This method of choosing a few officials or intellectuals as examples to keep a whole community in line had been used by the Soviet Union since the 1930s.

The harshest attack was on Wang Shih-wei – not only because he

12 Gregor Benton, translation of Wang Shih-wei, "Wild lily," in "The Yan'an 'literary opposition'" in *New Left Review*, 92 (1975), 101.
13 Ibid.   14 Wang Shih-wei, "Yeh pai-ho-hua" (Wild lily), *CFJP*, 13 March 1942, 4.

had been the most penetrating in his criticism, but also because he was involved in a factional struggle at the Central Research Institute with ideologues who were close to Mao. All campaigns have a factional as well as an ideological component. Wang was associated with the Soviet-trained student group, whereas the opposing faction was made up of Mao's personal secretary and ghost writer, Ch'en Po-ta, the historian Fan Wen-lan, and the ideologist Ai Szu-ch'i. This campaign gave them an opportunity to get rid of a persistent and annoying critic.

Wang and Ch'en had disagreed previously on a number of ideological issues. One of those issues was on national forms, another controversy left over from Shanghai, where in the mid-1930s Wang had sided with Lu Hsun and Lu Hsun's close associates Hu Feng and Feng Hsueh-feng in a debate with Ch'en Po-ta, Chou Yang, and others. Ch'en and company, following the lead of the Party's cultural leaders of the early 1930s, Ch'ü Ch'iu-pai and later Mao, argued that China's writers should repudiate the Western literary tradition and create their own style based on traditional literary forms such as short tales, songs, and simple drama, which would be far more effective in developing political consciousness and inspiring the masses. In response, Lu Hsun's group scorned the traditional literary forms as "feudal" and maintained that the internationalization of Chinese culture was a prerequisite for China's development. Wang and Ch'en resumed this debate in 1940–41. Essentially it was a conflict between Westernized May Fourth intellectuals and more populist, nationalist intellectuals.

Shortly after Wang's articles appeared, he became the focus of an ideological and factional campaign. In April 1942 the Party announced that there would be three months of ideological struggle. Within this time, virtually all work was to stop in Party units while comrades read documents and criticized one another in small groups. At the same time, there were large public meetings in May 1942 at which Mao delivered his two famous "Talks on literature and art."

Mao implicitly rejected the criticism of the *tsa-wen* writers and laid the foundation for the Party's policy on literature and toward intellectuals. Though not mentioning the writers by name, he attacked their attempt to stay independent of the encompassing role of the Party and rejected their demand that art be independent of politics. Artists and art must be subordinate to political tasks prescribed by the Party at any given time. Though he presented his views as original doctrine, Mao's views on literature were a combination of the Soviet theory of socialist realism and Ch'ü Ch'iu-pai's emphasis on national forms.

These views, which were among several debated in left-wing circles in the 1930s, now became prescribed doctrine. Literature was to be optimistic and heroic and written in the style the masses understood. The function of literature under the CCP was not to reveal the dark side of society as it had under the Kuomintang. Although Mao earlier had virtually deified Lu Hsun as "a hero without parallel in our history,"[15] in his Yenan talks he rejected what Lu Hsun represented. Whereas Lu Hsun had promoted Western literary styles and ideas, Mao urged writers to return to their traditional folk styles. Whereas Lu Hsun's work exposed the dark side of society in which the masses as well as the elite were derided for their apathy, backwardness, and injustice, Mao called for a literature that served the Party's goals and extolled the masses. No longer were writers to criticize reality as it was or as the individual saw it; they were to describe it as it would be and as the Party and Mao saw it.

Just four days after Mao's second Yenan talk, a series of mass meetings began at the Central Research Institute. They lasted from May to 11 June 1942, and were attended by more than a thousand ideological theorists and intellectuals in Yenan. Some defended Wang; others denounced him. Ai Szu-ch'i, who along with Ch'en Po-ta and Fan Wen-lan was one of the chief accusers, denounced Wang's "absolute egalitarianism"[16] as contrary to democratic central-ism and Party discipline. Wang was identified as a Trotskyite not only because he had been close to "Trotskyites" such as Ch'en Tu-hsiu in the past, but because he had called Stalin's purges "atrocities."[17] At first the majority refused to accept Wang's designa-tion as a Trotskyite and an anti-Party element, but unrelenting pressure at large meetings and small group sessions whittled away his support. Under increasing pressure, Wang's associates on the *Liberation Daily* denounced him.

On the last days of the struggle meetings, Ting Ling disavowed her own work and attacked Wang as an evil influence. Ai Ch'ing in a second self-criticism on 24 June also repudiated Wang. The ideologist Hu Ch'iao-mu and historian Fan Wen-lan had long sessions with Wang, and five Party members regularly visited him in an effort to make him write a public confession, but he refused. Wang was sent to work in a matchbox factory where a reporter who saw him in the

15 Mao, *SW*, 2.372.   16 Cheek, "Wild lilies," 36.   17 Ibid., 37.

summer of 1944 described him as mentally deranged.[18] He was executed in the spring of 1947 when the Red Army retreated from Yenan.

Although Mao in 1962 expressed regret about Wang's execution, the decision to execute Wang was made by the public security organization that in 1947 was in the charge of Mao's close associate K'ang Sheng. Wang's colleagues on the literary page of the *Liberation Daily* were sent to the countryside for labor reform, and their positions were taken by those who had denounced them in the 1942 rectification; Ai Szu-ch'i took Ting Ling's job as editor of the literary page. Chou Yang presented the definitive statement on the campaign – a role he continued in future campaigns.[19] He summed up Wang's ideological and political "errors," the negative aspect of the campaign, and set the tone for the positive aspect of the campaign by calling for an affirmative literature and "peasant" writers who depicted an optimistic view of peasant life under the Party.

Although the 1942 rectification was not on the scale or carried out with the intensity of later thought reform campaigns, it had the elements of later movements. The work of the person under attack was subjected to textual analysis and detailed criticism, which became the substance and material for the campaign. The victim was isolated from supporters. Those who dissociated themselves from the victim were treated more leniently, and those most prominent in attacking the victim enhanced their own positions in the official hierarchy. Massive struggle meetings, somewhat akin to the Stalin show trials of the 1930s, gradually silenced whatever supporters the victim had, along with anyone with similar ideas.

The 1942 rectification marks the beginning of the effort to suppress the pluralistic spirit and intellectual autonomy of the May Fourth movement and replace it with a Party-directed culture and Party-disciplined intellectuals. This effort did not end with the conclusion of the 1942 rectification. Ch'en Yun, in a speech on 29 March 1943, insisted that "a literary and art worker should regard himself as a Party member and not regard himself primarily as a cultural worker.... We hope that by studying and conducting criticism and self-criticism, all Party literary and art workers will strengthen their Party spirit and eliminate their evil habits."[20] Moreover, intellectuals

18 Ibid., 47.
19 *CFJP*, 28 June 1942, 4.
20 Ch'en Yun, "On the question of two tendencies among the Party's literary and art workers," NCNA, 22 May 1982, in *FBIS*, 24 May 1982, K8.

must subject themselves to the dictates of Party officials even when those who are directing them know less than they do. "To observe discipline, literary and art workers must obey the Party branch and next higher level even if people at that level are not as capable."[21] The Party's experience in Yenan has been described as laying the foundation for popular participation and egalitarian values, but the *tsa-wen* writers' criticism of the Party for disregarding such values and their ensuing repression belies this contention. On the contrary, the treatment of the *tsa-wen* writers in Yenan laid the foundation for the subsequent silencing of dissent and the encompassing Party control of intellectuals in general.

The 1948 campaign against Hsiao Chün

Although the Party had little time to concern itself with intellectuals as the struggle with the Kuomintang moved into its final stages, suddenly in 1948 it embarked on a campaign that was reminiscent of the one it had carried out against Wang and his colleagues in 1942. While the Party was ingratiating itself with non-Communist intellectuals whose services would be necessary for the modernization of China, it attempted to regiment and control intellectuals in its own ranks. In preparation for the end of the fighting, it sought to ensure that Party intellectuals were sufficiently disciplined to handle problems of social and political control. Along with its program of land reform in the late 1940s, it conducted a rectification among enclaves of left-wing intellectuals, particularly in Shanghai, Hong Kong, and Harbin.

The rectification that received the most attention was the one in Harbin against Hsiao Chün, author of a famous novel about the Manchurian struggle against the Japanese, *Village in August*. Hsiao had been a disciple of Lu Hsun and one of the Yenan *tsa-wen* writers. He was among the most recalcitrant intellectuals with whom the Party had to contend. Even before his 1942 *tsa-wen*, he had written letters to Mao pointing out shortcomings in Yenan that should be corrected. Mao replied by praising him as "a very frank and straightforward person," and acknowledged that his criticism merited attention. But Mao urged him "to pay attention to certain mistakes of your own and not to look at problems in terms of absolutes. We should ... purposely force ourselves to examine our own

21 Ibid., K10.

weaknesses."[22] This Hsiao refused to do. Hsiao had been the only one of the *tsa-wen* group who had not made a self-criticism other than Wang Shih-wei, whom he refused to denounce. Meetings presided over by Ting Ling were convened in October 1942, specifically to criticize Hsiao, but he still refused to respond to the Party's demand for a self-criticism.

After having been sent down for several years of labor reform in the countryside, Hsiao was returned to his native Manchuria in 1946 to help the Party solidify its control over the region. Despite his previous dissent, Hsiao, as an esteemed native writer, could be used to win popular support for the Party. The Party helped him set up a journal, *Wen-hua pao* (Cultural gazette), which was published weekly. But Hsiao soon became the first of the Yenan critics to resume the criticism of Party practices with which he disagreed. In addition to reiterating the May Fourth view that intellectuals, as the articulators of ideas and the conscience of the people, were as important for social change as political activists, Hsiao spoke out strongly against the Party's current political policies. He denounced the Party's sole reliance on the Soviet Union as its chief ally. He expressed the intense dislike of his fellow Manchurians for the Russians because of their repeated occupations, economic exploitation of Manchuria, and continued presence on Chinese soil. In several issues of *Cultural Gazette*, he denounced Soviet imperialism: "It does not matter what foreign nation it is, we should be treated with equality and respect. If it be Russians they should be even more respectful ... friendship without principles is irrational."[23]

Hsiao was also one of the few intellectuals to speak out against the violence that accompanied the land reform of the late 1940s. Here again, he appears to have expressed the latent dissatisfaction of part of the local population. While there was virtually unanimous support for land reform, the execution of landlords and violent class struggle in the countryside had aroused misgivings among some Party cadres and intellectuals. In a very strong statement, he asserted that "land is repeatedly divided, wealth distributed, and provisions taken away until the point is reached where people are destitute.... Why should the Communists be so unkind and heartless?" Even the policies of the Japanese and Manchus, he claimed, were not so tyrannical as those enforced by the Party.[24]

22 Reprint of Mao's letters in Peking newspapers, translated in *FBIS*, 24 May 1982, K2.
23 Liu Chih-ming, *Hsiao Chün ssu-hsiang p'i-p'an* (Criticism of Hsiao Chün's thought), 39.
24 Quoted in Yang Yen-nan, *Chung-kung tui Hu Feng ti tou-cheng* (The struggle against Hu Feng by the Chinese Communists), 179.

Hsiao's criticism of the Party's alliance with the Soviet Union and of land reform reached beyond the circle of students and intellectuals to arouse the ordinary Manchurian citizen. His articles fostered confusion and misunderstanding about the Party's political views and ideology among the literate population in Harbin. Thus, as the rectification, under way since January 1948, gained momentum, he was used to symbolize the disruptive, undisciplined forces the Party needed to purge from its own ranks in order to prevail.

In addition to his blatant nonconformity, factional reasons also played a role in Hsiao's selection as a scapegoat. Though the Central Committee initiated the rectification, its implementation was left to the Party's propaganda officials in Manchuria, primarily Liu Chih-ming, who had participated in the 1942 campaign against Hsiao and his colleagues and was close to Chou Yang. Moreover, the editors of another Party paper, *Sheng-huo pao* (Life gazette), which had been in fierce competition with Hsiao's journal, issued a barrage of articles against him from August to October 1948 and participated in the investigating teams that interrogated him.

The procedures in the Harbin rectification were similar to the ones in Yenan. Small group discussions and criticism and self-criticism sessions were combined with large-scale meetings in schools, factories, and the offices of Party organs. The propaganda apparatus in Harbin portrayed Hsiao as one who gave too much attention to nationalist goals and too little attention to class struggle. Since the war with Japan was over, Hsiao's nationalism no longer served a positive function and his disinterest in class struggle had a negative influence. Hsiao's denunciation of the Soviet Union received the most attention, probably because it reflected the sentiment of many Manchurians that the Party found difficult to dispel. Liu Chih-ming contended that Hsiao "cannot understand that the Soviet Union, unlike tsarist Russia, attempts to aid oppressed nations; she will never be an oppressor herself."[25] In contrast to Hsiao's questioning of Soviet intentions toward China, Liu in the 1948–49 rectification called for an unconditional alliance with the Soviet Union.

All kinds of pressure were put on Hsiao to make a self-criticism, in order to silence others with his views. The Party discontinued support for his journal, which left him not only without a means of livelihood but also without a platform from which to rebut the charges against him. Again his old colleagues were used against him.

25 Liu Chih-ming, "A criticism of the errors of Hsiao Chün and the *Cultural Gazette*," in Hualing Nieh, *Literature of the Hundred Flowers*, 2.303.

Ting Ling once more presided over a large meeting to criticize him. But despite all the pressure, Hsiao refused to make an acceptable . public criticism. He was sentenced to hard labor in the Fushun coal mines. In repudiating Hsiao, the Party treated his ideological differences as political opposition. The campaign against Hsiao went farther than the Yenan effort to set limits on criticism and instead treated criticism from intellectuals as political subversion. It was also extended to people and groups beyond left-wing intellectual and party circles. These measures were to become standard practice in future campaigns.

ESTABLISHMENT OF PARTY CONTROL OVER INTELLECTUALS, 1949–1955

After the establishment of the PRC there were in the 1950s about 100,000 higher intellectuals, defined as professionals, scholars, and creative artists, most of whom Chou En-lai characterized as having a degree of bourgeois idealism and individualism.[26] Nevertheless, in the very early days of the regime the Party slackened its drive to reform their thought in order to win their allegiance. Initially a large portion of the intellectuals welcomed the Party because of disgust with the Kuomintang and because of appreciation of the Party's ability to unite the country and provide financial security after decades of disorder.

Borrowing from the Soviet example, the Party paid the salaries and assumed responsibility for the living and working conditions of the intellectuals. Each professional group and each discipline was organized into a Party-controlled association. For example, the creative artists were incorporated into the All-China Federation of Literary and Art Circles. Within the federation, each discipline had its own organization, such as the Chinese Writers Union or the Chinese Stage Artists Union. The Chinese Writers Union had branches in all the provinces and major cities. The central office in Peking appointed the directors in the provinces and the editorial boards of the literary magazines. A similar pattern was followed in the other disciplines and professions.

Thus, despite a slackening of the drive for ideological conformity in the early days of the regime, the Party quickly imposed organizational control. It moved with more alacrity and deftness than the

26 *JMJP*, 30 January 1956, 1.

Soviets in organizing scholarship and the arts in the early years of its reign. The Soviets, because of lack of experience, made comparatively modest efforts in the first decade of their rule. By contrast, when the CCP assumed power, it not only had Stalin's example of the control of the Russian intellectuals; it also had its own experience in Yenan and Harbin and a core of trained cadres led by Chou Yang, Ch'en Po-ta, and Hu Ch'iao-mu. They were deputy directors of the Party's Propaganda Department, the ultimate source of ideological orthodoxy, headed by Lu Ting-i.

The Party's conciliatory policy toward the intellectuals was short-lived. In 1951 it initiated a campaign to reorient them away from the Western theories and scholarship in which most of them had been trained and toward Soviet theories and scholarship in all fields from biological research to the creative arts. The aim was to expunge Western liberal values and indoctrinate the intellectuals with Marxism-Leninism. Part of this effort was expressed in a campaign against the film "The Story of Wu Hsun," which told how a nineteenth-century educator who began as a beggar eventually became a landlord and used his money to establish schools. The Party characterized Wu Hsun as a negative symbol because he sought to change China through education and reform rather than through revolution.

Dovetailing with the Wu Hsun campaign was a rectification of literary circles, led by Ting Ling, whose prestige and powerful position as editor of *Wen-i pao* (Literary gazette), the authoritative journal of the Chinese Writers Union, rivaled those of Chou Yang in literary circles. In 1952, she became one of the chief editors of *Jen-min wen-hsueh* (People's literature), the preeminent fiction journal, and one of her close friends, Feng Hsueh-feng, took her place as editor of *Literary Gazette*. She virtually controlled two of China's most influential journals. Because of her prominent role in denouncing her former colleagues, she appears to have been fully pardoned for her rebellious past.

Yet Ting Ling's actions epitomized the schizoid nature of most intellectuals in the early days of the regime. She was motivated by a mixture of political opportunism and genuine enthusiasm for the Party in her vigorous implementation of its dictates. At the same time, she tried to maintain the independence and professional standards of the May Fourth era. At the very moment that Ting Ling was leading the rectification among her fellow writers, she urged writers to find their creative inspiration from their own feelings rather than from those imposed by others: "I am not against our present creative work being organized, but ... a writer is not a child who cannot leave his mother; he must be independent."[27]

These campaigns of the early 1950s were more subdued than the previous drives against Wang Shih-wei and Hsiao Chün. They were focused more on anticipating potential subversion than on stamping out any public expression of criticism. The Party was not yet ready to push ideological conformity with the zealousness of the previous drives. Although the intellectuals were subjected to efforts to change their Western liberal orientation, the Party was still wary of harsh measures that would alienate them. Moreover, the Party was primarily concerned with imposing ideological control over intellectuals in the arts and humanities. It allowed scientists more leeway. Because their work was more abstruse and more theoretical, the Party leadership admitted less understanding. It was also less prone to interfere with scientific work because it considered scientific skills more crucial to the Party's drive for economic modernization. Nevertheless, though most scientists felt the impact later and less severely, they were inevitably affected by the Party's thought reform campaigns. Similarly, in periods of relative relaxation, they felt the effects earlier and more generously, but relaxation affected all disciplines, as did thought reform campaigns. The Party was unable to isolate the scientists from other intellectual groups. The fortunes of most intellectuals usually rose and fell together, though in varying sequence.

Slight relaxation and the reemergence of thought reform campaigns, 1953–1954

The inauguration, though not the details, of the 1st Five-Year Plan (FYP) was announced at the start of 1953, but it immediately encountered problems of overambitious planning. As the Party's economic planners vacillated, so did its approach toward intellectuals. Conflicting directives were issued to cadres in the intellectual realm. They were told to tighten the Party's organizational control at the same time as they were to allow more leeway in the exercise of the intellectuals' individual talents in order to gain their active participation in modernization. The Party offered intellectuals a modicum of freedom in the expectation that they would reciprocate by being more productive and creative in their work. Since China was still

27 Ting Ling, *Tao ch'ün-chung ch'ü lo-hu* (Go into the dwellings of the masses), 102.

following the Soviet pattern, this relaxation may also have been due to the Soviet relaxation in the academic and artistic realm immediately after Stalin's death.

Similar in tone to the Party's exhortation in the early stages of the Yenan campaign, Party directives on the one hand encouraged intellectuals to criticize cadres and on the other instructed the cadres "to listen humbly to their criticisms and opinions and learn from them."[28] Several unorthodox ideas that hitherto had been muffled were allowed clear public expression. Among them was the demand that literature be allowed to break out of the confines of politically dictated material and prescribed forms. Again, there was a parallel with happenings on the Soviet literary scene where writers were demanding a fuller presentation of reality that drew from a wider range of subject matter and used a greater variety of literary styles. Another demand heard at this time in China and in the Soviet Union was for more professional standards in all fields.

In the latter half of 1954, however, the Party's measures to regiment intellectuals eclipsed the efforts to cajole them. Its previous contradictory approach of simultaneously letting go and tightening up had produced little result. More important, by the latter part of 1954, as the Party was about to announce the details of its 1st FYP, it was necessary to mobilize the population and ensure that nothing be allowed to divert attention from efforts for the economic program. Again the Party used a thought reform campaign to push its program, and once more it chose its scapegoats from the literary realm.

The movement began gradually with a relatively muted attack on the Western-oriented scholar Yü P'ing-po, who had been influenced by Hu Shih and had written an important interpretation of the great eighteenth-century novel *The Dream of the Red Chamber*. Unlike the May Fourth intellectuals, he had remained aloof from political conflicts. The drive against him was to mobilize non-Party intellectuals in preparation for the Party's revolutionary economic changes.

Yü had disobeyed the Party's order of 1953 to interpret Chinese classics in Marxist-Leninist terms by publishing an article in 1954 that presented the same interpretation of the novel as that which he had worked out in the early 1920s. He treated the novel not as a critique of the feudal system but as an autobiographical writing by its author, Ts'ao Hsueh-ch'in. The Party's conflict with Yü was not only because of his ideological dissent, but also because he had rejected

28 *JMJP* editorial, 25 March 1954, translated in *SCMP*, 77 (4–5 March 1951), 20.

Party direction. When Yü sent a draft of his 1954 article to Hu Ch'iao-mu for approval, Hu made some suggestions and asked Yü to rewrite it. Instead of revising it, Yü on his own initiative sent it to *Hsin chien-she* (New construction), where it was published, an indication that journals still were not fully controlled by the Propaganda Department. Although the campaign began with an obscure article written by two young students, Li Hsi-fan and Lan Ling, in a journal at Shantung University, after it was reprinted in *Kuang-ming jih-pao* (Kuangming daily) on 10 October 1954, and in *Jen-min jih-pao* (People's daily) on 23 October 1954, an avalanche of articles and editorials attacked Yü.

Although one purpose of the campaign was to use the *Dream* to indoctrinate the population in the Marxist historical view, the overriding purpose was to impose a political view of scholarship on China's intellectuals. It marked the beginning of a shift in emphasis from intellectual endeavor and professionalism to political orthodoxy and nonspecialization. Criticism of Yü was to demonstrate that the ideological militancy of Party-trained students represented by his two young critics was of greater value to the CCP than the scholarship and academic discipline represented by Yü. The campaign was an intensified effort to discredit Western scholarship in the social sciences and humanities. As in the 1951 drive against Western scholarship, the latter disciplines were the first to be affected; the natural sciences in mid-1954 still remained relatively exempt. Hu Shih's method of avoiding preconceptions became the main target of this aspect of the campaign. The Party claimed that to Hu Shih, "academic research is to satisfy one's own interest, not the needs of the country and the people."[29] The Party, through its attack on Yü and Hu Shih, sought to reverse this emphasis.

The criticism of Yü's work and Hu Shih was restrained in comparison to the campaign against Feng Hsueh-feng and other Party intellectuals that followed. When Feng became editor of the authoritative *Literary Gazette* in 1952, his influence had increased remarkably. His editorship, like his writings, expressed some divergences within a fairly orthodox framework. In the relatively relaxed period of 1953 and early 1954, he denounced China's current literature for falsifying reality and pointed to the Party's control over culture as being responsible. Ostensibly, the Party's virulent attack against Feng was because he initially refused to publish the criticism of Yü by the

29 Lu K'an-ju, "Hu Shih fan-tung ssu-hsiang" (Hu Shih's reactionary thought), *Wen-i pao*, 21 (1954), 4.

two young critics. More broadly, it was another effort to suppress the May Fourth spirit and subject intellectuals to strict Party command.

It was also a further demonstration of factional struggle, as Chou Yang and his associates attempted to displace Feng and his associates from positions of power in the cultural establishment and install their own people. Feng and his group were accused of building up "independent kingdoms" in which they suppressed free debate, as evidenced by Feng's unwillingness to publish criticism of Yü P'ing-po. What the Party now meant by its demand for open criticism was that the Party's view on intellectual questions should replace the Western-oriented views which hitherto had predominated. As expressed euphemistically by the writer-scholar and close associate of Mao, Kuo Mo-jo: "The minority must be listened to and permitted to uphold its own principles."[30] Feng was forced to make a public criticism and was replaced as editor of *Literary Gazette* by an editorial board dominated by Chou Yang's protégés. Ting Ling had left her position as editor of *People's Literature* in 1953 and into her place stepped one of Chou's closest followers, Shao Ch'uan-lin. By late 1954, Chou was in command of the Party's chief cultural journals and had dethroned and publicly silenced his old rivals.

At the concluding session of the struggle meeting against Feng, Kuo Mo-jo declared, "Not only literature, but also history, philosophy, economics, art, language, education, and even the natural sciences – all these fields should develop ... an ideological struggle."[31] Thus, by the end of 1954 the Party had set in motion a movement that had gone from Western-oriented scholars of classical literature through the left-wing intellectuals to the whole intellectual community.

The Hu Feng campaign, 1955

The thought reform campaign that began in mid-1954 reached its climax with the campaign of 1955 against Lu Hsun's disciple Hu Feng. It went beyond the intellectual community to indoctrinate the population as a whole and went beyond urban centers to become nationwide in scope. It was carried out with such intensity that it developed an emotional frenzy lacking in previous campaigns.

The choice of Hu Feng as a target had its origins in Hu's conflict with the Party's cultural authorities, particularly Chou Yang and his

30 *Wen-i pao*, 22 (1954), 46.   31 Ibid.

group, begun in the mid-1930s. The conflict continued into the 1940s, when the Yenan rectification was extended to left-wing intellectuals and cadres in Chungking in 1943, where Hu had gone with his disciples after the bombing of Shanghai. Like his counterparts in Yenan, he assumed that one of the purposes of the rectification was to generate genuine debate and criticize the dogmatism of Party officials. Consequently, he established a journal, *Hsi-wang* (Hope), in order to attack the doctrinairism of the Party's cultural officials. Subsequently he was criticized and his journal suppressed.

Hu's low-key conflict with the cultural authorities continued into the early years of the PRC. However, in the period of relative relaxation of 1953 and the first half of 1954, he was appointed to the editorial board of *People's Literature* and became a member of the executive board of the Chinese Writers' Union. Believing that the times were favorable for his criticism, he expressed his dismay at the stultification of intellectual life in a report to the Central Committee[32] reminiscent of literati memorials to the Ch'ing emperor. His purpose was not to overthrow the leadership or the existing system, but to point out that since 1949, China's culture had not been based on the principles of Mao and the Party, whose directives were distorted by a few cultural officials. Like the Ch'ing literati, he sought to demonstrate that the country's good and wise leaders had been deceived by unscrupulous officials. He criticized these officials because they forced writers to immerse themselves solely in the lives of the workers, peasants, and soldiers; to study Marxism-Leninism before they could write; to write in national forms; and to emphasize "bright things" and deemphasize backwardness and darkness, which Hu asserted meant writing what was false.

Hu proposed that writers reform themselves according to their own needs instead of being reformed by officials. To promote diversity, he suggested that the few official publications be replaced by seven or eight publications of writers' organizations that would edit their own journals. In this effort to loosen Party control, he sought to reinfuse Chinese culture with the May Fourth concern for professional and literary standards and intellectual pluralism. In Hu's view, his report only demanded a greater degree of freedom for writers to develop their individual talents within the present system. In fact, however, if Hu's view of the independent nature of artistic

32 "Hu Feng tui wen-i wen-t'i ti i-chien" (Hu Feng's literary opinions), supplement to *Wen-i pao*, January 1955.

creation had been put into effect, it would have undermined the whole system of controls the Party had imposed.

Nevertheless, Hu's demand for more autonomy cannot by itself explain the unprecedented zealousness and nationwide scope of the campaign against him. He was used as a tool in the campaign to bring the Party's collectivization of agriculture and nationalization of industry to fruition. Lu Ting-i announced that "our First Five Year Plan cannot be brought into realization in a calm, placid way. It demands a class struggle, an acute, complicated struggle."[33] Hu became one of the symbols against which this struggle was waged in order to instill the belief that the individual's first and only duty was to the state.

This campaign under the direction of the Propaganda Department, particularly Hu's old foe Chou Yang, was orchestrated by Mao himself. Hu's letters to his followers were confiscated and became the main evidence used against him. The introduction to a published collection of Hu's letters was written by Mao. In it Mao condemned the interference of intellectuals in politics. He said of Hu's group: "In the past it was said that they were a group of simple, cultural people. This is wrong because they have worked their way into the political, military, economic, cultural, and educational establishment."[34] Although Hu Feng's group was nothing more than a small literary coterie, by June 1955 the Party had accused it of building up bases and enlisting mass support to carry out counterrevolutionary activity. Anyone holding views diverging from the current orthodoxy was labeled "counterrevolutionary" and was purged not only from educational and cultural organizations but also from labor unions, mass organizations, and the armed forces.

The Party's enormous propaganda machine informed even the humblest peasant in the most remote frontier area about Hu Feng in order to ensure that any latent "Hu Fengism" – independent thinking and activity – would be eliminated. Even the favored scientists were finally affected by this campaign. But they were apparently slow to respond. As a radio broadcast pointed out: "The attitude among the natural scientists towards the Hu Feng case was one of 'It's none of my business.' This proves that their vigilance in the revolutionary cause is low."[35] They were charged with being contaminated with the same counterrevolutionary germs as other intellectuals.

33 *JMJP*, 27 July 1955, in *CB*, 350 (26 August 1955), 14.
34 Mao Tse-tung, "Supreme instructions," *CB*, 897 (10 December 1969), 32.
35 BBC, *Summary of world broadcasts*, 5. 472 (1955), 13.

By the summer of 1955 the Hu Feng campaign had developed a momentum that was difficult to control and had gone beyond the scope the regime had intended. It had evolved from an orderly Party instrument into a reign of terror, particularly among intellectuals. One observer described the pressure as so great that "suicides were frequent in cultural organs."[36] The effect of the campaign was to exacerbate the estrangement between China's intellectuals and the Party that had begun in the Yenan rectification. What happened specifically to Hu and his disciples was typical of what was to happen to outspoken intellectual critics henceforth. Their private papers were seized; they were isolated from their professional colleagues who denounced them; they were purged from their positions and professional unions; their wives and children were also denounced. Hu was imprisoned; his disciple Lu Ling was put into a mental institution; and others of his followers were sent down for labor reform. In prison, Hu continued his fight – he staged hunger strikes, asked for a press conference, and demanded a trial with legal counsel – until he finally had a nervous breakdown. All this punishment was incurred merely because he had pleaded for some degree of autonomy for the writer and intellectual.

THE HUNDRED FLOWERS CAMPAIGN

The first phase, 1956

As the Party foresaw the imminent completion of collectivization of agriculture at the end of 1955 and launched a new push in industrialization, it turned increasingly to the intellectuals and professionals for help. *Kuang-ming Daily* on 3 December 1955 announced, "A new situation has arisen in which intellectuals, particularly those of high standing in learning and technological accomplishment, must make greater contributions to society."[37] However, because of the ferocity of the Hu Feng campaign, a large segment of China's intellectuals did not respond to such entreaties; not only writers, but thinking people in all fields were intimidated and avoided work, innovation, and research. Confronted with a passive intellectual community and in urgent need of its services, the Party in 1956 granted intellectuals a degree of intellectual freedom in the academic

36 Robert Guillain, *Six hundred million Chinese*, 176.
37 *KMJP*, 3 December 1955, in *SCMP*, 1190 (16 December 1955), 5.

realm in order to win their cooperation in economic development. The Party's relaxation toward the intellectuals also reflected a general policy of relaxation in the economy as it allowed free markets in the countryside and paid more attention to light industry which had been neglected in favor of heavy industry.

During 14–20 January 1956, the CCP's central committee held a conference on the problems of intellectuals at which Premier Chou En-lai proposed certain reforms in order to arouse their enthusiasm. They were to be given more authority; their views were to be respected; and their professional research, valued. Moreover, they should be rewarded with greater monetary incentives, improved work conditions, and a more rational system of promotion. Mao endorsed Chou's views in his remarks at the end of the conference, and then took the dialogue with the intellectuals a stage farther. In a speech on 2 May 1956 he announced his famous slogan "Let a hundred flowers bloom, let a hundred schools contend," by which the relaxation came to be known. But since the speech was not published, Lu Ting-i's subsequent explanation of 26 May 1956 set the tone for the campaign. Lu called for another golden age of intellectual development like that of the Hundred Schools of thought of the late Chou era (722–221 B.C.). Lu's description of the golden age evoked the May Fourth era. "Unless independent thinking and free discussion are encouraged, academic life stagnates and conversely when they are encouraged, academic life speeds up."[38] He offered intellectuals the freedom to criticize, express, maintain, and reserve their own opinions on questions in the arts, literature, and science, areas of endeavor that he said should not be equated with politics. Debate was still not permitted in the political arena, but it was encouraged in the intellectual arena, where intellectuals were to have more leeway in choosing their subject matter and methodology.

While one aspect of the Hundred Flowers was to grant intellectuals a degree of freedom in order to gain their cooperation and improve their skills, another aspect was to allow them to criticize officials in order to improve the bureaucracy and increase its efficiency. This was a return to Mao's Yenan approach of reforming the bureaucracy and a reflection of his concern with bureaucratic privilege. It also paralleled the thaw in the Soviet Union after Stalin's death and speci-

38 Hualing Nieh, 1.20. Chou's 14 January speech is translated in *Communist China, 1955–1959*, 128–44; Mao's 20 January speech is translated in *Chinese law and government*, 11 (4), 71–81. Mao's Hundred Flowers speech has still not been published.

fically the criticism of dogmatism and oppressive controls following Khrushchev's secret speech denouncing Stalin at the Soviet Communist Party's Twentieth Congress in February 1956. Despite these different aspects of the Hundred Flowers, the relaxation for intellectuals and criticism of the bureaucracy went hand-in-hand, since the criticism would not have been possible without some leeway for free expression.

With Mao, Chou, and Lu Ting-i's encouragement, scientists and engineers began to question the competence of Party cadres to direct science and technology. They called for less interference by unskilled cadres, less time at political meetings, less Soviet academic dominance, and more access to Western publications. Various academic disciplines initiated significant debates; in genetics, a debate on Lysenkoism; in history, on periodization; in philosophy, on the role of Marxism-Leninism. A number of Western-oriented economists questioned the relevance of Marxist economic theories to China. They stated that classical Marxist writings could explain the happenings of a hundred years ago, but were not applicable to current economic development.[39] A number of social scientists argued the need for birth control in opposition to Marxist-Leninist doctrine that increased production can take care of increased population.

However, the May Fourth writers who had been the most outspoken in the past were more hesitant, most likely because of the fear of being trapped in one of the shifts in Party policy that had plagued writers more than any other intellectuals. With a few exceptions, such as Ai Ch'ing, the older, established writers in particular were conspicuous by their silence. However, when the writers did start speaking out by mid-1956, what they had to say hit more directly at the Party's political policies than the discussions of any other intellectual group. Among the most incisive were younger writers who had received most of their education under the Party and who were very much influenced by the intellectual ferment in the Soviet Union.

The Soviet influence evoked two contradictory trends. Some intellectuals, particularly those in the sciences and social sciences, criticized the domination in China of the Soviet academic approach and Soviet experts, but some of the writers patterned themselves after the more audacious Soviet thaw writers who forthrightly criticized the bureaucracy and its dogmatism. They did not quote from the

39 Ch'en Chen-han, Hsu Yueh-t'an, Lo Chih-chieh, Ku Ch'un-fan, Wu Pao-san, Ning Chia-feng, "Some of our views on current work in the science of economics," Appendix to *Ching-chi yen-chiu* (Economic research), 5 (1957), 123–33.

radical Soviet writers of the time such as Yevtushenko and Voz-
nesensky, but the more mainstream Simonov, Ehrenburg, and
Sholokhov. They used the Soviet criticism of socialist realism in order
to point out that socialist realist works bore little resemblance to
Chinese reality. Also, like their Yenan predecessors and Soviet
counterparts, their belief in Marxism-Leninism inspired them to
point out where the Party had deviated from the humanitarian ideals
they believed were embodied in their ideology.

In both China and the Soviet Union, criticism was presented in
official journals. The editors of literary journals played a pivotal role
in criticism of the bureaucracy and exposure of the Party's coverup of
real problems. There were comparable figures in China to Alexander
Tvardovsky, editor of the journal *Novy Mir*, who published such
works as Dudintsev's *Not by Bread Alone* and later Solzhenitsyn's
One Day in the Life of Ivan Denisovich. Ch'in Chao-yang, a protégé
of Chou Yang since Yenan days, editor of *People's Literature*, and
Huang Ch'iu-yun, an old leftist writer and Party member, editor of
Wen-i hsueh-hsi (Literary studies), the literary organ of the Communist Youth League, turned their journals into a major critical force
in the Hundred Flowers period. Like Tvardovsky, they were con-
scientious Party members and sought to express themselves within
the limits of the system. The process by which a work became
acceptable for publication is obscure, involving intricate negotiations
with the Propaganda Department. Nevertheless, in periods of relative
relaxation, individual editors were evidently given more responsibility in running their journals. These two editors solicited, revised,
edited, and published works that were to affect the course of the
Hundred Flowers movement.

Ch'in Chao-yang's *People's Literature* published stories based on a
Soviet prototype that depicted idealistic, resourceful young people,
committed to Communist ideals, who battled apathetic, inefficient,
cautious bureaucrats in order to improve the well-being of society.
Ch'in's views on literature were set forth in an article, "Realism — the
broad road," in which he insisted on an independent role for the
writer quite different from Mao's view in his Yenan talks. The writer
could not be in the service of every shift in political line and could not
be a tool of certain concepts. Great writers like Lu Hsun and Gorky
did not interpret policy regulations and mechanically fulfill a political
responsibility. "To present things which are not understood and not
observed, this is an important method which expresses the writer's
independent creativity and is a capability that every realist should

search for."[40] Ch'in pleaded with Chinese writers to look to their own literary past for inspiration: "How many masters of realism have emerged in our history! They all ... broke through outdated rules and clichés. Let us follow their example."[41]

Chi'n introduced several "masters of realism" in the pages of *People's Literature*. One of them, Liu Pin-yen, a writer and journalist, born in 1925 and a Party member since 1944, patterned his stories specifically on those of the Soviet writer V. B. Ovechkin, a writer of documentaries whom he had interviewed for *Literary Gazette* and had spent time with. He admired Ovechkin for facing conflicts squarely, particularly conflicts perpetrated by the bureaucracy. "Ovechkin is pitiless in his attacks against the bureaucracy in his documentaries and short stories."[42] Liu described the purpose of his own work thus: "Even if we refuse to recognize the contradictions in our society, they are still there. But when a contradiction is recognized, it becomes possible to resolve it."[43] His stories depict the conflict between bureaucratic mismanagement and Communist ideals.

The first story of this nature written in the Hundred Flowers period was "At the building site of the bridge," published in *People's Literature* in April 1956 with an editorial comment by its editor, Ch'in Chao-yang: "We have waited a very long time for such pointed criticism and satirical documentaries to appear."[44] The story describes the clash between Brigadier Lo, who is more interested in "not making mistakes" than in doing the right thing, and Engineer Tseng, who has expertise and enthusiasm and wants to double production and save materials. In this story, Liu Pin-yen lauds the Soviet willingness to reform in contrast to the unwillingness of Chinese officials to reform. In response to workers' criticism, Brigadier Lo replies: "China has Chinese characteristics. As an example, in the Soviet Union you can criticize the leadership, but in China this does not work.... If we want to criticize, this must be approved by the administration."[45]

---

40 Ho Chih (Ch'in Chao-yang), "Hsien-shih chu-i – kuang-k'uo tao-lu" (Realism – the broad road), *Jen-min wen-hsueh*, 9 (1956), 2, 8.
41 Ibid., 13.
42 *Wen-i pao*, April 1956, translated in Rudolf Wagner, "The cog and the scout: Functional concepts of literature in socialist political culture," in Wolfgang Kubin and Rudolf Wagner, eds., *Essays in modern Chinese literature and literary criticism*, 352.
43 Liu Pin-yen, "Presence of feeling in the absence of feeling," *Wen-i hsueh-hsi*, 3 (1957), in Hualing Nieh, 2.540.
44 Kubin and Wagner, *Essays*, 357.
45 Ibid., 348. *Jen-min wen-hsueh*, 4 (1956), 8.

Liu's next story, "Internal information of our newspaper," appeared in *People's Literature* in June 1956 and was edited and in part rewritten by Ch'in. It describes the press in terms similar to that of the censors of old. Just as the Manchu emperor K'ang-hsi described the censors as his "ears and eyes," so did Liu describe writers and journalists as the "ears and eyes" of the Party leadership. But at present, Liu complained, critical articles written by journalists and complaints written to the paper go into "internal information" because they are too critical to be published. The heroine of the story, Huang Chia-ying, a young journalist and Communist Youth League member, investigates and exposes the indifference and incompetence of the bureaucracy in order to improve its functioning, but her efforts end in frustration. Although she wins the support of some members of the staff, the newspaper continues to publish only what the Party bureaucracy approves.

The 22-year-old writer and Party member Wang Meng, in "Young newcomer in the Organization Department" (September 1956), depicts another idealist in conflict with bureaucratic rigidity. Ch'in also edited this story, highlighting its antibureaucratic orientation and playing down its original view that the leadership would be able to overcome the bureaucracy. Wang too was directly influenced by Soviet literature. In fact, his hero, Lin Ch'en, carries with him a work of Galina Nikolayeva's, "The director of the machine tractor station and the chief agronomist," with the aim of emulating its heroine, Nastasia, who struggles against bureaucratic inertia and procrastination in order to increase production.

Lin Ch'en, like Nastasia and Liu Pin-yen's heroine Huang Chia-ying, believed that officials should exemplify Party ideals. But when he is sent to investigate Party recruitment in a factory, Lin finds arrogant, lazy, incompetent managers and frustrated workers who want to increase production. He tries to take action against the managers and has the workers and basic-level cadres write complaints to the *Peking Evening News*. Both he and Liu's heroine had a Western view of the press as a relatively independent organ which can bring pressure on the leadership to reform. However, while middle-level cadres are punished, the higher-level officials remain in their jobs. Like Liu's heroes and those of his Soviet counterparts, Wang Meng's hero is an educated, idealistic youth whose efforts to realize his ideals and carry out Party policies are thwarted in practice. These stories implied that the Party bureaucracy had acquired so much power that even the most idealistic and courageous critics could make little dent.

The stories of these young writers received an immediate and enthusiastic response. They also evoked controversy, particularly within the Party bureaucracy, which regarded the relaxation as a threat to political and ideological unity. As a *People's Daily* editorial of 9 October 1956 explained: "Some are afraid argument and debate will cause disunity in inner-Party thinking."[46] Even more important, Party cadres considered the criticism a challenge to their own entrenched positions in the ruling system. The demand of intellectuals like the fictional Huang Chia-ying and Lin Ch'en for a more independent voice in affairs by virtue of their abilities clashed with the resolve of the Party cadres to defend their positions based on political reliability. *Kuang-ming Daily* of 17 April 1956 observed that the preferential treatment of intellectuals in the Hundred Flowers had made cadres "afraid that it would lead to the emergence of a privileged class with an undesirable sense of superiority."[47]

Cadres' resistance to the Hundred Flowers was expressed publicly early in 1957 by the deputy director of the Propaganda Department of the People's Liberation Army, Ch'en Ch'i-t'ung, along with three colleagues, in an article opposing the Hundred Flowers in literature in the *People's Daily*. While the pressure may have also come from the army, the fact that the criticism was published in the Party's official mouthpiece suggests that it had the support of some members of the top leadership. The article seemed aimed at Ch'in Chao-yang and the writers around him. Ch'en and his colleagues asserted that "the number of essays describing socialism have become less and less and the number of satiric pieces which voice dissatisfaction and disappointment is increasing."[48]

Subsequently in the early months of 1957 the Hundred Flowers movement was in suspension as criticism, which had been almost exclusively against dogmatism and bureaucratism, turned against liberalism and revisionism. Wang Meng's story became the focus of the effort to reverse the relaxation in literature and subsequently in the intellectual sphere in general. The debate over the story was carried in the pages of *Literary Studies*.

Although most of the articles in *Literary Studies* were condemnatory, calling the story an attack on the leadership cadres, a sizable

---

46 "Don't be afraid of opposing views," *JMJP* editorial, 9 October 1956, in *SCMP*, 1397 (25 October 1956), 5.

47 "Positively better the working and living conditions for teachers in institutions of higher education," *KMJP* editorial, 17 April 1956, in *SCMP*, 1279 (28 May 1956), 3–4.

48 Ch'en Ch'i-t'ung and others, "Some of our views on current literary and art work," *JMJP*, 7 January 1957, in *SCMP*, 1507 (9 April 1957), 18–19.

number vehemently defended Wang Meng and further criticized the bureaucracy and even Party policy. Its editor, Huang Ch'iu-yun, expressed some of the boldest criticism. In an article, "We must not close our eyes to the hardships among the people," published in *People's Literature* and edited by Ch'in, he described the reality of present-day China as quite different from the Communist society he had envisioned: "No one can deny that in our country at present there are still floods and droughts, still famine and unemployment, still infectious disease and the oppression of the bureaucracy plus other unpleasant and unjustifiable phenomena." He called on his fellow writers to expose the discrepancy between the ideal and the reality: "A writer in possession of an upright conscience and a clear head ought not to shut his eyes complacently and remain silent in the face of real life and the sufferings of the people. If a writer does not have the courage to reveal the dark diseases of society, does not have the courage to participate positively in solving the crucial problems of people's lives, and does not have the courage to attack all the deformed, sick, black things, then can he be called a writer?"[49]

In the early months of 1957 Huang Ch'iu-yun published articles by people who lived up to his definition of a writer. Prominent among them was the 22-year-old short-story writer and Party member Liu Shao-t'ang. Liu praised Wang Meng's story because it was "a stimulus to those who want to change all that is wrong and undesirable in our society. It hurts . . . those who regard life with unseeing eyes . . . and who perhaps with good intentions, pretend that all is well."[50] Liu asserted that the Party did not want lies to be told. "Those who conceal the truth of life or who do no more than offer superficial criticism of life . . . are deceiving themselves and others."[51] The purpose of exposing the ills of society was to remedy them. As stated in another article in *Literary Studies*: "An author should not shun mistakes, shortcomings, or weaknesses of Party members and cadres . . . not only because these things exist but because we want to correct them."[52] Despite such protest against the suspension of the

---

49 Huang Ch'iu-yun, "Pu yao tsai jen-min ti chi-k'u mien-ch'ien pi-shang yen-ching" (We must not close our eyes to the hardships among the people), *Jen-min wen-hsueh*, 9 (1956), 58.
50 Liu Shao-t'ang and Ts'ung Wei-hsi, "Hsieh chen-shih – she-hui chu-i hsien-shih chu-i ti sheng-ming ho-hsin" (Write the truth – the living core of socialist realism), *Wen-i hsueh-hsi*, 1 (1957), 17.
51 Ibid., 18.
52 Shao Yen-hsiang, "Curing sickness with bitter medicine," *Wen-i hsueh-hsi*, 1 (1957), 8.

Hundred Flowers, the voices of the intellectuals once again became muted. Huang described the literary realm at this time as overhung with a "frightening atmosphere."[53]

The second phase, April–June 1957

Confusion over Party policy toward intellectuals in early 1957 was suddenly clarified on 27 February 1957 with Mao's speech "On the correct handling of contradictions among the people" in which he presented his theory that nonantagonistic contradictions between leaders and led could exist in a Communist society. These contradictions were to be brought out into the open and resolved by "democratic methods" of discussion, criticism, reasoning, and education. Mao believed that indoctrination had made the intellectuals sufficiently loyal so that the Party could trust them to voice criticism aimed at improving rather than opposing the Party. Those outside the Party, particularly those "democratic" parties which were made up of intellectuals, were called upon to criticize and present differing views in order to prevent the bureaucracy from becoming rigid, unresponsive, and alienated. This was exactly what the young writers had been doing in the first phase of the Hundred Flowers, but now Mao implicitly gave their criticisms his imprimatur.

Mao went even farther than Soviet leaders at this time in encouraging discussion of political issues. His renewed summons to intellectuals to express criticism was in reaction to some Party officials who sought to limit the Hundred Flowers and in response to the Polish and Hungarian uprisings of 1956, which Mao attributed to the isolation of the Hungarian and Polish Communist Parties from the masses and to the repression of intellectuals. In another effort to reassure the intellectuals, Mao in a speech to the Propaganda Department on 12 March 1957 again called on "all people to express their opinions freely, so that they dare to speak, dare to criticize, and dare to debate."[54] Evidence that the Party bureaucracy was still reluctant to go along wholeheartedly with a wide-open campaign can be seen in the fact that the ideas contained in Mao's speeches of February and March 1957 were not immediately publicized in the official Party paper, the People's Daily.

---

53 Huang Ch'iu-yun, "Tz'u tsai na-li?" (Where is the thorn?), Wen-i hsueh-hsi, 6 (1957), 8.
54 Roderick MacFarquhar, The origins of the Cultural Revolution, 1, 188.

Under the circumstances, it is not surprising that intellectuals were slow to respond. Chang Po-chün, a leader of the China Democratic League and Minister of Communications, said, "Intellectuals are still groping for their way and speculate whether the policy is sincere or a gesture, whether it is an end or a means."[55] But as the nationwide campaign to rectify Party cadres from the local to the top levels got under way at the beginning of May (see Chapter 2), and as Chou Yang, an ardent implementer of Mao's policies since Yenan, gave the Hundred Flowers his full endorsement, criticism grew and spread. The non-Communist intellectuals, including such leaders of the Democratic League as Chang Po-chün and Lo Lung-chi, the minister of the timber industry, gave vent to bitterness stored up for six years. Criticism of specific bureaucratic practices expanded soon to criticism of the Party itself. Some maintained that it was not only the bureaucratic methods of the cadres but the privileged position of the Party itself that produced the contradictions between leaders and led. There were demands that the "democratic" parties be allowed independence from the CCP.

The editor-in-chief of the intellectuals' newspaper, *Kuang-ming Daily*, Ch'u An-p'ing, sent correspondents to large cities to organize forums where non-Party intellectuals expressed their views. Ch'u gave these forums full coverage in the *Kuang-ming Daily*, which emerged as a powerful force in demands for liberal political and cultural reforms. Ch'u An-p'ing's charge that the Party sought "to bring about the monolithic structure of a one-family empire"[56] became the battle cry of students and intellectuals who condemned the identification of Party and state and pronounced as a sham the coalition government that the Party had with the "democratic" parties. They demanded institutional changes in which decisions would be made according to legally established procedures and in which other parties would have a voice. While some invoked Western precedents, others invoked traditional ones. Lo Lung-chi had earlier asked that scholars be given a role in government like the literati of old: "During several thousand years of China's history, scholars have had some knowledge of the art of leadership."[57] As he had urged the

55 "Many scientists think the line of letting all flowers bloom should be further implemented," NCNA, 21 April 1957, in *SCMP*, 1529 (14 May 1957), 12.
56 "Refutation of the preposterous idea of 'Party Empire'," *Hsin chien-she* (New construction), 1 (January 1958), in *ECMM*, 123.3.
57 Lo Lung-chi, "Bind the non-Party intellectuals closer with the party," *JMJP*, 23 March 1957, in *CB*, 444 (3 April 1957), 17.

Kuomintang to allow intellectuals to participate in politics, he now called upon the Party to listen to intellectuals.

A number of intellectuals working in history and the social sciences as well as those in the sciences even questioned the relevance of the thought of Mao to academia. One historian said of Mao that he "does not have time to decide these problems for us. . . . Academic problems should be solved by the scholastic world. . . . The natural sciences are like this, the social sciences also should be like this."[58] Liu Shao-t'ang, the defender of Wang Meng, rejected Mao's Yenan talks as no longer applicable to China's intellectual life. He acknowledged that in the guerrilla days it was necessary to popularize and politicize literature, but since then people's lives had changed tremendously: "Works now created to serve politics and lacking a high level of artistic excellence can no longer fulfill the needs of the people." In fact, he insisted, they had a stultifying effect. "To insist on the same old theories and thought and the same old manner of leadership is a regressive rather than a progressive act."[59]

By mid-May 1957, these criticisms expressed by the intellectuals in the press and at forums were taken up by students at Peking University. They put up wall posters criticizing officials and the politicization of academic work. Their posters appeared on what became known as Democracy Wall, and the place where they gathered was known as Democracy Square. Peking University students went to other campuses to incite students there. The intellectuals' newspapers, *Kuang-ming Daily* and *Wen-hui pao* in Shanghai, reported on these happenings, thus encouraging emulation. A myriad of unofficial journals and pamphlets put out by university students revealed the lingering influence of Western ideas introduced in the May Fourth era. Though most called for little more than greater independence from Party interference in professional work, some demanded a system of laws that would protect their freedom to speak and criticize. A few went so far as to condemn the Party's monopoly of power and suggested its dissolution.

The student activists saw themselves in the tradition of the May Fourth movement. They were also influenced by Soviet de-Stalinization, Yugoslav reforms, and the Petöfi Circle (named after

58 "Kao-chi chih-shih fen-tzu tso-t'an Ma-lieh chu-i li-lun hsueh-hsi" (Higher intellectuals discuss the study of Marxist-Leninist theory), *Hsueh-hsi* (Study), 11 (1957), 6.
59 Liu Shao-t'ang, "Some thoughts on literary problems today," *Wen-i hsueh-hsi*, 5 (1957) in Hualing Nieh, 2.65.

the great nineteenth-century Hungarian poet), which was a debating club of a youth federation that participated in the Hungarian uprising. Moreover, they believed they were carrying out Mao's injunction to battle the bureaucracy in order to improve the Party and socialism. Of even more direct influence were the articles, and particularly the stories, of Liu Pin-yen and Wang Meng of the first phase of the Hundred Flowers. They stimulated critical thinking about the system as a whole and projected role models of independent youth questioning and challenging the status quo.

One of the most outspoken student leaders, Lin Hsi-ling of People's University, saw herself as Huang Chia-ying, the heroine of Liu Pin-yen's "Internal information of our newspaper," who supported the workers against the authorities. Lin led the movement to reopen the case of writers who had been victims of the Party's campaigns. Hu Feng became a cause célèbre. Lin and her associates argued that he had not attempted to overthrow the government as the Party claimed, but had presaged the Hundred Flowers. A wall newspaper at Tsing-hua University summoned students to fight for justice for Hu Feng in the way that French liberals had fought for Dreyfus. Lin Hsi-ling and her associates demanded a trial for Hu Feng in open court according to legal procedures, and she declared at student gatherings that history would judge Hu Feng to be one of the heroes of the age. Thus, despite the Party's unremitting campaign against Hu Feng, his example had inspired some educated youth.

The Hundred Flowers movement demonstrated that despite years of indoctrination, for some dating back to the early 1940s, an important segment of the Party and non-Party intellectuals had not abandoned the Western liberal ideas they had absorbed in earlier decades. Even more significant, young intellectuals and students, brought up by the regime, had also been influenced by Western ideas. Whether it be via Soviet channels or through the works of their predecessors, they continued the traditions of the May Fourth era.

THE ANTI-RIGHTIST CAMPAIGN

The Hundred Flowers movement had developed a momentum of its own that went far beyond the Party's intent. The Party had initiated and established the framework within which, at least in the beginning, intellectuals were to express themselves. But although the Party limited the scope and laid down the terms in which the criticism was to be expressed, it could not fully control the response. Criticism of the bureaucracy went beyond criticism of individual officials to criticism of the system itself. It released more pent-up dissatisfaction and bitterness than the Party had anticipated. The spread of the criticism, the coalescence of independent groups, and the demonstrations of students against Party authority in particular provoked the Party to stop the campaign and, on 8 June, launch a counterattack against its participants, who were labeled "rightists." The abrupt reversal in policy was also due to continuing economic difficulties that the regime attributed largely to the harmful effect of the intellectuals' criticisms, which had undermined the single-minded zeal required for economic development. The Party sought to channel discontent onto the intellectuals and away from the regime.

In mid-1957, regimes in all Communist countries tightened their controls, but the swing of the pendulum in China was sharper than elsewhere, an indication of the seriousness with which the leadership regarded the Hundred Flowers protest. The reaction may also have been greater because, having expected the intellectuals to be fully indoctrinated, Mao was disillusioned to find so much criticism of the Party. The Anti-Rightist Campaign marks Mao's abandonment of the intellectuals as the key to economic development and his increasing concern that educated youth, the next generation of leaders, had insufficient revolutionary consciousness.

Since the criticisms of the Hundred Flowers had transgressed the limits set by the Party, the Anti-Rightist Campaign followed the pattern of earlier thought reform campaigns, but it was conducted with much more thoroughness, and denounced many more people. Sweeping attacks were directed against those who had been most outspoken. A few important targets, representative of certain groups, were singled out as instigators. Their criticisms were interpreted as political subversion and they were subjected to unrelenting condemnation until at last they confessed. At first the Party pointed to the "democratic" leaders, Chang Po-chün and Lo Lung-chi, and the editor of *Kuang-ming Daily*, Ch'u An-p'ing, as the leaders of what it termed an anti-Communist plot. As in previous campaigns, their colleagues in the "democratic" parties denounced them. Although some intellectuals were able to remain silent in the Hu Feng campaign, virtually all intellectuals were forced to participate in the Anti-Rightist Campaign. Some participated in order to save themselves or to rise in the official hierarchy; others participated because there was no other choice. Once again, the "democratic" parties reverted to their passive role.

In addition to the leaders of the student activists, such as Lin Hsi-ling, the writer Liu Shao-t'ang was singled out as the most dangerous of the young rightists. Wang Meng was treated relatively leniently, at least in print. In fact, Wang was barely mentioned, perhaps because Mao in his 27 February speech ridiculed the attacks on his story. In an effort to reestablish the tighter control over journals and newspapers that had been loosened in the Hundred Flowers, Ch'in Chao-yang, editor of *People's Literature*, and Liu Pin-yen, whose "Internal information of our newspaper" demanded independence for journalists, were prime targets. Initially both men insisted that they had only been carrying out the Party's policy. As Liu described his critics, the cultural leaders were like "'chameleons' who in spring allowed the youth to oppose the bureaucracy and then in autumn called them anti-bureaucratic."[60]

Although the most outspoken participants in the Hundred Flowers were attacked, they were not the main focus of the Anti-Rightist Campaign. Once again the older left-wing writers, particularly Ting Ling and Feng Hsueh-feng, received the most attention. Most likely they were chosen because of their rivalry with Chou Yang. Despite criticism of Chou in the demonstrations and posters, he emerged in the Anti-Rightist Campaign as a virtual cultural czar and was finally able to eliminate his former foes. Besides factional reasons, there was evidence that Ting Ling still had considerable influence among younger writers, many of whom considered her their mentor. Shao Ch'üan-lin, one of Chou's major spokesmen in the Anti-Rightist Campaign, described Ting Ling's role: "Influenced by Ting Ling and her kind, a number of youth have taken the wrong path. They have refused Party leadership and supervision and have opposed the power of the Party group."[61] All those associated with Ting Ling in Yenan – Ai Ch'ing, Hsiao Chün, Lo Feng – were subjected to renewed attacks. Their Yenan *tsa-wen* were reprinted to be criticized once again, particularly by youth who had supposedly been deluded by Ting Ling and her associates.

Another of Chou's rivals, Feng Hsueh-feng, had said little during the Hundred Flowers, but was charged with collaborating with

60 *China Youth News*, "Liu Pin-yen exposed as a mouthpiece in the party for bourgeois rightists," in *JMJP*, 20 July 1957, in *SCMP*, 1583 (2 August 1957), 16.
61 Shao Ch'üan-lin, "Tou-cheng pi-hsu keng shen-ju" (The struggle must penetrate more deeply), *Wen-i pao*, 25 (1957), 5.

younger journalists to establish a magazine that would present alternative views. The fact that he and some associates planned to establish an independent magazine was not unusual in the Hundred Flowers period, but the reason that he and Ting Ling were made the focus of attack was because they were long-time, well-known Party members. They were treated as a greater threat than the non-Party and younger intellectuals. A *People's Daily* editorial explained that "the longer the rightists have had membership in the Party, the higher the positions they hold, the greater their threat to the Party."[62] They could use their authority to distort Party orders and to shape public opinion. The reason Ting Ling and her associates received much more attention than the more vocal participants in the Hundred Flowers was that their position and prestige could divert loyalty from the Party.

As in past campaigns, those who denounced the victims repeatedly and vociferously were able to move up the official hierarchy, some-times into positions vacated by their victims. Since a large number of intellectuals had been outspoken and then purged, the Anti-Rightist Campaign opened up many opportunities for advancement. A typical and portentous example of this upward mobility was the case of the young literary critic Yao Wen-yuan, later to become a member of the Gang of Four. In the mid-1950s he allied himself with the cultural bureaucracy around Chou Yang and parroted their line against Hu Feng in 1955 and in favor of liberalization in the spring of 1957. He was conspicuous in the Anti-Rightist Campaign in denouncing the old left-wing writers, several of whom had been friends of his father, the writer Yao P'eng-tzu, in Shanghai in the 1930s. By the late 1950s he was becoming an important official in the Shanghai propaganda bureaucracy.

By 1958, the Anti-Rightist Campaign had gone much farther than full circle to the tight political control over intellectual endeavor established in the Hu Feng campaign. As it merged with the Great Leap Forward (GLF), then getting under way, it took on a vociferous anti-intellectual stance. To a much greater degree than in previous campaigns, political reliability took precedence over professional competence. Reversing the priorities of the Hundred Flowers, the intelligence and creativity of the masses and the collective were

62 "Handle inner-party rightists sternly," *JMJP* editorial, 11 September 1957, in *SCMP*, 1616 (24 September 1957), 3.

lauded; the knowledge and prestige of the intellectual and the individual were denigrated. Whereas peasants and workers were capable of great achievements because they approached all questions as proletarians, intellectuals were bound to fail because they were imbued with the bourgeois values of individualism, liberalism, and anarchism. Even scientists were denounced because of their "attachments to professional tasks to the neglect of politics and attachment of greater importance to talent than to character."[63] Writers were considered the most dangerous because their critical view weakened confidence in the Party. Henceforth, Chou Yang declared, literature must praise, not criticize. "We do not want to be burdened with gloom and we require that literature be the inspiration of the people."[64]

The Anti-Rightist Campaign purged many more people than in previous campaigns. It is estimated that 400,000 to 700,000 intellectuals lost their positions and were sent to the countryside and factories for labor reform. A quota of 5 percent of the people in a unit were to be designated as rightists. Even in units with few intellectuals and where no one had spoken out, the quota had to be fulfilled. Those designated were denounced by their colleagues and families and forced to make self-criticisms. The chief targets of the campaign, such as Ting Ling, were treated most severely. They were expelled from the Party, lost membership in their professional unions, and had their works banned from libraries and universities. As intellectuals were undergoing labor reform, Party cadres took over their positions in culture and education, putting the Party more firmly in control of the intellectual realm than ever before. Though the Hundred Flowers had been designed to close the gap between the Party and the intellectuals, the Anti-Rightist Campaign widened the gap still further.

The population in general appears to have gone along wholeheartedly with the suppression of the intellectuals. The idea of intellectual autonomy and dissent had little understanding and support outside intellectual circles. The charges against the intellectuals of disloyalty and of hurting the Party had persuasive appeal to most of the population, which was still committed to the Party's and Mao's

63 *JMJP* editorial, 23 March 1958.
64 From Chou Yang's speech to the Chinese Writers Union; *Wen-i pao*, 29 November 1957, in Hualing Nieh, 1.256.

effort to transform China. The intellectuals were isolated from the population as a whole, and the state, with its power to intimidate by means of employment, campaigns, and labor reform, easily suppressed any support they might have had.

CHAPTER 6

FOREIGN RELATIONS:
FROM THE KOREAN WAR
TO THE BANDUNG LINE

On 1 October 1949 the broad united front that had supported
the Chinese revolution became the basis of the regime headed by
Mao Tse-tung. This newborn "people's democratic dictatorship" had
to tackle the urgent task of reconstructing the Chinese economy,
wrecked by foreign invasion and civil war. China was setting out
on the road to socialist transformation.

The newly established People's Republic was quickly recognized
by the Soviet Union, its East European satellites, and some Asian
nations including India. Britain followed suit early in 1950. The new
China was making a successful debut in the world.

China's top foreign policy goal was to develop good relations with
its socialist "elder brother," the Soviet Union. As early as December
1949, Chairman Mao personally led a delegation to Moscow in
pursuance of the "lean to one side" policy he had outlined that
summer. In February 1950, China and the Soviet Union signed a
treaty of friendship, alliance, and mutual assistance, as well as a
number of economic agreements. China initiated an economic development program on the Soviet model, with Soviet economic
assistance and under the banner of Sino-Soviet friendship.

However, the Chinese got less from the Soviet Union than they
had hoped. It is now known that they had long and difficult negotiations with the Kremlin leadership and that Stalin treated them rather
coldly. In this respect, the one-time myth of the monolithic unity
of Moscow and Peking certainly needs to be reexamined. In short,
while following the Soviet model had been taken by the Chinese
as a fundamental policy, there was tension between them and the
Russians from the start.

Following its foundation, moreover, the People's Republic of
China was soon faced with the outbreak of the Korean War in June
1950, and felt compelled to send "volunteers" to Korea in October in
order to halt the advance of the American-led UN forces. China was

thus back at war, and the regime launched a nationwide Resist America, Aid Korea Campaign. The Sino-American antagonism fueled by the Korean War set the pattern for the subsequent Cold War in Asia. Consequently the potential friction between China and the Soviet Union was played down by both sides.

Revolutionary China proclaimed a policy, adumbrated by Liu Shao-ch'i in 1949, of supporting and encouraging armed national liberation struggles by revolutionary forces elsewhere in Asia, including the Japanese Communist Party and Communist Parties in South and Southeast Asia. This was in step with the global strategy then followed by the Cominform. China also actively participated in the world peace movement and the international trade union organization backed by Moscow. But since the People's Republic was still young and preoccupied with the Korean War, the Chinese Communists did not venture on major diplomatic initiatives outside the framework of a somewhat simplistic revolutionary foreign policy posture.

Late in 1953, after the July truce in Korea, Peking finally set out on a full-scale economic development program. The 1st Five-Year Plan (FYP) (1953–57), based on Soviet aid and oriented toward heavy industry, was officially adopted in July 1955, but was actually in progress from 1953. China was on its way toward industrialization. Also in late 1953, "elections" were held to return delegates to the first National People's Congress (NPC), which adopted the Constitution of the People's Republic at its first session in September 1954. Its preamble laid down a "general line in the period of transition" aimed at a long-term progressive transformation of China toward socialism.

This basic policy of slow but steady economic development and social reform was reflected in Peking's diplomatic attitude. Indeed, it was during this period that an emphasis on peaceful coexistence became a feature of China's foreign policy, giving rise to a variety of new departures. In June 1954, Peking agreed to the famous Five Principles of Peaceful Coexistence in a Sino-Indian joint communiqué. In October, on the occasion of the fifth anniversary of the People's Republic, a delegation of Soviet leaders including Bulganin and Khrushchev agreed to eliminate Stalinist inequalities in Sino-Soviet relations. Along with Nehru's India and Nasser's Egypt, China was emerging as a leader of the newly independent nations of Asia and Africa. Chou En-lai, premier and foreign minister, was the principal executor of China's new policies and began to cut a large figure on the international stage.

The signing of the cease-fire agreement in Indochina in July 1954 and the success of the Bandung Conference of Asian and African Nations in April 1955, both attended by Chou, were two noteworthy developments that owed much to China's diplomacy under the rubric of the Five Principles of Peaceful Coexistence. In this mood of détente, official U.S.–Chinese ambassadorial-level talks began in Geneva in August 1955, and in June 1956, Chou En-lai's foreign policy speech to the NPC's annual session was remarkable for its reasonableness, most notably in its call for a "peaceful" liberation of Taiwan.

In the mid-1950s China's foreign policy thus followed what might be termed the Bandung Line of peaceful coexistence. China's prestige and influence rose steadily, and at one point Peking seemed to be emerging as the champion of the world's newly independent nations. Nor was there any major change in this external posture despite the more "leftist" direction in internal policies in 1955 when intellectuals came under renewed pressure in the Anti-Hu Feng Campaign and Mao personally set in motion a drastic speedup of agricultural collectivization.

With the victory of collectivization in sight by the beginning of 1956, the Chinese domestic scene became more relaxed, an appropriate background for the continuing Bandung Line. It was at this point that Stalin was criticized in Khrushchev's secret speech at the CPSU's Twentieth Congress in February 1956. The resulting demolition of the myth of Stalin followed by the revolt in Hungary in October 1956 had a considerable impact on the Chinese leaders. They issued a series of major theoretical documents, including "On the historical experience of the dictatorship of the proletariat" (April 1956), "More on the historical experience of the dictatorship of the proletariat" (December 1956), and Mao's speech "On the correct handling of contradictions among the people" (February 1957). In these, the Chinese expressed their own views as to how the evils of Stalinism should be overcome.

Moreover, as a result of the disturbances in Eastern Europe (in Poland as well as Hungary) caused by de-Stalinization, Soviet prestige was considerably reduced and China's rose concomitantly. In January 1957, Chou En-lai went specially to Eastern Europe to act as peacemaker, endeavoring to shore up Soviet leadership there.

Then came another drastic change in China's domestic policy. As part of a program to prevent Hungarian-type tensions' building up in China, Mao followed up his contradictions speech with a campaign to rectify the party's style of work and called on the intellectuals to offer criticisms, which they did in May–June 1957. But the response was far more extensive and bitter than anticipated, and on 8 June the Party suddenly counterattacked, launching the Anti-Rightist Campaign, aimed at removing "poisonous antisocialist weeds."

This was the most decisive turnaround in the political process of the People's Republic up to that time. As the struggle against the rightists grew rapidly in late 1957, Peking veered sharply away from its former policy of moderation at home and abroad. In November 1957, Chairman Mao made his second visit to the Soviet Union for the fortieth anniversary celebrations of the Bolshevik revolution. On this occasion, he laid out his thesis that "the East Wind is prevailing over the West Wind," in the light of the successful Soviet ICBM tests in August and the launching of the first Sputnik in October. He advocated a more militant foreign policy posture for the Communist bloc, even at the risk of war. Mao failed to carry his Soviet colleagues, but for its part China gradually abandoned the Bandung Line of peaceful coexistence. The Taiwan Straits crisis in the summer of 1958 and the Sino-Indian border clashes a year later were expressions of China's new stance in world affairs.

LEANING TO ONE SIDE:
MAO TSE-TUNG AND STALIN

Considering the long, delicate relationship between Mao Tse-tung and Stalin, and between the CCP and the CPSU, it is noteworthy that as early as December 1945 Mao instructed his comrades to build up a stronghold in the Northeast.[1] Of course, he had no option; this was probably the only area the CCP could hope to develop as a major new base. But conceivably, after suffering his first real blow from Stalin as a result of the Yalta Agreement, Mao may have thought that China should take precautions against possible Soviet action to detach the Northeast while he was deciding whether or not to deal with the United States. On 5 March 1949, when he was anticipating victory in the civil war with the Nationalists, Mao hinted at a conciliatory policy toward the United States. In his report to the Second plenum of the Seventh CCP Central Committee, he talked of

1 See Mao Tse-tung, "Chien-li kung-ku-ti tung-pei ken-chü-ti" (Build stable base areas in the Northeast) (28 December 1945), *MTHC* (Selected works of Mao Tse-tung), 4.277–80. Also see a signed article by Yen Chung-ch'uan in *Wen-hui-pao*, 11 May 1969.

allowing imperialist economic and cultural establishments to exist in the big cities, at least until nationwide victory had been won.[2] The Soviets began in late April to praise the forthcoming victory of the Chinese Communists. But on 15 June Mao made his conciliatory attitude toward the United States even more explicit, stating that the new Communist regime would be prepared to establish diplomatic relations with any foreign government if it severed relations with and ceased aid to Chiang Kai-shek. He added, "The Chinese people wish to have friendly cooperation with the people of all countries and to resume and expand international trade in order to develop production and promote economic prosperity."[3]

These remarks were, on one level, the common coin of new regimes, but in fact Mao's tone was extremely important. According to a report made public by the U.S. Senate Foreign Relations Committee on 21 January 1973, after the lapse of nearly a quarter of a century, in May and June 1949, the CCP had got in touch with the American ambassador to China, John Leighton Stuart, through one of his former pupils at Yenching University, Huang Hua.[4] Huang (a future foreign minister) was director of the Foreign Affairs Office of the CCP Military Control Commission, and went to see Stuart at Mao's request. Stuart was widely respected among Chinese for his vast knowledge of their country and his amiable personality, and his private teacher-pupil relationship with Huang was utilized by the CCP to explore the possibility of future negotiations with the United States, including diplomatic recognition by Washington.[5]

But on 1 July of that year, the very day on which Ambassador Stuart in Nanking received a telegram from Secretary of State Acheson instructing him to refuse to negotiate with Chinese Communist leaders, the *People's Daily* carried Mao Tse-tung's famous article "On the people's democratic dictatorship," written in commemoration of the twenty-eighth anniversary of the CCP. In this speech Mao laid

2 Mao Tse-tung, "Tsai Chung-kuo Kung-ch'an-tang ti-ch'i-chieh chung-yang wei-yuan-hui ti-erh-tz'u ch'üan-t'i hui-i-shang-ti pao-kao" (Report to the Second Plenum of the Seventh Central Committee of the Chinese Communist Party), *MTHC*, 4.1436; Mao, *SW*, 4.370.
3 Mao Tse-tung, "Tsai hsin cheng-chih hsieh-shang hui-i ch'ou-pei-hui-shang-ti chiang-hua" (Address at the preliminary meeting of the new Political Consultative Conference), *MTHC*, 4.1470; Mao, *SW*, 4.408.
4 U.S. Senate Committee on Foreign Relations, *The United States and Communist China in 1949 and 1950: The question of rapprochement and recognition.*
5 For details on this historic Stuart-Huang Hua negotiation, see Shigeru Usami, "Suchūato taishi no Pekin hōmon keikaku: ushinawareta rekishi no tenkanten" (Ambassador Stuart's plan to visit Peking: A lost turning point in history), *Kokusai mondai*, 198 (September 1976). See also Dorothy Borg and Waldo Heinrichs, ed., *Uncertain years: Chinese-American relations, 1947–1950*, 34–36, 207, 275.

down a policy of "leaning toward the Soviet Union," marking a radical shift from his earlier hints and ruling out Titoism.

Mao wrote: "'You are leaning to one side.' Exactly. The forty years' experience of Sun Yat-sen and the twenty-eight years' experience of the Communist Party have taught us to lean to one side, and *we are firmly convinced that in order to win victory and consolidate it we must lean to one side.* In the light of the experiences accumulated in these forty years and these twenty-eight years, all Chinese without exception must lean either to the side of imperialism or to the side of socialism."[6]

If, as we have seen, Mao Tse-tung was bitter about Stalin's line on China and in party-to-party relations, why did he abort the discussions with the United States initiated via the Huang-Stuart channel? Timing rules out the idea that he was reacting to Acheson's instruction. More likely, with the foundation of the People's Republic of China imminent, Mao must have felt that the new nation would badly need Soviet assistance in the massive task of economic reconstruction and development. In addition to this general consideration, however, a number of specific factors may have played a role.

First, there was a risk involved in the Chinese Communist's moving toward reconciliation with the United States at a time of cold war between Washington and Moscow. The former allies were harshly antagonistic toward each other as a result, on the one hand, of the Communist coup in Czechoslovakia and blockade of Berlin, and on the other, the American support for the Greek government against Communist insurgency and the formation of NATO. The Soviet Union was strong: China was weak. Mao may have been uneasy about Stalin's reactions, especially in view of his past attitude toward the CCP. This anxiety probably played an important role when the Chinese decided to lean to the Soviet side. Second, Mao may have felt it advisable to adopt a pro-Soviet line in order to consolidate his leadership of the Party.

The third and most important factor was probably Mao's concern about the integrity of China under his leadership. Under the Yalta Agreement and the 1945 Soviet Treaty of Friendship and Alliance with the Nationalist government, the Soviet government had recovered onetime tsarist rights in Manchuria – joint ownership and

6 Mao Tse-tung, "Lun jen-min min-chu chuan-cheng: chi-nien Chung-kuo kung-ch'an-tang erh-shih-pa chou-nien" (On the People's Democratic Dictatorship: In commemoration of the 28th anniversary of the Communist Party of China), *MTHC*, 4.1477–78; Mao, *SW*, 4.415; emphasis added.

operation of the Chinese Eastern and South Manchurian Railways (now known as the Chinese Changchun Railway), the internationalization of Dairen, and the use of Port Arthur as a naval base. If the CCP angered Stalin, this area of China might remain under Soviet domination. Such fears would have been confirmed in July 1949 when Stalin, apparently without consulting the Peking leadership, invited Kao Kang, chairman of the Communist administration in the Northeast, to Moscow and signed a trade agreement with him.[7] Mao's uneasiness about the growing intimacy between Stalin and Kao Kang may have influenced his "lean to one side" decision a great deal. He presumably hoped that his declared devotion to the Soviet Union would secure a generous response from Stalin.

Besides, at this early stage, Mao had almost certainly not freed himself from the conventional idea that the Soviet Union and its Communist Party represented the core and the leadership of a world Communist movement based on proletarian internationalism. In any case, Mao's strong criticism of the *China White Paper* published by Washington on 5 August 1949 reinforced the CCP's increasingly anti-American, pro-Soviet line.[8]

A review of the *People's Daily* in 1949 indicates that the Soviet Union was little covered in the first half of that year, whereas after Mao's pro-Soviet declaration on 1 July, coverage of the Soviet Union grew remarkably. It is clear that the CCP's important policy change was made around the time of the declaration.

After the foundation of the People's Republic on 1 October praise of Stalin in the *People's Daily* reached a climax with a publicity campaign for Stalin's seventieth birthday on December 9. Nor can this be taken as pro forma, for it was against this background that Mao Tse-tung personally led a delegation to Moscow later in the month. He presumably hoped that he would be warmly received by Stalin now that the CCP had proved itself with victory in the Chinese revolution. Significantly, when alighting at Moscow Station, Mao made a speech in which he called attention to the fact that "after the October Socialist Revolution, the Soviet Government, in compliance

---

7 For a more extended analysis of the Kao Kang affair, see above, Chapter 2; also see Mineo Nakajima, "The Kao Kang affair and Sino-Soviet relations," *Review* 44 (March 1977). For comment on the Yalta agreement and the Soviet-Nationalist treaty, see Charles B. McLane, *Soviet policy and the Chinese Communists*, 178–93. For the various texts, see A. K. Wu, *China and the Soviet Union*, 396–411.

8 Those five anti-U.S. articles written by Mao Tse-tung were all initially published as New China News Agency (NCNA) editorials, all contained in *MTHC*, 4.1487–1520; Mao, *SW*, 4.425–59.

with the policy of Lenin and Stalin, first abolished Tsarist Russia's unequal treaties with China," and said he expected much of Generalissimo Stalin's just foreign policy.[9] This was the first trip abroad Mao had ever made. On the surface, Stalin welcomed him cordially, granting him an interview on the very day he arrived in Moscow. But in reality Mao felt that the Soviet leader was even more frigid than he had been to T. V. Soong, the Chinese Nationalist foreign minister, when the latter had come to Moscow to negotiate the Friendship Treaty four and a half years earlier.[10]

In retrospect, one sign of the troubled course of the negotiations was when Mao, asked by a Tass reporter on 2 January 1950 how long he would stay in the Soviet Union, replied: "I intend to stay in the Soviet Union for several weeks. The length of my stay here will depend partly on how much time will be required to settle various matters concerning the interest of the People's Republic of China." In this interview with Tass, Mao Tse-tung referred for the first time to the ongoing Sino-Soviet negotiations, saying that the pending issues were "first of all, the current Sino-Soviet Treaty of Friendship and Alliance, Soviet loans to the People's Republic of China, trade and aid agreements between your country and ours, and other issues."[11] Mao's statement should have been noted more carefully at the time, as it allowed a glimpse of what was going on behind the scenes at the Moscow meeting.

Some years later, Mao Tse-tung recalled his Moscow negotiations and revealed that Stalin "was not willing to sign a treaty. After two months of negotiations he at last signed."[12] Clearly the widespread opinion among contemporary observers that the Sino-Soviet Treaty of Friendship, Alliance and Mutual Assistance symbolized a brotherly relationship between two socialist states, China and the Soviet Union, was only partially correct.

According to the subsequent account of the then-director of the Chinese Foreign Ministry's Soviet and East European Affairs Department, Wu Hsiu-ch'üan, Stalin suspected Mao of incipient Titoism; and the presence in the Chairman's party of non-Communist Chinese

---

9 *JMJP* (People's daily), 18 December 1949.
10 On this point, see Mineo Nakajima, *Chū-so tairitsu to gendai: sengo Ajia no saikōsatsu* (The Sino-Soviet confrontation and the present age: Reappraisal of the postwar Asia), 93–95.
11 "Mao chu-hsi ta T'a-ssu she chi-che wen" (Chairman Mao answers TASS correspondent's questions), *JMJP*, 3 January 1950.
12 Mao Tse-tung, "Tsai pa-chieh shih-chung ch'üan-hui-shang-ti chiang-hua" (Address at the Tenth Plenum of the Eighth Central Committee), 24 September 1962, *Wan-sui* (Long live Mao Tse-tung Thought) (1969), 432.

symbolizing the domestic unified front prompted fears that China would pursue pro-Western policies. It was only after Mao had been in Moscow a little while that there was any talk of a friendship treaty. At this point, Mao felt able to summon Premier Chou En-lai, Wu Hsiu-ch'üan, and other officials to conduct the actual negotiations. They arrived on 20 January.

A draft of the treaty was prepared by the Russians, and though the Chinese did not or could not change any of the principles, they did manage considerably to modify the wording. Chou ordered his staff to "study, deliberate and revise it item by item, sentence by sentence, and word by word." According to Wu, the Chinese premier and foreign minister "wanted to make sure there was not any catch in the draft which might later put us at a disadvantage." One article originally read: "In the event that one of the contracting parties was invaded by a third state, the other contracting party shall render assistance." To make it stronger, Chou insisted on adding at the end the words "by all means at its disposal."[13]

Mao witnessed the signing of the Sino-Soviet Treaty of Friendship, Alliance and Mutual Assistance by Foreign Ministers Chou En-lai and Andrei Vishinsky on 14 February and only then left for Peking, arriving there on 4 March. The Chinese leader had been willing to absent himself from the newborn People's Republic for more than two and a half months, so important did he consider his mission.

The treaty was basically a military pact designed to display the monolithic unity of China and the Soviet Union against any resurgence of Japanese militarism. Article 1 stated:

Both High Contracting Parties undertake jointly to take all the necessary measures at their disposal for the purpose of preventing repetition of aggression and violation of peace on the part of Japan, directly or indirectly, in acts of aggression. In the event of one of the High Contracting Parties being attacked by Japan or states allied with it, and thus involved in a state of war, the other High Contracting Party will immediately render military and other assistance with all the means at its disposal.[14]

This was taken in the West as evidence that China and the Soviet

---

13 For Wu's account, see his *Tsai Wai-chiao pu pa-nien ti ching-li* (Eight years' experience in the Foreign Ministry), 1–24. For a partial English version, see *Beijing Review*, 47 (1983), 16–21, 30. In fact, Wu misremembers the article, presumably deliberately, for there is no such reference to a "third state," only a far more forthright reference to Japan and its allies – i.e., the United States. But by the time Wu's memoirs were published, Japan and the United States were China's friends.

14 "Chung-hua jen-min kung-ho-kuo tui-wai kuan-hsi wen-chien-chi" (Collected foreign relations documents of the People's Republic of China), 1.75, translated in Grant Rhode and Reid Whitlock, *Treaties of the People's Republic of China*, 15b.

Union regarded Japan and, by extension, its patron, the United States, as hypothetical enemies. The treaty thus provided a theoretical justification for the 1951 San Francisco peace treaty between Japan and the Western allies as well as the U.S.–Japan Security Treaty signed shortly afterward.

As a result of the Moscow negotiations, China succeeded in obtaining concessions from the Soviet Union on some of the issues between them and was now better off in comparison with its position under the 1945 treaty between the Nationalist government and the Soviet Union. The Russians agreed to transfer the Chinese Changchun Railway gratis to China by the end of 1952, to withdraw Soviet forces from Port Arthur and transfer facilities there to China following the conclusion of peace with Japan and no later than the end of 1952 (with the proviso that the facilities should be used jointly by the two countries in the event of war), and to transfer gratis the property acquired by Soviet economic agencies in Peking.

On the other hand, Mao, like Chiang Kai-shek before him, had to agree to recognize the independence of "Outer" Mongolia, once Chinese (Ch'ing dynasty) territory; also to set up Sino-Soviet joint stock companies for the mining of oil and nonferrous metals in Sinkiang. These companies were patterned on those imposed by the Russians in Eastern Europe, which enabled the resources of the satellite countries to be exploited for largely Soviet advantage. This Stalin formula was later severely criticized by Khrushchev:

At one point Stalin concluded a treaty with China for the joint exploitation of mineral resources in Sinkiang. The treaty was a mistake on Stalin's part. I would even say it was an insult to the Chinese people. For centuries the French, English and Americans had been exploiting China, and now the Soviet Union was moving in. This exploitation was a bad thing, but not unprecedented: Stalin had set up similar "joint" companies in Poland, Germany, Bulgaria, Czechoslovakia, and Rumania. Later we liquidated all these companies.[15]

Thus, the 1949–50 Sino-Soviet summit must have given Mao Tse-tung only partial satisfaction. One can imagine how he felt when he was personally exposed to Stalin's attitudes, since he had based his foreign policy on leaning to the side of the Soviet Union and had praised Stalin a great deal. As early as 1957, Mao was already exposing to Party cadres what he had disliked about the Sino-Soviet summit. He told a meeting of provincial and municipal Party com-

15 Strobe Talbott, tr. and ed., *Khrushchev remembers*, 463. For a brief discussion of the imposition of the joint company system in Eastern Europe, see Zbigniew Brzezinski, *The Soviet bloc: Unity and conflict*, 125.

mittee secretaries: "Our opinions differed from Stalin's. We wanted to sign a Sino-Soviet Treaty but he wouldn't. We wanted the Chinese Changchun Railway but he wouldn't return it. However, one can pull the meat out of the tiger's mouth after all."[16] In March 1958, he stated at the Chengtu Conference:

In 1950, I argued with Stalin in Moscow for two months. On the questions of the Treaty of Mutual Assistance, the Chinese Eastern Changchun Railway, the joint-stock companies and the border we adopted two attitudes: one was to argue when the other side made proposals we did not agree with, and the other was to accept their proposal if they absolutely insisted. This was out of consideration for the interest of socialism. Then there were the two "colonies," that is, the North-East and Sinkiang, where people of any third country were not allowed to reside. Now this has been rescinded.[17]

Evidently Mao returned unhappy from the Moscow summit, and was especially angry about the establishment of the joint stock companies in Sinkiang. Long before Khrushchev's memoirs were smuggled out of the Soviet Union, Soviet leaders effectively criticized this Stalinist system, as may be seen in the speech of Anastas Mikoyan at the CPSU's Twentieth Congress in February 1956.[18]

Moreover, although Mao apparently worked very hard in Moscow to obtain Soviet aid, the total amount promised to the Chinese was only an interest-bearing credit of 300 million U.S. dollars over five years. This was less even than the 450 million U.S. dollars credit Poland had obtained from the Soviet Union a year before. Worse still, the devaluation of the ruble announced on 28 February 1950 further reduced the value of the credit by about a quarter, while the unfair ruble-yuan parity insisted upon by the Russians harmed Chinese trading interests.[19]

A month after the conclusion of the Sino-Soviet treaty, Secretary

16 Mao Tse-tung, "Sheng, shih-wei shu-chi hui-i tsung-chieh" (Summing up at a meeting of provincial and municipal committee secretaries) (January 1957), Wan-sui, 85. The long-awaited Volume 5 of MTHC was published in China in April 1977. Compiled by the CCP Central Committee's Editing and Publishing Committee for the Works of Chairman Mao Tse-tung, this fifth volume contains papers, speeches, and other works written by Mao between 21 September 1949 and 18 November 1957. But "Mao chu-hsi ta T'a-ssu she chi-che wen" (Chairman Mao answers TASS correspondent's questions) and other statements quoted in this chapter concerning Sino-Soviet relations and dealings with Stalin are heavily censored. A version of "Sheng, shih-wei shu-chi hui-i tsung-chieh" is found in volume 5 (pp. 330–62), but it does not contain Mao's reference to his argument with Stalin over the Sino-Soviet treaty.
17 Mao Tse-tung, "Tsai Ch'eng-tu hui-i-shang-ti chiang-hua" (Talks at the Chengtu Conference) (March 1958), ibid., 163–64, as translated in Stuart Schram (ed.), Mao Tse-tung unrehearsed,, 101.
18 "Speech by A. I. Mikoyan" (London: Soviet News, 1956), 8.
19 See Kang Chao and Feng-hwa Mah, "A study of the rouble-yuan exchange rate," CQ, 17 (January–March 1964); Wu Hsiu-ch'üan, "Sino-Soviet relations in the early 1950s," Beijing Review, 47 (1983), 20–21.

of State Acheson commented in Washington on the significance of the event. Heartily regretting this final pro-Soviet step taken by Peking, he also referred to the ruble devaluation as follows: "Thus, the Chinese people may find Soviet Russia's credit to be no more than 45 million dollars per year. They can compare this with a grant – not a loan – of 400 million dollars voted by the American Congress to China in the single year 1948."[20] As Acheson predicted, the Chinese did find out.

Lung Yun, vice-chairman of the National Defense Council, who had run Yunnan province under the Nationalist government, took advantage of the blooming of the Hundred Flowers in 1957 to state baldly: "The credit granted us by the Soviet Union has to be repaid within ten years. It is short-term, and interest-bearing. To ease its burden on our economy, I propose that its repayment term be extended to 20 or 30 years. This is what we have got for fighting for socialism."[21] At the time, Lung Yun was forced to criticize himself, but the Russians later revealed that his sentiments were general among the Chinese leadership. "In signing the Sino-Soviet Treaty of Friendship, Alliance and Mutual Assistance, the CCP leaders showed us mistrust and suspicion. Without bothering to remember that the Soviet Union itself had the difficult task of getting over the ravages of war, they complained that the credit they had got from the Soviet Union was 'only' $300 million."[22] Even in nominal terms, however, a credit of $300 million over five years was only $60 million a year, a rather insubstantial cash commitment in view of the massive propaganda extolling Sino-Soviet friendship. Sino-Soviet relations were thus soured from the very start.

THE KOREAN WAR

The Korean War was a civil war with an international background, reflecting the tragic history of the Korean people in modern times.

---

20 "Implications of the Treaty of Alliance and related agreements between the Soviet Union and Communist China: Address by the Secretary of State, March 15, 1950 [excerpt]," U.S. Department of State, *American foreign policy: Basic documents, 1950–55*, 2.2466.
21 "Lung Yun tai-piao-ti fa-yen" (Remarks by delegate Lung Yun), *Chung-hua jen-min kung-ho-kuo ti-i-chieh ch'üan-kuo jen-min tai-piao ta-hui ti-ssu-tz'u hui-i hui-k'an* (Minutes of the fourth session of the First National People's Congress of the People's Republic of China), 1403. Lung Yun also criticized the Soviet dismantling of factories in the Northeast after the war; see MacFarquhar, *The Hundred Flowers Campaign and the Chinese intellectuals*, 50.
22 O. B. Borisov and B. T. Koloskov, *Sino-Soviet relations 1945–1973: A brief history* (Translated from the Russian by Yuri Shirokov), 113. On the Soviet industrial construction projects, see note 46 below; see also the discussion in Chapter 3 of the present volume.

On the one hand, it solidified the division of the country; on the other, it dictated the international environment of postwar Asia. For this reason, it can be considered an epochal event in contemporary history.[23]

In January 1950, as the uneasy negotiations between Stalin and Mao Tse-tung were proceeding in Moscow, Washington came out with a series of important policy positions for Asia on the basis of its *China White Paper*. The Truman statement of 5 January made it clear that the United States did not intend to defend the remnant Nationalist Chinese regime on Taiwan. Secretary of State Acheson's speech at the National Press Club on 12 January stated that the American defense perimeter in Asia ran from the Aleutians through Japan and Okinawa to the Philippines, thus excluding the Republic of Korea and Taiwan from the area of vital strategic importance.

It is now known that these guidelines were issued as part of a process of rethinking America's Asian policies. Washington policy makers were responding to the "three losses": of the nuclear monopoly in August 1949, of China in October 1949, and of the prospect of Chinese Titoism after the conclusion of the Sino-Soviet Treaty in February 1950. But changes proposed in National Security Council (NSC) documents in April 1950 were far from ready for implementation. With respect to the Korean peninsula, these NSC documents saw no need for military intervention by the United States itself.[24]

What, then, was the philosophical basis underlying Washington's policy on Korea in particular and Asia in general before the Korean War? The United States had wanted to encourage Chinese "Titoism" ever since the publication of the *China White Paper* in the summer of 1949, and was even thinking of recognizing the new regime on the Chinese mainland. As a result, Washington was always careful not to provoke Peking when implementing its policy in Asia generally. The advent of the Korean War changed all this.

However much advance knowledge Mao and his senior colleagues may have had about the preparations for, and timing of, the war, they clearly did not envisage it as being of direct concern to them when hostilities broke out in the early morning of 25 June 1950. First, it

23 For a more extended analysis of the international background of the Korean War, see Mineo Nakajima, "The Sino-Soviet confrontation: Its roots in the international background of the Korean War," *The Australian Journal of Chinese Affairs*, 1 (January 1979).
24 NSC-48/1, 23 December 1949, *NSC papers*, Washington, D.C.; U.S. National Archives: NSC-48-2, 30 December 1949, ibid.: NSC-68, 14 April 1940, ibid.

should be noted that a Land Reform Law, conceived as one of the main pillars of the Chinese revolution, was promulgated in China on 30 June 1950, only five days after the Korean War began. Considering the long and assiduous preparations the Chinese Communists had been making for land reform and the tremendous importance they placed on it, one must assume they anticipated that the fighting on the Korean peninsula would be a sideshow that would be swiftly concluded by a victorious Kim Il-sung. Second, in early 1950 China's leaders were looking to reductions in expenditures on the military to buttress their economic recovery program. Indeed, in early June Mao ordered partial demobilization.[25]

Such evidence has led Western commentators to conclude that Mao could not possibly have intended that his nation should be involved in the war,[26] that "there is no evidence that it was instigated by the Chinese,"[27] and that "there is no clear evidence of Chinese participation in the planning and preparation of the Korean War."[28] Another scholar has suggested that the war was originally timed for August, after the PRC was to have recovered Taiwan, but that Kim Il-sung jumped the gun.[29] Certainly, the North Korean leader immediately displayed the utmost militancy. The day after the outbreak of the war, he declared in a radio announcement that the North Korean army had launched a decisive "counteroffensive" to sweep out the armed forces of the enemy.[30] On 26 June *Pravda* lost no time in accepting Kim's declaration as justified, stressing that the South Koreans had made the first attack and that the North Korean army had been instructed to repel the assault.

Peking's immediate concern, however, was not the struggle for the Korean peninsula but President Truman's decision on 27 June to interpose the U.S. Seventh Fleet in the Taiwan Straits as part of America's reaction to the new outbreak of hostilities in the Far East. While the Chinese press was explaining to its readers why the PRC would not be entering the Korean War, Chou En-lai was denouncing this "armed aggression" against Chinese territory.[31]

25 Allen S. Whiting, *China crosses the Yalu*, 17–18.
26 Schram, *Mao Tse-tung*, 263.
27 John Gittings, "The great power triangle and Chinese foreign policy," *CQ*, 39 (July–September 1969).
28 Whiting, *China crosses the Yalu*, 45.
29 Robert Simmons, *The strained alliance*, 102–68.
30 "Kim Il-sung's radio speech on the outbreak of the Korean War" (26 June 1950), in Kamiya, *Chōsen mondai sengo shiryō* (Documents on postwar Korean problems), 1. 309.
31 Simmons, *The strained alliance*, 149–50; Whiting, *China crosses the Yalu*, 58; Edgar Snow, *The other side of the river*, 654–55.

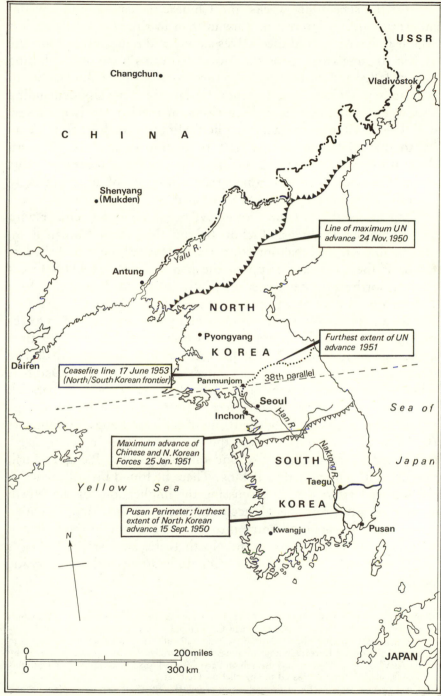

Map 6. Korean War

Over the succeeding weeks, the Chinese media continued to demonstrate greater interest in Taiwan than in Korea. China's leaders
appear to have involved themselves slowly and reluctantly in the fate
of Kim Il-sung's regime as the North Korean's hope of a lightning
victory faded and the tide began to turn in favor of the UN and South
Korean forces. On 20 August Chou En-lai cabled the UN demanding
PRC representation at any discussions on the Korean issue; a few
days later, a Chinese magazine explicitly linked North Korean security to that of China for the first time. But at the UN, Western
delegates rejected Soviet and Indian efforts to get Chinese diplomats
invited, and Soviet efforts to negotiate a way out of an increasingly
unpromising military situation also failed.

The successful UN counteroffensive began on 15 September with
an amphibious landing at Inchon behind the North Korean lines,
accompanied by a breakout from the defensive line established at
Pusan at the southeastern tip of the peninsula. As the UN forces
pushed northward, Stalin pessimistically informed Peking that Kim
Il-sung would have to set up a government in exile on Chinese soil.
But the Chinese, who had been regrouping forces in case of involvement almost from the outset of the war, warned the UN that they
could not sit idly by if North Korean territory were invaded. The
decisive moment occurred on China's National Day, 1 October,
when South Korean troops crossed the frontier at the 38th parallel.
On that day, Mao circulated a secret directive that Chinese troops
would enter the war, using the name of Chinese People' Volunteers
(CPV) as a device to try to limit the war to the Korean peninsula.[32]

Three days later, China's second-ranking general, P'eng Te-huai,
was urgently summoned to Peking. There he found his colleagues in
the top leadership already discussing the implications of the North
Korean retreat. From P'eng's account, it appears that Mao overruled
a majority who opposed entry into the war, on the grounds that it
was the PRC's duty to come to North Korea's assistance.[33] Mao's
views were later published in a joint declaration of the democratic
parties and the CCP:

---

32 Whiting, *China crosses the Yalu*, 68–93. For Chinese military preparations and Stalin's
pessimism, see Yao Hsu, "K'ang-Mei yuan-Ch'ao ti ying-ming chueh-ts'e: chi-nien Chung-
kuo jen-min chih-yuan-chün ch'u-kuo tso-chan san-shih chou-nien" (A wise decision to
resist America, aid Korea: Commemorating the 30th anniversary of operations abroad by
the CPV). *Tang-shih yen-chiu* (Research on Party history), 1980. 5, 5–14. According to this
source, the UN troops crossed the parallel on October 2.
33 *P'eng Te-huai tzu-shu* (P'eng Te-huai's own account), 257–58, translated as *Memoirs of a
Chinese marshal*, 472–74.

Historical facts teach us that a crisis in Korea has much to do with the security of China. With the lips gone, the teeth would be exposed to the cold; with the door broken, the house itself would be in danger. For the people of China to aid the people of Korea in their struggle against the U.S. is *not merely a moral responsibility but also a matter closely related to the vital interests of our own people, a decision necessitated by a need for self-defense.* Saving our neighbors at once means saving ourselves. To protect our own country, we must help the people of Korea.[34]

P'eng himself sided with Mao, concerned with the threat the United States represented to the Northeast (from Korea) and to Shanghai and East China (from Taiwan).

This chapter is not the place for a full account of the Korean War. But since the CPV's impressive performance established the new People's Republic as a formidable military power to be treated with respect, it is worth briefly recounting how that reputation was earned. According to the official war history of the U.S. Marine Corps:

Although the Chinese Reds were represented by a peasant army, it was also a first-rate army when judged by its own tactical and strategic standards. Military poverty might be blamed for some of its deficiencies in arms and equipment, but its semiguerrilla tactics were based on a mobility which could not be burdened with heavy weapons and transport. The Chinese coolie in the padded cotton uniform could do one thing better than any other soldier on earth; he could infiltrate around an enemy position with unbelievable stealth. Only Americans who have had such an experience can realize what a shock it is to be surprised at midnight with the grenades and submachine gun slugs of gnome-like attackers who seem to rise out of the very earth.

Press correspondents were fond of referring to "the human sea tactics of the Asiatic hordes." Nothing could be further from the truth. In reality the Chinese seldom attacked in units larger than a regiment. Even these efforts were usually reduced to a seemingly endless succession of platoon infiltrations. It was not mass but deception and surprise which made the Chinese Reds formidable.

The main shortcomings of the CPV as observed by their opponents were a primitive logistical system, leading to swiftly developing shortages of ammunition in battle, and a primitive communications system, which resulted in tactical rigidity, often with disastrous consequences: "A battalion once committed to the attack often kept on as long as its ammunition lasted, even if events indicated that it

34 "Ko min-chu tang-p'ai lien-ho hsuan-yen" (Joint declaration of the Democratic Parties) (4 November 1950), *JMJP*, 5 November 1950.

was beating out its brains against the strongest part of the opposing line. The result in many such instances was tactical suicide."

In his memoirs, Marshal P'eng Te-huai describes briefly the five "campaigns" of varying duration and importance that he fought between late October 1950 and July 1951, when truce talks began. The early campaigns were brilliantly successful, and the UN forces were pushed back to the 38th parallel frontier between the two Koreas. But by the end of the third campaign in January 1951, the CPV's lack of aircraft and anti-aircraft guns and its supply problems were beginning to tell. The Chinese forces had been reduced by nearly 50 percent. By February 1951, P'eng felt compelled to make a flying visit to Peking to explain to Mao what was clearly a desperate military situation.

By the end of the fifth campaign in mid-1951, the Chinese troops were exhausted and were suffering the greatest losses inflicted on them during the war. Western commentators later argued that had the military pressure been kept up at this time, the Chinese would have been forced to agree to an early armistice. According to the official U.S. Marine Corps history again, the CPV withdrawal was "a flight of beaten troops under very little control in some instances.... And where it had been rare for a single Chinese soldier to surrender voluntarily, remnants of platoons, companies, and even battalions were now giving up after throwing down their arms. There had been nothing like it before, and its like would never be seen in Korea again. The enemy was on the run."

But the UN forces relaxed the pressure with an agreement to initiate truce talks in July 1951, and P'eng Te-huai's battalions were enabled to dig in and strike back at regular intervals. The Americans suffered 60,000 casualties in the next two years before an armistice was signed.[35]

The Korean War imposed great sacrifices of blood and treasure on China as well as America. Certainly, the Resist America, Aid Korea Campaign launched domestically generated patriotism and assisted in the consolidation of the new regime, but this must be seen only as an incidental "by-product." The negative effects of intervention outweighed this bonus. China was isolated internationally and branded an "aggressor" by the UN, from which it would be excluded for two decades. It also had to postpone indefinitely its objective of liberating

35 *P'eng Te-huai tzu-shu*, 257–64; *Memoirs of a Chinese marshal*, 472–84; Alexander George, *The Chinese Communist army in action*, 1–12. Quotations from the U.S. Marine Corps history in preceding paragraphs are from ibid., 3–4.

Taiwan, because of the interposition of the U.S. Seventh Fleet. The Northeast remained Chinese, inviolate, but that was hardly a net gain.

In the light of these considerations, it is hardly surprising that there have been Chinese criticisms of the Soviet role in the Korean War. As early as 1957, Lung Yun publicly stated that it had been unreasonable for China alone to bear the cost of fighting America and aiding Korea. As China and the Soviet Union were still allies then, Lung Yun had to self-criticize, but it seemed likely that he was giving vent to widespread sentiment among senior Chinese. It is significant that Lung Yun made a quick comeback as a member of the Defense Council in December 1958, after a deterioration of Sino-Soviet relations. In 1963, after the Sino-Soviet rift had become open, the Chinese publicized their views on the Soviet role during the Korean War: "We have always made the necessary sacrifices and stood at the front-line in the defense of socialism so that the Soviet Union can remain in the second line."[36] The following year, in the "Letter of the Central Committee of the CCP to the Central Committee of the CPSU," the Chinese stated; "We made tremendous sacrifices and spent enormous sums of money for military purposes.... We have paid all the principal and the interest on the Soviet loans we obtained at that time, and they account for a major proportion of our exports to the Soviet Union. In other words, the military supplies provided China during the 'Resist America, Aid Korea' war were not free aid."[37] Lung Yun had been vindicated.

Subsequently there were other, similar statements, notably the one made by an official of the Sino-Japanese Friendship Association to a Japanese trade union delegation in January 1972: "The Soviet Union is a merchant of death. While China was sending volunteers and shedding blood in the Korean War, the Soviets stayed behind and merely sold weapons. They got payments for them with interest."[38] Since then, the Chinese have revealed that of a total of $1.34 billion borrowed from the Russians in the years after 1950, half the debt was incurred on account of the Korean War. Moreover, many of the

36 "Two different lines on the question of war and peace: Comment on the open letter to the Central Committee of the CPSU (5)," *JMJP*, 19 November 1963. For Lung Yun's remarks, see "Lung Yun tai-piao-ti fa-yen" (Representative Lung Yun's speech), *Chung-hua jen-min kung-ho-kuo ti-i-chieh ch'üan-kuo jen-min tai-piao-ta-hui ti-ssu-t'zu hui-i hui-k'an* (Proceedings of the fourth session of the First National People's Congress of the PRC), 1402–3.
37 "Letter of the Central Committee of the CCP to the Central Committee of the CPSU," 29 February 1964.
38 *Mainichi Shimbun*, 26 January 1972, report from Peking Correspondent Ando.

weapons sold them by the Russians were out of date. The total cost of the war to the Chinese was $10 billion.[39]

There are strong indications that this bitterness was not ex post facto. Surveying contemporary official reports, one notes that the Chinese leadership said nothing but good about the Soviet Union on Army Day (1 August 1950) but no longer praised the Soviets on that anniversary of the PLA in 1951 – that is, after the Chinese intervention in the Korean War.[40] From this fact, it is easily to imagine what China thought of the Soviet Union while it was fighting the war. Stalin had exposed the North Korean regime to the danger of liquidation and China to a hostile presence on a crucial frontier.

Stalin could not have foreseen American intervention followed by Chinese intervention in the Korean War. But according to Mao, Stalin "suspected that after we won the revolution, China would be like Yugoslavia, and I would be another Tito."[41] The Soviet leader, in unleashing Kim Il-sung, may have hoped to avert this danger by creating tension in the Far East that would almost inevitably set China and America at loggerheads. Whether by accident or design, the result was beneficial to Moscow. A Soviet study of Sino-Soviet relations has talked of "the Korean War ... cutting off for a long time the way to a collusion between the nationalistic CCP leaders and the U.S. ruling circles and compelling Chinese leaders to wider co-operation with the Soviet Union."[42]

One notes too that in and after January 1950, the Soviet Union refused to attend the UN Security Council, demanding the exclusion of the Nationalist Chinese delegation and admission of a delegation from the PRC before it returned. At that time, some observers already suspected that Moscow actually wanted the continued exclusion of Peking.[43] Now that we know that there was some uneasiness in Sino-Soviet relations, it is not inconceivable that the continued Soviet refusal to attend the Security Council until August, through

39 See Yao Hsu, *Tang-shih yen-chiu*, 1980. 5, 13. For Soviet figures on the debt, see below, note 46.
40 On Army Day in 1950, the Preparatory Committee of Various Circles in Peking for a Demonstration Rally in Celebration of the First of August Army Day and in Opposition to US Aggression in Korea and Taiwan announced a set of 35 slogans on the general theme of "Opposition to US aggression in Taiwan and Korea," of which No. 28 was "Long Live Generalissimo Stalin, Leader of all Peoples of the World!" A year later, in 1951, the General Political Department of the People's Revolutionary Military Committee of the Central People's Government announced a set of 18 Army Day slogans, none of which referred to Stalin or the Soviet Union or the CPSU.
41 *Wan-sui* (1969), 432.
42 Borisov and Koloskov, *Sino-Soviet relations 1945–1973*, 117.
43 Max Beloff, *Soviet policy in the Far East*, 82.

the most critical period following the outbreak of the Korean War, was to make use of American reinvolvement in the Far East to embroil Washington and Peking. Whatever Stalin's underlying aim, there can be no doubt that the Korean War, so costly to China, was an important factor in accounting for the bitterness of Peking's subsequent criticism of Moscow.[44]

China's foreign relations during and after the Korean War

China's efforts in the Korean War naturally helped to strengthen its standing in Stalin's eyes. In August–September 1952, a PRC delegation led by Chou En-lai visited Moscow for negotiations with Kremlin leaders, with apparently significant results. These talks were the second round of negotiations between Peking and Moscow, following the 1950 summit between Stalin and Mao. After nearly a month of talks with Stalin, Foreign Minister Vishinsky, and others, a communiqué was issued, along with an "Announcement concerning the transfer of the Chinese Changchun Railway to the Government of the People's Republic of China." At the same time, an "Exchange of notes concerning an extension of the term of the common use of the Port Arthur Naval Base in China" was signed.

In the case of the Changchun Railway, the 1950 agreement had laid down that all rights in its joint management and all property accessory thereto should be transferred gratis to the government of China by the end of 1952. On 31 December 1952, the final protocol on the transfer of the railway was signed in Harbin, after which the formal handover took place with appropriate ceremonies. The following day, 1 January 1953, Mao Tse-tung wired his thanks to Stalin.

With respect to the joint use of the naval base in Port Arthur – that is, the stationing of Soviet forces there – it had been agreed in 1950 that withdrawal of the Soviet forces and transfer of the facilities should take place after a peace was concluded with Japan, or by the end of 1952 at the latest. The San Francisco Peace Treaty had come

---

44 The Soviet boycott of the UN Security Council at that time has long been argued about. For detailed discussions of this issue, see Gaimushō chōsa kyoku daiikka, *Chōsen jihen no keii* (Process of the Korean War); Simmons, *The strained alliance*, ch. 4; Hajime Izumi, "Chōsen sensō o meguru Chū-Sō tairitsu: Soren no Kokuren anpoei kesseki no haikei" (The Sino-Soviet conflict in the Korean War: Centering on the Soviet boycott of the UN Security Council), *Gunji kenkyū*, 10.3 (March 1975). The United States had already decided on a rather flexible attitude toward the China issue at the UN. See "United States policy regarding problems arising from the representation of China in the organs of the United Nations," U.S. Department of State, *Foreign Relations of the United States 1950*, 2. 186–302.

into effect after April 1952, but during Chou's visit, the Chinese and Soviet negotiators agreed that it was a separate peace, hostile to them, and so they put off action on the Port Arthur issue until they too had signed a peace treaty with Japan. Soviet forces would stay in Port Arthur at Peking's "request."

These were the bare results of the 1952 Sino-Soviet negotiations. On the settlement of the long-pending railroad issue, the *People's Daily* carried an editorial titled "Congratulations on the transfer of the Chinese Changchun Railroad to our country!" in which it expressed satisfaction with this proof of the Soviet Union's "brotherly, unselfish assistance." But since the return of the railroad had been decided upon in the 1950 agreement, the clear implication is that the Chou delegation, despite its long stay in Moscow, had been unable to get any new concessions from the Soviets, be it economic aid or Soviet backing for a Korean truce.

The Chinese had been hinting their interest in a truce from time to time. But Stalin was then just organizing his final purge of political enemies and, preoccupied at home, it may be surmised that he found it advantageous to keep China and the United States bogged down in Korea a little longer. Hence his lack of enthusiasm for a Korean truce.

If, then, Peking and Moscow were at odds over the Korean truce issue, this must explain the extraordinary absence of any reference to the ongoing Korean War in the various speeches made by the negotiators during Chou En-lai's visit to Moscow or in the Sino-Soviet communiqué issued at its end. Confirmation is provided by the facts that the CPSU's Nineteenth Congress, which began on 5 October 1952, consistently ignored the Korean War and that it was also not mentioned at all in the congratulatory message delivered to the Congress by Liu Shao-ch'i on behalf of the CCP. All that was open to the Chinese was to sponsor an Asia-Pacific Peace Conference in Peking in early and mid-October 1952.

Sino-Soviet relations after Stalin

The death of Stalin on 5 March 1953 was bound to initiate a new phase in Sino-Soviet relations, and Peking, notwithstanding the obligatory official expressions of condolence, probably welcomed the event for that reason. Certainly, there was rapid movement on the Korean War issue. Progress toward a Korean truce, which had been very difficult, was suddenly expedited by diplomatic initiatives undertaken by Peking. In late March, agreement was reached to resume negotiations on the POW exchange issue on the basis of a Chou En-lai proposal in favor of free repatriation of POWs. On 11 April an agreement on an exchange of sick and wounded POWs was signed; on 26 April the Korean Armistice Conference resumed its regular sessions; on 8 June an agreement for the repatriation of POWs was signed; and finally on 27 July a Korean Armistice Agreement was concluded to mark the end of the hostilities in Korea. Thus the Korean War was brought to a close largely through Peking's diplomatic efforts after Stalin's death, Moscow being paralyzed by a serious succession struggle.

Having achieved the Korean truce, China found new opportunities to increase its international prestige. Developments such as the Chou-Nehru meeting of June 1954, with its advocacy of the Five Principles of Peaceful Coexistence, and the Geneva conference on Korea and Indochina held in April–July that year in which China played an active part, helped considerably. It was during the Geneva conference, on 5 June 1954, that the first U.S.–Chinese meeting at the ambassadorial level took place. But Secretary of State Dulles refused to shake Chou En-lai's hand and ensured that the courtesies were kept to a minimum.

The international environment after the Korean War, which was conducive to détente, was favorable for China. At home, the meeting of the first NPC in September 1954 and its adoption of a state constitution symbolized the stability of the new regime. At its fifth anniversary celebrations on 1 October 1954, Peking played host to the first top-level Soviet delegation ever to visit China. It was led by Khrushchev, CPSU first secretary; Bulganin, first vice-premier; and Mikoyan, vice-premier. This brought about a general change for the better in Sino-Soviet relations. The Soviet delegation signed ten documents, including declarations, communiqués, agreements, and protocols. It was agreed that the Soviet forces in Port Arthur should pull out without waiting for a peace treaty to be concluded with Japan by China and the Soviet Union. The Sino-Soviet joint stock company in Sinkiang, which Mikoyan and Khrushchev later acknowledged as a case of Soviet "exploitation" of China, was wound up.

The 1954 Sino-Soviet talks were thus fruitful for the Chinese, who may have felt for the first time that the "fraternal friendship" of the Soviet Union was a reality. Unlike Stalin, who never visited China (or, indeed, any of his allies), Khrushchev initiated the diplomatic practice of visiting Peking for talks. Previously, most treaties and agreements between the two countries had been signed or announced in Moscow. Now they began to be signed or announced in Peking too.[45] The impression was imparted that the Chinese had finally achieved "equality" in their relations with the Soviets.

How did this come about? Two major reasons suggest themselves. First, without Stalin, the Soviet Union had no option but to pay China the respect its increased international prestige and its role in the Korean War demanded. Second, factional struggle in the Soviet Union must have played a role. Conspicuous by his absence from the Soviet delegation to Peking was Foreign Minister Molotov.

Be that as it may, in his lengthy speech at the fifth anniversary celebrations, Khrushchev was full of praise for the PRC and its leaders, speaking highly of what China had been doing on the international scene, ranging from its participation in the Korean War through the pronouncement of the Five Principles of Peaceful Coexistence, and affirming that China was now an important power. Subtle differences remained between the two countries and later became important factors in the deterioration of their relations, but in 1954 there was a marked improvement in those relations, with the Chinese finally getting major assistance for their industrialization programs.[46]

45 A review of Sino-Soviet treaties, agreements, protocols, joint declarations, joint communiqués and other such documents signed and made public between the conclusion of the Sino-Soviet Treaty of Friendship, Alliance and Mutual Assistance in February 1950 and the Protocol of the Sixth Session of the Scientific and Technological Cooperation Committee in July 1957, indicates that those preceding the Sino-Soviet negotiations in October 1954 numbered 29, of which 24 were signed or released in Moscow and only 3 in Peking, with 2 in Harbin, whereas those dating thereafter, including those concluded as a result of those negotiations, numbered 37, of which 12 were signed or released in Moscow and 22 in Peking, with one in Port Arthur, one in Ulan Bator, and one released simultaneously in Moscow and Peking.

46 The Soviet Union extended to China between 1950 and 1957 a total of 8.1 billion rubles (old) in industrial construction assistance, covering the following 211 projects:

50 projects in April 1950	⎫	
91 projects in September 1953	⎬ 5.6 billion rubles	
15 projects in October 1954	⎭	
55 projects in April 1956	2.5 billion rubles	
Total: 211 projects	8.1 billion rubles	

(Source: *JMJP*, 18 February and 8 April 1956, 4 November 1957.)

In and after 1958, the Soviet Union continued to grant additional assistance, adding 47 projects to the above list in August 1958 and 78 projects in February 1959, or a total of 125 projects. In April that year these were combined with the previous 211 into 166 new projects. Thus, the total number of industrial construction projects to be completed by 1967 with Soviet aid increased to 291, worth 20 billion rubles (old). By early November 1957, however, only 37 of these projects had been fully completed (*JMJP*, 4 November 1957), and there were conspicuous delays in construction. After the deterioration of Sino-Soviet relations in 1960, the Soviet Union suddenly ordered home all its experts in July, and many of these industrial construction projects were left suspended. How many of them had been completed by the Soviets has been variously estimated. Soviet data mention 198 completed projects, whereas Western sources consider that 154 or 130 projects may have been

THE BANDUNG LINE

The adoption of a moderate, slow, but steady domestic development program in 1954–55 was reflected in China's foreign policy. Peaceful coexistence became the watchword.

In April 1954, China and India signed an agreement on Tibet under which New Delhi gave up extraterritorial privileges inherited from the British: a special status for Indian traders, the stationing of Indian military detachments on Tibetan soil, an Indian-owned telephone and telegraph system. The preamble to the agreement contained five rules of international conduct. These were reconfirmed as the Five Principles of Peaceful Coexistence at a Chou-Nehru meeting in June and subsequently became a main element of China's foreign policy pronouncements. When the Indochina truce agreement was signed at the Geneva conference in July 1954, it was partly Peking's pressure on Hanoi that made success possible. Returning home after the meeting, Chou En-lai, encouraged by widespread praise of China's performance at its first major international conference, declared confidently, "The outcome of the Geneva conference demonstrates that international conflicts can be settled through peaceful negotiations."[47]

The Afro-Asian conference held in April 1955 owed some of its success to Chou's emphasis on peaceful coexistence. Attended by government representatives from twenty-nine nations, practically the entire community of independent nations in Asia and Africa at that time, the conference took place from 18 to 24 April in the resort town of Bandung, Indonesia. Chou made a point of emphasizing China's policy of peaceful coexistence, or the Bandung Line, saying, "What our nations in Asia and Africa need is peace and independence. We have no intention at all of pitting the nations of Asia and Africa against those of other regions. On the contrary, we need to establish peaceful, cooperative relations with the countries of other regions as well."[48]

completed. Also, there have been various estimates (in U.S. dollars) of the amount of credit the Soviet Union had granted China by the summer of 1960, when their relationship openly deteriorated. Moscow has frequently mentioned a total amount of $2 billion, and points out that $500 million was granted during the Korean War, although it is not clear whether this $500 million is included in the $2 billion total. Some Western estimates are as high as $2.65 billion to $3 billion. All credits were in any case repaid by 1965.

47 See Chou En-lai's report on foreign policy at the Thirty-third Meeting of the State Council (19 April 1955), *Collected foreign relations documents of the People's Republic of China*, 3. For the text of the agreement on Tibet, see Ambekar and Divekar, *Documents on China's Relations with South and South-East Asia, 1949–1962*, 283–86.
48 See text of Chou En-lai's speech at the Afro-Asian Conference (19 April 1954), in *Collected foreign relations documents of the People's Republic of China*, 3.

At Bandung, Chou made use of his considerable personal charm and diplomatic adroitness to sap the hostility of leaders suspicious of China (like Prince Sihanouk of Cambodia) or of communism (like Prime Minister Mohammed Ali of Pakistan).[49] He thus laid the basis for his successful Asian tour eighteen months later and for a succession of friendly visits to Peking by Asian statesmen. The establishment of Chinese diplomatic relations with Yugoslavia early in 1955 also helped to smooth Chou's way, since many Afro-Asian leaders had good personal relations with Tito.

China's reasonableness was underlined for other participants by Chou's offer to defuse Sino-American tensions by setting up talks between the two nations. As a consequence, later in the year ambassadorial talks were initiated in Geneva. Only one agreement was ever reached – within a few weeks of the talks' starting, on the question of the mutual repatriation of civilians – but these talks, transferred later to Warsaw, became the major forum for Sino-American diplomacy for many years to come. Other Chinese gestures to Washington – notably an offer to exchange visits by journalists – were rejected by an unrelentingly hostile Dulles. Lack of progress in Sino American relations must have been a principal factor when Peking abandoned moderation for militancy in foreign policy in the second half of 1957.

Emergence of Sino-Soviet tension

China's new diplomatic line was also affected by developments within the Soviet Union. At the Twentieth CPSU Congress in February 1956, Khrushchev criticized Stalin and boldly revised Leninist doctrine on the inevitability of war. Ideological disputes would emerge between the CPSU and the CCP over the criticism of Stalin, the inevitability of war, and also over another innovation, the idea that Communist Parties could take power without resort to violent revolution. Of these issues, the one of greatest immediate import to Mao Tse-tung and other Chinese leaders concerned the criticism of Stalin and his "cult of personality."

The CCP's first comment on this issue was "On the historical experience of the dictatorship of the proletariat," published in the *People's Daily* on 5 April 1956. This article attempted to give a balanced presentation of Stalin's faults and merits to calm the confusion within the Communist movement provoked by Khrushchev's

---

49 For a description of the Bandung Conference and Chou En-lai's performance there, see George Kahin, *The Asian-African Conference.*

denunciation in his "secret speech." Mao had presumably found the criticism of Stalin welcome in the light of his own disagreements with the late Soviet leader. On the other hand, Mao could not but be wary of attacks on the "cult of personality," since it inevitably raised questions about his own position and cult (see Chapter 2). Internationally, the principal immediate issue was not theoretical but concrete: how to reestablish bloc unity and Soviet leadership in the wake of the confusion produced by de-Stalinization and the resultant unrest in Poland and revolt in Hungary. Faced with the Hungarian uprising, the Soviets resorted to force to reestablish control. By doing so, however, they considerably damaged their international standing and created serious fissures in the world Communist movement. The Chinese Communists stepped forward to buttress Soviet prestige and rally Communist parties behind the CPSU. Their own position was thus greatly enhanced.

At first, the CCP backed Eastern European parties seeking greater independence from Moscow's control. When Poland was in turmoil after an uprising in Poznan in June 1956, the CCP backed the new Polish party leader, Gomulka, against the Russians. But when the Nagy leadership threatened to take Hungary out of the Warsaw Pact, the CCP was unequivocal in its support of military intervention. On 29 December the *People's Daily* published its second major article on de-Stalinization and its repercussions: "More on the historical experience of the dictatorship of the proletariat." This document underlined implicitly China's emergence as potentially a rival source of ideological authority within the Communist movement. In early January 1957, Chou En-lai interrupted his Asian tour to lead a delegation to the Soviet Union, Poland, and Hungary, acting as a mediator, both to restore Soviet leadership and at the same time to tell Khrushchev and his colleagues that they could not run Eastern Europe in the old Stalinist style. Chou's visit to the Soviet Union and Eastern Europe impressed the world with the idea that China was beginning to play an important role in European affairs too, after establishing its key role in intra-Asian relations.

Despite their support for the CPSU, the Chinese Communists diverged from Moscow in their ideological analysis of the causes of the turmoil in Eastern Europe. Peking asserted in "More on . . ." that there could be contradictions between leaders and led even in a Communist country, a position the CPSU had never accepted, and one Khrushchev continued to deny.[50] On the basis of this position, in

50 For a discussion, see MacFarquhar, *The origins of the Cultural Revolution*, 1. 172–74.

February 1957, Mao expounded his theory on the correct handling of contradictions among the people, which became the basis of the CCP's party rectification campaign launched on 30 April. The Russians seemed uneasy about these developments and were almost certainly relieved when an outpouring of criticism resulted in the abrupt termination of the Hundred Flowers campaign on 8 June and a subsequent counterattack on critics under the rubric of the Anti-Rightist Campaign. Thus when Mao went to Moscow for the celebrations of the fortieth anniversary of the Bolshevik revolution, Chinese and Soviet domestic politics were more in tune, and the friendship stemming from the 1954 visit of the Soviet delegation to Peking could be said to be still in place.

Illustrative of the friendly relationship between the two countries at that time were two developments that preceded Mao's visit to Moscow (2–20 November). First, a Sino-Soviet military agreement with respect to new defense technology was signed in secret on 15 October 1957. Under it the Soviets apparently promised to make available to China a sample A-bomb and nuclear know-how. Second, a Soviet-Chinese Friendship Association, a counterpart of the Sino-Soviet Friendship Association established in China in October 1949 immediately after the foundation of the People's Republic, was set up in Moscow in October 1957.

In part these developments reflected Khrushchev's need for renewed CCP support after the purge of Malenkov, Kaganovich, and Molotov in the summer, and the subsequent ouster of Defense Minister Marshal Zhukov. But they also reflected increased interdependence and friendship between the two leaderships. Mao must have derived particular satisfaction from the defense agreement, since he placed great importance on the Soviet launching of an ICBM in August 1957, of Sputnik I in October, and of Sputnik II on 3 November. These Soviet achievements led Mao to make his famous appraisal of the current international situation: "The East Wind is prevailing over the West Wind."[51] It was also on the basis of this view

51 This slogan, which was to be severely attacked by Moscow in the course of the Sino-Soviet dispute, was first presented by Mao Tse-tung when he analyzed the current international situation by referring to the old Chinese proverb, "Unless the East Wind prevails over the West Wind, the West Wind will prevail over the East Wind." Mao said: "The Socialist camp should always have a head, which should be the Soviet Union. The Communist parties and labor parties of the various countries also should have a head, which should be the Communist Party of the Soviet Union. The unity of the international Communist movement and the Soviet launching of two man-made satellites mark a new turning point in the power relationship between the two camps. Forty years have elapsed since the October Revolution created a new world, and its power has already exceeded that of the old. Today

that he adjured the Moscow meeting not to fear thermonuclear war, arguing that mankind would not perish and that Communist society would emerge from the ashes of imperialism.[52] But the slogan and Mao's attitude toward thermonuclear war greatly perturbed many of his colleagues.[53]

In addition, the Chinese and the Russians clashed at the Moscow conference on the issue of peaceful transition to socialism, with Mao arguing that Communist Parties would come to power only via violent revolution. Once Peking's stand on this issue became known, it naturally led to a decrease in confidence among its non-Communist neighbors. The Bandung Line pursued by Chou En-lai seemed hollow, and this impression was subsequently confirmed in 1958 by China's response to the Middle East crisis and Peking's bombardment of the offshore islands, and became quite plain during the Sino-Indian border conflict in and after August 1959.

China and Japan

Finally, let us consider Peking's adherence to, and subsequent abandonment of, the Bandung Line as reflected in Sino-Japanese relations. As part of China's shift toward the Bandung Line, Peking switched its policy vis-à-vis Tokyo from earnestly encouraging the "anti-U.S. struggle of the Japanese people" to emphasizing peace with Japan in the light of such developments in the early 1950s as the post-Stalin change in the international Communist movement, the relaxation of international tension owing to the Korean truce, the success of the Five Principles of Peaceful Coexistence on the international scene, and a shift in Japan's attitude toward China under the Hatoyama and Ishibashi administrations.

After the Korean armistice agreement in 1953, Peking began to act in concert with Moscow to deal with Japan in a markedly different manner, stressing the importance of normalizing intergovernmental

there are 2.7 billion people in the world. The population of the Socialist countries is now close to one billion, that of the newly independent former colonies is over 700 million and that of the countries now on their way to independence or achieving complete independence is 600 million, whereas the population of the imperialist camp is only about 400 million. Moreover, they are split internally. At present, the West Wind does not prevail over the East Wind, but the East Wind prevails over the West Wind." (Chairman Mao Tse-tung's speech to Chinese students and trainees in Moscow: "The power of the new world has already exceeded that of the old," *JMJP*, 19 November 1957).

52 See Chinese government spokesman's statement: "Criticizing the Soviet government statement of August 21" (1 September 1963), *JMJP*, 1 September 1963.

53 See MacFarquhar, *The origins of the Cultural Revolution*, 2. 9–11.

relations with Japan and earnestly calling for contacts between China and Japan, arguing that the time was ripe for a rapprochement. In a Sino-Soviet joint declaration signed in October 1954, Peking and Moscow reaffirmed this approach, which subsequently became the basis of their policy toward Japan at that time. The CCP's former incitement of Japanese popular struggle against American imperialism and the Japanese government, to be led by the Japanese Communist Party, was downplayed.[54]

In the fall of 1954, Japanese notables in various walks of life were invited to China's national day celebrations in Peking and Madame Li Te-ch'üan of the Chinese Red Cross visited Japan. Contacts between the two countries increased in frequency and warmth. This flexibility in Peking's attitude toward Japan was symbolized by the fact that Premier Chou En-lai, asked by Japanese newsmen if they were right in assuming that abrogation of the Chinese (Taiwan) – Japanese Peace Treaty was not necessarily a precondition for expediting a normalization of relations between China (PRC) and Japan but should be viewed as a goal or a result of such a process, replied, "That won't make much difference."[55] Of course, this Chinese attitude toward Japan reflected not only the Sino-Soviet plan to undermine Japan's reliance on the United States, but also the fact that China's internal and external policies were moderate. In other words, it was a reflection of the Bandung Line adopted by the CCP.

Peking's calls for a rapprochement based on these motives did not, however, meet with a wholehearted response from Tokyo. The Hatoyama administration, inclined to refrain from any speech or action that might provoke Peking, adopted the attitude of a bystander watching private Sino-Japanese contacts and took no steps to fulfill Peking's expectations. The Ishibashi administration that came into being in December 1956 was warmly welcomed by the Chinese Communists but did not last long. The Kishi administration that followed was looked upon by the Chinese with growing suspicion.

Peking further hardened its attitude toward Japan as Premier Kishi visited six Southeast Asian countries and the United States in May–June 1957. In Taiwan especially, he expressed support for the Chiang Kai-shek regime and stressed Japanese-Taiwanese cooperation.

---

54 As the criticism of the JCP by the Cominform and the CCP showed in January 1950, the CCP, after the founding of the PRC, wanted to export "the way of Mao Tse-tung" and to lead a national liberation struggle in Japan and South and Southeast Asia.
55 On Sino-Japanese relations for this period, see Mineo Nakajima, *Chūgoku: rekishi, shakai, kokusaikankei* (China: history, society and international relations), 203–15.

Moreover, all this happened at a time when a critical turn took place in the PRC's domestic politics – the shift from the rectification campaign to the Anti-Rightist Campaign. This had a decisive influence on Peking's subsequent attitude toward Japan, which inevitably reflected China's abandonment of the Bandung Line.

The wheel had almost turned full circle. China's foreign policy in late 1957 was no longer based on the simplistic version of the two-camp theory prevailing in 1949–50. Its foreign relations were more subtly differentiated. But Peking's ideological militancy was once again at a high point, and was now reinforced by a growing self-confidence as well as an emerging sense of mission to keep the Communist bloc on the right course in the renewed struggle against imperialism.

PART II

THE SEARCH FOR A CHINESE ROAD, 1958–1965

CHAPTER 7

THE GREAT LEAP FORWARD
AND THE SPLIT IN
THE YENAN LEADERSHIP

AN OVERVIEW

The year 1958 began with the Chinese Communist leaders optimistic about their ability to lead the country up the path of rapid economic development and social progress. To be sure, not all Politburo members agreed on the best methods to use to accomplish these great tasks, but overall confidence was high and the degree of underlying unity clearly sufficient to enable the Chinese Communist Party (CCP) to act in a consistent and decisive manner. Seven years later, deep fissures had rent this leadership to the point where Mao Tse-tung himself stood on the verge of launching a devastating attack against many of the colleagues with whom he had worked for more than three decades. That attack would, in turn, launch China into a decade so tumultuous that even in the early 1980s leaders in Peking would look back to the eve of the 1958–65 era wistfully, as the time when the Party's power, prestige, and unity had reached pinnacles. The eight years between 1958 and 1965 were a period of major transition in the Chinese revolution.

To be sure, not all had gone smoothly for the Chinese Communists after 1949. There had been significant disagreement among the leaders over the pace and contours of the development effort. During 1953, for example, Finance Minister Po I-po had come under sharp criticism for advocating tax policies that would, Mao felt, slow down the development of the public sector of the economy. In 1955, Mao openly disagreed with his colleagues over the pace of the proposed collectivization of agriculture and effectively overturned the program they had adopted. His efforts in 1957 to encourage non-Party intellectuals to criticize the Party had brought bitter disagreement at the highest levels. And throughout this period there were repeated efforts to rectify what were seen as unhealthy tendencies in the Party and government bureaucracies as the new system of political power became consolidated.

The key point about the 1949–57 period, however, is that the conflicts were handled in a way that managed to preserve basic unity among the elite and maintain the élan of the revolutionary movement. Similarly, while many citizens dissented bitterly from the CCP's policies of this period, the overall prestige of the Party and of the new system remained high. The Communists could rightly proclaim that their policies were making China stronger and wealthier, even if they were forced to "break some eggs" to make their national omelette. It was precisely this prestige that the CCP lost during the 1958–65 period, with virtually catastrophic consequences. It is ironic that this period proved on balance to be so destructive, for it began with the Great Leap Forward (GLF), a program based on almost utopian optimism about what the Party, with its methods of mass mobilization, could accomplish.

During the spring and summer of 1958 Mao and his colleagues pushed the Great Leap idea as an alternative to the development strategy that had been imported from the Soviet Union for the 1st Five-Year Plan (FYP) of 1953–57. Needing some way to overcome bottlenecks that appeared to preclude a simple repetition of the 1st FYP strategy, the Chinese leaders settled on an approach that utilized the mass mobilization skills they had honed to a fine edge during the Anti-Japanese War years in Yenan. This new strategy (with its various component parts, including communization of the countryside), threw the country into a frenzy of production activity that lasted into 1959. Key elements in this strategy, however, ultimately made the production upsurge a prelude to economic disaster rather than to the anticipated time of plenty.

The Great Leap strategy entailed significant changes in the political situation. It stripped considerable power from the central government bureaucracy and transferred it in many cases to local Party cadres. It shunted technical specialists aside in production units and replaced them with political generalists good at firing up the enthusiasm of the workers. It raised the pervasiveness of political demands in all fields to a new level, as superhuman work motivated by political zeal was key to the successful implementation of this new developmental approach. And it introduced important new strains into Sino-Soviet relations, as it de facto decreased the authority of the many Soviet advisers in China and implicitly challenged the previously sacrosanct Soviet model.

Given the extent of these changes, serious problems naturally arose when the Great Leap began to falter. By the end of 1958 Mao and others were aware that extremism in the name of the Leap was already causing some damage, and they made appropriate modifications in targets and policies to keep the movement on track. But information about the actual results of state grain procurement in early 1959 revealed that the situation was worse than previously thought, and during that spring Mao led the effort to bring greater rationality and efficiency to the program. The movement proved difficult to bring under control, however, as those who had inherited greater power during 1958 continued to resist any retreat from the policies of that year.

During the summer of 1959 this problem of bringing the GLF under control became entangled in elite politics in a very damaging way. P'eng Te-huai, a leading military man who had long had a stormy relationship with Mao, returned from a trip to the Soviet Union and Eastern Europe in June and shortly thereafter made a biting critique of the "petty-bourgeois fanaticism" of the Great Leap at a major Party work conference convened at Lushan. The rationale for P'eng's actions at Lushan remains uncertain, but Mao chose to interpret it as a direct attack on his personal leadership and responded sharply. Mao demanded that P'eng and his supporters be removed from power, and he suggested that the Soviet Union had become involved in P'eng's challenge. The immediate results were twofold: The purge of P'eng swamped the efforts to rein in the Great Leap and produced a second upsurge in radical policies lasting into 1960, and relations between China and the Soviet Union became more strained.

Both these results bore bitter fruit in 1960. The Leap upsurge caused enormous further damage to the economy, to the extent that by late 1960 famine was stalking the land. Relations with Moscow continued to deteriorate to the point that in the summer of 1960 the Soviets suddenly withdrew all their assistance from China. Soviet aid was at that time still sufficiently crucial to a number of key industrial development projects that this action produced grave economic consequences in the PRC. It also distracted Peking's attention from the economic disaster that was looming in the countryside, thus delaying timely measures to salvage the situation there.

By the end of 1960, therefore, the GLF had produced economic disaster in the hinterland, and during 1961 this fundamental economic malaise spread through the cities. Peking now recognized the full gravity of the problem and drafted a series of programmatic documents to deal with the situation. During this year of crisis, there is every indication that Mao supported the far-reaching retreat from the

GLF that his colleagues devised. Indeed, in June 1961 Mao made a self-criticism at a key Party meeting in Peking,[1] and the Party as a whole adopted policies of retrenchment as official doctrine.

Once the crisis began to ease, however, tensions among the leaders rose as Mao sought to regain his position as the person who defined the basic tasks of the moment. His power and image had eroded as a consequence of his serious misjudgments during the GLF, and his concern about a potential waning of his influence had increased. He had reached the conclusion that recent events in the Soviet Union had demonstrated that under improper leadership, a Communist state could actually degenerate into a highly exploitative system. Substantively, Mao concluded that the Great Leap Forward had discredited the notion of making phenomenal economic progress by relying on mass mobilization, but he still firmly believed in the importance of mass mobilization for preventing the kind of bureaucratic degeneration of the revolution that had occurred in the Soviet Union.

Those of Mao's colleagues in direct control of the CCP apparatus disagreed with this latter judgment. They were anxious to restore internal CCP discipline and to pursue a path of economic development that made appropriate use of specialists and technical expertise. While they shared many of Mao's goals, therefore, they shied away from some of his methods. Given the distribution of executive power in the wake of the Great Leap, they probably would have carried the day – implementing Mao's basic agenda but modifying it in ways that made it compatible with their more bureaucratic approach – had Mao not found some key allies to boost his strength.

These allies were his wife, Chiang Ch'ing; the man he had put in to replace P'eng Te-huai, Lin Piao; and a key member of the security system, K'ang Sheng, who joined forces with the Chairman and his former secretary, Ch'en Po-ta, to overthrow the system that had emerged in the wake of the Great Leap Forward. The gradual formation of this coalition between 1962 and 1965 will be detailed farther on. Each member had personal reasons for joining the coalition, and all agreed on the desirability of changing the succession so that Liu Shao-ch'i (or someone else like Liu) would not eventually take over full power from Mao. The period thus became very much tangled up with coalition politics and intrigues over the succession.

The specific issues in contention, of course, changed over the years. During the early part of 1962 there was significant disagreement over

---

1 Since no full text of this confession is available, it is unfortunately not possible to characterize it as either thoroughgoing or perfunctory.

the degree of recovery that had already taken place in the country-side. Mao felt that recovery had gone far enough to permit Peking again to seize the initiative and reassert its authority. Liu Shao-ch'i, Teng Hsiao-p'ing, Ch'en Yun, and others disagreed, arguing that the Party must continue to implement emergency measures to salvage the situation. The question of rehabilitating those who in 1959 had warned about the dangers inherent in the Leap also arose then. Mao agreed that many of these "rightists" should now be rehabilitated, but he drew the line at bringing back P'eng Te-huai, to the chagrin of many of his colleagues (but not of Lin Piao).

By the fall of 1962 Mao had carried the day on the issue of the degree of recovery from the GLF, and the question now shifted to the best means to restore the regime's power and prestige in the country. Mao advocated a policy of rebuilding the Party in the countryside using means that entailed extensive political mobilization of the peasantry. His colleagues subsequently tried to achieve rural Party rectification through internal bureaucratic means instead. In his frustration with the bureaucratic biases of other Politburo leaders, Mao adopted two measures to enhance the role of his brand of politics in the system.

Starting in 1963, the Chairman increasingly promoted the People's Liberation Army as the model organization for Chinese to follow. The PLA had, under Lin Piao, acquitted itself well in technical military tasks, from progress toward building an atom bomb (the first Chinese atom bomb test took place in October 1964) to achieving an impressive series of victories in the border war with Indian forces in the fall of 1962. At the same time, Lin had promoted political work among the troops, centered on the study of Mao Tse-tung Thought as condensed and dogmatized in the *Quotations from Chairman Mao*. The PLA in Mao's eyes became an organization that had achieved the optimum synthesis of technique and politics, and Mao sought to expand its role in the political system. Lin Piao strongly encouraged this development – and the power of the Chairman on whom it depended.

Also beginning in 1963 Mao supervised the drafting of nine "letters" from the CC of the CCP to the CC of the Communist Party of the Soviet Union (CPSU). These polemical documents spelled out Mao's contention that the Soviet Union had degenerated into a non-socialist political system, a development Mao called going down the path of "revisionism." Mao used these letters to give wide publicity in China to the issue of revisionism and, essentially, to make his case (somewhat obliquely) against the policies of colleagues whom he opposed.

Between 1963 and 1965 Liu Shao-ch'i and the other Party leaders who later were to become the key initial targets of the Cultural Revolution carried out a very impressive program of economic recovery, bringing production in 1965 back up to the levels achieved on the eve of the Great Leap Forward in almost every sector (and, of course, ahead of these levels in some sectors). As noted, these leaders appear to have tried to accommodate many of Mao's demands while channeling them so as to make them less disruptive to the bureaucratic system they had reconstructed. The available documentation suggests that these leaders were not oblivious of the dangers lurking in the machinations of Lin Piao, Chiang Ch'ing, K'ang Sheng, and their followers, but there appears little reason to believe that before 1965 they saw these dangers as threatening in a fundamental sense.

Liu Shao-ch'i, Teng Hsiao-p'ing, and their colleagues of like mind seem to have regarded the situation as difficult but not impossible to manage. They were ultimately proved disastrously wrong in this evaluation. They had tried to meet Mao part way and to limit as much as possible the leverage of his eventual coalition partners in the system. Thus, for example, the attempt to enhance the power of the army by establishing military-type political departments in the civilian governing organs starting in 1964 met strong resistance, as did Chiang Ch'ing's repeated efforts to acquire authority over cultural policy. But as the middle of the decade approached, Mao himself saw this ongoing give and take less as the inevitable frictions of national politics and more in terms of a Manichean struggle of good against evil. This new perspective, of course, raised the stakes enormously, and an increasingly disturbed and restless Mao began to take the fateful steps that led to unleashing the Cultural Revolution in 1966.

This brief overview captures the highlights of a period in which four fundamental transitions took place: from a basically united leadership to one that was deeply divided; from a wholly legitimate CCP rule to one far less readily accepted; from a relatively disciplined and spirited CCP membership to one demoralized and uncertain; and from agreed-upon ways of handling intra-Party conflicts to disagreement over basic norms for resolving such tensions. In short, during 1958–65 the Chinese Communist movement lost some of its key political assets, both in terms of the organizational weapon it possessed in the Party and in terms of its reservoir of legitimacy among the population. These losses contributed to the deep divisions that led in turn to the Cultural Revolution. In greater detail, this story unfolded as follows.

ORIGINS OF THE GREAT LEAP FORWARD

Many forces contributed to the decision to adopt the policies collectively known as the Great Leap Forward. Among these, the most fundamental were the problems produced by the 1st FYP, modeled after the Soviet Union's development strategy. These problems were political, social, and economic, with the economic issues at their heart.

The Soviet strategy developed by Stalin and adopted by the PRC demanded two conditions: that a planning mechanism channel resources overwhelmingly into the development of heavy industry, with the metallurgical industry receiving first priority; and that the rural areas be starved for funds and exploited as needed to provide resources to permit the growth of heavy industry in particular and of the urban sector in general. The Chinese copied their planning apparatus so successfully from the Soviets that during their respective 1st FYPs, the Chinese managed to devote nearly 48 percent of their public capital investment to industrial development whereas the comparable Soviet figure was under 42 percent. The problem arose in the other part of the equation – the exploitation of the rural areas to support this urban industrial policy.

The Soviet Union had used agriculture during the 1st FYP both as a source of exports that would enable the government to import machinery and technology for industry and as a source of food for the rapidly expanding urban working force. Peasant deaths in the millions occurred either directly from Moscow's harsh imposition of the collective farm system or less directly from the resulting famine when the government maintained constant levels of agricultural procurement even as agricultural production fell more than 25 percent from 1929 to 1932–33. This approach assumed that there was a real surplus in agriculture and sought a way to make that surplus serve the goals of the political leadership.

The Chinese case differed in two fundamental respects from that of the Soviet Union. First and most important, per capita output in China in 1957 was only half that of the Soviet Union in 1928 in the production of grain (290 vs. 566 kg per person) and vegetable oils (1.7 vs. 3.0 kg per person). Thus, while the Soviets could debate how best to secure control over a consistent rural surplus, the Chinese had to develop a means first to create and enhance that surplus and then to gain control over its distribution. Second, while Soviet Party membership was more than 70 percent urban, the CCP was more than 70 percent rural in social composition. These differences in the social compositions of the two parties presumably made the CCP somewhat more reluctant to adopt a strategy premised on the misery of the countryside and the starvation of millions of country dwellers. Thus, in late 1957 China groped for a strategy that would enhance agricultural output while still permitting the rapid growth of capital-intensive heavy industry. The different elements of such a strategy, especially with regard to agriculture, were hotly debated at the Third Plenum of the Eighth Central Committee in September and early October of 1957.

The problem in agriculture was how to persuade the peasants to increase their output and marketings while Peking devoted state investment to the heavy industrial sector. There was clear recognition among the leaders that the formula followed up to then would not solve the problem. Mao Tse-tung wanted to utilize political and organizational tools to boost peasant output. Ch'en Yun, the fifth-ranking member of the Party and the highest-ranking economic specialist, however, premised his recommended solution on the assumption that the peasants would respond only to increased material incentives and not to either coercion or ideological exhortation. Material incentives required not only that the peasants receive good prices for their products but also that they have consumer goods available to purchase with the money they earned. State investment would, therefore, have to shift somewhat in the direction of light industry in order to provide the consumer goods necessary to make this rural strategy work. The light industrial sector would also produce relatively quick turnover on capital with a substantial profit rate, thus providing over time an adequate capital pool for the speedy development of heavy industry.

In this balanced approach, therefore, Ch'en argued essentially that each sector could help the others and that the Chinese need not view tradeoffs among sectors as a zero-sum game. He also pointed out the impossibility of feeding the large numbers of highly paid urban industrial workers if his advice were to be ignored (as, in fact, it was). In many ways, Ch'en Yun's policies in 1957 parallelled those of Nikolai Bukharin in the Soviet Union in 1927–28; and as Bukharin was brushed aside by Stalin, Ch'en was pushed from center stage by Mao.

Ch'en's policy recommendations, which amounted to the most

comprehensive developmental alternative put forward in the China of the 1950s, were defeated in part by simple impatience. Ch'en himself readily admitted that his formula for balanced growth would not produce any developmental miracles in the next few years. But the explanation for Chen's defeat is in fact more complex. His strategy presumed that the Chinese government, as distinct from the CCP, would continue to play the central role in running the economy. The system established under the 1st FYP placed enormous power in the central government ministries. While these were, like all bodies, under overall Party control, the greatest concentration of non-Communist experts was employed in the staffs of these ministries.

Ministerial work inevitably placed a premium on literacy, statistical skills, and the ability to deal in abstractions – all skills far more prevalent among the urban intelligentsia than among the peasant mass that had contributed so many stalwarts to the Party during the years in the wilderness. But the Hundred Flowers movement and the resulting Anti-Rightist Campaign in 1957 had largely discredited the urban intelligentsia and any development strategy that depended centrally on their contributions. Indeed, the harsh penalties exacted of the "rightists" in the wake of this campaign literally reduced the numbers of intellectuals outside of prison camps and thus changed the parameters of human capital that would inevitably shape the development strategy the government adopted.

The more radical, anti-intellectual atmosphere spread from the urban to the rural areas during the late summer and fall of 1957. In the countryside the Anti-Rightist Campaign was directed against those who had voiced doubts about the efficacy of the rapid cooperativization (essentially, collectivization) of agriculture that had swept China during the previous two years. Collectivization at China's low level of agricultural development and mechanization had itself been a policy signifying the primacy of human organizational factors in the country's economic growth. Thus, the Anti-Rightist Campaign in both urban and rural areas bolstered the position of those who believed that proper mobilization of the populace could accomplish tasks that the "bourgeois experts" dismissed as impossible. As such, the Anti-Rightist Campaign in the countryside facilitated the adoption of a policy of mass mobilization to build irrigation facilities during the winter of 1957–58. This policy proved highly successful, but it also highlighted several problems inherent in the rural organizational structure at that time.

First, a lack of appropriate organizational units to marshal people and resources hampered large-scale mobilization. Second, there was an absolute shortage of labor if the peasants were to put in millions of man-days at nonagricultural tasks such as dam building. Third, there was a continuing problem over establishing a good fit between basic-level government units and the economic units in the countryside. In 1956 the government had abolished the districts (*ch'ü*) and amalgamated the administrative villages (*hsiang*), but this had led to a series of escalating organizational problems that had not been resolved by the winter of 1957–58. The upshot of these issues was pressure in the countryside to devise a bigger unit that would be able to control large labor resources and also to fit neatly into the government administrative hierarchy.

The solution devised after some experimentation in early 1958 was the People's Commune (*jen-min kung-she*), which itself then underwent major organizational changes between 1958 and 1962. The initial communes were huge, centralized units embracing several standard marketing areas.[2] They served both as the basic-level government organs and the key economic units. Their size permitted them to take control over not only agricultural production but also local industry, commerce, education, and the militia. Under commune direction, moreover, the organization of agricultural labor changed dramatically, with many peasants now assigned to specialized work teams that traveled from one village to another to perform particular tasks.

These initial communes proved too large to manage, and their attempt to base members' incomes on the total production of units that embraced tens of thousands of peasants provided too few incentives for individual effort. Therefore, in a series of stages from 1959 to 1962, the effective level of collective organization became smaller. Within the communes, this evolution entailed the formation first of brigades and then of smaller units called teams, with the income of individual peasants depending on the total output of these successively smaller units. Also, by 1962 the communes themselves had been reduced in size, with the total number of communes increasing from the original 25,000 to 75,000. By 1962 these changes made many communes conform roughly to the former standard marketing areas

2 The standard marketing area included the villages that traditionally marketed their goods at the same periodic market. These areas had social as well as economic identities, as marriages often took place between peasants of different villages within the same SMA. See G. William Skinner, "Marketing and social structure in rural China," *JAS* (November 1964, February 1965, and May 1965). A June 1961 Central Committee decision had mandated that communes be reduced to the size of former *hsiang* or amalgamated *hsiang: Chung-hua jen-min kung-ho-kuo ching-chi ta-shih-chi* (Record of major economic events in the PRC), 306.

and made the most important economic unit within the commune, the team, coincide with either small villages themselves or with socially relatively cohesive neighborhoods within larger villages.

The shift from expertise toward mobilization in both urban and rural areas as of the conclusion of the Anti-Rightist Campaign meant that the apparatus best suited to mobilization efforts – the CCP – would assume a relatively greater role than it had under the Soviet-style strategy followed since 1953. This expansion in the span of control of the CCP would inevitably come at the cost of the government bureaucracy. Some administrative decentralization would strip power from central ministries. An important result of the discrimination against expertise would be the dismantling of the state statistical system, the bulwark of a development strategy that depended on expert calculation of possibilities and optimalities. And at the highest levels, the CCP apparatus directed by the Politburo and the Secretariat (headed by Teng Hsiao-p'ing) would play a far more important role, with the functions of the premier and the State Council reduced accordingly.

Two more sets of issues fed into the development of the Great Leap strategy. On a social level, the 1st FYP had adopted the Soviet approach to material and status differentials, with the result that Chinese urban society was becoming increasingly stratified by the mid-1950s. This stratification extended into the government bureaucracies, where the free supply system was replaced by a complex system of civil service grades in 1955. Similar grading systems were applied to various sectors of industry, commerce, and the educational system. The natural results were increasing status consciousness among the Chinese and encouragement of the type of careerism that was good for economic growth but rubbed against Mao Tse-tung's revolutionary grain. A strategy that relied more on ideological and coercive than on economic and status incentives might upset this unwanted social spinoff of the 1st FYP.

Second, Mao's own position in the system would be affected by the type of economic development strategy pursued. The Chairman's personal political strengths lay in the areas of foreign policy (especially toward the great powers), rural policy, and issues of revolutionary change (essentially, defining how rapidly change could be carried out, given the prevailing mood and conditions in the country). Urban economics, and especially the technicalities of finance and planning, were subjects about which he knew very little. Thus, Mao complained bitterly at the Nanning Conference in January 1958 that the Finance Ministry had for several years been sending the Politburo position papers so technical and complex that he simply had to sign them without even reading them. This situation naturally limited Mao's role in the system, and he determined to change it by forcing through a strategy of development that shifted the action from the areas in which he lacked strength to those where he felt more confident.

On the most fundamental level, finally, the motivations producing the Great Leap Forward strategy drew from very deep currents in the history of the Chinese Communist movement. Once before, when the revolution faced seemingly intractable odds, a creative set of military and political policies centered on mobilizing a wide range of forces had saved the day. The CCP had entered Yenan as a bedraggled remnant of what it had been in the mid-1930s. By the end of World War II the CCP and its army had vastly increased in size, strength, and vigor, even though the intervening years had witnessed almost constant military challenges from the Kuomintang or the Japanese. The CCP quite naturally tended in later years to idealize this time in the wilderness, seeing it as a period when the Party was truly close to the masses, when bureaucratism and social stratification did not tarnish revolutionary idealism, and when well-motivated leaders and their followers overcame seemingly insuperable odds to survive and eventually conquer. Given Mao's disgust with the sociopolitical results of the 1st FYP and the fundamental agricultural bottleneck that seemed to threaten the chances for the rapid industrial development that he craved, Mao and much of the rest of the top leadership seem to have harkened back to the Yenan spirit (and methods) as the source of their hope. Mass mobilization, social leveling, attacks on bureaucratism, disdain for material obstacles – these approaches would again save the Chinese revolution for its founders.

Thus, a broad range of forces pushed the leadership, and Mao in particular, toward adoption of a Great Leap strategy in 1958. A developmental dilemma, combined with dissatisfaction over the social consequences of the Soviet model, produced the search for a mobilizational alternative to previous practice. Organizational tensions between the Party and state apparatuses and between basic-level governmental and economic units in the countryside added to the stresses. Finally, beginning at the Tsingtao Conference in July 1957 and continuing through the following year, Mao began advocating a radically new approach toward making China strong and wealthy. This strategy, which was fleshed out during a series of meetings (at the Third Plenum in September–October, the Hangchow and Nanning conferences in January 1958, and the Chengtu Conference in March), called for use of organizational and mobilizational techniques to bring about simultaneous rapid development of agriculture and industry. The logical next step, the Great Leap Forward, was formally adopted at the Second Session of the Eighth Party Congress in May 1958. One of its most prominent features, the communization of agriculture, became official policy at the Peitaiho Conference in August of that year.

The Great Leap Forward strategy

Briefly, the strategy of the Great Leap had four key elements:[3]

1. To make up for a lack of capital in both industry and agriculture by fully mobilizing underemployed labor power. This approach would be especially important in the rural sector, where mass mobilization would produce essentially self-financed development that would solve the agricultural stumbling bloc to rapid overall growth and would provide inputs (especially food) for urban industrial growth. This, in turn, would allow China to accomplish the simultaneous development of industry and agriculture.

2. To carry out "planning" by setting ambitious goals for China's leading economic sectors and in essence simply encouraging any type of innovation necessary to permit the other sectors to catch up with these key sectors. "Bottlenecks be damned" captures the spirit of this approach.

3. In industry, to rely on both modern and traditional methods to enhance output. Thus, for example, major steel complexes would receive substantial new investment at the same time that "backyard" steel would be smelted by any group capable of doing so. Overall, the traditional sectors were to feed inputs into the modern sector while taking virtually nothing back in return.

4. In all areas, to disregard technical norms (and the specialists who stressed them) in favor of, in the lexicon of the times, achieving "more, faster, better, and more economical results." In practice the "more and faster" overwhelmed the "better and more economical."

This seemingly know-nothing approach appeared to work for a while. To an extent, of course, the appearances were false – the virtual destruction of the statistical system combined with tremendous pressure on cadres down the line to produce astonishing results. The

---

3 The economic strategy of the GLF is analyzed in Chapter 8.

not-too-surprising consequence was that an enormous amount of false reporting seriously misled the leadership as to the actual state of affairs in the country. Two elements did combine to make 1958 a year of substantial real economic achievements, however, and thus to lend some credibility to the Great Leap strategy.

First, the 1958 weather was exceptionally good, with the result that agricultural performance was better, other things being equal, than would normally have been the case. The organizational confusion attendant on the rapid formation of communes undoubtedly decreased agricultural yields, but the underlying weather conditions were sufficiently favorable to give at least the appearance of abundance throughout most of that fateful year.

Second, in the industrial sector many of the major projects that had been begun during the 1st FYP began to come on stream during 1958, producing impressive growth in industrial output. Again, objective conditions made it possible for a leadership that wanted to believe in the efficacy of the radical Great Leap strategy to find some support for its faith.

These various factors produced a rising crescendo of support for the GLF, both within the CCP and among the general populace, through the early and middle months of 1958. Foreign observers were astonished at the fervor of the popular efforts to leap into communism by performing shock-force work tasks. Groups of peasants put in incredibly long hours with virtually no rest and sustained this grueling pace for weeks on end. The leadership's claims for the efficacy of these efforts grew as the fervor built. In some areas, the newly formed communes began to do away with money as a medium of exchange, and by the fall the common assumption that the country's perennial food problem had been solved led to free supplies of food for many commune dwellers. In carrying out this mass mobilization strategy, the CCP cadres took over an increasing portion of the work from their government counterparts, and at the center the Party Secretariat under Teng Hsiao-p'ing assumed unprecedented power and authority. Had the GLF produced even a substantial portion of what was hoped, undoubtedly it would have further knit together the already impressive solidarity of the central leadership. But things did not turn out that way.

Politics of the Great Leap Forward

The record makes clear that Liu Shao-ch'i, Teng Hsiao-p'ing, and most other leaders supported the GLF strategy wholeheartedly throughout 1958. Indeed, the only obvious civilian dissenters at the Politburo level that year were Premier Chou En-lai and the top economic administrator, Ch'en Yun. Within the military, many army leaders did not like the new obligations to support the militia and to participate in civilian work that the GLF imposed on the PLA. Perhaps the most prominent among these military dissenters was Defense Minister Marshal P'eng Te-huai.

Liu Shao-ch'i and Teng Hsiao-p'ing had much to gain from the GLF. Both worked primarily in Party affairs and, as noted above, the CCP apparatus as a whole greatly expanded its power under the Leap. Teng personally had played a prominent role in the Anti-Rightist Campaign in 1957, and going back to the 1930s he could be considered to have been a part of Mao Tse-tung's personal clique in the Party. The GLF was primarily a Maoist alternative to the Soviet development strategy, and Teng identified himself closely with the success of this effort. He played a key role in managing the GLF via his position as head of the CCP Secretariat.

Liu Shao-ch'i had greater personal independence from Mao, but Liu also had to consider the succession. In the mid-1950's Mao had proposed that he should step back to the "second line," and by the beginning of 1958 he indicated that he would relinquish his position as head of state and remove himself from much of the day-to-day work in the Party leadership. In that way he could both determine the line of succession and devote himself more fully to working on the future direction of the Chinese revolution. During 1958 Liu Shao-ch'i probably had the succession very much on his mind, and personal support for Mao's plans would have been important in his strategy for obtaining the Chairman's blessing as the next in line.[4] Not surprisingly, therefore, Liu gave the keynote address on the GLF to the Second Session of the Eighth Party Congress, the meeting that formally adopted a Great Leap strategy for China. And in fact Liu did replace Mao as head of state when Mao relinquished that position in April 1959. In addition, of course, insofar as the GLF set China on the path of rapid progress toward communism, it would create an enviable situation for a successor to inherit. There is no indication that during 1958 Liu Shao-ch'i felt it would do anything other than this.

The concerns of the other three leaders mentioned above are easily understood. Ch'en Yun's opposition centered on strongly held views about the proper development strategy for China to pursue, views

4 Liu had formally obtained this in 1945, but that probably was not sufficient to make him fully confident as of 1958–59.

that differed fundamentally from the core elements of the Leap. Chou
En-lai certainly must have resented having his own organization – the
State Council – assume a diminished position in China's development
strategy, and Chou may very well in addition have believed in a
strategy closer to that advocated by Ch'en Yun. P'eng Te-huai had
differed with Mao over many issues since the 1940s. P'eng had taken
charge of the Hundred Regiments campaign against the Japanese
then and was subsequently sharply criticized by Mao for the conception and conduct of this offensive. P'eng Te-huai had led the Chinese
troops in Korea, and under his command Mao's son was lost when
his plane was shot down. At the conclusion of the Korean War,
relations between Mao and P'eng worsened. For these personal
reasons alone, P'eng may well have opposed a strategy so closely
identified with Mao as was the GLF.

But P'eng's opposition had stronger grounds than personal ani-
mosity. P'eng wanted a strong, modernized, professional military
organization, and he believed the Soviet Union was the only possible
source of the necessary weapons, equipment, technology, and aid.
P'eng sought good relations with Moscow and, not surprisingly,
modeled the PLA after the Red Army. Given his view of the
importance of Soviet military aid, he could do little else. Mao,
however, disagreed on all these counts. He felt that military spending
had to be curtailed and that the best way to accomplish this would be
to have the PLA enhance its capacity to wage guerrilla war (to defend
against invasion and prolonged occupation of the country) while at
the same time developing an indigenous nuclear weapons capability.
The latter would discourage the type of nuclear blackmail to which
the PRC might otherwise be susceptible. The nuclear component of
this strategy certainly put a premium on Soviet cooperation, but the
conventional side suggested that China should develop its own
military manuals and materials rather than rely on the Soviet model.

As noted above, Mao conceived of the GLF as a way to break
out of the Soviet economic development model's constraints, given
China's very different factor endowments. On the military side too,
Mao now sought to cast off the Soviet model, and he made this clear
at a prolonged enlarged meeting of the Military Affairs Commission.
It met directly after the Great Leap strategy was adopted by the
Second Session of the Eighth Party Congress in May and continued
until July 1958. Khrushchev had been supportive of Mao's desire for
nuclear aid (for reasons having more to do with Communist bloc
affairs than with Sino-Soviet relations), but this switch in China's

conventional military strategy increased the already rapidly growing strains in Sino-Soviet relations.[5] To add insult to injury from P'eng's perspective, the guerrilla conception of the role of the PLA demanded that the army create closer working relationships with the civilian population, a task that cut into military training and put the army in charge of the development and management of an enormous militia force.

Finally, at just this time Mao moved Lin Piao, long a close supporter and one of China's finest military tacticians, into a position on the Politburo that gave Lin a higher CCP rank than P'eng. The implications must have been clear – to both Lin and P'eng. During 1958 these tensions paled beside the overall enthusiasm of the bulk of the leadership for the GLF strategy; but when the Great Leap began to encounter serious problems, they rose to the surface to cause great resentment and prevent a timely shift in tactics for management of the GLF itself, ultimately producing a political and economic disaster of the first magnitude.

Inspection trips by the leaders during the fall of 1958 indicated that problems were brewing. In some places, peasant stories of food shortages belied the official statistics that showed abundance almost everywhere. In other areas, the excellent crops were not harvested fully and on time because too many workers had been shifted into local industry or had left to join the large state-run factories in the cities. Indeed, urban population growth skyrocketed during 1958. At the same time, the performance of the steel sector made clear that the original utopian goal of producing 30 million tons of steel in 1959 (1957 production had been 5.35 million tons!) could not be reached. Thus, by late 1958 Mao realized that adjustments were necessary, although he still felt the basic GLF strategy was sound.

Mao began to advocate these adjustments at the First Chengchow Conference in November and then followed this up at the Wu-ch'ang Central Work Conference and at the Sixth Plenum that followed it in November–December 1958. He called for the 1959 steel target to be reduced from 30 million to 20 million tons, and he also suggested that the government publicize grain production statistics that were lower than the highest internal estimates of the time. Mao himself characterized his approach in this period as having combined the revolutionary fervor of the August Peitaiho Meeting with practical spirit.[6] But soon the practical spirit – spurred on by alarming findings

5 On Sino-Soviet relations during this period, see Chapter 11 by Allen Whiting.
6 Mao, *Wan-sui* (1969), 258.

about the actual state procurement of grain at the end of 1958 – forced the Chairman to take stronger measures to rein in the increasingly obvious excesses of the GLF.

By the time the Chinese leadership gathered to map out strategy for 1959 at the Second Chengchow meeting in late February, Mao had decided that strong words were necessary to prevent the Leap from becoming a disaster. Focusing on problems in the rural communes, Mao declared himself in favor of "right opportunism." Essentially, he demanded that the level of communization be decreased, with more ownership rights being vested below the commune level itself. He called for a less cavalier attitude toward the interests of the basic-level cadres and peasants and threatened (for dramatic effect) to resign from the Party if appropriate reforms were not adopted. One senses here that Mao still fully believed in the correctness of the basic Great Leap strategy but that he worried that "leftist" errors among cadres carrying out the policy would produce a catastrophe that would do great harm both to China and to the Chairman's own position. During this same period, Mao invited Ch'en Yun to assume an active role in devising appropriate industrial targets and implementing related measures to make the Great Leap more rational and effective.

Events of the following few months made it clear that Mao was having trouble bringing middle-level cadres to heel in rectifying the errors of 1958. Some of the early stalwarts of the Leap, such as Wu Chih-p'u in Honan and Li Ching-ch'üan in Szechwan, showed little inclination to pull back on their earlier positions now. K'o Ch'ing-shih, the First Party Secretary in Shanghai and one of the key supporters of the backyard steel production drive, was reluctant to admit the problems of this effort. And more generally, sentiment in favor of going "all out" seemed to remain strong at the provincial through commune levels of the Party apparatus.

It is not completely clear just why this should have been the case. It may have reflected in part that these cadres had won increased power and influence as a result of the Great Leap strategy and yet had not worked at the basic levels, where they would feel more acutely the personal tensions the policy was creating. Also, the greater concentration of peasant cadres at the provincial through commune levels may partially explain this phenomenon, as the Great Leap had some of the atmosphere of a millenarian movement that would free the countryside from the chains of the cities and free the peasant cadres from the scrutiny of the urban-bred experts. In any case, all evidence suggests that Mao devoted much attention throughout the remainder of the spring of 1959 to reining in the excesses of the Great Leap in order to make his basic development strategy work.

The Tibetan revolt broke this concentration on development problems during the spring of 1959. This border region, whose society was so vastly different from the socialist community the Chinese sought to establish, had been smoldering for some time. While a truce of sorts had been worked out that had kept things calm in Tibet through the promised postponement of significant reforms, news of the Great Leap that came in from elsewhere significantly raised tensions. There had been revolts by Tibetans living in Szechwan in 1956 and in Kansu and Tsinghai provinces in 1958, with refugees from these areas living in Lhasa and contributing to the unease there. Some specific actions and missteps by Han soldiers and civilians in Tibet in early 1959 sparked an actual revolt in this tense atmosphere, and the Dalai Lama fled to India for safety.

The revolt evidently took the Chinese by surprise, and additional troops had to be sent in from outside the region to quell it. Although the main body of the revolt was put down with relative ease, the issue of how to handle the diplomatic and security fallout continued to trouble the leadership into the summer.[7] There is, however, no evidence suggesting that the leadership was divided over how to deal with this issue at the time.

THE LUSHAN CONFERENCE, JULY 1959

By July, when the top leadership gathered at the mountain resort of Lushan, the Tibetan revolt had been suppressed militarily, even if its diplomatic repercussions were just beginning. Mao and his colleagues now turned their attention back to reviewing the economic situation and mapping out a new strategy. Mao, at least, seems to have felt fairly well satisfied that his efforts at reining in the excesses of the Great Leap were achieving adequate results.

The Lushan Conference, however, lasted for almost the entire month of July and proved to be one of the most fateful in the history of the PRC. By the end of the meeting, Mao had launched a ferocious attack against P'eng Te-huai, China's defense minister and one of the ten marshals in the People's Liberation Army, and had set in motion

7 P'eng Te-huai subsequently recollected that he had the Tibetan question very much in mind as the Lushan Conference of July got under way: *P'eng Te-huai tzu-shu* (P'eng Te-huai's own account), 267.

the effort necessary to replace P'eng with Marshal Lin Piao. While still indicating that consolidation rather than expansion of the Great Leap was the order of the day, Mao had also launched an Anti-Right Opportunist Campaign that swamped the consolidation effort and itself produced a "second leap," with disastrous consequences. An enormous amount of data have been made available on the Lushan Conference over the years, but key questions about personal motivations and individual strategies still remain unanswered.

Indeed, the problems of interpretation extend back to before the conference itself. P'eng had traveled to several Warsaw Pact countries and returned to Peking on 12 June 1959. He had met with Khrushchev on this trip and may well have voiced his general consternation at the commune program and its effects on, among other things, the army and Sino-Soviet relations. In any case, almost immediately after P'eng's return to Peking, Khrushchev suddenly canceled the agreement under which Moscow was providing Peking with the nuclear aid so valued by Mao, and launched a public attack on the commune idea, the first such public criticism of the Chinese effort by the Soviet leader.

When Mao unleashed his counterattack against P'eng, he tried to suggest that Khrushchev and P'eng had colluded in a strategy that had Khrushchev pressure the Chinese over the Great Leap at the same time that P'eng attacked the policy privately at Lushan. To add further mystery to the situation, one of P'eng's close collaborators in his activities at Lushan was Chang Wen-t'ien, a vice-minister of foreign affairs who had long had close ties with the Soviet Union. MacFarquhar suggests, indeed, that it was Chang who put P'eng up to his critique of the GLF at Lushan.[8]

In any case, at Lushan itself P'eng Te-huai first voiced some criticisms of the Great Leap during small group discussions that overall seemed in keeping with the types of remarks Mao himself had been making during the previous few months. The one exception lay in a comment to the effect that Mao may not have fully understood what was going on in his own home village, as it appeared that the people there had received far more state aid than Mao had realized (an explosive assertion, given Mao's implicit claim that *he* understood China's rural situation better than any other leader).

On 14 July P'eng wrote a letter to Mao that summed up his feelings about the problems of the GLF. P'eng may have decided to take this

---

8 Roderick MacFarquhar, *Origins of the Cultural Revolution*, 2. 204–6.

action as a result of what he perceived to be a disturbing and continuing air of unreality at Lushan, or he may have been incited by Chang Wen-t'ien. Indeed, it is possible that P'eng's object was to embarrass Mao, and possibly to upset the succession to Liu Shao-ch'i that Mao had set in train. Under interrogation during the Cultural Revolution, P'eng claimed that he had intended the letter as a heartfelt and respectful communication to the Chairman for the latter's eyes only.[9] Much to his surprise, however, the Chairman had the letter printed and circulated to all participants at Lushan and gave it the rather formal sounding title of "P'eng Te-huai's letter of opinion" (*P'eng Te-huai ti i-chien shu*).

On 23 July Mao responded to the letter with a vengeance. Intervening comments by Chang Wen-t'ien and probably by others at the meeting may have convinced the Chairman he had a snowballing problem on his hands that he had better deal with quickly and decisively. Alternatively, it is possible that Mao had essentially "set up" P'eng once he had received the marshal's letter, using his actions as an excuse to replace P'eng with his own favorite, Lin Piao. If the latter is true, then Khrushchev's open criticism of the communes in a speech in Eastern Europe on 18 July played right into Mao's hands.

In any case, Mao's counterattack on 23 July drew a sharp line between permissible criticism and P'eng's "right opportunist" remarks. He claimed that P'eng sought to attack the Chairman rather than simply give advice on how to run the GLF better. He asked sarcastically why P'eng had not expressed his views at meetings earlier in the spring, since P'eng by then had already carried out the investigations that had led him to his negative conclusions. Mao reminded his audience that he himself had been sharply critical of the methods used in the GLF, but P'eng had held his silence. Now, at a major meeting designed to set the tone for policy over the coming months leading up to the tenth anniversary of the victory of the revolution in October, P'eng had chosen to launch an attack out of the blue, and evidently with substantial support from some quarters. The fact that P'eng lived in the house next to Mao's in the Chung-nan-hai compound in Peking must have added to the Chairman's sense of chagrin and betrayal. Mao's conclusion was clear – P'eng had so grossly violated permissible behavior that he and his "clique" would have to undergo rectification. Khrushchev's criticism of the commune movement opened P'eng to the accusation that he had

9 For P'eng's recollections of Lushan while under interrogation and the only authorized version of the letter to be published in China, see *P'eng Te-huai tzu-shu*, 265–287.

taken his criticisms to the Soviet leader to enlist his help before he had made them known to his fellow members of the Politburo.

Mao's biting presentation shocked his audience. P'eng himself did not sleep for nights afterward, reportedly being caught totally unawares by Mao's response. Given that much of what P'eng had to say had in fact been the type of language Mao himself had encouraged during the previous few months, others were evidently baffled by the vehemence of the Chairman's position. As noted, Mao did have a legitimate complaint about P'eng's previous silence. Also, some of P'eng's comments in the letter to Mao seemed in a subtle way to be direct and serious criticisms of the Chairman personally rather than simply of the policies the Chairman had encouraged (and about which P'eng had remained largely silent). Yet Mao's reaction was so contrary to normal practice that there may well have been some additional considerations at stake.

First, P'eng belonged to the group of marshals that in general had been disgruntled over the distribution of top posts after the communist victory in 1949. During the several decades of struggle for power, most of the key CCP leaders had been in the base areas, but some had spent much of their time either running the underground networks in China's cities (as had Liu Shao-ch'i) or doing formal liaison work with the Kuomintang (as had Chou En-lai). After 1949, the latter groups took a disproportionate share of top posts. The shadowy Kao Kang affair in 1954–55, the only Politburo-level purge before the Lushan meeting, seems to have involved a challenge by some of the former base area leaders (principally to Chou En-lai and Liu Shao-ch'i) for leading posts in the new regime. P'eng Te-huai was allegedly involved in that affair, but the desire to limit the damage produced a decision to hold the resulting purge to the smallest possible number of people. P'eng's actions at Lushan may, therefore, have been seen by Mao as his second attempt to position himself for higher office. The fact that Mao had recently moved P'eng's rival Lin Piao into a higher-ranking CCP post than P'eng's suggests that the Chairman had, by contrast, in fact been looking for a way to ease P'eng out of power. P'eng's criticism at Lushan may have provided an opportunity for Mao, with circulation of P'eng's letter as the first step in this maneuver.

Several months before Lushan, Liu Shao-ch'i had assumed the post that Mao relinquished as Chairman of the PRC. This reaffirmed Liu's claim to be the successor to Mao, and Liu's picture began for the first time to be given equal status with that of Mao in public displays. This transition may well have heightened the implicit contention over the succession issue and sparked P'eng to undertake more serious action than he otherwise might. It may also have increased Mao's own sensitivities to the succession dimension of the issue and made him see P'eng's criticism more readily in terms of a bid to weaken Mao's power (and Mao's ability to designate his own successor).

Chang Wen-t'ien also plays into this scenario. Chang had become the General Secretary of the Party during the Long March, but was later eased out by Mao in Yenan. A highly educated and articulate man, Chang had been demoted bit by bit since 1949. His close ties with the Soviet Union made him the natural choice for Peking's first ambassador to Moscow, but when he returned from that post he languished as a vice-minister of foreign affairs. Perhaps more important, he was demoted from full to alternate member status on the Politburo at the Eighth Party Congress in 1956 (he was formally removed from the Politburo altogether in 1961). Chang may well have viewed his rightful position as more exalted than the one to which he was being consigned, and with the tensions over the GLF and over the succession in 1959 he may have decided to act. His private conversations with P'eng Te-huai at Lushan could have sharpened his sense of opportunity, and he may have manipulated the less sophisticated P'eng into making the comments that the latter put forward. Through P'eng, Chang may have felt he could ally his personal ambitions with those of many of the old marshals. Also, P'eng was held in close affection among many top leaders, and Chang was not. In this scenario, then, P'eng may have been more a stooge than a plotter, used by Chang to create the atmosphere at Lushan that would justify Chang's own eloquent critique of the GLF. Chang delivered such a critique at length at the meeting on 20 July.[10]

Mao would probably have been highly sensitive to this type of maneuvering by Chang, and this may have determined the framework in which the Chairman viewed P'eng's criticism. This would also help explain the fact that Mao waited nine days after receipt of P'eng's letter before making a counterattack. Alternatively, of course, Mao may simply have wanted to circulate P'eng's letter and allow enough time for any sympathizers to show themselves in subsequent discussions before the Chairman made his own strong views plain. Should Mao have accepted the "Chang Wen-t'ien as

10 MacFarquhar presents the strongest case for the scenario involving Chang Wen-t'ien as a principal instigator: MacFarquhar, *Origins*, 2. 204–6.

instigator, P'eng Te-huai as stooge" scenario, the Chairman could still have decided to counterattack by aiming primarily at P'eng, for several reasons: his general desire to downgrade P'eng and promote Lin Piao; his need for a more well-known scapegoat; or P'eng's own discussions with Khrushchev, which may have made him the more vulnerable of the two.

One last possibility is that P'eng's challenge was implicitly more dangerous to Mao than Chang's. Unlike Chang, P'eng had close ties to a key constituency, the old marshals. Also, unlike Chang's, P'eng's position as minister of defense gave him unique access to information to understand the views of two key groups that Mao was anxious to keep firmly under his own aegis: China's peasants (whose views P'eng learned via military mail and other sources, as almost all conscripts in the PLA were from the countryside); and the PLA itself. Thus Mao may have felt it was imperative to train his fire on P'eng, even if Chang was the key figure behind the criticisms at Lushan.

The confrontation at the Lushan conference was then played out during the Lushan Plenum (the Eighth Plenum of the Eighth Central Committee) in August and an Enlarged Military Affairs Committee meeting in September. During the latter, P'eng formally lost his defense portfolio and was told to engage in study for several years. Chang Wen-t'ien and two others (Huang K'o-ch'eng, chief of staff of the PLA, and Chou Hsiao-chou, first secretary of Mao's home province of Hunan) were similarly purged as members of a (seemingly misnamed)[11] "military clique."

The consequences of Lushan

As suggested above, the long-term consequences of the Lushan Conference and the P'eng Te-huai affair were profound. One of the most significant was that Mao seems at Lushan to have broken the unwritten rules that had governed debate among the top leadership to that point. Before Lushan, it was accepted that any leader could freely voice his opinions at a Party gathering, and debate could be heated. Nobody would be taken to task subsequently for what he said, as long as he formally accepted and acted in accord with the final

---

11 P'eng several years later still expressed befuddlement as to why the four of them were called a "military" clique. Aside from P'eng's denial that any clique existed, two of the four were not connected with the military. But P'eng recalled that his detractors had been absolutely adamant in giving them this label. See *P'eng Te-huai tzu-shu*, 278–79.

decision reached. But Mao's actions at Lushan can be interpreted as having changed all that.

First, Mao labeled internal criticism by a top colleague "unprincipled factional activity." He then demanded that others choose between himself and his adversary, and that the loser be punished. At a minimum, this stance would hinder future free discussion among Politburo members. Given the fact that it required almost all other top leaders to take a stance[12] it undoubtedly sowed some personal bitterness that would later bear fruit. There is no evidence that any top-ranking leader voted against Mao after the Chairman had drawn the line at Lushan.

The P'eng Te-huai affair also produced some personnel changes of both short- and long-term significance. The most immediate result was Lin Piao's promotion to minister of defense. Lin, as noted, was a long-time follower of Mao's, and his new position gave Mao perhaps more secure control over the PLA than had previously been the case. Lin, in turn, was determined to keep P'eng from staging a political comeback that would threaten Lin's own power.[13] As will be seen below, this issue continued to fester in Chinese politics through the early 1960s.

Other personnel shifts took place in connection with Lushan. Lo Jui-ch'ing yielded his position as minister of public security to become PLA chief of staff. A more obscure change elevated Hua Kuo-feng to a higher post in Hunan province than he had previously held. Hua's promotion may have stemmed from an act of loyalty to Mao during the Chairman's time of need at Lushan. If so, Hua's service probably consisted of supporting Mao's version of developments in his home village of Shaoshan against the charges of P'eng Te-huai, backed up by Hua's superior, Hunan First Secretary Chou Hsiao-chou. Hua's willingness to undercut a long-time mentor in service to Mao stood him in good stead more than a decade later, when Mao again needed loyal subordinates to ferret out opposition in the wake of the Lin Piao affair.

Finally, as noted above, the dynamics of the Lushan meetings and the campaign against right opportunism that followed cut short the rectification and consolidation efforts Mao had set in motion during

12 Some, like Teng Hsiao-p'ing and Ch'en Yun, were absent from Lushan for different reasons.
13 P'eng in fact was designated to head the effort to develop a "third front" in Southwest China in 1965 in response to Mao's increasing sense of a security threat from the United States. But the Cultural Revolution cut short P'eng's effort. P'eng was summoned to Peking, where he endured Red Guard criticism, beatings, and incarceration until his death in 1974.

the previous half year. Opposition to opportunism swept the country during the fall of 1959, removing all those who had expressed doubts about the efficacy of the GLF policies during the previous months. Not surprisingly, this campaign effectively terminated the spring 1959 effort to rectify and consolidate the communes, and by early 1960 a new Great Leap was under way. Mao encouraged this development through, for example, his March 1960 endorsement of a new "constitution" for the Anshan Iron and Steel Works that replaced the previous management approach there (modeled after the steel works at Magnitogorsk) with one that put primary emphasis on politics. In April, the National People's Congress (NPC) formally adopted the Chairman's twelve-year agricultural program (a prominent feature of the brief "little" leap in the first half of 1956), and at the same NPC Mao's close supporter T'an Chen-lin again endorsed the commune program. Indeed, these spring 1960 months witnessed an attempt to organize urban communes and a renewal of the effort to "send down" (hsia-fang) cadres. It is not clear what occurred – other than the attack by P'eng Te-huai – that made Mao abandon his analysis of early 1959 in favor of renewed faith in a Great Leap strategy. The fact that during the first half of 1960 the leaders focused their attention primarily on Sino-Soviet relations permitted this "leap" strategy to mushroom to disastrous proportions.

The second Great Leap failed with a vengeance. According to figures released in 1981, agricultural output in 1960 was only 75.5 percent of that in 1958 (1961 output went down another 2.4 percent). Light industry uses primarily agricultural products as inputs, and thus light industrial shifts tend to lag one year behind those in agricultural output. In 1960, light industrial output decreased by 9.8 percent. It then declined by 21.6 percent in 1961 and another 8.4 percent in 1962. The cumulative impact was to produce a serious goods famine to match the food shortages. Heavy industrial output also declined sharply, going down 46.6 percent in 1961 as compared with 1960, and another 22.2 percent in 1962 over 1961.[14]

Overall, this renewed leap in late 1959 and 1960 produced the most devastating famine of the twentieth century in China (and probably in the world). The fundamental cause of this mass starvation was political, in that mistaken policies (such as insisting that the peasants leave land fallow in 1959 to avoid losses from not having enough

14 Figures from an article by Ma Hung in *JMJP*, 29 December 1981, 5, trans. in *FBIS*, 8 January 1982, 11–12. Ma Hung does not indicate how his percentages are calculated; presumably he used gross value of output each year.

storage facilities to handle the anticipated surplus) led inevitably to
serious food shortfalls. These shortfalls were exacerbated enormously
by the regime's blindness to the problem, to the extent that high
agricultural procurement quotas continued to drain the countryside
of available supplies into 1961. Bad weather and the mid-1960
withdrawal of Soviet technicians added to the difficulties, but neither
of these latter two elements would have produced the more than 20
million "excess" deaths (deaths over and above the normal death rate)
that occurred during 1959–61.[15]

The terrible consequences of the renewed Great Leap and the
rancor over the purge of P'eng Te-huai combined to unravel the
political consensus that had held the Yenan leadership together
through its days in the wilderness and its first decade in power. This
process of political deterioration developed through a range of issues,
any one of which in itself might have been manageable. But taken
together they set the stage for the final split of the Yenan leadership:
the Great Proletarian Cultural Revolution (GPCR). Six different
strands were woven into this tapestry of political decay during the
early 1960s.

First, Khrushchev's decision to try to bring a halt to the GLF and
demonstrate to China the great importance of its Soviet connection
by swiftly withdrawing Soviet advisors and aid at the height of the
1960 crisis had the unintended effect of shocking Mao into a fundamental reevaluation of the development of the Russian revolution.
To be sure, Mao had previously found much to fault in the evolution
of the Soviet Union and the actions of its leaders, but the Chairman
had not previously thought in terms of a fundamental degeneration of
the Soviet system. Khrushchev's crude pressure tactics raised this
possibility, and the thought was frightening. By implication, if the
Soviet revolution could change from socialist to fascist (or social
imperialist), then any socialist revolution was in theory reversible.
Given Mao's very much weakened position in Peking as a result of
the Great Leap fiasco, he evidently began to fear that his life's work in
China might have laid the basis ultimately not for the most just
society in the world but, rather, for an extremely exploitative system.

Mao thus began to devote a large portion of his energy to dealing
with the Soviet issue, and he brought K'ang Sheng, who had training

15 From 1959 to 1961 the total size of China's population fell by 13.5 million. The number of
"excess" deaths was, of course, far higher than this. State Statistical Bureau, comp.,
Statistical yearbook of China, 1984, 81. For a further discussion, see Chapter 8, notes 27
and 28.

in Marxism-Leninism and understood Soviet affairs well, to center stage to help him wrestle with Sino-Soviet relations. When within several years Mao began to have very serious doubts about the course his own successors were following, he then used the struggle with "Soviet revisionism" to give publicity in China to what amounted in reality to a critique of the policies of his own colleagues. Relatedly, K'ang Sheng had learned his approach to political in-fighting in the Soviet Union of the mid-1930s, and K'ang's ascendancy in Peking in the early 1960s therefore increased the tendency in the Forbidden City to wage struggles by Stalinist rather than more traditionally Maoist rules of the game.

Second, Mao's own prestige in the highest levels of the CCP suffered badly because of the GLF fiasco. Indeed, the Chairman made some form of self-criticism at a CCP Central Work Conference in Peking in June 1961. As noted earlier, Mao had in any case planned to retreat to the "second line" in the Politburo as of 1959 so that he could devote more time to major issues and be less involved in daily administrative affairs. But once the disasters of 1960–61 became fully evident, Mao found himself pushed more effectively out of day-to-day affairs than he would have liked. At the same time, some of his previous key supporters, such as Teng Hsiao-p'ing, no longer paid him the deference he felt was his due (Lin Piao proved to be the notable exception). Thus, for example, Mao complained during the Cultural Revolution that Teng had not listened to him since 1959. Teng had, as noted above, previously been a key supporter of Mao's. But when it came time to pick up the pieces from the Great Leap Forward catastrophe, Teng played a central role via his stewardship of the CCP Secretariat, and he did not fully agree with the Chairman over the proper remedies and the lessons to be drawn.

The third strand is precisely the fact that different leaders drew different conclusions from the utter failure of the Great Leap Forward. Mao personally recognized, as his subsequent actions showed, that political mobilization cannot itself produce rapid economic growth, and thus the Chairman did not proclaim major production increases as a goal of the Cultural Revolution. But as the GPCR also illustrates, Mao retained his faith in the efficacy of political mobilization to produce changes in outlook, values, and the distribution of political power. Most of Mao's supporters against P'eng Te-huai at Lushan, by contrast, concluded after their investigations of the situation in 1960–62 that large-scale political campaigns and the entire Yenan style of "high tide" politics had become counterproductive in virtually every way. Thus, while Mao no longer saw political movements as the basis for economic growth, many of his colleagues wanted to eschew campaign politics altogether.

Fourth, the CCP itself had taken charge of running the GLF, and the CCP suffered in prestige and organizational competence as a result of the failure of this monumental effort. The demoralization of the lower ranks of the CCP became still more acute as the country slowly pulled out of the Great Leap because in the end the cadres who had supported the second Leap were now purged for their "leftism," while Mao's own responsibility was carefully shielded to protect his legitimacy. For example, Mao's June 1961 self-criticism was never circulated to lower levels of the Party. Given the enormous strains on basic-level CCP cadres during 1960–62, it is not surprising that many lost their sense of revolutionary elan, thus giving the CCP apparatus to an extent feet of clay. The question of how best to rectify the basic-level CCP organs caused additional dissension in the upper levels, as various leaders proposed their own somewhat different methods of dealing with this important issue.

A fifth problem concerned disagreement over just how quickly China was recovering from the depredations of the GLF. Different assessments naturally justified different measures for bringing about a more normal situation. Mao tended to be more optimistic than many of his colleagues as this issue was debated in 1962, and indeed the Chairman seems to have begun to suspect that the pessimists were trying to limit his own flexibility and room for maneuver in the system. As Mao became more concerned with revisionism, this set of issues assumed increasing importance for him.

Finally, whatever one's views about the speed of China's recovery, there was no doubt about the extraordinary extent of the damage that the GLF (and especially its second stage) had done. In other words, the events of 1959–61 essentially vindicated what P'eng Te-huai had said and written at Lushan. To add insult to injury, P'eng carried out fairly extensive rural investigations during 1962, and that August he summarized his findings and submitted an 80,000-character document to the Central Committee justifying his rehabilitation on the grounds that his principled criticism at Lushan had been correct. But Lin Piao could not tolerate P'eng's rehabilitation, and Mao did not want it either. In addition, by 1962 Mao may already have been thinking about the need to rely increasingly on Lin and the PLA as his concerns about his other colleagues grew. Thus, Mao blocked P'eng's rehabilitation – and in so doing did further damage to the norms that had governed relations among the leaders to that date.

AFTER THE LEAP: THE LIU–TENG PROGRAM

In sum, the failure of the GLF left a full menu of problems on the plates of the central leaders. These varied from interpersonal relations among the top people to frayed institutional capabilities, to the relation of foreign to domestic policy. Basic political methods as well as immediate economic and other goals were at issue. All these concerns, moreover, interacted in a way that tended to heighten Mao's suspicions and make it more difficult to find agreed-upon solutions. In more detail, these issues arose as follows:

The leadership began to turn its attention to coping with the Great Leap disaster during a meeting at Peitaiho in July–August 1960. The termination of all Soviet aid to China that June forced Peking to think in terms of a self-reliant development effort and to take stock of the deteriorating situation in the countryside. Several types of initiatives flowed out of Peitaiho and subsequent deliberations over the following few months, as the magnitude of the summer crop failure became evident. First, the second Great Leap was formally terminated, and the guiding policy now became one of "agriculture as the base, industry as the leading factor," with "readjustment, consolidation, filling out, and raising standards" replacing the previous formula of "more, faster, better, and more economical results." Mao had first put forward the "agriculture as the base" formula in 1959, but it was not implemented until the fall of 1960. It became official CCP policy at the Ninth Plenum in January 1961.

Second, the CCP center sought to increase its control over its badly damaged nationwide apparatus through the re-creation of six regional bodies. (The parallel regional government bodies that had existed in the early postliberation years were not reestablished.) Relatedly, efforts were made to salvage the situation in the countryside through moving back toward a system that provided greater material incentives. The disastrous fall harvest drove home the magnitude of the problem to the extent that in November Chou En-lai presided over the drafting of an emergency measure on rural policy, called the Twelve Articles on People's Communes. This stopgap document essentially permitted great decentralization within the communes. Indeed, in Byung-joon Ahn's words, with the implementation of the Twelve Articles, "the GLF simply collapsed."[16]

16 Byung-joon Ahn, *Chinese politics and the Cultural Revolution*, 47.

Taking the pressure off cadres to implement GLF policies did not, however, make clear where the CCP should go from there. The specific reasons for the failure of the Great Leap remained unclear, and the CCP had not yet devised appropriate responses to put the country back on a long-term path of development. Rather, during the spring of 1961, local leaders were in general given great leeway to implement whatever measures – even including in many places a de facto dissolution of the communes – they felt were necessary to alleviate the famine that was devastating China. On a policy level, two types of responses were adopted. The first, initiated by Lin Piao and focused on the military, stressed renewed study of politics as a way to boost morale and increase discipline. The second, led by Liu Shao-ch'i and Teng Hsiao-p'ing, produced a series of investigations that provided the material used for programmatic policy documents in major spheres of work.

In the military, in September 1960, Lin called for a program of concentrated study of Mao's works. Famine in the countryside had produced considerable demoralization among the soldiers, and Lin felt it important to revive political work to combat this. Since this effort was directed in general toward barely educated peasant recruits, it inevitably involved a simplification and dogmatization of Mao's Thought. The attempt to make Mao's Thought comprehensible to simple soldiers eventually produced the *Quotations from Chairman Mao Tse-tung*, the "little red book," which would become the Bible of the Red Guards during the Cultural Revolution. During 1960–63, however, those responsible for work in urban China disparaged the idea that Lin's dogmatic exegesis of Mao's writing could serve any useful purpose outside the military.

Liu and Teng supervised the investigation and drafting process that culminated in a series of programmatic documents that are generally known by the number of articles in each. During 1961–62 the following major policy papers were produced: Sixty Articles on People's Communes; Seventy Articles on Industry; Fourteen Articles on Science; Thirty-five Articles on Handicraft Trades; Six Articles on Finance; Eight Articles on Literature and Art; Sixty Articles on Higher Education; and Forty Articles on Commercial Work. While, of course, the specifics concerning the drafting process varied for each of these policy papers, all shared some elements. In each case a Party leader took charge of the drafting process. Thus, Mao oversaw the drafting of the Sixty Points, Po I-po supervised the Seventy Articles on Industry (after preliminary work under the aegis of Li Fu-ch'un), Li Hsien-nien covered finance, Chou Yang and Lu Ting-i managed literature and art, P'eng Chen handled education, and so forth.

In addition, three broad policy groups were established under the Secretariat to oversee and coordinate policy toward major issue areas: Li Fu-ch'un and Ch'en Yun's group reviewed economic policies, P'eng Chen's took charge of cultural and educational affairs, and Teng Hsiao-p'ing's covered political and legal work. This mode of operation thus had Ch'en Yun, for example, make significant policy reports and pronouncements in the following areas in 1961: fertilizer production, foreign trade, urban population growth, agricultural policy, and coal production. In early 1962, as noted below, Ch'en became centrally involved in the overall evaluation of China's conditions and the policies to be pursued in the future.[17]

In drafting the various program documents, the person in charge typically first ascertained the actual situation and problems through carrying out on-the-spot investigations, often including (where appropriate) visits to units or locales with which he had ties from the past. In addition, meetings were convened with the experts or practitioners involved so as to mobilize their support and solicit their opinions. These documents went through a number of drafts, most of which reflected additional consultation both within the Party and among the non-Party experts. This presumption that experts could make valuable contributions conflicted sharply with the approach Lin Piao was taking at that very time in the military. To Lin, Mao's Thought contained both the answers and the source of any necessary inspiration. The division among top leaders in the wake of the Great Leap Forward disaster thus went beyond personal political likes and dislikes and included fundamental aspects of policy process and political calculation.

The substance of the policies developed by the apparatus under Liu Shao-ch'i and Teng Hsiao-p'ing also struck at the heart of the assumptions that underlay the Great Leap Forward. In fertilizer production, for example, Ch'en Yun called for construction of fourteen additional plants, each with a 50,000 ton per year capacity for

---

17 The precise institutional roles of various CCP and state organs in this process are not clear. The Secretariat under Teng Hsiao-p'ing seems to have assumed overall charge of the drafting of these documents. But key individuals involved, including Po I-po, Chou Yang, Lu Ting-i (until 1962), and Ch'en Yun did not themselves serve on the Secretariat. Evidently the Secretariat tapped the resources of a range of organs, including the pertinent State Council staff offices, to develop the policies noted. The role of the State Council in this drafting process remains unclear. It did, of course, become involved in the implementation of these policies once they had been approved by the Politburo.

production of synthetic ammonia. These plants would be large and modern, supplanting the inefficient small-scale chemical fertilizer production that had become so popular during the Great Leap Forward. They would also require substantial imports of key components from abroad, moving China away from its previous policy of self-reliance. Po I-po's Seventy Articles on Industry placed renewed stress on the role of experts and on the use of material incentives – almost directly contradicting the Anshan Iron and Steel Constitution that Mao had promulgated the previous year. The Eight Articles on Literature and Art promised the reintroduction of traditional art forms and permitted a broader range of topics to be explored by artists. The Sixty Articles on Education stressed quality of education and undercut many of the locally run (*min-pan*) schools that had been opened as a part of the GLF strategy. And the Sixty Articles on People's Communes articulated a detailed set of regulations that fixed the team as the basic accounting unit, made provision for private plots, and in general tried to shift agricultural production toward a system that provided greater material incentives for peasant labor.

These policies overall marked a dramatic shift from the priorities of the GLF. They brought experts and expertise back to center stage, produced greater reliance on modern inputs to achieve growth, reimposed central bureaucratic controls over various spheres of activity, and appealed to the masses more on the basis of material self-interest than of ideological mobilization. There is no evidence that Mao Tse-tung objected to these trends during 1961. Indeed, Mao himself had actively participated in drafting the Sixty Articles on People's Communes and had called for serious investigations to be carried out at the Canton meeting in March 1961. In June the Chairman had made a self-criticism at a central work conference in Peking. But as these investigations and consultations yielded to policy programs, Mao evidently became increasingly disconcerted – and he was not alone.

The Seven Thousand Cadres Conference, January–February 1962

The situation erupted during 1962, when basic disagreement arose as to how quickly the country was recovering and, therefore, over what future goals and time frames should be. In January–February a Seven Thousand Cadres Work Conference convened to review methods of leadership and to sum up the situation. There was more agreement on the former than on the latter. Liu Shao-ch'i made the key report and several other speeches to this conference, and he called for greater use of democratic centralism and less personal command by key individuals. In addresses on 26 and 27 January, he blamed much of the recent trouble on the Party center and stressed the importance of avoiding the kind of brutal purges and counterpurges that had racked the Party during the twists and turns of the previous few years. Liu specifically criticized the vehemence of the attack on "right opportunism" in the wake of the Lushan Conference, and he is reported to have called for the rehabilitation of P'eng Te-huai, among other "rightists." Mao's own talk to the conference on 30 January generally endorsed these themes, and Mao informed the cadres in the audience that he himself had made a self-criticism the previous June (he also warned them to be prepared to do the same). Thus, this conference in general helped to patch up the rather tattered decision-making apparatus within the Party.

But in other areas the conference failed to produce a consensus. In terms of what had caused the Great Leap disaster, Liu argued that wrong political decisions accounted for 70 percent, with the Soviet withdrawal of aid and the several years of bad weather accounting for the other 30 percent. Mao felt this stood the true situation on its head. Liu also felt that the economy still remained in a crisis and would take a long time to put back into shape. Mao argued, by contrast, that things had now largely returned to normal. Perhaps Mao meant his evaluation to apply only to the political and not the economic situation. Liu, in any case, appears to have harbored a far gloomier assessment of the general situation than Mao at this time. His more pessimistic evaluation would, in turn, provide a rationale for more far-reaching measures to salvage the situation.

Interestingly, Chou En-lai supported Mao at this meeting and seems to have given an overall positive assessment of the Great Leap Forward. On substantive issues later in 1962, by contrast, Chou strongly backed Liu Shao-ch'i and Ch'en Yun. Thus, the premier's performance at the Seven Thousand Cadres Conference evidently reflected his operational practice of siding with Mao whenever there was an open clash more than his substantive agreement with the Chairman's position. Chou is often compared by Chinese to a "willow branch," and his actions during the spring of 1962 reconfirm the appropriateness of a characterization that includes both strength and a graceful ability to bend with the wind. Not surprisingly, Mao also received strong verbal backing from Lin Piao at the conference.

Three other leaders were less clear in their positions. Teng Hsiao-p'ing reiterated the correctness of Mao Tse-tung Thought but then supported Liu Shao-ch'i on substantive issues such as the rehabilitation of rightists. Ch'en Yun had been asked to present a report on the situation in finance and trade, but he demurred on the basis that he had not yet fully clarified the situation in that sphere. Perhaps, however, P'eng Chen's performance sums up most clearly the difficult and uncertain position in which Politburo members found themselves in January 1962.

P'eng had ordered his subordinates in the Peking municipal hierarchy to investigate the real causes of the GLF disaster and prepare a report for him. It is not clear whether he did this on his own or as an integral part of a broader leadership effort to determine the lessons that should be drawn from the GLF. In any case, the initial investigation started in late May 1961, and in November P'eng issued a second order that all central directives between 1958 and 1961 should be reviewed as part of this effort. Teng T'o, a Peking Party secretary who had edited the *People's Daily* until 1957, assumed charge of this investigation. After convening a meeting at the Ch'ang-kuan-lou in December 1961, Teng T'o reported on the group's findings to P'eng Chen.

The report they made placed the blame for the disaster directly on the mobilizational politics of the GLF strategy. The center had approved and circulated too many false reports, had issued too many conflicting directives, and had virtually totally ignored economic reality in its calls for action by local cadres. In short, the GLF disaster must be laid largely at the doorstep of the Politburo. Given Mao's headstrong leadership of that body since 1958, there is little question that the Ch'ang-kuan-lou report in fact amounted to a severe critique of the Chairman's own work.

P'eng reportedly went to the Seven Thousand Cadres Conference in January 1962 prepared to spell out the case made in the Ch'ang-kuan-lou report. When he grasped the tenor of the meeting, however, he hesitated and in fact did not criticize the Chairman's leadership at this major conference. P'eng by then fully recognized the magnitude of the GLF catastrophe and certainly would not support that type of mobilizational effort again in the future. At the same time, he could not bring himself to confront Mao on the issue directly. This kind of lingering ambivalence meant, in turn, that even after the searing experiences of 1961, a current in support of GLF-type policies would remain strong within the Party throughout 1962 and thereafter.

Given the enormity of the problems engendered by the GLF, it is a tribute to Mao's inherent authority that he could still shape the outcome of conclaves such as the Seven Thousand Cadres Conference in 1962. This refects the unique position that the Chairman had assumed within the Chinese Party after 1949. Unlike other Communist parties in power, the Chinese created distinctive roles for the First Secretary (or General Secretary) and the Chairman. The former role was an integral part of the organizational hierarchy of the Party. The latter position stood apart from and above that hierarchy. It was a position whose formal authority evolved somewhat during successive Party constitutions but whose real power derived from the stature of the incumbent, who was regarded as virtually a philosopher-king. In the eyes of his colleagues, Mao had conceptualized the Chinese revolution itself. While people recognized that he could make serious mistakes and thus might try to vitiate his initiatives through bureaucratic devices, none had the courage (or gall) to question directly Mao's fundamental evaluation of the current situation and the priority tasks of the Party. There were, in short, no effective institutional curbs on Mao's power, and the Chairman used this advantage with great skill when he felt challenged or threatened.

Unfortunately, insufficient documentation is available from the Seven Thousand Cadres Conference to specify the dynamics of the discussions or the details of the final consensus at the meeting. It appears that on balance the conference left many issues only partly resolved. Indeed, the major issues with which it grappled continued to engender disagreement and tension among the leaders throughout the remaining years before the Cultural Revolution. These issues included the following. The rehabilitation of rightists: This meeting split the difference by agreeing that many should be brought back but that P'eng Te-huai and some other leading "rightists" should remain under a cloud. An evaluation of the current situation: This conference did not reach an agreement that would hold for more than a month or two. Mao seems to have forced a reasonably optimistic perspective on the conference, but this was challenged almost immediately and subsequently remained a contentious issue. Party rectification: While this conference made some progress toward accomplishing the vitally necessary task of reconstructing a disciplined and responsive Party apparatus, the issue of how best to carry out this task would continue to sow discord among the leaders. Thus, the January–February 1962 conference marked an uncertain transition from the desperation of 1961 to a more positive effort to shape events in 1962 and afterward. While the meeting reflected the fact that Peking was again ready to begin to seize the initiative, it also revealed the fissures within the central leadership that the traumatic previous three years had produced.

These fissures cracked open a bit wider under the strain of a Ministry of Finance projection, made available to Ch'en Yun just after the Seven Thousand Cadres Conference in February 1962, that the central government would face a budget deficit of 2 billion to 3 billion *yuan* that year under current plans and projections. Ch'en, always sensitive to the inflationary pressures budget deficits produced, prepared a wide-ranging report that cast the overall situation in gloomy terms and called for appropriate changes in plans. This included a significant scaling down of the production targets discussed during the previous month. Ch'en feared a deteriorating food situation and suggested emergency measures to increase marginally the supplies of fish and soybeans. He also argued that the poor agrarian situation demanded a revision of the recently adopted plans for recovery. This would entail designating 1962–65 as a period of recovery, where energies would remain focused on rural production, and growth in the metallurgical and machine-building industries would necessarily be held back.

With Mao in Wuhan, Liu Shao-ch'i had assumed charge of day-to-day affairs of the Politburo. He called the Hsi-lou Conference, named for the building in Peking in which it was convened on 21–23 February, to discuss Ch'en's views. The Hsi-lou meeting strongly endorsed Ch'en's sober assessment, which in any case seems to have come close to the picture that Liu himself had painted at the recently concluded Seven Thousand Cadres Conference. In addition, at Hsi-lou both Liu and Teng Hsiao-p'ing endorsed the various systems of "individual responsibility" in agriculture (a de facto partial decollectivization) that had been tried in hard-hit provinces such as Anhwei. These endorsements reflected a belief that the agricultural situation still had not "bottomed out" as of the time of the conference. Also, at Hsi-lou Li Hsien-nien admitted the accuracy of Liu Shao-ch'i's criticism of recent state financial work.

The Hsi-lou Conference decided to convene a meeting of Party core groups in the State Council to discuss this new assessment. They met on 26 February and, enthusiastically endorsing Ch'en's analysis, passed the issue to the Secretariat. Liu Shao-ch'i urged the Secretariat to circulate Ch'en's report as a Central Committee document, with an attached comment by the Standing Committee of the Politburo. Since (unnamed) people objected to the tone of the proposed document, Liu, Teng, and Chou traveled to Wuhan to report to Mao on its contents and background. Mao reportedly approved circulation of the document. After this, Ch'en had the Central Finance and Economics Small Group discuss the document and a related report on commercial work that also reflected Ch'en's views.

Following the Central Finance and Economics Small Group meeting, Chou En-lai took charge of this key body. Reportedly, Ch'en had to pull back from day-to-day involvement due to illness, although he evidently remained an influential counselor behind the scenes.[18] The Ministry of Metallurgy refused to accept Ch'en's analysis and continued to hold out for a larger steel target – placed at 25 to 30 million tons by 1970 – as the core of the new Five-Year Plan. Ch'en stressed instead the need for a recovery period followed by balanced growth. In early summer 1962 Chou En-lai brought together the secretaries of the six regional Party bureaus, along with members of the Politburo, to focus on Ch'en's ideas, which Chou put forward as the correct framework for CCP planning. K'o Ch'ing-shih, the Maoist stalwart from Shanghai who had been a key force in the backyard steel furnace drive of 1958, objected to Chou's position on the ground that the premier was characterizing the situation in terms far worse than those used at the Seven Thousand Cadres Conference. Chou countered that the budget deficit that sparked this revision became known only after the conference had been adjourned. Chou's speech was then circulated to a wider audience, evidently over K'o's strong objections.

Thus, two significantly different assessments of the situation emerged during the first half of 1962. Mao Tse-tung, supported at least by some provincial officials, by Lin Piao in the military, and by people in the heavy industry sector,[19] argued that the country was well on the way to recovery and thus that the time had come to begin to exercise some initiative in moving China farther along a socialist

18 In 1966 Liu Shao-ch'i "confessed" that during 1962 he had been overly influenced by Ch'en's views. Ch'en also seems to have attended the Tenth Plenum in September 1962, even though no other public appearances by him were recorded before the Cultural Revolution.

19 Mao's support almost certainly also came from others, such as T'an Chen-lin in agriculture, but the documentation to support this is lacking.

path. Mao thus opposed further decollectivization in agriculture and backtracking in other areas, such as culture. Mao's ruminations on the development of the Soviet revolution were spurring his concern over trends in China during these months, but overall he seems to have spent most of the time from February 1962 until the August Peitaiho Central Work Conference in partial seclusion in central China.

Liu Shao-ch'i, Teng Hsiao-p'ing, Ch'en Yun, and others, by contrast, had concluded by late February that the situation remained almost desperately bad and that a significant recovery period would be necessary before Peking could again really assume the initiative. The grim rural situation demanded further concessions to peasant material interests in the form of official endorsement of speculative activities by the peasants and the type of decollectivization referred to as "going it alone" (tan kan). The general social demoralization demanded that the regime yield to popular tastes in cultural fare, permitting the staging of old operas and plays and the composition of other works that played down revolutionary politics in favor of traditional favorite themes and characters. The desperate economic situation also demanded that the regime woo former capitalists and the technical intelligentsia into active efforts to revive the urban economy. Thus, while Mao felt the general situation permitted renewed efforts to move the country again toward his socialist ideals, many of his colleagues demurred. They thought the regime would have to retreat farther and nurse its institutional capabilities back to health before a more active strategy would be feasible.

The Peitaiho Conference and the Tenth Plenum

The clash between these two approaches came at the August 1962 Peitaiho meeting.[20] Liu and his confreres came to this meeting having spent the preceding months actively pursuing the policy implications of Ch'en Yun's analysis of China's situation. Thus, for example, in

20 This work conference began on 6 August and continued until the latter part of that month. These major summer central work conferences were more than simply business meetings, although they were extremely important in policy formulation. In addition, they were social gatherings, with wives frequently in attendance, evening entertainment provided, and time allowed for side trips and diversions. Key leaders might miss significant parts of the conferences, presumably reading the stenographic record to keep posted on the deliberations. Thus, conferences often appeared to drag on for one to two months and may even, as here, have shifted location part way through. Since these conferences generally were not covered in the press at the time, it is often impossible to establish precise dates for their opening and closing.

February they convened a National Conference on Scientific and Technological Work in Canton, and a month later they brought together a National Conference for the Creation of Dramas and Operas in the same city. Both meetings tried to mobilize support by yielding to the preferences of the groups of non-Party participants. As of early August, a related conference on short novels about the countryside was in session in Dairen. In the interim, Teng Hsiao-p'ing convened a meeting of the Secretariat to review the data on individual farming (*tan kan*), at which he pronounced his subsequently famous dictum "It does not matter whether a cat is black or white, so long as it catches mice." And, of course, the already recounted succession of events around Ch'en Yun's assessment was unfolding.

Mao Tse-tung approached this meeting in another frame of mind. He evidently felt increasingly isolated from the mainstream of decision making, even thought his signature continued to be sought on Central Committee documents before they were disseminated. Mao reportedly had ceased sitting in on Politburo meetings as of January 1958.[21] Originally, this had probably reflected his assumption of more independent decision-making authority at the start of the Great Leap; or it may have been part of a genuine effort to retire to the "second line" and give his colleagues more prestige. But over time it may well have taken on other significance for him, making him feel increasingly isolated and neglected by his colleagues. Mao clearly began in 1962 to search for ways to reassert himself in the system, and one of the most interesting dimensions of the politics of the period 1962–65 is the putting together of the coalition that would enable the aging Party Chairman to break into a position of dominance in 1966.

This search coincided with the development of the independent political ambitions of three key individuals – Chiang Ch'ing, Lin Piao, and K'ang Sheng. Others hovered in the background, at times playing important roles. Ch'en Po-ta, always the Maoist loyalist, was willing to encourage any move that would enhance the role of his patron. Wang Tung-hsing, a former bodyguard of Mao's, became involved in the byzantine palace security dimension. Chou En-lai played the political game cautiously, always keeping his lines open to both the Chairman and other members of the Politburo. At the crucial moment in 1966, however, Chou put himself squarely

21 *Yomiuri Shimbun*, 25 January 1981, trans. in *FBIS/PRC* Annex, 13 March 1981, 7.

on Mao's side, enabling the Chairman to complete the coalition necessary to launch the Cultural Revolution.

As Mao faced the Central Work Conference at Peitaiho in the late summer of 1962, however, he had yet to formulate fully either the challenge or his strategy. He was highly troubled by the events of the months since the Seven Thousand Cadres Conference, though, and he listened to the reports during the first days of the Peitaiho meeting with chagrin. Chu Te, one of the most respected of the old marshals, called for expansion of the individual responsibility system in agriculture and for other measures that put him solidly with Liu and Teng's evaluation of the problems in the countryside. Ch'en Yun reiterated his position on the rural situation and tasks. Other Politburo members reported on major issue areas,[22] but unfortunately no information is available on either the timing or the substance of their remarks. The timing is important, because on 9 August Mao addressed the meeting employing such biting sarcasm that his talk probably seriously affected the tone of the entire proceedings.

Mao bitterly attacked the Ministry of Finance, whose budget deficit projection had provided the basis for Ch'en Yun's February report and all that had followed from it. He then stressed the fact that China still faced the need for class struggle, and it was obvious that he felt the continuing retreat from socialist policies simply exacerbated the dangers in this sphere. He attacked directly the adoption of an individual responsibility system in farming and called for a campaign of "socialist education" to rectify the Party apparatus in the rural areas. And he warned against the possibility of capitalist or even feudal restoration in the PRC. Chiang Ch'ing subsequently revealed that she had been working on the Chairman to sensitize him to the "degeneration" of the arts and culture since 1959, and her proddings had found a reflection in Mao's stress on the need for proletarian ideology in his address to the Peitaiho meeting.[23]

Mao thus succeeded in turning the agenda around so that it at least in part reflected his own priorities. His commanding presence was most easily brought to bear at these central conclaves, and he took full advantage of his political resources there. Liu Shao-ch'i evidently challenged the Chairman's priorities in at least some respects at this

---

22 Ch'en Po-ta, only an alternate Politburo member at the time, reported on agriculture; Li Hsien-nien on commerce; Li Fu-ch'un (possibly with Po I-po) on industry and planning; and Ch'en I on the international situation. Liu Shao-ch'i also addressed this meeting.

23 Roxane Witke, *Comrade Chiang Ch'ing*, 304–5. Witke places this speech on 6 August, while other documentary sources give the 9 August date used in the text.

meeting, as Liu subsequently commented that he had "inclined to the right" at Peitaiho and had not begun to correct himself until the Tenth Plenum that convened on 24–27 September. What emerged was a patchwork compromise in an atmosphere of somewhat heightened political tension.

The Tenth Plenum revealed all the cleavages and contradictions that had boiled up at the Peitaiho meeting. Mao presided over this meeting, and his speech to the participants closely linked the degeneration of the Soviet Union to the fact that class struggle would still exist in China for decades to come. Mao was persuaded by Liu and others at this meeting, however, to make clear that the issue of class struggle should not be allowed to swamp other policy decisions coming out of the Tenth Plenum, as had happened after the Eighth Plenum at Lushan in 1959.[24]

Mao's general concern with class struggle reflected a more basic fear of his that the Chinese revolution was beginning to head down the path of "revisionism." A cynic might note that "revisionism" to Mao seemed to be anything that he disliked, but dismissing the term on this level would in fact be misleading. Mao was very concerned to shepherd the revolution along collectivist and relatively egalitarian paths. He distrusted urban-based bureaucracies and China's intellectuals as a whole. Even though many of his concrete policy proposals had the effect of exploiting the countryside to develop urban-based industry, he nevertheless seems genuinely to have thought of himself as a representative of China's poor peasants. While Mao believed in the efficacy of technological progress, he nevertheless distrusted the high culture and its carriers that were essential for nurturing technical development.

In the aftermath of the GLF tragedy, Mao could not argue as of 1962 that mass mobilization could restore the country's productive capacities. He therefore continued to yield to the entreaties that the Party make full use of material incentives and of technical expertise to recoup the situation. But Mao also as of the Tenth Plenum decided to draw the line. He resolutely opposed decollectivization in agriculture and insisted that the communes remain intact (or be restored where they had been abandoned). He also recognized that current policies would increase the strength of the groups in society that he trusted least – the former landlords and rich peasants in the countryside, former capitalists, technical specialists, and intellectuals in the cities.

---

24 *JMJP*, 15 January 1982, 5, trans. in *FBIS*, 25 (January 1982), K-22. A Partial text of Mao's speech is available in: *Chinese Law and Government*, 1.4 (Winter 1968–69), 85–93.

He also feared that a period of normality would nurture tendencies toward sluggish bureaucratism among the many middle-level cadres that had shown themselves so prone to this evil in the past. Thus, Mao called for measures to bring political issues onto the agenda (but without disrupting normal work). He also strengthened the organs responsible for handling those who slip into counterrevolution – the Public Security Ministry and the CCP Control Commission.

The Tenth Plenum embraced Mao's overall analysis in theory but in its concrete provisions kept close to the methods that had been worked out during 1961–62 to bring about a recovery from the Great Leap Forward. This compromise produced a communiqué that in some paragraphs echoed Mao's rhetoric and in others drove home the logic that Liu, Teng, and Ch'en had put forward. That this compromise was not put together easily is confirmed by reports that at this plenum Liu Shao-ch'i, Li Hsien-nien, Teng Tzu-hui, and Hsi Chung-hsun made self-criticisms. A subtheme that continued to rankle at this meeting was the P'eng Te-huai affair. As noted P'eng wrote and circulated an 80,000-character self-justifying report to provide a basis for his full rehabilitation. Mao demurred, agreeing only to assign P'eng some low-level work in the future. The Chairman argued that only those who fully recognized their errors would be rehabilitated – evidently unwilling to admit that in P'eng's case, the error was Mao's.

Much Chinese and Western historiography has portrayed 1963–65 as a time of two-line struggle between a Maoist camp, on the one hand, and a Liu–Teng headquarters, on the other. The real situation, though, was not so simple. The group that helped Mao launch the Cultural Revolution in 1966 consisted of diverse elements that had joined together for different reasons. Thus, one important desideratum of these years concerns how the various components of the Maoist coalition formed, and the impact each had on the politics of this era. The other key dimension is the evolution of Mao's own thinking as he came to grips both with his potential coalition partners and with the policies that Liu Shao-ch'i and his colleagues were implementing. The two key coalition groups were those headed by Lin Piao and Chiang Ch'ing. After analyzing these, we turn to Mao's direct attempts to deal with the major policy initiatives of Liu and company during 1963–65.

THE RISE OF LIN PIAO

Lin Piao faced two tasks after he became minister of defense in September 1959. One was to consolidate his position in the PLA, the other was to solidify his relationship with Mao Tse-tung and help Mao to enhance his own power in the Chinese political system. Lin executed a complex strategy for accomplishing these related tasks, one that eventually put him in a key position to help Mao launch and sustain the Cultural Revolution.

Lin began his reform of the PLA by bringing back into prominence the Military Affairs Commission (MAC) of the Party. This body had existed nominally throughout the period of P'eng Te-huai's stewardship, but in reality its role seems to have diminished with the increasing estrangement of P'eng and Mao. Lin revived the MAC, appointing to its standing committee seven of China's ten marshals (leaving out P'eng Te-huai and Chu Te, who allegedly supported P'eng in 1959).

Little is known about the composition of the MAC, as the Chinese have never published a full list of its members or details on its staff.[25] Before 1976, though, all individuals identified as being MAC members were uniformed members of the military, with the sole exception of Mao Tse-tung, its chairman. The Military Affairs Commission is formally a Party body and is the command vehicle through which the Party exercises control over the professional military. Party leaders such as Chou En-lai in fact addressed major meetings of the MAC. But the day-to-day leadership of this body generally resided in the Minister of Defense. And, given that Mao was the only civilian identified as a MAC member, it appears that this body's real purpose was to give the Chairman of the CCP[26] a special place in military decision-making. Thus, the revival of the MAC should perhaps more accurately be viewed as a reassertion of Mao's close association with the uniformed military command.

Lin not only moved the MAC to center stage, he also made personnel changes to assure his control over the Ministry of Defense. He quickly dropped three of the seven vice-ministers in office as of the time of his appointment and appointed six new vice-ministers of his own. Relatedly, he made virtually a clean sweep of the Chinese high command, reorganizing the former seven departments into three and appointing to each people who appeared to be his supporters (including Lo Jui-ch'ing, the head of the Public Security apparatus until the showdown at Lushan). These personnel changes in the ministry were probably linked to the revival of the MAC: The

25 The most complete account of the MAC available in the secondary literature is in Harvey Nelsen, *The Chinese military system*.
26 The chairmen of the CCP have been ex officio chairmen of the MAC until Teng Hsiao-p'ing stopped this practice during Hua Kuo-feng's tenure in these positions.

Military Affairs Commission formally makes all high-level appointments in the Ministry of Defense.

At about this time, Lin began, as noted, to stress the use of Mao Tse-tung Thought in the military. Many others in the PLA disagreed with this approach, but Lin made it a centerpiece of his reign as minister of defense. Lin's approach became official policy at the conclusion of the enlarged meeting of the MAC in September–October 1960. This occurred just as the fourth volume of Mao Tse-tung's *Selected Works* was being published. Whether or not the two were linked in planning and execution, there is little doubt that Lin's tack further endeared him to an increasingly beleaguered Chairman Mao.

Indeed, the fact that the propagation of the works of specific leaders was seen as an important political question is highlighted by the plans for publication of the *Selected Works* of Liu Shao-ch'i and of a collection of essays by Ch'en Yun, both of which were being put together in 1962. Neither appeared, reportedly because Liu himself objected to the publication of his works, and Mao essentially pigeonholed the Ch'en volume.[27] The question of the relative treatment of Mao and Liu had become a sensitive political issue after Liu took over the chairmanship of the PRC from Mao in April 1959.

Lin Piao then took a series of initiatives to enhance the role of the PLA in CCP affairs. He quickly began to increase the number of Party members in the military, perhaps because that would give him a greater say in national CCP affairs. During 1963–65, moreover, he worked to expand the PLA's organizational responsibilities, blurring at some points the boundaries between Party and military. These years saw the heads of the various military districts become secretaries in five of the six regional Party bureaus that had been formed in the wake of the Great Leap Forward. At the same time, at least half of the provincial Party first secretaries became political commissars in the military districts, putting them at least partially into the chain of command of the General Political Department of the PLA. This multiple officeholding in Party and Army could, in theory, have been used to increase Party control over the PLA, but experience indicates that the real effect was very much the opposite. These were essentially predatory moves by the PLA to increase its power vis-à-vis the Party. The PLA under Lin was also increasing its control over the civilian population. Mao in 1962 ordered the formation of a civilian mil-

27 On Liu, see *JMJP*, 15 January 1982, trans. in *FBIS/PRC*, 25 January 1982, K19–22. On Ch'en, see Teng Li-ch'ün, *Hsiang Ch'en Yun t'ung-chih hsueh-hsi tso ching-chi kung-tso* (Study how to do economic work from comrade Ch'en Yun), 8–9.

itia under military control, and the implementation of this order enhanced the military's contacts with the civilian sector.

Given these activities by the army, Mao increasingly pointed to the PLA as the type of organization that could successfully integrate politics and expertise – that could, in the terminology of the time, be both Red and expert. For during these same years Lin was bolstering the professional training and discipline in the ranks, and the military was heading the effort to develop China's atomic bomb. Also, in October 1962 the PLA acquitted itself well in the brief border war with India, thus adding to its prowess and prestige.

During 1963 the PLA generated several models of political rectitude, including a selfless soldier (Lei Feng) who had died in an accident and an outstanding military company, the Good Eighth Company of Nanking Road. Following initiatives to have people emulate these military models, in December 1963 Mao issued a general call for people to "learn from the PLA," a startling slogan given that the Party was supposedly the fount of all wisdom. In the Chairman's eyes, the problems with the 1st FYP had essentially demonstrated the inadequacies of the government adminstration, and the Great Leap catastrophe had substantially discredited the CCP. Thus, Mao began to look toward the military as the type of organization that might achieve the balance of political virtue and technical/organizational expertise that he regarded as vital for the PRC.

Soon Mao went from hortatory campaigns to learn from the PLA to a far more direct approach to increasing the military's leverage within the government and Party. In 1964, at Mao's direction, government units – and subsequently some CCP organs also – began to form political departments within the units. These were modeled after the political system within the army, and a number of the people who staffed them either went through training courses run by the military for this purpose or were themselves recently demobilized army personnel. These departments never became solidly established – partly because of resistance in the government and Party, partly because they could not define clearly their role, and partly because there were constant skirmishes over who would be the personnel to staff them. But the whole exercise again reflected the increasingly aggressive posture of the PLA vis-à-vis the Party and government – and Mao's encouragement of this trend.

In May 1965 Lin Piao took the unusual measure of having all ranks in the PLA abolished. This initiative again made the military appear to be the most "advanced" politically, since it alone was acting to implement the egalitarian ideals of the revolution. From the point of view of political power, moreover, this measure may in some degree have strengthened Lin's hand within the PLA. It meant, essentially, that a former officer's power now derived solely from his actual operational assignment. He would no longer have rank that could itself convey certain rights and privileges. Given that Lin held the top operational position within the army, the independent power of the other eight marshals (Lo Jung-huan had died in 1963) and of the officer corps itself should have been weakened somewhat by this measure.

Also in 1965 the PLA took direct control over the Public Security forces. Lo Jui-ch'ing, former minister of public security and a man with extremely strong ties in its apparatus, was at that time the chief of staff of the PLA. As we shall see later on, Lin turned against Lo in December 1965 and by May 1966 had him purged and vilified. One effect of the purge was to leave Lin in a better position to marshal the resources of the public security apparatus – one of the most powerful organizations in the country – to support Mao and Lin himself. He appears to have used these resources well once the Cultural Revolution began.[28]

The conflict with Lo Jui-ch'ing was broader than the issue of control over the public security forces, however. The year 1965 was a very bad one for China's foreign policy. Chou En-lai had hoped to put together an Afro-Asian Conference that would take an anti-Soviet line in the spring, but this effort failed. The PRC also tried unsuccessfully to influence the outcome of the August–September Indo-Pakistani war, while the Soviet Union proved in the final analysis to be able to play a constructive mediating role in that conflict. And the PRC's careful cultivation of the Communist Party of Indonesia (PKI) ended in disaster when in September 1965 the PKI supported a coup attempt against the military that failed. All these missteps produced a growing feeling of isolation and siege in Peking, just as the United States began to increase substantially its involvement in Vietnam, posing the possibility of a direct U.S. attack on southern China in the near future.

Within this troubling international context, Peking's leaders debated options and strategy. Lo Jui-ch'ing appears to have preferred an approach that would relieve some of the tension on China by seeking better relations with the Soviet Union – based on joint efforts to

---

28 As noted below, K'ang Sheng played a significant role vis-à-vis the Public Security apparatus, too.

combat the United States in Vietnam. Lo recommended the Soviet strategy of the eve of World War II, a strategy of projecting conventional force to engage the enemy well outside of the country's boundaries. This strategy demanded, in turn, that China maximize the output of its military-related heavy industry, striving for efficient industrial production as a high priority goal. Given the logistical demands of this strategy, it also presumed that China's cities would serve as the key production bases for the effort, and that Soviet help would be available to supplement the PRC's inadequate industrial base.

Lin Piao, by contrast, argued that Vietnam should basically fight the war itself, with indirect Chinese support but no direct intervention. He lauded the CCP's strategy against the Japanese, a strategy that required luring the enemy deep into the country and then wearing him down through guerrilla war techniques. This in turn demanded the dispersal of industry, a policy of regional basic self-sufficiency, playing up the role of the militia and of unconventional forces rather than of the regular army, and whipping up high political fervor among the population. It did not demand – and indeed it argued against – a strategy of rapprochement with the post-Khrushchev leadership of the Soviet Union. Lin laced his argument with quotations from Mao Tse-tung, and the strategy he advocated dovetailed neatly with a whole series of civilian, foreign policy, and military policy preferences of the Chairman's. Liu Shao-ch'i and Teng Hsiao-p'ing seem to have been opposed to many of these.

Thus, while building up his position in the military and enhancing the role of the PLA vis-à-vis the Party and government, Lin also carefully cultivated Mao and tried to support the Chairman's policy preferences in the system. In general terms, the Mao cult in the army redounded to the Chairman's overall political benefit. Indeed, starting in 1964, the book of Mao quotations that had been developed for use in the army was distributed among model youth to reward their accomplishments. On a more specific level also, as indicated by his wide-ranging strategic recommendations about Vietnam, Lin injected himself directly into the increasingly fractious relations that Mao had with Liu, Teng, and company. In some cases, his main purpose seems, indeed, to have been precisely to exacerbate tensions between Mao and his Politburo colleagues.

For example, at the September 1959 enlarged meeting of the Military Affairs Committee that formally stripped P'eng Te-huai of his post as minister of defense, Lin's attack on P'eng and characterization of the latter's errors were far harsher than those of Mao. Lin, trying to solidify his own newly acquired position, argued that P'eng was virtually irredeemable and that Mao Tse-tung Thought was the quintessence of Marxism-Leninism. Lin's position, finally accepted by Mao, helped to drive a wedge between the Chairman and the other members of the Politburo more sympathetic to P'eng. At the Seven Thousand Cadres Conference in January–February 1962, Lin leaped to Mao's defense (and that of the GLF itself) when debate occurred over the causes of the difficulties in which China found itself. Lin not only strongly supported Mao and the Three Red Banners (the GLF, the People's Communes, and the "general line"), but he also called on all present to study Mao Tse-tung Thought. Although documentary evidence is lacking to spell out Lin's role in other meetings involving the Party elite, it seems likely that he had continued to try both to build up the Chairman and to exacerbate Mao's relations with other leaders. For example, in May 1966 Lin spoke darkly about the chances of a coup against Mao and the need for the Chairman to protect himself against such a threat.

These activities indicate that Lin Piao was an ambitious man who had developed a clear political strategy soon after taking office as defense minister in 1959. That strategy was to link his fortune with that of Mao, and the disastrous effects of the Great Leap then required that Lin use his resources to bolster Mao's position in the system, in addition to simply solidifying his own position in the Chairman's eyes. Taken together, Lin's initiatives show that he was more than simply a puppet of the Chairman. Rather, while his interests overlapped with those of Mao, he also seems to have worked hard to prevent any improvement in relations between Mao and his colleagues on the Politburo. By the very nature of the situation, what were probably Lin's most effective efforts in this endeavor would remain known only to the few principal participants themselves.

Mao, it should be noted, never became fully a captive of Lin's initiatives. As noted elsewhere, for example, Mao perceived a major national security threat to China growing out of the potential escalation of the Vietnam War after the Gulf of Tonkin incident in 1964. In response, the Chairman undercut the original strategy for the 3rd Five-Year Plan and called instead for devotion of major investment resources to building a "third line" of industries in the remote hinterland of Southwest China. Mao created an informal State Planning Commission headed by Yü Ch'iu-li to oversee this new strategy. The body consisted basically of the people who in the 1970s would become known as the "petroleum clique," and during the Cultural Revolution it essentially merged with and superseded the formal State Planning Commission. The plan advocated by this group was the same one Lin Piao espoused for dealing with Vietnam. But Mao assigned P'eng Te-huai, Lin's nemesis, to take charge of the Szechwan-based headquarters for constructing the "third line."

Culture: Chiang Ch'ing

A second key component of the coalition that formed to launch the Cultural Revolution was Mao's wife Chiang Ch'ing and the group she put together in the cultural sphere. Indeed, in February 1966 Lin Piao and Chiang Ch'ing clearly linked up when Lin invited Chiang to stage a Forum on Literature and Art for Troops and made her the official cultural adviser to the military. This for the first time gave Chiang an official position that she could use as a base for pursuing her political goals.[29] But she obtained that help from Lin only because she had spent considerable effort over the preceding years building up her own resources in the cultural realm and winning her husband to her point of view.

Chiang Ch'ing had long held strong views about the directions in which cultural policy should move, and for an equally long time she had nursed hatreds against the Communist cultural establishment that kept her at arm's length. When Chiang Ch'ing had gone to Yenan and won Mao's heart, she replaced Mao's popular second wife Ho Tzu-chen, who had suffered terribly as one of the very few women on the Long March. Mao's colleagues obtained the Chairman's agreement that he would keep Chiang Ch'ing out of politics if they would not object to his having Chiang replace Ho in his bedroom.

Even in Yenan Chiang Ch'ing had advocated developing a new type of revolutionary cultural repertoire, and she had been active in the development of revolutionary plays during those years. A very bright, astute, and ambitious woman, she evidently felt acutely the ostracism imposed on her by the male-dominated cultural and propaganda apparatus. After 1949, Chiang remained very much in the background, owing in part to her continuing health problems and in part to the unwillingness of the cultural establishment to listen to her or give her an official place in the system. Chiang does, however,

29 Chiang had held a minor position in cultural affairs in the early 1950s.

seem to some extent to have served the Chairman as an informal political confidante. For example, she flew to Lushan when Mao informed her that trouble had erupted at the Lushan conference in July 1959. On that occasion Mao asked her not to come, but he evidently did not forbid her to participate, and indeed he called her from the meeting to discuss with her his response to P'eng's challenge.

The year 1959 seems to have been the start of a turning point in Chiang's health, and as her physical well-being became more assured, her energy for participating in politics and cultural affairs also grew. After the Lushan meeting, Chiang went to Shanghai to rest, and while there she had gone to a number of theaters. She was appalled at the content of the productions, finding that "old" themes and styles were very much in vogue and feeling that this should be rectified. Chiang gradually began to put together a faction of people who would help her carry out her plans to revolutionize Peking Opera and other aspects of Chinese culture.

Mao, of course, was central to Chiang's efforts, and she herself claims that by 1962 she had convinced him that the cultural sphere needed attention. Indeed, Mao instructed her in the spring of 1962 to draft a policy statement for the Central Committee on policy toward culture. Chiang's effort provided some of the background for Mao's call at the August 1962 Peitaiho meeting to promote "proletarian" culture. But Chiang's position paper did not become official policy until May 1966, when a considerably revised draft of it became one of the basic documents that led to the Cultural Revolution.

Chiang Ch'ing and K'ang Sheng

Chiang found a natural conjoining of interests with two others with whom she had ties from prerevolutionary days: K'ang Sheng and K'o Ch'ing-shih. K'ang Sheng came from Chiang's home town of Chu-ch'eng in Shantung province, and the two of them had known each other before Chiang went to Yenan. K'ang specialized in three areas of work: liaison with other Communist parties, public security, and higher education. What brought them all together was K'ang's evidently fairly sophisticated training in Marxism-Leninism while he was learning the finer points of police work from the NKVD in the Soviet Union in the mid-1930s, and his ongoing involvement with the issues of revisionism and counterrevolution.

K'ang had had major responsibility in public security affairs prior to the 1950s, and as a result took some of the blame when Khrushchev made his de-Stalinization speech to the Soviet Twentieth Party Congress. K'ang was dropped from full membership in the Politburo in September 1956, at the same time that the Party dropped Mao Tse-tung Thought as part of the guiding ideology specified in the CCP constitution. As of the early 1960s, however, things were moving in a direction potentially favorable to K'ang. With the Sino-Soviet dispute having reached a critical stage, Mao – who remained the dominant figure in handling the dispute on the Chinese side – needed a theorist with K'ang's knowledge to help him draft the CCP Central Committee's attacks on "Khrushchev revisionism." At the same time, K'ang – probably through his long friendship with Chiang Ch'ing – learned that Mao was planning to push for the proletarianization of Chinese culture. K'ang could play a useful role in that effort, especially if he could link it to counterrevolutionary activities to justify his involvement.

K'ang effected this linkage at the Tenth Plenum in September 1962, where he launched an attack on Hsi Chung-hsun for the latter's involvement in the production of a purportedly counterrevolutionary novel about Liu Chih-tan, one of the early communist guerrilla fighters in Shensi who had died in 1936. Claiming that the novel about Liu in fact vilified Mao, K'ang argued that using novels for purposes of contemporary political criticism was a new invention. He thus established an intellectual link with Chiang Ch'ing, who was trying to call Mao's attention to the political attacks against the Chairman that she had seen in the writings of intellectuals during the previous few years.

K'ang subsequently served as a bridge between Chiang Ch'ing and some of the radical intellectuals she brought to the fore in the early stage of the Cultural Revolution. K'ang's work in higher education gave him entrée to major educational units, and he took advantage of this to cultivate key individuals. The most prominent among these turned out to be Kuan Feng and Ch'i Pen-yü of the Research Institute of Philosophy of the Academy of Sciences, Nieh Yuan-tzu of the Philosophy Department of Peking University, and several people at the Higher Party School.[30] K'ang, like Lin Piao, was willing to foment trouble if need be to attain his purposes. For example, in the Higher Party School he attacked Yang Hsien-chen's theory of "two combine into one" as an anti-Maoist negation of the Chairman's philosophical premise that "one divides into two." Through

---

30 *Cheng ming* (Hong Kong), 34 (August 1980), 45.

such theoretical skulduggery, K'ang managed to purge Yang and to increase the influence of his followers in the Higher Party School. As of mid-1964, K'ang also heavily and personally involved himself in Chiang Ch'ing's efforts to revolutionize Peking Opera.[31]

K'o Ch'ing-shih, Shanghai's mayor, was an old friend of Chiang Ch'ing's. K'o had in 1958 been one of the most vociferous supporters of the Great Leap Forward and especially of the backyard steel furnace campaign. He was made a full member of the Politburo in the spring of 1958, and Shanghai became a major beneficiary of the Leap strategy.[32] As noted above, even in mid-1962 K'o had continued to support a Maoist interpretation of the current situation as opposed to the more pessimistic views of Ch'en Yun and others. K'o, then, like K'ang Sheng, Lin Piao, and Chiang Ch'ing, had good reason to want to bolster Mao's standing.

In late 1962 K'ang Sheng spoke with K'o about the need to have literature and art portray heroes drawn from the ranks of people who had emerged over the thirteen years since 1949, a line very much in tune with Chiang Ch'ing's own thinking. K'o during the GLF had already sided with Shanghai's "worker-writers" against the professional authors.[33] In January 1963 K'o made just such an appeal in Shanghai, calling on the local intelligentsia to abandon old repertoires, adopt the class struggle of the Tenth Plenum, and stage new dramas with heroes drawn from the ranks of post-1949 workers, peasants, and soldiers. Mao soon chimed in with support, calling the Ministry of Culture a "ministry of emperors and princes, generals and ministers, gifted scholars and beauties."

Chiang Ch'ing had been in touch with K'o in 1959 about cultural matters in Shanghai, and she remained in contact with him throughout the early 1960s (K'o died in 1965) on this issue. Through K'o, Chiang linked up with Chang Ch'un-ch'iao (who was in the cultural apparatus in Shanghai) and Yao Wen-yuan, a Shanghai critic. Yao, in turn, had cultivated good ties among the newly developing "proletarian writers" – workers who had taken up the pen during the 1950s – in Shanghai.[34]

Thus, Chiang Ch'ing during the early 1960s worked on her husband and began to put together her own coterie of advocates of a "revolutionization" of China's culture. The Ministries of Culture and Education and the Propaganda Department of the CCP, all manned

31 Ibid.
32 See Christopher Howe's contribution to Christopher Howe, ed., *Shanghai: Revolution and development in an Asian metropolis*, 173–79.
33 See Ragvald contribution to Howe, ed. *Shanghai*, 316.   34 See ibid., 309–23.

by old opponents of Chiang's, paid her no heed and scoffed at her efforts. Clashes occurred at national meetings dealing with culture such as the June–July 1964 Festival of Peking Opera on Contemporary Themes. Chiang had been developing her own model plays in Shanghai and through Mao kept up pressure to reform the cultural fare offered the Chinese people. Finally, in about June 1964 the Party Secretariat formed a Five-Man Group to coordinate efforts toward cultural reform. P'eng Chen, who conceivably was being considered by Mao as a potential replacement for Liu Shao-ch'i as the Party Chairman's successor, took charge of the group. K'ang Sheng was the member, however, who most clearly was loyal to Mao and Chiang Ch'ing, rather than to Liu Shao-ch'i or Teng Hsiao-p'ing.

To Chiang Ch'ing, the Five-Man Group proved more a hindrance than a force for positive changes in cultural policy. The group generally followed the preferences of the Peking cultural establishment (represented on the group by Lu Ting-i, the head of the Propaganda Department of the CCP). Chiang continued to seek other avenues for putting her priorities in the cultural and political spheres on the national agenda. The approach she adopted that eventually proved to have the greatest impact on national politics was to focus on the issue that K'ang Sheng had raised at the Tenth Plenum in 1962 – that novels and plays could be used for political purposes. Chiang particularly pointed to the play *Hai Jui dismissed from office*, written by Wu Han. This play concerned the upright actions of a Ming official in the face of unfair attacks from his political enemies, and Chiang argued to Mao that the play in fact represented a veiled defense of P'eng Te-huai. Chiang's specific accusation is plausible but probably wrong – Wu Han had begun work on a play about Hai Jui before the Lushan Conference, and he did so at the specific request of one of Mao's current secretaries, Hu Ch'iao-mu.[35] Nonetheless, in the increasingly suspicion-charged atmosphere of 1965, Chiang persuaded Mao to have Yao Wen-yuan write a critique of the play that raised the hidden political issues supposedly involved.

Yao's critique, published in November 1965, was important for three reasons. It cast the issue of cultural reform as a political rather than a purely academic matter, thus raising the possibility that the regime would again carry out a major political campaign against the intellectuals. It attacked a play written by a subordinate and close friend of P'eng Chen's, thus putting P'eng to the test as to whether

---

35 For an early examination of this problem, see MacFarquhar, *Origins of the Cultural Revolution*, 2. 207–12.

he would protect Wu Han or side with Mao.[36] And it came from Shanghai (where Mao was then residing), symbolizing Mao's decision that the leaders in Peking had moved so far away from his preferred positions that he would have to launch an attack on them that relied primarily on forces outside the central political apparatus. Chiang Ch'ing's group provided important resources for this effort.

But Chiang's contacts as of 1965, other than K'ang Sheng, were among radical intellectuals and people at lower levels of the system. Thus, when Chiang joined in the coalition to launch the Cultural Revolution, she brought in people unsympathetic to the bureaucratic values and practices that had developed since 1949. These were the people of ideas, not the people of organizational skills. Not surprisingly, therefore, they would prove themselves adept at manipulating ideas but disastrously inadequate at managing the economy.

The fact that Chiang's coalition included K'ang Sheng proved important for the politics of the 1960s. K'ang was ruthless and more than willing to destroy those who stood in his way. His movement toward the center of the political stage in and after 1962 permitted him to build on the bitterness of the P'eng Te-huai affair, with its damage to previous norms of intra-Party struggle, and contribute to changing completely the way the Party leaders dealt with each other in political disputes. The radical intelligentsia in Chiang's entourage had never been schooled in these intra-Party norms, and thus easily joined in wholesale violations of previous practice. Chang Ch'un-ch'iao was the only one in this group as of the mid-1960s who had enjoyed an extensive career as a bureaucrat outside secret police work. Not surprisingly, Chang also became the person in this group most sensitively attuned to the need to preserve order, build authority, and secure a bureaucratic base as the group acquired power.

Overall, Chiang Ch'ing wanted to change Chinese culture and to avenge the many years of slights she had suffered at the hands of Lu Ting-i and other leaders of the cultural establishment. Her coalition included people who were willing to wage ruthless struggles in order to destroy the Party establishment. Lin Piao had a more careful bureaucratic game to play, one that would lead to his replacing Liu

36 Actually, P'eng would lose either way. If he protected Wu Han (as he subsequently tried to do), he made himself vulnerable by that act. If he attacked Wu Han, however, he would also have been weakened by the acknowledgment that he had permitted an anti-Maoist to achieve high position in his own Peking municipal apparatus. Given the likely negative effect of this episode on P'eng Chen's career, one would like to know more about the real background to Yao Wen-yuan's article.

Shao-ch'i as Mao's successor. For this, he could utilize the destructive power of Chiang Ch'ing (and her ability to cultivate Mao's worst instincts), and thus in February 1966, as noted above, Lin cemented a coalition with Chiang by appointing her cultural adviser to the army. Chiang then used this position as a platform from which to make a wide-ranging attack against those who opposed her views on culture, whether related to the military or not.

RECTIFICATION

Let us now shift our focus from Mao's eventual coalition partners to the Chairman himself. As of 1962 Mao saw the revolution threatened by adverse forces at both the apex and the base of the political system. At the apex, his colleagues wanted to continue policies that Mao felt would simply strengthen the hands of the anti-Communist forces in the society. At the base, the Chairman recognized that the damage that the GLF had done to basic-level Party units, especially in the countryside, had been enormous. He determined, as Harry Harding has written,[37] to use rectification campaigns to remedy both problems. Rectification essentially allowed Mao to order the formation of a new hierarchy of temporary organs that would deal with the established institutions to remedy a problem. It was an ideal tool for Mao to use to enhance his leverage in the system.

Mao highlighted the need for Party rectification at the August 1962 Peitaiho meeting and at the Central Committee's Tenth Plenum that September. There was little argument over the need for rectification, but subsequent events would prove that there could be significant disagreement over the tools to be used. Experiments in rural rectification were carried out in selected spots following the Tenth Plenum, and the results of these provided the basis for the initial programmatic document of the rural rectification effort, the Socialist Education Campaign.

Mao personally played a determining role in drafting this document at central work conferences in February and May 1963. The resulting Former Ten Points called into being "poor and lower middle peasants' associations" to serve as a vehicle for exercising supervision over the erring basic level cadres. The problem, it turned out, was that poor and lower middle peasants had also suffered badly

37 Harry Harding, *Organizing China*, 196.

during the GLF, and many of them by 1963 were either disillusioned or corrupt. As this became evident during the course of the year, new measures (the Later Ten Points) were drafted by Teng Hsiao-p'ing and P'eng Chen and promulgated in September 1963.

The Later Ten Points recognized the problems in the "poor and lower middle peasants' associations" and called for stricter recruitment criteria for them. More significantly, this document worked on the assumption that they were by nature unable to supervise adequately the commune and brigade committees. It therefore called for the formation of urban-based work teams to carry out this rectification campaign. It further asserted that these teams should first take care of problems at the provincial, prefectural, and county levels before dealing with the basic-level cadres. Since these higher-level organs were located in cities, the document initiated an urban Five Antis Campaign to rectify the higher levels and lay an appropriate groundwork for follow-up work at the basic levels.[38] The effect of these shifts was to leave the peasants' associations essentially without a significant task to perform. Rectification had been shifted to a purely internal Party matter. Mao, however, had seen mobilization of non-Party people as one of the benefits of the rectification process, and in June 1964 the Chairman indicated his concern that the implementation of the Socialist Education Campaign was not involving sufficient mobilization of the poor and lower middle peasants.

During the first part of 1964, high-level cadres went down to the basic levels to carry out investigations of the conditions there. This method of acquiring data harkened back to the work style of the Yenan period and reflected the fact that the leaders knew they could not rely on the reporting that came up through normal channels. Thus, for example, Liu Shao-ch'i went to Honan province for 18 days – the province that had been a pacesetter during the Great Leap and had ended in a parlous state at the conclusion of the movement. Liu's wife, Wang Kuang-mei, spent five months incognito at the T'ao-yuan Brigade near her native city of Tientsin.

The Lius' findings made them deeply pessimistic about the situation in the rural areas. They ascertained that corruption was widespread and that many basic-level cadres opposed the Party (as did a large percentage of the peasants). As they came back from these trips they felt that counterrevolution had a grip on a large portion of rural

---

38 This Five Antis Campaign should not be confused with the other campaign of the same name that peaked in early 1952. See above, Chapter 2.

China and that draconian measures would be necessary to rescue the situation. Mao may well have agreed with this diagnosis – but he subsequently disagreed strongly with the measures taken to effect a later disagreed strongly with the measures taken to effect a cure.

The Revised Later Ten Points were drafted in September 1964 and reflected Liu's approach to the rectification campaign. They called for large work teams to go to selected communes and virtually take over the commune and shake it to the foundations in order to put it into shape. A work team would stay in one locale for appproximately six months and would deal harshly with those cadres who were found to have become lax and corrupt. While in the communes, these work teams would also carry out a new class categorization in the country-side – the first such effort since land reform at the beginning of the 1950s. The whole Socialist Education movement would, according to the calendar of the Revised Later Ten Points, take five to six years to carry out throughout the country.

Mao Tse-tung had three complaints about the implementation of the Revised Later Ten Points. First, they narrowed the target of attack from revisionism to corruption. Second, they imposed pen-alties that were too harsh on the cadres. And third, they involved the imposition of massive work teams on the communes rather than mobilizing the masses themselves to carry out the campaign. In short, the Socialist Education movement had been twisted around to the point where it no longer served as a vehicle for propagating Mao's ideas about revisionism but, rather, had become a relatively savage effort to reimpose discipline in the rural Party organs.

Mao's response to this set of trends was to seize the initiative with his own new program document for the Socialist Education movement. Issued in January 1965, Mao's Twenty-three Articles reoriented the campaign so that it would become a general education-al effort on the evils of revisionism at all levels of the Party. In the rural areas, this meant that the work teams pulled back, and many of the former cadres who had been severely punished by them were now rehabilitated – and their replacements removed. This simply increased the divisions among cadre ranks in the countryside on the eve of the Cultural Revolution.

Mao's efforts to use rectification as a means of forcing his political agenda on the society, then, proved only partially successful. As in his attempt to bring his version of politics more directly to bear through the formation of political departments in government and Party organs starting in 1964, the ruling bureaucracies proved capable of protecting their right to handle their own organizational affairs themselves. The Revised Later Ten Points were harsh, but they were also an approach that kept the rectification problem within the Party and precluded large-scale use of non-Party bodies to rectify the CCP. But it was precisely Mao's growing concern about the directions of policy within the CCP – a concern nurtured by Chiang Ch'ing, K'ang Sheng, and Lin Piao (along with Ch'en Po-ta and others) – that made the Chairman increasingly determined to enhance his leverage over this core political organization.

A changing Mao

Mao personally did not share the sense of personal insult that haunted Chiang Ch'ing, and there is no reason to believe that he felt comfortable with the notion of Lin Piao as his successor at any point before the late 1960s, if then.[39] It appears, in fact, that during 1963–65 Mao had been toying with the notion of building up P'eng Chen as the replacement for Liu as his successor. Thus, as suggested above, Mao gradually put into place a coalition of partners to launch the Cultural Revolution, but he fully shared the goals and perspectives of none of them. How, then, did the Chairman himself arrive at the conclusion that it was necessary to launch a frontal assault on his colleagues in the Politburo?

Three elements appear crucial to understanding Mao's psychological evolution during the critical years of 1959–66: his changing understanding of the potential evolution of the Chinese revolution; his continuing concern with the problem of succession; and his related sense of impending death. All of these intertwined in a way that escalated his fear that his life's work had produced a political system that would, in the final analysis, turn away from his values and prove as exploitative as the one it replaced.

Mao's concerns about the future of the revolution cannot be separated from his evolving analysis of the degeneration of the Soviet political system. To be sure, Mao had spent much of his career fighting Soviet influences in the Chinese Communist Party, and in both substance and style he was the least Soviet of the Chinese leaders. During the mid-1950s he had launched concerted efforts to move China away from the Soviet model of development, and starting in 1958 he had included the military and military doctrine in this effort. But whereas before 1959 Mao had felt that the Soviet leaders had often been overbearing and lacking in understanding

39 Indeed, at the height of Mao's reliance on Lin during 1966, he is said to have written to Chiang expressing his distrust of Lin.

of the Chinese situation, after 1959 he began to wrestle with the question of whether the Soviet revolution itself had not gone fundamentally astray and changed its nature.

Essentially, as the Soviet Union began to try to interfere in Chinese internal affairs, to declare that its own revolutionary era was over, and to seek a more stable accommodation with the United States, Mao began to wonder whether the victory of socialism in a country ensured that there could not be a resurgence of capitalism in that society. Many things contributed to this intellectual shift. Mao thought he saw Khrushchev attempt to establish leverage over the Chinese navy in 1958, and perceived another attempt by Khrushchev to interfere in Chinese affairs via cancellation of the nuclear sharing agreement and collusion with P'eng Te-huai in 1959. In that year also Mao saw Khrushchev's declaration that the Soviet Union had become a "state of the whole people" rather than a "dictatorship of the proletariat";[40] his Camp David summit with the United States and the related effort toward peaceful coexistence with the West; Moscow's seeming neutrality in the 1959 border tensions between Peking and New Delhi; and the Soviet withdrawal of advisers from China in mid-1960. These were but a few examples.

Growing out of this new concern, Mao began a period of study of Soviet political economy, and he concluded that even Stalin had made some fundamental errors in this central theoretical sphere. He instructed Chinese delegations to debate the Soviets on the issues on which there was disagreement, and the Soviet responses increased his concerns. Chiang Ch'ing noted that the swift withdrawal of Soviet advisers in 1960 had "shaken" Mao,[41] and probably from that point on he determined that at a minimum Khrushchev himself must be ousted in order to put the Soviet system back on solid ground. The refusal of the Soviet leadership to remove Khrushchev simply increased Mao's anxiety.

Having waged struggles with Khrushchev at meetings since 1958, Mao in 1963 decided that it was time to make the polemics open. On this central ideological plane, his Politburo colleagues evidently could not deny him the lead. Thus, during 1963–64 Mao supervised the writing of nine polemics, each of which was given wide publicity in

---

40 By calling the Soviet Union a "state of the whole people," Khrushchev indicated that the exploiting classes had been destroyed and class struggle had ended in the Soviet Union. A "dictatorship of the proletariat," by contrast, is the form of dictatorship used by a Communist Party in power to wage class struggle against the remnants of the exploiting classes.
41 Witke, *Comrade Chiang Ch'ing*, 304.

China. As noted above, Mao enlisted K'ang Sheng's talents in writing these pieces, at a time when K'ang had already become involved in the struggle against revisionism in the cultural arena at home.

It appears in retrospect that Mao used the nine polemics as a device for giving publicity to his political thinking within China. These polemics raised all the issues on which Mao in fact disagreed with his colleagues on the Politburo, and they provided a vehicle for identifying the Chairman's political views with the anti-Soviet struggle then being waged. This linkage of Chinese nationalism with Mao's political critique of "revisionism" proved a potent mixture – so potent, in fact, that Mao subsequently had the Chinese media attack Liu Shao-ch'i during the Cultural Revolution simply as "China's Khrushchev."

But beyond the shrewd politics in this approach there lay a human tragedy. There is no reason to suspect that Mao himself did not believe what he was saying about the degeneration of the Soviet revolution. He evidently could see the same forces under way in China, where his colleagues now argued (as they had in 1956) that class struggle must be subsumed under the overriding importance of the struggle for production. Inevitably, if these trends were allowed to continue, the younger generation would grow up with a revisionist perspective. Undoubtedly, history would then prove to be as unkind to Mao as it had been to Stalin after his death. Mao was a man with a keen sense of China's history, who compared himself in 1965 with the country's greatest emperors. He could now see the possibility of being remembered as a man who had in fact led the country astray. Equally disconcerting, his legacy to China might be a political system that exploited his beloved countryside and colluded with imperialism. Thus, Mao's observations of the evolution of the Soviet revolution significantly raised the stakes for him as he saw the trends in China during the first half of the 1960s.[42]

Mao's changing role in the Chinese political process also contributed to his sense of urgency. As noted above, the Chairman reportedly had stopped his regular attendance at Politburo meetings in January 1958.[43] After that, he still received reports on Politburo

---

42 Parenthetically, the fact that the Soviet leadership did not change Moscow's position on the issues in dispute with China in the wake of Khrushchev's ouster in October 1964 confirmed to Mao that it was the system and not simply an individual that had degenerated. This also helps to explain the vehemence of Mao's opposition to Lo Jui-ch'ing's suggestion in the spring of 1965, noted above, that China cooperate with the Soviet Union to oppose the escalating U.S. commitment in Vietnam.

43 After that date, Mao only attended those Politburo meetings that he wanted to address. Otherwise, he relied on reports of what had happened at the Politburo meetings.

discussions, and he had to approve all documents issued in the name of the Central Committee before they could be circulated as official documents.[44] The same stricture evidently did not, however, apply to the documents issued by the Party Secretariat headed by Teng Hsiao-p'ing, and the Secretariat assumed a major role in the policy process of the first half of the 1960s. Mao subsequently complained, as noted above, that Teng did not consult with him on policy matters after 1959. While this complaint may well have been exaggerated for effect, the sense of grievance undoubtedly was there.

More fundamentally, when Mao had pulled back from regular participation in Politburo meetings, it in fact marked the beginning of a period in which he dominated the political system more than at any time previously. Mao at that point indicated also that he would like to give up his role as head of state so that he could concentrate on the larger issues of the development of the revolution. On both the Party and state sides, therefore, in 1958 Mao saw himself as moving to a somewhat more Olympian role, in firm control over the central directions of policy while at the same time moving into place successors in whom he would have confidence. The greater responsibilities acquired by Liu Shao-ch'i, Teng Hsiao-p'ing, and Lin Piao in 1958–59 reflect the implementation of this strategy.

But after the collapse of the GLF, Mao found that in 1962 he was not able to assume full control of the basic directions of policy again. Rather, Liu and Teng now appeared to restrict his access to the policy flow and to twist the meaning of his directives, such as those on rectification. Thus, although Mao had wanted to step back to the "second line" in 1958–59, he was dismayed as that changed its meaning in the wake of the GLF. He then began to test his proposed successors to determine whether they would support the general policies he believed to be central to the future of the revolution. The more he tested, the more they (with the exception of Lin Piao) demonstrated their inadequacy.

The heart of this growing disparity between Mao's priorities and those of his successors lay in the different lessons they drew from the GLF. Mao, as noted above, learned that mass mobilization is not the key to rapid economic development. But at the same time, he retained his faith in mass mobilization as an instrument of ideological renewal, social change, and rectification. Mass mobilization was not, however,

44 Documents issued by the Politburo were said to be issued by the Central Committee, so this rule in fact enabled the Chairman to ride herd on all official documents sent out by the Politburo.

a policy that could be carried out by central ministries in Peking. Rather, by its very nature it relied on the skills of CCP generalists rather than technical specialists, and demanded tolerance of sufficient decentralization to permit the flexibility this strategy inevitably entailed. Thus mass mobilization was to an extent an inherently anti-intellectual and anti-bureaucratic approach, although it could be implemented without totally dismantling a centralized, specialist-dominated political system.

Liu Shao-ch'i and his colleagues concluded from the Great Leap that China had progressed beyond the point where mass mobilization was any longer a useful tool of policy. Given the parlous state of the country's economy and political institutions in 1962, they felt that strong measures must be taken to put control over the economy back in the hands of experts in the central ministries and commissions, and related efforts must be made to rebuild disciplined Party and state organizations that would link the center to the basic levels. The "high tide" politics inherent in major political campaigns could only disrupt the effort they were making to salvage what they could from a bad situation. The campaign approach had served the CCP well in the days in Yenan and the early 1950s, but it was no longer suited to the complex task of governing the country in the 1960s.

Mao tried to nudge the system back toward his own priorities through a series of measures. Some, like the use of rectification campaigns to bring mass mobilization back into the system, are detailed above. Aside from these, the Chairman periodically indicated specific policy preferences in various fields that had the effect of attacking the urban orientation and technical premises of the Liu-Teng strategy. In culture, egged on by his wife and K'ang Sheng, he demanded that writers and artists go to the grass roots in order to understand life through living with average people, especially in the countryside. In medicine, he leveled a series of blasts at the Ministry of Health and demanded that the best doctors of the country leave the cities and practice in the rural areas.[45] In education, he advocated a shorter curriculum, more concentration on applied studies rather than theory, and the integration of manual labor with the academic curriculum in a significant way. He also wanted school textbooks rewritten to take better account of local needs and conditions.[46] In all these areas, the Chairman's recommendations would have the

45 For details, see David Lampton, *The politics of medicine in China*, 129–92.
46 For details, see Seybolt, *Revolutionary education in China*, Introduction and 5–62.

effect of undercutting the control exercised by the authorities in the relevant ministries in Peking.

Mao also objected to the economic centralization and specialization inherent in the program of forming specialized national companies to run major sectors of the economy. Calling these companies "trusts," Mao argued instead for greater regional self-sufficiency. As noted above, this approach also tied in neatly with Mao's preferred strategy for coping with the escalating threat from the United States in Vietnam in 1965.[47]

The results in virtually every area were largely the same. In each case Liu Shao-ch'i and others accepted the general thrust of Mao's critique of current policy and took some measures to implement his ideas. But at the same time, these measures fell far short of the type of drastic restructuring of the system Mao had in mind. As a result, Mao increasingly saw his colleagues as running a bureaucratic leviathan that gobbled up his pressing demands and turned them into relatively innocuous reforms that did little to affect the basic functions and trends of the system.

Finally, Mao's concerns about these issues grew rapidly in 1964–65 because, as his available speeches and interviews indicate, he began to focus on his own mortality. Beginning in 1964, he made repeated references to "going to see Karl Marx" and the inevitable mortality of any man. He also revealed these concerns in startling fashion in an interview with André Malraux in early 1965. While it is impossible to be precise about Mao's mental state at the time, it seems reasonable to conjecture, as Robert Lifton has, that the Chairman increasingly saw his physical life coming to a close and his fundamental identity as defined by the fate of the revolution he had fathered. In other words, Mao thought he could achieve immortality only through the continuation of his revolution along proper paths,[48] but what the Chairman saw as he looked around him was the subversion of that revolution through the revisionism of his chosen successors. The psychological and political stakes for him thus became so high that he felt compelled eventually to launch a brutal frontal assault on the Party he had spent his life creating.

The split in the Yenan leadership

This analysis has focused on the different components that came together to launch the Cultural Revolution in 1966. It has said

---

47 On trusts, see Ahn, 139–44.
48 Robert Lifton, *Revolutionary immortality*.

relatively little about the targets of that major campaign. Much could be written about the policies and developments of 1962–65, a time of impressive economic recovery and policy initiatives in a range of areas related to the economy. But the economic side of this analysis belongs in another chapter, and on a political level it appears that the leaders tried to reestablish the system that had developed by late 1956: a system of clear division of responsibility, with a powerful Secretariat serving the needs of the Politburo, with extensive ministerial direction of the government and the use of wide-ranging State Council commissions to prevent the system from becoming too fractionated along functional lines, and so forth.[49]

It seems too that the leaders of this system did not see themselves as approaching a showdown with Mao. They continued to respect him and tried to accommodate what they must have felt were his somewhat misguided policy demands. But they were concerned overwhelmingly with putting the country back on its feet after the GLF and recapturing the initiative in their dealing with Chinese society. In this, as noted, they disagreed with Mao's more optimistic assessment of the situation as of 1962 – and probably thereafter. And they were almost certainly aware of the potential dangers of allowing Mao's future coalition partners to realize their ambitions. Thus, as noted, they tried to limit the PLA penetration of other organs and attempted to keep Chiang Ch'ing out of power in the cultural arena. Unfortunately, too little data are available to specify what, if any, measures were taken against K'ang Sheng's growing power.

Indeed, so much of our information on the period from the Great Leap to the Cultural Revolution comes from the polemical literature of 1966–76 (and the often almost equally biased material from after 1976) that it is important to bear in mind the issues that remain in doubt about the history of these eight years. The key unknowns or areas of significant doubt are the following:

First, what did the various members of the leadership who did not join the Cultural Revolution coalition think about the Chairman and his policy preferences during these years? The record presented during the Cultural Revolution is almost wholly negative, but it is also highly selective. For example, while the propaganda apparatus purportedly tried to play down Mao's preferences, in point of fact the official media of the day gave enormous prominence to the cult of Mao and the critique of revisionism. Also, even though a range of

---

49 As of 1965, the number of State Council ministries and major commissions stood at 55, the same number as existed at the height of the 1st Five-Year Plan, before the streamlining of the government during the Great Leap Forward.

indicators suggests that through much of the later part of this period
Mao was purposely elevating P'eng Chen, virtually every quotation
from P'eng made available during the Cultural Revolution had him
disparaging Mao's health policies, Chiang Ch'ing's attempts to reform opera, and the like. Indeed, on substantive issues it appears that
the leaders around Liu always tried to meet Mao more than halfway
(although they were understandably less tolerant of Chiang Ch'ing
and more wary of K'ang Sheng[50] and Lin Piao). By about 1964 Mao
may, therefore, have begun to distort reality quite seriously in his
own mind, his suspicions fed by his wife and others who hoped to
gain by a reordering of the leading organs. While Liu and colleagues
clearly did not fully share Mao's sense of priorities and methods, the
Chairman's changing mental state and concerns about his mortality
may have caused him to turn normal types of policy disagreements
into a moral struggle between the forces of good and evil.

Second, one important dimension of this story – the role of the
public security apparatus and of Mao's personal security forces – is
unfortunately too well hidden from public view to be told. Both
K'ang Sheng and Lo Jui-ch'ing, as noted, had been key figures in
the public security system. When Lo left the Ministry of Public
Security to move into the PLA in the wake of Lushan, he was
replaced by Hsieh Fu-chih, who in turn rocketed to political power
during the early part of the Cultural Revolution. Hsieh's meteoric
rise in 1966–67 suggests that the Ministry of Public Security played a
key part in the conflicts leading to the Cultural Revolution, but the
details are not available. The former head of the CCP's General
Office, Yang Shang-k'un, was formally purged in 1966, and he was
said to have planted listening devices in Mao's private quarters. Once
Yang was out of the way, Mao's personal security force (the 8341
Division, which also provided security for other ranking leaders),
under the Chairman's long-time bodyguard Wang Tung-hsing,
moved quickly to take over the former functions of the General
Office. This same unit assumed charge of the detention of ranking
leaders during the Cultural Revolution. But little concrete can be said
about the role of Wang Tung-hsing and the entire security apparatus
during the years before 1966.

Third, the role of Chou En-lai remains somewhat obscure, even
though the premier maintained a high profile throughout these years.

50 For example, Wang Chia-hsiang prevented K'ang Sheng from gaining full access to the
materials on the CCP's relations with other Communist Parties: *Kung-jen jih-pao* (Worker's daily), 4 February 1981, trans. in *FBIS/PRC*, 26 February 1981, L-9.

Chou's entire career suggested that he would lean toward Liu Shao-ch'i's preferences on policy issues during 1962–65, and yet in the summer of 1966 Chou's support proved crucial to Mao's launching of the Cultural Revolution. Chou's 1966 performance, in turn, raises questions about his real role during the previous years. Did he himself begin to think of replacing Liu Shao-ch'i as Mao's successor? If so, did he quietly contribute to the Chairman's distrust of his colleagues? Perhaps Chou simply adhered to a rule that he would support Mao in any showdown, even though he might try to curtail some of the Chairman's policy thrusts with which he disagreed. Unfortunately, Chou is such an important figure that the different hypotheses about him support considerably different interpretations of these crucial years – and the data necessary to discriminate among them are missing.

In sum, for all the years that have passed and the data that have become available, the period from the Great Leap Forward to the Cultural Revolution remains at best partially understood and will be so for some time to come. Much more can be pieced together now that the "moderates" are having their chance to contribute to the literature, but these additions to the record leave uncomfortably large gaps. On the basis of what can be learned at this point, however, there is a clear answer to the question, "What caused the split in the Yenan leadership?" The answer is that it was a combination of three factors: different lessons drawn from the catastrophic consequences of the Great Leap Forward; the tensions arising from the issue of the succession to Mao, which was constantly on the agenda after 1958; and the growing fears of an aging and possibly increasingly senile leader. Too much information is missing, though, to enable us to judge the relative weight and influence of each of these factors.

CHAPTER 8

THE CHINESE ECONOMY UNDER STRESS, 1958–1965

At the start of the 2nd Five-Year Plan (FYP) (1958–62) there was no consensus within the leadership of the Chinese Communist Party (CCP) on the lessons of the 1st FYP and their implications for China's evolving development strategy. The years from 1953 through 1957 had brought unprecedentedly rapid economic growth, but the strategy of the 1st FYP was being seriously questioned from 1956 onward. Growth in the 1st FYP was quite imbalanced, with an industrial output rising almost five times more rapidly than that of agriculture.[1] Lagging performance in agriculture had allowed less than a 3 percent increase over five years in average per capita consumption of food grains, the source of about 90 percent of total caloric intake, and had substantially constrained the growth of manufactured consumer goods, since they were heavily dependent on supplies of raw materials from the farm sector.

From the point of view of the planners, the continued decline after 1954 in the absolute quantity of grain they were able to extract from the countryside, either in the form of taxes in kind or compulsory sales at fixed prices, was even more critical than the slow growth of output. The reopening of private rural markets in the second half of 1956 had increased the difficulty of fulfilling procurement quotas. Although private market transactions were supposed to be restricted to subsidiary products and items not subject to compulsory quotas for delivery to the state, the scope of the markets quickly expanded to include grain, oil-bearing seeds, and cotton.

Competition between state and market became so severe that in the face of the grain shortages that emerged in the summer of 1957, the State Council issued regulations in August prohibiting the sale of

---

1 Measured in terms of value added (rather than gross value) and in comparable prices, the growth rates of industry and agriculture in the first plan were 18.7 and 3.8 percent per year, respectively. Yang Chien-pai and Li Hsueh-tseng, "Nung, ch'ing, chung chieh-kou" (The structure of agriculture, light industry, and heavy industry), in Ma Hung and Sun Shang-ching, eds., *Chung-kuo ching-chi chieh-kou wen-t'i yen-chiu* (Research on problems in China's economic structure), 106.

grain, edible vegetable-oil seeds, and cotton (all subject to compulsory quotas for sale to the state) in rural markets. In the 1957 grain year (ending 30 June 1958), however, the quantity of cereals procured by the state fell slightly below the level of 1956 and remained less than in either 1954 or 1955, suggesting that the prohibition on market sales was not widely enforced and that peasants were able to withhold grain from the state.

While the quantity of grain controlled by the state was declining, demand was rising considerably. The urban population, for whose grain supply the state assumed the entire responsibility, had grown significantly, especially during 1956. Moreover, in 1957 the Chinese for the first time had to maintain an export surplus in their trade with the Soviet Union, their largest single trading partner. Since Chinese exports to the Soviet Union were almost exclusively agricultural products, minerals, and other raw materials, sustaining that trade surplus placed additional demands on the agricultural resources controlled by the state. While the initial export surplus required in 1957 was small, about 130 million U.S. dollars, the refusal of the Soviets to respond positively to China's request in 1957 for credits beyond those extended up through 1955, meant that the required surplus of agricultural exports would grow in the years ahead as more prior loans came due.[2]

Ultimately the most fundamental issue surrounding the 2nd FYP was the prospect for increasing the rate of growth of Chinese agriculture. The conservative view of Premier Chou En-lai, Li Fu-ch'un, head of the State Planning Commission, Li Hsien-nien, minister of finance, Ch'en Yun, the ranking Politburo member concerned with economic issues, and many others was that the rate of growth of agricultural output could be increased somewhat, but that this would require an increase in the share of state investment funds allocated to agriculture and an increased allocation of industrial investment to the chemical fertilizer industry and to manufacture of certain types of agricultural machinery. That view, which was embodied in the proposals for the 2nd FYP, implicitly rejected the contention that further changes in the organization of the producing units in agriculture could provide the basis for more rapid growth. Indeed, by the beginning of 1958, it was increasingly clear that contrary to expectations, agricultural growth had slowed since collectivization. Grain

2 State Statistical Bureau, *Chung-kuo t'ung-chi nien-chien 1983* (Chinese statistical yearbook 1983) (hereafter *TCNC*), 359.

output, for example, expanded by more than 4 percent annually in the first three years of the 1st FYP, but by less than 3 percent annually in the last two years, after higher-stage Agricultural Producers' Cooperatives (APCs) had become universal.[3]

Mao Tse-tung had an entirely different perspective. He had fought against what he regarded as the excessively cautious view of the planners on the pace of collectivization and more broadly on the pace of development, particularly of industry, during 1956. Although he had suffered a seeming setback when his mobilization strategy was curtailed by mid-1956, his fundamental outlook was unchanged. He still was predisposed to the belief that organizational changes, particularly when combined with resource mobilization campaigns, could provide a dramatic breakthrough to a path of more rapid development.

As indicated in Chapter 7, Mao's effort to replace what he regarded as the conservative approach embodied in the proposed 2nd FYP unfolded over a period of several months in late 1957 and early 1958. It was initiated at the Third Plenum of the Eighth Central Committee in the fall of 1957. There Mao spoke of the two methods of doing things, "one producing slower and poorer results and the other faster and better ones,"[4] and objected to the constraints that had been imposed on his mobilization campaign of 1956. In an effort to bypass the more cautious approach of the planners toward agriculture, at that time he also revived his twelve-year program for agricultural development, which had been quietly shelved in 1956. In November, the *People's Daily* published an editorial reviving the slogan of the leap of 1956 – "more, faster, better, and more economically."[5] While in Moscow in the same month Mao, almost certainly without consulting his colleagues in the Politburo, announced that Chinese output of major industrial products would surpass that of England within about fifteen years.[6]

When mobilization slogans and discussion of the twelve-year plan were revived, the planners were slow to respond. The few FYP targets set forth by the Chairman of the State Planning Commission in December 1957 were if anything actually even more cautious than those initially proposed by Chou En-lai at the Eighth Congress the

3 State Statistical Bureau, *Ten great years*, 119.
4 Roderick MacFarquhar, *The origins of the Cultural Revolution*, 2. 16–17.
5 Ibid., 17.
6 Po I-po, "Ch'ung-ching ho huai-nien hsien-kei tang tan-sheng ti liu-shih chou-nien" (Respect and remembrance – marking the sixtieth anniversary of the founding of the Chinese Communist Party), *Hung-ch'i* (Red flag), 1981, 13, 66.

previous year. The proposed targets for grain and cotton, for example, were scaled back, grain from 250 to 240 million metric tons and cotton from 2.4 to 2.15 million metric tons. Hence Mao, at an important Party meeting in Nanning in January 1958, directly criticized Chou En-lai, Ch'en Yun, and Li Hsien-nien for their refusal to support his efforts to raise growth targets substantially.

This criticism too failed to produce much change. Shortly after the close of the meeting in Nanning, Po I-po presented the 1958 annual plan to the National People's Congress for approval. The planned level of grain output of 196 million metric tons implied a rate of growth of 5.9 percent, not significantly above the long-term annual rate of 5.4 percent implicit in the 2nd FYP target of 240 million metric tons for 1962 presented by Li Fu-ch'un the previous December.[7]

The upward spiral of production targets for 1958 was finally launched by Mao at a meeting with members of the Central Committee and of local party committees in the early spring in Chengtu, Szechwan. There Mao cautiously endorsed a grandiose agricultural development program devised in Honan Province that promised, among other things, to double grain output in a single year. Mao's caution was, however, undermined by his own encouragement of interprovincial competition in raising cereal output.

THE ECONOMIC STRATEGY OF
THE GREAT LEAP FORWARD

The Great Leap Forward (GLF) was predicated on Mao's misunderstanding of the constraints facing Chinese agriculture. Contrary to the evidence from 1956 and 1957 that indicated otherwise, Mao continued to believe that larger agricultural producing units would capture significant economies of scale. He also believed that mobilization of existing resources, primarily labor, within the rural economy would provide a breakthrough to more rapid growth.

In large part the labor mobilization strategy was directed toward water conservancy and irrigation projects that were expected to raise crop yields substantially. Although there was a modest increase in the allocation of state funds to support agricultural development, in large measure the agricultural development strategy was to be a bootstrap operation.

7 Po I-po, "Kuan-yü 1958 nien-tu kuo-min ching-chi chi-hua ts'ao-an ti pao-kao." (Report on the draft of the 1958 national economic plan) in *Jen-min shou-ts'e, 1959* (1959 People's handbook), 240.

The industrial component of the GLF strategy was distinctly different. Great attention has been given to the program of "back-yard" steel furnaces and other smaller-scale industrial plants that embodied the spirit of "walking on two legs." But the GLF strategy for industry was predicated on a massive infusion of capital goods, in part based on imported machinery and equipment. In short, the industrialization strategy was primarily a further intensification of the capital-intensive development approach already evident in the 1st FYP, while agricultural development was predicated on a strategy of massive reorganization and mobilization.

The intersection of these two strategies came in 1958. In the winter of 1957–58 an unprecendentedly ambitious program of water projects was undertaken in the countryside. This reflected the revival of the twelve-year program for agricultural development that placed increased emphasis on small-scale projects which could be undertaken locally by collective units with little state coordination or state-provided resources. By the end of January 1958, Po I-po reported that the intense efforts of 100 million peasants had been successful in providing irrigation systems to 7.8 million hectares.[8] By the end of the year the claimed increase was 32 million hectares, more than ten times the area targeted at the time of a joint directive of the State Council and the Central Committee in September 1957.[9] The claimed increment represented almost a doubling of the total irrigated area.

The massive mobilization of labor for water conservancy projects led to the major organizational change in the countryside during the late 1950s – the formation of People's Communes. Although APCs were still the endorsed form of organization, as the demands of the water conservancy campaign increased, local and seemingly spontaneous mergers of APCs began to occur. These mergers were implicitly endorsed at the Chengtu meeting in March 1958, leading to an acceleration of mergers and ultimately within a matter of months to the emergence of the communes. As in the socialist transformation of 1955–56, the new organizational form quickly became universal.

---

8 Ibid., 235.
9 State Statistical Bureau, *Ten great years*, 130. MacFarquhar, *The origins of the Cultural Revolution*, 2. 34. CCP Central Committee and the State Council, "Kuan-yü chin-tung ming-ch'un ta-kuei-mo ti k'ai-chan hsing hsia nung-tien shui-li ho chi-fei yun-tung ti chueh-ting" (Decision concerning the development this winter and next spring of a movement to develop large scale initiation and repair of agricultural water conservancy projects and the collection of manure), in *Jen-min shou-ts'e, 1958* (1958 People's handbook), 533–34.

By the end of 1958, 99.1 percent of all households were members of communes.[10]

Communes had several distinct features. Most important, they were geographically large and subsumed the functions of government that previously had been lodged at the township (*hsiang*) level. Initially on average there were about 5,500 households per commune, about 25 times the size of the higher-stage APCs formed in 1955–56. The commune assumed the responsibilities for population registration, tax collection, and police administration, as well as for the provision of some services such as primary and lower middle school education and health services.

Second, the mix of private and collective activities was shifted decisively toward the latter. Private farming plots, a major source of subsidiary food for household consumption and for marketable products, particularly pigs, were eliminated under the commune system. Rural periodic markets were also widely curtailed, further reducing opportunities to earn cash income from the sale of handicrafts and other items of household production. Many other consumption-related activities such as cooking, washing, and child-rearing were shifted from a household to a communal basis, in part to release female labor for work in farming activities. These shifts toward more collective activities entailed the widespread confiscation of private agricultural tools and, to a lesser extent, personal household property.

Third, principles of income distribution were fundamentally altered. In higher-stage APCs, net income (gross earnings less the costs of purchased inputs and deductions for taxes, and retentions for welfare and investment funds) was distributed to APC members according to their labor contributions. In the communes, by contrast, a large share of net earnings was distributed on a per capita basis, consistent with the ideology of the period which promoted communes as a manifestation of the evolution away from socialist and toward communist principles of distribution. Even the small share of output distributed according to labor contributions was now distributed on the basis of a system in which workers were classified in labor grades and paid wages. The overall effect was to compress sharply the income differentials within communes.

The commune movement was accompanied by the perception of a massive increase in grain output. T'an Chen-lin, who had effectively

10 State Statistical Bureau, *Ten great years*, 43.

replaced Teng Tzu-hui as the head of the CCP's Rural Work Department, reported in August 1958 that record summer crops had been harvested and that total annual cereal production would reach at least 240 million metric tons and perhaps as much as 300 million tons.[11] By December, in the communiqué of the Sixth Plenum of the Eighth Central Committee, the reported grain output for 1958 was 375 million metric tons, double the 1957 level of 185 million metric tons. That figure was confirmed in April 1959 in the communiqué of the State Statistical Bureau.[12]

These totally unrealistic figures were the consequence of the campaign atmosphere evident in agriculture since the early months of 1958, the enhanced power of the Chinese Communist Party, particularly the key role played by the CCP committees at the commune level, and the widespread disruption of the statistical system. Given the breakdown of the statistical collection and monitoring system at the basic level and the intense pressure generated from above to report dramatic production breakthroughs, political cadres at the commune level reported highly inflated output figures which were then passed up the administrative hierarchy with no attempt to verify their accuracy. When the data were aggregated in Peking they were accepted, at least initially, as confirming the validity of Mao's judgment on the possibility of a dramatic acceleration of the pace of the agricultural development.

Acceptance of these data on agricultural output had several major repercussions. It provided the impetus for an increase in the rate of investment and a substantial acceleration of industrial growth. China's political leadership came to believe that the persistent problem of providing adequate food supplies for the growing urban population had been solved and that it was, therefore, possible to ease existing constraints on the growth of the nonagricultural population.

Moreover, the spurt in output would substantially increase the margin between production and the subsistence level of consumption in rural areas, providing the basis for a substantial increase in the mobilization of investment funds, to be utilized largely to support industrial investment. The image of rural prosperity also made it possible to envisage successfully implementing the supply system in communes, along with communal eating facilities. Finally, the acceptance of inflated output reports as real led to mistaken reductions in grain sown area, a policy that contributed to substantial food shortages.

Industry in the Great Leap

The rising target for steel production in 1958 exemplifies the evolution of the Great Leap in industry. The initial target in February 1958 by Po I-po was 6.2 million metric tons, a 19 percent increase over the 5.35 million metric tons of the previous years.[13] Three months later the Politburo raised the target to 8.0 to 8.5 million metric tons, and by August, in the wake of the higher assessment of the probable 1958 agricultural harvest, Mao persuaded the Politburo to endorse a target of 10.7 million metric tons.[14] Within a few weeks, Mao was proposing a target of as high as 12 million tons.

Capital investment targets were similarly raised throughout the course of 1958. The target proposed at the beginning of the year of 14.577 billion yuan, a modest 2.2 billion more than the estimated investment of 1957, was quickly superseded by more ambitious goals.[15] Ultimately investment in state-owned units reached 38.6 billion yuan, almost twice the level of 1957.[16] Although small-scale industry was a highly visible part of the investment drive, most increases were channeled into medium and large-scale state projects. In 1958, 1959, and 1960 the number of such projects started (1,587, 1,361, and 1,815, respectively) annually surpassed the 1,384 large and medium-scale projects undertaken in the entire 1st FYP.[17] For example, 157 large and medium-scale enterprises were initiated in the metallurgical sector, 61 in coal, 200 in electric power, 85 in chemicals, 80 in construction materials, and 180 under the First Ministry of Machine Building.[18]

The increases in construction associated with the investment drive and the increases in output of steel, machinery equipment, and other industrial goods were accompanied by an unprecedented increase in the nonagricultural labor force. In 1958 alone, the number of

13 Po I-po, "Kuan-yü 1958 nien-tu kuo-min ching-chi chi-hua ts'ao-an ti pao-kao," 230.
14 MacFarquhar, *The origins of the Cultural Revolution*, 2. 89–90.
15 Po I-po, "Kuan-yü 1958 nien-tu kuo-min ching-chi chi-hua ts'ao-an ti pao-kao," 237.
16 *TCNC 1981*, 295.
17 Ts'ui Chieh, "Chi-pen chien-she ti t'iao-cheng" (Readjustment of capital construction), in Liu Sui-nien, ed., *Liu-shih nien-tai kuo-min ching-chi t'iao-cheng ti hui-ku* (Recalling the readjustment of the economy in the 1960s), 73. Hereafter Liu Sui-nien, *Liu-shih nien-tai*.
18 Wu Ch'ün-kan, "Kuan-yü 'ta yueh-chin' shih-wu ho t'iao-cheng ti li-shih ching-yen," (Historical experiences concerning failures in and readjustment of the Great Leap Forward), in Liu Sui-nien, *Liu-shih nien-tai*, 26.

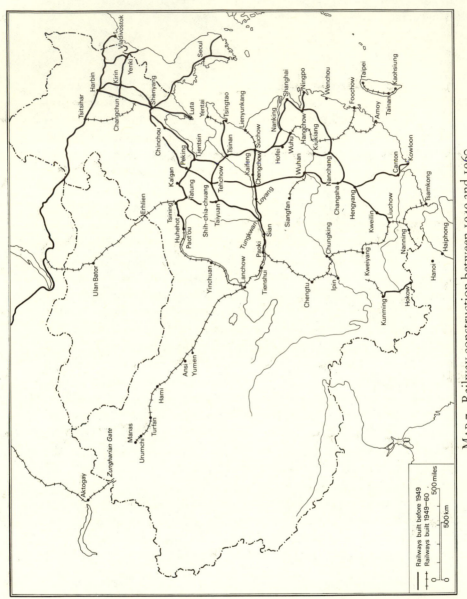

Vladivostok
Yenki
Kirin
Harbin
Changchun
Shenyang
Seoul
Tsitsihar
Chinchou
Luta
Yentai
Tsingtao
Lienyunkang
Nanking
Shanghai
Ningpo
Wenchou
Foochow
Taipei
Kaohsiung
Peking
Tientsin
Tsinan
Suchow
Hangchow
Amoy
Tainan
Erhlien
Kalgan
Tsining
Tatung
Kaifeng
Chengchow
Hofei
Wuhu
Kiukiang
Canton
Kowloon
Huhehot
Shih-chia-chuang
Tehchow
Loyang
Wuhan
Nanchang
Paot'ou
Taiyuan
Tungkwan
Sian
Siangfan
Changsha
Liuchow
Tsamkong
Ulan Bator
Yinchuan
Lanchow
Paoki
Tienshui
Chungking
Hengyang
Kweilin
Nanning
Haiphong
Yumen
Ansi
Chengtu
Ipin
Kweiyang
Hanoi
Hami
Manas
Turfan
Urumchi
Kunming
Hokow
Zungharian Gate
Aktogay

Railways built before 1949
Railways built 1949-60

500 miles
500 km

MAP 7. Railway construction between 1949 and 1960

workers and staff in state units rose by almost 21 million, an increase of 85 percent compared with 1957. An additional 5 million were added in 1959 and 1960. The peak level of employment in state units was 50.44 million at the end of 1960, more than double the number in 1957.[19]

The unprecedented increase in the modern sector labor force placed unusual demands on the state for rationed cereals and on the market for supplies of other food products. Although many of the additions to the work force were either single males or contract and temporary workers who had left their families behind in rural areas, the urban population grew by 31.24 million, and the number of persons for which the state assumed responsibility for the provision of cereals through its grain-rationing system rose by 28.0 million.[20] The share of the population eligible for grain rationing rose by a third from about 15 to about 20 percent between 1957 and 1960, with more than half the increase occurring in 1958.[21]

Both the massive increase in investment and the huge increase in the urban population led the state to place an unprecedented demand for grain on the rural population. In 1958 taxes in kind and compulsory deliveries to the state rose by more than 10 million metric tons over the average of 1956 and 1957. In 1959 procurement reached an all-time high of 67.4 million metric tons. Moreover, since grain production fell by 25 million tons compared with 1957, deliveries constituted 39.7 percent of total production. Although some of this grain was resold to peasant consumers, state purchases in 1959, net of resales, absorbed 28 percent of production, substantially above the 17 percent net procurement rate of 1957.[22]

Finally, the acceptance of inflated food grain output figures in 1959 led to a massive miscalculation in the 1959 plan for agriculture. Given the huge increase in grain yields in 1958, planners decided to cut back on the total sown area and allocate a somewhat higher share to cotton, edible oil seeds, and other nongrain crops. The result was that total sown area in 1959 was 10 percent less than in 1957 and that grain sown area was off by 13 percent. In reality, unit yields in 1959 were not distinguishably different from 1957, and production fell by 13 percent, some 25 million metric tons.[23]

Although the mistake of reducing sown area in 1959 was partially

19 *TCNC 1981*, 107.
20 *TCNC 1983*, 103.
21 Hsu Ti-hua, "Ching-chien chih-kung ho ch'eng-chen jen-k'ou" (Reducing the number of workers and staff and the urban population), in Liu Sui-nien, *Liu-shih nien-tai*, 123–24.
22 *TCNC 1983*, 393.
23 Lardy, *Agriculture in China's modern economic development*, 42.

reversed the following year, production continued to fall. In part the reduction in output was due to the mismanagement of agriculture brought about under the commune system. Most notably, many of the irrigation projects undertaken during the GLF were poorly designed and reduced rather than raised yields. This was particularly true on the North China Plain, where the failure to provide adequate drainage meant that irrigation led to increased soil salinity and thus a drop in yields. Agricultural production was also adversely affected by the substantial shrinkage of the agricultural labor force. Between 1957 and 1960 the corollary of the rapid growth of the numbers of nonagricultural workers and staff was a 22.91 million reduction in the agricultural labor force, a loss of more than 10 percent.[24] Finally, in 1960 adverse weather may have further reduced output. The net result was a 1960 grain harvest of 143.5 million metric tons, 26 percent below the 1957 harvest and the lowest level since 1950.

Other food crops also suffered catastrophic declines. Oil-bearing crop output in 1960 was less than half the 1957 output and lower than any other year since the CCP rose to power. Output of sugarcane and sugar beets was falling precipitously and would reach by 1962 a level one-third or less that of 1957. By 1962 the output of meat was only half the level of 1957.[25]

The decline in food production and a breakdown in the system of distribution set off a famine of proportions unprecedented in the twentieth century. According to official data the mortality rate, which had averaged 11.1 per thousand in 1956–57, rose to 14.6 per thousand in 1959 and reached a peak of 25.4 per thousand in 1960. Mortality declined sharply in 1961 to 14.2 per thousand, but was still well above the level of 1956–57. The increased mortality in 1960 was so large that over the course of that single year, China's population fell by 10.0 million.[26] The cumulative increase in mortality, over and above the number of normally expected deaths, has been estimated to be from 16 to 27 million.[27] In part this was the result of a sharp

24 *TCNC 1983*, 122.
25 Ibid., 158.
26 Ibid., 103–5.
27 The smaller figure results from applying the official data on increased mortality to the official series on the total population. But the consensus of Western demographers is that Chinese data significantly undercount mortality for the entire period since 1949. That conclusion is drawn because Chinese data on the age structure and on age-specific fertility rates cannot be made consistent with the published population totals unless one accepts mortality rates higher than those published. Coale estimates that 63 percent of all deaths between 1953 and 1964 were recorded and that this share rose to 85 percent between 1964 and 1982. When allowance is made for underreporting, Coale estimates 27 million excess deaths between 1958 and 1963. Ansley Coale, *Rapid population change in China 1952– 1982*, 70.

increase in infant mortality.[28] The ultimate demographic consequences were much larger than these numbers suggest, since the
birth rate fell from 33.0 per thousand on average in 1956–57 to a
trough of 18.0 per thousand in 1961.

In comparative historical terms, these data suggest a loss of life far
surpassing that of other crop failures or natural disasters in China in
the twentieth century. The major drought famines of the twentieth
century in China were in north and northwest China in 1900,
1920–21, and 1928–30. The famine of 1920–21 was probably the
most severe, both in duration and in geographical scope, and rendered at least 20 million peasants destitute. But the famine was
partially relieved by government and private efforts, and the death
toll was limited to an estimated 500,000.[29] A much larger number, in
excess of 2 million, perished in the great famine of 1928 that affected
Honan, Shensi, and Kansu.[30] The greater loss of life, as compared
with 1920–21, is generally attributed to the disruption of rail traffic
caused by Chiang Kai-shek's Northern Expedition, which effectively
curtailed relief operations.

One must move back in history to the prerailway era and the
famine of 1877–78 to find disaster on the scale of the Great Leap. In
that famine, which was concentrated in Shensi and Shansi, but also
affected Honan, Hopei, and parts of Shantung, government and
private efforts to move grain inland from coastal areas were stymied
by poor transport facilities. An estimated 9 to 13 million perished
from hunger and ensuing epidemics.[31]

One modern demographic catastrophe approaching the magnitude
of the Great Leap crisis occurred during and after Soviet agricultural
collectivization. The consensus estimate of the number of lives lost,
primarily from famine conditions created by government policy, is
about 5 million, roughly 1 out of 25 Russian peasants.[32] The Chinese
famine, by comparison, took from three to five times that number of

---

28 Chinese infant mortality data are widely believed to be persistently understated, presumably
    accounting for a large share of unrecorded deaths (see note 27). A reconstruction of Chinese
    population dynamics using the officially reported age structure, age-specific fertility rates,
    and population totals shows that infant mortality more than doubled between 1957 and the
    peak year of 1960. Judith Banister, "An analysis of recent data on the population of China,"
    Population and development review 10, 2 (June 1984), 254.
29 Marie-Claire Bergère, "Une crise de subsistence en Chine (1920–1922)" *Annales ESC*, 38.6
    (1973), 1361–1402.
30 Ibid., 1398, estimates the number of deaths as "in excess of 2 million." Ho Ping-ti, *Studies
    on the population of China 1368–1953*, 233, estimates 3 million deaths occurred in Shensi
    alone.
31 Ho Ping-ti, *Studies on the population of China, 1368–1953*, 232.
32 Dana G. Dalrymple, "The Soviet famine of 1932–1934," *Soviet Studies*, 15.3 (January
    1964), 259.

lives and even surpassed the Soviet famine in proportional terms if Western estimates of excess mortality are used in place of the official figures.

THE INCIDENCE OF THE CHINESE FAMINE

Little is known about the incidence of this massive famine, but two hypotheses can be advanced. First, the famine was disproportionately a rural phenomenon. Second, even within rural areas, deaths were highly concentrated regionally.

Several types of empirical evidence suggest that the famine was disproportionately rural. First, as shown in Table 5, the decline in grain consumption on average was far more severe in rural areas. By 1960 rural consumption of cereals had fallen 24 percent, while urban consumption had fallen less than 2 percent. In 1961, when average national consumption reached its lowest point, rural consumption had fallen 52 kilograms or 25 percent, while urban consumption was off only 15 kilograms or 8 percent. In absolute terms, consumption of vegetable oils and pork fell by more in urban than in rural areas, but the urban consumption of these items remained twice that of rural areas. Moreover, since caloric intake was derived so overwhelmingly from direct consumption of cereals, there is little doubt that urban consumers suffered less deprivation than peasants.

Second, Chinese data which divide mortality into "municipal" and "county" components suggest that deaths occurred disproportionately in rural areas during the famine years. Even in average or normal times, "county" mortality rates, which include deaths in rural areas as well as in small towns, were from 30 to 60 percent higher than those in municipalities. Data in Table 6 show that in 1960, the year of peak national mortality, deaths registered at the county level rose to a level more than twice as high as the mortality rate recorded in municipalities.

Even these figures almost certainly understate the degree to which the differential between urban and rural mortality rates widened during the Great Leap Forward. The county data aggregate mortality in towns, where a large share of the population was eligible for grain distributed through the rationing system, and in the surrounding countryside, where government-supplied grain was generally not available.

The empirical data on consumption, disaggregated into its urban and rural components, and on mortality, disaggregated into its

TABLE 5

Urban and rural grain consumption, 1952–1965
(kilograms per capita)

Year	National	Urban	Rural
1952	197.5	—	—
1957	203.0	196.0	204.5
1958	198.0	—	201.0
1959	186.5	—	183.0
1960	163.5	192.5	156.0
1961	—	180.8	153.5
1962	164.5	—	—
1963	—	—	159.5
1964	—	—	178.5
1965	184.0	—	177.0

Notes: Consumption is measured in units of "trade grain," which in Chinese statistical practice includes rice and millet in unprocessed form (original weight) and other grains in processed form. Grain is, in Chinese statistical practice, inclusive of cereals, tubers (at grain equivalent weight), and soybeans and other legumes. – indicates data not available.
Sources: Lardy, *Agriculture in China's modern economic development*, 150, 158. Wang P'ing, "'Ta-yueh-chin' ho t'iao-cheng shih-ch'i ti jen-min sheng-huo" (People's livelihood during the Great Leap Forward and readjustment), in Liu Sui-nien, ed., *Liu-shih nien-tai kuo-min ching-chi t'iao-cheng ti hui-ku*, 163, 169. Hsieh Tu-yang, "Hui-ku liu-shih nien-tai ch'u nung-yeh ti t'iao-cheng" (Remembrances of agricultural readjustment during the beginning of the 1960s) in ibid., 64.

"municipal" and "county" components, are supported as well by other types of evidence showing that the famine may have been predominantly rural. First, the rare references in published Chinese sources to famine invariably refer to famine in the villages (*nung-ts'un chi-huang*) and omit reference to urban mortality.[33] Second, the pressure on rural consumption standards is borne out by a sharp decline in animal stocks. Pigs were slaughtered first, since they were raised for food and the cash income they generated through the sale of pork in rural markets. The number of pigs dropped sharply – by more than 70 million head, or 48 percent, between 1957 and 1961. But peasants also slaughtered more than 30 percent of their draft animals,

33 The most authoritative references to "rural famine" are those of Hsueh Mu-ch'iao and Lo Keng-mo. At the onset of the Great Leap Hsueh was vice-chairman of both the State Economic Commission and State Planning Commission and director of the State Statistical Bureau. By 1961 he retained only the vice-chairmanship of the State Planning Commission. Lo at the time of the Leap also was a vice-chairman of the State Planning Commission. Hsueh Mu-ch'iao, *Tang-ch'ien wo-kuo ching-chi jo-kan wen-t'i* (Some current problems of China's economy), 14. Lo Keng-mo, "Kuan-yü wo-kuo chi-hua ching-chi ti hsing-ch'eng chi ch'i fa-chan ti ch'ü-che kuo-ch'eng ti fen-hsi" (An analysis of the formation of China's planned economy and its course of development), *Ching-chi yen-chiu* (Economic research), 1981. 2, 42.

TABLE 6

Mortality rates, 1956–1962 (deaths per thousand)

Year	National	Municipal	County
1956	11.40	7.43	11.84
1957	10.80	8.47	11.07
1958	11.98	9.22	12.50
1959	14.59	10.92	14.61
1960	25.43	13.77	28.58
1961	14.24	11.39	14.58
1962	10.02	8.28	10.32

Notes: "Municipal" (*shih*) refers to deaths registered in "established municipalities" (*ch'eng-li shih*), a designation made by the State Council for cities that function as major administrative and economic centers. In 1958 there were 185 municipalities, of which Peking and Shanghai were under the direct administration of the central government. "County" (*hsien*) refers to deaths registered in areas other than municipalities; that is, in towns and villages.
Source: State Statistical Bureau, *Chung-kuo t'ung-chi nien-chien, 1983,* 105.

a significant loss of farm assets in the pre-tractor era.[34] These declines are comparable with the loss of animal stocks during the Soviet collectivization campaign and the ensuing famine crisis.

Third, acute shortages of food in rural areas led after 1959 to a massive shift of cultivated area out of cash crops and into cereals. Total economic crop area declined by 35 percent between 1959 and 1962, when the share of farm area allocated to nongrain crops reached its lowest level. The largest share of the decline was accounted for by a collapse of the area sown to cotton, China's most important nongrain crop.[35] The sown area of less important cash crops declined by even larger proportions.

Fourth, the extraordinary pressure on rural living standards is suggested by the persistence through 1962 of starvation levels of food supplies in certain rural areas. As late as the spring of 1962 the grain consumption of 70 percent of the population in Tunhuang, Yümen, Chiuch'üan, and Chint'a counties in northwestern Kansu was less than one-quarter of a kilogram daily, a level about half what is sometimes stated to be the "semi-starvation" standard. Cereal consumption of half the rural population in Changyeh county, Kansu, was even lower – 3 ounces per day.[36] Examples such as this suggest

34 *TCNC 1983,* 177.
35 *TCNC 1981,* 138–39.
36 Wang P'ing, "'Ta yueh-chin' ho t'iao-cheng shih-ch'i ti jen-min sheng-huo" (People's living standards during the Great Leap Forward and the period of readjustment), in Liu Sui-nien, *Liu-shih nien-tai,* 169–70.

that even though the national data show mortality dropping back to the level of 1957, famine conditions persisted in 1962, particularly in more remote areas.

Finally, shortages of food in rural areas are reflected in an extraordinary increase in rural market prices of available foodstuffs. In the second half of 1959 the Central Committee of the CCP sanctioned the reopening of rural markets that had been closed at the onset of the commune movement in 1958. Initially these markets were restricted to commodities not subject to unified state procurement. But that prohibition was not widely enforced as early as 1960. As a consequence of the acute shortages, by the second half of 1960 the rural market prices of most agricultural products had shot up to a level two to three times the prices paid by the state. But the prices of cereals had soared to ten times the state fixed price, and in 1961 this gap widened.[37] The rural free market price of grain was from 2 to 4 yuan per kilogram, a 15- to 30-fold multiple of the procurement price for all cereals, which averaged .13 yuan per kilogram. Pork prices rose to 10 yuan per kilogram on the market, a 14-fold multiple of the state procurement price.[38] These price increases for foodstuffs substantially exceed recorded increases in other cases of severe famine, lending further support to the demographic data discussed above.[39]

Historically unprecedented rates of extraction of cereals from the countryside by the government, published references to famine in the

---

37 Chao Hsing-han and Ts'ao Chen-liang, "Ch'ien t'an nung-ch'an-pin shou-kou-chung ti i-wu to chia" (A preliminary discussion of high prices for the procurement of some agricultural commodities), *Chia-ko li-lun yü shih-chien* (Price theory and practice), 1982. 4, 26. Hsiang Ching-ch'üan, "Liu-shih nien-tai t'iao-cheng shih-ch'i wen-ting chia-ko ching-yen ch'u-t'an" (A preliminary assessment of experience in commodity price stabilization in the period of readjustment in the 1960s), ibid., 2. 22.

38 Hsueh Mu-ch'iao, "Kuan-yü i-chiu-wu-pa – i-chiu-liu-liu nien kuo-min ching-chi chien-she ti ch'ing-k'uang ho ching-yen" (China's experience and situation in economic construction from 1958 to 1966), *Ching-chi ts'an-k'ao tzu-liao* (Economic reference materials), 1. 13–14. Lardy, *Agriculture in China's modern economic development*, 225.

39 In the Bengal famine of 1943, in which approximately 3 million died of starvation and related causes, the price of rice, the major staple food, rose by May–August 1943 to a peak of four to five times the level of 1941. A national prohibition on interstate rice trade instituted in 1942, the year before the famine, effectively prevented an inflow of cereal that otherwise would have mitigated the cereal price spiral in the state of Bengal. Not until the national Indian government instituted a centralized program of interstate grain movements was the price spiral broken in the last months of 1943. The Bangladesh famine of 1974 provides another example where the increases in the price of cereals were far less than in China. The retail price of rice rose to a peak in October 1974, 210 percent greater than the level in December 1973. In the most severely affected famine district, Rangpur, the peak retail rice price was 265 percent above the level of December 1973. Although the official government estimate of deaths due to famine was 26,000, independent estimates place the toll many times higher. See A. K. Sen, *Poverty and famines: An essay on entitlement and deprivation*, 64, 66.

villages, the drop in animal stocks, the shifting pattern of cropping, and the sharply higher rural market prices for food all suggest that the famine was predominantly rural. But even within rural areas, it appears that famine deaths were concentrated in certain regions. That supposition rests on two a priori observations and limited data. First, national cereal output exhibits relatively small year-to-year fluctuations because national output is produced over widely varying climatic and cropping conditions. But fluctuations are much more substantial if one looks at regions such as the North China Plain, the Northwest loess plateau, and even larger if we look at the provincial level. For example, grain output in Liaoning Province in 1960 fell to a trough of 3.1 million metric tons, half the level of 1958 and 40 percent below the level of 1957, declines substantially greater than the national average.[40]

In the 1950s the central government redistributed substantial quantities of grain interregionally not only to support specialized cropping patterns or provinces with large urban populations but to alleviate localized food shortages due to flood, drought, or some other natural disaster. Liaoning, for example, because it was the most urbanized province, during the 1st FYP annually received about 1.66 million metric tons of transferred grain, the largest amount of any province.[41] In the GLF these interregional commodity flows were curtailed. In 1958, for example, the amount of grain moving interprovincially was reduced by 1.5 million metric tons.[42]

In part that curtailment occurred because local self-sufficiency was an integral part of the ideology of the commune movement, but it also occurred because extreme political mobilization made it difficult for local political leaders to request food assistance from the center. Indeed, there are reasonably documented cases in which local political cadres suppressed the flow of information on local food shortages because it was inconsistent with the "bumper harvests" they had reported previously. Because the interregional flows of commodities that normally alleviated local food shortages were curtailed, regions with unusual shortfalls in production were less able to rely on transferred grain.

Chinese sources refer to "abnormal deaths" in 1960 in localities in Shantung, Honan, Shansi, Anhwei, and Kiangsu provinces.[43] Of

40 *Liao-ning ching-chi t'ung-chi nien-chien, 1983* (Liaoning economics and statistics yearbook, 1983), 424.
41 Kenneth R. Walker, *Food grain procurement and consumption in China*, 87.
42 Lardy, *Agriculture in China's modern economic development*, 41.
43 Liu Sui-nien, *Liu-shih nien-tai*, 180.

these, Anhwei probably was the most severely depopulated. In 1960 the provincial death rate soared to 68 per thousand, more than 3.5 times the national average. Since the birth rate in 1960 was 11 per thousand, the population of the province must have declined by almost 6 percent, or more than 2 million persons, in a single year.[44] The population decline in Anhwei alone would account for fully 20 percent of the officially reported decline in national population in 1960. It is noteworthy that the increase in the death rate in Anhwei in 1960 far surpassed that which occurred in the Indian state of Bengal during the massive famine in 1943.[45]

Second, famine deaths must have been more severe in regions that traditionally specialized in nonfood crops. Under normal conditions, peasants in these areas bought grain in local rural markets or relied on grain purchased from the government. At the outset of the GLF, local rural trade was disrupted by widespread market closures. Even after these markets had reopened, the terms of trade effectively moved sharply against these peasants. Where grain could be purchased, its price had increased manyfold while the prices of fiber crops – tobacco, sugarcane, and so forth – that they might be able to sell either directly to the government or in rural markets increased little or perhaps even fell. Those dependent on grain sold by the government may have been still worse off because of the chaotic conditions of the period and an emphasis on self-sufficiency that curtailed government resales.

In either case, the ability of producers of nongrain food crops or animal husbandry products to trade their output for cereals that normally provided a less expensive source of calories was reduced, while producers of fibers and other nonfood crops were also less able to obtain cereals. Similar concentrations of deaths among rural non-food producers are commonly observed in famine conditions. The validity of this supposition for the Chinese famine appears to be borne out by qualitative evidence. Some peasants from northwest

44 Thomas P. Bernstein, "Stalinism, famine, and Chinese peasants: Grain procurements during the great leap forward," *Theory and Society*, 1984. 3, 344.
45 In 1943, the peak year of famine deaths in Bengal, Greenough estimates there were 3.7 million deaths, of which 1.7 would have occurred in the absence of famine conditions. These deaths were overwhelmingly rural, and the initial rural population of Bengal was 55.2 million. Thus the 1943 mortality rate was 67 per 1,000, a little more than twice the normal mortality rate of 30 per 1,000. Although the peak year mortality rates in Anhui (Anhwei) Province and the State of Bengal were virtually identical, the normal mortality rate was probably about half that of Bengal – thus the increase in the death rate was far greater in Anhwei. Paul R. Greenough, *Prosperity and misery in modern Bengal: The famine of 1943–1944*, 200, 309.

Shantung, a traditional cotton-producing area that was devastated during the Great Leap, survived the early 1960s by traveling to areas south of the Yellow River, where they were able to barter their clothing and other possessions for grain.[46] That phenomenon suggests a breakdown of government redistribution of available cereal supplies.

Peasants unable to travel or living farther from regions with surplus grain fared less well. One example is Ku-yuan county in southern Ninghsia, a remote pastoral county where rural prosperity in the 1950s was achieved in large measure through the sale of hides, meat, and wool. Mortality was so high that the population, 275,000 in 1957, fell in both 1959 and 1960.[47] Qualitative accounts of adjacent counties within Ku-yuan prefecture suggest starvation was even more widespread than just in the one county. Famine in animal husbandry areas of the Northwest bears many similarities to the Ethiopian famine of 1972–74 in which the hardest hit areas were pastoral regions within Wollo province in the northeast, especially in the Afar' and within Harerghe province. In these cases, the declining price of livestock and livestock products relative to the price of grains effectively diminished the ability of pastoralists to sell animal products to buy grain, which in prefamine times was the major source of caloric intake.

THE PARTY'S RESPONSE TO THE FAMINE CRISIS

The crisis created by the Great Leap Forward posed the most severe challenge the Party had faced since coming to power in 1949. Yet the course of political events not only made it difficult for the Party to anticipate the magnitude of the crisis but led to policy decisions that exacerbated the famine. Even more startling is the fact that once incontrovertible evidence of widespread famine was in hand, the Party remained paralyzed, unable or unwilling to formulate a timely and cohesive response to the most massive famine of the twentieth century.

Evidence of the failure of the agricultural mobilization strategy was

46 The depths to which conditions had sunk in the four prefectures of Ho-tse, Te-chou, Liao-ch'eng, and Hui-min is extraordinary. By 1961 production of cotton was less than 10 percent the level of the 1st FYP and cereal output had fallen to fewer than 1 million metric tons, compared with averages of 3 million metric tons in 1956–57, 2.25 million metric tons in 1959, and 1.6 million metric tons in 1960. Lardy, *Agriculture in China's modern economic development*, 177.
47 Chung-kuo k'o-hsueh yuan ti-li yen-chiu-so ching-chi ti-li yen-chiu-shih (Chinese Academy of Sciences, Geography Research Institute, Economic Geography Research Office), *Chung-kuo nung-yeh ti-li tsung-lun* (A treatise on China's agricultural geography), 366.

available as early as the winter of 1958–59. It was clear to members of the Central Committee at the time of the Wu-ch'ang Plenum in November and December 1958 that there was precious little basis for the announcement that 1958 grain output was 375 million metric tons and cotton output was 3.5 million metric tons. The account by P'eng Te-huai, then a member of the Politburo and minister of national defense, of the discussions at that meeting shows that the statistical system had deteriorated to the point where it was impossible to know the actual harvest level with any degree of confidence. According to P'eng, some comrades at the meeting thought that the harvest was in excess of 500 million tons and that regardless of the precise amount, "industry is now vastly behind agriculture." P'eng challenged the accuracy of the reported levels of output. According to P'eng, Mao personally made the decision to announce a figure of 375 million metric tons.[48] The published output figures thus reflected a political rather than a statistical judgment.

Although those figures became the basis for agricultural planning for 1959, at least two members of the Politburo challenged the veracity of substantial increases in reported cereal production. P'eng Te-huai, some time after the conclusion of the Wu-ch'ang Conference, traveled to Hunan province for a firsthand examination of rural conditions. He found that conditions in the countryside where he visited were grave and concluded that the output figures previously submitted to the center were inflated. Not waiting until he could return to Peking and report his findings directly, and fearing that "the masses are in danger of starving," he sent an urgent cable to the Central Committee requesting that the province's tax and compulsory delivery quota be reduced by one-fourth.[49]

Ch'en Yun, the fifth ranking member of the Party and by far the most senior on economic affairs, also distrusted the reports being submitted to Peking and in the spring of 1959 pointedly chose to visit Honan, the province that had played such a path-breaking role in the water conservancy campaign in the winter of 1957–58 and subsequently in the formation of communes. He too found that local political cadres were out of touch with conditions in the rural areas of the province, lacked adequate data on the true grain situation, and were deluded by the inflated reports submitted from the grassroots

48 Nicholas R. Lardy and Kenneth Lieberthal, *Chen Yun's strategy for China's development*, xxv.
49 Ibid., xli. Li Jui, "Tu 'Peng Te-huai tzu-shu'" (Reading P'eng Te-huai's own account), *JMJP*, 30 March 1982, 5.

level.[50] It is not clear how Ch'en brought his findings to the attention of other members of the Politburo, but it is implausible to argue that he kept the information to himself.

The reports of P'eng Te-huai and Ch'en Yun in the winter and spring of 1959 signaled that the fundamental strategy of the GLF was flawed. Organization of large-scale communes and massive political mobilization had not raised agricultural output in 1958 even with weather conditions that, on balance, were more favorable than in either 1956 or 1957.[51]

P'eng personally posed a dramatic challenge to the strategy of the Great Leap Forward and, more important, to Mao's leadership at the crucial party meeting convened at Lushan in July 1959. But P'eng's broadside was decisively rebuffed by Mao, and the GLF entered a new upsurge in which criticism of policy became impossible. Far more significant, the intensive mobilization of resources for indus-trialization accelerated. During 1959 the rate of investment rose to an all-time peak of 43.4 percent of national income. The state supported this drive in large measure by increasing its extractions of cereals, vegetables, and fiber crops from the peasantry. The effect of rising cereal procurement on the rural population is shown in Table 7. In 1959 retained grains, which included amounts that had to be utilized for livestock feed and seed for the following year's crop, fell dramati-cally to 223 kilograms per capita, only three-quarters of the level of 1957. Similarly, even though production was down, the state's pro-curement of oil-bearing seeds rose by one-quarter in 1959 compared to 1957. A growing quantity of agricultural goods were exported to the Soviet Union in payment for the stepped-up imports of machin-ery and equipment that were a key component of the higher rate of investment.

Most astounding, even as the mortality rate was rising in 1959, Chinese exports of cereals, shown in Table 8, were reaching peak historical levels. Exports (primarily rice and soybeans) in 1959 reached a level twice the average of the 1st FYP, while imports (mostly wheat) fell to the lowest level in six years. Thus net exports in 1959 were more than double the average annual level of the 1st FYP. Similarly, in 1959 cotton yarn and cotton cloth exports were double

---

50 Teng Li-ch'ün, *Hsiang Ch'en Yun t'ung-chih hsueh-hsi tso ching-chi kung-tso* (Study how to do economic work from comrade Ch'en Yun), 54–55.
51 The sown area suffering losses of 30 percent or more due to calamities and natural disasters in 1958 was 13.73 million hectares. In 1956 and 1957 the area suffering similarly was 15.23 and 14.98 million hectares, respectively. *TCNC 1983*, 212.

TABLE 7

Grain production and government transactions with the
rural sector, 1953–1965

Year	Production[a]	Procurement[a]	Resales[a]	Rural retentions[a]	Rural retentions per capita[b]
1953–57 (average)	181.614	48.699	15.456	148.371	280.5
1957	195.045	48.040	14.170	161.175	294.6
1958	200.000	58.760	17.035	158.275	286.4
1959	170.000	67.405	19.840	122.435	223.3
1960	143.500	51.050	20.155	112.605	211.9
1961	147.500	40.470	14.665	121.695	229.0
1962	160.000	38.145	12.425	134.280	241.4
1963	170.000	43.465	15.045	141.080	245.2
1964	187.500	47.425	15.580	155.655	270.5
1965	194.520	48.685	15.090	160.925	270.5

Notes: [a] Millions of metric tons. [b] Kilograms. All measured in terms of unhusked weight (i.e., "original weight"). Rural retentions equal production less procurement plus resales. Procurement and resales data are for the production year, the second half of the calendar year plus the first half of the following calendar year.
Source: State Statistical Bureau, Chung-kuo t'ung-chi nien-chien 1983, 103, 393.

TABLE 8

Grain exports and imports, 1952–1965 (thousands of metric tons)

Year	Exports	Imports	Net exports
1952	1,528.8	.1	1,528.7
1953	1,826.2	14.6	1,811.6
1954	1,711.0	30.0	1,681.0
1955	2,233.4	182.2	2,051.2
1956	2,651.2	149.2	2,502.0
1957	2,092.6	166.8	1,925.8
1958	2,883.4	223.5	2,659.9
1959	4,157.5	2.0	4,155.5
1960	2,720.4	66.3	2,654.1
1961	1,355.0	5,809.7	−4,454.7
1962	1,030.9	4,923.0	−3,892.1
1963	1,490.1	5,952.0	−4,461.9
1964	1,820.8	6,570.1	−4,749.3
1965	2,416.5	6,405.2	−3,988.7

Notes: Exports and imports are measured in terms of unhusked grain ("original weight").
Source: State Statistical Bureau, Chung-kuo t'ung-chi nien-chien 1983, 422, 438.

and almost double, respectively, the levels of 1957. In value terms, Chinese exports to the Soviet Union rose 50 percent between 1957 and 1959 and in 1959 made up 60 percent of China's exports.[52]

Moreover, at the height of the GLF crisis in 1958–62, government expenditures for rural relief averaged less than 450 million yuan per year, or about eight-tenths of a yuan annually for each individual in collective agriculture,[53] while the market price of grain in shortage areas had reached 2 to 4 yuan per kilogram. The internal welfare funds of collective units did not provide an effective alternative source of support for starving rural people. In 1960, the peak of the mortality crisis, internal welfare funds totaled only 370 million yuan.[54]

The only policy responses to the famine visible in 1960 were meager, given the magnitude of the crisis. Cereal procurements were scaled back by more than 16 million tons (Table 7). But since resales to peasants did not increase over the previous year and total production fell by more than 25 million tons, the grain retained in the countryside fell even farther from the already low levels of 1959, and rural mortality rates skyrocketed. Second, exports were scaled back and the Chinese opened discussions for large-scale wheat imports. But exports in 1960 remained well above the average level of the 1st FYP (Table 8), and the decision to import appears to have been more related to an emerging crisis of urban consumption standards than a response to the rural crisis that by the time contract negotiations opened, had been going on for a year and a half. Urban consumption standards had been maintained in 1958 and 1959 not only through record levels of procurement but in part by drawing down state-controlled grain inventories. In an effort to conserve the small remaining stocks, in September 1960 the amount of grain supplied to urban residents through the rationing system was reduced by one kilogram per capita per month.[55] In October, contracts for wheat imports were negotiated and signed.

Finally, changes in rural policy were contained in a document drafted by Chou En-lai entitled "Urgent directive on rural work." That directive, approved by the Central Committee in November 1960 despite the opposition of some Party members, sought to alleviate the rural crisis by changing the internal organization of

52 State Statistical Bureau, "Chung-kuo ching-chi t'ung-chi tzu-liao hsuan-pien" (A compilation of Chinese economic statistics), in Hsueh Mu-ch'iao, ed., Chung-kuo ching-chi nien-chien 1982 (Chinese economic yearbook 1982), viii–38, viii–47, viii–59.
53 Lardy, Agriculture in China's modern economic development, 131.
54 TCNC 1981, 195.
55 Liu Sui-nien, Liu-shih nien-tai, 180.

agriculture. It formally endorsed a shift of the locus of decision making from the commune, an organization that was too large to provide adequate incentives and effective management of labor intensive agricultural processes, downward to the brigade, the smaller intermediate-size unit in the three-level rural organizational structure. In some ways the directive also sought to enhance the power of the lowest-level units, the production teams.

While the decision to import cereals and to shift the locus of decision making and income distribution to lower levels of the commune may have partially alleviated the disincentives associated with the commune system, it was not until late 1960 that a comprehensive reevaluation of the GLF strategy was initiated and a more cohesive response to the crisis began to emerge. The initiative was led by Chou En-lai, who revived the Finance and Economics Small Group, a crucial policy-making organization, to take the lead in the formation of a recovery strategy. A key element of Chou's reconstitution of this group was his personal invitation to Ch'en Yun to return to play an active role in economic policy formulation. Ch'en had fallen from sight after the first half of 1959 prior to the convening of the Lushan Conference, perhaps for reasons of health but more likely because of his opposition to policies of the GLF. In the early 1960s, he reemerged as the central figure in designing the recovery strategy.

The core of Ch'en's view was that sustained recovery was possible only with a more balanced growth strategy. While he naturally supported a reduction in the degree of socialism in the countryside, Ch'en argued that internal changes in agricultural organization could not provide an adequate basis for either recovery or sustained growth in the future. Ch'en's strategy embodied more far-reaching changes: more active use of price policy; increased specialization in agricultural production based on comparative advantage in cropping patterns and interregional trade; the development of a modern chemical industry to supply fertilizers to agriculture; a restoration of normal marketing channels; a substantial reduction in the rate of investment and a shift in its composition away from metallurgy and machinery toward consumer goods and selected industrial goods that could be used to support agricultural production; and the resettlement in rural areas of almost 30 million persons who had migrated to cities after 1957, initially because of the increased numbers of urban jobs available and subsequently to seek food.[56]

56 Teng Li-ch'ün, *Hsiang Ch'en Yun t'ung-chih hsueh-hsi tso ching-chi kung-tso*, 8.

Among the highest levels of Chinese leadership, Ch'en Yun had the deepest understanding of the problems of China's agriculture. His views seem clearly to have been shaped by the experience of collectivization in 1955–56, which showed that whatever economies of scale existed in production were far from sufficient to offset the disincentive effects of large units where the high costs of monitoring individual work under conditions of dispersed production make it difficult to reward individual productivity. Ch'en thus differed profoundly from Mao Tse-tung, who had continued to seek agricultural growth primarily through increased mobilization of labor and other inputs within agriculture. Moreover, Ch'en in 1955–56 had opposed the closure of rural markets, which reduced opportunities for peasants to earn extra income. Finally, Ch'en advocated a lower rate of investment – in sharp distinction to Mao, who seemingly oblivious of the problems created by the excessive rate of investment of the GLF, as late as 1960 continued to believe that an investment rate of about 30 percent could be sustained.[57]

But because of continued opposition it would take more than two years for Chou, Ch'en, and others to secure the approval and implementation of these policies. Initially, the debate focused on agricultural policy. Rural investigations during 1961 by Ch'en Yun and others strengthened the hands of those seeking reforms more fundamental than were entailed in the 1960 "Urgent directive on rural work." Ch'en, in his investigation of his native Ch'ing-p'u county, near Shanghai, found even in this relatively prosperous Yangtze Valley area, where there had been no reported natural calamities, that "there is not enough grain to eat," that mismanagement by Party cadres undermined incentives, and that exaggerated production claims were still being reported to higher authorities. Ch'en recommended further strengthening of household production, expansion of private plots, and less interference in the determination of cropping patterns by rural political cadres.[58]

Chen's concerns about agriculture were not based only on investigation of individual local areas. He was also alarmed by the continued drawdown of state grain reserves and the difficulty of reviving interregional grain transfers. By the middle of 1961 state grain

57 Kjeld Erik Brodsgaard, "Paradigmatic change: Readjustment and reform in the Chinese economy, 1953–1982," *Modern China*, 1983. 2, 255–56.
58 Ch'en Yun, "Ch'ing-p'u nung-ts'un tiao-ch'a, i-chiu-liu-i nien pa yueh" (An investigation of rural Ch'ing-p'u (August 1961)) in *Ch'en Yun t'ung-chih wen-kao hsuan-pien, i-chiu wu-liu-i-chiu liu-erh* (Selected manuscripts of comrade Ch'en Yun, 1956–1962), 130–46.

reserves, which had stood at 21.35 million and 18.20 million metric tons in mid-1956 and mid-1957, respectively, were depleted to little more than working stocks.[59] In December 1960, as Peking, Tientsin, Shanghai, and other major cities, as well as areas incurring major natural disasters, were hard-pressed to maintain food supplies, the central government issued an urgent directive requiring those provinces with surplus to mobilize all available manpower to ensure the fulfillment of provincial responsibilities to transfer grain.[60] Yet the amounts to be transferred were negligible compared to the 1st FYP or even to the latter half of 1959 and the first half of 1960, when the self-sufficiency policy of 1958 was abandoned and interregional grain transfers revived.[61]

Even maintaining modest levels of procurement was difficult, since peasants were increasingly less willing to sell to the government. In part, that reflected low levels of per capita production and rural starvation. But in many regions with surplus grain peasants were unwilling to sell grain, even at the higher prices instituted in 1960, because of the acute shortage of consumer goods in the countryside. With the decline in the output of manufactured consumer goods and the collapse of the distribution system, peasants fortunate enough to have surplus grain above their own consumption needs were interested in acquiring real goods, not increased quantities of money whose purchasing power was rapidly eroding. To get peasants to part with their grain, beginning in the winter of 1961 the state not only had to pay higher prices but also had to guarantee rights to purchase goods no longer available in sufficient quantities in the countryside. In exchange for selling 750 kilograms of cereals at the new higher fixed procurement price, peasant producers were given the right to purchase, at prevailing retail prices, 15 feet of cotton cloth, 1 pair of rubber shoes, 20 feet of knit goods, 1.5 kilograms of sugar, 2 cases of cigarettes, and 400 grams of cotton for padding in quilts and jackets.[62]

The positive incentive provided by improved access to scarce consumer goods was reinforced with sanctions. In March 1962, in an effort to force more grain into government hands, a new directive was issued strictly forbidding the sale and purchase of grain on rural

59 Lardy and Lieberthal, *Chen Yun's strategy for China's development*, xxix–xxx.
60 Liu Sui-nien, *Liu-shih nien-tai*, 181–82.
61 Kenneth R. Walker, *Food grain procurement and consumption in China*, 155, 158.
62 Chao Hsing-han and Ts'ao Chen-liang, "Ch'ien t'an nung-ch'an p'in shou-kou-chung ti i-wu to chia," *Chia-ko li-lun yü shih-chien*, 1982. 4, 28. Wang P'ing, "Ts'ai-mao fang-mien t'iao-cheng ti ch'ing-k'uang ho ching-yen" (Our experience and the situation in the financial aspects of readjustment), in Liu Sui-nien, *Liu-shih nien-tai*, 148.

markets.[63] However, as shown in Table 7, procurement recovered only slowly.

These continued problems in the agricultural sector led Ch'en Yun and others to seek further reforms. That effort was reflected in Liu Shao-ch'i's report at the Seven Thousand Cadres Conference in January 1962, which portrayed a continuing grim rural situation. Debate, however, continued. The proponents of the GLF, which included a large number of cadres beyond Mao and his closest supporters, argued in 1962 that the policies of adjustment had set the stage for a new leap forward, which they sought to embody in the 3rd FYP, scheduled to begin in 1963. Chou En-lai, Liu Shao-ch'i, Ch'en Yun and other moderates favored an extension of the period of readjustment through 1965 that would entail continued priority for agricultural development and a deferral of the ambitious industrialization program being pushed by Wang Ho-shou of the Ministry of Metallurgy and other continued strong supporters of an industrialization strategy based on heavy industry.[64] This ongoing debate is fascinating, since it suggests that the rectification campaign of 1960–61, which removed a number of leftist provincial and lower-level political leaders who lacked "sufficient understanding of the distinction between socialism and communism," was not sufficiently far-reaching to reestablish a consensus on economic policy.[65]

The scale and pattern of investment

The first priority of Ch'en Yun, Li Fu-ch'un, and others was drastically to control the level and rate of investment. The sharp increases in the rate of capital formation, from an average of 24 percent during the 1st FYP to an average of 34 percent in 1958–60, had placed severe demands on the economy and precipitated a dramatic decline in efficiency in the use of resources. Shortages of materials and the difficulties of coordinating so many key projects caused the amount of time required to complete projects to increase considerably. The result was a huge rise in the wage bill, largely for construction

63 Liu Sui-nien, *Liu-shih nien-tai*, 195.
64 Lardy and Lieberthal, *Chen Yun's strategy for China's development*, xxxiii. Wu Ch'ün-kan, "Kuan-yü 'ta-yueh-chin' shih-wu ho t'iao-cheng ti li-shih ching-yen," in Liu Sui-nien, *Liu-shih nien-tai*, 35. Liu Sui-nien, "'T'iao-cheng, kung-ku, ch'ung-shih, t'i-kao' pa-tzu fang-chen ti t'i-ch'u chi chih-hsing ch'ing-k'uang" (The proposal and implementation of the eight character policy of readjustment, consolidation, filling out, and raising standards), *Tang-shih yen-chiu* (Research on Party history), 1980. 6, 29.
65 Frederick C. Teiwes, *Politics and purges in China*, 448–50.

workers, but no corresponding increase in manufactured goods. The problem of higher wages not matched by increased output of manufactured goods was, of course, compounded drastically by the simultaneous decline in agricultural output.

The imbalance was also reflected in the government budget, which was the source of finance for most investment projects. As early as 1958 the budget incurred a deficit. By 1960 it had grown enormously, exceeding 8 billion yuan, about 15 percent of revenues. These developments led to substantial excess demand and inflationary pressure. By 1961 investment outlays and government expenditures were undergoing a drastic shrinkage. Expenditures fell by 29 billion yuan in 1961 and a further 6 billion yuan in 1962. By 1962 there was a budget surplus of almost a billion yuan. State investment fell even more dramatically, from 38.9 to 7.1 billion yuan, between 1960 and 1962. Accumulation as a share of national income fell to a low of 10.4 percent.

In part, the decline in investment reflected the economic collapse of the GLF, but especially after 1960 it also reflected the ascendancy of the Finance and Economics Small Group in policy formulation. Steel output, for example, was cut back from 18.66 million metric tons in 1960 to 6.7 million metric tons in 1962; coal production from 397 to 220 million metric tons; cement from 15.65 to 6.0 million metric tons; metal-cutting machine tools from 153,500 to 22,500; and so forth.

Simultaneously with the reduction in investment, tens of thousands of construction and manufacturing enterprises were closed, and almost 30 million urbanites were forcibly resettled in the countryside. Specifically, during 1961, as construction projects were reduced and 25,000 state industrial enterprises were shut down, 5.470 million industrial workers and 2.956 million construction workers lost their source of wage income, and about 10 million urban residents were resettled in the countryside. Although it was fiercely contested, at the insistence of the Finance and Economics Small Group another 18,000 state industrial enterprises were shut down in 1962 and 4.19 million industrial workers and 1.57 million construction workers lost their jobs, while 20 million urbanites were moved to the countryside.[66]

The cumulative effect of this massive forced resettlement program was substantial. The industrial labor force in state enterprises was reduced by 45 percent; and the number of construction workers, by

---

66 Liu Sui-nien, "T'iao-cheng, kung-ku, ch'ung-shih, t'i-kao' pa-tzu fang-chen ti t'i-ch'u chi chih-hsing ch'ing-k'uang," 27. *TCNC 1983*, 126.

35 percent. By the middle of 1963 the urban population had been cut by 26 million and the nonagricultural population, those entitled to receive cereal through the state rationing system, had been reduced by 28 million.[67] The shrinkage of the labor force reduced the wage bill in state-owned industries from 11.41 million yuan in 1960 to a low of 8.20 billion yuan in 1963, it also reduced the state wage bill in construction by 2.14 billion yuan, or 52 percent, reducing the inflationary pressure caused by excess demand. Moreover, the closure of industrial enterprises suffering financial losses increased budget revenues. Losses sustained by state industrial enterprises, which had peaked at 4.6 billion yuan, were reduced to 1.2 billion yuan by 1963, in large measure by closing those enterprises sustaining losses.[68]

Agricultural policy

Although the initial response to the agrarian crisis brought on by the GLF was shockingly inadequate, more substantial policy changes were evident by 1961. These changes sought to respond to the immediate welfare needs of rural China and to provide a sound basis for agricultural recovery and sustained growth. The single most significant change was a sharp reduction in compulsory deliveries of cereals to the state. By 1961 these had dropped to 40.5 million metric tons, compared to 67.4 million metric tons in 1959. Even more critically, the share of output retained in the countryside rose to 82.5 percent, about the same share as during the 1st FYP. The reduction in the rate of procurement broke the precipitous decline in rural consumption that had begun in 1958. The financial impact of these reductions was maximized because most of the reductions in procurement were of the tax grain which farmers delivered to the state without any financial compensation. Thus, the share of the deliveries for which compensation was paid (so-called quota procurement) was increased. The financial effect of these changes was an 11.3 billion yuan reduction in the agricultural tax. The rate of compensation (the so-called quota purchase price) for cereal deliveries was raised by 27 percent in 1961. Procurement prices of most other agricultural products were raised by lesser amounts in 1962 ȯr 1963. The state raised the

67 Hsieh Tu-yang, "Hui-ku liu-shih nien-tai ch'u nung-yeh t'iao-cheng" (Recalling the readjustment of agriculture at the beginning of the 1960s), in Liu Sui-nien, *Liu-shih nien-tai*, 60.
68 Wu Ch'ün-kan, "Kuan-yü 'ta-yueh chin' shih-wu ho t'iao-cheng ti li-shih ching-yen," in Liu Sui-nien, *Liu-shih nien-tai*, 4.

price it paid for oil-bearing seeds by 19 percent in 1961 and for cotton by 10 percent in 1963.[69] Finally, welfare expenditures in rural areas were increased to provide more income and goods to low-income rural residents. In 1963–65 annual per capita rural welfare expenditures, while still low in absolute terms, were three times the level prevailing in 1958–62.[70]

More far-reaching measures were taken to facilitate agricultural recovery and lay the basis for sustained growth. In large measure these policies reduced the role of the Party in management of agriculture, but they included positive actions as well. Among the most important was the lessening of the constraints on private rural marketing and the restoration of small private plots. As early as the fall of 1959 periodic rural markets were reopened in some locations, increasing peasant income-earning opportunities. In mid-1961 private plots were officially sanctioned, for the first time since the beginning of the commune movement in the fall of 1958, although they had been reestablished earlier in many regions. Five to 7 percent of the cultivated land was to be allocated for this purpose. Simultaneously, the state eliminated the prohibition on private household subsidiary production that had been imposed during the formation of communes. This allowed the revival of private household raising of pigs, sheep, chickens, ducks, and other domestic animals; household weaving, sewing, embroidery, and other handicrafts; and foraging for wild plants (e.g., mushrooms), fishing, hunting, beekeeping, and sericulture. Most of the products of these activities could be sold in private rural markets.

The role of the Party was also curtailed by the formal transfer in 1961–62 of decision-making authority to the lowest level of the three-tiered commune-brigade-team structure and by the reduction in the size of the team to 20 to 30 households, on average, comparable to the lower-stage APCs that had been the predominant form of agricultural organization prior to the winter of 1955–56. That change essentially divested Party cadres, lodged primarily at the brigade and commune levels, of a large share of their decision-making power.

Moreover, the previous practice of the arbitrary requisition and allocation of agricultural funds by Party cadres was reduced. The share of total income that teams could set aside for investment and collective welfare was limited to 3 to 5 and 2 to 3 percent, respectively. Moreover, expenditure of these funds was to be made by the

69 Ibid., 46.   70 *TCNC 1983*, 453.

decision of each team, rather than by the decision of higher-level cadres.[71] These measures largely restored the connection between work and rewards that had been effectively destroyed when the basic accounting had been transferred to very large units under direct control of Party cadres.

In some areas of rural China, where changes went beyond those officially approved, there was a complete collapse of collective farming. Land was divided up among the members of the local community, and private farming was restored. Individual households were obliged to meet sales quotas to the state but otherwise were free to make their own decisions on cropping patterns, use of inputs, and the like. Over significant areas, the presence of the Party in rural economic activity declined abruptly.[72]

Positive actions to support long-term agricultural growth focused on investment and on policies to support specialization in farm production. The share of state investment allocated to agriculture, water conservancy projects, and the like rose to more than one-quarter in 1963, compared with 7.8 percent in the 1st FYP and 10.5 percent in 1958 and 1959. Moreover, the pattern of investment within industry was shifted to support agriculture. There was, for example, a special allocation of materials such as steel, wood, and bamboo to be used for increasing the production of medium and small implements, hand tools, carts, and boats. By the end of 1962 the availability of these items was restored to the precommune level, making up for the substantial loss of tools, boats, and carts due to destruction or deterioration that had occurred between 1957 and 1961.[73]

More far-reaching changes went beyond simply restoring the assets of the farm sector that had been destroyed during the Great Leap. In 1961 Ch'en was instrumental in pushing through the Party decision-making apparatus a major program for the expansion of the chemical fertilizer industry.[74] This represented a fundamental shift from the 1st FYP, when minuscule investment resources had been allocated to

---

71 Hsieh Tu-yang, "Hui-ku liu-shih nien-tai ch'u nung-yeh ti t'iao-cheng," in Liu Sui-nien, Liu-shih nien-tai, 57.
72 C. S. Chen, Rural people's communes in Lien-chiang, 81–122.
73 Between 1957 and 1961 about 75 percent of small iron tools, 35 to 40 percent of tools made from bamboo and wood, 40 percent of traditional medium-scale farm tools, 35 percent of agricultural boats in south China, and 30 percent of the carts in North China were lost. Hsieh Tu-yang, "Hui-ku liu-shi nien-t'ai ch'u nung-yeh ti t'iao-cheng," in Liu Sui-nien, Liu-shih nien-tai, 54.
74 Ch'en Yun, "Chia-su fa-chan tan-fei kung-yeh (i-chiu-liu-i nien wu-yueh)" (Speed up the development of the chemical fertilizer industry [May 1961], in Ch'en Yun t'ung-chih wen-kao hsuan-pien, 108–15.

develop that industry. It reflected Ch'en's conviction that labor mobilization could not provide the basis for sustained growth of agriculture. Moreover, the scale of plants constructed under Ch'en's program was many times that of the small-scale plants constructed during the GLF as part of a strategy frequently referred to as "walking on two legs." This program of industrial support for agricultural development was a fundamental departure from the policy of the first decade of CCP rule.

Longer-term agricultural growth also was encouraged by the adoption of a policy of specialization. At the height of the GLF crisis, area sown to noncereal crops collapsed, and in the early 1960s in some quarters it was proposed that local self-sufficiency in cereals form the basis for agrarian recovery. Ch'en Yun argued decisively against that course because of the substantial inefficiency it would introduce. Curtailment of economic crops, he argued, had already proceeded too far. If the state commercial system could not supply diversified agricultural products to areas with a comparative advantage in grain production, these regions would take land out of grain, in turn reducing their sales to the state.[75] At first sight, self-sufficiency might appear to provide a basis for growth, but Ch'en pointed out it would simply lead all regions to produce more of their noncomparative advantage, high-cost products.

By 1963, Ch'en's approach was embodied in the "high and stable yield" area policy.[76] Under that program, regions with good water control and actual or potential high grain yields were encouraged, via special provision of fertilizers and other inputs, to concentrate on cereal production. These regions were to become the source of a large share of the cereals procured by the state, primarily to feed the urban population. Traditional comparative advantage producers of fiber and oil seed crops, tobacco, and the like were also encouraged to return to their historic cropping patterns.

ECONOMIC RECOVERY, 1963 – 1965

Agricultural response

On balance, the agricultural recovery program was only moderately successful. From a low point of 143.5 million metric tons of cereals in 1960, output grew by 1965 to a level just below that of the pre-GLF

75 Lardy, *Agriculture in China's modern economic development*, 45.
76 Liu Sui-nien, *Liu-shih nien-tai*, 207.

peak year of 1957. But with the population having increased by 80 million since then, production remained well below the pre–Great Leap levels in per capita terms. That meant that the goal adopted by the Central Committee in 1962 of gradually reducing grain imports over a five-year period had met with little success (Table 8).[77]

The level of output of fiber crops, sugarcane and sugar beet, and some other noncereal crops, which had without exception fallen proportionately more than that of cereals, had by 1965 surpassed the pre-GLF levels. But oil-seed crops were the conspicuous laggard, largely because sown area remained depressed. By 1965, unit yields of many important crops were above the pre-GLF levels: grain by more than 10 percent, cotton by almost 50 percent, rape seed by almost 60 percent. These data suggest that the specialization policy embraced in the early 1960s had contributed to growth of productivity in the ensuing years. The output of animal husbandry and fruit products did show a strong pattern of recovery. Production of meat and timber each rose to a level 40 percent above the level of 1957.[78]

While not all crops had recovered to the 1957 levels, agriculture was better positioned to benefit from the short-stalk fertilizer-responsive rice varieties that were to be grown on a widespread basis after the mid-1960s. The quantity of land under irrigation rose to 33 million hectares in 1965, up 6 million from 1957. More significantly, mechanized pumping (via either electric or gasoline-powered pumps) had been adopted on fully a quarter of the total irrigated area, up from a mere 4 percent in 1957. That provided improved irrigation control, so essential to the pattern of multiple cropping that accompanied the new high yield rice varieties.

Industrial response

Industrial recovery was far more rapid than that of agriculture. Light and heavy industrial output grew at 27 and 17 percent a year, respectively, in 1963–65. By 1965, the level of output of such major products as steel, electric power, cement, and heavy trucks was more than double that of 1957. Manufactured consumer goods output also had risen substantially. The output of sewing machines and bicycles, for example, quadrupled and more than doubled, respectively, between 1957 and 1965.

More impressive than the expanded levels of output of standard

77 Ibid., 200.   78 TCNC 1983, 162–64, 171–72, 178, 245.

products was the emergence of major new sectors of industrial activity and the completion of a number of major investment projects that had been set back by the withdrawal of Soviet technical support in mid-1960. Notable examples were petroleum and petrochemicals. In the 1950s the Chinese had been heavily dependent on imports of petroleum and petroleum products from the Soviet Union. Annual crude oil production in the mid-1950s was limited to about 20,000 barrels per day, primarily from the Yümen oil field in Kansu province, in the Northwest, which had been developed before 1949. Because of limited production and refining capacity, China was dependent on imports. In 1955-57, for example, imports were roughly double domestic production.[79] During the 1950s the Chinese launched a vigorous petroleum exploration program that led to the discovery, in the late 1950s, of the Sungliao Basin, in the Northeast, the place where Ta-ch'ing, China's most famous oil field, was developed.

The results of these efforts led to a sustained growth of crude oil output. While the output of most heavy industrial products fell substantially in the early 1960s, the output of crude oil rose every year throughout the GLF and the entire recovery period. By 1965 annual output was over 200,000 barrels per day, almost ten times the level of the mid-1950s. The output of natural gas also rose continuously, reaching an annual rate of 1.1 billion cubic meters in 1965, forty times the highest level of the 1st FYP.

There was a parallel development of oil refining and the related petrochemical, chemical fertilizer, and pharmaceutical industries. Refining was limited to minor facilities, with annual distillation capacity averaging a little over a million tons (20,000 barrels per day) during the 1st FYP. After the construction and opening of major large-scale refineries at Lanchou in Kansu in 1958 and at Ta-ch'ing in 1963, the quantity and variety of refined products rose enormously. The average volume of refined products in 1963-65 was seven times that of the 1st FYP, and imports of crude and refined products as a share of domestic production declined sharply. Chou En-lai proudly proclaimed China's basic self-sufficiency in petroleum in late 1963, and by 1965 imports were down to a million tons, only 10 percent of domestic output.

The synthetic fiber industry was in its infancy in 1957, with only 200 tons produced annually. By 1965, the level of output was 50,100

79 A. Doak Barnett, *China's economy in global perspective*, 460.

tons annually. Chemical-based pesticide output was only 2,200 tons in 1957 but rose to 10,500 tons by 1965. Similarly, chemical fertilizer output was a mere 151,000 tons in 1957 and 1.73 million metric tons by 1965.

New industrial products were not limited to producer goods such as chemicals, but included consumer goods as well. The clock industry delivered its first products in 1957 – 400 watches. In the ensuing years, output rose continuously (with no setbacks during the early 1960s), and annual production exceeded a million units by 1965.

Thus, despite a sharp reduction in industrial investment during the first half of the 1960s, priority sectors continued to develop, sometimes rapidly. In no small part this restructuring was made possible by China's independent completion of major plants, such as one for producing petroleum-refining equipment, initiated with Soviet support in the mid or late 1950s but then delayed after the withdrawal of Soviet technical and engineering help in mid-1960.

Price stability

The recovery of production and other measures led to the reestablishment of price stability, particularly in rural markets. At the peak of the market shortages in 1961, the index of market prices stood at a level 4.92 times that of 1957, and even prices in state-controlled retail outlets rose significantly.[80] As an almost emergency measure to absorb excess purchasing power, Ch'en Yun devised a plan to import in excess of 1 million tons of sugar annually in 1961 and 1962 (a ten-fold increase over average annual imports in the 1950s) to be manufactured into candy that was sold at high prices, primarily in urban markets. Restaurants in urban areas also received allocations of increased food supplies, particularly delicacies that could be resold at substantial markups.[81]

Beginning in 1962, prices began to drop, in part because of these measures but more fundamentally from the partial recovery of agricultural production. By 1964 rural market prices had fallen to a level only twice that of 1957. The cost of living index of state workers also was reduced. The prices they paid rose more than 20 percent in 1961 and 1962, a rate of inflation six times more rapid than in the 1st FYP.

80 Hsiang Ching-ch'üan, "Liu-shih nien-tai t'iao-cheng shih-ch'i wen-ting chia-ko ching-yen ch'u-t'an," 22.
81 *TCNC 1983*, 439. Ch'en Yun, "Mu-ch'ien ts'ai-cheng ching-chi-ti ch'ing-k'uang ho k'o-fu k'un-nan ti jo-kan pan-fa (i-chiu-liu-erh nien erh-yueh)" (The current financial and economic situation and some methods for overcoming difficulties, February 1962), in *Ch'en Yun t'ung-chih wen-kao hsuan-pien*, 169.

The cost of living index fell in 1963–65, in part because of the decline in urban market prices and in part because of reductions in state-controlled prices of retail commodities, which had also shot up in 1961 and 1962.

Summary

The recovery of industrial and agricultural output is reflected in China's national income. In real terms (after accounting for changes in the price level), aggregate national income in 1965 was 29 percent ahead of 1957 and 51 percent above the trough of 1962. In comparative terms, both the drop in national income and the pace of recovery exceeded the fluctuations in national income in the United States during the Great Depression of the 1930s. Per capita national income dropped 32 percent in the United States between 1929 and the depths of the Depression in 1933, compared to a 35 percent decline in China between 1959 and 1962. Due to the U.S. economy's deep structural problems, the 1929 level of output was not reattained in the United States until 1940, a decade after the onset of the Depression and seven years after the trough. In comparison, the pre–Great Leap levels of aggregate output in China were reattained by 1964, a short two years from the low point, because the setbacks were primarily due to faulty policies. Once these were corrected, recovery could begin.

Although the recovery was rapid in terms of national income, this should obscure neither the catastrophe of the GLF nor the failure of some elements of the leadership fully to grasp the implications of the depths into which the country had plunged. The growth of national income over the entire period 1958 to 1965 was only 3.2 percent per year, a sharp decline from the 8.9 percent achieved under the 1st FYP.[82] More drastically, the GLF led to the most massive famine of the twentieth century and subsequently the forced resettlement of almost 30 million individuals. Moreover, while national income in per capita real terms was, by 1965, 15 percent ahead of the level of 1957, personal consumption had not yet recovered to the levels achieved in the 1st FYP, in large measure because of the failure of agriculture to reattain the pre–Great Leap levels of per capita output of the most important consumption goods. As reflected in Table 5, per capita cereal consumption remained almost 10 percent below the level of 1957 and was also actually less than in 1952. Rural consumption was even more depressed, remaining 13.3 percent less than 1957 (Table 5).

82 *TCNC 1983*, 23.

Similarly, consumption of cotton cloth in 1965 remained 8.7 percent less than in 1957 and again, the burden was borne disproportionately by the rural population, whose consumption remained 17.1 percent less than in 1957. Consumption of edible vegetable oils also was down, since per capita production remained almost one-fourth less than in 1957.[83] Consumption in rural areas was particularly low, only 1.1 kilogram per person annually, 40 percent below the level of 1957 and, astoundingly, one-quarter below the depressed level of 1960.[84]

In part, these figures reflect the severity of the effect of the GLF in the farm sector. But also they reflect the ongoing debate on the appropriate growth strategy and the difficulties in ensuring resources adequate to sustain agricultural growth. Chou En-lai, Ch'en Yun, and other moderates ultimately had been successful in extending the period of readjustment through 1965 and deferring the beginning of the 3rd FYP to 1966. They had been noticeably successful in the critical debate on the magnitude of the target for steel production, scaling back the originally proposed 25 million and 30 million metric ton options to 20 million.[85]

In a broader sense, however, they had only slightly altered the imbalanced growth strategy of the GLF and had not succeeded in fully implementing the strategy of "agriculture first." Indeed, by the end of 1965, fixed assets in state industry reached 96 billion yuan, 3.5 times the level of 1957.[86] There was sustained pressure for a resumption of economic growth based on heavy industry.[87] The character of the forthcoming 3rd (1966–70) and 4th (1971–75) Five-Year Plans was evident in several policies.

First, during the last three years of readjustment, the rate of investment rose sharply. As a share of national income, which itself was growing rapidly, accumulation rose from 10.4 percent in 1962 to an average of 22.7 percent in 1963–65.[88] Second, the share of investment allocated to agriculture dropped from a peak of 21.3 percent in 1962 to 14.6 percent by 1965, a harbinger of the decline that would continue for more than another decade.[89] Moreover, between 1962

83 Wu Ch'ün-kan, "Kuan-yü 'ta-yueh chin' shih-wu ho t'iao-cheng ti li-shih ching-yen," 37.
84 Wang P'ing, "'Ta-yueh chin' ho t'iao-cheng shih-ch'i ti jen-min sheng-huo," in Liu Sui-nien, *Liu-shih nien-tai*, 173. Liu Sui-nien, "'T'iao-cheng, kung-ku, ch'ung-shih, t'i-kao' pa-tzu fang-chen ti t'i-ch'u chi chih-hsing ch'ing-k'uang," 24.
85 Lardy and Lieberthal, *Chen Yun's strategy for China's development*, xxxiii–xxxiv.
86 TCNC 1983, 12.
87 Liu Sui-nien, "'T'iao-cheng, kung-ku, ch'ung-shih, t'i-kao' pa-tzu fang-chen ti t'i-ch'u chi chih-hsing ch'ing-k'uang," 29.
88 TCNC 1983, 25.
89 Minstry of Agriculture Policy Research Office, *Chung-kuo nung-yeh ching-chi kai-yao* (An outline of agricultural economics in China), 103.

and 1965, in part to make more resources available for industrial development, the state, on average, reduced by 6 percent the prices it paid peasants for agricultural products they were required to deliver to it.[90] Finally, the role of the Party in the countryside was again expanding. As early as 1962, Mao Tse-tung was working for a new upsurge in "class struggle" in the countryside to counter what he regarded as the revival of capitalism. Within a short time, that led to the reestablishment of Party control of agricultural production, a curtailment of rural marketing, and the resulting stagnation of farm productivity.

Tragically for the Chinese peasantry, the major lessons of the Great Leap Forward were not fully comprehended by enough of China's highest political leaders. An imbalanced growth strategy came strongly to the fore, a policy that would produce a decade of rapid industrial growth (except for a brief setback in 1966–67) but much more modest results in agriculture.

90 *TCNC 1983*, 455.

CHAPTER 9

NEW DIRECTIONS IN EDUCATION

According to the conventional periodization of post-1949 China, the Great Leap Forward of 1958 marks the end of direct Soviet influence and the beginning of a new Chinese road to socialism. Ironically, one of the major principles underlying the changes introduced into Chinese education at this time might well have been inspired by the critique of the "Stalin model" of education that developed in the Soviet Union after his death in 1953. Resolutions first adopted there in 1956 concerning the role of labor in education were not widely promoted in Soviet education until they were officially decreed in 1958. Known as the "Khrushchev reforms," they aimed at closing the gap between education and practical life. In promoting them, Khrushchev complained that senior secondary school graduates who did not gain admission to college were unprepared for production work. "There are even certain young people," he remarked, "who are unwilling to go to work in industry or farming, thinking it beneath them."[1]

The Soviet reforms of 1958 were therefore designed to prepare all secondary students for work regardless of when they terminated their schooling, and production training was included in the curriculum. At least 80 percent of the new students admitted to Soviet institutions of higher learning each year were to be enrolled from among those who had worked at least two years after finishing secondary school.[2]

The Khrushchev reforms were never successfully integrated into the Soviet educational system, and did not survive the political demise of their chief advocate. In China, where a similar debate over labor education was also developing in the mid-1950s, the changes of 1958 had a more complex history. This was partly because the demise of

---

1 Quoted in Jan-Ingvar Lofstedt, *Chinese educational policy*, 61.
2 George Z. F. Bereday, William W. Brickman, and Gerald H. Read, eds., *The changing Soviet school*, 86–100, 290–1; Jaan Pennar, Ivan I. Bakalo, and George Z. F. Bereday, *Modernization and diversity in Soviet education*, 102–17; Nigel Grant, *Soviet education*, 96–103.

their leading promoter came much later, giving them a longer life, and partly because they were launched with considerably more sound and fury, in accordance with the mass movement method of policy implementation. This "method" was another innovation from the rural pre-1949 experience that together with the Yenan model of development, the Chinese Communist Party (CCP) sought to adapt for national use.

By the mid-1940s, Mao had already discovered the many uses to which mass energy and emotion could be put in overcoming resistance to major social changes. This discovery had served the Party well in many areas, including land reform, the transformation of agriculture, and the campaigns against various adverse manifestations of the "bourgeois mentality" in the early 1950s. Among the costs of the mass movement method were the excesses that usually occurred in the process. But "in correcting wrongs," Mao had written in a frequently reprinted passage from his 1927 report on the Hunan peasant movement, "it is necessary to go to extremes or else the wrong cannot be righted." Yet the costs had always been contained and the excesses corrected during the final "consolidation" phase of a mass movement. At that time, they might be blamed on a few misguided individuals who ran too far ahead and did not pull back when the signal came, or who maliciously tried to make trouble "behind the scenes." In 1958, however, the technique was put to its most ambitious use yet in order to launch the "general line for socialist construction," better known as the Great Leap Forward (GLF). This time, the excesses were not so easily contained, nor was ultimate responsibility so easy to deflect.[3]

The new Chinese strategy did not really abandon the Soviet model but, rather, tried to devise an acceptable accommodation with it. The result was the concept of "walking on two legs," which promised to achieve greater, faster, and better results by the simultaneous use of modern and traditional or indigenous methods. The latter were in spirit and form derived from the Party's Yenan experience, except that now the entire society and economy were being mobilized to apply simultaneously and somehow to integrate the principles of uniformity, quality, and planning, together with those of flexibility, quantity, and local self-reliance. Even in education, therefore, the

---

3 The theme of the mass movement as a method of policy implementation is based on an analysis of the mass movement during land reform that appeared in intra-Party documents during the late 1940s (Suzanne Pepper, *Civil War in China: The political struggle, 1945–49*, 254–60, 264–74, 294–97, 312–27). See also Chapter 4, note 41.

aims of the 1958 reforms went far beyond those introduced in the Soviet Union at the same time.

THE GREAT LEAP IN EDUCATION: 1958

The key document for education was the "Directive on education work" issued jointly by the CCP Central Committee and the State Council on 19 September 1958.[4] The directive called for a cultural revolution and criticized education for the errors of neglecting politics, CCP leadership, and productive labor. It called for a determined struggle against such bourgeois ideas as "education for education's sake," "the separation of mental and manual labor," and "education can only be led by experts."

To strengthen CCP leadership, the directive outlined a number of changes that would soon be implemented throughout the system and remain integral features of it, just as many features taken over from the Soviet system would persist long after the policies that launched them had passed into history. All institutions of learning led by ministries and departments of the central government were to be placed under the direct political leadership of their *local* Party organization. Within all institutions of higher learning, the responsibility system of the college or university affairs committee, under the leadership of the school's Party committee, was to be established. This was because the single president system, or one-man management, had proved inadequate since it tended to deviate from Party leadership.

The University Party Committee was to assign Party members to positions of academic and administrative leadership within the school, while the CCP committee members, including the committee secretary, would try to teach politics courses. In promoting teachers, attention was henceforth to be paid first to their political qualifications, their level of knowledge, and their practical abilities. Formal academic credentials and seniority were to be treated as secondary. In assessing students, attention was similarly to be paid first to their political awareness and practical abilities, and last to their grades.

In order to make final the break with bourgeois academic domination over teaching, research, and administration within each school, six measures were advanced. These were designed to institutionalize the participation of the "masses," including the students, in various

4 *JMJP*, 20 September 1958, 1.

aspects of school management. The first of the six "mass line work methods" was the "free airing of views" and writing big character posters. In conducting courses, people with practical experience were to be invited to lecture together with the professional teachers. Students were to participate in assessing the performance of their classmates. Leadership personnel, including Party and Youth League cadres, were instructed to fraternize as much as possible with the students in life and labor, and teachers were to maintain close contact with the students and establish relationships with them based on "democratic equality."

Productive labor was to be introduced into the curriculum in all schools at all levels, and every student would be required to participate as stipulated. To promote the new work-study movement, schools would begin to run farms and factories with the guidance and assistance of the governments in their localities. Students could work in these or in the established factories and cooperatives. These, in turn, were called upon to set up schools for their own personnel.

The quantitative goals were as extravagant for education as for the economy. Within three to five years from 1958, illiteracy was to be basically eradicated and primary schooling universal. Within the same time, every Agricultural Producers' Cooperative (APC) (or presumably its equivalent-level unit under the new commune system just then being created) would have a secondary school, and there would be nurseries and kindergartens for all preschool children. Within fifteen years, college education would be available for everyone with the necessary qualifications who wanted it; the quality of higher education could then be improved during the fifteen years thereafter.

The single, unified nationwide objective was to produce laborers with socialist consciousness and culture. But many different forms of schooling would be used in pursuit of that single aim, including schools run by the state and those run by collectives; general education and vocational training; education for children and for adults; full-day schools, work-study schools, and spare-time schools; and schools that charged tuition as well as those that did not.

More specifically, the task of rapidly universalizing education for the masses and raising the technical level of industry and agriculture was given to the half-work half-study and to the spare-time schools. This was because these schools could be run on a self-supporting basis without financial assistance from the government. They also did not require a professional staff, but could rely on the principle of "whoever is capable can teach." Such schools would over time gradually become more complete in their curricula, teaching staff, and facilities. The distinctions between spare-time and work-study schools would disappear, and all would become tuition-free.

The September 1958 directive also stipulated that some of the established regular schools should have the responsibility of raising the quality of education. Such schools were to maintain a complete curriculum and pay attention to raising the quality of their own teaching and research. "Where their own original levels will not be harmed," said the directive, "they should energetically help with the work of setting up the new schools; but if their level is lowered it will not be beneficial to the larger educational enterprise."

The same directive contained all the elements that would motivate educational development in one way or another for the next two decades, while the search continued for an acceptable equilibrium along which the line might stabilize. It was said in 1958 that the main dispute then was with "some bourgeois educators," and "some of our comrades" who agreed with them, in proposing to restrict the extent and speed of educational development. They also allegedly advocated one type of school system only: state-run and state-funded, with regular schools, teachers, and methods of instruction. These "erroneous suggestions" were opposed. Mao's strategy of "walking on two legs" was adopted as the only means of popularizing education among the worker-peasant masses within a reasonable period of time.

Lu Ting-i explained the new strategy further, saying that without it, "our country would find it very difficult to institute universal primary and secondary education ... because it has no way of carrying the huge burden of expenditure involved without heavy damage to production." For this reason, he declared, "we Communists do not agree with the bourgeois pedagogues."[5]

A decade later, the "erroneous suggestions" would be referred to as "the revisionist educational line represented by Liu Shao-ch'i and the vestigial education systems millenniums old."[6] It was probably for more specific reasons that Liu was later appointed the symbolic

5 Lu Ting-i, "Education must be combined with productive labor," *Hung-ch'i* (Red flag), No. 7 (1 September 1958), in *CB*, 516 (2 September 1958), 4; also Lin Feng, "All-out effort in Cultural Revolution to promote education among worker-peasant masses, and labor performance by intellectuals," NCNA – English, Peking, 1 June 1960, in *CB*, 622 (28 June 1960), 13.
6 "Chronology of the two-road struggle on the educational front in the past seventeen years," *Chiao-yü ko-ming* (Education revolution), 6 May 1967, in Peter J. Seybolt, ed., *Revolutionary education in China*, 29.

representative of a line stretching back a thousand years. Certainly there is no evidence, except for the inconsistent accusations made during the Cultural Revolution, that Liu Shao-ch'i actually sided with the bourgeois pedagogues in the 1950s, when they advocated walking on one leg only.

For one thing, it was the bourgeois educators themselves who consistently opposed importing the Soviet educational model, which Liu was also later accused of favoring. To complicate the matter further, the September 1958 directive was accepted as a revolutionary document by Liu's accusers – yet it contained clear instructions to promote two different kinds of education: quality schooling in the regular system and popular education in the work-study stream. This was reflected in the key slogan of the period, "walking on two legs." This "two-track system" was, however, later to be denounced as the dominant feature of Liu's revisionism in education.[7]

That the bourgeois academics opposed the new line when it was launched seems certain. They were relieved of having to emulate the Soviet Union in all things. But this burden was lifted from them only to be replaced by others equally onerous, and the basic Soviet-style structure of higher education remained essentially unchanged. In fact, most of their complaints, voiced in May 1957 and before, were swept away in the course of the Anti-Rightist Campaign and the subsequent Great Leap Forward. The conditions they had been protesting were actually intensified. The truth of the later accusations against Liu Shao-ch'i is compromised by their implausibility, since it would appear logically impossible for him to have all at the same time: promoted the Soviet model, sided with the bourgeois academics who opposed that model but wanted a single-track regular form of education, advocated a two-track system, and opposed the "walking on two legs" policy spelled out in the September 1958 directive.[8]

Given the irreconcilable contradictions in that later accusation, the most plausible interpretation of the 1958 directive and the policy that flowed from it is that they represented just what the Party at the time said they did – namely, an attempt to popularize education within the foreseeable future, while simultaneously trying to maintain the quality of the existing system. To make sense of the later accusations, it is necessary to consider instead how the policy outlined in

7 Ibid., 31–33.
8 For a similar conclusion based on other data, see Roderick MacFarquhar, *The origins of the Cultural Revolution*, 2. 108–13.

1958 was implemented and how the education system was reshaped in the process.

In the countryside, the communes superseded the Agricultural Producers Cooperatives during 1958, and the expansion of education accompanied the movement to create this new form of rural organization. Sixty million persons were said to have taken part in the "high tide of the elimination of illiteracy" movement in 1958. "Scores of millions" attended newly established spare-time schools for adult peasants. In many areas, this spare-time study "fell into stagnation" during the final quarter of 1958, owing to the combined pressures of the autumn harvest season and the upsurge of activity that accompanied the national campaign to smelt iron and steel in home-made furnaces and foundries. The communes were directed to reactivate the study programs the following spring.[9]

Primary schools also "sprouted like bamboo shoots after a spring rain" in 1958. By September 337,000 new primary schools had been set up, and the nation's total primary school enrollment had jumped from 64 million in 1957 to 84 million, according to one report. According to another published a month later, primary school enrollment was actually 92.6 million and the number of primary schools was close to 1 million.[10] As before, the medium that made this possible was the *min-pan* school. These were set up in ever increasing numbers as part of the mass movement sweeping the countryside, and in urban areas as well.

Also both in city and countryside, the *min-pan* idea was now applied to the secondary level. This made it possible for total secondary enrollment to double from 7 million in 1957 to 14 million at the start of the 1958 autumn semester. The agricultural middle school, combining the *min-pan* concept with a work-study curriculum, was the innovation of the period. These schools represented the first attempt to promote mass secondary schooling in the countryside. According to official statistics, there were in 1955 an average of only 1.7 middle schools per county throughout the country. Urban secondary schools were calculated separately.[11]

9 "Directive of the Central Committee of the CCP and the State Council concerning the continual wiping out of illiteracy and the consolidation and development of after-work education programs in the rural areas," 24 May 1959, trans. in *Compendium of laws and regulations of the People's Republic of China* (hereafter, *Compendium of Laws*), Joint Publications Research Service (hereafter, JPRS), General Series: 14,346 (2 July 1962), 321.

10 "Never so many at school," *Peking Review (PR)*, 30 (23 September 1958), 4; and "Third quarter results: Still faster growth," *PR*, 33 (14 October 1958), 14.

11 The 1958 enrollment figure is from "Third quarter results," 14; The earlier school statistics are from *Shih-shih shou-ts'e* (Current events), 23 (10 December 1956), trans. in *Extracts from China Mainland Magazines (ECMM)*, 71 (1956), 27.

The new agricultural middle schools were vocational in orientation; courses in the techniques of agricultural production were taught
along with the basic language, math, and politics. The training was
terminal for the junior secondary age group, and designed to prepare
students for the lives they would be living as agricultural producers.
These schools were usually run on a work-study basis and were
intended to be largely self-supporting through the proceeds from the
students' work projects. Buildings and land were contributed by
cooperative farms and later communes. Subsequent expenses were
met primarily by earnings from the students' productive undertakings, the most important being the cultivation of land allocated to the
school by the collective for this purpose.

Officials were quick to advertise the economical nature of these
schools. One set of figures from Kiangsu Province showed the costs
to the state per student per year as being 187 yuan in the ordinary
junior middle schools, and only 13 yuan in the agricultural schools.
Exuberant claims as to the numbers initially set up were made, in
keeping with the spirit of the times. By 1960, after the consolidation
phase of the movement, there were approximately 30,000 such
schools, averaging about one per commune, with a total of 2.9 million
students.[12]

Less successful was the *min-pan* concept applied at the tertiary
level and aimed at the goal of universalizing higher education within
15 years. By August 1958 it was claimed that the number of institutions of higher learning had risen to 1,065 from the 227 existing in
1957. The number of students had risen from 400,000 to 700,000. In
addition, 23,500 spare-time "Red and expert" colleges and part-work
part-study universities had been set up by autumn 1958.[13]

The spare-time "colleges" were run by factories and communes for
adult workers and peasants. These schools claimed to offer more
advanced instruction in a variety of subjects, both technical and
general, and relied on whoever might be qualified to serve as instructors. The majority appear not to have survived the period of consolidation and the years of economic hardship that followed, and
little was subsequently heard of them.

Nevertheless, the experiments in applying the *min-pan* concept

12 Robert D. Barendsen, "The agricultural middle school in Communist China," *CQ*, 8
(October–December 1961), 106–34; and an updated version of this article by the same
author: *Half-work half-study schools in Communist China*, 6.
13 For the 1957 figures, see Table 4 in Chapter 4. The 1958 figures are from, "Never so many at
school," *PR*, 30 (23 September 1958), 4, and "Third quarter results," *PR*, 33 (14 October
1958), 14.

combined with work-study proliferated at all levels in 1958. Among the most creative and successful of these experiments – perhaps because of the high-level sponsorship it enjoyed – was the Kiangsi Communist Labor University (Kiangsi Kung-ta), also established in 1958. This school survived the consolidation period and went on to become a national model. Among the national leaders to associate themselves personally with this experiment in agricultural education were Mao himself, Chu Te, and Chou En-lai. The then top provincial leaders responsible for establishing the school were Kiangsi Governor Shao Shih-p'ing (regarded as the university's founder), a provincial Party secretary named Liu Chün-hsiu (the first president of Kung-ta), and Deputy Governor Wang Tung-hsing (the Party secretary of the main campus, who would soon return to Peking, take up public security duties again, and rise to the Politburo during the Cultural Revolution). The university was established by the Kiangsi provincial leadership in collaboration with the central Ministry of State Farms and Land Reclamation (Nung-k'en-pu) and the provincial Land Reclamation Department.

Kiangsi Kung-ta was characterized by a network of branches set up throughout the province on land reclamation sites, with the branches becoming an integral part of the reclamation work. The main initial work-study activities of students (and staff) were reclaiming barren wastelands that were otherwise uncultivable and restoring forest lands or planting trees under contracts allocated by the provincial Land Reclamation Department. School buildings were also constructed with student and staff labor. Between 1958 and 1962, the time students devoted to study and work was about 60 percent and 40 percent, respectively. After 1962, when the university's basic construction had been completed, study time increased to about 70 percent.

The student body was primarily in the secondary school and college age brackets. The first class in 1958 contained many cadres who had been sent down to the land reclamation bases where the branches were set up, but adult cadres and workers never constituted the main source of students. The university recruited primarily within Kiangsi, but between 1958 and 1965 students were enrolled from elsewhere as well. Many thousands, for example, came from Shanghai. The students were recruited in a variety of ways and initially, at least, came from widely varying educational backgrounds. These ranged from "semi-literacy" through senior secondary school. Branches were soon established throughout the province, with at least one per county, in addition to prefectural-level branches and the main campus located in the suburbs of Nanchang, the provincial capital. Together they offered instruction in a variety of programs at all academic levels from junior secondary through college. The branches were all guided and led in academic and policy matters by the parent campus, and the entire complex was devoted primarily to agriculture and forestry specialties.

Of the 200,000 students who had been graduated from Kung-ta by 1980, most eventually became "basic-level cadres in agriculture," although they were not necessarily assigned as such upon graduation. Two different principles governed job allocation for Kung-ta graduates. The students in the county-level branch schools usually returned to their own communes to work following the *she-lai she-ch'ü* (from the commune to the commune) principle and were subsequently assigned work as needed by the locality in question. Many of these later became production brigade and team leaders.

Graduates from the prefectural-level branches and the main campus, which had many out-of-province students before 1965, sometimes followed the *she-lai she-ch'ü* method and sometimes regular job assignment plans and procedures. Graduates assigned according to the latter method became cadres in the county and provincial bureaus and departments responsible for agriculture, forestry, land reclamation, and also other areas in which Kung-ta at times offered courses of instruction. Many of these graduates later became commune Party secretaries. Kung-ta students were usually assigned to work in Kiangsi, although some of the outsiders did return to their home provinces.

Kiangsi Kung-ta was never entirely self-sufficient (able to survive without state subsidies in some form), but the entire complex throughout its history continued to rely for a considerable portion of its income on student labor and the school's productive enterprises. In time these grew to include, in addition to land reclamation and afforestation, factories, forestry centers, orchards, and livestock farms. These, in turn, required an extensive network of county and prefectural-level support for the allocation of unreclaimed land, the assignment of money-earning work projects, and the guaranteed allocation of supplies, transport, and sale of finished products. But according to administrators at the school, one reason the local authorities were willing to sustain the support network in the face of competing demands for scarce resources was the high-level sponsorship it initially had and the attention it subsequently generated. In their opinion, the political and administrative support network was a crucial feature of the university's success.

Despite political and economic vicissitudes, including the closure of half its branches during the economic depression of the early 1960s, the school's status was confirmed by Mao's 30 July 1961 directive praising its work-study orientation. It retained that status until 1979, when the parent campus became a full-time regular agricultural university and was divested of its branches. This was done because its work-study orientation was held to be producing a kind of student no longer recognized by China's newly restandardized system of higher education.[14]

The Kiangsi Communist Labor University was a unique institution not only because it was so successful but also because of its province-wide scope and its continuing reliance on a part-work part-study curriculum. Regular full-time secondary and tertiary schools responded in a variety of ways to the 1958 directive that every student must participate in manual labor. Initially, during the latter half of 1958 backyard steel smelting was the fashion. Participation in farm work by cadres, intellectuals, and students was also undertaken with much fanfare at this time. In addition, by the end of 1958, secondary and tertiary level schools were operating more than 150,000 factories and workshops, and 10,300 farms. Of the factories and workshops, 7,200 were being run by colleges and universities, 21,500 by technical secondary schools, and 122,800 by middle schools.[15]

That the GLF strategy for educational development did not so much abandon the Soviet model as try to seek an accommodation with it is nevertheless suggested by the emphasis that was placed on the self-supporting nature of all these innovations. Their economic implications were stressed equally with the practial and ideological significance of integrating labor with learning. As indicated by the budgetary allocations for the agricultural middle schools, the dominant portion of the state's education budget continued to be allocated to the regular full-time school system. This was also acknowledged in a report on financial work in education and culture issued toward the end of 1958. During that year, the number of college students was

14 From interviews conducted by the author during a week-long stay at Kiangsi Kung-ta in October 1980, shortly before its name was officially changed to the Kiangsi Agricultural University. See also John Gardner, "Educated youth and urban-rural inequalities, 1958–66," in John Wilson Lewis, ed., *The city in Communist China*, 250–53, and Barendsen, *Half-work half-study schools*, 39–56.

15 "Education: in a nutshell," *PR*, 2 (13 January 1959), 5; Ling Yang, "Schools run factories," *PR*, 39 (25 November 1958), 15.

said to have increased by 78 percent, middle school students had doubled, and primary enrollments had increased by 70 percent, all largely as a result of the innovations in locally run work-study schooling. The state's financial outlays had increased during that same period by only 5 percent.[16]

Nevertheless, the new line of 1958 initially appeared to leave little room for compromise with the "rightist" academic critics. As noted, the newly specialized structure of higher education was retained, and so was the teaching-research group as the basic unit of organization. Many lesser features of the Soviet-style system were abandoned or modified at this time, but they were replaced by others little more to the conventional academic's liking. The Ministry of Higher Education was abolished, as were the new graduate degree programs, the latter not to be revived until the late 1970s. Students already enrolled in these programs were given job assignments without their degrees in 1959.

The "three-three" formula was introduced in institutions of higher learning. This was a rotation system wherein at any given time, one-third of the teaching staff was supposed to be engaged in teaching, one-third in research, and one-third in social investigation. The purpose was to train faculty members to perform the three tasks equally well.[17]

The rewriting of teaching plans and textbooks began at once in order to incorporate the new requirements for student labor and a more practical orientation to subject matter. But these revisions were supposed to be done in a "democratic" manner, with students and technicians participating along with the professional educators. One of this writer's interviewees in Hong Kong was a young college instructor in Peking in the late 1950s. He told how they had rewritten the college teaching materials for basic chemistry courses, describing it as a fairly rational effort to delete and simplify. By contrast, a Russian scientist was scandalized to find beginning chemistry students at the teacher training college in Kunming rewriting their organic chemistry textbooks as they went along. The Chemistry Department there had also decided to abandon the "bourgeois"

16 "The Report of the Ministry of Finance, Ministry of Culture, Ministry of Education and Ministry of Health on the National Conference for the Interchange of Experiences in Financial Work concerning Culture and Education, 5 November 1958," trans. in Compendium of Laws, JPRS, General Series: 14,335 (2 July 1962), 315. On the education budget in the 1950s, see Leo A. Orleans, Professional manpower and education in Communist China, 14–17.
17 Suzanne Pepper, "China's universities," Modern China, 8. 2 (April 1982), 162.

method followed in both the United States and the Soviet Union of teaching students specializing in inorganic chemistry to identify all the common elements. Instead, they were concentrating on the study of copper, since there was so much of it in Yunnan.[18]

A new form of college admissions was also adopted in 1958. The national unified college entrance examinations were not held that year. Instead, institutions of higher learning individually or jointly gave their own separate examinations as they had prior to 1952, although guidelines for the examination subjects were issued by the Education Ministry. But 1958 also marked the intensified use of political criteria in college admissions, applied both positively and negatively. Young people with certain kinds of family backgrounds – mainly those from capitalist and landlord families and particularly those among them who had been singled out as targets during the previous campaigns – were discriminated against to varying degrees.

If the problem was serious enough, the individual could be prevented from entering college altogether. One such case was that of the son, interviewed by the author in Hong Kong, of a Kiangsi capitalist-landlord Kuomintang military officer who had fled to Taiwan. With this the worst of all possible family backgrounds, the son was not permitted to study at the Kiangsi Communist Labor University in 1958, although he had taken and passed its entrance examination that year. Nor could he study at any other college in the region. He was finally able to enroll in a technical institute in Harbin only after an elaborate attempt to disguise his true origins. People with less serious political problems might be admitted to college, but only to less popular or prestigious schools such as teacher training institutes.

By contrast, candidates of worker-peasant origin and cadres who had participated in revolutionary work were given priority in admission. More specifically: In 1958, workers, peasants, graduates of the worker-peasant accelerated middle schools, and cadres could be admitted to college on the basis of recommendation, without having to take any written entrance examinations.[19] Large numbers of students were apparently admitted in this manner. The proportion of students from worker-peasant backgrounds in China's institutions of higher learning had increased gradually each year, from 19 percent in 1951 to 36 percent in 1957. As a result of the new admissions

18 Mikhail A. Klochko, *Soviet scientist in Red China*, 137–40.
19 *KMJP*, July 3, 1958, 1, 2.

priorities, they rose to 48 percent in 1958, and to 50 percent in 1959–60.[20]

Scientific plans were also affected. The timetable for completion of the twelve-year plan was shortened by five years, and research institutes rushed to complete their assignments ahead of schedule. In addition, hundreds of new institutes were set up and thousands of new projects promoted. The disaffected "bourgeois" intellectuals, sceptical that China could "leap forward with flying speed," saw their ranks diluted by working-class colleagues. Thousands of skilled workers were promoted to the ranks of engineers and technicians, while similar numbers of peasants became scientists. Many of the latter were appointed to positions in agricultural research institutes and agricultural colleges. It was reported that 45,000 Shanghai worker and peasant scientists had joined the Scientific and Technical Association there by 1960, making up half its membership. These scientists were lauded as new intellectuals who, unlike their old-style counterparts, continued to engage in productive labor and did not treat their intellectual work as private property.[21]

THE AFTERMATH: 1959–1960

The high tide of the mass movement in all sectors was over by the end of 1958, when the usual retrenchments and recriminations began. As had occurred many times in the past, the "law of the mass movement" proceeded on course. The players found themselves rearranged to the right or left, depending on their interests and inclinations, as events developed. P'eng Te-huai took a stand in opposition at the CCP's Lushan conference in July 1959, and fell from power as a result. Mao held his ground but not, according to later accounts, without having to accept responsibility for some of the economic excesses that had occurred the preceding year.

Educational statistics, unlike those for industry and agriculture, did not have to await the Lushan Conference to be revised downward. Without actually acknowledging that they had been overassessed, Chou En-lai, in his report to a National People's Congress (NPC) meeting in April 1959, presented 1958 enrollment figures considerably lower than those issued a few months previously. His figures

20 State Statistical Bureau, *Ten great years*, 200; and Hong Yung Lee, *The politics of the Chinese Cultural Revolution*, 79.
21 Chu-yuan Cheng, *Scientific and engineering manpower in Communist China, 1949–1963*, 61–67.

were 660,000 at the college level, 12 million at the secondary level, and 85 million primary school students (for summary figures, see Table 9, on page 427).

Pointing the way to the future, Chou En-lai commented in his report, "Last year, schools at all levels all made great progress; now it is time to tidy up, consolidate and raise up their level on the basis of this great development." Indicating further the fateful course on which the Party's education policy was about to embark, he continued:

Full-time regular schools at all levels should make it their constant and fundamental task to raise the quality of teaching and studying; in the first place, we must devote relatively more energy to perfecting a number of "key" schools so as to train specialized personnel of higher quality for the state and bring about a rapid rise in our country's scientific and cultural level.[22]

The new Education Minister, Yang Hsiu-feng, addressed the same session of the NPC in more explicit terms. Due to inexperience in 1958, he said, schools had cut out too many classes for the sake of their productive labor activities. Efforts were now being made to correct this by formally including labor in the curriculum, but with the objectives clearly defined. Reiterating the point made in the September 1958 directive on the need for a division of labor between the mass-level work-study schools and the quality-oriented full-day schools, he continued: "We must raise the quality of the full-day schools as well as raise the work quality of a selected group of these schools to a particularly high level so as to enable them to become the backbone of our educational undertakings." He praised this selective development as a way of "utilizing reasonably our limited strength" making it possible to "popularize education simultaneously with raising standards."[23]

The line of unequal development was thus clearly articulated. But it followed directly from the "revolutionary" directive of September 1958, which had unambiguously called for a division of labor between the work-study schools and others. This two-track system and the social inequalities inherent in it were later alleged to be the chief points of divergence between Liu Shao-ch'i and Mao over education

22 Chou En-lai, "Report on Government Work," 18 April 1959, reprinted in Robert R. Bowie and John K. Fairbank, eds., *Communist China, 1955–1959*, 517. One of the highest assessments for 1958 (*PR*, 33 [14 October 1958] 14) had claimed enrollments at those three levels to be 700,000, 14.0 million, and 92.6 million, respectively.
23 NCNA–English, Peking, 28 April 1959, in *CB*, 577 (14 May 1959), 14.

policy. If indeed that was so, then the two men must have diverged on this issue at some later date, or else the clause on quality schools was inserted in the otherwise revolutionary September 1958 directive against Mao's will. The differences probably emerged as the full social implications of "walking on two legs" became apparent. And this could not occur until the system actually began to function in the manner prescribed, that is, after the mass movement had run its course and the principles it was designed to launch had begun to be institutionalized.

Toward this end, a series of joint CCP Central Committee and State Council directives were issued in May and June 1959, following the April meeting of the NPC. A directive on institutions of higher learning acknowledged that more than seven hundred new schools had been set up in 1958 by provinces, cities, and central government departments. "Some of the schools correspond to the standard of the institutions of higher learning and can be continued," noted the directive. It went on to list the specific criteria to be used in determining whether or not a school should be allowed to continue in operation and, if so, the precise name that should be given to it, for example, college, technical school, or cadre training class.

Another directive concerning the experimental revision of the school system noted that many schools had carried out such experiments in accordance with a central directive issued in October 1958. The new directive in May 1959 placed strict limits on the experiments, which involved curriculum changes, teaching methods, and a reduction of combined primary and secondary schooling from 12 to 10 years. (The 12-year system was based on the pre-1949 system, which in turn was based on American practice; the Soviet Union followed a 10-year system.) Henceforth only a small number of specially designated primary and middle schools in each province and city were to continue these experiments, which were to be brought under the control of the Ministry of Education. Pending its decisions on the experiments expected to continue until 1961, all other full-day schools were ordered to continue operating under the existing system. Reports by Lu Ting-i and Education Minister Yang Hsiu-feng in 1960 indicated that the experiments were quality-oriented and aimed at maintaining high standards despite the attempt to reduce the length of regular schooling.

Yet another May 1959 directive stipulated labor and study time for full-day schools at all levels. Labor time was fixed at two to three months per year in college, and the Education Ministry was granted the authority to specify the total number of hours within the curriculum to be devoted to major courses. Labor time was fixed at eight to ten hours per week for senior middle school students; six to eight hours per week at the junior secondary level; and four to six hours per week for primary school students from the age of 9. These schedules constituted the basis of more formal regulations drafted during 1961–62 for the full-time schools. Promulgated in 1963, the new regulations reduced slightly the amount of labor time to one month per year at the secondary level and half a month per year in senior primary school.

The national unified college entrance examinations were restored in 1959 and given every year thereafter until the Cultural Revolution began in 1966. In 1959, however, workers, peasants, and cadres could still be admitted on the basis of recommendation and an assessment by the institutions they wished to enter, without having to take the national entrance exams.[24]

Details of an early retrenchment in science and technology, if it occurred, are not available. The previously mentioned Russian scientist who had worked in China in 1958 noted little difference in the organization and performance of scientific research when he returned in 1960, except that more people were at work in their laboratories and at their desks than before. After his second trip and subsequent defection to the West, he summarized his views of China's scientific research in two related points. The first was that China had modeled the enterprise too closely on the contemporary Soviet system without considering either its defects or whether it was appropriate in all respects for a less developed scientific environment.

The second point was that the Party's decision makers had a poor grasp of the particular problems associated with scientific work. They followed Soviet advice and concentrated scientific research in specialized institutes rather than universities. This spread the existing meager supply of scientific talent too thin, since there were not enough trained scientists even to staff the institutes. Meanwhile, these scientists were not reproducing themselves, and the universities had been deprived of the ability to train the next generation. Newly built research institutes compared favorably in their physical aspects with

24 The 1959 directives are translated in *Compendium of Laws, JPRS*, General Series: 14,346 (2 July 1962), 318–43. On the teaching experiments, see reports by Lu Ting-i (NCNA–English, Peking, 9 April 1960) and Yang Hsiu-feng (NCNA–English, Peking, April 8, 1960) both in *CB*, 623 (June 29, 1960). The school regulations are translated in Susan Shirk, "The 1963 temporary work regulations for full-time middle and primary schools: Commentary and translation," *CQ*, 55 (July–September 1973), 511–46.

Soviet counterparts, but there were not enough trained personnel to guarantee the progress of teaching and research.

In the view of this Soviet observer, the personnel problem was compounded in many ways by bad leadership. The Academy of Sciences and its provincial branches were led not by scientists, but by Party bureaucrats who had no understanding of the prerequisites for scientific development, namely, time and thorough preparation. Work was constantly interrupted for political activities and meetings; research projects were started and stopped, seemingly on a whim, before any results could be achieved. Even more than their Soviet mentors in their own earlier phase of development, the Chinese leaders disparaged pure science in deference to practical application.

In addition, the older generation of trained scientists were treated with suspicion as class enemies, while laymen were encouraged to engage in research whether trained or not. Finally, he cited the secrecy the Party bureaucrats imposed on all scientific research. Not only were all contacts with the outside world forbidden; so were scientific exchanges between different branches of the scientific community within China itself.[25]

Significant adjustments on the scientific front were apparently not registered until 1961–62. Acknowledging then that it had been overextended during the GLF, official policy called for many of the newly established research institutes to be merged or abolished in order to improve quality and concentrate research in those with the best facilities. It was also acknowledged that the scientific enterprise required skill, training, and a stable, well-organized scientific community. Mass-line participation had perhaps been an "oversimplification."[26]

WALKING ON TWO LEGS INTO THE 1960S

The difficulty of trying to use the concept of the "law of the mass movement" as a framework for analyzing policy implementation is that it assumes a leader who stands above the fray. As initiator, he not only sets the movement in motion but later determines the point at which it has peaked and the consolidation phase can safely begin. This is a crucial step. Resistance must have been sufficiently intimidated so as no longer to present a threat, and new leaders must be

25 Klochko, *Soviet scientist in Red China*, 28–31, 102–4, 130–1, 135–40, 176, 194–213.
26 Cheng, *Scientific and engineering manpower in Communist China*, 31–33.

ready to begin implementing the new policies for which the movement was launched in the first place.

This is the point at which costs are calculated and excesses can be
corrected. Naturally, not all errors can be easily reversed, particularly
when physical violence is involved. Naturally too, some participants
refuse to respond to the signals that are sent out as the movement
progresses from one phase to the next. This is an easy mistake to
commit, since the rules of the game are never announced in advance.
These few individuals who have not yet learned the laws of the
movement or at least the value of opportunism – usually the younger,
less experienced participants who are prone to interpret the initial
mobilization phase too literally – represent part of the cost of the
mass movement method. They are regularly sacrificed to it and pay
the heaviest price, together with the formal targets of the movement
against which its excesses are directed.

Assuming he is still in power, the initiator also has the right to
interpret the movement's twists and turns afterward so as to portray
himself to best advantage. But he will not actually have been able to
control all the twists and turns themselves as the movement develops.
If it is a true mass movement, based on the mobilized-spontaneous
participation of many people outside the regular channels of leader-
mass contact, it will for a time have been allowed to develop in an ad
hoc fashion and take on a certain life of its own. This is necessary
because it is precisely when the movement is pushed out of control
that excesses are committed. And only in that way, according to Mao,
can wrongs be corrected and resistance overcome. These conditions
also make it virtually impossible for everyone else to separate fact
from fabrication in the subsequent interpretation and to determine
who was actually responsible for what at any given time.

This is, of course, what made the mass movement such a useful
instrument for Mao as a method of policy implementation. It gave
him as the initiator, at least temporarily, an overwhelming advantage
of mass strength against the forces of opposition, whoever or whatever they might be. And it was also possible for him – so long as he
remained in control of the Party center and its propaganda apparatus
– to camouflage responsibility for errors and excesses by deflecting it
onto the actual perpetrators of wrongdoings committed during the
course of the movement.

As initiator, he therefore retained the right of defining what was
and was not a wrongdoing and also of changing the standards of the

definition as events developed. For example, violence might be inevitable and therefore beneficial at one stage but harmful at another. In this manner, political allies became enemies, and what was advocated as correct for one period was cast aside and condemned during the next. Particularly complex was the consolidation phase of the movement, when whatever forces of opposition remained might regroup in various ways in an attempt to recoup some of their losses.

In the process of initiating the next major movement, the Cultural Revolution of 1966, the events of the intervening years since the Great Leap Forward were interpreted as a progressive perversion by Liu Shao-ch'i and his allies of Mao's correct line in education as advanced in 1958. A more plausible explanation, however, is that developments in education progressed during the early 1960s – after the high tide of the mass movement in 1958 and its consolidation phase in 1959 – very much *in accordance with* the line launched in the September 1958 directive, albeit disrupted by the unanticipated economic difficulties of the period. The movement having progressed in that manner, the contradictions inherent in the line also developed accordingly.

For example, the decision to develop the key schools and the regular full-time system, together with the work-study schools, may have initially been thought to "give equal emphasis to quality as well as quantity," as the education minister had asserted in early 1959. But during the implementing of that line, the distinctions between the two kinds of schooling and, more important, between the two kinds of people receiving them became sharper.

It must have been within this developing context, which contained a number of other contradictions as well, that Mao himself by the mid-1960s abandoned his "walking on two legs" (*liang-t'iao-t'ui tsou-lu*) slogan as it had been applied to education, reinterpreting it in negative terms as Liu Shao-ch'i's pernicious and unequal "two-track" or dual education system (*liang chung chiao-yü chih-tu*). But however stylized, attempting to build an education system based on a division of labor between two separate forms of schooling actually served to reinforce the differences between them.

The "failure" of the work-study concept

Contemporary data from official sources on education, particularly from the national perspective, is scarce to nonexistent for the early

1960s.[27] This is probably a reflection of the havoc wrought upon the upward flow of statistical indicators in all sectors by the economic difficulties of the period. Most of the available information for those years was published after the fact, both in the official press and in unofficial Red Guard publications between 1964 and 1968, during the prelude to and onset of the Cultural Revolution. While biased to reflect the Maoist interpretation then prevailing, the Red Guard materials in particular produced a wealth of previously unavailable data.[28] They are now supplemented by an even greater wealth of data garnered from essentially the same source but via a different medium, interviews conducted by scholars in Hong Kong with former student members of the Red Guard generation, primarily from Canton.[29]

According to these later accounts, the agricultural middle schools suffered a precipitous decline in the early 1960s. They had numbered, by official count, 30,000 nationwide in 1960, with 2.9 million students. By 1962, they had declined to 3,715 schools with a total enrollment of 260,000 students. Primary schools were also closed during this period until only 56 percent of school-age children were attending at the primary level, compared with 80 percent claimed in 1958.[30]

The decline may well have been due to economic causes. But the work-study concept was revived in 1964–65, when it was introduced at the primary level as well. And the official press promoting it at that time revealed more basic reasons for the lack of success. The target group such schools were intended to serve regarded them as a second-rate alternative to the "real" education offered by the regular, full-time school system. Traditional attitudes about the division of mental and manual labor still prevailed, reinforced by the economics of daily life in a subsistence-level rural economy.

27 See, for example, Barendsen's update on the agricultural middle schools based on these data: *Half-work half-study schools*, 28–38.
28 Accounts based largely on these materials are Gardner, "Educated youth and urban-rural inequalities, 1958–66"; and Hong Yung Lee, *The politics of the Chinese Cultural Revolution*.
29 The studies now or soon to be available are Anita Chan, "Images of China's social structure: The changing perspectives of Canton students," *World politics* (April 1982), 295–323; Anita Chan, *Children of Mao: Personality development and political activism in the Red Guard generation*; Anita Chan, Stanley Rosen, and Jonathan Unger, "Students and class warfare: the social roots of the Red Guard conflict in Guangzhou," *CQ*, 83 (September 1980), 397–446; Stanley Rosen, *Red Guard factionalism and the Cultural Revolution in Guangzhou*; Stanley Rosen, *The role of sent-down youth in the Chinese Cultural Revolution: The case of Guangzhou*; Susan L. Shirk, *Competitive comrades: Career incentives and student strategies in China*; Jonathan Unger, *Education under Mao: Class and competition in Canton schools, 1960–1980*.
30 Gardner, "Educated youth and urban-rural inequalities, 1958–66," 246.

A simple fact, revealed in interviews conducted in Hong Kong with former teachers from rural Chinese schools, is that given a choice between sending their children to a regular full-time middle school in the county town – typically there were then only one or two per county – or to a work-study middle school nearer home, most rural parents would choose the former. This was because they knew that it was qualitatively better and that an education there offered a chance for their children to escape a life of agricultural labor. In fact, the vast majority of rural children had no chance of attending a regular secondary school. These were filled mainly with the county town children and those of the rural elites. But given the choice between sending their children to the new work-study agricultural middle school and allowing them to work full-time at home to supplement the family income, most rural parents would choose the latter course. Why go to school to prepare for a life of labor, the peasants reasoned, and why labor at school for nothing when that could more profitably be done at home? These were the typical questions that emerged from the cost-benefit calculations of rural families.

Since agricultural labor was still uniformly regarded as the lowest rung on the ladder of human productivity, everyone continued to regard the work-study agricultural school as an inferior version of the regular variety, which offered a route upward and outward. If a peasant youth attended such a school and still had to return to agricultural labor, this was regarded by all as an injustice or at least a waste. Given this environment, local cadres and teachers – without the spur of higher-level backing that allowed the Kiangsi Communist Labor University to persevere and prosper – failed to build their own work-study schools into an acceptable alternative.[31]

Here in another form was the developmental problem first acknowledged in 1957 – namely, how to provide equitable forms of secondary education that would be college preparatory for some and terminal for the majority. When there are no secondary schools at all, the problem does not arise. When secondary schools begin to appear but in two different forms, among a people long sensitized to every manifestation of unequal advantage, contradictions of necessity sharpen.

31 On the problems of this period, see also Julia Kwong, "The Educational Experiment of the Great Leap Forward, 1958–59," *Comparative Education Review*, 3 (October 1979), 443–55; Julia Kwong, *Chinese education in transition: Prelude to the Cultural Revolution*, 81–129; Unger, *Education under Mao*, 48–65. On rural attitudes toward agricultural labor, see William L. Parish and Martin King Whyte, *Village and family in contemporary China*, 110–11.

Nevertheless, during April 1965, the Education Ministry convened the first national conference on rural work-study education. It was lauded for achieving "More, faster, better and more economical" results in paving the way toward universal primary schooling and the expansion of secondary education in the countryside. The conference reported many shortcomings in the regular full-time schools and called for their rectification. But the conference acknowledged that the "two kinds of education systems," that is, full-time and work-study, would continue to exist side by side for a fairly long time to come, although work-study represented the long-range direction for the development of socialist education. At the secondary level, work-study schooling would become the mainstay of the system.[32]

In November 1965, an urban work-study conference was held. Liu Shao-ch'i did figure prominently at both conferences and at both proclaimed that the development of two kinds of educational systems was in keeping with the policy of "walking on two legs." But the inferior status of the work-study stream was clearly acknowledged. In the cities, it was promoted as the means whereby those primary school graduates who could not gain admission to regular junior secondary schools could be organized for labor and study. In addition, only a few city youth would henceforth be able to go on with their studies or find employment in cities; the great majority would have to accept work assignments in the countryside. The work-study schools were seen as a means of preparing urban youth for that life.[33]

It was this clear development of two separate and unequal education systems – and not the work-study concept itself – that Liu Shao-ch'i was later accused of promoting. He was said to have robbed the concept of its "revolutionary soul."

The "success" of the regular full-time system

Professional academics, whether influenced by liberal Western learning, forced into the more specialized Soviet mold, or obliged to adopt a new Chinese socialist orientation, were nevertheless academics and intellectuals still. They used the opportunity provided by the "walking on two legs" policy and the acknowledged need to restore order and quality to education after the GLF to build their leg into a system that completely dominated the other not only in their own eyes but in the eyes of everyone else as well.

32 *JMJP*, 30 May 1965, 2.   33 Ibid., 6 December 1965, 1.

Institutionalized at the apex of the pyramid were the elite keypoint (*chung-tien*) schools, which were developed at all levels of the full-time school system from kindergarten through university. The history of the keypoint schools appears lost in the mists of time. Interviews in 1980 with administrators at a dozen universities in China and many secondary schools as well produced no clear responses concerning the precise origin of the system and who was responsible for it. An Education Ministry spokesman gave the most detailed answer, parts of which were also given by others and none of which was contradicted elsewhere. He denied that the system had been inspired in any way by examples from Soviet education. Rather, the system owed its origins to the keypoint concept, which was the basis of the CCP economic development strategy during the Anti-Japanese and civil wars of 1937–49. This strategy concentrated manpower and material for the purpose of economic construction in the impoverished rural base areas.

The concept was subsequently applied to education. The earliest example of this was the "central school," which was promoted as part of the 1942 Yenan reforms. The promotion of the concept after 1949 is now traced to a widely cited directive issued by Mao in 1953 to run keypoint middle schools well, although the directive was not publicized at that time. Nor was it until 1959, following Chou En-lai's April 1959 Government Work Report cited above, that keypoint schools began to be established in a systematic fashion. They were used as a means of maintaining quality within the context of the rapid expansion of mass education that occurred during the GLF.[34] Despite the existence of key schools from the mid-1950s onward – often simply the most prestigious schools from pre-1949 days were so designated – the system was not developed in a concerted fashion throughout the country until the 1960–66 period.

Whereas the function of the developing urban work-study schools was by 1965 to produce talent for the countryside, the primary function of the urban-based keypoint system was from the start to produce talent for institutions of higher learning. The key schools were defined immediately as the college preparatory stream, and the lives of everyone associated with them revolved around that aim. Secondary schools in the inner city and near-suburban districts of Canton, for example, were ranked in 1962 on the basis of their

---

34 Suzanne Pepper, *China's universities: Post-Mao enrollment policies and their impact on the structure of secondary education: A research report.*

promotion rates to university. The schools were divided into three categories. At the best of the first category schools, as many as 70 to 90 percent of graduating students might be admitted to college in any given year, and the majority of Canton's college students came from the first category secondary schools. Category two schools generally achieved pass rates of 15 to 30 percent or less. Third-ranking schools included the *min-pan* and agricultural middle schools; their students did not usually go on to college.

Schools with the highest pass rates from junior to senior middle and on to college were designated as keypoints, ensuring that they would receive the best teachers, the most generous financial appropriations, the best equipment, and a continuing supply of the best primary and junior middle graduates. Students who scored highest on their secondary school entrance exams were channeled into the first category schools, and so on down the scale of academic achievement. Officially announced and publicized in the local press only in 1962, the rank order nevertheless continued to be used internally and was refined in the public mind thereafter as the basis for evaluating these schools.[35]

All sources indicate that this ranking system for middle schools and primary schools was not limited to Canton but became a nationwide phenomenon during the early 1960s. In neighboring Fukien, for example, geography and the proximity of several good schools originally established before 1949 with Overseas Chinese funding in neighboring towns along the coast contributed to a provincial system of examination competitions. These culminated each year in the college entrance examinations, and Fukien gained national recognition for the pass rates these schools achieved. Provincial Education Bureau head Wang Yü-keng threw the weight of her position and prestige behind the effort and personally visited the coastal towns and schools with high promotion rates. She urged them on in the race for the red flags of achievement awarded to the winners. So intently was the contest pursued, according to one former student interviewed in Hong Kong, that in his school during the economic depression years the younger students were asked to contribute a portion of their monthly grain ration to the graduating seniors. This not only bolstered their physical strength during the tense pre-exam cram period but also drew the entire student body into the struggle to win recognition and "glory" for the school.

35 Rosen, *Red Guard factionalism*, 18–22.

As to whose offspring were being accommodated where in this new hierarchy of achievement, Rosen and Unger found that in a random sample of Canton secondary schools, "good" class worker-peasant youth predominated in the poorer regular junior middle schools with the lowest promotion rates. These tended to be newer schools established in working-class neighborhoods that had previously had none. At the best key junior middle schools, by contrast, only 11 percent of the students were of worker-peasant background; 48 percent were the children of "revolutionary cadres." This was another "good" category designating those who not only were ranking officials in the bureaucratic hierarchy but had joined the Party and the revolution before 1949.

The proportions were almost exactly reversed in the neighborhood junior middle schools, with only 8 percent revolutionary cadre students and 42 percent of worker-peasant background. The children of intellectuals constituted 20 percent of the students in the poorer schools and 32 percent in the elite institutions. At the senior secondary level, where places were fewer, competition more intense, and academic standards therefore higher, the proportion of cadre children apparently declined. At the best key schools, they constituted 27 percent of the student body, and worker-peasant youth 12 percent. The children of intellectuals amounted to 34 percent, while those of other middle-range nonintellectual classes constituted 16 percent.[36]

The survey referred to a five-year period, 1962–66. In looking more closely at changes during that time, Rosen concluded that the education system was becoming increasingly bifurcated as conflicts over policy objectives mounted. In 1961 and 1962, the emphasis on academic achievement and entrance examination scores was restored in order to promote quality after the experiments with worker-peasant admissions by recommendation in 1958 and 1959. Ch'en I's famous speech set the tone. "It is the political duty of the student to learn his specialized subject," he had said in 1961. The post–Great Leap adjustments were reaffirmed the next year, as indicated by Chou En-lai's April 1962 report to the third session of the Second NPC. He emphasized that the government would continue to adjust cultural, educational, and scientific research and public health undertakings and improve the quality of their work.[37]

36 From a survey conducted jointly by Rosen and Unger among former Canton students living in Hong Kong in the mid-1970s: Rosen, *Red Guard factionalism*, 26; Unger, *Education under Mao*, 26–27.
37 "Press communiqué on the National People's Congress," *PR*, 16 (20 April 1962), 6.

The promotion of quality in the regular schools was not the whole picture, however. In 1961, Mao had written a directive praising the work-study orientation of the Kiangsi Communist Labor University, and in 1962 he issued his celebrated injunction "Never forget class struggle."[38] This call marked the reaffirmation of the doctrine of class struggle at the Tenth Plenum of the Eighth Central Committee in September 1962, as spelled out in Mao's address to the Plenum and in its communiqué.[39]

This reaffirmation also heralded the advent of the Socialist Education campaign, which eventually merged into the Cultural Revolution in 1966. This campaign began as an education and indoctrination movement intended to correct certain "unhealthy tendencies" such as corruption among rural cadres and spontaneous inclinations toward capitalism among the peasants that had grown up during the "three bad years" following the Great Leap.[40] By 1964, this campaign had escalated into a major rectification movement directed against rural cadres and was accompanied by a new nationwide emphasis on politics.

From 1963, renewed stress was placed on politics and class background as criteria for admission to senior middle school and college. "Socialist education" for everyone but especially for young people intensified, focusing on Marxism-Leninism, class viewpoint, class struggle, and direct participation in labor. For primary and middle school students who had no memories of pre-1949 China, the key theme was to compare the bitterness of exploitation and hardship in the old society with the sweetness of life in the new. Old workers and peasants, each with a bitter story to tell, became regular guest speakers at school assemblies and forums. This exercise was of pointed significance, since the country was just emerging from the economic depression that followed the GLF and young people might have difficulty making the correct comparisons. One early theme of social education in Canton, for example, was "to recall and compare the different situations between the old and new societies in years of serious drought." Kwangtung was then, in May 1963, in the midst of

38 "Outline of the struggle between the two lines from the eve of the founding of the People's Republic of China through the Eleventh Plenum of the Eighth CCP Central Committee," trans. in CB, 884 (18 July 1969), 20.
39 "Communiqué," PR, 39 (28 September 1962), 7; and, "Speech at the Tenth Plenum of the Eighth Central Committee," 24 (September 1962), in Stuart Schram, ed., Mao Tse-tung unrehearsed, 189–90.
40 Richard Baum and Frederick C. Teiwes, Ssu-ch'ing: The Socialist education movement of 1962–66; and Richard Baum, Prelude to revolution.

a serious drought, the latest in a succession of natural calamities suffered for "several years in succession."

As part of their political education, college students and faculty members were sent down to the countryside for months at a time in 1964–65, where they joined the work teams investigating rural cadres, reclassifying peasant households, and gaining firsthand knowledge of peasant life. By mid-1965, the intensifying political activity was being referred to as a "deep-going socialist revolution on the cultural front." "When the economic base and the political system have changed," noted one commentator, "culture, as a form of ideology, must also change accordingly." Otherwise the socialist revolution risked being abandoned halfway, with all its achievements lost.[41] This theme in turn heralded the onset of the 1966 Cultural Revolution.

In early 1964 at the Spring Festival forum, Mao had also issued the first of his later much publicized commentaries criticizing the pedantic and impractical nature of the education offered by the regular primary and middle schools. The twelve-year system was too long; the subjects were too many and too complicated; the examinations were too rigid; and the students had difficulty finding jobs after graduation, since they were prepared only to continue their studies, not to engage in labor.[42] This too heralded themes that would be more fully developed during the Cultural Revolution.

Yet the emphasis on academic achievement was retained in uneasy combination with the developing political activity. The Ministry of Higher Education was restored in 1964, indicating the continued concern with quality at the elite level. The following year, the

41 Tien Chu, "Fruits of the Cultural Revolution," *PR*, 42 (15 October 1965). On the socialist education campaign for youth, see, for example, *Yang-ch'eng wan-pao*, Canton, 28 May 1963, trans. in *Survey of China Mainland Press – Supplement (SCMP–S)*, 116 (28 January 1964), 1–3; *Pei-ching jih-pao*, 30 (November 1963), trans. in *SCMP–S*, 123 (21 August 1964), 23–26; *Pei-ching jih-pao*, 4 May 1964, trans. in *SCMP–S*, 126 (18 September 1964), 4–7; *Pei-ching jih-pao*, 12 October 1964, and *Wen-hui pao*, Shanghai, 12 September 1964, both trans. in *SCMP–S*, 133 (12 February 1965), 13–18.

42 "Remarks at the Spring Festival," 13 February 1964, in Stuart Schram, ed., *Mao Tse-tung unrehearsed*, 201–11. Mao's comments, widely publicized after 1966 as a basis for criticizing the regular schools, were interjected during a talk on education given by a Comrade XXX subsequently discovered to have been Teng Hsiao-p'ing. Although the criticism by both men was directed against the regular schools, Teng and another unidentified comrade also spoke in favor of diversifying the system and "walking on two legs" at the primary and secondary levels. They specifically advocated two separate streams, one college preparatory and the other vocational. Mao did not elaborate on this point except for a single assenting sentence. Only Teng commented on the need to improve quality. Mao was clearly preoccupied with reforms that would undermine it at least in terms of the conventional standards then obtaining within the regular school system.

minister acknowledged that college admissions requirements were actually following the pre-1958 formula of giving priority to worker-peasant youth only when their examinations scores were otherwise competitive.

Caught between these conflicting demands, the regular school system tried to serve both. Political study and emulation campaigns, such as the movement to learn from the socialist hero Lei Feng in 1963–64, were introduced into school lives still dominated by the preoccupation with pass rates. This preoccupation extended even to ordinary schools, which also threw themselves into the competition, devising stratagems along with the best to push up their scores and thus enhance their reputations. In these circumstances, the main beneficiaries at the elite level of the renewed emphasis on class background had to be the revolutionary cadre children, with their impeccable class credentials, and the high-scoring offspring of the intelligentsia and other middle-class elements. Young people from bad or exploiting class backgrounds found it increasingly difficult to gain admission, regardless of their academic standing.

Despite their good class background, worker-peasant youth could not hold their own in the competition. The districts where they lived tended to be served by the newest schools, many only recently built and not even including senior secondary sections. Indeed, there was little expansion at the senior secondary level after 1961–62. Hence working-class youth were at an academic disadvantage. They were also more inclined for economic reasons to terminate their regular education at the end of junior middle school in order to seek employment, perhaps after attending a vocational school. In 1964–65, Canton set up 31 new vocational schools, mainly operating on a work-study basis.[43]

Susan Shirk carries the analysis a step farther to discover what student life was like within this competitive school structure. Of the young people she interviewed in Hong Kong, half had been students at the best keypoint secondary schools. The others had been students of regular full-time city schools. Two-thirds of her interviewees had attended schools in Canton; the others had received their education in other towns in Kwangtung province and elsewhere. About half were of middle-class background, mainly the children of teachers, doctors, and other white collar workers; almost all the rest were from exploiting class backgrounds; very few were good class, worker-

43 Rosen, *Red Guard factionalism*, ch. 1, passim.

TABLE 9

Numbers of schools and students, 1958–1965

	Tertiary		Secondary			Primary	
Year	Schools	Students	Schools		Students	Schools	Students
1958		660,000	general specialized agric. & vocational		8,520,000 1,470,000 2,000,000		86,400,000
1959		810,000 (full-time) 300,000 (spare-time)			12,900,000		90,000,000
1960		955,000					
1961		819,000					
1962		820,000					
1963		680,000					
1964		700,000					
1965	434	674,000	80,993 (incl. 61,626 agric. & voca- tional)		14,418,000 (incl. 4.4 million in agric. & vocational)	1,681,900	116,000,000

Sources: 1958: State Statistical Bureau, *Ten great years,* 192. *1959:* Yang Hsiu-feng, "Actively carry out the reform of the school system," NCNA, Peking, 8 April 1960, in *CB,* 623 (29 June 1960), 11. *1960–64:* Robert Taylor, *China's intellectual dilemma,* 138. *1965:* Total student enrollments from *Peking Review,* 5 (3 Feb. 1978), 16–17; number of schools and agricultural and vocational school enrollments from *Chung-kuo pai-k'o nien-chien 1980,* 535–36.

peasant youths. Only a third had been politically active, as indicated by their applications to join the Communist Youth League. All had attended secondary school between 1960 and 1966.

Even among this group, who had left their homeland for Hong Kong, there was a general acceptance of egalitarian and collective ideals. But in addition, they revealed patterns of student behavior, particularly at the senior secondary level – among 16- to 19-year-olds – that were the antithesis of those ideals. Coexisting with them was an informal student subculture dominated by the objective of winning a coveted place in college or, as second best, assignment to a city job upon graduation from middle school. The time devoted in American high schools to dating, sports, and extracurricular activities was used in this Chinese context to induct students into the adult world of "mutual-use" relationships and intense individual competition.

In the process, students also learned to value the opposite kinds of behavior, but not for the "right" reasons. Nonactivists tended to avoid activists, rather than share confidences with them that might later be used to harm career prospects. Private friendships, far from being destroyed by such tensions, were actually strengthened. Students sought out like-minded mates who could be trusted not to use friendly candor for personal or political gain. Students also tended to transform the regular peer-group assessment sessions into rituals of mutual protection. These young people had learned to distinguish at an early age between sincerity and hypocrisy among activists; perfidy and loyalty among classmates; and between true friendship and self-serving alliances.

Shirk's findings suggested, however, that students probably behaved differently in different kinds of schools. In the full-time technical secondary schools (*chung-teng chuan-yeh hsueh-hsiao*), for example, student behavior appeared to be closer to the official ideal, and student activists were admired by their peers. Students in those schools were already resigned to the ordinary technical jobs that were guaranteed them upon graduation. The stakes were at once higher and more uncertain in the college preparatory stream, where success meant a secure and respected future, while failure could result in banishment to a rural work assignment.[44]

Rosen found similar differences. Because individual political activism was a criterion that was also weighed along with inherited class background and achieved examination scores, the desire to demonstrate activism was much more evident in elite schools than in ordinary ones. Youth League membership was regarded as a stepping stone to university, and membership rates were accordingly highest in schools which fell along the upper ranges of the academic rank order.

The political study and emulation campaigns were only minimally successful in moderating this environment of competition and careerism. The campaigns did generate a good deal of student activism, both real and feigned. In the process some students, even whole classrooms, resolved not to sit for the college entrance examinations and to volunteer for settlement in the countryside. But so long as the examinations and the college careers they led to remained the recognized pinnacle of achievement for the regular school system, it also remained difficult to distinguish students who were studying "for the

44 Shirk, *Competitive comrades*, 59–60, and passim.

revolution" from those following the bourgeois path of individual gain and glory.

In this climate, a rural work assignment was the least desirable of all possible post secondary school options. It was, nevertheless, promoted increasingly from 1961 on, as urban employment opportunities declined relative to the number of new entrants in the job market. Aside from those who could be mobilized to volunteer for rural work through the enthusiasm generated in a mass campaign, almost everyone apparently viewed working in the countryside as a fate to be avoided by whatever means possible.

The notion that the countryside was a dumping ground for urban rejects was given credence by the manner in which this alternative job assignment was made between 1961 and 1965. As the Urban Work-Study Conference in 1965 had affirmed, youth who were able to continue their studies or obtain jobs could stay in the cities. The remainder, the great majority, would have to go to the countryside. A rural work assignment had become a means of punishment for youth of bad class background, and carried in addition the stigma of failure within the urban hierarchy of status and achievement.[45]

In many respects, therefore, China's educational system, as of 1965, made a mockery of the GLF's ideal: to "promote education among the worker-peasant masses and labor for the intellectuals." Yet the perversions of the ideal were logical results of Mao's "Walking on two legs" policy. This conclusion is based especially on the assumption that the keypoint school concept was not a distortion but an integral feature of the 1958 reforms.

The *min-pan* and work-study schools were direct descendants of the 1944 strategy for popularizing education. The difference was that the CCP domain now encompassed the entire country and not just the backward border regions. Hence Mao reached back to his pre-1949 experience again, but in a different way, to adapt the keypoint concept as an alternative to perform the function of guaranteeing quality. The enthusiasm of the mass movement, also adapted from pre-1949 experience, was the vehicle for launching the new two-legged model into Chinese society.

The results should have been foreseen by the drafters of the

45 Thomas P. Bernstein, *Up to the mountains and down to the villages: The transfer of youth from urban to rural China*; Rosen, *The role of sent-down youth in the Chinese Cultural Revolution*. On the job preferences of urban youth, see D. Gordon White, "The Politics of *Hsia-hsiang* Youth," *CQ*, 59 (July–September 1974), 491, 517.

September 1958 directive, but apparently they were not. The Yenan model may have functioned well enough in the isolated environment for which it was originally designed. But when grafted onto a modern regular school system run by and for academic professionals, no amount of political tinkering and ideological reform could make the system appear other than the divided structure it was. To assign the work-study system the task of educating the rural-peasant and working-class sectors, while the regular system imparted quality education to those most in a position to benefit from it, proved but a new means of institutionalizing all the old cleavages at once. The education system that had grown out of the "walking on two legs" policy was actually serving to reinforce the divisions between elites and masses, between mental and manual labor, and between the peasants and everyone else.

By 1964, these consequences were inescapable. It was probably only then that Mao decided to destroy the system he had created before it could develop further, blaming in the process the "bourgeois educators" responsible for building it. Certainly, he now had reasons enough for wanting to destroy the system over which they presided. The peasants themselves looked down on the work-study agricultural middle schools. Young people of worker-peasant origin remained largely excluded from the elite college preparatory stream that had sprung to life almost immediately after the signal was given in 1959.

But perhaps the most telling blow was that the successor generation, that is, the offspring of the very same cadres who had made the revolution, were congregating within the best keypoint schools. There these good class background successors were being infected by the same "bourgeois" individualism, intellectual interests, and career aspirations that Mao and the CCP had been trying to expunge from the Chinese intellectual community for at least two decades.

Mao and his comrades had lived in the countryside most of their lives. The most important lessons of the Party's history had been derived from that experience. In the meantime, however, they had all moved to the city, and their children had become urban youth. As such, they regarded rural life with the same distaste that city people had always shown for it. For the time being, they were protected by their class credentials. Otherwise, they would be devising all manner of personal strategies to avoid a rural work assignment as others, less privileged by birth, were already doing. Like the typical peasant youth who joins the army and then demands a nonagricultural job upon demobilization, the revolutionary cadres had also changed. But the basic urban-rural contradictions within Chinese society that they had pledged to overcome remained as sharply drawn as ever.

These considerations gave some substance to the Maoist charge of 1966 that "capitalist roaders" had invaded the Party itself and were threatening the successor generation. The solution was to attempt to destroy altogether the bifurcated and competitive structures that had developed during the 1960s. This could be accomplished in the course of yet another mass movement. Replacing those structures with something that might effectively and more equitably integrate the contradictory urban-rural and elite-mass goals the education system was expected to serve would prove more difficult.

CHAPTER 10

THE PARTY AND THE
INTELLECTUALS: PHASE TWO

THE DENIGRATION OF INTELLECTUAL ENDEAVOR
IN THE GREAT LEAP FORWARD

The suppression of specific intellectuals in the Anti-Rightist campaign turned into anti-intellectualism in general in the Great Leap Forward (GLF). The leadership's hope of using the intellectuals as key figures in China's modernization had been dashed when both intellectuals and students criticized the Party in the Hundred Flowers. After a decade of indoctrination and ideological remolding campaigns, intellectuals still questioned Party policies. The leadership's disillusion with the intellectuals was reflected in Propaganda Director Lu Ting-i's statements in the GLF period. Whereas in the Hundred Flowers he had used Mao's slogan to encourage intellectuals with Western learning to participate actively in the nation-building, effort, in a *Kuang-ming Daily* article of 13 March 1958 he rejected Western learning as "poisonous weeds": "There is bankruptcy in bourgeois philosophy, science, social sciences, literature and arts. The only value in studying them is that we can learn to recognize them as 'poisonous weeds' and by weeding, use them as fertilizer."

Even though the intellectuals in the GLF were less direct objects of attack than in the Anti-Rightist Campaign, their relative position in Chinese society deteriorated further. In contrast to the Hundred Flowers period, the GLF emphasized political reliability rather than professional skill. A new slogan was advanced, calling on people in all walks of life, including intellectuals, to be "Red and expert," with the emphasis on "Red." As the movement gained momentum, the emphasis shifted almost wholly to redness. Intelligence was equated with political commitment and was no longer regarded as the monopoly of the few, and this change presaged the Cultural Revolution. Party cadres armed with the ideological weapons of Marxism-Leninism and Mao Tse-tung Thought were praised as superior to intellectuals and professionals trained in Western methods and ideas. Moreover, to a much greater extent than ever before, the creativity and intellectual capacities of the masses were idealized and accepted as articles of almost mystical faith. Peasants and workers, just emerging from illiteracy, were praised as scientists, philosophers, and poets, capable of virtually any achievement because of their "proletarian" consciousness. By contrast, intellectuals were denigrated because they were imbued with the bourgeois concepts of individualism, liberalism, and anarchism.

Scholarship was treated as purely functional and coordinated with industrial and agricultural production. The importance of science and engineering increased still more in relation to the social sciences and humanities, but even scientists and engineers were ordered to learn from the achievements of ordinary peasants and workers. Academic standards were watered down. The study of math and scientific theory, crucial to modernization, was slighted in favor of mastery of technical skills.

Almost all the older urban intellectuals and students were sent to the countryside and smaller towns for a period of labor reform, where they were to be reeducated by doing manual labor and mixing with the masses. Their positions in universities and research centers were filled by younger, more politically indoctrinated Party cadres who were able to insert themselves into the intellectual establishment at this time. Older intellectuals who managed to remain at their institutions were relegated to subservient or even menial positions. The old textbooks were dispensed with and new ones were written as collective works by Party cadres and younger scholars and graduate students. Like the rest of the population, intellectuals were ordered to produce whatever they did in great quantities for the sake of the revolution. Quantity was exalted at the expense of quality.

The harnessing of literature for the GLF exemplified what happened in other fields of intellectual and creative endeavor. Writers were given grandiose plans that had to be completed in 1958. The eminent writer Pa Chin, who had produced little since the Party's accession to power, pledged to write one long novel, three medium-length novels, and several translations within the course of a year. The Writers Union announced that China's professional writers would produce seven hundred stories, plays, and poems, all of which would be easy to understand and conducive to the emergence of new heroes and new phenomena. Despite the extraordinary demands placed on professional writers, more emphasis was given to unskilled, politically committed writers. As in other fields, the distinction between the professional and amateur was blurred. The number of "writers" jumped from fewer than a thousand in 1957 to more than two hundred thousand in 1958. Thousands of loyal amateurs even became members of the elite Writers Union.

The anti-intellectual and collectivist spirit of the GLF was expressed in the creative activity of anonymous groups of amateurs. They produced the most distinctive cultural products of the GLF – poems and songs of workers and peasants created at large meetings. Party cadres suggested themes and ideas and wrote down the lines as the masses spoke them out. The Party manipulated these poetry-writing sessions into expressing the Party's will and then used the poems to stimulate mass enthusiasm for rapid economic advances.

The CCP had used such methods of indoctrination and mobilization since the late 1930s, but never on such an intensive, widespread scale as in the GLF, when poems and songs were incessantly broadcast over loudspeakers and ubiquitously pasted on walls. China's foremost literary journal, *Jen-min wen-hsueh* (People's literature) gave itself over entirely to publishing the writings of workers and peasants.

China's cultural czar, Chou Yang, provided a theoretical framework for the literature and art of the GLF – the combination of revolutionary realism and revolutionary romanticism. Although this theory was introduced as an original concept of Mao Tse-tung, it was a restatement of the Soviet concept of socialist realism. In fact, as early as 1934 the Soviet cultural chief, Zhdanov, had advocated revolutionary romanticism, defined as the description of characters and events as they will be in the ideal state of communism. At a time of worsening relations with the Soviet Union, the CCP, in the GLF, tried to dissociate its cultural policies from their Soviet derivation, and from the Soviet emphasis in the post-Stalin era on realism rather than socialism, by presenting the Soviet literary theory under another name. Yet, just as before the GLF, at a time when relations with the Soviet Union were better, literary works were to capture in ordinary life a vision of the future and arouse enthusiasm for Party policies.

THE INTELLECTUAL RELAXATION IN THE AFTERMATH OF THE GREAT LEAP FORWARD

As a result of economic chaos in the late 1950s and early 1960s, the Party modified the commune system, allowed private plots, sanctioned private service trades, and permitted material incentives in order to repair the economic damage of the GLF. It also relaxed its grip on the intellectuals in order to win their cooperation in this endeavor. The period of relative relaxation that began in 1961 and extended through the autumn of 1962 was similar to, and yet different from, the Hundred Flowers. Both interludes of a more moderate, more tolerant approach toward intellectuals were in part a by-product of prior periods of intellectual repression.

The Anti-Rightist Campaign and GLF had silenced and demoralized a larger number of intellectuals than the Hu Feng campaign of 1955. A substantial number had become increasingly passive in the face of intensive criticism and enforced labor reform. Scholars in the social sciences, humanities, arts, and even the more general sciences were reluctant to innovate and participate. In addition to this dialectical process, the shift from repression to relative relaxation was governed by political and economic considerations. Confronted with an economy in shambles and the withdrawal of Soviet scientific and technical experts due to the Sino-Soviet split of 1960, the Party was in desperate need of the services of the intellectuals. Thus, it offered them intellectual and material incentives in the expectation of reactivating them.

The moving force behind the 1961-62 relaxation was Liu Shao-ch'i and the Party bureaucracy rather than Mao, who had been so instrumental in initiating the Hundred Flowers. Whereas Liu and most of the bureaucracy had gone along reluctantly with the Hundred Flowers, they now led the effort to rejuvenate the intellectual community. Like Mao, they had no interest in liberalizing China's intellectual life or making it more pluralistic. But they were willing to encourage a degree of intellectual ferment and criticism if it created a more favorable climate for scientific, technical, and economic development and did not weaken political control.

Superficially, the relaxation of 1961-62 had many of the same trappings and slogans as the Hundred Flowers. It was heralded by several high officials. Vice-Premier Ch'en I, in a speech given in August 1961, reminiscent of the one Chou En-lai had given in January 1956 to usher in the Hundred Flowers, sought to invigorate the intellectual community by urging that greater respect be shown to the scholar and higher regard be given to his contribution to the nation. Ch'en explained, as Mao had during the Hundred Flowers period, that years of Party indoctrination had rendered the intellectuals politically trustworthy. In fact, Ch'en had so much confidence in the transformation of the intellectuals that he believed they need no longer spend time in political sessions and manual labor to the neglect of their own work. He declared, "As long as experts show results in their profession and contribute to the construction of socialism, there should be no objection to their taking only a small part in political activity." Furthermore, he announced that an intellectual need not be thoroughly versed in Marxism-Leninism and completely committed to the Party ideology. In Maoist jargon, that meant that one could be more expert than Red.

Ch'en redefined communism in terms closer to Khrushchev's pragmatic interpretation than to the Chinese Communist Party's more ideological approach. The intellectual demonstrated his political spirit, Ch'en declared, not by constantly professing his devotion to the regime or to its political system, but by contributing to the development of modern industry, agriculture, science, and culture. In Ch'en's view, such activity was "a manifestation of the politics of socialism." He feared that unless there were these changes in attitudes toward intellectuals, "Our country's science and culture will lag behind for ever."[1]

Chou En-lai also encouraged greater freedom of speech, particularly in a talk on 19 June 1961 that was not published until 1979 but whose ideas must have been known in the intellectual community. He went so far as to sanction criticism of decisions that had already been accepted by Party leaders. "Even things officially approved and passed by the working conference, convened by the Party's Central Committee, can be discussed and even revised."[2] Although Chou did not call for legal guarantees of the right to speak, he advocated an approach more in tune with Western attitudes than previous Party treatment of intellectuals. As long as one's work was not against the Party and against socialism, it should be permitted. There should also be a separation between intellectual activities and political activities. He discarded as well the emphasis on political reliability, characteristic of the GLF, in favor of expertise.

Chou's view of the early 1960s was that one who was skilled in his work was much more valuable to the development of socialism than one who was versed in politics but unskilled. Even Mao expressed the general feeling at this time that intellectuals should be allowed to

1 *KMJP*, 3 September 1961, 2.
2 Chou En-lai, "On literature and art," *Wen-i pao* (Literary gazette), February 1979, *Peking review* (30 March 1979), 9.

work relatively unhindered by political considerations. On 30 January 1962, at the Seven Thousand Cadres Conference, Mao pointed out that intellectuals need not be revolutionary: "As long as they are patriotic, we shall unite with them and let them get on with their work."[3] In apparent support of the relaxation, he urged people to present their views without fear of punishment so long as they did not violate Party discipline and engage in secret activities.

The Party made a special effort to win the cooperation of the scientists. To remedy the lowering of scientific standards during the GLF, in January 1961 the Ninth Plenum of the Eighth Central Committee called for improvement in the quality of scientific work. Scientists were assured sufficient time for their own research and given added material incentives. They were also given more responsibility in directing their work. Administrators at all levels were directed to heed the advice of scientific and technical personnel on technical matters. A scientist was to be judged by his expertise, not by his ideology. The *Kuang-ming jih-pao* stated on 5 November 1961; "We should not judge a scientist's achievement in natural science by the standard that he is a materialist or an idealist in his philosophical thinking. A scientist who is philosophically an idealist may attain great achievements in natural science."

As during the Hundred Flowers, courses were given in Morgan genetics, and such formerly deprecated scientists as Newton, Copernicus, and Einstein were spoken of favorably. More attention was also given to providing students with a broader theoretical scientific education rather than just specialized technical training. With scientists and technicians given wider discretion in meeting their obligations to the state, the Party had created the conditions for the emergence of a new class of specialists whose decisions would be based on more apolitical standards and whose activities might represent a potential challenge to Party control.

Even in the social sciences, intellectuals were given more latitude. Social scientists were encouraged to explore different methods of research, conduct various experiments, and raise different assumptions. Several articles in the authoritative journal *Hung-ch'i* (Red flag) advised social scientists that they need not concentrate on subjects directly related to the political and class struggle. With such urging, some unprecedented discussions occurred, particularly in the field of economics. Several economists offered suggestions that paralleled the

3 Stuart Schram, ed., *Mao Tse-tung unrehearsed*, 169.

ones being made by reformist economists in the Soviet Union. They, like their Soviet counterparts, called for a pragmatic rather than an ideological approach to economic problems. They urged that profitability and efficiency instead of political criteria be made the basis of investments and that the marketplace rather than administrative decisions determine prices. In addition to the profit and price mechanisms, some economists also recommended the use of mathematical methods, differentiated rent, economic accounting, and interest on capital as means for promoting China's modernization.

The latitude granted to writers in 1961–62 was similar in scope to that granted them in previous periods of relaxation. Writers, as in earlier interludes, were urged to use a variety of styles and methods of expression. Socialist realism and revolutionary romanticism were no longer prescribed, as they had been in the GLF, as the only literary forms. In addition, there was emphasis on more professional literary standards and on the intrinsic value of art. This more creative approach was not merely tolerated but was actively promoted by Party leaders. As in the Hundred Flowers, writers were allowed diversification not only of style but also of subject matter and theme. An editorial in *Wen-i pao* declared, "A writer, according to his different circumstances, [should] freely select and arrange the material with which he is most familiar and which he enjoys."[4] No longer did writers have to depict construction projects or even the class struggle; they were now allowed to describe family life, love affairs, nature, and the small details of everyday living.

Yet unlike the Hundred Flowers, the few intellectuals who did speak out in 1961–62 limited their statements to a parroting of the official line. Though the debate by the economists certainly had political implications, the regime refrained from counterattack at this time. The anxiety of Party leaders during this period of economic crisis was evident from their willingness to explore, or at least permit, the publication of comparatively radical economic suggestions that might lead to more efficient use of scarce resources.

Even an apparently bold article by the novelist Pa Chin, "The writer's courage and responsibility," written in commemoration of the twentieth anniversary of Mao's Yenan "Talks on literature and art," conformed to the Party line. Although his arguments were strongly stated, they coincided with the regime's attack on the bureaucracy's suffocation of China's cultural life. His essay began on

4 *Wen-i pao*, 3 (1961), 3.

a note of sadness as he expressed anxiety over growing old without having created anything he considered worth while. This anxiety must have been shared by most May Fourth writers who had produced few literary works after 1949. Instead of fulfilling his responsibility as a writer, he lamented, "I have spent myself on all kinds of things. I have advanced much politically, but I have written little and moreover have written it badly." What prevented him from carrying out his duty as a writer, Pa Chin asserted, was the literary bureaucracy, which dictated what he could write.

He described these bureaucrats as "people with a hoop in one hand and a club in the other who go everywhere looking for persons who have gone astray.... They enjoy making simple hoops ... and wish to make everyone jump through them.... If there are people who do not wish to go through their hoops and if there are some who have several kinds of flowers blooming in their gardens ..., these people become angry, raise up their clubs, and strike out."[5] He did not draw the obvious conclusion that the existence of bureaucrats with hoops and clubs was due to the Party's policies. Speaking in more general terms, he stressed the need, as did the regime at this time, for greater unity between leaders and led. He proposed that this be done by the democratic method of expressing diverse viewpoints, rather than by the authoritarian method of frightening people with different opinions into submission.

Outwardly, therefore, this period of relaxation appeared to be in the spirit of the original Hundred Flowers campaign. In actual fact, it was not. Although many of the same techniques were employed and several of the same terms were used, from the very start its scope was restricted to scientific and academic subjects. The Party was unwilling to allow the wide-open discussions of spring 1957. As soon as the relaxation began, it called for a clear-cut distinction between contention in the academic sphere and contention in the political arena. Some intellectuals had previously demanded this separation so they could express themselves more freely in their own fields without the imposition of political criteria. The Party now demanded it so that the intellectuals would not interpret the Party's tolerance of freer discussion in academic subjects as a sanction to examine political issues as had happened in 1957.

The restricted nature of this relaxation is seen in the speech by Ch'en I that urged intellectuals to contend. Besides emphasizing

5 *Shang-hai wen-hsueh*, 5 (1962), 3.

intellectual merit and deemphasizing political reliability, he insisted on the need for continued ideological indoctrination. The concession was that thought reform was to be carried out in a different manner than in the more intense periods of regimentation. The Party sought to indoctrinate the intellectual by making acceptance of Marxism-Leninism a voluntary rather than an enforced act. This aim was clearly stated by Ch'en I when he declared, "Since thought reform relies chiefly on the individual's consciousness, the individual must come to conclusions himself. Therefore, it is not feasible to use forceful measures and exert popular pressure."[6]

Thought reform sessions were to be conducted in an atmosphere that was psychologically less threatening. The Party called these sessions of the early sixties "meetings of the immortals" to distinguish their more easygoing approach from the intense pressure applied during the criticism and self-criticism sessions of preceding campaigns. The meetings were to leave an ethereal feeling, as if one were immortal; instead of reforming the intellectual by coercion, they were to wash him with "gentle breezes and mild rain."

This phrase had also been used in the Hundred Flowers campaign, but for a different purpose. It was the method to be used by the intellectuals in criticizing the cadres, not the reverse. The meaning of this phrase in practice was described by Ch'en I when he stated that in reforming another individual, one must "not hurt his feelings or deal blows to his soul. One must be patient and understanding."[7] As before, the intellectuals were divided into small study groups, but the discussions in these groups were to be conducted as informal chats rather than as confessions extorted by the cadres. If ideological "mistakes" were made in the course of a chat, the individual was not to be ostracized but was to remain part of the group and be treated in a comradely fashion. The Party's aim, as stated in the *People's Daily*, was that "by exchanging thoughts and helping one another, all people will naturally ... acquire an identical, definite understanding of right and wrong."[8]

The Party's call for a clear division between debate in academic and in political spheres was meant to confine the intellectuals' discussions to the academic realm, but it was not meant to confine the Party to the political realm. The Party, as in the past, sought to exert its

6 *KMJP*, 3 September 1961, 2.
7 Ibid.
8 Lin Kuo-chün, "Meetings of Immortals drive the intellectuals forward in self-remolding," *JMJP*, 16 May 1961, *SCMP*, 2.513, 11.

control over scholarship, particularly in nonscientific fields. Only academic discussion useful to the Party was allowed. Contradictory goals continued to characterize the Party's policy toward the intellectuals. It sought to foster intellectual and scientific endeavor while at the same time it maintained ideological control. Scholars were urged to look for the truth, but the truth could not be contrary to Mao's teaching or to the Party's current program. The printing of unofficial journals and wall posters and the formation of independent groups engaging in a spontaneous exchange of ideas, as in the spring in 1957, were not permitted.

The uniqueness of the relaxation of 1961–1962

With a few exceptions, most intellectuals and non-Party people were reluctant to participate because of the undefined nature of the new freedom and because of their past experience. They feared that the movement was designed to investigate their minds rather than to enrich culture and science. Pointing to the ambiguity between the line dividing debate in the political and in the academic spheres, several refused to express their own opinions. They claimed their views on academic questions would be construed as opinions on political issues. Still others excused themselves from the debate with the plea of insufficient knowledge.

Unlike the Hundred Flowers, when criticism came principally from the intellectual community and students, the criticism that was heard in 1961–62 came from intellectual-officials high in the Party hierarchy, principally in the Propaganda Department and the Peking Party Committee, the very organizations instrumental in implementing the relaxation. They used the more indirect Confucian style of criticism through literary and historical allusions rather than the more forthright Western style of the Hundred Flowers. Moreover, whereas in the spring of 1957 the "democratic" leaders and students challenged the one-party rule of the CCP, in 1961–62 the intellectual-officials did not attack the Party in which they had prominent positions. Rather, they subtly criticized Mao and his policies of mass mobilization, economic leaps forward, and thought reform campaigns. They also defended former Defense Minister P'eng Te-huai, whom Mao dismissed for criticizing the GLF in July 1959.

Yet the easier atmosphere of the early 1960s, increasing disillusion with the GLF, and concern over the capabilities of China's aging leader still do not fully explain why these intellectual-officials, who were well aware of the consequences of dissent, chose to criticize publicly. There is little proof for the charges made in the Cultural Revolution that Liu Shao-ch'i and Teng Hsiao-p'ing were the behind-the-scenes manipulators. They were linked more directly to the head of the Peking Party Committee, P'eng Chen, who had special jurisdication over intellectuals and the director and deputy director of the Party's Propaganda Department, Lu Ting-i and Chou Yang. Yet it is unlikely that these politically astute officials would have allowed the attack on Mao and his policies unless they had support from Liu and Teng, who could not explicitly criticize Mao themselves without shattering the façade of a coherent, unified leadership. Liu had, in fact, gone along with the GLF and had seconded Mao in implementing it. However, in his report in January 1962 at the Seven Thousand Cadres Conference, he expressed disillusion with the GLF's methods of revolutionary exhortation and episodic upheaval. Such methods had been appropriate to the guerrilla days, but now he condemned them as detrimental to building a modern, industrialized society. This view gave implicit sanction to the criticism of the intellectual-officials.

The Peking Party Committee intellectuals

In May 1961, P'eng Chen instructed his closest deputies in the Peking Party Committee to evaluate the GLF. Under the direction of Teng T'o, head of the Peking Party Committee Secretariat, about a dozen members of the committee gathered to study the Central Committee directives of the GLF. As a result of their deliberations, they not only presented P'eng Chen with a critique of the GLF but also burst forth with criticism, albeit oblique, of Mao, and a defense, similarly veiled, of P'eng Te-huai in the theater, newspapers, journals, films, lectures, and discussions in Peking. Whether P'eng Chen specifically called for such attacks is not clear, but it is obvious that they could not appear in his domain without his sanction or at least his tolerance. Given his past political orthodoxy, it is unlikely that he identified entirely with the intellectual-officials ideologically. Yet when P'eng read some of their articles, he was quoted as saying, "They are rich and colorful" in content and "highly welcome."[9]

9 Wu Tung-hui, "Destroy the black backstage manager of 'The three-family village,'" *KMJP*, 18 June 1967, *SCMP*, 3977, 14.

Teng T'o was the leader of the intellectual-officials associated with the Peking Party Committee. A journalist, historian, poet, and classicist, he set the intellectual standard of the group with his Marxist critique of the GLF, combined with the reassertion of Western liberal values of the May Fourth era and some of the traditional values of Confucianism, particularly a concern for the plight of the peasant. Between 1952 and 1957 he was editor-in-chief of the *People's Daily*, and from 1954 to 1960, president of the All-China Journalists Association. In 1957 he was dismissed as editor-in-chief of the *People's Daily*, perhaps because he, along with his patron P'eng Chen, had reluctantly gone along with Mao's Hundred Flowers and supposedly had refused to publicize Mao's ideas on the correct handling of internal contradictions. His old associate P'eng Chen then appointed him to the Peking Party Committee, where he established a theoretical journal called *Ch'ien-hsien* (Front line).

He worked closely with a vice-mayor of Peking, Wu Han, a major historian of the Ming dynasty, who represented a different intellectual strand. In the 1930s and 1940s, he was active in the democratic parties and had associated with Westernized academics such as Hu Shih and Feng Yu-lan. Another collaborator was the writer Liao Mo-sha, one of the luminaries of the Shanghai literary world of the 1930s, who was the director of the United Front Work Department of the Peking Party Committee and also in the Propaganda Department. These men came from different backgrounds but had a long personal association and had agreed on certain principles.

Their sharpest weapon was the *tsa-wen*, the short, subtle, satirical essay form that Lu Hsun had used so effectively against the Kuomintang and his ideological enemies in the 1930s and his followers had used in Yenan. Teng T'o, Wu Han, and Liao Mo-sha were masters of this form. Under the pen name Wu Nan-hsing, they published sixty-seven *tsa-wen*, called "Notes from a three-family village" in *Front Line*. Teng T'o also published his own series, "Evening talks at Yen-shan," in the *Peking Evening News* (*Pei-ching wan-pao*) and the *Peking Daily* (*Pei-ching jih-pao*).

What the bureaucratic leaders supposedly said behind closed doors they expressed allegorically, yet vividly, in the public arena. Because of their subtlety and sophistication, it is unlikely that they were fully appreciated by a wide audience. But it is likely that their indirect messages were understood by the political and intellectual elite cognizant of Party concerns. Using ancient characters and historical incidents, Teng T'o in particular obliquely criticized contemporary

people and events. On the surface his essays appeared to be mild
social and historical commentaries, but in reality they were devastating, though subtle, criticisms of Mao's leadership and policies. Like
Lu Hsun's *tsa-wen*, the essays were written in an Aesopian language
intended to be understood by a limited circle of like-minded intellectuals and leaders.

Several of the *tsa-wen* appeared to denounce the personality cult of
Mao. They pointed out that it was impossible for one man or even a
small group to understand everything and command everything. In
one of their essays, "A special treatment for amnesia," they implied
that Mao suffered from a form of mental disorder that led him to
irrational behavior and decisions. "People suffering from this disease
... often go back on their word and do not keep their promises. . . .
It will not only bring forgetfulness, but will gradually lead to
abnormal pleasure or anger ... easiness to lose one's temper and
finally insanity." The advice, obviously directed to Mao, was that
under such conditions "a person must promptly take a complete rest.
. . . If he insists on talking or doing anything, he will get into a lot of
trouble."[10]

Perhaps Teng T'o's most daring criticism of Mao was in "The royal
way and the tyrant's way." He contrasted the ancient historian Liu
Hsiang's definition of the royal way, which was "combining human
sentiments with law and morality," with the tyrant's way, which
"relied on authority and power, used violence and coercion, ordered
others about and robbed people by force or by tricks." In terms of
the present, he said, the royal way would be called following the mass
line, whereas the tyrant's way would be called "arrogant, subjective,
dogmatic, and arbitrary."[11]

As sharply as Teng questioned Mao's ability to rule, he attacked his
policy of the GLF. In "The theory of treasuring labor power," he
protested against the forced use of peasant labor for large-scale
construction projects. Once again he used the example of ancient
rulers to criticize the present one. He wrote, "Even as early as the
Spring and Autumn period and the Warring States, our great politicians already understood the meaning of caring for human labor.
The *Book of rites* states that the labor power of the people can be
requisitioned no more than three days a year." He concluded, "We
should draw new enlightenment from the experience of the ancients

10 Wu Nan-hsing, "Notes from a three-family village: A special treatment of amnesia,"
   Ch'ien-hsien (Front line), 14, 1962, *CB*, 792, 4.
11 Ma Nan-ts'un (Teng T'o), "The royal way and the tyrant's way," *Yen-shan yeh-hua*,
   4. 13–16.

and take care to do more in every way to treasure our labor power."[12]

In another essay, on the German philosopher Ernst Mach, he allusively criticized Mao's voluntarist view of development by lamenting the belief of Mach and his followers that they could accomplish whatever they wished. The result was that they ran up against the limitations of reality and in the end destroyed themselves. In an essay entitled "This year's spring festival," he directly referred to the food shortages caused by the GLF by pointing out that whereas traditional governments had guarded against these shortages, the present one had not fulfilled its responsibility to the people.

While attacking Mao and the GLF, he defended P'eng Te-huai. In obvious allusions to P'eng, several of his *tsa-wen* described courageous, incorruptible officials who had been accused unjustly of crimes for protesting against injustice. He described one, Li San-ts'ai, a high official of the Ming who, because he boldly exposed the crimes of the eunuchs at court, was dismissed from office. Li submitted memorial after memorial requesting a personal hearing from the emperor, but he was refused. Li then reportedly said, "Unable to contain myself, I take up 100 pieces of silk to point out my misery in all its detail,"[13] perhaps an allusion to Peng's own 80,000-word defense of himself, which it was rumored he was writing at the time. Teng published this essay on 29 March 1962 in the *Peking Evening News*. P'eng's defense was finally presented to the Party's Central Committee in June 1962.

However critical these *tsa-wen* were of Mao and the GLF, they generally conformed to the view of the bureaucratic leadership. Other *tsa-wen*, however, were not necessarily in conformity with the leadership. They asked for a degree of autonomy and a voice for scholars in political decision making that was not sanctioned by the leadership. They described Sung, Ming, and Ch'ing scholars, poets, artists, and advisors who were courageous and honest in criticizing harsh rulers no matter what the cost. Teng also praised traditional rulers who "welcome miscellaneous scholars," by whom he meant intellectuals with unorthodox approaches. "It would be a great loss to us if we now failed to acknowledge the general significance of the wide range of knowledge of 'miscellaneous scholars' for all kinds of leadership as well as for scientific research."[14]

Teng often cited the Tung-lin scholars in the late Ming dynasty as

12 Teng T'o, "Treasuring labor power," ibid., 1, 58.
13 Teng T'o, "In defense of Li San-ts'ai, ibid., 3, 150.
14 Teng T'o, "Is wisdom reliable?" ibid., 4, 17–19.

the paradigm of a group of intellectuals engaged in politics. In direct contradiction to Mao's disdain for learning in officials or for scholars advising on politics, Teng declared: "To be learned without being interested in politics is just as wrong as being politically inclined without being learned."[15] He concluded by asking why, if one's ancestors understood these truths, those who lived now could not understand and try to emulate them. He also admired the Tung-lin because they risked death to right the wrongs they saw in society. He printed a verse that depicted their courage:

> Do not think of them as mere intellectuals indulging in
>   empty talk
> Fresh were the bloodstains when the heads rolled
> Fighting the wicked men in power with abiding will
> The Tung-lin scholars were a stout-hearted generation.[16]

This was an epitaph that could also have been written later for Teng T'o and his associates.

Despite a relative silence after the establishment of the PRC in 1949 and an active role in attacking rightists in 1957, Wu Han suddenly began to write articles in 1959 about the upright Ming official Hai Jui. At Party meetings in April–May 1959, Mao had urged emulation of Hai Jui's criticism of bureaucratic misdeeds. The Chairman's secretary Hu Ch'iao-mu asked Wu Han as a Ming historian to write about him. But one of Wu Han's writings, a play which dealt with the dismissal of this famous magistrate from office, was later attacked as an indirect criticism of Mao's policies, the GLF, and the dismissal of P'eng Te-huai.

It focused on the plight of the Soochow peasants who complained to Hai Jui that their lands had been confiscated by local officials. Despite threats and bribes from local officials, Hai Jui demanded that illegally confiscated land be returned, that grievances be redressed, and that arbitrary acts be stopped in an effort to restore prosperity and stability to the area. He also ordered the death of a landlord's son because he had killed an elderly peasant. The local landlords and officials appealed to the emperor to spare the landlord's son and dismiss Hai Jui, which the emperor did. Though presented in a historical context, this play denounced policies that impoverished and disregarded the wishes of the peasants and could be interpreted as defending P'eng Te-huai's efforts to help the peasants. Although

15 Teng T'o, "A concern for all things," ibid., 2, 60–62.
16 Teng T'o, "Sing the praise of Lake T'ai," *KMJP*, 7 September 1960.

the play, staged in February 1961, received good reviews, it was suspended after a few performances.

The May Fourth writers associated with the Party's Propaganda Department

Views similar to those of the intellectual-officials in the Peking Party Committee were expressed by a group of writers, playwrights, literary critics, poets, and journalists who held high positions in the Party's propaganda bureaucracy. These groups had been closely associated since the 1930s in the long struggle to bring the Party to power. They had worked together in the leftist cultural and journalist community at different times in Japan, Shanghai, Yenan, Chungking, and Hong Kong. Within the group associated with the Propaganda Department were some of China's most famous May Fourth writers such as T'ien Han, Hsia Yen, Yang Han-sheng, Pa Chin, and Mao Tun. The Party leaders of this group were Chou Yang and a coterie of close associates formed in Yenan in the 1940s.

Although Chou Yang's main function since Mao's 1942 Yenan "Talks on literature and art" was to ensure ideological orthodoxy and carry out a series of relentless campaigns and purges, in the early 1960s he was a member of the group that questioned Mao's infallibility in directing China's development. He was a leader of the retreat from the GLF's educational revolution and the revival of intellectual and cultural endeavor. In his public statements, he sanctioned more creative, more diversified styles and less ideological subject matter. In talks before small meetings and to his associates, he encouraged a more Westernized approach to culture. In the Cultural Revolution, it was charged that he had expounded a liberal, bourgeois view all along, but in reality up until the early 1960s he had been unswerving in his implementation of Mao's cultural policies.

It could be that as the bureaucracy and Mao diverged after the GLF, Chou Yang, the quintessential Party organization man, went along with the bureaucracy and unquestioningly carried out its policies as previously he had carried out Mao's. But his diversion from Mao was more than factional or organizational. In addition to his disillusion with Mao's policies, he also diverged from the anti-intellectual, antiprofessional approach exhibited during the GLF. Though a cultural bureaucrat par excellence, he was also an urban, Westernized intellectual steeped in a tradition that included the great writers of nineteenth-century Europe. Although he was a leader in

the GLF movement to promote collectivized amateur writing inspired by native folk tales, he retained a conventional Westernized
view of literature and scholarship.

He and his colleagues in the early 1960s sought to lessen the effects
of the GLF on culture and reinvigorate China's intellectual life. At a
literary forum in 1961, Chou recommended a deliberate depoliticiza-
tion of culture as a way to lessen the strains caused by the GLF. To
advocate apolitical creativity in such a highly politicized society was a
significant political act, but one in conformity with the Party's efforts
to lessen the political zeal of the previous period.

Chou also downplayed class orientation as a criterion for judging
literature. With the exception of the reactionaries, literature should
appeal to all classes, not just to workers and peasants. A *People's
Daily* editorial "Serve the broadest masses of people," in celebration
of the twentieth anniversary of Mao's Yenan talks, explained that
because the times had changed since Yenan, it was also necessary to
change the culture so that it could serve a more sophisticated
audience.[17]

Although intellectuals were allowed to turn away from Marxism-
Leninism, they could not look outward as they had in the Hundred
Flowers because of the break with the Soviet Union and alienation
from the West. Thus, they revived plays and films written in the
relatively free Shanghai of the 1920s and 1930s. One play that was
revived was "The death of Taiping general Li Hsiu-ch'eng," by Yang
Han-sheng, a vice-chairman and Party secretary of the All-China
Federation of Literary and Art Circles. It had first been performed in
1937 as a product of national defense literature, the cultural policy of
the united front, and had been officially endorsed by the Party at that
time. It was revived in 1956 and restaged in February 1963. In the
1930s the play advocated class collaboration against the common
enemy, but in the context of the early 1960s it appeared to symbolize
the conflict between P'eng Te-huai and Mao. Li was depicted as a
courageous figure who dared to risk his own life to challenge the
leader of the Taipings, Hung Hsiu-ch'üan, who was portrayed as unwilling to listen to the advice of this associates, adhering stubbornly
to a policy which led to the defeat of the Taipings.

The characters in the novels and stories of the 1930s re-created on
the screen and in the theater in the early 1960s were questioning,
agonized, ambivalent people caught in the midst of revolution and

17 *JMJP*, 13 May 1962.

uncertain which way to turn. It was as if they were presented in opposition to the idealized heroes and villains of the GLF literature which, like traditional Chinese literature, taught values and norms through the models of fictitious heroes and villains.

A variation of these 1930s characters was the "middle character" depicted in stories in the late 1950s and early 1960s. These also were ambiguous protagonists caught between the old society and the new, whose contradictions were more within themselves than between them and other classes. They were the topic of a conference held in Dairen in August 1962, presided over by Chou Yang and discussed by Chou's chief lieutenant, Shao Ch'üan-lin. Though originally a short story writer, Shao was known primarily as a powerful literary bureaucrat. After 1949 he rapidly made a name for himself as a leader of the thought reform campaigns. Yet at the Dairen Conference he asserted that the "middle character" represented the ordinary Chinese peasant, who was not the perfect hero the Party portrayed but a person in an intermediate stage between "backward" and "advanced" thinking, and with both positive and negative elements within himself. Instead of depicting heroic and villainous extremes, he urged writers to portray the vast majority of people, who were as yet uncommitted to the revolution.

Shao's approach struck directly at the Party's basic political and ideological teachings. He exposed the differences between the official view of reality and what actually existed, and implied that millions of Chinese workers and peasants, supposedly the bulwark of the revolution, were not the exemplary revolutionaries officially pictured. In reality, those who wavered between the "progressive" and "backward" paths were not just a small number of bourgeois and intellectuals, as the Party claimed, but the vast majority of the population.

Because writers had been forced to use ideological stereotypes rather than write with tough-minded realism, Shao lamented that model people had been "described to an inordinate degree in the GLF," which meant that "we lose touch with reality."[18] The peasants' latent communist motivation had not emerged in the GLF as Mao and the Party had anticipated. The overestimation of the ideological readiness of the peasants for revolution, Shao believed, had contributed to the failure of the GLF.

Critics of Mao's policies had thus gone beyond the criticism sanctioned by their political backers. Liu and the bureaucracy may

18 *Wen-i pao*, 8/9 (1964), 15–18.

have wanted criticism of the GLF, mass mobilization, and economic irrationalities. They even desired more intellectual and cultural "blooming" and a loosening of ideological restraints on scholarship and creative work to help resolve some of the problems brought on by the GLF. But in the charges later hurled against the Party's bureaucratic leaders in the Cultural Revolution, there is no evidence that they were willing to give up political and ideological control over scholarship – particularly humanistic scholarship of the type Teng T'o and Wu Han were requesting. Furthermore, Liu and the bureaucracy were as unwilling as Mao to allow intellectuals a voice in policy-making or public criticism of their policies through regular procedures. Nor were they willing to allow questioning about the basic commitment of peasants and workers to the revolution. That the leadership encouraged specific criticisms and a relative relaxation of control did not mean it would tolerate pluralism, diffusion of its power, or doubts about its mass support.

RESISTANCE TO MAO'S IDEOLOGICAL CLASS STRUGGLE

At the Tenth Plenum, held in September 1962, Mao announced a shift from the relative relaxation of the early 1960s to increased control over intellectual activity. He called for ideological class struggle, which was an implicit summons for an attack on his critics. He expressed concern that public opinion, greatly influenced by ideas and even by works of fiction, could overthrow political power, a reflection of his increasing obsession with ideological consciousness. The Tenth Plenum marked the beginning of Mao's effort to stop criticism of his policies, halt the slowing down of revolutionary momentum, and implement a cultural revolution. He sought to do this first through the Party bureaucracy.

In academic circles, however, Mao's call for ideological class struggle activated a new form of dissidence. Party as well as non-Party intellectuals engaged in debates over class struggle in which the underlying ideological basis of Mao's thought was questioned. Although the dissidence took different forms, a unifying theme was the desire for less rather than more polarization – a diminution rather than intensification of class struggle and a reconciliation rather than accentuation of the differences in Chinese society.

A number of eminent scholars spoke of the need to unite the country to strive toward goals shared by all classes of society. They sought to find in Chinese tradition ethical and aesthetic values relevant not merely to certain times and certain classes but to all times and all classes. By looking for the middle ground in their respective fields – history, philosophy, and aesthetics – their debates implicitly subverted Mao's call for ideological class struggle. The Socialist Education movement launched in the countryside in 1963 to halt the spontaneous trend toward individual farming did not spread into the intellectual community.

How then could divergent ideas be expressed in the period when Mao called for ideological struggle and tighter control over the intellectual community? Those with responsibility for tightening up, the Propaganda Department and the Peking Party Committee, were the very organizations that had presided over the relaxation of the 1960s. Verbally they went along with Mao's demand for renewed ideological class struggle, but actually they were reluctant to embark on a new campaign for fear it would lead to disruptions like those of the GLF. Disillusion with Mao's previous policy left the leadership less responsive to his new demands. Furthermore, since their baili-wicks were the centers of dissidence, they were not anxious to pursue a campaign that would ultimately redound on them.

Also, as Mao later charged, a growing process of bureaucratization had occured in the various cultural hierarchies, as is inevitable in any totalitarian organization after the end of the revolutionary phase. The cultural officials were entrenched, held together by close personal ties developed in the freer atmosphere of Shanghai in the 1930s and the civil war of the 1940s. They also were concerned with the erosion of revolutionary spirit, but exhausted and embittered by previous campaigns, they were reluctant to launch again the nationwide, inten-sive thought reform campaigns they had engineered in the past. Hence, though their rhetoric called for class struggle, their tone was moderate. They may not have agreed with some of the intellectuals whose views were as opposed to theirs and Liu Shao-ch'i's as to Mao's, but they permitted some genuine ideological debates to take place. The result was a watering down of Mao's demand for a class struggle. In the aftermath of the GLF, cultural officials as well as intellectuals shared a desire for a period of unity rather than of conflict.

These officials played a major role in the return of China's univer-sities to conventional educational practices after the GLF. The Party Secretariat put Chou Yang in charge of selecting materials for the liberal arts courses in the universities. He sought to reverse the GLF stress on politics, Mao Tse-tung Thought, and mass research and to reintroduce professional and academically oriented education to help in China's modernization. He pointed out: "If we train all students to be political activists, then we will have too many political activists. These will become empty-headed politicians without professional knowledge."[19] As part of the move to raise academic standards, the salaries of the older Western-trained professors were increased considerably over the younger teachers spawned in the GLF. Chou Yang also appointed a number of outstanding Western-trained scholars to head the committees that would select the liberal arts texts to replace the materials prepared by the younger teachers and students in the GLF. These intellectuals also dominated the major academic journals as the May Fourth writers dominated the literary journals. In their pages raged intellectual debates that ultimately touched on the fundamental ideological questions facing China's leadership.

Another aspect of the retreat from the revolutionary practices and severe disruption of the GLF was a more positive view of Confucianism because it embodied universal and enduring moral values. This effort to reassess Confucianism in universal terms had begun during the Hundred Flowers. Resurrected in the aftermath of the GLF, it had gained a certain momentum by 1963. Scholars couched their reevaluation in Marxist terminology, much as the nineteenth-century Chinese literati couched their introduction of Western thought in orthodox Confucian doctrine. The philosopher Feng Yu-lan, for example, pointed to a small portion of early Marxism, *The German ideology*, as the authority for his view of the universality of Confucianism. Although Feng presented Confucius as representing the emerging new landlord class as China moved from a slaveholding to a feudal society, Confucianism, Feng believed, had meaning for all nonruling classes – peasants, artisans, merchants – as well as for the landlords. In the struggle with the slave masters and the nobility, it was necessary for the landlords to endow their ideology with a "universal pattern."[20] Feng claimed that the Confucian concept of *jen*, benevolence or human kindness, has a class character, but also embodies a universal ethic for all classes because the landlords used it to gain broad support.

19 "A Collection of Chou Yang's counter-revolutionary revisionist speeches," *SCMM*, 648, 11, 15.
20 Feng Yu-lan, "Criticism and self-criticism in discussion about Confucianism," *Che-hsueh yen-chiu* (Philosophical research), 1963. 6 in IASP, *Chinese Studies in History and Philosophy* 1. 4 (Summer 1968), 84.

Another impetus to a more positive evaluation of Confucianism was a conference convened in November 1962, just a month after Mao's Tenth Plenum speech. Attended by noted scholars from all over China, it became a platform for a variety of non-Marxist interpretations of Chinese history. Among the most controversial was the view of Liu Chieh of Chungshan University in Canton that China's history had a different pattern than that of the West. Whereas class struggle may have governed Western historical development and may explain contemporary events, it had not governed China's development. Because the theory of class struggle was formulated in modern times by Marx and Engels, Liu insisted that the thinkers of ancient times could not have understood this concept. "We must not improperly impose on the ancients the problems of our times."[21]

In addition to challenging the Marxist class view of history, a number of historians questioned the Maoist view that peasant rebellions were revolutionary movements in Chinese history. Some argued in strictly Marxist terms that the peasantry was a conservative force and did not desire a new order but wanted only wealth and power like those of the upper classes. Although their arguments were couched in historical terms and were filled with Marxist jargon, they, like those who upheld the concept of the "middle character," contested the Maoist glorification of the peasant as a revolutionary and presented another form of criticism of the GLF. They argued that political elites as well as peasants made history and warned against exaggerating the role of peasant rebellion. Though their criticism was supported in part by the official Marxist denigration of the peasant's revolutionary potential, it was also influenced by the Confucian tradition of concern for the peasants and by the Western academic tradition of letting historical facts determine analysis. These facts had shown, they said, that peasant rebellions against the ruling class were spontaneous, improvised actions against repression, not an organized revolutionary movement.

For a number of years and in discussions in 1963, the chairman of the Peking University history department, Chien Po-tsan, presented the concept that came to be called the concession theory. It implicitly questioned revolution as the impetus for improving the lot of the Chinese peasant. After a dynasty was overthrown, the new unifying dynasty temporarily relaxed its suppression of the peasants. It offered concessions to them, such as reducing taxes, parceling out small plots

21 IASP, *Chinese Studies in Philosophy* (Fall–Winter 1972–73), 18.

of land, and opening up new land. These actions were not revolutionary; on the contrary, they prevented revolution by contributing to the peasant's welfare. Therefore, it was class reconciliation rather than class struggle that improved the peasants' lives.

Feng Yu-lan, in line with his view of the common interest between classes, also pointed out: "Ruling class thinkers, for the sake of the long-range interest of their own class, often advocated that some concessions be made to the interests of the ruled classes in order to diminish the latter's opposition."[22] Peasant discontent with the threat of insurrection gave an impulse to the working together of opposing classes of society, which in turn advanced society. The amelioration, not the intensification, of class struggle was regarded as the motivating force of history and as the impetus to the peasants' betterment.

A number of economists in the Economics Institute of the Chinese Academy of Sciences also questioned Mao's effort to intensify class struggle in the economic sphere in the Socialist Education movement. The most prominent of these was Sun Yeh-fang, director of the Economics Institute. A Party member since the 1920s, he had studied in the Soviet Union and had visited Moscow again in the early 1960s, at the time the Liberman economic reforms were being dicussed. Upon his return, he suggested similar reforms such as giving more autonomy to the operation of an enterprise and allowing a portion of the profit to remain with the enterprise to be used as a bonus to stimulate increased production and better management. As scientific knowhow was to replace mass movements, profit rather than political consciousness was to be the determinant for investment and development. Sun saw profit as the most sensitive indicator of technological feasibility and competent management. In the rural economy, he favored restoration of the individual family economy and prescribed output targets to each peasant household. He and his colleagues did not question the principle of socialist planning or the regulatory role of the state, but they pointed out that disregard of material incentives was economically irrational and harmful.

More directly critical of Mao's policies was Sun's characterization of the commune as a "mistake of rash and reckless advance." In a talk to a cadre training class, he noted: "We want to reach heaven in one step and so think the bigger [the project] the better, and as a result we have encouraged blind direction. . . . We have forgotten productivity

22 Feng Yu-lan, "Criticism and self-criticism," 86–87.

and over-exaggerated man's subjective initiative."[23] He restated the traditional Marxist view that revolution depends on the increase of production and technological progress. Only when productivity is developed to a high degree is it possible to put into effect the principle of distribution according to everyone's needs. Although Liu Shao-ch'i was accused in the Cultural Revolution of parroting Sun's ideas, Liu had not called for "profits in command" as charged, and his material incentives policies were relatively narrow in comparison with those of the 1st Five-Year Plan.

Nevertheless, the criticisms and suggestions made by Sun as well as by other academic and cultural figures played a role in creating the climate of opinion for the broad, far-reaching economic, educational, and cultural shift away from the policies of the GLF. They also provoked Mao to enlist another group of intellectuals to refute their criticisms and propose different solutions.

THE RADICAL INTELLECTUALS

As Mao's old comrades and the Party bureaucrats questioned his leadership after the GLF, Mao became increasingly suspicious of them and turned more and more to a handful of trusted intimates, particularly his wife, Chiang Ch'ing; his former secretary-ghostwriter Ch'en Po-ta; and K'ang Sheng, who had a long association with the Party's security apparatus. They, in turn, developed close contacts in the early 1960s with a group of young radical intellectuals who played a conspicuous role in condemning the views of the older, established intellectuals. Comprising two distinct but overlapping groups from the philosophy and social sciences department of the Chinese Academy of Sciences and the Shanghai Party Committee's Propaganda Department, they too were skilled in intellectual debate. Though academically trained, they differed from the senior intellectuals in that they had a more Marxist-oriented education and were lower in the academic hierarchy. They also had less experience in organization and administration. Their opposition to the senior intellectuals was generational, personal, and opportunistic, as well as ideological.

Chang Ch'un-ch'iao was the elder of this group. He was born in

23 Kung Wen-sheng, "Sun Yeh-fang's theory is a revisionist fallacy," *JMJP*, 8 August 1966, *SCMP*, 3766, 17.

1910 into an intellectual family. Like his intellectual rivals, he was active in left-wing literary circles in Shanghai in the 1930s and did propaganda work in the border areas in the 1940s. It was not until after 1949, however, that he began to achieve important positions. In the GLF, he was active in articulating Mao's policies, and shortly after he was made a member of the Shanghai Party Committee and of its standing committee. His contact with high Party officials came in 1963–64 when K'o Ch'ing-shih, a Politburo member, First Secretary of the Shanghai Party Committee and confidant of Mao, gave Mao's wife, Chiang Ch'ing, the opportunity she was denied in Peking by the Party Propaganda Committee and the Peking Party Committee: to reform the Peking-style opera. The Shanghai Propaganda Department, particularly Chang and his younger colleague Yao Wen-yuan, was mobilized to help her.

Yao had first made a name for himself by allying with the literary bureaucrats around Chou Yang in the Propaganda Department.[24] Although he was active in the campaigns against Hu Feng, Ai Ch'ing, Ting Ling, and Feng Hsueh-feng and the rightists, he was particularly conspicuous in the late 1950s for his attacks on the literary theorist Pa Jen for his view that there were elements of human nature common to all people, and Pa Chin, whom he labeled a "reactionary" shortly after his works had been reprinted in 1958. He came to be known as "the stick," one who suppressed writers by calling them names. His criticisms so infuriated the older May Fourth writers that Chou Yang and his assistant Lin Mo-han personally intervened to stop his attacks on them.

Having been rebuffed by the cultural bureaucracy, Yao, Chang, and Chiang Ch'ing joined together as natural allies. Their link with a group of young philosophers and historians associated with the philosophy and social sciences department of the Chinese Academy of Sciences – the leading ones being Kuan Feng, Ch'i Pen-yü, Lin Yü-shih, and Lin Chieh – added substantial intellectual substance to their challenge to the views of the senior intellectuals.

Chang had been associated with a few of them, at least as early as the GLF, when he and the philosopher Kuan Feng and another colleague Wu Ch'uan-chi wrote articles calling for restrictions on material incentives in the manner of war communism and the Paris Commune. In fact, Chang's article pushing Mao's GLF views supposedly caught Mao's attention. It was published in *People's Daily*

24 See Lars Ragvald, *Yao Wen-yuan as a literary critic and theorist.*

with an editorial note by Mao that did not fully endorse its ideas, but urged readers to use it as a starting point for discussion.[25]

The articles and speeches of the radical intellectuals in the early 1960s were on a variety of subjects, but a common denominator was that they drew more from the radical aspects of Mao's thought than from traditional Marxism. They continued to expound Mao's beliefs as articulated during the GLF, but now expressed in ideological and political rather than economic terms. Like their mentor, they insisted that socialist transformation of the economy did not automatically transform bourgeois ideology. It was necessary to wage ideological class struggle against the bourgeois superstructure that survived and exerted influence, even though its means of production had been eliminated. The subjective will that had been aroused to overcome the forces of nature and economic limitations in the GLF was now to be aroused against bourgeois and revisionist ideological forces. Equating the subjective will with revolutionary zeal, they sought to mobilize the subjective will of the masses against the prevailing bourgeois superstructure and particularly against the senior intellectuals.

The arguments, rhetoric, and symbols used in the 1963–64 debates with the senior intellectuals provided the ideological underpinnings for the Cultural Revolution. In their protest against the existing intellectual and bureaucratic establishment, they were China's New Left. Their arguments not only expressed their own ideological disagreements and personal rivalries, but also reflected genuine socioeconomic grievances of a segment of the population, particularly educated youth, against the lack of mobility in the hierarchy and the inequalities between the well-trained older and the less well-trained younger.

Their contention with famous intellectuals gave them some support among radical intellectuals and students and gained them prominence and notoriety that could be used by political leaders seeking to undermine the establishment. To what extent Mao instigated this group and to what extent they instigated him is not yet clear. In the pre-Cultural Revolution period, Mao and his confidants Chiang Ch'ing, Ch'en Po-ta, K'ang Sheng, and K'o Ch'ing-shih often suggested the general themes and symbols, but they did not directly supervise their writing until the start of the Cultural Revolution – and even then, the radical intellectuals could not be fully controlled.

25 *JMJP*, 13 October 1958. See also Parris Chang, *Radicals and radical ideology in China's Cultural Revolution*, 81.

In contrast to the senior intellectuals, the radicals took up Mao's call for ideological class struggle quickly and energetically after the Tenth Plenum speech. Though the senior intellectuals dominated the editorial boards of the scholarly journals, the radicals were able to publish in them. Their general criticism of the senior scholars was that they had spread the idea that classes had common interests, when in reality there was only class struggle. But their intellectual and ideological disagreements with the senior intellectuals in 1963–64 were not as polarized as they would become in the Cultural Revolution. Positions had not hardened enough to cause an irrevocable split between Mao and the Party bureaucracy, or between them and the senior intellectuals. Although the radicals echoed Mao's call for class struggle, their arguments in 1963–64 were not the simplified clichés that they were to become. They used a wide range of references and acknowledged the complexities of the questions. They engaged in lively exchanges and debated on an academic level and, for the most part, in a nonbelligerent, balanced manner. At this point they were not yet in opposition to the Propaganda Department, but constituted a faction within the cultural organization.

Among the younger intellectuals at the philosophy and social sciences department, the philosopher Kuan Feng was perhaps the best known. Since the early 1950s he had written a number of erudite articles on ancient Chinese philosophers such as Chuang-tzu, Hsun-tzu, and Confucius. Several were written in collaboration with two other colleagues, Lin Yü-shih and Lin Chieh. He became prominent in the late 1950s and early 1960s for his criticism of Feng Yu-lan for disregarding class characteristics and promoting supraclass interpretations of philosophical concepts. His attack on such a well-known philosopher may have been motivated partly by a desire for fame, but it was also consistent with his previous views that stressed in a scholarly fashion the class character of philosophical and social theory. Kuan and one associate asserted that class struggle and development were inseparable: "The history of objective civilized society is a history of class struggle."[26] In their rebuttal of Chien Po-tsan's view that peasant uprisings were spontaneous acts against oppressors, they asserted that to deny that uprisings against landlords were against feudalism was to deny the revolutionary character of the peasants. In an article published a bit later, the radical historians

---

26 Kuan Feng and Lin Yü-shih, "Some problems of class analysis in the study of the history of philosophy," *Che-hsueh yen-chiu* (Philosophical research), 6 (1963) in IASP, *Chinese Studies in History and Philosophy*, 1. 4 (Summer 1968), 66.

Ch'i Pen-yü and Lin Chieh insisted that it was not concessions to the peasants, as Chien claimed, but the peasants' "revolutionary struggles against the landlord class [that] have impelled historical development."[27]

With this view of history, the authors concluded, "It is necessary to adhere firmly to the theory of class struggle and to wage a tit-for-tat struggle against the class enemy."[28] They charged that scholars like Chien Po-tsan not only opposed using class struggle to interpret history, but opposed using historical research to serve present-day politics. This rebuttal presaged the Cultural Revolution and more specifically the attack on intellectuals who refused to obey Mao's summons to struggle, whether it be in the context of one's research or against one's colleagues.

The radical intellectuals also used historical figures as analogies to criticize current leaders. Ch'i Pen-yü used the character Li Hsiu-ch'eng, the last general of the Taipings, in a way diametrically opposed to his use by Yang Han-sheng in his play. Whereas Yang had depicted Li as a courageous figure challenging an arbitrary leader, Ch'i depicted him as one who had abandoned the revolutionary struggle and betrayed its leader. Given the current effort to rehabilitate P'eng Te-huai and criticize the GLF, Ch'i's portrayal could be analogous both to P'eng's criticism of Mao and to Liu's and the Party leaders' subsequent rejection of Maoist policies. Ch'i did not deny that Li had taken part in a revolutionary struggle, "but his participation and his position as a commander could not negate the facts about his surrender and desertion at the last minute." We must "despise those who deserted their revolutionary cause under adverse conditions." The desertion was not just a shortcoming or a mistake, but counterrevolutionary. Li therefore cannot be pardoned, because "the foremost question about revolution is to distinguish between friend and foe."[29] Ch'i argued against any tolerance of critics of revolutionary policies.

Although the radical intellectuals criticized prominent scholars such as Feng Yu-lan and Chien Po-tsan, they did not publicly attack those well connected to the Peking Party Committee or the Party Propaganda Department. Some of Wu Han's ideas on history were

27 Ch'i Pen-yü and Lin Chieh, "Comrade Chien Po-tsan's outlook on history should be criticized," *Hung-ch'i* (24 March 1966), 19–30, JPRS, 35, 137.
28 Ibid.
29 Ch'i Pen-yü, "Comment on Li Hsiu-ch'eng's autobiography," *LSYC*, reprinted as "How should we look at the surrender of Li Hsiu-ch'eng?" *JMJP* and *KMJP*, 23 August 1963; also in *Pei-ching ta-kung pao*, JPRS, 26, 631. 13–14, 15.

criticized, but no public mention was made of his *tsa-wen* or his use of the Hai Jui figure. In 1964, Ch'i Pen-yü, Kuan Feng, and Lin Chieh wrote criticisms of Wu Han's play, but their articles were blocked from publication by the Peking Party Committee and the Propaganda Department. It was only when the Peking intellectual-officials and their political backers were about to be overthrown that these criticisms were published in April 1966.

It was charged in the Cultural Revolution that there was a deliberate effort to keep these debates within a strict historical and philosophical context in order to prevent attacks on specific individuals and specific policies. Consequently, the debates had the appearance of academic discussions, rather than of the surrogate political and ideological struggles they were. Both sides, even the radicals, cited a range of Western as well as Chinese historical sources and acknowledged complexities and qualifications. Their arguments were to be turned into slogans in the Cultural Revolution, but in the period before, they were seemingly scholarly and knowledgeable.

The reform of Peking Opera

The other flank of the radical attack on the cultural establishment was the effort to reform Peking Opera. It is not surprising that Chiang Ch'ing should take the lead in this endeavor, because that was the area of her own experience.[30] Although she regarded herself as an intellectual, her formal education was not extensive. She graduated from junior high school and studied at the Shantung Experimental Drama Academy. In the early 1930s she went to Shanghai, where she played bit parts in low-grade films. At that time the May Fourth writers T'ien Han, Hsia Yen, and Yang Han-sheng, who were later to become the leaders of theater and screen in the PRC, were among the major screen writers and film directors in left-wing circles. Unappreciative of her dramatic talents, they refused to give her important parts, apparently instilling in her a hostility toward them that she was later to avenge during the Cultural Revolution.

When the Japanese bombed Shanghai in 1938, she, along with many Shanghai intellectuals and students, made her way to Yenan. There she was befriended by K'ang Sheng, who came from her county of Chu-ch'eng, in Shantung. He helped her get a position in the Lu Hsun Academy of Arts. She also married Mao after his

---

30 See Roxane Witke, *Comrade Chiang Ch'ing.*

divorce from his third wife. Because of the protests of some members of the Party hierarchy, she was made to promise that she would not engage in political activities in the early years of the PRC. Her old "enemies" from Shanghai moved into powerful positions in the cultural sphere, while her role and contacts were limited to membership in the Film Guidance Committee of the Ministry of Culture, which censored films.

She was relatively inactive until the early 1960s, when the indirect criticisms of Mao and the GLF activated her. She claimed she had brought these criticisms to Mao's attention. She has said of her role at this time, "In the field of education and culture, I was a roving sentinel. . . . My job is to go over some periodicals and newspapers and present to the Chairman . . . things . . . which are worthy of attention."[31] She also reviewed more than a hundred plays and had K'ang Sheng transmit to her old adversary Hsia Yen, the head of the theater in the PRC, her views that the bulk of recently performed plays were bad and that Wu Han's *Hai Jui dismissed from office* should be withdrawn. Hsia appears to have paid little heed. Although Wu Han's play was banned, traditional, historical, and ghost plays continued to be performed. Again in December 1962, she criticized the theatrical repertoire and called this time for the banning of ghost plays. But although ghost plays subsequently were banned, traditional and historical plays continued to be staged.

With such resistance from the propaganda bureaucracy, Chiang Ch'ing turned her attack on Peking Opera. This dominant form of the traditional Chinese theater is called opera because it combines singing, acting, mime, recitation, and acrobatics. Its stereotyped characters and plots, which dramatize the confrontation between good and evil, were an effective medium for communicating ideological teachings and moral values to the illiterate masses, as well as to the cultural elite. Chiang Ch'ing sought to transform the traditional relationships into class struggle confrontations between worker, peasant, and soldier heroes and landlord and bourgeois villains.

In contrast to stories portraying "middle characters," her operas projected a world of heroes and heroines with no doubts, weaknesses, sorrows, or disorders, thoroughly infused with ideological goals, carrying out superhuman feats for the revolution. Her effort to reform China's traditional opera dispensed with its content but used

31 Chiang Ch'ing, "Do new services for the people," *Tung fang hung* (The east is red), 3 June 1967, *SCMP–S*, 192, 7.

its formalized techniques and styles, combined with Chinese folk dances and revolutionary songs. She repudiated Western culture but injected the most banal, conventional Soviet-style dance, music, and song. These devices, together with the content of class struggle, military conflict, and heroic characters for emulation, presaged the official culture that would dominate the Cultural Revolution.

She had Mao's support in this effort. Since Yenan he had been concerned with transforming traditional opera, but it had proved resistant to change. Even during the GLF, when most of the creative arts depicted contemporary class struggle, Peking Opera troupes continued to perform the traditional repertoire. In the early 1960s, Peking Opera, as well as regional operas, was flourishing. In November 1963, Mao lashed out at traditional opera not only because it was resistant to change but also because it was being used to criticize him. He also attacked the cultural officials responsible for staging the operas: "The Ministry of Culture cares little about culture. Operas abound with feudal emperors, kings, generals, ministers, scholars, and beautiful women, but the Ministry of Culture doesn't care a bit."

In another speech at about the same time, he called for immediate action on this matter: "In the field of culture, particularly in the sphere of drama, feudal and backward things predominate while socialist things are negligible.... Since the Ministry of Culture is in charge of cultural matters, it should pay attention to problems arising from this respect, conduct investigations, and put things right in real earnest. If nothing is done, the Ministry of Culture should be changed into the Ministry of Emperors, Kings, Generals, Ministers, Scholars, and Beauties or the Ministry of Foreign Things and the Dead." Mao's words also signaled the rhetoric of the Cultural Revolution. Yet he still left open an opportunity for change by adding, "If things are righted, no change of name will be made."[32]

With Mao's imprimatur, Chiang Ch'ing embarked on her program to produce model revolutionary operas. The purposes of the program were stated at the East China Drama Festival from 25 December 1963 through 26 January 1964 under the auspices of the Shanghai Propaganda Department. K'o Ch'ing-shih opened the festival by restating publicly Mao's directive of the previous month and decrying the influence on the masses of "the unhealthy bourgeois atmosphere and reactionary, erratic, superstitious plays." By contrast, "socialist

---

32 "Chairman Mao's important instructions on literature and art since the publication of 'Talks at the Yenan Forum on Literature and Art' (1942–1967)," Wen-i hung-ch'i (Red flag of literature and art), 30 May 1967, SCMP, 4000, 23.

literature and art are ideological weapons to educate and rally the people and criticize and destroy the enemy."[33] New model revolutionary operas were to perform that function.

The cultural establishment responded sluggishly to Mao's pressure and Chiang Ch'ing's reform efforts. But to depict the controversy over this issue as a two-line ideological struggle, as it would be described in the Cultural Revolution, is not exactly accurate. The cultural establishment, like Chiang Ch'ing and her associates, also advocated reform, but it tried to reconcile reform with its own bureaucratic imperatives. Still, although this was not yet a direct confrontation between two explicitly opposed lines, it did not mean that there was no conflict between the two groups. The fact that Chiang Ch'ing was only listed as a speaker in the discussions on opera reform and that there was no record of her speeches in the press at this time suggests, as she later charged, that the bureaucracy refused to give her media coverage.

Although some cultural officials were somewhat reluctant to reform Peking Opera, conflict between her and the bureaucracy was not so much over the need to reform as over who would do the reforming. It was more a factional than an ideological struggle. The rebuffs given her by the cultural officials were not so much because they were unwilling to go along with Mao's demand for opera reform as because they resented her interference in their domain. Only when these officials were purged in the Cultural Revolution was she given a free hand to revolutionize the opera and turn it into China's main cultural fare.

PARTY RECTIFICATION, 1964–1965

Since Mao's call for ideological class struggle and suggestions for opera reform were being echoed in the media and at meetings but not being carried out in fact, in late 1963 and 1964 he went beyond criticism of specific art forms such as opera and fiction to attack the cultural bureaucracy itself. On 12 December 1963 he declared, "Problems abound in all forms of art.... In many departments very little has been achieved so far in socialist transformation. The 'dead' still dominate.... The social and economic base has changed, but the arts as part of the superstructure which serve this base, still remain a serious problem. Hence we should proceed with investigation and

33 Editorial, *CFJP*, 25 December 1963, 3.

study and attend to this matter in earnest. Isn't it absurd that many Communists are enthusiastic about promoting feudal and capitalist art, but not socialist art?"[34] The following day he expressed even harsher criticism in his 13 December instruction to the Central Committee, in which he charged some members with being "conservative, arrogant, and complacent."[35] He blamed this on the fact that they talked only of their achievements, but did not admit their shortcomings or dealt with them superficially.

The extreme anti-intellectualism of the Cultural Revolution was foreshadowed in his February 1964 speech at the Spring Festival on Education: "Throughout history, very few of those who came in first in the imperial examinations have achieved great fame." He pointed out that the only two emperors of the Ming who did well were barely literate. He disparaged the role of intellectuals in China's development. "In the Chia-ch'ing reign [1522–67], when the intellectuals had power, things were in a bad state, the country was in disorder. . . . It is evident that to read too many books is harmful."[36] He ordered that "actors, poets, dramatists, and writers" be "driven out of the cities" and government offices. They should periodically go down in groups to the villages and factories. He even threatened harsh sanctions. "Only when they go down will they be fed."[37]

The cultural officials either did not understand, misinterpreted, or chose to ignore Mao's statements. They may have felt sure enough of their bureaucratic patronage to pay lip service to Mao's views but not actually carry them out except in a perfunctory manner. They did, as Mao asked, send groups of intellectuals, cultural cadres, and students to the countryside and factories. However, they disregarded his instructions of December 1963 to implement an "ideological transformation" in their domain and investigate their own departments "in earnest."

Implicitly rejecting Mao's major criticism of them for obstructing the revolution, they accepted his lesser charge of not carrying out his policies energetically enough. Chou Yang, at a meeting convened in early January 1964, conceded "failure on some occasions to exercise a tight enough grip on work" and "failure to make enough effort in

34 Mao Tse-tung, "Comment on comrade K'o Ch'ing-shih's report," *Long live Mao Tse-tung Thought*, in *CB*, 901, 41.
35 Mao Tse-tung, "Instruction of the Central Committee on strengthening of learning from each other and overcoming conservatism, arrogance, and complacency," *Long Live Mao Tse-tung Thought*, in *CB*, 892, 15.
36 Schram, *Mao Tse-tung unrehearsed*, 204.
37 Ibid., 207.

cultivating . . . the new things of socialism."[38] But this criticism of his department and colleagues was halfhearted. His resistance to Mao's demand for ideological struggle may have been bolstered by the knowledge that Liu Shao-ch'i, shortly after Mao's 1963 announcements, enunciated a view of the superstructure diametrically opposed to Mao's. Whereas Mao believed the superstructure lagged behind changes in the economic base, Liu was reported to have said that "work in the superstructure corresponds to the economic base these days."[39] Chou had official justification for his weak response to Mao's summons to transform the cultural arena.

With the cultural bureaucracy sidestepping his orders, Mao on 27 June 1964 issued a more emphatic and accusatory directive. Again his anger was directed not so much at the intellectuals engaged in these debates as at the cultural officials who permitted the debates to take place. "In the last fifteen years, these associations, most of their publications (it is said a few are good), and by and large the people in them (that is not everybody) have not carried out the policies of the Party. They have acted as high and mighty bureaucrats, have not gone to the workers, peasants, and soldiers and have not reflected the socialist revolution and socialist construction. In recent years they have slid right down to the brink of revisionism. Unless they remold themselves in real earnest at some future date, they are bound to become groups like the Hungarian Petöfi Club."[40]

But the rectification they launched in the summer of 1964 was not due only to Mao's pressure; it also expressed their own concern with the deterioration of ideological discipline. While some of the senior intellectuals continued to press for relaxation, the bureaucracy sought to tighten controls. They had allowed the intellectuals to criticize for practical reasons, not because they were advocates of intellectual freedom. Since economic recovery was under way, they did not want too much criticism, which might be just as disruptive to orderly development as Chiang Ch'ing's effort to circumvent regular Party procedures. The divergence between the bureaucracy and Mao was not so much on the need to reimpose tighter controls as on how to do it. Whereas Mao was calling for a large-scale mass campaign that would reach the top levels of the cultural establishment, the

38 "The tempestuous combat on the literary and art front," *Shou-tu hung-wei-ping* (Capital Red Guards), 7 July 1967, *CB*, 842, 17.
39 "Hail the Victory of the Mao Tse-tung Line on Literature and Art," NCNA, 17 May 1967, *SCMP*, 3950, 13.
40 "Instructions concerning literature and art," *Long live Mao Tse-tung Thought*, in *CB*, 891, 41.

bureaucracy carried out a rectification limited to the literary and academic sphere. It touched only superficially on a very small number of "the high and mighty" cultural officials whom Mao had denounced.

It was carried out by the usual managers of thought reform campaigns – the officials in the Propaganda Department, Ministry of Culture, and Peking Party Committee. In the spring of 1964 the Party Secretariat had set up a high-level task force known as the Five-Man Group to coordinate the cultural reform. It was headed by P'eng Chen and had Lu Ting-i, K'ang Sheng, Yang Shang-k'un, director of the Central Committee's General Office, and Wu Leng-hsi, editor-in-chief of the *People's Daily* and director of the New China News Agency, as its members. The only one of the group close to Chiang Ch'ing and her associates was K'ang Sheng; the rest were identified with the cultural establishment. Mao's confidants and the radical intellectuals through K'ang Sheng were able to inject themselves into the rectification, but they played a minor role.

The army also played a minor role in the campaign. After Lin Piao replaced P'eng Te-huai as minister of defense in 1959, the PLA had become increasingly conspicuous in cultural activities. It set up opera, literary, and art groups in the PLA, but at this time they were to parallel – not to replace – the Party groups. Political officers of the PLA were inserted into the cultural, propaganda, and educational bureaus, as they were inserted into the economic and administrative bureaus, in an effort to revitalize the bureaucracy, with Mao's Thought. This network, however, was under the control not of the General Political Department of the PLA but of the Party Central Committee. The Party leadership was very much in charge of the rectification and determined to keep it from exploding into a mass movement that could be turned against itself. Actually, the Party's rectification, launched in the summer of 1964, was not one hard-hitting campaign, but a series of mini-campaigns against a number of famous intellectuals just below the top echelon of cultural officials.

As if in an effort to divert attention from itself, the bureaucracy chose as its foremost target an intellectual outside its inner circle. He was Central Committee member and leading Marxist theoretician Yang Hsien-chen. He had spent twenty years in the Soviet Union, where he had studied at the University of Toilers of the East in Moscow in the 1920s and was head of the Chinese department of the Soviet Foreign Languages Institute in the 1930s. Given the regime's increasingly anti-Soviet invective, Yang was a convenient target. He also had been in factional conflict with Ch'en Po-ta at the Higher Party School. Perhaps more important, he presented concepts that were in opposition to Mao's current stress on struggle.

As the campaign against him unfolded in the media, Party schools, universities, and research institutes focused on countering the desire for compromise, as expressed in a slogan associated with Yang that "two combine into one," in opposition to Mao's slogan "one divides into two," which stressed class struggle. Mao had also talked of the union of opposites in the concept of nonantagonistic contradictions in "On the correct handling of contradictions among the people" and in the interrelation of opposites in "On contradiction." But whereas Mao emphasized that the transformation of one force by another in endless struggle was more fundamental than union, Yang emphasized that the union did not dissolve the opposites but each remained separate, held together by mutual need. He advocated seeking common ground with opposing ideologies, but allowing differences to remain. The implication of this concept for the PRC was the toleration of a diversity of viewpoints and classes within a unified nation.

In addition to silencing the demand for compromise, criticism of Yang was also used to stifle criticism of the GLF, still echoing into 1964. In the GLF, Yang had initiated a debate in academic circles called "the question of thinking and being" that could be interpreted as implicit criticism of Mao's policies. He argued that no one, no matter how omniscient, could afford to disregard the inexorable laws of history or oppose his will to the built-in limitations of the objective situation. Implicit in Yang's argument was the Marxist orthodoxy that a society must go through economic stages of development and could not leap into communism. Since China was an economically backward country, radical changes were counterproductive because they were not in accord with China's reality.

As in the attack on the concept of "two into one," these ideas were attributed to Yang largely on the basis of unpublished articles. In 1958, after a visit to the countryside, he had written an article that questioned the revolutionary nature of Chinese society and denied the dynamic role of the masses in the GLF. He warned that "the abandonment of objective laws and one-sided discussion of subjective function means metaphysics and this can only be changed into the theory of sole obedience to the will."[41] As in the discussion of the

---

41 Ts'ung Wei, "Yang Hsien-chen and the 'Identity of thinking and existence,'" *KMJP*, 11 December 1964, *SCMP*, 3380, 5.

"middle character," Yang attributed the failure of the GLF to the discrepancy between Mao's revolutionary vision and the reality of nonrevolutionary peasants.

Yang's main critic was an old ideological opponent, Ai Szu-ch'i, who chastized Yang and people like him who were not fully committed to continuing struggle. His words already hinted at the imminent Cultural Revolution attack on Party colleagues who sought moderation. He pointed out that the line "one divides into two is not only between friend and foe but also among friends – distinguishing the closest friends from the vacillating ones." He warned that if the Party tolerated those who vacillate, then socialism will not be achieved. "Instead of distinguishing friend from foe, we mix them up and desist from waging struggle among friends, but 'only seek agreement and reserve differences.' [We] may lead the revolution astray and cause it to fail."[42] While concern with vacillating comrades and continuing struggle was only one among a number of strands of the 1964 rectification, it was to become a keynote of the Cultural Revolution.

The rectification also attacked Yang's traditional Marxist view that policy must conform to the unfolding stages of history in order to create the conditions for socialism. The discussion resembled a number of Western ideological and philosophical debates in the nineteenth and early twentieth centuries between those who believed in the existence of immutable laws of history and those such as Lenin who believed in man's ability to shape his own history. Mao's latest statement in the Leninist tradition was in May 1963 in "Where do correct ideas come from?" in which he wrote: "Once correct ideas ... are grasped by the masses, these ideas turn into a material force which changes society and changes the world." The question whether one knows if he correctly reflects the laws of the objective world is not proved until "the stage leading from consciousness back to matter in which they are applied in practice."[43] Thus, Mao insisted that one must act in order to know if one accurately reflects the objective world.

In contrast to Mao's belief that ideas depended on action, Yang was charged with believing that ideas were only a passive reflection of material progress. He was criticized for rejecting subjective initiative

---

42 Ai Szu-ch'i, "Surreptitious substitution of the theory of the reconciliation of contradictions and class for revolutionary dialectics must not be permitted," *JMJP*, 20 May 1965, *SCMP*, 3475, 7.
43 Mao Tse-tung, "Where do correct ideas come from?" *Four essays on philosophy*, 134–35.

and revolutionary spirit. In actuality Yang did not reject the subjective and revolutionary spirit, but he maintained that it had to be combined with a sober respect for objective limitations. Undoubtedly, he and several members of the Party hierarchy who shared his views felt they were acting in good Leninist, as well as Marxist, tradition. Even Lenin's emphasis on the subjective factor and revolutionary will was accompanied by a genuine effort to comprehend "objective reality" accurately.

The discussion of Yang's ideas was primarily an ideological debate between the orthodox Marxist view of sequential stages of development and the Rousseauian-Jacobin voluntarist view transmitted through Marxism-Leninism to Mao. For the most part, the Party bureaucracy appears to have taken a middle course on this issue. Yang was removed from his position as vice-chairman of the Higher Party School to be replaced by his old rival, Ai Szu-ch'i. But Yang was not denounced with the fervor and epithets meted out to intellectual targets in previous campaigns. Most of the criticism was more academic than political, more balanced than polemical.

As Yang's views had criticized the regime for projecting future utopias rather than dealing with present realities, so did Shao Ch'üanlin's view of the peasant as a "middle character" rather than as a revolutionary imply that the bureaucracy as well as Mao did not understand the real needs of the peasantry. Thus, another purpose of the rectification was to reject Shao's concept of the "middle character." Instead of confronting this issue, the regime threw Shao's criticisms back at him by charging that it was he and a number of fiction writers, such as Chao Shu-li, Chou Li-po, and Ma Feng, who showed themselves out of touch with the peasants by depicting them as vacillating and ambivalent.

But Shao was the main target of the campaign against the "middle character." Even though there was pressure from Mao and his associates, the choice of someone like Shao, directly connected to the cultural bureaucracy as head of the Party group in the Chinese Writers' Union, appears to have been made by the bureaucracy itself in order to hold onto its power. Narrowing the attack to one important official protected his colleagues, particularly Chou Yang. Thus Shao became the scapegoat for the "failings" of the cultural establishment.

Chou Yang personally supervised the campaign against Shao. He himself revised a number of the criticisms and sought to keep the discussion limited to literary matters and away from political matters.

Under Chou Yang's guidance, the drive quickly moved from the negative stage of denouncing Shao and the "middle character" to the positive stage of defining new behavior patterns, new values, and new beliefs for a new socialist man. In contrast to Shao's image of the peasant as suspicious of the revolution, riddled with conflicts and desirous of material benefits, the regime depicted the peasant as a hero of unqualified optimism, unstinting self-sacrifice, and abiding faith in the revolution.

Despite Chou Yang's efforts to control the campaign, the radical intellectuals, most prominently Yao Wen-yuan, injected themselves into this discussion. Their public views at this time were not too different from those of the cultural establishment. Even Yao admitted indirectly that the majority was still nonrevolutionary, but to write about the majority meant "a fundamental exclusion and suppression of new things which are germinating or developing, and an extension of protection to old things which superficially still exist extensively."[44] He therefore advised writers to depict not the majority but the few. "Mold energetically, richly and vividly the heroic characters . . . thus enlightening and encouraging the people."[45]

Several heroic figures were molded in this period to contrast with the "middle character." The shift from a number of nonheroic literary characters of the late 1950s and early 1960s to heroic figures of the mid-1960s reflects the shift from recognition of human and economic limitations to the belief that self-sacrificing new men could overcome all obstacles. The main literary protagonists changed from ordinary peasants and workers whose commitments were ambiguous to "ordinary" heroes, usually from the PLA, such as Lei Feng, whose commitment to the Maoist virtues of sacrifice, selflessness, and devotion to Mao was unswerving.

Accompanying this shift was a move away from conventional literary forms of the novel and short story, written by individual writers, to the more controllable semi-fictional diary presented almost as myth, written by committees, such as *The diary of Lei Feng*. Less and less was published by the established writers still writing in the late 1950s and more and more by anonymous groups, attached primarily to the Propaganda Department of the PLA, an indication of the increasing intrusion of the PLA into the cultural realm.

44 Yao Wen-yuan, "A theory which causes socialist literature and art to degenerate," *KMJP*, 20 December 1964, *SCMP*, 3374, 9.
45 Ibid., 4.

There was a carryover of the campaign against the "middle character" into the cinema. Not only had the cinema portrayed nonheroic protagonists, particularly in the films based on the literary works of the 1930s, but it was directed by Hsia Yen and Yang Han-sheng, who had antagonized Chiang Ch'ing. She had tried to insert herself into films as into the opera. She pointed out to Lu Ting-i and Chou Yang a large number of films she claimed Mao wanted repudiated. But only a few were criticized. True, the films that were criticized were associated with her old enemies, but the criticism itself, under the supervision of the Propaganda Department, was generally mild. The film that received the most attention was *The Lin family shop*, based on a story by Mao Tun and adapted for the screen by Hsia Yen. Though well received when it was first shown, in 1959, it was criticized in 1964 because the principal protagonist's relationships were not based on sharp class conflict. It was acknowledged that the story had had a positive influence in the 1930s because it showed the difficulties of the petty bourgeoisie and gained their support for the revolution. But now it was regarded as inappropriate because it was no longer necessary to have cooperation between workers and bourgeoisie.

Generally, rectification of the cinema was relatively restrained. This film plus a few others were criticized, but there was no mass campaign or large-scale meetings to repudiate them. Instead, there were bland critiques by colleagues who were closely connected with the people who had written and produced these films. Yet a few criticisms gave hints of the kinds of attacks that would pour down on the May Fourth writers in the Cultural Revolution. One, for example, asserted that Hsia Yen represented the type of intellectuals who, though Party members, still had "a bourgeois realm hidden deep in their hearts."[46] Moreover, it was charged that their bourgeois ideas had a corrosive influence on the young.

The rectification was similar to other thought-reform campaigns in its use of the media, criticism and self-criticism sessions, and the selection of personalized targets. But its approach was different. Though for the most part the same group from the Propaganda Department that conducted the Hu Feng campaign of 1955 and the Anti-Rightist Campaign of 1957–58 were in charge, the rectification was less direct, less thorough, and more tolerant of its victims. Probably this group was just as anxious as they had been previously

46 Su Nan-yuan, "*The Lin family shop* is a picture for prettifying the bourgeoisie," *JMJP*, 29 May 1965, CB, 766, 9.

to stop what Mao called "a slide toward revisionism," but there were factors that held them back – increasing bureaucratization, the fear of another full-scale campaign reeling out of control, and the questioning of Mao's policies. Moreover, a rectification in which the masses were activated would not only be a threat to themselves personally, as it was in the Hundred Flowers, but a threat to the Party as a whole.

As a result, there appears to have been in some cases genuine, in other cases deliberate, misinterpretation of Mao's wishes. Mao's speech before the national propaganda work conference on 12 March 1957, in the midst of the Hundred Flowers Campaign, which had not previously been published, appeared in June 1964 just as the rectification was to be launched. Though some of the language appears to have been revised, this speech, given at a time when Mao was less disillusioned with the intellectuals and the Party, called for criticism with restraint and understanding. He cautioned that criticism of intellectuals must be "fully reasoned, analytical, and convincing and should not be brutal, bureaucratic, or dogmatic." Furthermore, he advocated a gradual approach toward dissenting intellectuals: "Such people will remain for a very long time to come, and we should tolerate their disapproval."[47] This speech, together with Mao's short directives, were ambiguous on how the rectification was to be implemented and, if anything, advocated persuasion rather than coercion.

Whether purposely or not, the propaganda bureaucracy chose to interpret Mao's words as an order for a limited rectification. As in the past, personalized targets served as vehicles for transmitting ideological messages. But this time, instead of one specific target as in the Hu Feng campaign of 1955 or one specific group like the Ting Ling clique or the China Democratic League in the Anti-Rightist Campaign, several different campaigns, launched simultaneously against several related but different targets, tended to diffuse the movement.

In addition to Yang Hsien-chen and Shao Ch'üan-lin, the rectification criticized the philosopher Feng Ting for emphasizing instincts common to all people, the writer Ou-yang Shan for describing love without class content, and the aesthetician Chou Ku-ch'eng for talking of a "unified" consciousness. It was a broad campaign, touching philosophy, history, literary theory, the arts, and ideology, but it was

47 Mao Tse-tung, "Talk at the national conference on propaganda work of the CCP," CB, 740, 10.

not thorough – there was a gap between the rhetoric and the reality, between the enunciation of policy and its implementation. Moreover, the revolutionary fervor of previous movements was missing; those affected were a small group of Party intellectuals in the large cities. As opposed to the Hu Feng campaign, which affected the masses as well as the intellectuals, there was little effort to involve ordinary workers and peasants. There were no big struggle meetings or large wall posters, features that characterized past and future campaigns.

Most of the rectification was carried out quietly behind closed doors, primarily in the Ministry of Culture and the All-China Federation of Literary and Art Circles. In contrast to the publication of Hu Feng's letters or the republication of Ting Ling's stories and essays in the Anti-Rightist Campaign, there was what appeared to be a deliberate paucity of material so that it was difficult to generate large-scale criticism. Except for disconnected quotations from Shao Ch'üan-lin's speech at Dairen, there was no real record of anyone else speaking there. Chou Yang supposedly stopped their publication. Except for the slogan "one into two, two into one," little effort was made to simplify the ideological themes to ensure that they could be understood by the uneducated. Most of the criticism had the character of an abstruse, intellectual exercise filled with Marxist abstractions, as if to distract from its political implications. Though the rectification was implicitly political, the substance was explicitly academic.

The personalized targets were treated leniently. They were referred to throughout as "comrade," an appellation that Hu Feng and Ting Ling had lost with the initial charges leveled against them. Unlike the past, the rectification ended without abject self-criticisms published throughout the land as a source of further indoctrination. No public confessions came forth from Yang Hsien-chen, Shao Ch'üan-lin, or the others. The people and journals that had not recognized their "mistakes" did not suffer to any extent. In contrast to the purge of Feng Hsueh-feng and his associates from the *Literary Gazette* in 1954 for rejecting student criticism of Yü P'ing-po, *Chinese Youth* issued a mild self-criticism for its turning down the initial attack on Feng Ting, and that was all.

Nevertheless, there were signs that Chou Yang and the cultural establishment were under pressure. Not only Shao Ch'üan-lin, but Chou Yang's close colleagues and Chiang Ch'ing's old enemies T'ien Han, Hsia Yen, and Yang Han-sheng were removed from office. Mao Tun stepped down as minister of culture. The journal with which Chou Yang and his associates were closely identified, *Literary Gazette*, published a number of articles criticizing itself for having praised writers like Chao Shu-li and Ou-yang Shan, who had portrayed "middle characters." One critic accused *Literary Gazette* of being revolutionary in words but revisionist in implementation. Another accused it of relying on a small group of professional writers without allowing input from the masses. These were the main charges to be leveled against the cultural bureaucrats in the Cultural Revolution.

The removal of some of his close colleagues and the challenge from Chiang Ch'ing appeared to mark the beginning of the end for the cultural bureaucracy that Chou Yang had built up for almost thirty years. Yet although the cultural bureaucracy had gone a long way to placate Mao by removing some of its most famous names and reshuffling its leadership, its operation continued intact. Although Mao had accused the majority of cultural officials of revisionism, as opposed to the earlier campaigns when all the disciples, as in the case of Hu Feng, and all the associates, as in the case of Ting Ling, suffered a fate similar to that of their leader, the criticism stopped with a small number of colleagues and the charges against them for the most part were limited to a few specific misdeeds. As later described in the Cultural Revolution, they were like "the castles" that were sacrificed to protect "the king" – Chou Yang. Chou's other close colleagues, Lin Mo-han, Yuan Shui-po, and Ho Ch'i-fang, were not even criticized at the time.

Chou's superior, Director of Propaganda Lu Ting-i, took over from Mao Tun as minister of culture. By the spring of 1965 criticism of Hsia Yen, Yang Han-sheng, and T'ien Han had waned. Chou was able to shelter most of his apparatus from attack. Furthermore, he appears to have protected it from the infiltration by the PLA that had affected other bureaucracies. Whereas by the end of 1964 the establishment of political departments on the model of the PLA commissar system had made some headway in the economic ministries, there was little evidence of this system in the Ministry of Culture.

Although those selected for criticism were not, as in the past, well-known intellectuals, but Party members with long careers in propaganda and ideology, they were not at the very top of the cultural hierarchy. Moreover, they were not the ones who had most sharply criticized Mao and the GLF. When one member of the Three Family Village group, Liao Mo-sha, had written a self-criticism, he had made no mention of his participation in the Three Family Village or of his criticism of Maoist programs. Most likely, P'eng Chen protected the Three Family Village as Chou Yang sought to ensure mild criticism of his cronies. A hard-hitting campaign against their underlings would have ricocheted onto them as their sponsors. Nothing was said, as in past campaigns, about the fact that the errors of the subordinates reflected those of their leaders.

Perhaps the most important difference from previous campaigns was that there was no unanimity of views in the negative appraisal of the scapegoats and in the imposition of one definitive line. This time there was a diversity of views, with some defense of the victims and some divergence from the line being imposed. The attackers dominated, but the defenders and modifiers did not vanish from the scene as they had in other campaigns. The themes that were to dominate the Cultural Revolution were all present in the 1964 rectification – class struggle, transformation of consciousness, concern over the deterioration of the revolutionary spirit among youth and Party leaders. But the discussion was contradictory, reflecting again the differing views of the cultural authorities, which in turn reflected division within the political leadership.

Another distinctive feature of this rectification was that as it was unfolding, there was open criticism of some of the critics, particularly the radical intellectuals. Yao Wen-yuan was censured in 1964 for his earlier comments on the aesthetician Chou Ku-ch'eng. A *People's Daily* article on 2 August 1964 termed Yao's criticism "self-contradictory" and "not in correspondence with the facts of history." In perhaps an indirect criticism of Mao, a few critics described Yao's approach as based on rigid formulas that distorted reality.[48] These countercriticisms reflected the still dominant position of the cultural bureaucrats. Yet they were not pushed too far, because Mao likewise protected the radical intellectuals.

By the beginning of 1965, Chou Yang quickly sought to bring the rectification to a formal close. He had suspended it earlier, in November 1964, in the various unions of the All-China Federation of Literary and Art Circles on the grounds that the cadres were needed elsewhere. At the end of February 1965, he called a meeting of editors and journalists where he denounced recent criticism in the rectification as dogmatic, simplistic, and exaggerated. Subsequently, the rectification faded away. As was his custom in previous campaigns,

48 Chin Wei-min and Lin Yun-ch'u, "Some queries on the spirit of the times," *JMJP*, 2 August 1964, *CB*, 747, 25.

on 15 and 16 April 1965 he summed up the results and announced its conclusion.

Chou admitted once again, in his final report, that he had been slow in criticizing revisionism and implementing rectification. But he did not admit to any serious shortcomings as Mao had demanded in his 13 December 1963 directive. In reference to some of his colleagues, Chou agreed that they did some things for which they should be criticized, but he insisted, "The Party does not regard them as rightists. Our contradictions with and our struggle against them remain to be a contradiction among the people and an inner-party struggle."[49] They might have deviated in the cultural sphere, but were not guilty of revisionism in the political sphere. Moreover, Chou Yang claimed they had already ceased holding some of these views and, therefore, should no longer be criticized.

In the sciences, as well as in the arts and humanities, Mao's directives were disregarded and in some cases resisted. In the Spring Festival in Education speech of 13 February 1964, Mao had praised Benjamin Franklin and James Watt as examples of scientists who made discoveries in the course of their everyday work. In contrast, a number of university science departments were merely gathering places where "bourgeois ideology exists in serious proportion."[50] Ai Szu-ch'i argued in a new section in *Red Flag*, "Natural science and dialectic materialism," that scientific achievement depended on the use of the Marxian dialectic and denounced those who refused to apply it to scientific research.

Yet in 1965 *China Youth News* published a set of articles urging youth to become "expert" without being "Red." It advised them to disregard the Marxian dialectic and work in research centers rather than in fields and factories. At a forum on "Red and expert," some even encouraged the use of bourgeois experts precisely because they were motivated by bourgeois values. "Some bourgeois technical experts whose world outlook has not been remolded can still serve socialism under proletarian leadership. Had they spent too much time on Marxism-Leninism, their expertness surely would have suffered."[51]

A *China Youth News* editorial held that a person's "Redness" is

49 "The tempestuous combat on the literary and art front," *Shou-tu hung-wei-ping*, 7 June 1967, CB, 842, 27.
50 Schram, *Chairman Mao talks to the people*, 208.
51 Tien Ho-shui, "When one cannot be both red and expert," *Chung-kuo ch'ing-nien pao*, 26 December 1964, CB, 757, 6.

not expressed by attendance at meetings and political study. For a scientist, it is expressed by devoting the greater part of one's time to professional activity. It warned, "Under no circumstances should we critically regard devotion to study and energetic effort to conduct intensive research and professional work as a manifestation of individualism."[52]

There was reason, therefore, for Mao to be dissatisfied with the 1964–65 rectification. Instead of swelling into a major mass movement, it had petered out, becoming a relatively low-key, inconclusive affair that became the medium for a variety of views, some diverging from his own. Whereas the PLA was infusing its ideological efforts with revolutionary fervor and action, the Party's rhetoric intensified but its actual implementation was superficial. The very organization Mao had empowered to carry out the ideological transformation he deemed so necessary resisted and even opposed his demands. By the fall of 1965 he had abandoned his reliance on the Party to carry out a cultural revolution and launched his own with his intimates Chiang Ch'ing and Ch'en Po-ta, the PLA, and the radical intellectuals. In contrast to the Party's rectification, Mao's Cultural Revolution would compel unanimity in ideology, activation of the masses, and a thorough purge of those who did not follow his orders.

The concerns expressed by the intellectuals since the early 1960s for a period of stability and reconciliation, for professional and intellectual standards, for concurrence between ideology and reality, and for recognition of the genuine demands of the peasants were pushed underground. Their advocates were purged, and some of them were killed in the Cultural Revolution. But in the post-Mao era, the Teng Hsiao-p'ing leadership as well as a small number of intellectuals and youth would seek to carry out reforms that addressed these same concerns.

52 "Redness and expertness is what the era demands of our youth," editorial, *Chung-kuo ch'ing-nien pao*, 24 July 1965, *SCMP*, 3517, 5.

CHAPTER 11

THE SINO-SOVIET SPLIT

In 1958–64, the Sino-Soviet dispute became the overriding problem for Chinese foreign policy.[1] During the first half of the 1950s, Peking's preoccupation with Sino-American relations had been manifest in the Taiwan problem, the Korean War, exclusion from the United Nations, and the American economic embargo. These issues were primary, involving such matters as sovereignty, national security, and economic development. Sino-Soviet relations had been in this sense a function of Sino-American relations because of China's dependence on Moscow for defense and development.

None of these issues disappeared from the agenda in Peking; however, after 1958 they became secondary to the Sino-Soviet dispute. Except for brief periods of tension in 1958 and 1962, the Taiwan Strait stabilized as a relatively inactive point of confrontation. Similarly, Korea remained divided in a status of "no war – no peace." China's rapidly expanding relations with European, African, and Asian countries obviated much of the substantive, if not the symbolic, deprivation of remaining outside the United Nations. Expanded foreign trade provided access to European and Japanese technology, diluting the impact of the American embargo.

By contrast, the two Khrushchev-Mao encounters in Peking in 1958 and 1959, together with the multiparty Communist conferences in Bucharest and Moscow in 1960, fueled a growing dispute in the Sino-Soviet alliance that ultimately blew it apart in all but the formal sense. The Soviet withdrawal of all economic assistance in 1960 and the rising level of border incidents thereafter transformed the relationship from qualified friendship to tempered hostility. Chinese

---

1 The volume of literature on the Sino-Soviet dispute is both large and impressive. The main works upon which I have relied include Zbigniew K. Brzezinski, *The Soviet bloc* (hereafter *Bloc*); Alexander Dallin et al., eds. *Diversity in International communism*; John Gittings, *Survey of the Sino-Soviet dispute*; William E. Griffith, *The Sino-Soviet rift*; William E. Griffith, *Sino-Soviet relations, 1964–1965*; G. F. Hudson et al., *The Sino-Soviet dispute* (hereafter *Dispute*); Kurt London, ed. *Unity and contradiction*; and the classic Donald S. Zagoria, *The Sino-Soviet conflict, 1956–1961*.

accusations of Soviet intervention in domestic affairs, at the elite level in 1959 and among Sinkiang minorities in 1962, added a particularly volatile dimension to the usual differences between allied states over their conflicting external priorities. Finally, Mao's anathematizing of Khrushchev as an ideological heretic provided the ultimate blow to the much vaunted "monolithic unity" that purportedly had characterized Sino-Soviet relations during Stalin's time.

Yet despite its salience, the Sino-Soviet split defies simple historical recapitulation. Multiple factors drove Moscow and Peking apart. At the individual level, the personalities of Nikita Khrushchev and Mao Tse-tung proved wholly incompatible with the standard alliance requirements of consultation, compromise, and collaboration. The two autocrats' idiosyncratic behavior also transformed normal differences of policy into mutual hostility.

These differences embraced political, economic, and military affairs. Difficult relations between the two Communist Parties extended back to the mid-1920s. The ability of the Chinese to carry their revolution to victory independently and against Stalin's advice provided Mao and his colleagues with a unique preeminence, in comparison with other Communist leaders after Stalin's death. The asymmetry of power in Moscow's favor was therefore at least politically offset by the asymmetry of prestige in favor of Peking.

These conflicting weights of power and status coexisted with a total Chinese dependence on Soviet economic and military aid during the first half of the 1950s. The terms of trade and aid, together with the implications of China's military dependence in the nuclear era, raised practical and psychological problems for both sides that became increasingly evident in the latter half of the decade. The staggering scope of China's economic and military developmental needs compounded the strain on Soviet resources imposed by the devastation of World War II and the postwar needs of the Eastern European satellites. The resulting conflict of priorities in Moscow was understandably perceived differently in Peking.

Beyond these essentially bilateral matters, third-country relations confronted the alliance with major problems of coordination. Soviet-American summitry at Geneva in 1955 and Camp David in 1959 contrasted with the absence of diplomatic recognition between Peking and Washington. A Soviet emphasis on "peaceful coexistence" was accompanied by warning against the risks of war in the nuclear age. This implied Soviet acquiescence in the American defense commitment to Taiwan, which shielded the Chinese Nationalists from final defeat in their civil war with the Communists. In South Asia, Moscow wooed New Delhi while the latter's border dispute with Peking flared into armed clashes associated with rebellion in Tibet. Farther afield, Chinese pretensions to leadership in Afro-Asian councils collided with Soviet ambitions in the newly independent Third World. Even Eastern Europe, a Soviet *glacis* acquired at considerable cost, was not beyond Peking's reach as one or another Eastern European leadership, particularly in 1956–57, sought to gain leverage on Moscow with Chinese assistance. By the early 1960s, this led to Peking's open championing of Albania's cause against the Kremlin.

Within the Marxist-Leninist framework, the two Communist giants competed for theoretical and practical influence among communist parties and national liberation movements throughout the world. Advocacy of the Soviet parliamentary versus the Chinese revolutionary path to power was backed by actions in pursuit of one or the other strategy. As a related issue, support for bourgeois regimes as an alternative to their communist opposition revived historic debates over the united front from below against one from above. This abstract and somewhat esoteric debate over theory masked real contests for power and influence, which in turn exacerbated Sino-Soviet relations at the highest level.

But it would be wrong to explain all of Peking's behavior abroad as spurred by the dispute with Moscow. Many actions were entirely separate, either initiated toward or reacting to other countries independently. The arc of Asia was a primary focus for Peking, as compared with its secondary role for Moscow. India and Indonesia demanded attention in their own right, apart from their contribution to Sino-Soviet competition. In addition to this independent external dimension of foreign policy, domestic politics provided an important context within which China's relations with the outside world were determined. Similarly, the impact of economic factors, whether at the general level of demography and development or with the specific results of the Great Leap Forward (GLF), cannot be ignored.

The multiple aspects of Sino-Soviet relations pose severe problems of analysis and presentation. We have little reliable, direct evidence on precisely how and why the alliance came apart. The eventual flood of polemical literature on both sides was sometimes reliable and revealing, but much remained partially distorted or wholly concealed.

One final caveat deserves brief attention. The terms "China," "Peking," and "the leadership" imply a unanimity on foreign policy that almost certainly did not exist. Such references finesse the question of which individuals, factions, or groups held which views. In most instances this troublesome question cannot yet be answered. We therefore must resort to verbal shorthand without, however, assuming unity on a particular policy at any given time.

Because the Sino-Soviet dispute came to preoccupy Chinese foreign policy between 1958 and 1964, it offers a leitmotif around which we will relate other developments. As such, its antecedents in the November 1957 Moscow conference of communist parties in power require recapitulation in order to place the subsequent split in perspective.

PHASE ONE: 1958

Redefining Sino-Soviet relations: November 1957

The fortieth anniversary of the Bolshevik Revolution provided a forum within which a new general line for international communism and relations among ruling communist parties was hammered out. It was also the context for Mao's second visit to Moscow and his second public meeting with Khrushchev. The timing was opportune for Mao on several counts. Soviet-Yugoslav disagreement on Moscow's status vis-à-vis ruling communist parties had prompted Tito to boycott the conference, although a strong Yugoslav delegation did attend. Tito's absence embarrassed Khrushchev, who had invested considerable personal prestige in attempting to close the breach caused by Stalin. Domestically, Khrushchev had triumphed over a majority in the Party Presidium, which had moved to oust him as First Secretary the previous June. However, it had been a close call, with some of Khrushchev's critics remaining in positions to challenge him further should the opportunity arise.

For his part, Mao had survived the short-lived and embarrassing experiment in allowing a "hundred flowers" to bloom, and a "hundred schools" to contend, which loosened restrictions on intellectual and political criticism in China. After a storm of public criticism, a harsh Anti-Rightist Campaign that summer restored tight Party control. Meanwhile, publication of Mao's celebrated speech "On the correct handling of contradictions among the people" in June 1957 had won worldwide attention, particularly in Eastern Europe. It was a unique acknowledgement that "nonantagonistic" conflicts of interest existed normally under socialism and did not warrant their authoritarian suppression. On balance, Mao's international prestige profited from these developments, disruptive as they proved to be in China at the time.

One more event, seemingly in Khrushchev's favor but shrewdly exploited by Mao, occurred on the eve of the conference. On 4 October 1957, the Soviet Union launched the first artificial satellite, Sputnik, into orbit. Following the earlier announcement of a successful ICBM test on 26 August, this symbolized Soviet ability to match American achievements in strategic nuclear weapons. But recognition that it was still some time before symbol would become substance prompted the Kremlin to temper its triumphant propaganda so as not to throw down the gauntlet before a still-superior United States. No such caution constrained Mao, who confidently proclaimed, "The characteristic of the situation today is the East Wind prevailing over the West Wind."[2] Thus Mao, in effect, challenged Khrushchev to press the psychological advantage of Sputnik through a more assertive, if not more aggressive, posture against the "paper tiger" of "U.S. imperialism."

The conjunction of circumstances permitted Mao to insert the Chinese view on critical areas of controversy at the Moscow Conference. Formulations which asserted that "the forces of peace have so grown that there is a real possibility of averting wars" were offset by Mao's warning that "so long as imperialism exists there will always be soil for aggressive wars."[3] The accompanying text clearly came down more heavily on the prospects for the latter. Again, after a lengthy elaboration of the "peaceful path" to power stressed by Khrushchev, attention was paid to the "nonpeaceful transition to socialism" – "Leninism teaches, and experience confirms, that the ruling classes never relinquish power voluntarily." With regard to the debate over loosening or tightening domestic and intraparty control, the conference statement firmly asserted: "The main danger at present is revisionism, or, in other words, right-wing opportunism."

In general, the softer language reflected Khrushchev's preferred emphasis, although the differences were not so clear-out as they became later. Nor was Mao alone in his advocacy of a harder line both domestically and in foreign policy. In addition, Mao backed Khrushchev against Gomulka, whose Polish path to socialism and assertions of implied independence from Moscow's *diktat* challenged standard Soviet definitions of the correct line. This support, which

2 Brzezinski, *Bloc*, 299.   3 Full text in Hudson, *Dispute*, 46–56.

proved critical in solidifying Khrushchev's position at the conference, paralleled Mao's assertion that a new "turning point" had been reached internationally by Soviet technological and weaponry achievements. The resulting responsibility for bloc leadership fell on Moscow, but defining bloc policy required Peking's concurrence. Thus, making the Soviet Union *primus inter pares* did not consign China to a passive role.

More than verbal bargaining marked Sino-Soviet exchanges in Moscow. On the eve of the conference, the Soviet Union agreed to provide the PRC with assistance in developing nuclear weapons. As subsequently claimed by Peking, an "agreement on new technology for national defense" was concluded on 15 October 1957, and Khrushchev allegedly promised "to provide China with a sample of an atomic bomb and technical data concerning its manufacture."[4] This explains why Mao was accompanied by his minister of defense, Marshal P'eng Te-huai, and joined on 6 November by a military "goodwill" mission that did not depart until 29 November. Simultaneously, Kuo Mo-jo headed a scientific and technical delegation, together with a group from the Chinese Academy of Sciences, for meetings with their Soviet counterparts. On 11 December, a five-year Sino-Soviet scientific cooperation agreement was signed in Moscow, along with a protocol on scientific cooperation for 1958.

To anticipate, these negotiations resulted in a major contribution to China's nuclear weapons program, as revealed later through U.S. intelligence.[5] Although Moscow never confirmed the Chinese claims, its assistance to Peking was substantial, albeit terminated in 1959–60. Construction of a gaseous diffusion plant near Lanchow duplicated standard Soviet facilities, at least in external appearance. At the Lop Nor nuclear test site, the supporting infrastructure was configured according to Soviet designs. A missile identical with those of the Soviet Union was sighted nearby, although whether it was a mockup or operational could not be ascertained. Thus, while a "sample atomic bomb" per se may or may not have been actually promised, these indicators of a substantive sharing in nuclear weapons technology suggest that the 1957 accords significantly advanced China's research and development program.

4 "A comment on the Soviet government's statement of August 3," *PR*, 6 (16 August 1963), 7–15.
5 The following paragraph draws on the author's access to U.S. government information during his tenure in the Department of State's Bureau of Intelligence and Research, 1961–66.

In sum, Sino-Soviet interaction during the fall of 1957 seemingly strengthened the alliance, although the seeds of subsequent tension were also sown at this time. Thus Mao's assertion that "the socialist camp must have a head, and this head is the USSR," as well as that "the Communist and workers' parties of all countries must have a head and that head is the CPSU" carried potentially troublesome as well as favorable implications.

Similarly, his exaggeration of Soviet missile achievements may have been disconcerting, but it did not threaten adventuresome action on the part of China at the moment. More worrisome was Mao's cavalier dismissal of a nuclear war in which although "half of mankind died, the other half would remain while imperialism would be razed to the ground and the whole world would become socialist." Yet however disturbing Mao's rhetoric was to his Soviet audience, it did not deter Khrushchev from agreeing to share nuclear weapons technology. Although the Soviet leader would subsequently come to rue and ultimately to reverse this decision, he showed no such restraint at the time. Thus, Chinese foreign policy entered 1958 in the context of newly defined Sino-Soviet relations framed through favorable negotiations at the highest level.

1958: an overview

Years later, Mao identified 1958 as a benchmark in China's post-revolutionary development: "From 1958, we decided to make self-reliance our major policy and striving for foreign aid a secondary aim."[6] The implications of this remark for Sino-Soviet relations were borne out on both the domestic and foreign policy fronts, with far-reaching consequences.

Domestically, the GLF evoked open as well as private criticism from Khrushchev for its alleged emulation of "war communism." This in turn irritated Chinese sensibilities as interference in internal affairs and public humiliation of an ally. Mao's flagrant disregard for Soviet economic methods in 1958 totally ignored Soviet advisers, whose exclusion from any effective role contributed to their ultimate withdrawal in 1960. Finally, hyperbolic claims of GLF successes and assertions that the commune offered a shortcut to communism, leapfrogging Soviet developmental stages, implicitly challenged the

---

6 Mao Tse-tung, "Talk at an enlarged Central Work Conference," 30 January 1962, in Stuart Schram, ed. *Chairman Mao talks to the people* (hereafter *Talks*), 176–78.

Kremlin's assumed role as ideological and economic leader of the socialist camp.

Externally Chinese attacks against "revisionism" in Eastern Europe consistently went beyond Soviet positions, particularly with respect to Yugoslavia in the spring of 1958. In July, Khrushchev's cautious handling of the Middle East crisis when U.S. Marines landed in Lebanon evoked a harsher line from Peking that called for a more militant response. Shortly thereafter, the two leaders met secretly for three days in the Chinese capital, accompanied by a high Soviet military official. During their rendezvous, however, Mao failed to inform Khrushchev of his impending bombardment and blockade of the offshore island of Quemoy later that month. This unilateral action triggered a massive American naval and air deployment to the Taiwan Strait and, according to authoritative Soviet sources, prompted Khrushchev's decision to cancel the nuclear weapons technology agreement concluded only the previous year.

This brief overview of 1958 suggests the magnitude as well as the complex interaction of domestic and foreign developments. Scholarly analysis has probed for causal linkages to test one hypothesis that explains both aspects of Chinese policy with a single factor. This approach stresses internal politics represented by the ascendancy of a "left" or "radical" faction over a "moderate" or "right" faction in the aftermath of the "blooming and contending" experiment and its Anti-Rightist epilogue.[7] Yet despite monographic research, sufficient evidence for this holistic explanation of Chinese behavior on both fronts has not been found. While allegations and revelations during and after the Cultural Revolution threw partial light on isolated events, they fail to explain the full range of considerations that underlay the Taiwan Strait actions and the ideological challenge to Moscow.

This does not deny the hypothesis. But it cautions against attributing an overall causal explanation for both domestic and foreign policy where logical inference and plausible reconstruction must substitute for direct evidence. Indeed, in the case of Quemoy it is not only necessary but perhaps justified to separate domestic from foreign affairs so far as policy origins are concerned. The Taiwan Strait situation was a function, at least in part, of Sino-American relations with a history extending back to the first offshore island crisis in 1954–55. As such, it deserves attention in its own right, especially

7 Zagoria, *Conflict*, esp. ch. 2.

given the suspension of Sino-American ambassadorial exchanges in December 1957, and the failure of Peking's effort to achieve a modus vivendi on the Taiwan issue during the previous two years.

Similarly, the strident attack on Yugoslav "revisionism" was in part a reaction to Tito's decision to formalize his "separate path to socialism" in a major statement in March 1958. This brought to a head issues which had first arisen in 1948 with the Cominform denunciation of Belgrade and which had persisted to plague Belgrade's relations with Moscow, as well as Peking, to a varying degree thereafter.

A second hypothesis prominent in analysis of the times alleges that Soviet missile achievements prompted Peking to assert its positions vigorously across the entire range of issues from Eastern Europe to East Asia. But this argument also remains unproved. The antecedents of events in 1958 provide sufficient explanation in themselves without requiring a more holistic hypothesis. Insofar as policy can be attributed to a single individual, namely, Mao, it is plausible to identify a single factor as determining various actions that offer a common appearance. But it is questionable to what degree all decisions, domestic and foreign, were made by Mao personally and alone. This question is particularly relevant in view of his resignation that fall as Chairman of the People's Republic while remaining Chairman of the CCP. Deferring causal explanation until more evidence is available, in the meantime we can place events in a sequence of development. Sequentially, but not in order of importance, we examine the handling of the Lebanon crisis, the Peking summit meeting, and the Quemoy bombardment. Finally, the spillover effects of the GLF deserve mention.

Lebanon and the Peking summit

The secret Peking meeting of 31 July–3 August 1958 between Khrushchev and Mao came after a buildup of differences in the polemical postures struck by the two sides, first with regard to Yugoslavia and then with respect to the landing of U.S. Marines in Lebanon. These political atmospherics set the context within which the two leaders exchanged views. In March, the Yugoslav Communist Party released a 230-page draft program formally enunciating a wide range of domestic and foreign policy positions which openly challenged those advocated by Moscow and endorsed at the November 1957 conference of ruling communist parties. The circulation of this document throughout the communist world to invite comment evoked strong reactions. Its advocacy of nonalignment and neutrality countered the Warsaw Pact principles. Its attitude toward socialists in the West and the Third World implicitly ruled out a leading role for communists there. Its emphasis on internal autonomy and the equality of all communist parties countered the long-standing concept of Moscow as *primus inter pares*.

Not surprisingly, the Kremlin led the other parties in announcing a boycott of the forthcoming Yugoslav Party Congress. Yet, despite a detailed critique of the program by *Kommunist* only three days before the congress convened, Moscow maintained a measure of restraint by referring to the Yugoslav "comrades" and publicly vowing to "be friends with Yugoslavia – always."[8]

Peking showed no such restraint. After the congress had closed, the *People's Daily* avoided a "comradely" tone, instead denigrating the "leading group" of the Yugoslav Party, together with their "out and out revisionist" program, as acting to reverse course or risk a break in relations with the bloc.[9] Peking also asserted that the 1948 Cominform resolution against Tito's alleged heresies remained valid. This was China's first endorsement of Stalin's initial attack. His second move, a 1949 Cominform resolution tying Tito to "U.S. imperialism," had already been withdrawn as a result of Khrushchev's peacemaking trip to Belgrade in 1955.

Over the following month, Moscow persistently responded more slowly and less harshly than Peking while gradually stepping up its attack. In addition, the Soviet Union maintained normal state relations with Yugoslavia. Belgrade, however, withdrew its ambassador from China after he was refused access to the leadership there. Khrushchev continued his references to "comrade" Tito, although Peking employed the derogative term "the Tito clique." Thus, while Soviet criticism challenged Tito at virtually every point, its choice of language made credible Khrushchev's express desire to "preserve some spark of hope and to search for acceptable forms of contact on certain questions."[10] By contrast, the Chinese polemic seemed deliberately designed to destroy this possibility for the Soviet Union as well as for the PRC.

It has been suggested that Mao's motives were twofold: First, to strengthen bloc unity against the threat of neutralism or ideological

8 Zagoria, *Conflict*, 180.
9 "Modern revisionism must be condemned," *PR*, 11 (13 May 1958).
10 Zagoria, *Conflict*, 182.

diversity posed by Belgrade so as to confront imperialism more vigorously; and second, to inhibit Khrushchev's tendency toward détente with the West by attacking Yugoslav views on peaceful coexistence and the easing of East-West tensions. This analysis is buttressed by Chinese statements at the Warsaw Pact meeting in May 1958. Echoing Mao's remarks at Moscow the previous November, Ch'en Yun declared, "'U.S. phobia' is entirely groundless. It is extremely erroneous and harmful to overestimate the imperialist forces of war and underestimate the forces of peace and socialism." More pointedly, he continued, "If formerly, for instance, at the time after the October Revolution, Lenin, the Soviet Communist Party, and the Soviet people, confronted with the encirclement of the capitalist world and the armed intervention of the fourteen countries, were not afraid, why should there be any fear toward imperialism when the socialist camp has absolute superiority?"[11] By contrast, Khrushchev's report depicted the destructive consequences of nuclear war in graphic terms, called for unilateral and mutual reductions of armed forces, and urged "meetings between responsible statesmen that will lead to a solution of controversial issues."

Almost simultaneously Mao addressed the second session of the Eighth Party Congress in May 1958 in terms that combined Khrushchev's dark portrayal of nuclear war with the Chairman's celebrated assurance that China could survive the loss of half its population. His remarks warrant extended quotation as a reflection of Mao's own views when presented to a private audience. In a section subtitled "preparation for the final disaster," he warned:

Now my talk will be a little dark. We must prepare for great disaster and great difficulty.... If the war maniacs use atom bombs what is to be done? Let them use them. So long as warmongers exist then this is a possibility....

Of war and peace, the possibility of peace is greater than the possibility of war. Now the possibility of struggling for peace is greater than in the past. The strengthening of the socialist camp is greater than before ... But there is also a possibility of war and we must prepare for the possibility of a madman, of imperialism seeking to escape from economic crisis....

If we prepare and if they really strike, what is to be done? We must talk about this problem. If they strike then they strike. We will exterminate imperialism and afterwards once again construct. From that point there cannot again be a world war....

If war breaks out it is unavoidable that people will die. We have seen wars kill people. Many times in China's past half the population has been wiped out.... We have at present no experience with atomic war. We do not

11 Ibid., 188.

know how many must die. It is better if one-half are left, the second best is one-third.... After several five-year plans [China] will then develop and rise up. In place of the totally destroyed capitalism we will obtain perpetual peace. This will not be a bad thing.[12]

Mao backed up his analysis with a recapitulation of China's repeated loss of life in the tens of millions, from the Han through the T'ang dynasties. But he did not assert the superiority of the socialist camp, as he had at Moscow or as Ch'en Yun did at Warsaw. Nor did he introduce his subject in a belligerent or defiant context. Least of all did he imply a readiness to test American resolve by Chinese action. Seen in these terms, the private Chinese posture could not be characterized as reckless or adventurist, much less contriving to trigger an East-West conflict in which a Soviet-American nuclear exchange would be likely.

Nonetheless, China's public rhetoric and polemics, whether ostensibly targeted on Yugoslavia or obliquely phrased at Warsaw, betokened Sino-Soviet differences over the proper strategy and tactics for confronting imperialism. These differences became evident during the Middle East crisis which began with a revolt in Iraq that took that country out of its Western alliance and ended with U.S. Marines in Lebanon and British troops in Jordan.

Khrushchev's response to these events was to propose an immediate summit conference of the United States, Britain, France, the Soviet Union and India, in Geneva or elsewhere. His letter to President Eisenhower of 19 July raised this unique prospect in appropriately moderate language: "We address you not from positions of intimidation but from positions of reason.... The statesmen of countries must seek solutions not by means of fanning war psychosis, but reasonably and calmly."[13] This rejected the *People's Daily* position of only two days previous: "There cannot be the slightest indulgence or tolerance toward American imperialism's act of aggression.... If the American aggressors are permitted to do as they wish, then not only will the people of the Middle East be enslaved, but a new world war would be inevitable.... Therefore let the people of the world take emergency action."[14]

Worse, Khrushchev's proposal excluded China, while including

12 Mao Tse-tung, "Second speech to Second Session, Eighth Party Congress," 17 May 1958, *Mao Tse-tung ssu-hsiang wan-sui* (Long live Mao Tse-tung Thought), hereafter *Wan-sui* (1969), 207–8.
13 Zagoria, *Conflict*, 198.
14 Ibid.

India. Peking finally endorsed it three days later and thereafter muted its public differences of emphasis. Khrushchev further antagonized Peking on 23 July when he agreed to a Western counterproposal that the five-nation summit meet within the Security Council, thereby including Taiwan's representative while excluding the PRC.

On 3 August, a joint Sino-Soviet communiqué revealed that Khrushchev, accompanied by Soviet Defense Minister Malinovsky, had met with Mao and his colleagues secretly since 31 July. Malinovsky's failure to attend or to address PLA anniversary celebrations on 1 August, together with the international context, suggested this summit was hastily called for emergency purposes. The timing also had possible domestic implications. On 25 July Peking announced that more than a thousand high-ranking officials had attended an "enlarged conference" called by the CCP Military Affairs Commission from 27 May to 22 July. Mao and his top generals had addressed the principles for development of China's military capabilities and questions of national defense in the light of current developments.

Unfortunately, no detailed accounts have ever been released on either event, although subsequent Chinese and Soviet references agree on two points: First, Mao's impending bombardment of Quemoy was not discussed with Khrushchev; second, some sort of shared Sino-Soviet military facilities in the PRC proved to have been the subject of considerable contention and ultimate disagreement. These two points deserve amplification, if necessarily speculative, for their contribution to subsequent Sino-Soviet strains.

Speaking privately to a select audience in late November 1958, Mao asserted, "The Sino-Soviet talks . . . did not contain a word about the question of the Taiwan situation."[15] Subsequent Soviet allegations of not having been consulted in advance, "as was required by the spirit of the Treaty of Friendship, Alliance, and Mutual Aid," therefore seem valid.[16] References to "the spirit" of the Sino-Soviet treaty, rather than to the treaty itself, highlights a fundamental difference in approach to the relationship. For Mao, Quemoy was a purely internal matter that lay wholly within China's discretion to dispose of as it wished. Consultation with Moscow was not only unnecessary and

---

15 Mao Tse-tung, "Record of talk with directors of various cooperative areas," 30 November 1958, in *Wan-sui* (1969), 255.
16 M. I. Makarov et al., *Vneshnava politika KNR* (Foreign Policy of the People's Republic of China), 28, cited in Jonathan Pollack, "Perception and action in Chinese foreign policy: The Quemoy decision" (Ph.D. dissertation, University of Michigan, 1975), 347; also A. S. Whiting, interview with M.S. Kapitsa, 10 June 1975.

perhaps unwise, but also undesirable, as inviting foreign intervention in a domestic matter.

For Khrushchev, however, the American commitment to Chiang Kai-shek and the American military presence in the Taiwan Strait could not but concern the Soviet Union. At the very least, a Sino-American confrontation there could complicate the timing and tactics of another Soviet push against Berlin. At worst, it could escalate through the patron-client ties on both sides whereby local exchanges between Chinese Nationalist and Communist forces could incrementally involve their respective superpower supporters. This might not lead to a Soviet-American conflict, but it would jeopardize the chances of a summit conference toward which Khrushchev had been maneuvering.

To anticipate the outcome of the Quemoy bombardment that began on 23 August 1958, the early American response, both in the area and in Washington, prompted Peking to propose Sino-American negotiations on 6 September. The next day Khrushchev sent a letter to Eisenhower warning that an attack on China "is an attack on the Soviet Union." Privately, however, he reportedly decided at this time that Mao's behavior warranted termination of the Soviet nuclear sharing agreement, although formal communication of that decision did not occur until the following June.[17]

Khrushchev may have already doubted the wisdom of nuclear sharing as a result of the acrimonious exchanges over proposed military cooperation at the Peking summit meeting. These could not have been more untimely, given a renewed Chinese emphasis on "self-reliance" and against dependence on foreigners (the Soviets) during the previous months. This domestic development coincided with and reinforced strains in the alliance already manifest in the divergent postures on Yugoslavia and the Middle East.

In the first half of 1958, Mao gave a series of talks which focused on the need to arouse and to mobilize the Chinese people for undertaking the GLF.[18] In this context he repeatedly attacked the "slavish mentality" that "worships foreign things," specifically rejecting wholesale reliance on the Soviet Union. The following excerpts illustrate the overall tenor of his remarks:

17 Whiting interview with Kapitsa.
18 See "Speech at the Supreme State Conference," 28 January 1958; "Talks at the Chengtu Conference," March 1958; and "Speech at the group leaders' forum of the enlarged meeting of the Military Affairs Committee," 28 June 1958; in Schram, *Talks*.

(10 March 1958): To import Soviet codes and conventions inflexibly is to lack the creative spirit.... Since we didn't understand these things [heavy industry, planning, banking, and statistics] and had absolutely no experience, all we could do in our ignorance was to import foreign methods.... I couldn't have eggs or chicken soup for three years because an article appeared in the Soviet Union which said that one shouldn't eat them. Later they said one could eat them. It didn't matter whether the article was correct or not, the Chinese listened all the same and respectfully obeyed. In short, the Soviet Union was tops....

The greater part of Soviet planning was correctly applied to China, but part of it was incorrect. It was imported uncritically ... we understood still less the economic differences between the Soviet Union and China. So all we could do was to follow blindly. Now the situation has changed. Generally speaking, we are now capable of undertaking the planning and construction of large enterprises. In another five years we shall be capable of manufacturing the equipment ourselves.[19]

(28 June 1958): In wartime it will not do to implement orders according to Soviet army regulations. It is better for us to have our own regulations.... In the documents of the Eighth Congress, there is a passage dealing with the problem of technological reform. From the point of view of present conditions this is inappropriate because it over-emphasizes Soviet aid. It is very necessary to win Soviet aid, but the most important thing is self-reliance.... The main aim of this conference is to overthrow the slave mentality and to bury dogmatism....

We have rich experience, more than the Soviet Union. We should not regard our own experiences as worthless. This is wrong.... Nowadays the stuff produced by the Soviet military advisors [combat plans and ways of thinking] all deal with the offensive and are all concerned with victory. They have no defensive material and do not provide for defeat. This does not conform with real situations.[20]

Mao's secret speeches elaborated on themes more elliptically suggested in public articles which implied a lessening reliance on Soviet aid. In May, PLA Air Force Commander General Liu Ya-lou forecast major military weapons improvements based on indigenous, not Soviet, resources: "China's working class and scientists will certainly be able to make the most up-to-date aircraft and atomic bombs in the not-distant future. By that time ... we can use atomic weapons and rockets made by the workers, engineers, and scientists of our country."[21]

These hints in private and public statements of lowered expectations for Soviet assistance run counter to the logic of the 1957 atomic

19 Ibid., 103.   20 Ibid., 125–30.
21 Alice Langley Hsieh, *Communist China's strategy in the nuclear era*, 112.

sharing agreements, which were already being implemented. One explanation may lie in Khrushchev's proposals for Soviet-American negotiations on a nuclear test ban. His 4 April letter to world leaders, including Chou En-lai, noted that with only the Soviet Union, the United States, and Great Britain possessing nuclear weapons, a test ban agreement "is comparatively easy to reach," whereas when "after some time other countries may become possessors of nuclear weapons ... it will be a more complicated matter to reach an agreement on the discontinuance of these tests."[22] On 22 April, he agreed to President Eisenhower's suggestion of a Soviet-American technical study on how to police a test cessation.

In addition to understandable Chinese resentment at this apparent move against Peking's ultimate nuclear capability, a Sino-Soviet disagreement arose over other areas of proposed military cooperation. Indeed, this may have been the immediate issue which prompted the Peking summit meeting. Post hoc accounts of what actually was offered or requested on each side differ, but they agree on an argument over the joint use of naval, air, and communications facilities in China.[23] Differences persisting at lower levels over previous months apparently prompted an attempt at resolution in Peking. No agreement was reached, however. Instead, the two sides probably parted on worse terms than before. Whether Khrushchev expected access to joint facilities in return for nuclear sharing or Mao demanded a wider range of modern weapons without conceding to Soviet demands cannot be determined on the available evidence. But Chinese sensitivity over a foreign military presence, coupled with Mao's renewed emphasis on "self-reliance," produced an impasse that subsequently embittered both sides.

The Quemoy bombardment

On 23 August 1958, Chinese Communist batteries unleashed an estimated 41,000 shells against the Quemoy Island complex, the

22 MacFarquhar, *The origins of the Cultural Revolution*, 2. 66.
23 Pollack, "Perception," 350–52, reviews Soviet and Chinese sources, including interviews with Kapitsa by American scholars, and lists Soviet demands as possibly including naval access to Chinese ports, communications facilities for the Soviet navy, a joint Sino-Soviet fleet along the Chinese coast, a Soviet tracking station in China to monitor U.S. missiles, and Soviet interceptor air bases in China. Possible Chinese demands were for extensive Soviet submarine construction help, including eventual nuclear subs, Soviet air defense wings under Chinese control, and various kinds of air and ground assistance against Quemoy.

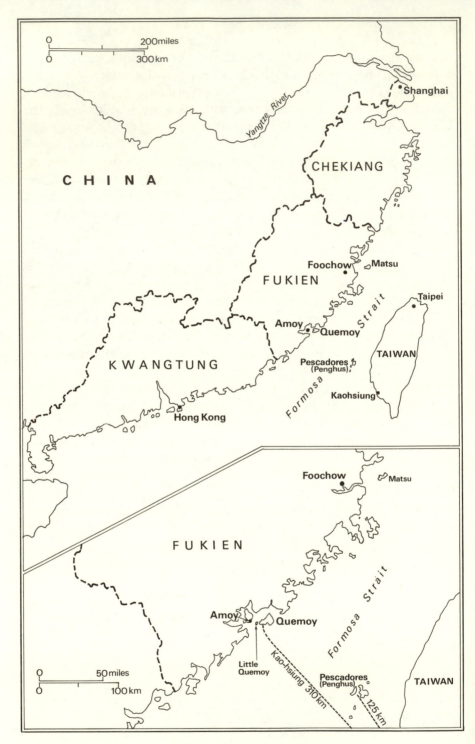

MAP 8. Offshore islands

highest total in nearly ten years of recurring hostilities.[24] The targets lay within a few thousand yards of mainland artillery on three sides. The approximately 80,000 Nationalist troops, together with a civilian populace of 40,000, basically depended on seaborne supplies from 125 miles away in Taiwan to maintain the offshore bastion, one of the last legal territorial remnants of Chiang Kai-shek's sovereignty. The threat to nearby shipping posed by the Quemoy garrison's guns effectively blocked access to the major port of Amoy, visible across the harbor.

During the following week, the Fukien provincial radio station blared surrender ultimatums to Quemoy, while an intermittent bombardment of varying intensity hit the island complex.[25] Isolated bombing and strafing by MIG-17s struck at military targets, while naval units interdicted supplies from Taiwan. On 28 August the *People's Daily* gave front-page attention to a Ministry of Defense commendation for the sinking of a Nationalist ship four days previously, claiming that this "showed the power of the Chinese People's Navy, severely threatening marine contact between the Chiang Kai-shek army now entrenched on Quemoy Island and Taiwan and increasing the difficulty of its situation."[26] The directive ordered the navy "to make further efforts and be ready to deal heavier blows to reinforcements of the traitorous Chiang Kai-shek army at any time in close coordination with land and air force units at the front."

But after 27 August, the tempo and level of military action decreased sharply. This was only partially attributable to the impact of typhoons. American responses to the bombardment suggest an additional explanation. Within days of the first shelling, the U.S. Seventh Fleet in the western Pacific and the U.S. Fifth Air Force in Japan went on alert status. The aircraft carrier *Essex* and four destroyers from the Sixth Fleet in the Mediterranean were ordered to the Taiwan area. The Taiwan Strait patrol was strengthened with two additional aircraft carrier groups, and an American air defense exercise was held over Taiwan. U.S. military commanders from the Pacific theater met on the island to supervise a previously announced joint Sino-American amphibious exercise in early September, which would

---

24 Ibid., 117. Pollack's data are based on declassified U.S. government documents in addition to a thorough review of press reports and Chinese sources, Nationalist and Communist.
25 The initial surrender demand threatened "landing on Quemoy" as well as total blockade; *China News Service* in Mandarin, Fukien Front, 28 August 1958, as quoted in ibid., 128–29. Subsequent ultimatum broadcasts omitted the invasion threat. Shelling intensity varied from 3,000 to 36,000 shells per day.
26 Ibid., 122.

involve 3,800 U.S. Marines. By 29 August, more than 50 American ships, including 6 aircraft carriers with more than 500 fighters and bombers, were either in or on their way to the Taiwan area. The next day Seventh Fleet units prepared to escort Nationalist supply ships to Quemoy.

American political statements, albeit more ambiguous, left sufficient room for involvement to add concern in Peking. On the day the bombardment began, Secretary of State Dulles released a letter responding to a congressional inquiry over the meaning of recently increased mainland military activity near the offshore islands, noting, "I think it would be highly hazardous for anyone to assume that if the Chinese communists were to change this situation by force and now to attack and seek to conquer these islands, that it could be a limited operation."[27]

On 27 August, President Eisenhower claimed that with one-third of the Nationalist forces on the islands, this created "a closer interlocking between the defense systems of the islands with Formosa than was the case before," in 1954–55.[28] He thereby invoked the 1955 Formosa Resolution, which had authorized the president to use force beyond the 1954 Mutual Defense Treaty limits of Taiwan and the Pescadores if he determined this were necessary to the defense of Taiwan. He also cautioned that "the U.S. will not desert its responsibilities" were the islands to be invaded. Four days later in Taipei, U.S. Secretary of the Army Brucker warned Peking not to "underestimate" American warnings.

The concatenation of actions and words apparently countered Mao's own expectations. Speaking privately to the Supreme State Conference on 5 September, he confessed, "I simply did not calculate that the world would become so disturbed and turbulent" from "firing a few rounds of artillery at Quemoy and Matsu."[29] Although he blamed the "turmoil" on the fact that "people fear war, they are afraid that America will rush into calamity everywhere," he did not disguise his surprise at his miscalculation.

On 6 September, Chou En-lai publicly proposed resumption of the Sino-American ambassadorial talks, suspended since the previous December. Although his speech followed immediately after the most explicit American commitment to date in support of the Nationalists,

27 Ibid., 157–58.
28 Ibid., 158.
29 Mao Tse-tung, "Speech to Supreme State Conference," 5 September 1958, in *Wan-sui* (1969), 233.

delivered by Secretary Dulles on 5 September, a close reading of Chinese words and behavior suggests that a decision to reduce the risk of war came well before Dulles's press conference. One month later, on 6 October, Marshal P'eng Te-huai announced a one-week suspension of the bombardment and blockade. After another three weeks, he declared a unique program of shelling only on even-numbered days. Tension abated, and no further action occurred.

Central to Chinese calculations in planning the Quemoy bombardment was the anticipated American response. Mao's secret self-criticism stated that he did not expect it to be so vigorous. But Chinese officials claimed success immediately after the bombardment ended, alleging that its goal had actually been to involve American forces so as to preclude abandonment of offshore islands in a "two-China" move.[30] This latter explanation appears to have been a post hoc rationalization. The ultimatums initially broadcast to the Quemoy garrison demanded that it surrender. Moreover, on 8 September Mao, addressing the Supreme State Conference, called on Dulles and Eisenhower "to take the initiative and gradually disengage.... What way of disengagement is there? Simply for 110,000 men [his estimate of the Kuomintang forces on Quemoy and Matsu] to get away."[31] Mao specifically denied that the "trap" of Quemoy and Matsu was closed to "escape."

This suggests that a range of goals underlay the move, which at best, might have resulted in capture of the islands while American power was concentrated on the Middle East crisis. At worst, the bombardment might have forced Washington to resume the ambassadorial talks with due regard for Peking's claims on Taiwan. Pertinent in this regard are certain developments during the previous year.

In 1957, after two years of effort by Peking to negotiate a modus vivendi with Washington, relations sharply worsened. That May, the United States revealed its intention to deploy the nuclear-capable missile Matador, with a 650-mile range, on Taiwan. In June, Secretary Dulles delivered an unusually hostile and uncompromising address on China policy. In December, Peking suspended the Sino-American ambassadorial talks when transfer of Washington's representative elsewhere resulted in a lower-level officer's replacing him.

Chou's February 1958 review of foreign policy to the National

30 Anna Louise Strong, "Chinese strategy in the Taiwan Strait," *New Times*, 46 (November 1958), 8–11.
31 Mao, "Speech to Supreme State Conference," 8 September 1958, in *Wan-sui* (1969), 239.

People's Congress responded to these developments in kind, omitting previous references to a "peaceful liberation of Taiwan" and excoriating Washington for its alleged "two-China" plot. On 30 June Peking publicly demanded that the United States name an ambassadorial representative to the suspended talks within fifteen days, or the PRC would "consider that the United States has decided to break [them] up."[32] Washington, refusing to submit to an ultimatum, deliberately delayed its designation of the U.S. ambassador to Poland as participant. Meanwhile, the Lebanon crisis erupted.

Speaking months later to the Supreme State Conference, Mao linked these two developments:

In the past the Americans insulted us. Before the Middle East incident they openly published a memorandum and spoke ill of China, saying China is the worst one.... They also cut off the Geneva talks. Not until the end of the Middle East incident did their documents come and they postponed by several days our time limit. Our deadline was the 15th and their letter requesting talks was the 17th. We did not publish this at the time because we did not care about that document and we wanted to shell.[33]

Suddenly the Chinese introduced "liberate Taiwan" themes into the mass demonstrations over Lebanon and accelerated the movement of jet fighters, artillery, and troops opposite the offshore islands and Taiwan. On 22 July, the main military newspaper, Liberation Army News, ostensibly marking the fifth anniversary of a battle that had foiled a Nationalist invasion of an island south of Quemoy, claimed that "the Chinese People's Liberation Army coastal defense forces have all pledged themselves to ... prepare to liberate our country's territory of Taiwan, Quemoy, Matsu, and other coastal islands."[34] The People's Daily repeated this dispatch the next day.

On 29 July, MIG-17s made their first combat appearance along the coast, shooting down two Nationalist fighters on patrol south of Quemoy. Airfields built a year or more before became operational with deployments in late July and early August. A 500-mile railroad to Amoy, the first to be built in Fukien, had been completed in February, and it now serviced some 400 artillery pieces targeted on Quemoy and more than 300,000 troops assembled along the Fukien front.

Thus, Peking's relations with Washington had deteriorated badly

32 Pollack, "Perception," 89.
33 Mao to Supreme State Conference, 15 April 1959, in Wan-sui (1969), 290.
34 Pollack, "Perception," 89.

beginning in mid-1957. Its adamant stand on the ambassadorial talks dated from December 1957. Its military activity opposite the offshore islands began in late July 1958, triggered by the Middle East crisis. This suggests a series of decisions and their implementation in advance of the abortive Khrushchev-Mao meeting. Combining the emphasis on "self-defense" with the consistent definition of Taiwan's "liberation" as an "internal affair," it would appear that Mao hoped the Quemoy attack would prompt the garrison to surrender without an American response, thereby demonstrating to Khrushchev Peking's resolve, Washington's impotence, and Moscow's irrelevance.

However, Mao's admitted miscalculation not only brought about a Sino-American military confrontation but also seriously worsened Sino-Soviet relations. On 5 September, Foreign Minister Andrei Gromyko arrived in Peking, accompanied by his top China specialist, M.S. Kapitsa, for consultation on the Quemoy affair. The next day, Chou called for Sino-American ambassadorial talks. On 7 September Khrushchev wrote to Eisenhower: "An attack on the People's Republic of China, which is a great friend, ally, neighbor of our country, is an attack on the Soviet Union. Loyal to its duty, our country would do everything to defend, jointly with People's China, the security of both countries."[35] He defended Peking's actions as "striving to liberate its own territory" with "every legitimate right" and "a lawful measure of self-defense."

Privately, however, the Soviet leader apparently was angered by Mao's unilateral action. According to Kapitsa, Khrushchev rejected his colleagues' opposition to publicly backing Mao, arguing that the alliance required him to respond once Eisenhower had intervened, but after tension abated it would be necessary to review the relationship.[36] Mao's reportedly cavalier dismissal of the escalatory risks of nuclear warfare in his meeting with Gromyko further provoked the Soviet decision to renege on the 1957 nuclear agreement.

The public polemics between Moscow and Peking which emerged in the mid-1960s included Soviet claims of having deterred an American attack during the Quemoy affair and a Chinese denial that such an attack had been imminent, least of all by the time Khrushchev sent his letter to Eisenhower.[37] The absence in Mao's speeches immediately after the event of any charges of inadequate Soviet support makes it

35 Ibid., 230–31.
36 Whiting interview with M. S. Kapitsa, 10 June 1975.
37 Soviet government statements, 21 August and 21 September 1963; Chinese government statement, 1 September 1963; in Griffith, *The Sino-Soviet rift*, 365, 382, and 439.

unlikely that the subsequent exchanges reflect the actual cause of tension at the time. Chinese actions neither invited nor required Soviet intervention and, on the contrary, ruled it out on principle. But the role of Quemoy in the Soviet decision to suspend nuclear assistance, whether genuine or feigned, proved important.

The Great Leap and Soviet criticism

During the bombardment of Quemoy, Peking mobilized the country in the so-called Great Leap Forward (GLF). On 29 August, an enlarged session of the Politburo of the CCP passed a resolution "Concerning the establishment of the People's Communes," which declared that these "basic social units of Communist society" were to "accelerate the speed of socialist construction and the purpose of building socialism is to prepare actively for the transition to Communism. It seems that the attainment of communism in China is no longer a remote future event. We should actively use the form of the people's communes to explore the practical road to transition to communism."[38]

Although the primary implications and importance of this development were domestic, the spillover into Sino-Soviet relations contributed further to friction in the alliance. On the Chinese side, the communes, together with their free supply system, communal mess halls, and nurseries, were authoritatively hailed as "a major event, not only in Chinese history but in world history" and "an event of world significance."[39] In contrast, Soviet ceremonial speeches, messages, and official statements relating to China studiously avoided public reference to the communes throughout the fall. Speaking to Senator Hubert Humphrey, Khrushchev dismissed the communes as "reactionary."[40] He likened them to Moscow's abortive experiment with communes after the revolution which had failed because "you can't get production without incentive." Publication of his remarks violated the Chinese sense of appropriate conduct among allies.

On 10 December 1958, a CCP plenum resolution backtracked on the timing in the earlier statement, citing "fifteen, twenty, or more years to complete" the building of socialism, with communism even

38 Text in PR, 29 (16 September 1958); quoted in Zagoria, Conflict, 97.
39 Chu Te in JMJP, 9 September 1958, and Li Hsien-nien in Hung-ch'i, 16 October 1958; quoted in ibid., 102–3.
40 Ibid., 99, 126.

more distant.[41] It declared that "pay according to work" would "occupy an important place over a long period," as opposed to distribution according to "need" which, if introduced prematurely, would be "undoubtedly a utopian concept that cannot possibly succeed."

This retreat from the positions advanced in late August did not end the controversy over the GLF either within China or between the PRC and the Soviet Union. Soviet skepticism continued over the economic consequences. Soviet advisers became frustrated over the flouting of their warnings.[42] Soviet officials resented the increased demands for deliveries to China. Soviet leaders bristled at implications of Chinese ideological superiority. Although basically an internal affair, Mao's reckless economic experiment inevitably involved foreign relations, as had his decision to bombard Quemoy – also ostensibly an internal matter.

The Quemoy bombardment ended in humiliation for the PLA. Mao's repeated injunction to "strategically despise, tactically respect" had failed to restrain his hand. Similarly, the GLF ended in the economic catastrophe of 1960–61. Mao's ignorance of economics, which he belatedly admitted, had failed to rein in his hubris. Seen from Moscow, the magnitude of miscalculation in both instances suggested megalomania. This perception was eventually to provoke a Soviet withdrawal of aid in 1960, thereby making a necessity of the "self-reliance" program announced in 1958.

PHASE TWO: 1959–1960

Overview

Strain in the Sino-Soviet alliance neared the breaking point in 1959–60 as a result of Khrushchev's meeting with Eisenhower in the United States, Moscow's public neutrality in the Sino-Indian border dispute, Peking's challenge to the Kremlin's ideological leadership, the withdrawal of Soviet economic aid, and the polemical exchanges at multiparty conferences in Bucharest and Moscow. But dramatic and far-reaching as were these developments in their implications for national, regional, and global politics, other relationships also re-

41 Ibid., 125–26.
42 For a recapitulation of Soviet advisors' experiences and criticisms during 1958–59, see O. B. Borisov and B. T. Koloskov, *Sino-Soviet relations, 1945–1973: A brief history*, 144–45.

quired China's urgent attention. A Tibetan revolt forced the issue of control over high Himalayan passes through which guerrillas could flee and also return. This made Sino-Indian relations contentious – whereas previously they had been avowedly friendly, if actually competitive.

Sino-Indian tensions, in turn, affected Sino-Burmese border differences because the disputed McMahon Line continued throughout the area. In addition, Communist insurgency in Burma tested Peking's willingness to support "people's war" in neighboring countries. Laos also challenged revolutionary rhetoric when the 1954 Geneva Accords brought a neutralist regime that in 1958 gave way to an anticommunist government under American sponsorship. Farther away, Indonesia posed unique problems. First, an American effort to topple Sukarno through a Sumatran rebellion failed. Then anticommunist interests, led by the army, sought to break Sukarno's pro-Peking orientation and his association with the Indonesian Communist Party (PKI) by exploiting anti-Chinese sentiment to provoke Peking into an overreaction.

These developments loaded the PRC foreign policy agenda with questions that required answers, if not action. Ideological and theoretical formulations could guide polemical exchanges with Moscow on a general line for the socialist bloc and the international communist movement. They were, however, an inadequate guide for coping with specific cases. Mao may personally have supervised major statements on general policy that drove Soviet relations to the breaking point in 1960. But otherwise it appears that Chou En-lai and the Ministry of Foreign Affairs adhered to the more restrained posture adopted at the 1955 Bandung Conference with the "united front from above" against "imperialism and colonialism" evident in most of the important confrontations that arose during 1959–60.

Laos

Developments in Laos revealed Peking's priority between cautious diplomacy and revolutionary violence. The former prevailed through much of this period. In May 1958, the Communist front in Laos placed first in elections managed by the International Supervisory and Control Commission (ICC) established under the 1954 Geneva Accords. Neutralist premier Souvanna Phouma thereupon asked the ICC to leave, its mission ostensibly completed. By the time it did so in July 1958, Souvanna had resigned and the left-neutral coalition had

been replaced by an anticommunist coalition under Phoui Sanani-
kone. His leadership resulted in a Taiwan consulate's being opened in
January 1959, at which time Phoui Sananikone declared the Geneva
Accords no longer binding and openly threatened to ally with the
United States. Peking charged correctly that Washington had already
been manipulating events behind the scenes. Its concern over the
Taiwan link arose from remnant Kuomintang (KMT) forces in the
hill and jungle border area causing trouble in Yunnan province.

In February Ch'en I formally accused "U.S. imperialism" of
violating the Geneva Accords and plotting aggression in Indochina.
He also demanded that the ICC enforce the accords. In March the
Southeast Asian Treaty Organization (SEATO) held maneuvers
against a hypothetical Chinese attack, and included nuclear weapons
in the exercise. Chinese media reacted with charges of a "tripartite
military alliance" linking Thailand, Laos, and South Vietnam, but did
not call on the Pathet Lao to take countermeasures.

By March the PRC felt compelled to admit "disturbances" within
its borders, attributing espionage and riots in Yunnan to American-
Laotian airdrops of supplies to KMT troops.[43] Anxiety was probably
heightened by eruption of the Tibetan revolt the same month,
resulting in the flight of the Dalai Lama to India, together with tens of
thousands of refugees who were potential future guerrillas. The
CIA-KMT network of support for the Tibetan revolt made credible
Peking's charges about Laos.[44]

Fighting broke out in May when Phoui Sananikone ordered the
two Pathet Lao battalions, numbering 1,500 men, disarmed. One fled
and, with help from Communist North Vietnam, began attacking
Vientiane's forces. Meanwhile Peking sharpened its tone. It hit the
Laotian and Thai foreign ministers' joint statement which approved
Laos's joining a regional organization and once again called on the
ICC to remedy the situation. Secretly, however, Peking began to cooperate with Hanoi. It provided modest amounts of military aid,
advisers, training, and recruitment among ethnically related groups in
support of the Pathet Lao.[45] That summer, a Laotian-French agree-
ment legitimized American supplies and training for Vientiane's army.
Peking responded in August by formally demanding return of the

43 Chae-jin Lee, *Communist China's policy toward Laos: A case study, 1954–67* (hereafter
Laos), 52.
44 Allen S. Whiting, *The Chinese calculus of deterrence: India and Indochina*, ch. 1, details the
evidence of clandestine activity in Tibet.
45 Lee, *Laos*, 55.

ICC, withdrawal of all American military involvement, and restoration of the status quo ante based on the Geneva Accords.

The arrival of a United Nations investigatory group in mid-September apparently inhibited both sides, as evidenced by a marked decline in reported casualties and a reduction in the sporadic fighting. The UN report claimed evidence of Chinese material assistance in the form of weapons, uniforms, and medical supplies, but implied this was secondary to North Vietnam's role. The military situation thereupon stalemated.

The right-wing coup at the end of 1959 provoked Peking's denunciation of it as a "fascist and military dictatorship," and strongman Phoumi Nosavan's continued attack on Pathet Lao forces won Peking's pledge to resist "U.S. imperialist adventures to extend the civil war in Laos."[46] But no Chinese action followed. In May 1960 Chou En-lai's visit to Hanoi produced a joint statement that merely called for the resumption of ICC activity and faithful adherence to the Geneva Accords.

Peking's relative passivity seemed justified in August 1960 when Kong Le, a neutralist army officer, seized power in Vientiane for the avowed purpose of ending American intervention and restoring Souvanna Phouma as premier. But Chinese efforts to reestablish a united front between Souvanna and the Pathet Lao were countered by Phoumi Nosavan's rival organization at Savannakhet, backed by the United States and Thailand. Then in mid-December Phoumi's forces seized Vientiane, driving Souvanna into refuge in Cambodia. Resumption of civil war brought the two superpowers into an open proxy confrontation as American advisers, tanks, and artillery supported Phoumi against Kong Le and the Pathet Lao, who were supplied by Soviet airlift as well as by North Vietnam.

Ch'en I talked tough in warning that because the "biggest armed intervention" by "U.S. imperialism" in Indochina since 1954 was a "scheme" for an ultimate attack on China and Vietnam, the PRC might have to take "proper measures."[47] But Peking continued to endorse Hanoi's proposal that the 1954 Geneva Conference be reconvened and the ICC return to Laos. Thus the year closed with no substantive change in China's public position, which favored negotiations over fighting and only minor change in its clandestine support for the Pathet Lao forces.

46 *JMJP*, 8 January; Radio Peking, 11 January; *JMJP*, 22 January, and *Ta-kung pao*, 23 January; in ibid., 65–66.
47 Ibid., 74.

Cambodia, Thailand, and Burma

Chinese policy toward the noncommunist neighbors of Laos similarly eschewed a radical revolutionary line, in contrast to its polemic with Moscow. The Cambodian relationship began informally and personally when Prince Norodom Sihanouk visited Mao in 1956 and then publicly rejected SEATO's protection. A few months later Peking's first aid grant to a noncommunist country gave Cambodia $22.4 million for plywood, cement, textile, and paper factories. That December Chou En-lai visited Phnom Penh, but formal diplomatic relations began only in July 1958.

Suspicion that the Chinese economic mission in Cambodia was subsidizing left-wing newspapers and promoting leftist influence in Chinese schools and clubs prompted the regime to restrict foreign participation in certain professions dominated by Chinese and to place controls over the schools while abolishing the clubs.[48] In 1960 several hundred Chinese reportedly were arrested for subversion, among other things, and several dozen were deported to China following another visit by Chou in May. However, to what degree these activities aimed at a genuine revolutionary movement as compared with Peking's effort to convert the Chinese community from its previous pro-Taiwan orientation has never been determined. So far as Cambodian left-wing activities were concerned, French, and to a lesser extent Soviet, influence was much more evident until 1961.

In contrast with Laos, 1960 ended on a positive note for Peking when Liu Shao-ch'i's visit to Phnom Penh resulted in signing of a Treaty of Friendship and Mutual Nonaggression. Although no substantive changes occurred, this symbolized a relationship that was to become increasingly close in the future.

Chinese relations with Thailand were virtually nonexistent during these years. Bangkok viewed Sino-Cambodian ties as implicitly hostile, evidenced by its October 1958 directive banning all Chinese imports, as well as striking against communist and leftist activity. In 1959–60 Sino–North Vietnamese–Pathet Lao cooperation was seen to pose a potential threat to Thai security should Laos come under communist control. Bangkok reacted by strengthened support for Phoumi Nosovan and cooperation with clandestine American programs.

For its part, Peking responded with rhetoric to Thai activities in and around Laos but did little to challenge Bangkok on its own

48 Melvin Gurtov, *China and Southeast Asia – The politics of survival* (hereafter *Survival*), 62.

soil. The Thai Communist Party remained a minuscule and minor annoyance until the mid-1960s. Its only visible relationship with China at this time was a congratulatory telegram on the PRC tenth anniversary, wholly bereft of any revolutionary reference. The large and economically powerful Chinese community, in contrast with Cambodia, maintained its Taiwan orientation.

Burma, the third noncommunist country adjoining Laos, posed three problems for Peking. Remnant KMT bands in Burma threatened Yunnan. A border dispute involved the troops of both countries. The Burmese Communist Party, specifically the so-called White Flag faction, resisted Rangoon's rule with guerrilla warfare along the Chinese border. The KMT presence was less serious than in Laos and Thailand. More than half the force had been evacuated to Taiwan in previous years, and the rest were more interested in the opium trade than in anticommunist activity. Meanwhile, communist insurgents appeared to receive little help from China, as evidenced by the fact that from 1954 to 1958 Rangoon reported no evidence of Chinese arms.[49]

The Sino-Burmese border, however, had been a sticking point since 1954. After a minor clash in 1956, the reciprocal withdrawal of forces from disputed sections in the Wa and Kachin states had reduced tension, but negotiations from 1956 to 1958 had proved fruitless. The issue was a sensitive one in Rangoon, faced with a 1,350-mile frontier to control and separated from much of it by rebellious Shan, Karen, and Kachin minorities, as well as White Flag remnants.

Burma's assiduous pursuit of neutrality benefited the PRC, however, in excluding a potential American presence. Its political value emerged in October 1959 when Burma abstained on a UN resolution condemning China for the use of force on the disputed Sino-Indian frontier. This facilitated Ne Win's visit to Peking in January 1960, which produced a more generous border agreement than might have been expected from the imbalance of Sino-Burmese power.[50] Only the western portion remained undefined, where the trijuncture of China, Burma, and India rested on the disputed McMahon Line.

Indeed, it was probably the Sino-Indian dispute itself that

49 John H. Badgley, "Burma and China," in A. M. Halpern, ed. *Policies toward China: Views from six continents*, 308.
50 China won three villages with 59 square miles plus 73 square miles in the Wa area; Burma won four of six villages on "the 1941 line," plus 85 square miles in the Namwan Tract. Gurtov, *Survival*, 95.

prompted Peking to settle with Rangoon, not only as a reward for Burma's abstention in the UN vote but also as a signal to New Delhi that compromise was possible. In this regard it was no coincidence that China concluded boundary and economic aid agreements with Nepal on 21 March 1960, followed by a friendship treaty with Kathmandu on 28 April, between which dates Chou met with Nehru in New Delhi. A similar motive undoubtedly underlay Ch'en I's trip to Afghanistan and the conclusion of a Treaty of Friendship and Nonaggression in Kabul on 26 August 1960. China was willing to compromise territorial disputes; but should India not follow suit, it might face political isolation from its neighbors.

Indonesia

Lacking any adjacent or nearby land connection to China, in contrast with the countries discussed above, Indonesia might be considered a special case. But it too forced a choice on Peking during 1958–60 between a "united front from above," which made state-to-state relations primary but which required a compromise of Chinese interests, and a harsher stance of confrontation and pressure, possibly involving revolution.

As in Laos, Peking vacillated briefly in 1959, experimenting with a tougher stance. But ultimately it gave in to Jakarta in 1960. Again as in Laos, the bilateral relationship intertwined with the U.S.–Taiwanese tie, on the one hand, and Soviet policy, on the other. Indonesia did not involve China's security. In addition, Peking had a stronger and somewhat more reliable friend in Sukarno than in Souvanna.

In early 1958 a rebellion in Sumatra challenged Jakarta's rule. The next month the U.S. Seventh Fleet appeared off Indonesia's coast, ostensibly to safeguard American lives if necessary. But a SEATO hint of possible support for the rebellion, evidence of Chinese Nationalist arms flown in American B-26s from bases in the Philippines, and capture of an American pilot based on Okinawa combined to reveal the Washington-Taipei linkage.[51]

In April 1958, Peking sought to capitalize on this fact with a $16 million credit to Indonesia for the purchase of rice and textiles. The next month it publicly linked Taiwan with the rebellion to posit a joint security interest between China and Indonesia. Peking's pledge

51 David Mozingo, *Chinese policy toward Indonesia: 1949–1967*, 141–45.

of unspecified help was accompanied by a private offer which reportedly included "volunteers."[52] This favorable international context was reinforced by the participation in power of the growing Indonesian Communist Party, although its orientation was implicitly more toward Moscow than toward Peking, and in any event it was beholden to Sukarno for a role in his "guided democracy."

Once the Sumatran rebellion was brought under control, however, the situation rapidly changed. After breaking up pro-Taiwan groups because of Taipei's activity, Indonesian interests turned to the remaining Chinese as a target of control. Army commanders stood to gain as they took over Chinese ventures, while civilians would benefit from lessened Chinese competition in finance and manufacturing. Most important, conservative military leaders wanted to move Sukarno from his pro-Peking stance back toward the West and at the same time to break the PKI before it became more powerful and independent of Sukarno. For his part, Sukarno refused to face down the army, which had suppressed the rebellion and was essential to his plans for expansion and dominion first over West Irian and then over Malaysia.

Thus in May 1959 the Indonesian Ministry of Trade announced that all alien trading licenses would be revoked in rural areas by December. A central army decree also approved local commanders removing aliens from their residence "for security reasons." A West Java colonel thereupon ordered all aliens into urban areas by December. These developments opened the door to discrimination against and confiscation of Chinese business interests throughout the countryside.

Such steps were legally within Jakarta's purview. Although they went against the sense of the 1955 Sino-Indonesian Dual Nationality Treaty, Jakarta had yet to ratify it. Lacking any formal basis of protest, in September Peking proposed "quiet diplomacy," to which Foreign Minister Subandrio responded with a visist in October. But he was reportedly harangued and threatened with a boycott of Indonesian goods by the Singapore dockworkers if the discriminatory steps were not ameliorated.[53] Shortly after his return, the trade ban was modified somewhat and West Java exempted Chinese aliens who had applied for Indonesian citizenship before May.

But the situation became tense when the West Java colonel took preemptory action to expel the Chinese, often with rough treatment.

52 Ibid., 146.   53 Ibid., 165–66.

Chinese embassy personnel went to the area and mobilized resistance by leaflets and meetings. Officials reacted by arresting local Chinese and barring all embassy figures. In December Ch'en I called for immediate ratification of the treaty, the protection of Chinese nationals and their interests, and voluntary repatriation after the sale of property. The next day Peking began a systematic campaign to persuade all Chinese, whether foreign or locally born, to leave for the PRC.

Thousands responded to the appeal, fearful for their lives as well as their fortunes. Inflation resulted from the hoarding of consumer goods against a possible pogrom, and from the purchase of foreign exchange. More basic disturbance of the economy was threatened by the possible departure of Chinese essential to the processing and marketing of key exports such as copra, oil, rubber, and tin, as well as those who bridged rural and urban marketing while providing credit to farmers.

Peking's pressures grew but Jakarta remained firm, refusing to permit property or foreign exchange to be removed from the country. The growing sense of confrontation between the two capitals threatened the PKI, which could not afford to go down with the Chinese but alternatively could not afford to lose a main source of financial support.[54] This dilemma was precisely what the decrees had been designed to produce. To complicate matters further for Peking, in February 1960, at the height of the dispute, Khrushchev visited Jakarta and provided a $250 million credit.

This concatenation of contrary pressures persuaded Peking to back down on virtually all the issues, signaled by Chou En-lai's remarks to the National People's Congress on 10 April 1960. His specific reference to "revisionist" plots against Sino-Indonesian relations suggested that the decision had been finally forced by fear of Moscow's exploiting the dispute so as to be preeminent with Sukarno, the army, and the PKI. In addition, the timing coincided with the border agreements associated with the Sino-Indian dispute.

India

Sino-Indian relations became critical in 1959-60, affecting China's other relationships, particularly with the Soviet Union. Beginning in 1954, Peking and New Delhi publicly espoused the Five Principles of

54 Ibid., 180ff.

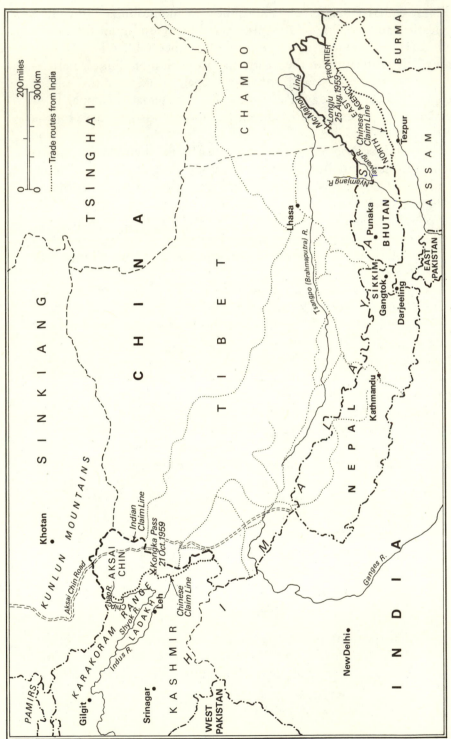

MAP 9. Sino-Indian border

TSINGHAI

CHAMDO

200 miles
300 km
Trade routes from India

McMAHON Line

FRONTIER

Longju
25 Aug. 1959

NORTH EAST FRONTIER AGENCY

Chinese Claim Line

BURMA

Tezpur

Tawang R.

Nyamjang R.

ASSAM

Lhasa

BHUTAN

Punaka

SIKKIM

Gangtok

EAST PAKISTAN

Darjeeling

Tsangpo (Brahmaputra) R.

SINKIANG

CHINA

TIBET

Khotan

KUNLUN MOUNTAINS

Aksai Chin Road

AKSAI CHIN

Indian Claim Line

Kongka Pass
21 Oct. 1959

Chagra R.

Shyok R.

KARAKORAM RANGE

LADAKH

Leh

Chinese Claim Line

Indus R.

KASHMIR

PAMIRS

Gilgit

Srinagar

WEST PAKISTAN

NEPAL

Kathmandu

HIMALAYA

Ganges R.

New Delhi

INDIA

Peaceful Coexistence while privately differing over the border, as depicted on their respective maps. But with the western section in Ladakh virtually unpopulated and mutual observance of the eastern section along the Northeast Frontier Agency (NEFA), the issue remained dormant.

Then, in 1958, Peking disclosed a newly completed highway linking Sinkiang with Tibet and traversing the Aksai Chin plateau, which New Delhi's maps showed as Indian. Patrols sent to examine the situation were captured and detained for a month, prompting India to protest. That December Nehru reasserted his position in a letter to Chou without reference to the highway. Chou replied in January, stating that the border had never been delimited and that the highway was in PRC territory.[55] He proposed that although the McMahon Line in the east was illegal, both sides should continue to observe the status quo there. Nehru's reply in March restated India's demand that China return to its side of the border at all points.

Meanwhile, a long-simmering revolt by the militant Khambas in eastern Tibet spread to Lhasa's jurisdiction. On 10 March 1959, a mass demonstration in the capital attempted to dissuade the Dalai Lama from fleeing to India. In its aftermath, however, the PLA opened fire, riots followed, and His Holiness fled during heavy fighting. Peking protested New Delhi's open sympathy for the Tibetans, but on 31 March the Dalai Lama won asylum, together with thousands of his refugee supporters. This provoked further press attacks in Peking and a formal demarche on 16 May accusing India of "interference in China's internal affairs."[56]

Control over the high Himalayan passes came into question because they provided access to Tibet for guerrillas as well as to India for refugees. In August 1959 PLA efforts to close off this flow resulted in a clash with Indian patrols at Longju in the eastern sector, and an Indian soldier was killed. The Indians abandoned this position to Chinese occupation. On 8 September, Chou defended the PLA actions as aimed at stopping remnant armed Tibetan rebels from crossing the border back and forth.[57] But he reiterated his proposal that the border differences be settled through negotiations and that until then both sides should observe the status quo.

In the meantime, on 6 September, Chinese officials had told the Soviet chargé d'affaires that New Delhi had provoked the border

55 Harold C. Hinton, *Communist China in world politics*, 285.
56 Ibid., 287.   57 Ibid., 289.

dispute. They had warned Moscow against being "taken in by Nehru who was striving to put pressure on China by utilizing the Soviet Union."[58] Three days later, however, the Soviet chargé transmitted the text of a Tass statement to be issued on 10 September that implicitly rejected the Chinese position by taking a completely neutral stand on the "incident" which it termed "certainly deplorable."[59] Tass blamed "certain political circles and the press in the Western countries" for trying "to obstruct a relaxation of international tension and to complicate the situation on the eve" of Khrushchev's visit to Eisenhower.

According to Peking's subsequent polemic, Moscow issued the Tass statement against China's express admonition to the contrary, "thus revealing the differences between China and the Soviet Union . . . without first distinguishing between right and wrong."[60] Moreover, on 13 September 1959, Moscow signed an agreement to extend more than $375 million for India's 3rd Five-Year Plan, negotiations for which had begun in July. By doubling its total previous aid to India, the Kremlin signaled its preferred side in the escalating Sino-Indian confrontation.

The issue apparently triggered a sharp exchange between Khrushchev and the Chinese leadership during his appearance in Peking following his trip to the United States. Peking's account claims Khrushchev "did not wish to know the true situation . . . but insisted that anyway it was wrong to shoot people dead."[61] More dead resulted, however, on 21 October, from fighting at Kongka Pass, at the trijuncture of Tibet, Sinkiang, and Ladakh, where nine Indians were killed and ten taken prisoner. Sino-Indian exchanges of notes over the next month did not bring agreement on the PRC proposal for a mutual withdrawal to 20 kilometers from the McMahon Line and for talks before year end, but did lead to a cessation of border patrols, thereby reducing the risk of further clashes.

Finally in April 1960 Chou En-lai met with Pandit Nehru in New Delhi, but after six days he left, having reached no agreement on any aspect of the border dispute. The security of Tibet precluded Chinese compromise on the road through Ladakh and particular pass points. Likewise, the passions of Indian nationalism expressed within Nehru's own Congress party, as well as by the vocal opposition, blocked acceptance of the status quo in Ladakh as Peking pro-

58 *JMJP*, 2 November 1963, in Gittings, *Survey*, 114.
59 Tass, 9 September 1959, in ibid., 326.
60 Ibid., 114.   61 Ibid., 115.

posed, although this would have included Peking's acceptance of the McMahon Line.

Meanwhile, Sino-Indian relations continued to trouble Sino-Soviet relations. Back in Moscow, Khrushchev publicly decried the border clashes as "sad" and "stupid," causing him "regret" and "distress," but without taking China's side even by implication. Privately Peking made successive protests to the Soviet ambassador, claiming this "strict neutrality" actually worked against China and in favor of India. Nevertheless, "in a verbal notification" of early February 1960, the CPSU informed the CCP that Peking's behavior was "an expression of a narrow nationalist attitude" and that New Delhi, "which is military [sic] and economically immeasurably weaker," could not "really launch a military attack on China and commit aggression against it."[62] This locked the position on both sides into irreconcilable difference.

Soviet-American versus Sino-Soviet relations

During Khrushchev's successive visits to the United States and the PRC in September–October 1959, the theoretical issue of the general line of "peaceful coexistence" versus "armed struggle" and the practical issue of Taiwan linked Soviet-American and Sino-Soviet relations. Neither issue involved any immediate choice of action, either in the form of war with the United States or an attempt to seize Taiwan. However, Khrushchev's trip forced Peking to respond to his various statements. Given the context of Tibet, the Sino-Indian border, Laos, and Indonesia – all simultaneously threatening PRC interests – it is no wonder that Khrushchev's words provoked vigorous Chinese criticism.

Peking's polemic, issued through *Red Flag*, targeted the Khrushchev-Eisenhower meetings immediately after their initial announcement in August and on the eve of their occurrence in September 1959. Its main theme was an attack on those who "could not clearly perceive the true nature of imperialism and entertained various illusions about it. Hence they often lost their bearings." Worse, they thought "the U.S. imperialists" would "lay down their butcher knife and become Buddhas," that a hard, long-term anti-imperialist struggle was no longer called for, and that "the imperialists would no longer proceed with their disruptive schemes."[63]

62 Ibid.   63 *PR*, 22 September 1959.

Khrushchev countered this line in Peking on 30 September 1959. Ostensibly celebrating the PRC's tenth anniversary, he declared, "The leaders of governments in some capitalist countries have begun to show a certain tendency toward a realistic understanding of the situation," noting his impression that "President Eisenhower ... understands the need to relax international tension. ... Therefore we on our part must do all we can to exclude war as a means of settling disputed questions, and settle these questions by negotiations."[64] Any attempt to "test by force the stability of the capitalist system would be wrong."

Addressing the Supreme Soviet on 31 October, the Soviet leader implicitly compared Mao with Trotsky. Khrushchev contrasted Lenin's "flexible foreign policy" at the time of Brest-Litovsk in 1918 with Trotsky's "notorious slogan of 'neither peace nor war' by which he played into the hands of the German imperialists."[65] China had the "legal and moral right" to recover Taiwan, for which Khrushchev expressed sympathy and support, but he avoided addressing its "liberation." As for Laos, the "skirmishes taking place could soon be eliminated" with a "sensible approach"; therefore, the Soviet Union opposed "even the smallest source of war in Laos which could give food to the aggressive forces."

In short, Peking and Moscow differed fundamentally as between confrontation and compromise in coping with "U.S. imperialism." Although Taiwan won no specific mention in the public exchanges between Khrushchev and Eisenhower, the Soviet leader's remarks implicitly but clearly opposed the use of force in its attainment by the PRC. The same conflict of view arose with respect to the Sino-Indian border dispute. Moreover, in each case divergent positions of principle paralleled divergent positions of interest. Beyond the territorial questions involved in Taiwan and the border, both of which aroused nationalistic sensitivities in Peking, there was the question of status and prestige. Khrushchev could meet with Eisenhower as his equal in diplomatic standing, but Mao was beyond the pale so far as U.S. recognition and UN membership were concerned. Similarly, by taking a neutral stance in the border dispute, Moscow could advance its influence in New Delhi while Peking's would diminish.

These conflicts of interest in foreign affairs combined with sharp differences over China's domestic development to create a near-total impasse in the alliance. Khrushchev's intervention in internal affairs

64 Ibid., 6 October 1959.   65 Zagoria, *Conflict*, 282.

through criticism of the communes and the GLF insulted Mao's personal leadership. Soviet obstruction of China's nuclear weapons program hobbled its future defense potential. Linkage between these two problems is, on the basis of presently available evidence, only circumstantial. But the coincidence in timing of key developments was sufficient to reinforce Mao's suspicions of Khrushchev's duplicity. In addition, of course, there may have been secret information to strengthen such suspicion.

Thus the Soviet letter of 20 June 1959, abrogating the 1957 nuclear assistance agreement, came one week after Minister of Defense P'eng Te-huai returned from a "military goodwill mission" through Eastern Europe and Mongolia. P'eng was in Poland when the Warsaw Pact members met. He was reported to have had a friendly talk with Khrushchev during their simultaneous visits in Albania. The two men met again in Moscow on P'eng's way back. On 14 July, P'eng sent Mao his subsequently celebrated letter attacking the GLF and by implication, the Chairman himself. On 18 July, Khrushchev broke a six-month moratorium on public criticism of China by excoriating those who had advocated communes in the 1920s as having "a poor understanding of what Communism is and how it is to be built." Small wonder that Peking later charged P'eng's attack at the Lushan Conference with having "the support of the Khrushchev revisionist clique."[66]

Whether Khrushchev colluded with P'eng or acted independently to exploit sensed opposition to Mao at the conference, the coincidence of the two positions permitted Mao to imply conspiracy. It was tolerable if nettlesome for Khrushchev to lecture Mao critically on the Great Leap in private during their August 1958 summit.[67] It was intolerable, however, to lobby through PRC politics, adding injury to insult by suspending help in China's atomic bomb program. These developments appeared to exercise economic pressure for political intervention in China's internal affairs.

Sino-Soviet differences aired

In February 1960, the Warsaw Pact members issued a declaration that claimed, "The main problem of international life in our day [is] whether it will be possible to rule out completely the possibility of

66 *PR*, 1 July 1966.
67 Soviet government statement, 21 September 1963, in Gittings, *Survey*, 96. According to this, "the Chinese leaders turned a deaf ear."

a new war, which in the present conditions would lead to the death of hundreds of millions of people and the annihilation of whole states."[68] Two months later the *Red Flag* editorial, "Long live Leninism," admitted that "imperialist war would impose enormous sacrifices upon the peoples of various countries," but reassuringly asserted, "On the debris of a dead imperialism, the victorious people would create very swiftly a civilization thousands of times higher than the capitalist system and a truly beautiful future for themselves."[69]

These two statements captured the contradictory postures of Moscow and Peking on the general line to be adopted toward the United States and its associates. Their publication for multiple audiences revealed the willingness of both sides to expand the dispute from bilateral to multilateral confrontation. In the process, however, the specific problems of 1958–59 were muted, and greater stress was given to ideological and theoretical issues. This, in turn, betokened a struggle for leadership of the international Communist movement, initiated by Peking in a defiant challenge to Moscow.

The year 1960 was one of unprecedented public polemics and bitter private exchanges between the two Communist capitals as they waged their dispute through reams of articles and weeks of conferences. At the February Warsaw Pact meeting, China's delegate, albeit only an observer, spoke in obvious disagreement with the declaration. Then in April both *Red Flag* and the *People's Daily* offered lengthy exegeses of Lenin's writings to prove that Peking's position was not only correct for the moment but also fully consonant with the founding father's teachings. By implication, the heavily documented line of argument rebutted Khrushchev's well-known positions as "modern revisionism." At the World Federation of Trade Unions (WFTU) conference in June, the Chinese used their position as host to lobby delegates from various countries against Moscow's general line, thereby moving the bilateral dispute into a multilateral forum.

Moscow met Peking's challenge head on in a lengthy ideological counterattack delivered by a Politburo member for the ninetieth anniversary of Lenin's birth. Further exchanges in June followed the WFTU meeting, but the first major personal confrontation before a selected audience occurred at the Rumanian Party Congress, 20–26 June 1960, in Bucharest. An authoritative account of the secret

68 Text in Hudson, *Dispute*, 66.   69 Ibid., 93–94.

speeches revealed the extent to which the two sides traded verbal blows in the presence of delegates from fifty communist parties.[70]

Khrushchev criticized the Chinese on global strategy and domestic economic development. He claimed they could not be trusted with nuclear weapons, and compared Mao with Stalin – as vain and isolated from reality. The Chinese responded, accusing Khrushchev of betraying Marx, Lenin, and Stalin. The Soviet leader chided those who "act like children who, studying the alphabet, compile words from letters" and "mechanically repeat now what Vladimir Ilyich Lenin said many decades ago."[71] A CCP statement distributed as the meeting adjourned accused Khrushchev of being "patriarchal, arbitrary, and tyrannical."[72]

The CCP statement came as an immediate rejoinder to a Soviet Party letter to the Chinese of 21 June that Khrushchev distributed at the conference opening. The CCP statement claimed he had launched a "surprise attack of putting forward a draft communiqué" without prior consultation or full discussion at the meeting. The Chinese further declared that "when the occasion arises" they would "carry on serious discussions with the CPSU and other fraternal Parties on our differences with Comrade Khrushchev." The Soviet letter would also be responded to in due course. Bucharest thus proved to be the opening round in a new series of exchanges, both public and private.

As a flurry of press polemics emerged that summer, however, Moscow suddenly informed Peking in mid-July that all Soviet technicians would be withdrawn by early September. Peking subsequently claimed that 1,390 experts departed, 343 contracts were "torn up," and "257 items for scientific and technical cooperation were abolished."[73] Moscow denied that any substantive role for the experts had been possible since the beginning of the GLF and cited its suggestion in 1958 that they leave then.[74] Although they had probably become superfluous, their withdrawal, taking "thousands" of blueprints and technical papers, according to Peking, could only

---

70 *The Sino-Soviet dispute and its significance*, Central Intelligence Agency, 1 April 1961, TS #142274-b (hereafter cited as *Significance*). Originally Top Secret, this study drew on first-hand accounts of the three confrontations in 1960 at Bucharest, Moscow, and the pre-Moscow drafting session. Much of the material was subsequently confirmed in the open polemical exchanges of 1963.
71 N. S. Khrushchev, "Speech at the Third Congress of the Rumanian Workers' Party," 21 June 1960, in Gittings, *Survey*, 346–47.
72 Ibid., 350.
73 *PR*, 6 December 1963, in Gittings, *Survey*, 142.
74 Soviet statement of 14 August 1964, in ibid., 137–39.

inflame Chinese nationalism and cement support for Mao's vaunted program of "self-reliance." Peking reacted by publicly asserting its ability to "rely on our own efforts . . . in socialist construction." Privately it responded to the 21 June Soviet letter on 10 September, charging Moscow with having exerted pressure through the technicians' withdrawal, but concluding defiantly: "Truth cannot be bought."[75]

From 30 September to 22 October, delegates from 26 communist parties met in Moscow to draft a declaration for a fuller conference where 81 parties were represented, from 10 November to 1 December 1960. The two assemblages witnessed hours of charges and counter-charges exchanged between Khrushchev, Suslov, and other Soviet leaders on the one hand, and Teng Hsiao-p'ing on the other. Mao did not attend, he and Kim Il-sung being the only bloc leaders absent. Liu Shao-ch'i said little at the meetings, but met privately with Khrushchev at Ho Chi Minh's instigation in a successful last-minute effort to negotiate agreement on a conference statement.[76]

The Soviet side focused mainly on theoretical questions concerning the proper attitude toward wars – general, local, "national liberation," and revolutionary. The Chinese answered in kind but went beyond this to review specific policy disputes between the two capitals. Teng recapitulated the events of 1956–59, including alleged Soviet demands for military facilities in China, Moscow's reaction to the Sino-Indian fracas, its public criticism of the GLF and communes, Khrushchev's supposed remarks on China to Eisenhower, the anti-China Soviet press campaign, which included threats to the PRC, the technicians' withdrawal, and unspecified "border encroachments."[77]

Of the 81 parties present, a handful supported Peking, and of these, only Albania went all the way in attacking Soviet policy and practice. On several issues the Australian, Japanese, North Korean, North Vietnamese, and Indonesian delegates sided more or less with the Chinese. Essentially, however, Khrushchev succeeded in mobilizing overwhelming support against Mao in absentia. The conference unanimously approved a compromise document whose tortured merger of the divergent positions forestalled the embarrassment of an open break but did little to advance the vaunted "unity" to which all present pleged support. Combined with Moscow's pulling out its economic advisers and assistance, the public and private polemics of

75 *Significance*, Annex, 4.   76 Ibid., Annex, 33.   77 Ibid., Annex, 25–26.

1960 virtually ended the Sino-Soviet alliance as a working relationship. The personalization of the dispute by Khrushchev, manifest in his taking the harshest line against Mao's individual leadership, added an extra dimension of confrontation that would foreclose any reconciliation at least until his removal four years later.

PHASE THREE: 1961–1962

Nothing new was added to China's foreign policy agenda in 1961–62, but previous problems took new turns, generally for the worse. Sino-Soviet differences added Albania as a point of contention, became more heated over India, and burst into the open with the Cuban missile crisis of October 1962. India's emulation of Chinese probing tactics along the disputed Himalayan border triggered a brief war wherein the PLA swept down to the undisputed borders in Ladakh and the Northeast Frontier Agency. Taiwan posed a perceived threat of invasion as Chiang Kai-shek sought to exploit the GLF economic disaster, whereupon the PLA moved counter-deployments and Peking summoned Washington to an emergency ambassadorial meeting at Warsaw. Almost simultaneously, a massive exodus across the Sinkiang border prompted Peking to accuse Moscow of seeking to detach that vast Central Asian area. In neighboring Laos a mounting confrontation between communist and noncommunist forces ended in another Geneva conference where the major protagonists and their proxies compromised their differences sufficiently to defuse the crisis and to camouflage the growing contest over all of Indochina.

What made 1961–62 different, however, was the staggering consequences of the GLF, worsened by the withdrawal of Soviet advisers and assistance. Statistics released twenty years later showed an absolute decline in China's population as a result of increased deaths from famine and disease, combined with decreased births from lowered conception and heightened infant mortality. Secret PLA records captured at the time revealed declining troop morale because of desperate economic conditions in home villages and entire provinces under martial law to stop the looting of granaries and the killing of cadres.

This domestic context for foreign policy contributed to a heightened sense of external threat perceived as responding to China's economic difficulties. In mid-1962 the threat became manifest on three sides – in the west, south, and east – with the two superpowers directly or indirectly involved on one or more of these fronts. Although none of these problems was new, their impact on the Chinese leadership was unprecedented, prompting one well-informed diplomat to characterize the leadership as "panicky."[78]

The Sino-Soviet dispute

Enver Hoxha refused to be fenced in by the 1960 Moscow statement or cowed by Moscow's threat of political intervention in Albanian politics. Instead, he joined Mao in a diatribe against Soviet "revisionism." An incipient Sino-Albanian entente emerged at the February 1961 Party Congress in Tirana, after which Moscow withdrew its economic advisers and assistance. In October, at the twenty-second CPSU Congress, sharp attacks on Stalin and Albania prompted Chou En-lai to a dramatic walkout. Khrushchev thereupon broke diplomatic relations with Albania and in 1962 expelled Albania from the principal organizations linking the Soviet Union and Eastern Europe, the Council for Mutual Economic Assistance and the Warsaw Pact. That spring Moscow mended the break with Belgrade through words and deeds supporting "socialist" solidarity, in direct refutation of Peking's polemic to the contrary. In September 1962 the Soviet head of state, Leonid Brezhnev, visited Yugoslavia to confirm the rapprochement.

Closer to home, a perceived threat of Soviet subversion arose in Sinkiang. In 1961–62 economic dislocations similar to those prevalent elsewhere in China prompted the flight of non-Han peoples across the Soviet border to join ethnic kinsmen with higher living standards. The number of migrants reached between sixty thousand and eighty thousand. Much of it was done with tacit official encouragement, as occurred simultaneously along the Hong Kong border. The growth and pace of the exodus, however, apparently caused alarm in Peking, and in May 1962 restrictions were suddenly imposed. Because the migration required the connivance of Soviet consulates issuing travel visas, local riots and their suppression by the PLA inevitably involved the Soviets. Chou En-lai reportedly apologized to Moscow for the disturbances, but in July new restrictions forced the closing of all Soviet consulates in Sinkiang and the transformation of the border into a depopulated security zone.

---

78 Information available to the author at the time. For a comprehensive treatment of the period and these problems, see Whiting, *Calculus*, chs. 1–5.

Subsequently, Peking publicly accused Moscow of having attempted to "detach" Sinkiang. This charge did not arise at the time but may well have been believed by one or more groups in the regime. It further fueled the dispute, recalling as it did Russian occupation of the Ili Valley in 1871 and Soviet sponsorship of the East Turkestan Republic in 1944—49.

Meanwhile, a slowly emerging Soviet-Indian military relationship seemed to foreshadow a more substantive anti-Chinese alignment in the subcontinent. In April 1961 Moscow sold eight four-engine troop transports which New Delhi intended for use in Ladakh. Moscow next provided helicopters capable of lifting men and supplies to altitudes of 17,000 feet. By June 1962 Soviet-Indian discussions were under way on the eventual manufacture of jet fighters in India based on Soviet-provided factories.

A third development pertinent to China's national security came in August 1962 when Moscow informed Peking it had accepted an American proposal to halt nuclear proliferation by banning the transfer of nuclear knowhow to nonnuclear countries. These countries would also agree to remain nonnuclear. Peking promptly demanded that Moscow not formalize this agreement by treaty and threatened public denunciation.

Against this background of substantive differences came the October 1962 Cuban missile crisis. During the week-long confrontation, Chinese restraint led to a government statement pledging support for Moscow. But no sooner had the crisis ebbed than Peking publicly accused Moscow of "adventurism" for having put intermediate-range missiles in Cuba and "capitulationism" for agreeing to pull them out under the American ultimatum. Mass rallies excoriated Soviet behavior and defended Cuban sovereignty.

Peking's short-lived support of Moscow came during the first week of Sino-Indian fighting on the high Himalayan frontier and may have reflected uncertainty over the Soviet reaction. *Pravda*'s simultaneous backing of the Chinese position reciprocated this gesture. But in parallel with Peking's changing stance on Cuba once the Sino-Indian war was over, Khrushchev addressed the Supreme Soviet on 12 December 1962, disparaging claims of Indian belligerence and disputing China's contention of national security's being involved in the border disagreement.

In contrast with the ideological argument waged in open journals and closed conferences, the confrontation over Albania and the conflict of national interests involved in war and near-war situations pitted Moscow against Peking on issues of truly vital importance.

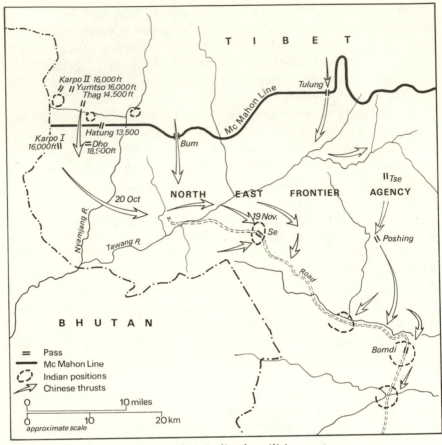

MAP 10. Sino-Indian hostilities, 1962

This further strain finally dissolved the Sino-Soviet alliance for all practical purposes.

The Sino-Indian war

During the spring and summer of 1962, Indian patrols advanced into disputed areas of the Himalayan frontier to establish outposts similar to, and often behind, those advanced by the PLA previously. If presence was to determine ownership, as Peking claimed, two could play that game. The resulting confrontations, protests, and incidents gradually raised the level of public acrimony and quickened the pace of private diplomacy in the late summer and early fall. In mid-September Peking warned New Delhi against "playing with fire" and proposed that discussions without preconditions take place one month later. The deadline lapsed without Indian compliance, and in the meantime more serious incidents caused casualties on both sides. On 20 October, after an Indian crossing of the McMahon Line into undisputed Tibetan territory, the PLA launched a coordinated offensive against alleged "large-scale, all-out attacks" in the eastern and western sectors of the frontier.

After one week the PLA suspended its offensive while Peking assessed the reactions of New Delhi, Moscow, and Washington. Indian intransigence, stiffened by the nationalistic response to foreign attack, coupled with relative passivity on the part of the two superpowers, preoccupied with their own dispute, prompted a resumption of the Chinese attack three weeks later. On 20 November, exactly one month after the initial offensive, Peking announced a unilateral ceasefire and a troop withdrawal to 20 kilometers behind the line of actual control as it had existed on 7 November 1959, provided that the Indian forces also stopped fighting and did not attempt to recover positions held before the conflict began.

The PLA proved superior on every count. Holding the high ground and well-supplied by truck routes, PLA firepower easily decimated the Indian offensive, which was uphill and supplied only by porters climbing over rough terrain at high altitudes. The Chinese expelled Indian forces from all the territory claimed by Peking but did not cross any undisputed boundary. The PLA took 3,968 prisoners of war; the Indians took none. New Delhi claimed its casualties reached 1,383 killed and 1,696 missing in action. Peking released no comparable statistics, but Chinese losses undoubtedly were much lower, given the nature of the fighting. Many Indian units fell under surprise attack, and others fled. Politically, Peking capped New Delhi's humiliation by gratuitously returning not only the entire NEFA but also all prisoners, together with a meticulously itemized inventory of trucks, guns, and ammunition. Last but not least, in tacit contrast with Khrushchev's handling of Cuba, Mao was neither "adventurist" nor "capitulationist." His unique termination of hostilities foreclosed any action on behalf of Nehru by "imperialism" or "revisionism," while retaining the strategic Aksai Chin plateau through which ran the Sinkiang-Tibet highway.

Tension from Taiwan

On 29 May 1962, Foreign Minister Ch'en I spoke at length in a press interview on China's foreign policy problems with the United States and India. He referred repeatedly to the possibility of a U.S.-

supported invasion from Taiwan exploiting serious economic problems on the mainland. Admitting that opponents of communism in China "may amount to several million," Ch'en noted that "a disturbance by Chiang Kai-shek would mean another reason for an attack on the government by them."[79]

Peking's alarm responded to indications from Taiwan of preparations for an attack, seemingly encouraged by high-level American visits. In March Taipei called up recruits a year ahead of schedule and delayed demobilization indefinitely beyond the initial terms of service. It also organized sea transport into "mobilization groupings." In May an "invasion preparation tax" levied a heavy tariff on industries. At the same time, Washington appointed a former World War II admiral with amphibious combat experience as its ambassador to Taiwan.

Meanwhile, throughout May 1962 tens of thousands of refugees streamed across the Hong Kong border, seeking relief from economic chaos. This drew worldwide attention to China's domestic crisis, resulting in emergency food shipments to Hong Kong from the United States, Great Britain, and Canada, plus an American lifting of Chinese immigration quotas. Under these circumstances the PLA rushed more than 100,000 troops into Chekiang and Fukien provinces opposite Taiwan during the first three weeks of June. On 23 June Peking convened the Sino-American ambassadorial meeting in Warsaw on twenty-four hours' notice to warn against supporting Chiang Kai-shek in an invasion of the mainland, pointedly alluding to the Korean War as a reminder of the consequences for the United States.

In addition to the American ambassador's denial of any such intention, President Kennedy four days later publicly confirmed U.S. policy as "opposed to the use of force in this area." These reassurances proved sufficiently credible for the PLA deployment to be reversed, and the crisis passed. The episode, however, contributed to the sense of threat from India because of cooperation with Taiwan and the CIA in providing refuge and supplies for Tibetan guerrillas. The linkage won attention in a *People's Daily* report on an Indian press reference to the prospect of China facing "war on two fronts." Thus the coincidence in timing of the Sinkiang exodus, Soviet military aid to New Delhi, advancing Indian patrol activity, and preparations on Taiwan for invasion all merged into a coordinated threat as seen from Peking in the summer of 1962.

Laos: Geneva II

In response to this threat, Peking resorted to militancy and belligerence in Sinkiang, the Taiwan Strait, and Tibet. Diplomacy proved sufficient in Laos. In early 1961 the Kennedy administration had debated armed intervention but finally accepted the British proposal that a second Geneva conference arrange for the ICC to supervise a ceasefire, followed by a neutral coalition government under Souvanna Phouma.

Peking thereupon dropped its objections to the ICC role and supported the Geneva negotiations while covertly strengthening the Pathet Lao with military supplies and advisers. Chinese policy aimed at reducing the threat of American intervention, removing Laos from the SEATO treaty's protection, and relieving Hanoi as well as the Pathet Lao of the need for Soviet assistance. Negotiations dragged on into 1962, when suddenly right-wing forces attacked the Pathet Lao. A sharp Communist counterattack threatened the local power balance, whereupon President Kennedy sent more than 5,000 Marines to the Thai-Lao border, joined by British, Australian, and New Zealand air units, in response to a SEATO meeting.

While Moscow adopted a low posture, Peking publicly threatened intervention. Privately, however, Chinese advice apparently brought Pathet Lao restraint, and the three factions finally agreed to a coalition government that won immediate PRC recognition. On 23 July 1962 the Geneva Conference ended by confirming Laotian neutrality, albeit guaranteed only by joint consultation among the fourteen signatories. The ceasefire had never proved effective during negotiations, and it dissolved thereafter, as the three factions retained their respective armed forces. Peking's careful mixture of public rhetoric, diplomatic compromise, and covert support for the Pathet Lao had succeeded in showing up Moscow and deterring Washington without risking open confrontation.

PHASE FOUR: 1963–1964

Overview

Having stabilized its collapsing economy and fended off the perceived threats in Sinkiang, Tibet, and the Taiwan Strait, Peking was less pressured by domestic and foreign crises in 1963–64. But no outstanding issues were resolved, and some worsened. The Sino-Soviet dispute burst into an open exchange of accusations and revelations communicated through lengthy, detailed letters and statements released by both sides. Mao added fuel to the fire by hinting he might demand the return of all territory ceded by treaty to tsarist Russia. Incidents multiplied along the frontier as Chinese insistence on disputed boundaries prompted bilateral discussion. Finally, after Moscow signed a nuclear test-ban treaty with Washington, Peking detonated its first atom bomb.

Indochina gradually increased in importance as the United States drastically expanded its military presence in South Vietnam and threatened to bomb North Vietnam if it did not cease supporting communist insurgents in the south. In August 1964, American aircraft struck North Vietnamese patrol boat bases after an alleged attack on American destroyers in the Gulf of Tonkin. Peking thereupon sent MIG jet fighters to Hanoi as a token of support, while Moscow avoided direct involvement.

Laos became entangled in the Vietnam War as communist infiltration routes from north to south came under air attack from U.S. bases in Thailand. This, in turn, prompted Peking to step up its presence in Laos and encourage the militancy of the Thai Communist Party. The year 1964 ended with the fall of Khrushchev, an abortive trip to Moscow by Chou En-lai to test the new leadership, and the threat of a possible Sino-American confrontation over Indochina. Amid these negative developments, France's granting recognition to the People's Republic provided a positive sign of diplomatic progress that somewhat offset a series of setbacks for Chinese tactics in the Afro-Asian arena. China's relations with Pakistan, Cambodia, Burma, and Indonesia continued to improve as diplomacy prevailed over revolutionary rhetoric. In the case of Japan, trade increased considerably as the Chinese economy recovered from the disastrous GLF and Peking realized it had more to gain economically and diplomatically from high-level "unofficial" economic agreements than from futile earlier attempts to pressure or manipulate Tokyo into a reappraisal of its ties with Taipei and Washington.

The Sino-Soviet rift widens

During the winter of 1962–63, the dispute between Moscow and Peking surfaced in Eastern European Party congresses, followed by fierce Chinese attacks on third parties which served as surrogates for the actual Soviet target. Anxious appeals for compromise from concerned communists in Asia and Europe prompted both sides to agree they would meet in July 1963. But in June Peking broke its pledge to "temporarily suspend" polemics, publicly listing twenty-five points of principle to be discussed at the bilateral talks. These began as scheduled on 5 July, but eight days later the *People's Daily* resumed its anti-Soviet editorials. Moscow reacted immediately with a lengthy public recapitulation of the origin and history of the dispute.

On the surface China appeared intransigent, initiating greater tension in bilateral relations. But secretly Soviet policy had taken an important step in the multilateral area of nuclear arms negotiations aimed at restricting China. This issue had lain dormant but potentially divisive ever since Khrushchev's short-lived unilateral test suspension in March 1958 and his January 1959 proposal for an atom-free zone in Asia. Peking had supported both moves, albeit slowly. More recently, however, it had repeatedly warned Moscow in private against "any sort of treaty between the Soviet government and the United States which aimed at depriving the Chinese people of their right to take steps to resist the nuclear threats of U.S. imperialism."[80]

Despite Peking's demarches, on 15 July 1963, in the midst of Sino-Soviet talks, Khrushchev began negotiations with the United States and Great Britain on the prohibition of nuclear tests in the atmosphere. On 21 July the Sino-Soviet talks adjourned "until some later time," and on 25 July, the Test Ban Treaty was signed.

Khrushchev's timing could not have been more provocative, and Peking responded accordingly. Government statements, editorials, and correspondence between the two parties proliferated in the Chinese and Soviet press, documenting in detail accusations of ideological heresy, political betrayal, and direct threats to the national interests, including security, of both countries. In addition to actions and events dating back to the Twentieth Party Congress and the Quemoy bombardment, a new point of controversy emerged concerning the Sino-Soviet border and the land tsarist Russia had taken from China.

The territorial question initially emerged almost as an aside in December 1962 when Khrushchev, lashing back at Chinese criticism of his Cuban missile crisis behavior as "capitulationist," chided Mao for continuing to tolerate Portuguese and British rule over Macao and Hong Kong, respectively. In March 1963 Peking responded to the American Communist Party's replay of Khrushchev's line by citing

80 Statement by spokesman of Chinese government, 15 August 1963, in Gittings, *Survey*, 186–87.

the many instances of Chinese territory's being lost to nineteenth-century imperialism, including three "unequal treaties" whereby Russia took much territory in the west, north, and northeast. The *People's Daily* editorial ended, "In raising questions of this kind, do you intend to raise all the questions of unequal treaties and have a general settlement? Has it ever entered your heads what the consequences will be? Can you seriously believe that this will do you any good?"[81]

In its version of the dispute's origin and history, Peking accused Moscow of having "enticed and coerced several tens of thousands of Chinese citizens into going to the Soviet Union" while subverting Sinkiang in 1962.[82] Moscow responded: "Beginning with 1960, Chinese servicemen and civilians have been systematically violating the Soviet border. In the single year of 1962, more than 5,000 violations . . . were registered."[83] The statement charged Peking with refusing to consult on border problems to avoid some misunderstandings, while "making definite hints at the unjust demarcation of some sections . . . allegedly made in the past."

On 25 February 1964, the two sides met in Moscow on this issue. Four days later, Peking charged that "in recent years the Soviet side has made frequent breaches of the status quo on the border, occupied Chinese territory and provoked border incidents."[84] But the statement declared, "Although the old treaties relating to the Sino-Russian boundary are unequal treaties, the Chinese Government is nevertheless willing to respect them and take them as the basis for a reasonable settlement of the question."

This definition of the situation did not last long. On 10 July Mao gave to some Japanese an interview that threatened to reopen the entire territorial question, noting:

The Soviet Union has an area of 22 million square kilometers and its population is only 220 million. It is about time to put an end to this allotment. . . . About a hundred years ago, the area to the east of [Lake] Baikal became Russian territory, and since then Vladivostok, Khabarovsk, Kamchatka, and other areas have been Soviet territory. We have not yet presented our account for this list.[85]

81 *JMJP*, 8 March 1963, in Dennis J. Doolin, *Territorial claims in the Sino-Soviet conflict*, 30.
82 Joint *JMJP* and *Hung-ch'i* editorial, 6 September 1983, in ibid., 32.
83 Soviet government statement, 20 September 1963, in ibid., 32.
84 Letter from the Central Committee of the Chinese Communist Party, 29 February 1964, to the Central Committee of the Communist Party of the Soviet Union, in ibid., 37–38.
85 *Sekai Shuho*, 11 August 1964, in ibid., 43–44. An authoritative but unofficial Chinese text in *Wan-sui* (1969), 540–41, confirms the Japanese account.

Subsequently Chou En-lai claimed that "there were some incorrect comments by the Japanese press concerning Chairman Mao's statement," but he did not repudiate any specific part of the reported interview. Soviet media fully exploited Mao's words as proof of Chinese "expansionism." Privately his statement probably contributed to decisions that increased the Soviet forces opposing China, evidence of which emerged in 1965 and mounted during the following years.

On 14 October 1964, Khrushchev suddenly fell from power in a virtual coup, which installed Leonid Brezhnev and Alexei Kosygin as leaders. On 16 October China exploded its first atom bomb. This coincidence of events provided an auspicious background to Chou En-lai's 5 November visit to Moscow for the first high-level talks since July 1963. But his return to Peking on 14 November without any joint statement left Sino-Soviet relations essentially where they were before Khrushchev's ouster.

The Indochina War intensifies

The flimsy Laotian accords fashioned at Geneva failed to contain fighting among the factions, and the situation worsened as Hanoi and Washington escalated their covert struggle over South Vietnam. North Vietnam's use of Laos for infiltrating troops and supplies to the guerrilla war in the south prompted American attacks through Laotian and Thai intermediaries on the infiltration routes and Pathet Lao bases. In June 1964 these attacks hit the Chinese mission in Khang Khay, killing one and wounding five. Peking protested but took no overt action.

In August two American destroyers on an electronic intelligence mission in the Gulf of Tonkin associated with covert South Vietnamese attacks on North Vietnamese radar installations were fired on by Hanoi's torpedo boats without suffering significant damage or any casualties. Two days later the destroyers returned at night and again reported they were under attack. (It was subsequently discovered that the reports had been in error.) President Johnson immediately ordered air strikes against six North Vietnamese naval bases. Moscow proposed that the incident be taken up at the United Nations, contrary to Hanoi's will, but Peking dispatched a squadron of MIG-15s and MIG-17s flown by Vietnamese trained in China.

Publicly China warned, "Whenever the U.S. imperialists invade

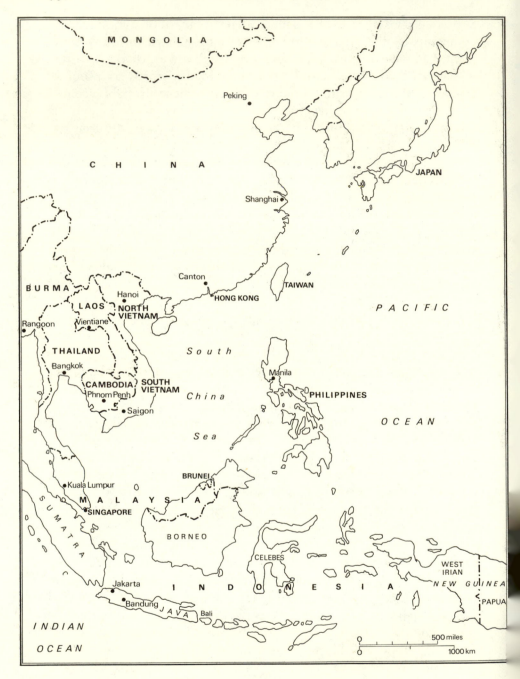

MAP 11. China and Southeast Asia

the territory, territorial waters, or air space of the Democratic Republic of Viet Nam, the Chinese people without hesitation will resolutely support the Vietnamese people's just war against the U.S. aggressors. . . . Should it dare to launch an attack on the Democratic Republic of Viet Nam, the Chinese people will absolutely not stand by with folded arms or sit idly by without lending a helping hand."[86] Privately Peking increased the quality of jet fighters in its southern region and constructed three new airfields immediately north of Indochina, two of which seemed designed to support the air defense of North Vietnam.[87]

By the end of 1964, the number of American military personnel in Thailand had reached 6,500, mostly Air Force personnel. Sorties from secret Thai bases accompanied CIA-led Laotian ground and air attacks on the Pathet Lao and the so-called Ho Chi Minh Trail in eastern Laos. On 1 October, the Communist Party of Thailand's message to Peking on the PRC national day, calling for the overthrow of the Bangkok regime, was unprecedently militant. Precisely one month later, the clandestine radio station Voice of the Thai People, broadcasting in Chinese, launched the Thai Independence Movement with the avowed aims of ousting "U.S. imperialism from Thailand and toppling the Thanom government."[88] At the same time, Radio Peking increased its Thai programming from 14 to 21 hours a week.

None of these moves committed Peking to any specific action. The various measures, overt and covert, were aimed at deterring Washington from carrying out its threatened air attacks on North Vietnam, and Bangkok from participating in the Laotian struggle. But though basically limited to signaling possible future steps, these moves qualitatively changed China's involvement in Indochina. Peking's pledge to Hanoi implied some future Chinese response should the United States make good its threat to bomb the North. Failure to respond would discredit later Chinese deterrence efforts and provide Moscow with an advantage in the Sino-Soviet contest for influence in third countries. In addition, Peking's encouragement of communist militancy in Thailand changed a posture of moderation dating back to the 1955 Bandung Conference. Unleashing of local insurgents could be difficult to reverse without losing ground to Hanoi as a rival patron of the Thai Communists, quite aside from the potential damage to China's revolutionary reputation elsewhere.

86 *PR*, 32, 7 August 1964.   87 Whiting, *Calculus*, 176–77.   88 Gurtov, *Survival*, 12–13.

The Afro-Asian world

That revolutionary reputation had already suffered contradictory pressure from China's diplomatic aims, especially in the Third World, then subsumed under the Afro-Asian rubric. In early 1964 Peking defined a "vast intermediate zone" in the international system as "composed of two parts. One consists of the independent countries and those striving for independence in Asia, Africa, and Latin America.... The second part consists of the whole of Western Europe, Oceania, Canada, and other capitalist countries.... While their ruling classes are exploiters and oppressors, these countries are themselves subjected to U.S. control, interference, and bullying.... In this regard they have something in common with the socialist countries and the peoples of various countries."[89]

This formulation came just one week before the first major power recognition of the PRC since 1950. On 27 January 1964, France and China established diplomatic relations, thereby justifying the second category of this "intermediate zone." Although President de Gaulle's action provoked debate in Japan, Prime Minister Ikeda showed no inclination to follow his example and step out of line with the United States. The takeover of Eisaku Sato as prime minister in November 1964 at first seemed to promise a strengthened relationship, but the Chinese soon came to regard him as being as hostile to their interests as his brother Prime Minister Kishi in the late 1950s. They had to be satisfied with the de facto diplomatic ties established as a result of the 1962 Liao-Takasaki trade agreement, which led to the posting of Foreign Ministry and trade officials in the "unofficial" Japanese trade office in Peking.

In the first category within the "intermediate zone," the PRC won recognition from Kenya, Burundi, Tunisia, Congo (Brazzaville), the Central African Republic, Zambia, and Dahomey, all between December 1963 and November 1964. This brought to a total of 52 those countries with which the PRC had diplomatic relations.

The prominence of newly independent African states in this process underscored the importance accorded Chou En-lai's tour of ten African countries from 14 December 1963 to 4 February 1964. His multiple mission was to explain China's refusal to sign the nuclear test-ban while detonating its own atomic device, encourage anti-Soviet positions and "self-reliance" in economic affairs, and raise

89 *JMJP* editorial of 21 January 1964 in *PR*, 4, 24 January 1964.

revolutionary rhetoric to a level inconsistent with Chou's status as premier and his reputation as diplomat. All this got mixed results.

Peking's policy in Africa operated at three levels: official, individual, and revolutionary. Token grants and loans symbolically rivaled Western and Soviet aid programs but could not compete substantively. Militant individuals and potential opposition leaders that Chou met through the Afro-Asian People's Solidarity Organization (AAPSO) won subsidies and trips to China, often to the annoyance of local governments. Insurgents received overt propaganda and covert money, arms, and advice.

But when Chinese protégés targeted black governments, as in Rwanda, Cameroun, and the Congo (Leopoldville), African reaction tended to be critical, in contrast with the Chinese assistance to anticolonial guerrillas in Angola and Portugese Guinea. Thus Chou's assertion in Somalia that "an excellent revolutionary situation exists in Africa" was countered by lectures delivered to him in private and public from such different leaders as President Bourguiba of Tunisia and Emperor Haile Selassie of Ethiopia.

A particular problem for Chou was African unwillingness to take sides in the Sino-Soviet dispute and disillusionment over China's effort to manipulate AAPSO toward this end. The February 1963 AAPSO conference in Tanganyika polarized the participants into factions supporting either Moscow or Peking. The Chinese prevailed on several key points aimed against the Soviet and Indian positions and dominated subsequent meetings of AAPSO affiliates. One result was lack of support for another Bandung Conference, as advocated by Peking. Instead, most African leaders called for a second nonaligned conference that would exclude the Sino-Soviet disputants. Plans for the latter emerged in March 1964; Mali refused to attend, the only success of Chou's lobbying. The actual meeting in July adopted resolutions favoring peaceful coexistence and opposing nuclear weapons production, acquisition, and testing, all in rebuttal of Peking's position.

Individual instances of successful state relations in the Afro-Asian world somewhat mitigated these setbacks. Peking's close ties with the leftist regime in Zanzibar survived the merger of Zanzibar and Tanganyika in April 1964, with the new state of Tanzania receiving one of China's larger credit lines of $42 million, together with a grant of $2.8 million in June 1964. That August, President Julius Nyerere announced he had invited Chinese instructors to train the Tanzanian army. Chinese mortars, heavy machine guns, and antitank guns were publicly paraded the following February.[90]

In Southern Asia, Sino-Pakistani relations steadily strengthened. Although Pakistani leaders explicitly denied any alliance, their hints of an informal entente won low-key support in Peking in 1964 when Chinese statements shifted to Pakistan's side in the Kashmir dispute with India. The joint communiqué issued in February, after Chou's trip to Rawalpindi, called for a settlement "in accordance with the wishes of the people of Kashmir," a majority of whom were Muslim. Foreign Minister Ch'en I's statement during the visit advocating "Asia for Asians" accommodated that of his counterpart, Foreign Minister Bhutto, whose ambivalent attitude toward SEATO underlay his description of Pakistan as "being both aligned and non-aligned."[91]

In July, China granted Pakistan a $60 million long-term, interest-free loan to be repaid with jute, cotton, and manufactured goods, while Pakistan purchased Chinese cement, sugar mills, and machinery. In October the New China News Agency asserted that the two countries shared a "common cause of opposing foreign aggression and intervention." This fell well short of an explicit commitment but suggested an evolving relationship between Peking and Rawalpindi juxtaposed against that between Moscow and New Delhi.

In Cambodia, China also pledged support but left undefined its actual content. After Phnom Penh's renunciation of American economic and military aid in November, 1963, Peking declared, "If the Kingdom of Cambodia ... should actually come under armed incursions planned by the United States and its lackeys, the Chinese Government and the Chinese people will steadfastly stand on the side of Cambodia and moreover will give her full support."[92] But the following October Prince Sihanouk revealed he had been unable to win Peking's agreement to a mutual defense treaty or a declaration that an attack on Cambodia equalled an attack on China. His trip to Peking had also failed to pressure Premier Pham Van Dong into North Vietnamese acceptance of the existing border; Chinese sponsorship of the negotiations did not provide leverage on Cambodia's behalf. Within these limitations, however, Peking solidified its patron-client relationship with Phnom Penh against Washington's alliance with Bangkok and Saigon.

90 J. D. Armstrong, *Revolutionary diplomacy*, 224.
91 Khalid B. Sayeed, "Pakistan and China," in Halpern, *Views*, 258–59.
92 Gurtov, *Survival*, 65.

After Rangoon refused to side with New Delhi against Peking in the Sino-Indian conflict, Burma benefitted from China's preferring diplomacy over revolution. In April 1963 Liu Shao-ch'i arrived in the Burmese capital with an agreement to complete ten aid projects, including bridges, hydroelectric plants, and manufacturing facilities for plywood, paper, sugar, and textiles. Chinese statements on "national liberation struggle" carefully omitted reference to the Communist Party of Burma, and the month of Liu's visit saw Rangoon announce a general amnesty and offer unconditional negotiations for all insurgents. Senior White Flag cadres returned from China that summer. Peking's influence apparently helped to start discussions between a White Flag mission and the Burmese government in September.[93]

The collapse of these discussions and Rangoon's banning of all political parties in March 1964 – except the officially sponsored one – did not change Chinese policy. Visits to Rangoon by Chou and Ch'en I during February and July 1964 revealed differences on various matters, but sufficient agreement existed to permit continuation of aid projects and a muting of critical comment in the Chinese press. When the Burmese Communist Central Committee decided during the summer and fall of 1964 to take a more militant line aimed at "winning the war, seizure of power, and total elimination" of the Rangoon regime, Peking remained silent. The Thai Communist Party's call for the overthrow of Thanom was embodied in its PRC National Day message on 1 October, but the Burmese message made no such demand, despite the recent decision to fight. Instead it praised "the government's foreign policy of peace and neutrality."

Sino-Indonesian relations similarly prospered from China's emphasis on governmental rather than Party ties. In March 1964 Peking offered to transfer the Bank of China assets in Indonesia to Jakarta's control. Since the bank had been seen as providing leverage over the Chinese business community for funding the PKI, this seemed to signal sincerity on Peking's part in foreswearing interference in Indonesian affairs. Sukarno, rebuffed at the October 1964 nonaligned conference in Cairo over his bid for support in confrontation with Malaysia, flew to Shanghai on 4 November for talks with Chou En-lai. Three weeks later, Ch'en I arrived in Jakarta for a week of discussions, which resulted in a joint press release of unprecedented agreement on a wide range of issues, including the struggle to "crush"

93 Ibid., 100.

Malaysia.[94] China also extended a credit of $50 million for foreign exchange reserves and economic development.

Peking's pursuit of a tacit coalition within the "vast intermediate zone" as identified in its public analysis of world affairs made governmental relations primary and revolutionary relations secondary. Ayub Khan, Sihanouk, Ne Win, and Sukarno won major attention from Liu Shao-ch'i, Chou En-lai, and Ch'en I, who also brought modest economic assistance that carried considerable symbolic weight in view of China's obviously straitened circumstances. In addition to exploiting local grievances of these leaders and regimes against their immediate neighbors, PRC policy carefully cultivated seeds of anti-Soviet or anti-American attitudes that might strengthen China's position against the two superpowers. Thus, despite the ideological thrust of the Sino-Soviet polemic which cast Peking in the role of a radical revolutionary championing Marxism-Leninism, Chinese foreign policy in 1963–64 resembled that of the celebrated Bandung Conference nearly a decade earlier, except where the escalating Vietnam War threatened China's self-defined interests.

1964: a watershed year

From several points of view, 1964 marked a watershed in Chinese foreign relations. Qualitative changes in key areas posed new problems and prospects for the immediate future. First and foremost, the Sino-Soviet dispute deepened and broadened. Second, American escalation of the Vietnam War prompted Peking to increase its support for Hanoi's defiance of Washington. Third, China's detonation of an atomic bomb elevated the PRC to membership in the small group of nuclear powers without, however, increasing its defense capacity for some years to come. It even raised the possible threat of a preventive attack by the Soviet Union, the United States or both.

The gradual deterioration of Sino-Soviet relations accelerated with Mao's July interview publicly challenging the legitimacy of Russian control over much of Siberia and the Soviet Far East. In that same month was published "On Khrushchev's phony communism and its historical lesson for the world," the ninth in the polemical series by the editorial departments of *People's Daily* and *Red Flag*. Broadening the attack beyond the Soviet leader, it alleged, "The revisionist Khrushchev clique are the political representatives of the Soviet bourgeoisie and particularly of its privileged stratum [which] has gained control of the Party, the government, and other important organizations."[95]

Yet four months later, Chou En-lai went to Moscow to see whether Khrushchev's removal could improve relations. Ironically, Peking's July analysis proved correct, at least insofar as Khrushchev's associates maintained the hard line on Sino-Soviet relations. This foreshadowed a long and bitter confrontation that was not likely to be ameliorated by any leadership changes in Moscow.

The worsening situation in Vietnam further complicated Sino-Soviet relations. So long as the Moscow-Peking dispute had remained mainly political, whether over ideology or strategy, the controversy had not been central to China's vital interests, specifically its national security. To be sure, border incidents and minor differences over demarcation of the frontier might broaden to require a greater defense commitment. Basically, however, the virulent polemical exchanges in the press and at communist party conferences involved words, not action.

But the Gulf of Tonkin events raised the prospect of American air attacks on North Vietnam and a widening American presence in South Vietnam. This, in turn, forced Peking to strengthen its commitment to Hanoi, both to reassure North Vietnam and, possibly, to deter the United States. In this context, the Sino-Soviet dispute threatened the security of China as well as that of Vietnam. At the very least, it could complicate the transportation of military assistance to Hanoi. At the worst, it could encourage Washington to invade North Vietnam as it had North Korea and, if necessary, to interrupt or damage China's ability to help its ally. Attacks on China by the U.S. Air Force might not be inhibited by the Sino-Soviet alliance as they had been in Korea, now that the two partners had allowed their quarrel to appear irreparable.

The ultimate threat to China's national security lay in the prospect of Soviet-American collusion to forestall Peking's imminent possession of an operational nuclear capability. In 1959 Moscow had reneged on its promise to provide Peking with a sample atomic bomb. In 1963 Moscow and Washington had reached agreement against atmospheric tests. With both superpowers opposed to China's nuclear future, either or both could attack the nascent production facilities to cripple, perhaps permanently, this scarce source of

95 *PR*, 17 July 1964.

strength. The October 1964 test explosion thus was a cause for Chinese concern as well as pride.

At a lower level of importance, the prospect of China's recapturing its Third World role of the mid-1950s appeared badly dimmed. Efforts to promote a Second Bandung Conference stalled amid Afro-Asian internecine differences and a general reluctance to allow Sino-Soviet rivalries to factionalize further the various organizations. Then Indonesia's sudden withdrawal from the United Nations on 5 January 1965 prompted Chou En-lai to demand that the United Nations be "thoroughly reorganized" or, failing that, "another United Nations, a revolutionary one, may well be set up."[96] This added to Peking's problems with other Third World regimes whose membership in the world body was a universally accepted status symbol.

Last but not least, the interrelated problems of Sino-Soviet relations, the Indochina War, and China's interaction with the Third World moved rapidly toward a critical juncture just as domestic politics were about to take a dramatic and ultimately destructive turn that would threaten the very existence of the People's Republic as a cohesive entity. The entangling of domestic and foreign policy had already proved hazardous. In 1959 P'eng Te-huai's challenge to Mao's management of the economy had coincided with Khrushchev's denigration of the communes and reneging on the nuclear sharing agreement. This precedent augured poorly for the rational disposition of internal and external issues confronting Mao as 1964 drew to a close; the full ramifications of this problem were to become acutely manifest in the subsequent eighteen months. Indeed, seen from this perspective, 1964 closed a chapter in China's foreign relations, which were to experience increasing risk and tension for a number of years to come. The period of 1958 to 1964 would seem relatively calm by comparison, Quemoy and the Sino-Indian War notwithstanding.

96 Ibid., 29 January 1965, speech by Premier Chou En-lai at banquet for Indonesian Foreign Minister Subandrio, 24 January 1965.

EPILOGUE

By the mid-1960s, the record of the Chinese Communist regime was a mixture of triumph and tragedy. Its early years had witnessed a startlingly successful nation-building effort. The authority of the new government had been quickly established, assisted by universal relief at the restoration of peace and unity. The economy was rehabilitated and inflation brought under control. Land reform and a succession of campaigns in the cities exhibited the regime's willingness to use various forms of coercion, including execution, to eliminate opponents and intimidate potential critics. The Party state swiftly came to dominate all sections of society.

Despite the immensity of these tasks, the Chinese leaders had felt confident enough to take on the United States in the Korean War. In the event, the war effort assisted the consolidation of the regime and cemented relations between the Chinese and their hitherto somewhat wary Soviet allies. By the time an armistice was signed in 1953, China's leaders were initiating their 1st Five-Year Plan, on the Soviet model and with Soviet assistance. In 1955–56, at Mao's command, the Chinese Communist Party (CCP) demonstrated its organizational virtuosity by collectivizing China's 500 million peasants within months (a process that had taken the Russians years and cost countless lives).

This victory of the socialist revolution (quickly reinforced by similar achievements in industry and handicrafts) permitted domestic relaxation as the regime switched focus from ideological to economic goals and sought to mobilize the broadest possible coalition in the interest of development. But when Mao, reacting to Soviet de-Stalinization and the Hungarian revolt, attempted to moderate further the Party's methods of rule with the Hundred Flowers and Rectification campaigns, the experiment exploded in his face. The subsequent Anti-Rightist Campaign of 1957 put a large proportion of China's intellectual and technical leadership out of action. Nevertheless, by the end of the 1st FYP, in that year, the Chinese could congratulate themselves on an impressive start along the road to wealth and power. Despite exclusion from the United Nations, the People's Republic was already seen by its Asian neighbors as a superpower in embryo.

But the Chinese leaders, Mao particularly, were misled by their earlier successes. Impatient with the slow pace of development, they attributed it to Soviet methods rather than China's backwardness. Their revolutionary victory had taught them that people could win against apparently overwhelming odds. The decisive factor was the inspiration of "the masses" with the will to win, and after the victory of 1949 the CCP's techniques of popular mobilization had been raised to new levels in a relentless series of mass campaigns sanctioned by the concept of "class struggle." Economic and political life in China's towns and villages had been transformed. We shall examine the impact of the changes on China's urban and rural population in our final volume. Disillusioned with the Soviet model of industrialization and swept by nostalgia for their simpler, less urban and centralized life in Yenan, Mao and his colleagues conceived of a strategy that would use China's vast human resources to achieve economic development. If China's disciplined millions were mobilized in the newly devised communes, could not nature be tamed as effectively as the armies of the Kuomintang?

The tragedy of the Great Leap Forward (GLF), with the millions of deaths it caused, was the price of this monumental hubris. In its dark aftermath, China's leaders seemed agreed on the overriding importance of engineering economic recovery. The disastrous policies of the GLF were abandoned; the commune system was drastically modified. By 1965, the main economic indicators had been brought back to the level of 1957. Years as well as lives had been lost, but perhaps the chastening experience would serve the regime well in the future. The political trauma engendered by the GLF had resulted in the disgrace of a few leading comrades of the Long March and loss of face by Mao as its chief progenitor. He removed himself from administration but was distressed by his colleagues' drive to achieve economic growth through material incentives. At the apex of the Chinese leadership, however, the broad unity that had served the Communist movement so well in the past seemed on the surface intact. The proved resilience of the Chinese people suggested that a new start was possible.

It was not to be. During the GLF, simmering disputes between Peking and Moscow on a variety of policy issues had come to a boil.

When the Chinese insisted on their right to question Moscow's global strategy, the Russians abruptly withdrew their technical assistance personnel. Soviet highhandedness reawakened in China's leaders the anger engendered by a century of humiliation at the hands of stronger powers. Soviet neutrality in the Sino-Indian border dispute seemed a betrayal of international communist solidarity. The signature by the United States, the United Kingdom, and the Soviet Union of the partial test ban treaty in 1963 was a confirmation in Chinese eyes that Soviet leaders had abandoned China – and Leninism – in favor of appeasement of American imperialism. Peking's polemics talked darkly of a restoration of capitalism in the homeland of the revolution.

Probably all of China's top leaders were incensed at the Soviet Union's treatment of their nation. Almost certainly, they were agreed also that something had to be done domestically to restore the morale of Party and people after the disasters of the GLF. Only Mao seems to have drawn the lesson that without radical and urgent measures, China would follow the Soviet Union down the heretical path of revisionism.

Although few of Mao's old comrades could have realized it, the Long March–Yenan generation had reached a parting of the ways. For the great majority of China's leaders, the experience of the first decade and a half of the People's Republic had bred a belief that economic development and the well-being of the people had to take precedence over social engineering. The expanding war in Vietnam threatened to involve China in conflict with the United States again; domestic strife was to be avoided.

But Mao, by now apparently increasingly conscious of his own mortality, feared that without radical surgery the revolution so intimately associated with his name would become a mockery of all for which he had striven. In our final volume, we shall trace the evolution of his thinking, chronicle the Great Proletarian Cultural Revolution he unleashed on China, and analyze the impact of those ten years of storm on the Chinese people and the leaders who succeeded him.

In the present volume, certain historic Chinese themes have emerged: the crucial role of the founding ruler as he attempts to shape the new regime in his image and distance himself from the comrades who helped him create it, the overriding importance of unifying the Chinese realm as the ultimate justification for assuming the Mandate of Heaven, the imperative of an ideological legitimation claiming to explain man's place in the world, the need for a bureaucratic elite to expound the ideology and implement its teachings.

But the People's Republic, it was already clear by 1965, was not simply the old imperium writ large. Restoration was the myth if not the reality of traditional China; change was the watchword of the nation's new rulers. The technology of modern communications gave them control over the people undreamed of by the most megalomaniac of emperors. Their drive to modernize was undermining traditional society; and even if the transformations came more slowly than they wished, it was above all their impatience – Mao's in particular, but that of his colleagues too – that shattered the rhythms of the past. For China, they realized, was no longer the central kingdom, setting its own pace in splendid isolation. There was a wider world, not marching to Peking's drumbeat, to be overtaken. But in the mid-1960s China's leaders were committed to the belief that they could accomplish that task alone. Their own follies, combined with external dangers, finally brought them to the realization that this was not so. That end of innocence will be a major theme of our final volume.

BIBLIOGRAPHICAL ESSAYS

POLITICS TAKES COMMAND: AN ESSAY ON THE STUDY OF POST-1949 CHINA

This essay precedes several bibliographical essays on specific aspects of the People's Republic of China. It traces the evolution of scholarly writings on China by identifying the major sources on contemporary China, portraying their main limitations, and assessing the effect of the changing mix of sources available to the foreign researcher.

Researchers into the politics, economy, society, and culture of the post-1949 era confront many serious constraints. The student of contemporary China learns to use a diversity of sources: the mainland press in Chinese and in translation, accounts by émigrés and Western residents, interviews with émigrés and Chinese citizens abroad, fiction, analyses by foreign governments (sometimes partly based on clandestinely obtained information), and information derived from personal observation and field research in China. Because of the limitations inherent in each of these sources, the essence of research on China is to search for convergence among diverse sources. Where the various sources point in a similar direction, the researcher can be somewhat confident of the validity of the conclusions, but when the sources point in disparate directions, analysts must qualify their judgments and seek to reconcile the apparent discrepancies.

Before turning to these issues, however, a few more general observations about the difficulties of doing research on the People's Republic are appropriate. Chief among these have been the secrecy of the Chinese government, the inability of most foreign scholars to do research in China until 1979, the need therefore to rely on alternate, imperfect sources to study the living society, and the extraordinary discontinuities in availability of various sources. The extent to which the available sources distort as well as illuminate China has posed major methodological problems for thirty years.

The penchant for secrecy was manifest in the refusal of the Chinese government to publish any reliable statistical series from 1959 to 1978. Reluctance to disclose the extent of the failures of the Great

Leap Forward, an intense concern with national security, the destruction of the statistical network during the Cultural Revolution, and a deeply rooted cultural preference for secrecy combined to make developments in China a genuine puzzle for over two decades. Production statistics, population figures, government revenue and expenditure figures, data on personal income and consumption, information on foreign trade, employment statistics, records of major Party and government meetings, legal compendia, notices of official appointments and dismissals, and biographical information on political and military officials were unavailable. Foreign governments and Western scholars devoted great effort to generate these kinds of data, the existence of which are ordinarily taken for granted. Since 1978, the Chinese government has gradually been reporting statistics and has attempted to reconstruct data for the intervening years. Yet many vital statistics at the national level are still unavailable, data for the provincial level remain scarce, and many of the available statistics are misleading or inaccurate.

Foreign scholars confronted another major problem: China was simply closed for research purposes until 1979. To be sure, several Western and Japanese newspapers had posted correspondents to Peking by the mid-1960s, and some Western academics studied in Chinese universities at almost all times from 1949 on. Western diplomats also occasionally published their impressions of Peking. But the Westerners were isolated, without access to research libraries and unable to travel freely or to reside outside Peking for sustained periods of time. A Western community did reside in China, employed by the government, but their writings were rather uncritical and superficial. For all practical purposes, until 1979 China had to be studied at a distance. Alternative sources for understanding the living society had to be fostered.

To compensate, Western scholars developed a research base in Hong Kong, where major research archives were assembled at the Union Research Institute (URI) and the Universities Service Centre (USC). Research in these archives was then interwoven with interviews of Chinese émigrés to generate monographs on various facets of contemporary China.[1] Interviewing of Hong Kong informants

---

1 Thomas Bernstein, *Up to the mountains and down to the villages: The transfer of youth from urban to rural China*; Jerome A. Cohen, ed., *The criminal process in the People's Republic of China, 1949–1963: An introduction*; Richard Solomon, *Mao's revolution and the Chinese political culture*; Ezra F. Vogel, *Canton under communism: Programs and politics in a provincial capital, 1949–1968*; and Lynn White, *Careers in Shanghai: The social guidance of personal energies in a developing Chinese city, 1949–1966*.

itself became a sohisticated art, with researchers aware of the strengths and weaknesses of the émigrés. Among their limitations was the preponderance of informants from south and coastal China, the lack of higher-level officials among them, the difficulty of assessing their reliability, and their possible antiregime biases. Most of these deficiencies could be taken into account through imaginative yet rigorous interview procedures, but the relatively small number of available informants at any one time and the inability to place the informants in the context of their residence and workplace imposed limitations on this source of information. However, the opening of China to research by foreigners in 1979 did not extend to allowing social scientists to interview statistically significant samples of the population or to observe the living society for sustained periods of time. Interviewing émigrés to Hong Kong remains a major if imperfect source on contemporary China.

Another difficulty has been the discontinuities in source materials. Few publications have continued through the entire thirty-five years of the People's Republic. The *People's Daily* (*Jen-min jih-pao*), the Shanghai *Wen-hui pao*, and the government gazette *Hsin-hua yueh-pao* (New China monthly), published as *Hsin-hua pan-yueh-k'an* (New China semi-monthly) from 1956 through 1961, are the only three that come to mind. Many journals and newspapers ceased being available to foreigners after the Great Leap Forward, and other publications ceased during the Cultural Revolution.

Partially offsetting these discontinuities, a series of unique and illuminating sources has become available at different times and had a significant effect on research: (1) Chinese prisoners-of-war who chose repatriation to Taiwan rather than the People's Republic after the Korean War and who shed light on the People's Liberation Army (PLA);[2] (2) the American victims of Chinese brainwashing techniques who were released in the mid-1950s and whose accounts illuminated Chinese techniques of manipulating small group pressures;[3] (3) the outpouring of views about the regime during the Hundred Flowers campaign in 1957;[4] (4) the availability of the *Kung-tso*

---

2 See William Bradbury, *Mass behavior in battle and captivity: The Communist soldier in the Korean War*; and Alexander George, *The Chinese Communist army in action: The Korean War and its aftermath*.

3 Robert J. Lifton, *Thought reform and the psychology of totalism: A study of "brainwashing" in China*; Edgar H. Schein, "The Chinese indoctrination program for prisoners of war," *Psychiatry*, 19.2 (May 1956), 149–72; and Edgar H. Schein et al., *Coercive persuasion*.

4 Dennis Doolin, *Communist China: The politics of student opposition*; Roderick MacFarquhar, *The Hundred Flowers Campaign and the Chinese intellectuals*; and Hualing Nieh, *Literature of the Hundred Flowers*.

t'ung-hsun, an internally circulated journal of the PLA, obtained by Taiwan for much of the year 1961;[5] (5) an influx of refugees into Hong Kong in 1962;[6] (6) the documents about Lien-chiang county in Fukien and Pao-an county, Kwangtung, during the Socialist Education campaign in 1962–64;[7] (7) the Red Guard newspapers during the Cultural Revolution of 1966–68;[8] (8) the secret 1972 documents of the Central Committee describing the Lin Piao affair;[9] (9) the documents condemning the policies of Teng Hsiao-p'ing during his 1975 ascendancy, which the opponents of Teng distributed in 1976;[10] (10) the popular opinions expressed during the T'ien An Men incident of 1976;[11] (11) the secret 1977 documents of the Central Committee describing the evils of the Gang of Four;[12] (12) the handbills and journals distributed during the Democracy Wall movement of 1978–79;[13] and (13) the indictment released during the trial of the Gang of Four and of Lin Piao's accomplices in 1980–81.[14]

Each of the sources attracted considerable attention, but it is not clear whether the insights they provided are limited to the time, place, and issues with which they were concerned or whether they have more general applicability. The lack of continuity in sources and the enormous impact of sources of short duration have probably caused

5 J. Chester Cheng, *The politics of the Chinese Red Army: A translation of the Bulletin of Activities of the People's Liberation Army*; John Wilson Lewis, "China's secret military papers: 'Continuities' and 'revelations,'" *The China Quarterly* (hereafter CQ), 18 (April–June 1964), 68–78; and Ralph L. Powell, *Politico-military relationships in Communist China*.

6 Barnett and Vogel, *Cadres, bureaucracy, and political power in Communist China*; Cohen, ed., *Criminal process*; Lucian Pye, *The spirit of Chinese politics: A psychocultural study of the crisis in political development*; Richard Solomon, *Mao's revolution*; and Vogel, *Canton under communism*.

7 Maurice Freedman, *Chinese lineage and society: Fukien and Kwangtung*; and S. C. Chen and Charles P. Ridley, *The rural people's communes in Lien-chiang*.

8 Hong Yung Lee, *The politics of the Chinese Cultural Revolution: A case study*.

9 Michael Y. Kau, ed., *The Lin Piao affair: Power, politics, and military coup*.

10 Kenneth Lieberthal et al., *Central documents and Politburo politics in China*.

11 *Ko-ming shih ch'ao* (A transcript of revolutionary poems), 2 vols.; Xiao Lan, ed., *The Tienanmen poems*.

12 Wang Hsueh-wen, "The 'Gang of Four' incident: Official exposé by a CCPCC document," *Issues and Studies*, 13.9 (September 1977), 46–58.

13 James Tong, ed., "Underground journals in China," *Chinese Law and Government*, Part I, 13.2–3 (Fall-Winter 1980–1981), and Part II, 14.3 (Fall 1981); James Seymour, *The fifth modernization: China's human rights movement, 1978–1979*; and David S. G. Goodman, *Beijing street voices*.

14 Tsui-kao jen-min fa-yuan yen-chiu-shih (Research Office, Supreme People's Court), ed., *Chung-hua jen-min kung-ho-kuo tsui-kao jen-min fa-yuan t'e-pieh fa-t'ing shen-p'an Lin Piao, Chiang Ch'ing fan-ko-ming chi-t'uan an chu-fan chi-shih* (Record of the trials of the principal criminals of the Lin Piao and Chiang Ch'ing cliques before the Special Tribunal of the Supreme People's Court of the People's Republic of China); *A great trial in Chinese history: The trial of the Lin Biao and Jiang Qing counter-revolutionary cliques, Nov. 1980 – Jan. 1981*.

China to appear to be more unstable, unsteady, and volatile than has really been the case. The discontinuities in sources make it very difficult to chart trends accurately.

Another problem, which this essay is intended partially to redress, concerns obtaining bibliographic control over primary and secondary sources. Bibliographies of the major translation services that record Chinese radio broadcasts are generally unavailable. In recent years, many Chinese books with the *nei-pu* (internal use only) designation have appeared in the West, but no centrally coordinated system exists to indicate what is available. Various sorts of ephemeral materials – diaries and reports from trips to China, protocols from Hong Kong interviews, newsletters of organizations dealing with China – are available at many university centers for Chinese Studies, but they are usually not catalogued and their contents usually do not appear in bibliographies.

Obtaining control over secondary sources is a major challenge – if not impossible. As a result of these problems, knowledgeable scholars in the field are inveterate footnote readers. They first examine the footnotes of a new book or article to identify its sources and to ascertain whether the work plunges into new data.

THE BASIC SOURCES AND THEIR LIMITATIONS

The Chinese press

The Chinese press provides the staple for research on China: books, journals, and newspapers. These sources come from diverse institutions throughout the political system. The Central Committee of the Chinese Communist Party (CCP) began to publish the *People's Daily* soon after the Party established itself in Peking, and since 1958 the Party has published *Red Flag* (*Hung-ch'i*) as its leading theoretical journal. The State Council has published a gazette containing its principal directives.[15]

A publication usually follows a major national meeting, such as those of the National People's Congress, the CCP's national party congress or its Central Committee's plenum, the Youth League, or the Federation of Literary and Art Circles. A pamphlet gathers the principal documents from the meeting: speeches of the top leaders,

---

15 *Chung-hua jen-min kung-ho-kuo kuo-wu-yuan kung-pao* (Gazette of the State Council of the People's Republic of China), published by the State Council, 1955 to present, irregular.

directives, resolutions, and so on. Central ministries, provinces, universities, research academies, and mass organizations such as the Women's Federation and the Communist Youth League typically have their own publishing houses which, except for disruptions during the Cultural Revolution and its aftermath (1966–76), churn out books, pamphlets, journals, and newspapers. Initiated during the 1950s, and discontinued in the immediate post-Great Leap era, many special districts (*ti-ch'ü* or *chuan-ch'ü*) and counties (*hsien*) published newspapers. In the post-Mao era, local presses began to publish local histories, local fiction, and some journals.

Establishing bibliographical control

The challenge to the researcher is to establish bibliographical control over the books, journals, and newspapers published in the People's Republic. Two bibliographies published in China are helpful aids: The *Ch'üan-kuo hsin shu-mu* (National bibliography of new books), a periodical, and the *Ch'üan-kuo tsung shu-mu* (Cumulative national bibliography), published annually. These series catalogue books and pamphlets published on the mainland and group titles according to broad topical categories. Major libraries outside China hold most issues in these two series, and the total series are easily available in libraries in mainland China. But the two series have serious limitations.

Many of the titles are simply not available in Western libraries and frequently cannot be located in mainland libraries. Further, some of the most interesting and useful books and pamphlets printed on the mainland are not contained either in the *Ch'üan-kuo hsin shu-mu* or the *Ch'üan-kuo tsung shu-mu*. These publications bear the designation *nei-pu*. They contain material that for various reasons either the authors or the regime consider to be sensitive, and hence are not allowed to circulate among non-Chinese or are not legally permitted to leave the country. Such classified and secret materials are, for most of the post-1949 era, not listed in mainland bibliographies. Compiling a list of attractive titles from Chinese bibliographies is therefore of limited use. Bibliographical control over books and pamphlets, in the end, can be established only through diligent combing of library catalogues both inside and outside China, through securing access to the stacks, and through the assistance of Western and Chinese scholars who have their own private collections of useful materials.

Establishing bibliographical control over journal and newspaper articles is another matter. Most major newspapers publish extensive indexes. Articles in the *People's Daily* and *Kuang-ming jih-pao* (Kuang-ming daily) are classified in the *Jen-min jih-pao so-yin* (Index to *People's Daily*) and *Kuang-ming jih-pao so-yin* (Index to *Kuang-ming Daily*). Several regional and provincial newspapers, such as the *Nan-fang jih-pao* (Southern daily), also publish indexes. Except for the index to the *Jen-min jih-pao*, which is available in its entirety, Western libraries usually have partial holdings, but libraries on the mainland frequently contain the entire series.

Another extremely useful index is the *Ch'üan-kuo chu-yao pao-k'an tzu-liao so-yin* (Index to national important periodical materials). It classifies articles according to rather refined topical categories, and for many of its issues it even refers to articles from *nei-pu* journals. Western libraries hold complete runs of this publication for 1955 to 1959 and sporadic issues for the 1960s and 1970s, but access to the entire series can be secured in many mainland libraries. Use of this valuable bibliography in Chinese libraries which have extensive holdings of provincial newspapers and periodicals becomes an effective way to do research on well-defined topics.

A major challenge in the use of Chinese newspapers and periodicals is to discover their existence. Many contain the *nei-pu* classification and therefore are not always mentioned in the *Ch'üan-kuo tsung shu-mu*. Nor does this catalogue describe the nature of the publication. *Contemporary China: A research guide*, published in 1967, remains a unique guide to the Chinese periodical press, listing many of the ministerial journals of the 1950s and 1960s; many of these periodicals ceased publication during the Cultural Revolution and resumed in the 1970s.[16]

Once armed with a list of pertinent periodicals, the researcher confronts a new problem: Where are the journals and newspapers located? No union catalogue currently exists for PRC newspaper and periodical holdings in the West. Several partial catalogues do exist,[17] but these are now outdated. Researchers have little choice but to search among principal collections on contemporary China: in Australia, the Australian National University and the Australian National Library; in Britain, the British Museum and the School of Oriental and African Studies; in France, the Bibliothèque Nationale (Paris); in West Germany, the Institut für Asienkunde (Hamburg); in Hong Kong, the Universities Service Centre, the Chinese University,

16 Peter Berton and Eugene Wu, *Contemporary China: A research guide*.
17 See especially G. Raymond Nunn, comp., *Chinese periodicals, international holdings, 1949–1960*; and Bernadette P. N. Shih and Richard L. Snyder, *Communist Chinese serials*.

and the Hong Kong University; in Japan, the National Diet Library, the Institute for Developing Economies, and the Tōyō Bunko; in Sweden, the Universitets Bibliotek (Stockholm) and the University Library of Lund; in Taiwan, the Institute of International Relations and the Bureau of Investigation; and in the United States, the Library of Congress (Washington), the Center for Chinese Studies Library of the University of California (Berkeley), the Far Eastern Library of the University of Chicago, the East Asian Library of Columbia University (New York), the Harvard-Yenching Library of Harvard University (Cambridge, Massachusetts), the Asian Library of the University of Michigan (Ann Arbor), the Hoover Library of Stanford University (Palo Alto, California), and the Far Eastern Library of the University of Washington (Seattle).

The other alternative is to use Chinese libraries. The Peking Library (Pei-ching t'u-shu-kuan) and the Shanghai Municipal Library are principal repositories, and the social science library of the Chinese Academy of Sciences and several university libraries also have sound collections. The Peking Library has published a useful catalogue of its holdings of newspapers from the post-1949 era which reveals extensive holdings of national, provincial, and even subprovincial newspapers.[18]

Three valuable collections or compendia of articles from newspapers and periodicals merit mention: the *Fu-yin pao-k'an tzu-liao*, the URI clipping files, and *Hsin-hua yueh-pao*. Jen-min ta-hsueh (People's University) compiles and publishes an annual file of important or revealing articles on a wide range of topics. This series, the *Fu-yin pao-k'an tzu-liao* (Duplication of press materials), reproduces clipping files maintained at Jen-min ta-hsueh. The publication apparently began after 1978 and in 1980–81 was open to foreigners. The series was designated *nei-pu* in 1982–83, when it continued to be distributed to many libraries throughout China, and was reopened to foreigners in 1984. Outside China, the URI maintained a clipping service in its Hong Kong archive. The service remained active from the early 1950s until the late 1960s, after which it gradually atrophied. Many Western libraries acquired the files on microfilm, and the original archive was acquired by the Hong Kong Baptist College. This archive is particularly strong for the 1950s and early 1960s, when the URI had an aggressive and well-funded program for acquiring

---

18 *Pei-ching t'u-shu-kuan kuan-ts'ang pao-chih mu-lu* (Catalogue of newspaper holdings at the Peking Library).

Chinese publications and an adequate staff to clip and file the articles. Indeed, the URI clipping files provided a substantial portion of the documentation in the monograph work done in the 1960s and early 1970s.[19]

The Chinese publish a periodical compendium of major newspaper and journal articles. *Hsin-hua yueh-pao* has appeared on a monthly basis since 1949 (on a semi-monthly basis from 1956 through 1961, when the series was entitled *Hsin-hua pan-yueh k'an* [New China semi-monthly]). This hefty publication, which has averaged between 200 and 250 pages in length, contains the major directives, speeches, editorials, commentaries and news dispatches, as well as a chronology of major events of the month. In 1979, *Hsin-hua yueh-pao* became exclusively a journal of record, a semi-official gazette of government and Party policy, while an accompanying new monthly, *Hsin-hua yueh-pao wen-chai-pan* (later *Hsin-hua wen-chai*) reprinted articles on history, economics, philosophy, culture, and politics, as well as short stories and poetry from newspapers and periodicals throughout China.

Limitations and opportunities of the Chinese press

Use of the Chinese press involves severe problems and constraints. The press is controlled by the state and serves the purposes of the rulers and diverse organizational interests of the bureaucracies which control the various publishing houses. China lacks a strong tradition of independent, critical, and responsible journalism and of detached social science scholarship. The press serves an avowedly propagandistic role, publicizing current policies (usually in a favorable light) and denigrating previous, rejected policies. A considerable portion of domestic newspaper reporting is not "news" in the Western journalistic sense, but rather presents essays expounding current policy (which may subtly disagree with portions of it) and accounts from model units that have successfully implemented state policy and from localities whose failure to heed policy has led to obvious difficulties. Reporting on foreign affairs also tends to hew to official policy.

Only in the post-Mao era have books and periodicals begun to appear in any number which analyze the effect of domestic policies in a systematic fashion or which illuminate political, social, and economic processes. For example, *Liao-wang* (Outlook), a widely

19 Examples are John Wilson Lewis, *Leadership in Communist China*; Franz Schurmann, *Ideology and organization in Communist China*; and James Townsend, *Political participation in Communist China*.

distributed periodical published by the New China (Hsin-hua) News Agency since 1981, has reported on the personal activities and deliberative processes within the Chung-nan-hai, the seat of government in Peking. Numerous reminiscences by higher level officials have provided glimpses into the personalities, styles, and policy debates of the Party from the 1920s to Mao's death. Pamphlets and journal articles have begun to recount the evolution of high-level policy struggles since 1949. Collections of speeches and writings of high-level officials other than Mao have begun to appear; for example, the selected works of Chu Te, Ch'en Yun, Chou En-lai, Liu Shao-ch'i, Tung Pi-wu, and Teng Hsiao-p'ing are now available. Increasing numbers of social science journals have begun to detail aspects of current policy choices and reveal the contending opinions of clashing bureaucracies. Pamphlets are appearing that are genuinely intended to inform an interested reader about some facet of China, rather than to instruct someone as to why that facet is beneficial.

All these are recent developments, however, and during most of the post-1949 era effective use of the press as a reliable source of information was a form of art. Scholars outside China developed various techniques to decode the esoteric Chinese press in more rigorous fashion. For example, observers of Chinese foreign policy carefully reviewed all Chinese statements in the media to understand the evolution in attitudes toward such key issues as China's entry into the Korean War, Chinese behavior during the 1958 Quemoy-Matsu crisis, the Sino-Indian border war of 1962, and the Sino-Soviet dispute.[20] Out of these studies has come an understanding of the way Chinese signal their intent, Chinese crisis behavior, and the conduct of China's bilateral relations. Students of elite-level politics scrutinized the appearances, absences, and positioning of leaders in photographs in the *People's Daily*, the different order which leaders used to enunciate the slogans of the day (for example, did the leader say, "grasp revolution and boost production" or "boost production and grasp revolution"?), the patriarchs whom a leader might choose to quote (was Mao the sole leader quoted? was Liu Shao-ch'i cited? and so on), and news that a leader previously in a different area was performing new responsibilities (with no formal announcement that

20 See Allen S. Whiting, *China crosses the Yalu* and *The Chinese calculus of deterrence*; Jonathan Pollack, "Perception and process in Chinese foreign policy: The Quemoy decision"; and Donald Zagoria, *The Sino-Soviet conflict*. These studies interweave a careful reading of the Chinese press with a study of diplomatic and military activity.

the previous incumbent had been dismissed or the new incumbent had been appointed). Out of such myriad clues came Western interpretations of the debate over agricultural collectivization in 1955–56, the dispute over policy toward intellectuals in 1956–57, and the cleavages among the top leaders toward the Great Leap Forward.[21] Remarkably, subsequent revelations during the Cultural Revolution and in the post-Mao era have shown these interpretations to have been correct in broad outline if not in every detail.

Similarly, strategies began to be employed for analysis of policy implementation or for sociological analysis. One obvious method is to read all available material about a specific locale and to examine that locale in detail, with the researcher enriching the data through interviewing.[22] Another approach is to study the evolution of a specific policy and its implementation over time.[23] Yet another strategy is to examine one or a set of institutions, using all the material available about that organization: legal enactments about it, speeches and articles describing its role, articles about its subordinate agencies, and so on.[24] Such research usually relies heavily on the press under the control of the agency under scrutiny – for example, study of the Youth League draws largely on materials from the youth press; the trade unions, from the trade union press; and so on. (Studies

21 For examples of Pekingological studies, see Byung-joon Ahn, *Chinese politics and the Cultural Revolution: Dynamics of policy processes*; Parris H. Chang, *Power and policy in China*; Merle Goldman, *China's intellectuals: Advise and dissent*; and Roderick MacFarquhar, *The origins of the Cultural Revolution*, vols. 1 and 2.
22 Lynn T. White III, *Careers in Shanghai*; Dorothy Solinger, *Regional government and political integration in Southwest China, 1949–1954: A case study*; Kenneth G. Lieberthal, *Revolution and tradition in Tientsin, 1949–1952*; Donald McMillen, *Chinese Communist power and policy in Xinjiang, 1949–1977*; Gordon Bennett, *Huadong: The story of a Chinese people's commune*; and Vivienne Shue, *Peasant China in transition: The dynamics of development toward socialism, 1949–1956*.
23 On education: Robert I. Taylor, *China's intellectual dilemma: Politics and university enrollment, 1949–1978*. On public health: David M. Lampton, *The politics of medicine in China: the policy process, 1949–1977*. On agricultural mechanization: Benedict Stavis, *The politics of agricultural mechanization in China*. On industrial management: Stephen Andors, *China's industrial revolution: Politics, planning, and management, 1949 to the present*; Chong-wook Chung, *Maoism and development: The politics of industrial management in China*. On science and technology: Richard P. Suttmeier, *Research and revolution: Science policy and societal change in China*. On bureaucratic management: Harry Harding, *Organizing China: The problem of bureaucracy, 1949–1976*. On national minority policy: June Teufel Dreyer, *China's forty millions: Minority nationalities and national integration in the People's Republic of China*. On grain management: Kenneth R. Walker, *Food grain procurement and consumption in China*.
24 George N. Ecklund, *Financing the Chinese government budget: Mainland China, 1950–1959*; Katherine H. Hsiao, *Money and monetary policy in Communist China*; Choh-ming Li, *The statistical system of Communist China*; and Benedict Stavis, *People's communes and rural development in China*.

of the PLA are an exception; publications by the military are usually highly classified and unavailable.) Whether the focus is on a specific locale, policy issue, or institution, reliance on the press presents problems. The press describes structure rather than process and focuses more upon the formal rather than the informal dimensions. It conveys a sense that Chinese organizations are efficient and effective, it implies that policy and reality coincide, and it suggests a national uniformity. Although these impressions accurately convey the perception from Peking, the reality frequently departs significantly from policy. China is much more heterogeneous than its national elite has usually acknowledged – at least during the Mao era.

The result is to encourage another strategy for using the press: to aggregate data, to place cases in their appropriate contexts, and to draw upon the enormous variation of China to develop verifiable hypotheses. For example, in studies of enterprise management, Stephen Andors and Andrew Walder used 187 examples of management gleaned from the press to identify which types of factories used particular forms of management over time. Andors and Walder wanted to know which types of industries (heavy, light, or chemical) were more prone to adopt worker participation in management or cadre participation in labor.[25] Richard Baum carefully plotted the geographical location of Kwangtung newspaper references to the consequences of the Cultural Revolution in the countryside to ascertain what kind of communes and production brigades were suffering from turmoil in 1966–69.

In different studies, John Burns and Elizabeth Perry scanned the press for accounts of peasant political behavior. Burns developed a typology of how peasants pursue their political interests, while Perry traced the evolving circumstances under which peasants engage in violent protest.[26] Frederick Teiwes scanned the provincial press to measure the degree of responsiveness of provinces to various central programs and then sought to explain the responsiveness through reference to certain political and economic conditions in the province. He sought to identify correlations between the rank ordering of

25 Andors, *China's industrial revolution: Politics, planning, and management, 1949 to the present*; Andrew Walder, "Press accounts and the study of Chinese society," *CQ*, 79 (September 1979), 568–92; Richard Baum, "The Cultural Revolution in the countryside: Autonomy of a limited rebellion," in Thomas Robinson, ed., *The Cultural Revolution in China*, 367–476.
26 John Burns, "Chinese peasant interest articulation, 1949–1974." Columbia University, Ph.D. dissertation, 1979; Elizabeth J. Perry, "Rural violence in socialist China," *CQ*, 103 (September 1985), 414–40.

provincial responsiveness and the rank order in such dimensions as strength of the Party apparatus in the province or level of economic development.[27]

These and other research efforts carefully accumulate many instances, cases, or examples of behavior or practices (types of factory management, provincial response to central directives, or peasant pursuit of interest) which the researcher wants to understand. Typologies of the behavior are then developed, and the recorded cases are classified according to the typology. Using a classic method of the social sciences, these practices are treated as the dependent variable. The task of the analyst is to explain the distribution of cases among the various types of behavior through reference to the different contexts in which the behavior took place. That is, for all its deficiencies, the mainland press can be used to try to explain variation in particular phenomena over time and place. Yet these analyses remain somewhat unsatisfying. The press does not provide a representative sample; the cases that can be gleaned from the press usually are sufficiently small in number that they do not permit sophisticated quantitative analytical techniques; and not enough is known about the context to identify and measure all the relevant independent variables.

Translations from the Chinese press

The Chinese press is the indispensable source of information for most questions. To be sure, certain subjects simply have been excluded from extensive treatment in the press: natural disasters and colossal policy blunders, such as the extent of starvation and malnutrition during 1960–62 or of terror and death during the Cultural Revolution; the policy process at the higher levels of the Party; the organization and roles of the public security system; the personnel system (how appointments, promotions, and dismissals are made); the way prices are set and modified; and the structure, functions, and processes of the intermediate levels of the state – province, special district, municipality, and county. The press reveals more about the top and the bottom of the system, whether in economics, politics, or culture, than about the intervening levels. Apart from these significant lacunae, the press has enabled students of China to acquire a general sense of current policies, policy differences among the lead-

27 Frederick Teiwes, "Provincial politics in China: Themes and variations," in John M. H. Lindbeck, ed., *China: Management of a revolutionary society*, 116–92.

ers, and developments at the grassroots level. Nonetheless, even on these topics the press is inadequate by itself to illuminate these topics in any depth. As a result, researchers must combine the press with other sources.

A significant portion of Chinese-language publications is available in translation. The Foreign Languages Press in Peking and other companies publish materials aimed for consumption abroad in a wide variety of foreign languages. For example, *People's China* was published semi-monthly from 1950 to 1957 and was then succeeded by the weekly *Peking Review* (now *Beijing Review*) published in over twenty foreign languages since March 1958. The Chinese government publishes a daily English-language compilation of dispatches from *Hsin-hua hsin-wen-she* (New China News Agency). In 1981 the English language *China Daily* began publication in Peking.

The Foreign Languages Press provides access to Chinese fiction through the numerous novels it has translated and the Chinese short stories that appear in *Chinese Literature*. Further, major government and Communist Party pronouncements, important speeches, and compendia are routinely translated and published in pamphlet or book form. Thus, the *Selected Works of Mao Tse-tung*, the *Selected Works of Deng Xiaoping*, the documents from each National People's Congress, and the communiqués of Central Committee Plenums were distributed by the Foreign Languages Press soon after the Chinese-language versions appeared.

Foreign governments incorporate some of the Chinese translations into their own translation series, and translate additional news dispatches, journal articles, and books for these series. The British Broadcasting Corporation, for instances, publishes its daily *Summary of World Broadcasts (Far East) (SWB/FE)*, series that antedates the establishment of the People's Republic of China and contains either the entire texts or excerpts of major news items from China, including translations of provincial news broadcasts. The United States government has published several translation series. From 1950 until 1979, the United States Consulate General in Hong Kong maintained a large press monitoring unit which distributed several series: *Survey of the China Mainland Press (SCMP)* (after 1974, the *Survey of the People's Republic of China Press*), the *Extracts from China Mainland Magazines (ECMM)* (later, *Selections from China Mainland Magazines (SCMM)* and after 1974, the *Survey of the People's Republic of China Magazines*), and *Current Background*, a grouping of articles dealing with a similar topic. The Consulate General provided an excellent, detailed topical index to these three translation series. But the index did not refer to the supplementary series, which carried a low-level security classification and was released to the general public only later. The *SWB/FE* was available by subscription and is on microfilm, and hence can be obtained in many libraries. The Consulate General series, during much of its life, was distributed to a limited number of libraries specializing in East Asia. It is thus not as widely available as *SWB/FE*, although it is much more extensive in coverage.

The United States government Foreign Broadcast Information Service (FBIS) provides a daily compilation of monitored radio broadcasts from China. This compilation appears in a separate pamphlet as part of global coverage by FBIS. Until 1967, the China portion of the monitored radio broadcasts appeared in the Asia pamphlet, and in 1968 *FBIS (China)* appeared as a separate edition. As a courtesy it was distributed to a few libraries and scholars, but later it became available only by subscription. With the closing of the Hong Kong press monitoring unit, *FBIS* included some of the materials previously contained in the *SCMP-SCMM* series.[28]

The third United States government translation series is the Joint Publication Research Service (*JPRS*), which has provided English-language renditions of Chinese books, journals, and newspaper articles (especially from provincial presses) since 1957. The history of this series, as well as the various efforts to sustain an index to it, is extraordinarily complex. Suffice it to say that *JPRS* was reorganized on several occasions, and hence contains several subseries of varying duration on such topics as agriculture, science and technology, local politics, energy, and education, as well as a subseries which translates the entirety of each issue of *Red Flag*. With the termination of the United States government translation series based in Hong Kong in June 1979, the JPRS series was titled *China Report* and was reorganized into six subseries: agriculture; economic affairs; political, sociological, and military affairs; plant and installation data; science and technology; and *Red Flag*. No convenient and continuous index exists to provide easy entry into the JPRS series for its entire variegated life span. One single index covers the years 1957 to mid-1960, while another editor compiled a periodic index from 1962 to 1970.[29] Since 1979, some of the subseries occasionally

28 *Index Foreign Broadcast Information Service Daily Report: China* (New Canaan, Conn.: NewsBank, 1975–). See Bibliography for a full description of this publication.
29 See Richard Sorich, ed., *Contemporary China: A bibliography of reports on China published by the Joint Publications Research Service*; Theodore Kyriak, ed., *Bibliography-index to US JPRS research translations*, Vols. 1–8.

group the tables of contents of previous issues into a separate publication.

Three other useful translation series deserve mention. From 1955 to 1977, the Union Research Institute in Hong Kong published *Union Research Service (URS)*, which grouped translations on a particular contemporary topic. Beginning in 1968, M. E. Sharpe, Inc., began a series of quarterly journals, each devoted to translation in specific areas: *Chinese Law and Government, Chinese Economics, Chinese Education*, and *Chinese Sociology*. Issues in these different series frequently are devoted to special topics. For example, *Chinese Law and Government* has focused separate issues on the Lin Piao affair, the Party constitution, personnel management, and so on. The Regional Information Office, the Hong Kong branch of a British government agency, monitored provincial broadcasts in its *Provincial Radio Broadcasts*, a weekly publication distributed to a few libraries, journalists, and scholars from 1963 to 1974. This fine series frequently contained items found in neither *FBIS* nor *SWB/FE*.

In addition to these regular translation series of Chinese language materials, many special compilations have appeared on limited topics. For example, original documents on such topics as Chinese educational policy,[30] agricultural policy,[31] economic organization,[32] military directives,[33] Sino-American relations,[34] the Sino-Soviet dispute,[35] major policy pronouncements during select time periods,[36] leadership doctrine,[37] and selections of short stories on special topics[38] have been assembled in edited volumes.

---

30 Stewart Fraser, *Chinese communist education: Records of the first decade*; and Peter J. Seybolt, ed., *Revolutionary education in China: Documents and commentary.*
31 Chao Kuo-chün, *Agrarian policies of mainland China: A documentary study, 1949–1956.*
32 Chao Kuo-chün, *Economic planning and organization in mainland China: A documentary study, 1949–1957.*
33 Ying-mao Kau, ed., *The People's Liberation Army and China's nation-building*; and Kau, *The political work system of the Chinese communist military.*
34 Roderick MacFarquhar, *Sino-American relations, 1949–1971*, and Gene Hsiao and Michael Witunski, *Sino-American normalization and its policy implications.*
35 G. F. Hudson, Richard Lowenthal, and Roderick MacFarquhar, *The Sino-Soviet dispute*; David Floyd, ed., *Mao against Khrushchev*; Alexander Dallin, ed., *Diversity in international communism*; John Gittings, *Survey of the Sino-Soviet dispute*; and William Griffith, *Albania and the Sino-Soviet rift, The Sino-Soviet rift*, and *Sino-Soviet relations, 1964–1965.*
36 Robert R. Bowie and John K. Fairbank, eds., *Communist China, 1955–1959: Policy documents with analysis*; Union Research Institute (URI), *CCP documents of the Great Proletarian Cultural Revolution, 1966–1967*, and *Documents of the Chinese Communist Party Central Committee*; H. Hinton, ed., *The People's Republic of China, 1949–1979.*
37 John W. Lewis, *Major doctrines of Communist China.*
38 Perry Link, ed., *"People or monsters?" and other stories and reportage from China after Mao, by Liu Binyan.*

In short, the effort to provide access to the Chinese-language media through translation has been extensive. Yet the coverage is highly uneven, and to do serious research on most topics requires use of Chinese-language sources. While the major articles and editorials in the leading national newspapers, speeches by top leaders, and major national directives are easily available, the provincial newspapers, ministerial journals, and book-length monographs are not extensively translated. Since governments – Chinese, American, British – finance and operate the major translation services, they tend to serve immediate government interests and purposes, and these do not always coincide with the long-term interests and objectives of historians and social scientists. The *FBIS* series, for example, is widely used within the American intelligence community. Although its contents include reports on a wide range of topics, including family life, social conditions, and local politics, its task is to inform its readers about China's intentions, capabilities, and strategies in world affairs. The *JPRS* series contains more information than *FBIS* about social conditions, local politics, and economics, but it also strongly emphasizes scientific developments in China and issues of commercial concern to the United States. On balance, then, the translation series are more extensive in coverage of such topics as national-level politics, foreign policy, military affairs, and science, and are less satisfactory in their reporting of articles on Party history, literature, philosophy, local politics, culture, and social life. The extent of translation has varied enormously over time.

Further, while precise measures are not available, the percentage of Chinese-language publications available in English translation probably was at a low ebb during two points: first, from 1949 to 1954, when the Western monitoring and translation services were just being formed, and second, from 1978 to the present, during which time the number of newspapers, journals, and books published in China has risen dramatically, without a commensurate increase in translation facilities. The apex of coverage probably was reached in the late 1950s, when the translation services hit their stride, and again in the Cultural Revolution years (1966–69), when the Chinese press dramatically reduced the number of publications, repetition was extensive, and much that was published was also translated. The early 1960s and the early and mid-1970s present a mixed picture, since many previously open publications were classified for internal use (*nei-pu*) and were not allowed to leave the country.

Memoirs and travelogues

Many Chinese and Western former residents of China have published reflections, memoirs, diaries, or autobiographical accounts of their experiences on the mainland: a technician in the UN relief effort in the late 1940s who observed land reform in a rural village; an American student couple who remained in Peking in 1949 and were imprisoned as foreign agents; a Catholic priest who suffered religious persecution during the Communist revolution; a Chinese journalist who escaped to Hong Kong in the 1950s; a student who experienced the transformation of her university; an American captured during the Korean War who chose to remain in China until 1965; the son of a Chinese woman and a French man who spent years in Chinese prisons and labor camps before finding his way to freedom; a Soviet scientist in China who ultimately defected to the West; a Swedish diplomat who witnessed the worst years of post-Great Leap Peking; an African student in China who was exposed to Chinese racism; a Canadian journalist who reported from Peking during the mid-1960s; a young Chinese diplomat in Africa who defected to the United States; an Australian hired as an English-language teacher whose institute was at the vortex of the Cultural Revolution in Shanghai; the son of the foreign minister in Sun Yat-sen's Canton government who was a long-time employee of the Foreign Languages Press and who chronicled the Red Guard attacks upon the foreign affairs system; a young participant in the Cultural Revolution in Hunan province who married his American language teacher and moved to the United States; an English diplomat who was involved with the Democracy Wall movement in 1978–79; and several American, British, and Canadian journalists who reported from Peking in the early post-Mao era. This partial listing of well over a hundred such accounts conveys the extraordinary range of participant-observer stories about life in China.[39]

39 William Hinton, *Fanshen*; Allyn and Adele Rickett, *Prisoners of liberation*; Carlo Suigo, *In the land of Mao Tse-tung*; Eric Chou, *A man must choose*; Maria Yen, *The umbrella garden: A picture of student life in Red China*; Maurice R. Wills, *Turncoat*; Bao Ruo-wang and Rudolph Chelminski, *Prisoner of Mao*; Mikhail Klochko, *Soviet scientist in Red China*; Sven Lindqvist, *China in crisis*; Emmanuel John Hevi, *An African student in China*; Charles Taylor, *Reporter in Red China*; Tung Chiping and Humphrey Evans, *The thought revolution*; Neale Hunter, *Shanghai journal*; Jack Chen, *Inside the Cultural Revolution*; Liang Heng and Judith Shapiro, *Son of the revolution*; Roger Garside, *Coming alive: China after Mao*; Fox Butterfield, *China: Alive in the bitter sea*; Richard Bernstein, *From the center of the earth*; Jay and Linda Mathews, *One billion*; David Bonavia, *The Chinese*; John Fraser, *The Chinese*.

These narratives provide valuable supplements to the Chinese press. They frequently deal with topics which the press either does not treat or treats inadequately: the prison system; the harsh inequities of life in China, the violence, oppression, and volatility of the society; the rigidities of CCP control and the opportunities to evade the control. Occasionally participant-observers were involved in politically significant events, such as the Hundred Flowers campaign in May 1957 at Peking University or the T'ien An Men incident of 5 April 1976. Participant-observers partook of the life cycle in China. observing birth, marriage, worship, childrearing, job hunting, aging, and death.

Since the Chinese press tends not to dwell on these facets of China and since Chinese fiction tends to depict life in excessively glowing terms, personal accounts provide especially important material for the sociologist and social historian. For example, Martin Whyte's article in volume 15 of the *Cambridge History of China* draws heavily on participant-observer accounts. Yet these accounts have severe limitations. Obviously, they are no better than the astuteness of the observer, and many of the authors were not very precise, perceptive, or inquisitive. Memories are often imperfect. Many Western observers spoke no Chinese and were captives of their interpreters. Many discovered the China which they wished to find. Many Chinese report on a China about which they believe the Westerner – or at least the sponsor of the publication – wishes to hear. Others use the occasion as a way to justify their lives, either to themselves or to the readers. In short, participant-observer accounts about China suffer from all the inherent deficiencies of the genre. Added to this are the problems of acquiring a broad perspective in a highly segmented society, where members of one work and residential unit may know little about developments elsewhere and where life is in constant flux due to changing policies. The result is that the validity of personal observations is often bound by time and place, and it is difficult to know whether the insights provided in such accounts can be easily generalized.

A related genre is the accounts of short-term visitors to the People's Republic. Until the opening of China in the 1970s, these reports – often by journalists – were a popular way for academics and the public to peek behind what was called the Bamboo Curtain. Typically the result of a one- to two-month trip to Peking, some provincial capitals, and several showplace factories and communes, the travelogues attempted to capture the mood of China. The titles capture their tone: *I saw Red China, When China wakes, No flies in China, The anthill, The yellow wind, The other side of the river.*[40] Influential in shaping images of China at the time, a survey of these books is a reminder of how misleading contemporary reporting from China can be, particularly if the traveler enters China without adequate preparation. The problems, complexity, and diversity tend to be missed, while the current successes and the superficial uniformity of China frequently are stressed. For a period in the 1970s, the opening of China saw an increase of this type of reporting, as visitors were swept away by euphoric reactions to the land they were newly discovering. Those who arrived at a more somber and accurate assessment frequently either did not report their reactions or circulated their impressions privately, aware that negative accounts would jeopardize their Chinese hosts and friends. Even academic China specialists for the most part failed to capture the extent of economic difficulties, political terror, and tensions among the elite during the last years of the Mao era.

But one type of travelogue has proved useful, namely, the disciplined report about a limited aspect of China by a qualified professional observer.[41] For instance, the Committee on Scholarly Communication with the People's Republic of China (CSCPRC) in the United States sent a number of scientific delegations to China to survey the state of particular fields. Delegations of social scientists, humanists, and, where appropriate, engineers and technicians also went. Various organizations in other countries undertook similar studies. Corporations that began to come in contact with China in the early 1970s also began to develop profiles and assessments of Chinese organizations in their areas of endeavor. Some – such as Pullman-Kellogg, which built several large-scale turnkey fertilizer plants in the early 1970s – had an extensive exposure to China. The expatriate employees in China frequently wrote extensive and fascinating accounts of their experiences. The results are numerous benchmark monographs and private papers on particular fields of scholarly and commercial endeavor against which continuities and changes in the

---

40 Lisa Hobbs, *I saw Red China*; Robert Guillain, *When China wakes*; G. S. Gale, *No flies in China*; Susan Labin, *The anthill*; William Stevenson, *The yellow wind*; Edgar Snow, *The other side of the river: Red China today*.
41 Examples of such reports include S. D. Richardson, *Forestry in Communist China*; W. R. Geddes, *Peasant life in Communist China*; Barry Richman, "Capitalists and managers in Communist China," *Harvard Business Review* (January 1967), 57–78; Geoffrey Oldham, "Science in China: A tourist's impression," *Science*, 147.3659 (February 1965), 706–14.

post-Mao era can be measured.[42] Members of these delegations also frequently kept diaries or wrote accounts of their observations for private dissemination. These materials are likely to be quite useful to future research on China in the 1970s.

Equally valuable observer accounts are the memoirs of political figures, diplomats, and soldiers who negotiated with the Chinese. Two accounts of the Korean War by Matthew Ridgway and C. Turner Joy, American participants in that struggle and the Panmunjom peace talks, provide raw material on these topics. The memoirs of the Indian ambassador to China in late 1950 yielded important information on China's effort through diplomacy to deter American forces from approaching the Yalu River.[43] Indian diplomat Arthur Lall provided insight into Chinese behavior at Geneva in 1962.[44] Particularly noteworthy are the memoirs of Richard Nixon, Jimmy Carter, Henry Kissinger, Cyrus Vance, Zbigniew Brzezinski, Alexander Haig, William Safire, and Robert Haldeman, which describe Sino-American relations from 1972 to 1982 and portray various Chinese leaders. Nor have the memoirs been limited to the more voluble American and Indian officials. British, Canadian, Dutch, French, Japanese, and Soviet officials have also recorded their encounters with Chinese officials. Such accounts are not always accurate, and some are rather self-serving; yet they contain unique information and insight.

A major problem confronting the researcher is to obtain bibliographical control over this disparate and often ephemeral material. Few academic libraries systematically purchased all the personal accounts of former residents, travelers, and officials, and bibliographical entries in the catalogues usually neither reveal the genre of the book nor tell much about the author. Nor is it possible to identify whether a book summarizes interviews with high-level Chinese

---

42 See, for example, the reports prepared by the Committee on Scholarly Communication with the People's Republic of China and published by the National Academy of Sciences assessing the state of various sciences in China: plant studies (1975), solid state physics (1976), insect control (1977), pure and applied mathematics (1977), paleoanthropology (1977), oral contraceptives and steroid chemistry (1977), wheat (1977), astronomy (1979), earthquake engineering and hazards reduction (1980), oceanography (1980), nuclear science (1980), and animal agriculture (1980). See also Yu Ying-shih, ed., *Early Chinese history in the People's Republic of China, the report of the Han Dynasty studies delegation*; CSCPRC, *Traditional and contemporary painting in China*; Anne Thurston and Jason Parker, eds., *Humanistic and social science research in China*; Frederic Wakeman, Jr., ed., *Ming and Qing historical studies in the People's Republic of China*; CSCPRC, *Report of the CSCPRC economics delegation to the People's Republic of China*; The American Rural Small-Scale Industry Delegation, *Rural small-scale industry in the People's Republic of China*.
43 K. M. Pannikar, *In two Chinas*; Matthew Ridgway, *The Korean War*.
44 Arthur Lall, *How Communist China negotiates*.

officials. These can be quite helpful to political historians, even though the significance of the information conveyed in the interview may have escaped the reporter at the time. For example, in retrospect the many interviews Chou En-lai gave to Westerners from 1971 to 1973 contain subtle information on the Lin Piao affair and on his domestic political struggles. Only a few of these interviews were fully and accurately recorded, however, and no single compilation of them exists in the West.

Obtaining control over the ephemeral materials is even more difficult, although three American collection efforts are helpful with respect to the United States. The National Council for U.S. – China Trade maintained its own organizational records detailing its early contacts with Chinese commercial and industrial organizations in meticulous fashion and developed an extensive file of articles by visitors chronicling various aspects of the Chinese economy. These files are deposited at the President Gerald R. Ford Library at the University of Michigan. The CSCPRC developed extensive files on the academic and research communities, which are available through the National Academy of Sciences. Finally, the Bentley Historical Library at the University of Michigan, under a foundation grant, established an archive on Sino-American relations which attempted to collect all available trip reports, including private diaries, by Americans who visited China in the early 1970s.[45]

The creative arts

Scholars of most foreign societies usually find the creative arts in that society to have intrinsic aesthetic merit, but the arts tend not to flourish when the artist is subject to terror and political control. So too for the People's Republic, where few creative works that have come to public attention since 1949 are likely to have enduring value. The intense emotions, heroism, and deprivations the Chinese people experienced during the Maoist era make the stultification of the arts all the more lamentable. An era of epic proportions in history has been inadequately captured in the arts.

Nonetheless, students of Chinese society do find the arts useful for many research purposes. Perhaps the most underutilized source of information is fiction: novels, short stories, drama, opera, and poems.

---

45 *Americans in China, 1971–1980: A guide to the University of Michigan National Archive on Sino-American relations.*

Other creative arts reveal much about the society: poster art, movies, radio and television stories, paintings, advertisements, comedy routines, and so on. Such material is perhaps less immediately relevant to the economist or political scientist than to the anthropologist, sociologist, or cultural historian, but it is increasingly being employed by all the social sciences as they seek ways of understanding the formation and expression of popular culture. (We see here the direct and indirect influences of French sociologists and social historians, including Lévi-Strauss and Braudel, on the China field; that is, we see an increased interest in identifying the shared mentality of the population and its effect upon the elite.) But because the state has directed, censored, and controlled the creative arts, such diverse art forms as novels, children's stories, and poster art do not so much reflect popular values – although the work must sufficiently embody the existing culture so that its message can be understood – as portray the beliefs and goals of the political leaders.

Consequently, most research based on the creative arts uses the material to illuminate the evolving beliefs and values the leaders have been attempting to inculcate in the populace. Sociologist Mary Sheridan, for instance, used fiction to trace the evolving attributes of the model heroes the Chinese people have been encouraged to emulate,[46] and in separate studies, Charles Ridley and Eileen Blumenthal analyzed the themes of children's readers to ascertain the evolving values conveyed to preteenagers.[47] Joseph Huang has examined the Chinese novel as a reflection of life.[48] The literary world has served as a battleground for high-level political strife, particularly during Mao's reign, and several scholars have examined the contested areas, particularly the operas Chiang Ch'ing sought to transform, and the allegorical plays and commentaries of the early 1960s.[49]

A few scholars have sought to derive sociological data from fiction. Their contention is that fiction bears some relationship to modal patterns of conduct and that even the idealized accounts portrayed by socialist realism reflect reality concerning, for example, the socioeco-

46 Mary Sheridan, "The emulation of heroes," CQ, 33 (January–March 1968), 47–72.
47 Eileen Blumenthal, "Models in Chinese moral education: Perspectives from children's books." University of Michigan, Ph.D. thesis, 1976; Charles Ridley, Paul Godwin, and Dennis Doolin, The making of a model citizen in Communist China.
48 Joseph Huang, Heroes and villains in Communist China: The contemporary Chinese novel as reflection of life.
49 See Merle Goldman, China's intellectuals; Clive Ansley, The heresy of Wu Han; James Pusey, Wu Han: Attacking the present through the past; and Colin Mackerras, Amateur theatre in China, 1949–1966 and "Chinese opera after the Cultural Revolution (1970–1972)," CQ, 55 (July–September 1973), 478–510.

nomic profile of local leaders, the dynamics of small group behavior, and the mechanisms of conflict resolution in China.[50] Finally, a few Chinese authors have captured the nature of Chinese bureaucratic practices and the pathos of the Cultural Revolution in as moving and insightful a fashion as any social scientist. Novelist Wang Meng has detailed personnel practices within the Party. Investigative journalist Liu Pin-yen has revealed power relations within the *tan-wei*. Chen Jo-hsi conveyed the harshness, hypocrisy, and wounds of the Cultural Revolution. The bitter poems posted in the T'ien An Men in 1976 powerfully conveyed the cynicism and bitterness of many urban residents in the mid-1970s. Such works are as essential for understanding the People's Republic as are Solzhenitsyn or Pasternak for understanding Stalinism and its legacy.

The creative arts, then, provide important supplementary avenues to understanding aspects of elite and mass cultures. In the 1980s, the Chinese began to publish many research guides and bibliographies in the cultural area. But in spite of these aids, bibliographical control is difficult to obtain over these materials. One English-language source, *Chinese Literature*, is particularly helpful. Probably the only way to follow Chinese literature at a distance is through the principal literary publications, such as *Wen-i pao*, but these are the mainline journals, and some of the more interesting and innovative work appears in less well known and local journals. To navigate the treacherous shoals of the Chinese artistic world, with its factionalism, petty jealousies, and convoluted allegorical references, most researchers need some assistance from Chinese participants – although that assistance is only cautiously rendered and can be self-serving. By the mid-1980s, however, many foreign scholars of Chinese literature had met Chinese colleagues through conferences, and maintained direct contact with them. With their assistance, translations of recent Chinese fiction and research on modern Chinese literature has become one of the most active and stimulating areas in Chinese studies.[51]

50 See especially Frederick Gaenslen, "Culture and decision making: Social influence in China, Japan, Soviet Russia, and the United States." University of Michigan, Ph.D. thesis, 1984.
51 See, for example, Perry Link, ed., *"People or monsters?"*; Perry Link, ed., *Stubborn weeds*; Perry Link, ed., *Roses and thorns*; Eugene Eoyang, ed., *Selected poems of Ai Qing*; and Susan Wolf Chen, trans., *Feng Jicai: Chrysanthemums and other stories*. Analysis is in Bonnie S. McDougall, *Popular Chinese literature and performing arts in the People's Republic of China, 1949–1979*; Yi-tse Mei Feuerwerker, *Ding Ling's fiction*; and Jeffrey C. Kinkley, ed., *After Mao: Chinese literature and society, 1978–1981*.

Interviews with former PRC residents

Systematic interviews of former residents of China have been a major source of information since 1949. Several factors explain the importance of émigré interviewing. The inability of scholars to study the living society is certainly the principal factor. Not only was focused research in China practically impossible until the post-Mao era, but the opening of China to research has not extended to the ability to do field research. Except for a brief time from 1979 to 1981 and in a few other unusual circumstances, foreign sociologists and anthropologists have not been able to employ the research techniques of their disciplines: prolonged residence in a living community and the administration of closed and open questionnaires to random samples of the populace they are studying.

Even where the opportunity to observe and interview exists, the scholar bears the burden of doing research in an authoritarian political system. Dangers always exist that the confidentiality of one's informants cannot be maintained. Most researchers believe it necessary to take unusual steps to protect their informants from political persecution, particularly if they provide data or interpretations the regime does not like. Moreover, field research in China to date has been arduous and circumscribed in terms of questions that are welcomed, the length of stay permitted, and the access the researcher has to documentary material in order to sharpen the inquiry. This means most researchers prefer to enter China well prepared; the preliminary research is done outside China.

The substantial numbers of Chinese who have migrated to Hong Kong, Taiwan, India, and Western countries, moreover, have provided an attractive pool of informants. The émigrés come from all over China, although the vast majority come from Kwangtung and the urban coastal cities (especially Shanghai). While intellectuals constitute a substantially higher percentage than they do in the overall population, the émigrés also include peasants, workers, and youths, thereby permitting studies of different occupational and generational sectors. Although a few former Party, public security, and PLA members have left the country, the biggest deficiency among the émigrés is the relatively few officials who have held major positions. Unlike the Soviet Union and Eastern Europe, China has not suffered a single high-level defector. But particularly among the 1962 émigrés to Hong Kong who fled the harsh economic conditions, there were a few lower-level bureaucrats who illuminated Chinese organizational practices.

Some casual observers wonder whether those who left China can provide any useful information, since they would be biased against the regime. This skepticism appears unwarranted. Many of the émigrés did not flee the mainland out of fear of or repugnance for the regime. Rather, they left to join relatives or to seek economic improvement, and they retain considerable patriotic sentiment toward the People's Republic. Further, while many were alienated from the regime, these sentiments did not intrude in their descriptions of political institutions, economic practices, or social customs in China. In short, careful interviewing procedures and well-constructed questionnaires can minimize the effect of informant bias. The limitations of the émigré informant concern not so much bias as imperfect and fading memories, the difficulty of verifying the information they provide, and the problems the researcher faces in identifying the right questions to ask. A great advantage of field research is that, immersed in the community, the observer begins to adjust the inquiry and pursue a modified set of questions. Interviewing informants away from the research site, the researcher finds it more difficult to ascertain what the informant should know and what the best and most pertinent questions are. On the other hand, the informant, unbound from obligations to the community, may discuss topics that would be sensitive at home.

On balance, then, interviewing former PRC residents has been an essential ingredient of research on China. The enterprise was facilitated with the establishment of the Universities Service Centre in Hong Kong in 1963. Since then, literally several hundred research projects involving interviewing and the use of the USC and URI libraries have been undertaken, reaching a high point from the mid-1960s to the mid-1970s. While informants have moved to Hong Kong throughout the history of the PRC, three clusters attracted special attention: urban intellectuals and businessmen who left in the early and mid-1950s after experiencing persecution; Kwangtung peasants and others who sought refuge from the 1960–62 depression; and youths in the late 1960s and early 1970s who escaped the turmoil of the Cultural Revolution. Each of these informant pools provided opportunities for specific research efforts.

Governments also maintained interview projects in Hong Kong. Until the late 1970s, the British and American governments conducted an extensive program to ascertain economic conditions in

China from recent Hong Kong arrivals. Some of these interviews, which served as the basis of U.S. Department of Agriculture estimates of Chinese agricultural production, are available on microfilm. The Japanese government interviewed Japanese who had remained on the mainland after 1949. They often were knowledgeable technicians, married to Chinese, who held responsible engineering positions in factories or even municipal governments. The URI also interviewed on current conditions on the mainland, and the protocols are available on microfilm.

Since the mid-1970s, two new types of informants have appeared: Chinese sojourners abroad and foreigners who resided in China on diplomatic or business assignments. The former includes Chinese diplomats, commercial representatives, journalists, visiting scholars, and students. No longer under tight surveillance and discipline, as in the Mao era, the number of citizens from the People's Republic residing abroad has risen dramatically in the 1980s. No major research project has been launched using this informant pool, but on an informal, off-the-record basis, many Chinese are willing to be very helpful to foreigners trying to understand their country. They frequently are better placed and more knowledgeable than the émigrés who formed the Hong Kong pool. It is gradually becoming possible even to piece together obscure aspects of high-level politics. The problem the foreign observer faces, however, is how to verify the information to meet scholarly standards of documentation. The advantage of these sources is the light they shed on the informal and personal dimension of Chinese politics and on certain facets of social life which neither the press nor Hong Kong émigrés reveal (such as marriage patterns and family life among the elite).

Foreigners with extensive exposure to limited aspects of China are also a growing source for the 1980s. Foreign-language teachers, businessmen, scientists, philanthropists, journalists, athletes, development specialists, lawyers, students, tourist guides, managers of joint ventures, diplomats, military officers, and artists have all had extensive professional contacts with their Chinese counterparts since the late 1970s. A few, as we have noted, have recorded their experiences, but more have not done so. A substantial amount of information now exists, in scattered fashion, about diverse aspects of the Chinese bureaucracy, the economy, and certain officials. The World Bank, for example, has accumulated considerable expertise about significant portions of the Chinese economy; multinational energy corporations possess unique insight into the petroleum, coal, gas, and nuclear power industries; and foundation representatives have become well acquainted with the leaders of the influential Chinese Academy of Social Sciences. With a few exceptions, analysts of China have not sought to aggregate this information in systematic fashion. Based on interviews of American businessmen who traded with China, Lucian Pye's pioneering study *Chinese commercial negotiating style* is indicative of the potential here.

Can bibliographical control be established over the interviews of émigrés, sojourners, and foreigners? The question is pertinent on two grounds. First, does any record exist as to the informants for specific monographs? The answer is "no," and students must therefore read the secondary literature at their peril. For example, descriptions of the public security system in the 1950s and 1960s are contained in several works by A. Doak Barnett, Ezra Vogel, Jerome Cohen, Victor Li, and Stanley Lubman.[52] Rather than the similarity in secondary accounts breeding confidence in the accuracy of the findings, the similarity is attributable to a limited number of Hong Kong émigrés these scholars all interviewed from 1963 to 1966. The overlap was not perfect, but nonetheless a relatively small number of émigrés who served in the public security system in Fukien and Kwangtung provinces were the source of all these accounts. Similarly, Victor Falkenheim, Gordon Bennett, and this author have written along very similar lines concerning Chinese bureaucratic practices, particularly in the financial realm.[53] Not surprisingly, the conclusions converged, as all scholars relied to varying degrees on the same, quite knowledgeable former cadre in the Kwangtung finance and trade system. A somewhat similar but not as acute situation existed for research on youth, where the émigré informant pool was larger, but where there was still an undeterminable overlap among the sources used by USC-based scholars in the early 1970s.

The professional standards of the social sciences generally demand that interview sources be precisely footnoted and that interviews be well recorded. Ideally, the transcripts or notes would be deposited in

52 See Cohen, ed., *The criminal process*; Stanley Lubman, "Mao and mediation: Politics and dispute resolutions in Communist China," *California Law Review*, 55:5 (November 1967), 1284–1359; Victor Li, "The Public Security Bureau and political-legal work in Hui-yang, 1952–1964," in Lewis, ed., *The city in communist China*; and Barnett, *Cadres, bureaucracy, and political power in communist China*.
53 Victor Falkenheim, "County administration in Fukien," *CQ*, 59 (July–Stepember 1974), 518–43; Gordon Bennett, ed., *China's finance and trade: A policy reader*; and Michel Oksenberg, "Methods of communication within the Chinese bureaucracy," *CQ*, 57 (January–March 1974), 1–39.

archives for secondary analysis. Future scholars would benefit from being able to read the protocols of émigré interviews conducted in the 1950s and 1960s. Here is the baseline for measuring the evolution of Chinese practice. Unfortunately, with some exceptions, the China field has not abided by these standards. Ezra Vogel deposited the very useful set of interviews derived from his study of Kwangtung in the mid-1960s at the East Asian Research Center at Harvard University. Audrey Donnithorne graciously has shared her many interviews concerning financial practices in China. I have done the same for my 1964–65 interviews on rural local government and those of 1971–72 on Chinese bureaucratic practice. Martin Whyte has deposited his interviews on local social organization. These are at the Bentley Historical Library at the University of Michigan. To the best of my knowledge, no other similar sets of interview data have been deposited for secondary analysis, to the long-term detriment of the field.

In spite of these problems, monographs based on émigré interviews have withstood the acid test: The China that scholars found after its opening to research did not depart significantly from the China that was discovered via Hong Kong research. Three very different research strategies, all based heavily on émigré interviews, merit mention. In 1964–65, A. Doak Barnett interviewed three middle- and lower-ranking bureaucrats intensively and several others more superficially to portray the structure of a ministry, a county, and a commune. The book turns out to be remarkably useful as a starting point for understanding Chinese institutions in the 1980s. Martin Whyte and William Parish collaborated to interview hundreds of former residents from thoughout China to generate aggregate data on rural and urban social life in the late 1960s and 1970s. They used their data to establish modal patterns of life, to identify differences and the range of behavior, and to explain variance. Their monographs will affect the research agenda for many years. Finally, Anita Chan, Richard Madsen, and Jonathan Unger interviewed several informants from the same rural village, cross-checking the information they obtained, to reconstruct the political history of the community from 1962 to 1983. The consequence of these and other monographs based on émigré interviews is that the scholarly understanding of Chinese social, political, and economic processes at the grassroots level probably exceeds the understanding of most socialist societies in Eastern Europe, certainly of the Soviet Union, and of many developing countries where field research is circumscribed.

Field research

Since 1979, Western and Japanese scholars have had the opportunity to undertake field research in China. A handful of anthropologists, sociologists, and political scientists were able to live in rural China for extended periods from 1979 to 1981, after which Chinese authorities imposed restrictions on such activity.[54] In addition, shorter stays in the countryside, repeated visits to the same rural locale, survey research in urban areas through administration of open-ended or closed questionnaires, and interviews of Chinese officials have all been possible. With rare exceptions, urban field research through extended observation of residential areas or work units has not been possible to date.[55] In addition to these opportunities, scholars have undertaken research in conjunction with teaching assignments in China. For example, even with the ban on field research, anthropologists have carried out village studies while teaching at provincial universities. Lawyers, sociologists, and economists have investigated their specialities while affiliated with universities and research institutes, and political scientists have used ties their universities developed with Chinese institutions to undertake attitudinal surveys.

To cite some examples, field research has been undertaken on village life, care of the aged, the status of women, post-Mao university administration, the development and allocation of water resources in Hupei Province, the budgetary process at national and provincial levels, the demographic profiles of select areas in Szechwan and Liaoning provinces, local leadership in rural counties near Nanking, Shihchiachuang, and Wuhan, the structure of the foreign policy apparatus, recent developments in ideology, and personal life during the Cultural Revolution.[56] In fact, most research published since the early 1980s on contemporary cultural, social, political, and economic

54 The early results of such research are reported in Margery Wolf, *Revolution postponed: Women in contemporary China*; Steven Mosher, *Broken earth*; and the articles in William Parrish, ed., *Problems in China's rural development: Evolving issues*.
55 An exception is Gail Henderson and Myron Cohen, *The Chinese hospital*.
56 Examples include Suzanne Pepper, *China's universities*; Deborah Davis-Friedmann, *Long lives: Chinese elderly and the Communist revolution*; several articles in David M. Lampton, ed., *Policy implementation in post-Mao China*; Tyrene White, "Implementing the 'one child per couple' population program in rural China: National goals and local politics," in David M. Lampton, *Policy implementation*; Steven Butler, *Conflict and decision making in China's rural administration, 1969–1976*; A. Doak Barnett, *The making of foreign policy in China*; Stuart Schram, "Economics in command?' Ideology and policy since the Third Plenum, 1978–84," *CQ*, 99 (September 1984), 417–61; and Anne Thurston, "Victims of China's Cultural Revolution: The invisible wounds," *Pacific Affairs*, Part I, 57.4 (Winter 1984–85), 599–620, and Part II, 58.1 (Spring 1985), 5–27.

issues has been based, to varying degrees, on personal observation and interviews in China.

No convenient list exists of all scholars who have undertaken substantial research in China. The study of contemporary China is a worldwide enterprise, and scholars from Australia, Britain, Canada, Denmark, France, Germany, Japan, New Zealand, Sweden, the Soviet Union, and the United States – to mention only the major countries – either have carried out anthropological studies or engaged in interview projects. Arrangements for such research are frequently made through nongovernmental auspices, and even within individual countries no central records are kept. By the mid-1980s, it was not unusual for a foreign scholar to interview a bureaucrat or scholar, only to learn that the same Chinese had been interviewed by another foreigner on roughly the same subject a few days earlier. Certain Chinese officials and researchers were spending a substantial portion of their time meeting foreigners.

Few researchers have deposited in archives the raw data from their fieldwork – the interview protocols, the notes, the statistical series, and unit descriptions. Unless a massive effort is soon launched to gather such original research materials, they are likely to be lost for secondary analysis.[57] Just as the raw data derived from studies by J. L. Buck or Sidney Gamble in the 1920s and 1930s or from Japanese social surveys in the 1930s and 1940s have proved invaluable to current researchers, gathering the data from current research in China within a single archive, even under terms of highly restricted access, is highly desirable.

Research in China has been beneficial in many ways. Scholars gain a visual sense of their study. Abstract notions acquire a reality. The production brigade of a commune had a daunting, efficient tone to it, but knowledge that most brigades were actually impoverished, sleepy, dusty traditional villages put things in a different perspective. Analysts find it harder to write about the humming machinery of disciplined Chinese bureaucracy when they have walked along the dank, ill-lit corridors of ministries in Peking and seen the over-crowded offices where bureaucrats nap at their desks. Visual impressions can be misleading, however, and more has been secured from research in China than mental snapshots.

While the empirical findings cannot be easily summarized, several

---

57 One exception is Steven Butler, who has shared his raw data on a Hopei commune. Lewis Putterman has prepared these extraordinary data for computer usage.

conclusions pervade the writings to date. First, a considerable gap exists between the policy that is enunciated in Peking and elaborated in the press and its actual implementation at the local level. Distortions may be excessive and go beyond the desires of Peking, or may be lethargic and fall far short of Peking's intent. Nor do statistics and newspaper reports adequately capture the diversity and heterogeneity of Chinese reality. Not only is reporting inaccurate and distorted in order to suggest compliance with central directives, but even accurate quantitative data do not easily capture qualitative distinctions. For example, primary school enrollments available for provinces reveal near-universal educational opportunities for children in the Chinese countryside. Differences do exist among provinces and among counties within provinces, but the statistics reveal that upward of 80 percent of rural children are enrolled in primary schools everywhere, an impressive record for a developing country. However, these figures disclose nothing about the quality of schooling. Similar problems exist with data on doctors and health care, diet, industrial production, and so on. Personal observation has encouraged caution among scholars in interpreting Chinese data and heightened sensitivity to the diversity of the country.

The China revealed through field research and interviews is also more "Chinese," like Taiwan, Hong Kong, and pre-1949 China, than the China manifest through other sources. Particularly as the masks of informants are slowly stripped away, the concerns, motivations, and beliefs of mainland Chinese are reminiscent of Chinese in other parts of the cultural area: the emphasis on family, the stress on propriety in interpersonal relations, the sense of obligation and loyalty to those individuals who are part of the web of social relations in which one is enmeshed, the preference for harmony and fear of disorder, and the low ability to handle conflict situations.[58] Such concepts as *p'ai* (faction), *kan-ch'ing* (feeling of intimacy), *kuan-hsi* (relationship), *li-mao* (courtesy), and *te* (virtue) are as central to understanding contemporary society and culture as in the past. Not all Chinese attach equal primacy to these traits. Indeed, another find-

---

58 J. Bruce Jacobs, "A preliminary model of particularistic ties in Chinese political alliances: *Kan-ch'ing* and *kuan-hsi* in a rural Taiwanese township," *CQ*, 78 (June 1979), 237–73; Lucian Pye, *Spirit of Chinese politics*; Richard Solomon, *Mao's revolution*; Richard W. Wilson, *Learning to be Chinese: The political socialization of children in Taiwan*; Margery Wolf, *The house of Lim: A study of a Chinese farm family*; and Morton Fried, *The fabric of Chinese society: A study of social life of a Chinese county seat*.

ing from field research involves the diversity in the culture. Some individuals esteem educational attainment, while others denigrate it. Some avoid disorder (*luan*), while others appear to seek it out. Field research has yielded both a greater hesitancy to generalize about Chinese culture and personality and a realization that nonetheless China retains its distinctive range of societal attributes. We see a more complex society than the previously available sources portrayed; yet Mao's revolution did not remold the society in his image.

The third overwhelming impression researchers have gained is of a segmented political system in which bargaining, consensus building, and bureaucratic politics are rife. At issue is whether this finding pertains exclusively to the post-Mao era or whether this facet of Chinese politics, while perhaps less intensive and obtrusive, has characterized Chinese politics since 1949 (as it did before 1949). At least since the Great Leap and even during the Cultural Revolution, many individual bureaucracies and local units (*tan-wei*) have enjoyed guaranteed sources of revenue that provided them some influence. It would not be correct to view these lower-level agencies as independent or autonomous; they still depend on supplies allocated by higher-level units. At the same time, these lower-level units control resources that the higher-level units need to meet their objectives. Thus, based largely on interviews from field research in China, the old research question of whether the Chinese economy and polity is highly centralized or cellular has been recast through the finding that, in many important areas, the system has been dominated neither by center nor locality, but rather has been characterized by mutual dependence. The research task has become to understand the interdependence of center, province, and locality, the bargaining that is associated with it, and the variation in central-provincial-local relations depending on the region and the functional area involved. That is, the central government's relations with Shanghai, Szechwan, and Tsinghai, to take three examples, are qualitatively different, and the center, province, and locality interact quite differently in, for instance, the spheres of public security, energy, education, and water resource management.

These and other insights into the nature of contemporary China, underscored through field research and interviews of Chinese officials, have not been acquired easily. The obstacles to research in China are formidable. Informants easily may place themselves in jeopardy within China through disclosures that run counter to current policy or that security officials conclude violate sometimes ill-defined secrecy regulations. To protect sources, academic researchers use the information for background, seeking confirmation from the press and citing references to open sources. Or the researchers disguise the source, sometimes even changing details such as the locale or institution involved. The scholar, in short, of necessity ceases to abide by the canons of the profession, namely, the rigorously precise reportage of sources in order to make knowledge cumulative, verifiable, and replicable. Rather, academic researchers in China are driven to adopt the equally honorable but different canon of the journalist, which is to ascertain the facts accurately through the ability to protect the anonymity of sources when necessary.

Another problem with research in China is that major aspects of the system remain closed to investigation. To date, crucial aspects of the system are closed to study by foreign scholars: the Party and its Organization Department, the military, the public security apparatus, and the decision process within the large Chung-nan-hai complex, China's equivalent of the Kremlin or the White House compound, where the State Council and Central Committee offices are located. That is, researchers have learned more about the substance of public policies than about economic, social, and political processes.

Because of these and other impediments, researchers find that interviews and field research usually supplement and enrich findings derived from other sources, but they do not replace the need for documentary research and, when possible, Hong Kong interviews. Research in China is significantly enhanced when the researcher embarks on the field research after considerable preparation outside China. The questioning is then sharper, and the answers can then be placed in a broader context. Some social scientists, evidently reflecting disciplinary traditions that disdain relying on the press in favor of trusting personal observations, report findings (frequently shortcomings and excesses of the regime) that are seemingly "new" but that in fact are being simultaneously reported in the press. Indeed, one wonders if the excesses would have been revealed to the foreign investigator were higher authorities not acknowledging them.

THE ENGLISH-LANGUAGE SECONDARY LITERATURE

We have noted the diverse sources that sustain research on China. The accessibility of each source has varied over time, with the consequence that the range of sources available for any particular time differs from the sources available for preceding and subsequent time periods. The discontinuities in primary sources constitute a fundamental aspect of the study of China and pose serious methodological and analytical challenges. Given the shifting data base, how does one measure continuity and change? New data on previous time periods, such as the Cultural Revolution revelations about elite strife in the late 1950s and 1960s, necessitate continual reinterpretation of previous developments. Novices in the China field may conclude that analysts disagree in their interpretations of past events, whereas the difference really is to be attributed to the availability of new information.

In oversimplified terms, Western interpretations of China have passed through distinctive stages, and it is very difficult to ascertain the extent to which the changing interpretations are due to developments in China or are attributable instead to discontinuities in the available information. Further, in spite of the reinterpretations of the past, once an initial impression of an era has been formed – based on the distinctive combination of information available at that time – that image tends to persist, and new information which challenges the first impression frequently is greeted with great skepticism, even though the new information may be no less reliable than the initial sources. In short, contemporary Chinese studies is a field in perpetual ferment and change; scholars continually are called upon to readjust their interpretations, as they incorporate the latest data about past developments. While most analysts have been sensitive to the data problems, the field has also exhibited occasional maladies. For one, some analysts have become enamored with the new research finds and seek totally to reinterpret the past in light of the latest revelations. For example, the documentation researchers obtained in 1966–70 illuminated the growing conflict between Mao Tse-tung and Liu Shao-ch'i from the mid-1950s and the reasons for the rupture in their relations in 1965–66. Seizing exclusively on this material and ignoring the long record of cooperation between these two titans of the Communist Party, some analysts began to portray their relationship as essentially adversarial from a very early date.

The other extreme is the temptation to reject or explain away new material. For instance, the unmistakably despotic and even sadistic streak in Mao Tse-tung became totally clear only in the later years of his life, through descriptions of his behavior by erstwhile associates and through revelations about the policy process under his aegis.

While some interpretations seize upon this material to portray Mao as a tyrant from his ascendancy to power within the Party, others tend to limit Mao's dark side to his declining years and to preserve a lacquered image for the early period.

Even more of a challenge in reinterpretation of the past is the information obtained in the post-Mao era about the depth of the economic depression of the post–Great Leap era (1960–62) and about the extent of the terror during the Cultural Revolution. The malnutrition and starvation in the Chinese countryside following the establishment of the communes were more extensive and pervasive than the outside world generally understood at the time. The Cultural Revolution and its aftermath rent the fabric of intellectual and social life in the urban areas. Social and cultural interpretations that do not adequately reflect these searing experiences and their consequence upon popular attitudes toward officialdom are missing major dimensions of China's modern evolution. Yet until the 1980s not enough was known to probe these developments and to reflect them in the analysis. The conclusion for the casual student of China is obvious: *When* a book was written and what sources were available at the time are at least as important in shaping the contours of the analysis as the inevitable bias and unstated assumptions which the writer brought to a subject. It is useful, therefore, before surveying the secondary literature on China, to recall the stages in the development of the field.

The 1950s and early 1960s: the ascendancy of the totalitarian model

The initial image of the Chinese regime came from two sources: the Chinese press and émigré interviews and accounts. A significant portion of the latter described thought reform and the coercive dimension of the Chinese system.[59] As the Chinese statistical system began to take shape and produce reliable production data, moreover, the Chinese press began to chart with some precision the economic progress of the nation. The publication of the 1st Five-Year Plan (1953–57) in 1955 gave further indication of an economic and political system that was functioning smoothly and effectively. With the exception of the Kao Kang affair, American scholars failed to detect

59 Edward Hunter, *Brain-washing in Red China*; Lifton, *Thought reform and the psychology of totalism: A study of "brainwashing" in China*; and Edgar Schein with Inge Schneier and Curtis Barker, *Coercive persuasion*.

divisions at the top. Rather, the monolithic quality of the Chinese press and the absence of major purges implied that the leadership was cohesive and collegial, and decision making was a collective process. The Sino-Soviet alliance and the extensive Soviet presence in China further encouraged analysts to stress the Sovietlike qualities of the new regime: the adherence of its leaders to Marxism-Leninism, the totalitarian grip of the top political leaders upon the entire society and culture, and the centrally planned economy in which resources were allocated through political command.

Several key topics which intrigued scholars and which generated polemical exchanges flowed naturally from this image of China. One was whether Mao Tse-tung had made original contributions to Marxist-Leninist theory.[60] A second was to what extent Chinese Communist doctrine and practices drew upon strands of thought in traditional China.[61] A third focused on how the mechanisms of control and mobilization actually worked, particularly toward the intellectuals who experienced the harshness of Communist rule in the early 1950s.[62] Several broad works are representative of scholarship in the heyday of the totalitarian model: W. W. Rostow et al., *The prospects for Communist China*; Richard Walker, *China under communism: The first five years*; Yuan-li Wu, *An economic survey of Communist China*; A. Doak Barnett, *Communist China: The early years, 1949–55*; Li Choh-ming, *Economic development of Communist China*; Peter S. H. Tang, *Communist China today*; and the U.S. Senate Committee on Government Operations, *National policy machinery in Communist China*. It is instructive to reread these works with the advantage of twenty years' hindsight. The sources on

---

60 See Benjamin Schwartz, "The legend of the "Legend of Maoism,'" *CQ*, 2 (April 1960), 35–42; "On the 'originality' of Mao Tse-tung," *Foreign Affairs*, 34.1 (October 1955), 67–76, and *Chinese communism and the rise of Mao*; Karl Wittfogel, "The legend of 'Maoism,'" *CQ*, 1 and 2 (January and April 1960), 72–86 and 16–31; and Arthur A. Cohen, "How original is 'Maosim'?" *Problems of Communism*, 10.6 (November 1961), 34–42, and *The communism of Mao Tse-tung*.

61 See Franklin Houn, *Chinese political traditions*; David S. Nivison, "Communist ethics and Chinese tradition," *JAS*, 16.1 (November 1956), 51–74; Arthur F. Wright, "Struggle vs. harmony: Symbols of competing values in modern China," *World Politics*, 6.1 (October 1953), 31–44; and Charles Hucker, "The traditional Chinese Censorate and the new Peking regime," *American Political Science Review*, 45.4 (December 1951), 1041–57.

62 See S. B. Thomas, *Government and administration in Communist China*; Kuo-chün Chao, *The mass organizations in Communist China*; H. Arthur Steiner, "Current 'mass line' tactics in Communist China," *American Political Science Review*, 45.2 (June 1951), 422–36; Wen-hui C. Chen, *Wartime "mass" campaigns in Communist China*; Commission Internationale Contre le Regime Concentrationnaire, *White book on forced labour and concentration camps in the People's Republic of China*; Wen-ch'i Wei, *Courts and policy in Communist China to 1952*; Theodore Hsi-en Chen, *Thought reform of the Chinese intellectuals*; and Chalmers Johnson, *Communist policies toward the intellectual class*.

which they were based did not yield glimpses into the ceaseless competition over scarce resources at all levels of the hierarchy, the imperfections in the control apparatus, and the persistence of certain cultural and social patterns. To a remarkable extent, although to varying degrees, these works also exhibited a hostility or repugnance for the developments in China. Achievements, when recognized, were acknowledged in grudging fashion. The international politics of the day clearly had their effect upon scholarship. (One wonders whether readers of this volume twenty years hence will have a similar reaction.) Yet, these works retain significant scholarly value, for recent Chinese historiography has begun to portray the 1950s as the halcyon years of Maoist rule, marked by regularity, predictability, rationality, effectiveness, and even a measure of benevolence toward the populace. The secondary literature of the time provides a convenient reminder of the uncertainty, tentativeness, harshness, and even messiness of those years.

The dominance of the totalitarian model persisted into the 1960s, modified however by the changes in the nature of the Soviet system in the post-Stalin era and by the increased sophistication in understanding Communist regimes. The introduction of the *China Quarterly* in 1960 gave the field a forum through which analysis was toughened. Younger scholars trained in comparative law, economics, sociology, and political science began to enter the field, and major research centers on contemporary Chinese studies began to flourish not only in the United States but in Great Britain, Australia, and India as well. In 1963, the Universities Service Centre in Hong Kong opened its doors, thereby facilitating émigré interviewing. Moreover, the numerous refugees in 1961–62 included former bureaucrats, peasants, and intellectuals who were less alienated from the system. Finally, owing to the disasters of the Great Leap, the regime ceased releasing statistics on its economic performance, and previously available provincial newspapers and ministerial journals could no longer be obtained in the outside world. The database had undergone a significant change, away from the heavy reliance on the Chinese press and toward a balanced use of the less informative press and émigré interviewing. Meanwhile several unique sources – the outpouring of criticism during the 1957 Hundred Flowers movement, the previously unavailable *Bulletin of activities* of the People's Liberation Army, information about the purge of Defense Minister P'eng Te-huai, and documents from county offices – illuminated previously veiled political problems, processes, and policies.

As a result of these developments, the research agenda evolved, although still largely within the context of the totalitarian model. Hong Kong interviews revealed Chinese society persisted under totalitarian control, leading to renewed scholarly interest in questions about the interaction between state and society and the mechanisms through which the Communists had reunified the disintegrated nation.[63] The availability of former officials enabled interviewing on the structure of Chinese bureaucracy, although the paucity of high-level officials precluded definitive study of the policy process.[64] The abundance of émigrés from Kwangtung province adjacent to Hong Kong enabled detailed work on the relations between that province and the central government.[65] The polemics from the Sino-Soviet dispute and China's departure from the Soviet model prompted comparisons of Chinese and Soviet communism.[66] The Hundred Flowers movement, the Anti-Rightist Campaign, and the arrival in Hong Kong of intellectuals affected by them sparked an interest in the intelligentsia.[67] With the completion of the 1st Five-Year Plan, the careful sifting of data from China's first decade of development, and the gathering of journals and legal compendia describing economic performance and practice, economists began to publish more so-phisticated analyses of the economy. Especially noteworthy was the encyclopedic institutional survey by Audrey Donnithorne entitled *China's economic system*. Not surprisingly, national income esti-mates and institutional descriptions of specific sectors of the eco-nomy received the initial attention.[68] The army *Bulletin of Activities* and the P'eng Te-huai affair spurred the work on the military.[69] The combination of Chinese press and émigré informants also facilitated

63 Schurmann, *Ideology and organization in Communist China*.

64 See Barnett, *Cadres, bureaucracy, and political power in Communist China*.

65 Vogel, *Canton under communism*.

66 Kurt London, ed., *Unity and contradiction: Major aspects of Sino-Soviet relations*; Donald Treadgold, ed., *Soviet and Chinese communism: Similarities and differences*.

67 D. W. Fokkema, *Literary doctrine in China and Soviet influence, 1956–1960*; and Goldman, *Literary dissent in Communist China*.

68 T. C. Liu and K. C. Yeh, *The economy of the Chinese mainland: National income and economic development, 1933–1959*; Walter Galenson, Alexander Eckstein, and Ta-chung Liu, eds., *Economic trends in Communist China*; W. W. Hollister, *China's gross national product and social accounts, 1950–1957*; Kenneth Walker, *Planning in Chinese agriculture: Socialization and the private sector, 1956–1962*; Alexander Eckstein, *The national income of Communist China*; Dwight Perkins, *Market control and planning in Communist China*; and George Ecklund, *Financing the Chinese government budget: Mainland China, 1950–1959*.

69 Ralph Powell, *Politico-military relationships in Communist China*; John Gittings, *The role of the Chinese army*; Ellis Joffe, *Party and army: Professionalism and political control in the Chinese officer corps, 1949–1964*; Alice Langley Hsieh, "China's secret military papers: Military doctrine and strategy," *CQ*, 18 (April 1964), 79–99.

work on political participation, the Chinese legal system, and the dynamics of the small political study groups.[70] What is striking about this partial listing of the major publications of the era is its focus on the state and its control of the populace, facets of China which the available sources illuminated. The congruence between the available data and the research agenda derived from the totalitarian model persisted until the mid-1960s.

To be sure, other important intellectual currents informed the field. In particular, students of Chinese intellectual history, their writings frequently informed by knowledge of Marxism-Leninism, focused on ideological and philosophical currents in the People's Republic. Benjamin Schwartz, for example, traced intellectual developments in Maoist China in a series of brilliant essays, placing these developments in the context of traditional Chinese thought.[71] Stuart Schram wrote the standard biography of Mao Tse-tung, focusing on his intellectual development and tracing some roots of his thought to traditional Chinese influences.[72] Joseph Levenson sought to place the emergence of Marxism as China's seemingly dominant belief system in the context of the evolution of Confucianism in the modern era.[73] These and other works by historians that dealt with the People's Republic but not exclusively or primarily so placed the first fifteen years of Communist rule in perspective and conveyed an understanding of the underlying intellectual issues with which Mao and his associates were wrestling: how to modernize China while preserving China's distinctiveness.

Another perspective came from anthropologists interested in religion, rural society, and family organization.[74] Eschewing the totalitarian model and drawing instead on traditional patterns of interaction between state and society, the anthropologists cautioned about the capacity of the state to remold the society. The problem

---

70 Jerome Cohen, *The criminal process in the People's Republic of China, 1949–1963*; James R. Townsend, *Political participation in Communist China*; Martin Whyte, *Small groups and political rituals in China.*

71 These essays are collected in Schwartz's *Communism and China: Ideology in flux*; see also his *In search of wealth and power: Yen Fu and the West.*

72 See his books, *Mao Tse-tung* and *The political thought of Mao Tse-tung*. See also Jerome Ch'en, *Mao Tse-tung and the Chinese revolution.*

73 See especially his trilogy, *Confucian China and its modern fate*. See also his book *Liang Chi-ch'ao and the mind of modern China.*

74 G. William Skinner, "Marketing and social structure in rural China," *JAS*, 24.1, 2, 3 (November 1964, February and May 1965), 3–44, 195–228, 363–400; Ching-kun Yang, *A Chinese village in early Communist transition, Religion in Chinese society*, and *The Chinese family in the Communist revolution*; and Maurice Freedman, *Lineage organization in southeastern China* and *Chinese lineage and society: Fukien and Kwangtung.*

was a good deal more complicated, as the society had the capacity to absorb the lower rungs of the state apparatus or present effective challenges to it. Finally, a few analysts, drawing on modernization theory, warned that the economic and political transformation Chinese leaders had been directing from 1949 to the mid-1960s was not unique to China; the modernization process elsewhere had generated both conflict among the elite and severe social tensions among the populace. China's continued stability should not be taken for granted, these analysts warned on the eve of the Cultural Revolution.[75] The research agenda of the historians, anthropologists, and modernization theorists derived not so much from the available data as from disciplinary theories. Perhaps it is worth noting that their writings have better stood the test of time, in my opinion, than the work of those whose research agenda basically was determined by the availability of the data.

The late 1960s and the 1970s: the ascendancy of conflict models

The Cultural Revolution and its aftermath profoundly affected the secondary literature on China. Ironically, China was never more totalitarian than during the 1966–76 period, for the politicization of all aspects of the society, culture, and economy reached its apogee at that time, the deification of the leader climaxed in a cult of personality rarely attained before in history, and terror became a way of life. Yet with a few exceptions, the field tended to move from the totalitarian model toward more complex ways of interpreting Chinese phenomena. In part, there was general disenchantment with the model and especially its inability to account for change. Further, the totalitarian model posited a disciplined political hierarchy relatively unaffected by conflict. If the Cultural Revolution revealed anything, it was that China was conflict-ridden – not just after the movement was launched, but before as well.

Not only the fact of the Cultural Revolution but, as important, the new materials obtained after 1966 had major consequences for analysis of China. In particular, the Red Guard newspapers and other ephemeral materials released in the organized chaos of the time provided hitherto unknown information about high-level policy

---

75 See especially Lucian Pye, "China in context," *Foreign Affairs*, 45.2 (January 1967), 229–45.

since the mid-1950s. The texts of crucial directives, the existence of which frequently had not even been known before, came to light. Major materials on such crucial gatherings as the 1959 Lushan Plenum and the January 1962 central work conference surfaced. Valuable collections of speeches and writings of Mao Tse-tung and other leaders were circulated within China, and some of these filtered to the outside world. The revelations were related to the efforts of the warring factions to besmirch the reputations of their adversaries.

Meanwhile, the flow of refugees to Hong Kong continued, increasingly composed of disenchanted, articulate youth – many ex-Red Guards – who had been sent to the Chinese countryside. Significantly, the quality of the Chinese press deteriorated. Policy debates were increasingly waged through reference to obscure historical allegories. Even Chinese journalists could not draw upon reliable statistics to inform their reporting. Indeed, it is unclear how well the top leaders were informed about their own economy and polity, as the State Statistical Bureau had been abolished and monitoring of the quantity and quality of production became exceedingly difficult. In oversimplified terms, the principal sources from 1966 to 1976 consisted of Hong Kong interviews, special Cultural Revolution revelations, and an increasingly arid press. (The declining quality of, and access to, the press led Western scholars to rely increasingly on American and British monitoring of radio broadcasts.) The importance of the Hong Kong listening post increased, and journalists and diplomats on the scene were the first to write lengthy accounts of the Cultural Revolution.[76]

The reality and these sources pointed to a society in conflict: leaders afflicted by internecine strife; parts of the elite, linked with parts of the society, tormenting other portions of the society; and local units bitterly divided and attacking one another. The key descriptive topics were to identify when the conflicts actually erupted, what caused the disintegration of the system, and what the process of conflict entailed. Soon, researchers differed on all these questions. Some attributed the origins of the Cultural Revolution to the mid-1950s, others to the Lushan Plenum, while others focused on Mao's growing discontent with the policies and institutional arrangements of the early 1960s. Other eschewed the entire debate, developing instead a more complicated argument about evolving differences

76 Stanley Karnow, *Mao and China: From revolution to revolution*; and Edward E. Rice, *Mao's way*.

among shifting coalitions which reached a crisis stage in 1964–65.[77]

As to the sources of the conflict, some focused on Mao's effort to transform China; others stressed the structural flaws and cleavages of the Maoist system; yet others attributed the chaos to deep flaws in the political culture; a few looked to the external pressures upon China brought on by the Vietnam War and their domestic ramifications; and still others examined internal social and economic stresses. The third essentially descriptive task was to capture the process of Cultural Revolution conflict: how Red Guards were organized and battled with each other, what happened with specific units, and so on. That scholarly task is still in early stages; some exemplary works are now available, but at this writing the full dynamics of the Cultural Revolution as a social movement are still only dimly understood both in China and in the West.[78]

Beyond description, the effect of the perception of a China in conflict was to spur analysis of the distribution of power and authority in China and on the policy-making process; the new sources enabled work on both topics. The sources also stimulated interest in public policy in China. Mao's innovations in education, public health, agriculture, public security, culture, industrial management, military affairs, control of the bureaucracy, and the efforts of the state to alter the system of stratification encouraged external interest in the substance of Mao's policies. In addition, the Cultural Revolution saw many articles both in the Red Guard media and in the official press detailing an alleged "two-line struggle" between "revisionists" and "socialists" that had been waged since 1949. The accounts purported to show how Mao's supporters in each of these areas had been opposed, thwarted, or sabotaged by the agents of "capitalist roaders" Liu Shao-ch'i and Teng Hsiao-p'ing. Thus P'eng Chen and Lo Jui-ch'ing had supposedly enforced Liu's "black" line in public security, Teng Tzu-hui had been his nefarious stooge in agriculture, and Po I-po and Ch'en Yun were the chief culprits in the economic realm. Such revelations became meat for foreign researchers eager to trace the evolution of policy in particular spheres.

More precisely, new issues came to dominate the field. By the mid-1970s, a lively debate was being waged over the nature of the

77 Byung-joon Ahn, *Chinese politics and the Cultural Revolution*; Lowell Dittmer, *Liu Shao-ch'i and the Chinese Cultural Revolution: The politics of mass criticism*; and MacFarquhar, *The origins of the Cultural Revolution*.
78 See, however, Hong Yung Lee, *The politics of the Chinese Cultural Revolution*, and Stanley Rosen, *Red Guard factionalism and the Cultural Revolution in Guangzhou*.

policy process at the center.[79] Some portrayed the policy process as largely dominated by Mao; the Chairman induced the conflict within the system. Others used the new data to argue that the system was endemically faction-ridden, with Mao and his allies one of several contenders; the dynamics of the system arose from the efforts of competing factions to survive, expand their power, and triumph over their rivals. Yet others stressed that political conflict was waged over substantive, complex issues, and that the differences between the leaders did not necessarily pit the same clusters against one another in issue after issue. Still others refused to be drawn into the fray, arguing that the policy process varied over time and from issue to issue. The proliferation of viewpoints indicates that the new data were sufficient to stimulate more telling questions than had been posed before, but the quality of the data did not permit rigorous testing of alternative interpretations.

The same situation existed with respect to another issue: the relationship between the center and the provinces. Some characterized the economic system as center-dominated, while others termed it a "cellular economy" in which lower-level units – provinces, counties, and communes – enjoyed considerable autonomy and capacity to ward off the center. Cultural Revolution charges against various provincial officials provided ammunition to both sides in this particular polemic. In any case, the clearly differentiated response of various provinces to different policy initiatives emanating from Peking from 1966 to 1976 and the striking differences in the thematic content and emphases of various provincial broadcasting stations spawned a cottage industry among foreign China specialists seeking to explain the variance.[80]

The completion of the *Biographic Dictionary of Chinese Communism, 1921–1965*, by Donald Klein and Anne Clark, a major confer-

---

79 See, for example, Andrew Nathan, "A factionalism model for Chinese Communist Party politics," *CQ*, 53 (January–March 1973), 1–33; the debate between Andrew Nathan and Edwin Winckler, "Policy oscillations in the PRC," *CQ*, 68 (December 1976), 720–50; and Tang Tsou, "Prolegomenon to the study of informal groups in Chinese Communist Party politics," *CQ*, 65 (March 1976), 98–114.

80 Audrey Donnithorne, "China's cellular economy: Some economic trends since the Cultural Revolution," *CQ*, 52 (October–December 1972), 605–19; Nicholas Lardy, "Centralization and decentralization in China's fiscal management," *CQ*, 61 (March 1975), 25–60, and *Economic growth and distribution in China*; Audrey Donnithorne and Nicholas Lardy, "Comment: Centralization and decentralization in China's fiscal management," and "Reply," *CQ*, 66 (June 1976), 328–54; Robert M. Field, Kathleen McGlynn, and William B. Abnett, "Political conflict and industrial growth in China: 1965–1977," *The Chinese economy post-Mao*, 1.239–84; and Frederick Teiwes, "Provincial politics in China."

ence on elites in the People's Republic of China, and the greater availability of biographical files accumulated by the U.S. government, as well as the considerable elite mobility generated through the promotions and purges of the Cultural Revolution, stimulated interest in studies of elite mobility.[81] Another reason for the surge of interest in quantitative analysis of the Chinese elite was the lack of hard data on other topics; this area attracted interest because, on a relative basis, the opportunities were greater than elsewhere. A lively debate erupted in this area too concerning the sources of elite mobility. What best explained promotions and demotions: informal patron-client ties, objective abilities, formal bureaucratic position, or ideological and policy preference? If patron-client ties were significant, what was the basis of the patronage: common geographic origin, shared revolutionary experience, old school ties, shared obligation toward an even more senior sponsor? If the criterion for advance was objective ability, what skills were requisite to success? Proponents of various views argued their cases, but in the end the quality of the data precluded any but the most murky of findings. Many factors were involved, and the weighting of the factors varied according to time, organization, place, and level of the hierarchy. The criteria for career success differed in the 1950s and the 1960s, varied in the Party and the army, differed in Shanghai and Hunan, and helped to distinguish politics within a commune, at the provincial level, and within the central committee.

Although this finding may be unsurprising, it underscored the need to be sensitive to the diversity of China and avoid simple generalizations. The data were beginning to permit, and indeed to demand, a more richly differentiated picture of Chinese politics and society. The result was an increase in carefully researched monographs that were specific to time, locale, and sector of society. Sensitivity to the differentiated nature of Chinese society and the disenchantment with the totalitarian model in turn prompted two additional questions. What was the pattern of stratification and the overall nature of Chinese social structure? How did the different sectors of society interact with the political systems, and what strategies did these sectors

81 Monte Ray Bullard, "PRC elite studies: A review of the literature," *Asian Survey*, 19:8 (August 1979), 896–910; Robert A. Scalapino, ed., *Elites in the PRC*; William Ting, "Longitudinal study of Chinese military factionalism," *Asian Survey*, 19:8 (August 1979), 789–800; Paul Wong, *China's higher leadership in the socialist transition*; and D. Michael Lampton, *Paths to power: Elite mobility in contemporary China*.

employ to influence public policy? Here too, the data permitted the raising of sophisticated issues, but the research findings remained tentative and often unsatisfactory.[82]

The data from the Cultural Revolution era and its aftermath, in sum, permitted a maturation in the questions which political scientists and sociologists posed. They sustained an explosion in the literature, but a scrutiny of this literature reveals an appropriate modesty in the conclusions advanced in monographs based on often sketchy data. Firm findings enabling the aggregation of knowledge did not pervade the field. Economists and anthropologists were worst off. The only reliable statistics about China came from third countries that reported on their trade with the People's Republic. Not surprisingly, analysis of Chinese foreign trade became one of the preferred topics of economists, who also labored valiantly to construct estimates of China's economic performance.[83] Partly to compensate for lack of firm data, they also sought insight by placing China's development experience in comparative and historical perspective.[84] In spite of these undertakings, the blunt fact is that the study of the Chinese economy was seriously hampered by the paucity and unreliability of Chinese statistics. Anthropologists were in even worse shape. Denied access to the People's Republic, they concentrated on Hong Kong and Taiwan.

Reluctant to tackle the bewildering Cultural Revolution and appropriately skeptical of the reliability of the Red Guard materials, historians proved more hesitant to write about contemporary China in the late 1960s and 1970s than they had been earlier.[85] Their perspective was sorely missed in a secondary scholarly literature that

---

82 See Victor Falkenheim, *Citizens and groups in contemporary China*; David Goodman, ed., *Groups and politics in the People's Republic of China*; Victor Nee and David Mozingo, eds., *State and society in contemporary China*; James Watson, ed., *Class and social stratification in post-revolution China*.

83 Alexander Eckstein, ed., *Quantitative measures of China's economic output*. Particularly noteworthy is the series sponsored by the Joint Economic Committee of the United States Congress: *An economic profile of mainland China*, two vols.; *The People's Republic of China: An economic assessment*; and *China: A reassessment of the economy*. Also, Alan P. L. Liu, *Political culture and group conflict in Communist China*.

84 Dwight Perkins, *Agricultural development in China, 1368–1968*; Dwight Perkins, ed., *China's modern economy in historical perspective*; and Robert Dernberger, ed., *China's developmental experience in comparative perspective*.

85 Exceptions are John Fairbank, *China: The people's Middle Kingdom and the U.S.A.*; Maurice Meisner, *Mao's China: A history of the People's Republic*; John Israel, "Continuities and discontinuities in the ideology of the Great Proletarian Cultural Revolution," in Chalmers Johnson, ed., *Ideology and politics in contemporary China*; James P. Harrison, *The long march to power: A history of the Chinese Communist Party, 1921–1972*; and Richard C. Thornton, *China: The struggle for power, 1917–1972*.

came to be dominated by journalists and political scientists engrossed in issues concerning political conflict, elite mobility, the policy process, and the diversity and differentiation within China. As with totalitarian China, many of the analysts tended to elucidate the present situation with such persuasiveness that the literature seriously underestimated the potential for change in China. The difficulty was compounded by the impact in the early 1970s of a new source – the short visit to China – which prompted excessively optimistic assessments of the effectiveness of Mao's policies and camouflaged popular disenchantment with the regime. Missing were the perspectives historians should have provided concerning the ways in which the Cultural Revolution departed from the mainstream of China's development and which economists could not provide concerning the accumulating obstacles to sustained high rates of economic growth.

Four noteworthy exceptions deserve mention. In his *Uncertain passage*, A. Doak Barnett assessed the range of problems that would confront Mao's successors. Rejecting a conflict model of Chinese politics and assuming rationality would have to prevail over the long run, Barnett concluded that changes in economic, national security, and social policies were inevitable in the post-Mao era. Franz Michael drew upon the Hong Kong/Taiwan assessments of Mao to develop a harsh indictment of the Chairman.[86] The inescapable impression which a reader acquired from that study was that a fate similar to that of Stalin certainly awaited the contemporary Chinese despot. In a series of trenchant essays which employed the totalitarian model and incorporated a historical perspective, Tang Tsou argued that the extreme politicization of the society and the persecution of the intellectuals were not in keeping with the dominant intellectual trends since the May Fourth movement.[87] Further, Tsou posited that the factional struggles in China entailed life-and-death struggles; victors would eliminate their defeated rivals. Implicit in Tsou's dynamic analysis was the possibility of a sudden reversal of policy by a victorious faction acting in congruence with long-term trends in Chinese society. Finally, Richard Lowenthal, a student of comparative communist revolution, early on argued that mobilization regimes based on utopian vision do not long sustain themselves and inevitably yield to more pragmatic, bureaucratic rule.[88] As with analysis in the

---

86 Franz Michael, *Mao and the perpetual revolution.*
87 Tang Tsou, *The Cultural Revolution and post-Mao reform: A historical perspective.*
88 Richard Lowenthal, "Development vs. Utopia in Communist policy," in Chalmers Johnson, ed., *Change in Communist systems*, 33–116.

1950s and early 1960s, analysts were well served by not allowing the available data and the events of the moment totally to dictate their research agenda but by approaching the data with a dynamic model in mind, informed by historical and comparative perspectives.

To conclude, the field has not developed in a typically cumulative fashion, with new research building upon previous findings. A major implication of our analysis is that many publications on post-1949 China become dated as new information becomes available, and reinterpretation of previous findings is continually necessary. As a result, a selective survey must give preference to the latest and best analyses and slight prior monographic work, even though it was admirable scholarship and advanced the field at the time. The bibliographical essays that follow were compiled with this principle in mind.

BIBLIOGRAPHICAL ESSAYS
FOR CHAPTERS

In his immediately preceding analytic survey of comprehensive proportions, Michel Oksenberg sets forth the essential sources for research on the People's Republic of China (PRC) and major books resulting from it. Inevitably, the following essays, geared to the chapters in this volume, repeat many of the references in that overview.

We believe this repetition may be helpful because the contributors present their own selections of the works important to their subjects, whereas Professor Oksenberg focuses mainly on China's political problems.

1. THE REUNIFICATION OF CHINA

One approach to this protean subject can begin with the comparison of dynasties, especially their founding and demise. There is less literature on this subject than one might expect. In 1944, sixteen Kyoto and Tokyo scholars joined in a project for a collaborative survey of the "dynasties of conquest," among which Japan at that time was trying to take its place. During the China Incident, a historical view of previous cases might be of use. In 1943 the Tōa Kenkyūjo published a 300-page volume, *Iminzoku no Shina tōchi gaisetsu* (Outline of the rule of alien peoples over China). This surveyed the Northern Wei, Chin, Yuan, and Ch'ing as to origin, official and military systems, economic and religious institutions and policies toward China and Inner Asia. In 1952 was published a similarly path-breaking volume by Professor Ch'ien Mu of New Asia College in Hong Kong, entitled *Chung-kuo li-tai cheng-chih te-shih*. The topics analyzed are the government organization, examination system, and economic system of the Han, T'ang, Sung, Ming, and Ch'ing dynasties. This interesting though brief survey work has now been translated by Chün-tu Hsueh and George O. Totten III in *Traditional government in Imperial China: A critical analysis* (Chinese University Press, Shatin, Hong Kong, 1982). An important aid to making dynastic comparisons has been published by Charles O. Hucker, *A dictionary of official titles in imperial China* (Stanford, 1985). It expands the old Chinese handbook, *Li-tai chih-kuan piao*, and provides sensible English equivalents of the Chinese titles.

For accounts of the founding of dynasties and their reunifications of

China, see the studies by Arthur F. Wright on the Sui, Howard J. Wechsler on the T'ang, Edmund H. Worthy, Jr., on the Sung, Edward L. Dreyer and John W. Dardess on the Ming, and Joseph F. Fletcher, Jr., on the Manchus, to be combined with Frederic Wakeman's new study of the Ch'ing conquest, *The great enterprise* – all as noted in note 23 in Chapter 1. On the founding of Ch'in and Han, see Chapters 1–5 of *CHOC*, Volume 1. Once investigated, the literature on dynastic foundings will be enormous, but the number of overall and comparative studies still seems surprisingly small.

2. ESTABLISHMENT AND CONSOLIDATION OF THE NEW REGIME

The study of the 1949–57 period must be based primarily on contemporary PRC publications. In these years, especially the mid-1950s, these materials are rich in terms of both availability and relative detail and candor. In addition to complete runs of such key central newspapers and periodicals as *Jen-min jih-pao* (People's daily), *Kung-jen jih-pao* (Workers daily), and *Hsueh-hsi* (Study), many provincial newspapers and, from the mid-1950s, specialized ministerial journals are available, albeit with considerable gaps in the various holdings. The most extensive holdings of these publications are in the Library of Congress, and a useful and wide-ranging clipping file drawn from such sources was compiled by the Union Research Institute (URI), Hong Kong. English translations of the Chinese press and journals were provided on a fairly extensive basis by the various series of the United States Consulate General, Hong Kong – especially *Survey of China Mainland Press, Extracts* (later *Selections*) *from China Mainland Magazines* and *Current Background* – and starting in 1955 by URI's *Union Research Service*.

Various collections of contemporary official documents are also available. Particularly useful are the annual *Jen-min shou-ts'e* (People's handbook) and the periodic *Chung-hua jen-min kung-ho-kuo fa-kuei hui-pien* (Compendium of laws and regulations of the PRC). The major collections in English are: *Communist China 1955–1959: Policy documents with analysis; Eighth National Congress of the Communist Party of China;* Roderick MacFarquhar, ed., *The Hundred Flowers;* and Harold C. Hinton, ed., *The People's Republic of China, 1949–1979: A documentary survey.*

Contemporary documents are supplemented by several additional sources: the personal accounts of both foreigners and Chinese who experienced at first hand developments during the PRC's early years; information published during the Cultural Revolution in 1966–69; and data emerging in the post-Mao period. All these sources provide further perspectives and information but have their own biases, which require careful evaluation against existing contemporary sources. First-hand accounts of Chinese émigrés have been incorporated in various secondary works, notably for the period in question in Ezra F. Vogel, *Canton under communism: Programs and policies in a provincial capital, 1949–1968.* Major works on the period authored by émigrés are: Chow Ching-wen, *Ten years of storm: The true story of the Communist regime in China*; Robert Loh with Humphrey Evans, *Escape from Red China*; and Mu Fu-sheng, *The wilting of the Hundred Flowers: The Chinese intelligentsia under Mao.* Books by foreigners in China during 1949–57 include: Derk Bodde, *Peking diary, 1948–1949: A year of revolution*; Allyn and Adele Rickett, *Prisoners of liberation*; and Maurice Wills, *Turncoat: An American's 12 years in Communist China.* In addition, A. Doak Barnett's *China on the eve of Communist takeover*, while dealing only briefly with actual Communist rule, provides invaluable insights into the situation the CCP inherited in 1949.

Cultural Revolution sources that appeared in 1966–69 are essentially of two types: highly polemic "revelations" about the alleged crimes of various leaders in the pre-1966 period, and purportedly original pre-Cultural Revolution documents that were only then made available. The revelations are found not only in official publications from 1966–69 but especially in so-called Red Guard sources – newspapers and pamphlets produced unofficially by various "rebel" groups but generally with the assistance of high-level factions within the CCP. Collections of such materials are held in various major libraries, and extensive translations are found in the various series of the United States Consulate General, Hong Kong. In addition, revelations from radio broadcasts can be located in *Foreign Broadcast Information Service: Communist China; British Broadcasting Corporation, Summary of World Broadcasts: Far East;* and *News from Chinese Provincial Radio Stations.*

Of still greater value were documents from 1949–57 made available largely through Red Guard sources in 1966–69. Textual analysis creates a high degree of confidence in these documents, the most important of which are various speeches and directives by Mao Tse-tung to inner Party audiences. The most significant Mao collections are: *Mao Tse-tung ssu-hsiang wan-sui* (Long live Mao Tse-tung Thought); *Miscellany of Mao Tse-tung Thought*; Jerome Ch'en, ed., *Mao*; Jerome Ch'en, ed., *Mao papers: Anthology and bibliography*; and Stuart Schram, ed., *Mao Tse-tung unrehearsed, talks and letters: 1956–71.*

The period since Mao's death has also produced an official volume of his writings over the 1949–57 period, *Selected works of Mao Tse-tung*, Volume V, which provides both some previously unavailable documents and some different (but compatible) versions of speeches unofficially released during the Cultural Revolution. Another important collection is *Ch'en Yun wen-hsuan (1949–1956)* (Selected works of Ch'en Yun, 1949–1956). In addition, the official media and a substantial array of memoirs, chronologies, and Party histories have reviewed various developments between 1949 and 1957. The current (early 1980s) official view of the period is laid down in the "Resolution on certain questions in the history of our Party since the founding of the People's Republic of China," *Beijing Review*, 27 (1981), and less authoritatively in Liao Kai-lung, "Historical experiences and our road of development," *Issues & Studies*, October and November 1981. The Liao article is but one of a growing number of articles, books, journals, and documents for internal (*nei-pu*) distribution within official Chinese organizations which shed important light on this and other periods of PRC history and which are now becoming available externally and included in Western library collections. Finally, increasing scholarly interchange with China has opened up opportunities for discussions with PRC scholars and participants in major post-1949 events.

A quite considerable secondary literature covering the 1949–57 period has now developed. Major guides to this literature are: Peter Berton and Eugene Wu, *Contemporary China: A research guide* (which also includes primary sources); Michel C. Oksenberg with Nancy Bateman and James B. Anderson, comps., *A bibliography of secondary English-language literature on Contemporary Chinese politics*; G. William Skinner et al., eds., *Modern Chinese society: An analytical bibliography* (which covers Western, Chinese, and Japanese language publications); and the annual *Bibliography of Asian Studies*.

Until the mid-1960s monographic studies on the early and mid-1950s, as well as contemporary China generally, were few; the most notable publications were of a general nature: A. Doak Barnett, *Communist China: The early years, 1949–1955*; Peter S. H. Tang, *Communist China today*; and S. B. Thomas, *Government and administration in Communist China*. Beginning in the mid-1960s, however, a new generation of scholars began to produce studies of considerable scope and sophistication. A number of major works on Chinese politics include substantial segments on the 1949–57 period: Harry Harding, *Organizing China: The problem of bureaucracy 1949–1976*; Franz Schurmann, *Ideology and organization in Communist China*; Frederick C. Teiwes, *Politics and purges in China: Rectification and the decline of Party norms, 1950–1965*; James R. Townsend, *Political participation in Communist China*; and Vogel, *Canton under communism*.

Several studies focusing on ideological issues contain important sections on the period: Arthur A. Cohen, *The communism of Mao Tse-tung*; Stuart R. Schram, "Introduction: the Cultural Revolution in historical perspective," in his *Authority, participation and cultural change in China*; Benjamin I. Schwartz, *Communism and China: Ideology in flux*; and John Bryan Starr, *Continuing the revolution: The political thought of Mao*. In addition, various monographs dealing with specialized areas throw light on aspects of 1949–57. Some of the most significant of these are: Jerome Alan Cohen, *The criminal process in the People's Republic of China, 1949–1963: An introduction*; June Teufel Dreyer, *China's forty millions: Minority nationalities and national integration in the People's Republic of China*; John Gittings, *The role of the Chinese army*; Ellis Joffe, *Party and army: Professionalism and political control in the Chinese officer corps, 1949–1964*; David M. Lampton, *The politics of medicine in China: The policy process, 1949–1977*; Benedict Stavis, *The politics of agricultural mechanization in China*; and Martin King Whyte, *Small groups and political rituals in China*.

Monographic studies of considerable quality dealing exclusively with various aspects of the first eight years of the PRC have appeared in the past decade and a half. The best study of the process of consolidating power in urban China is Kenneth G. Lieberthal, *Revolution and tradition in Tientsin, 1949–1952*; it can be usefully supplemented by the concluding chapters of Suzanne Pepper, *Civil war in China: The political struggle, 1945–1949*. The nature of regional administration after liberation is examined by Dorothy J. Solinger, *Regional government and political integration in Southwest China, 1949–1954: A case study*. The politics of industrial organization in the immediate post-1949 period are analyzed in William Brugger, *Democracy and organisation in the Chinese industrial enterprise (1948–1953)*. Frederick C. Teiwes, *Elite discipline in China: Coercive and persuasive approaches to rectification, 1950–1953*, presents a more detailed examination of Party reform movements in the early years than is provided in *Politics and Purges*.

The major rural transformations, land reform in 1950–52 and cooperativization in 1952–56, are examined in several major volumes. An excellent study from the late 1950s is C. K. Yang, *A Chinese village in early communist transition*. More recent studies are: Thomas Paul Bernstein, "Leadership and mobilization in the collectivization of agriculture in China and Russia: a comparison"; Vivienne Shue, *Peasant China in transition: The dynamics of development toward socialism, 1949–1956*; and John Wong, *Land reform in the People's Republic of China: Institutional transformation in agriculture*. In addition, there are several important articles on these matters: Geoffrey Shillinglaw, "Land reform and peasant mobilization in Southern China 1947–1950," in David Lehmann, ed., *Agrarian reform and agrarian reformism: Studies of Peru, Chile, China and India*; and Kenneth R. Walker, "Collectivisation in retrospect: The 'socialist high tide' of autumn 1955 – spring 1956," *The China Quarterly*, 26 (1966).

Two unpublished Ph.D. dissertations shed considerable light on the policy-making process in the mid-1950s. Charles Thomas Fingar, "Politics and policy-making in the People's Republic of China, 1954–1955," examines the interrelation of various policy areas as the PRC moved into its most highly bureaucratized phase. A study which extends into the Great Leap Forward, Michel C. Oksenberg, "Policy formulation in communist China: The case of the mass irrigation campaign, 1957–58," reveals much about the political, technical, and administrative factors shaping CCP programs.

The key political developments of 1956–57 – political liberalization, debates on economic policy, the Eighth Party Congress, and Party rectification – are most extensively dealt with in Roderick MacFarquhar, *The origins*

of the Cultural Revolution 1: Contradictions among the people 1956–1957.
Further insights and varying interpretations of these matters are found in the
relevant sections of: D. W. Fokkema, *Literary doctrine in China and the
Soviet influence 1956–1960*; Merle Goldman, *Literary dissent in Communist
China*; Richard H. Solomon, *Mao's revolution and the Chinese political
culture*; and Teiwes, *Politics and purges.*

Several research aids are worthy of note. The Hong Kong newsletter,
China News Analysis, has since 1953 provided invaluable summaries of data
on varied topics. Kenneth Lieberthal, *A Research guide to central Party and
government meetings in China 1949–1975,* draws on both contemporary
and Cultural Revolution sources to pinpoint conferences where major
decisions were made after 1949. Biographical data is provided by a number
of volumes including: Donald W. Klein and Anne B. Clark, *Biographic
dictionary of Chinese communism 1921–1965; Gendai Chūgoku jimmei
jiten* (Modern China biographical dictionary); and *Who's who in Communist China.*

3 AND 8. THE ECONOMY

The policy of releasing few or no economic data and the suppression of
serious economic analysis within China between 1960 and 1978 have inhibited analysis of China's economic development not only for more recent
times but for the years prior to the onset of the Cultural Revolution as well.
That situation was reversed dramatically with the publication in 1979 of the
first State Statistical Bureau communiqué in two decades and a subsequent
flood of new materials, both quantitative and qualitative, covering contemporary and historical developments. Among the statistical materials, the
most significant are the statistical yearbooks, *Chung-kuo t'ung-chi nien-
chien,* published annually since 1981 in both Chinese and English editions,
by the State Statistical Bureau. These provide not only current statistics but
also a mass of data going back to 1950, much of it previously unpublished.
The 1981 yearbook (published in 1982), for example, included annual data
on the quantities of a large number of import and export products for the
years 1950–81, as well as the value of imports from and exports to 26 major
trading partners during the same period. Subsequent volumes have disclosed
new data for earlier years, as well as providing an annual updating of many
series.

In addition, since 1981 the Chinese have published a massive *Chung-kuo
ching-chi nien-chien* (Chinese economic yearbook), which provides full texts
of major economic documents, economic policy statements, and laws and
decrees related to economic development; detailed analyses of each sector of
the economy; and surveys of economic developments in each of the provinces and provinical level municipalities. Also published are several important sector yearbooks such as *Chung-kuo nung-yeh nien-chien* (Chinese

agricultural yearbook), published annually beginning in 1981, and *Chung-kuo mei-t'an kung-yeh nien-chien* (Chinese coal industry yearbook), published annually beginning in 1983. All of these contain materials that deal with the long-term as well as recent developments.

Among the most important volumes providing Chinese analysis or texts of speeches are: Ma Hung and Sun Shang-ch'ing, eds., *Chung-kuo ching-chi chieh-kou wen-t'i yen-chiu* (Research on issues in China's economic structure); *Ch'en Yung wen-kao hsuan-pien 1949–1956* (Selected manuscripts of Ch'en Yun, 1949–1956); this volume was subsequently published openly in China under the title *Ch'en Yun wen-hsuan 1949–1956* (Selected works of Ch'en Yun, 1949–1956); *Ch'en Yun t'ung-chih wen-kao ksuan-pien 1956–1962* (Selected manuscripts of comrade Ch'en Yun 1956–1962); this volume was subsequently published openly under the title *Ch'en Yun wen-hsuan 1956–1985* (Selected writings of Ch'en Yun 1956–1985); *Ma Yin-ch'u ching-chi lun-wen hsuan-chi* (Selected economic essays of Ma Yin-ch'u) and, most important for contributing to our understanding of the aftermath of the Great Leap Forward: Liu Sui-nien, ed., *Liu-shih nien-tai kuo-min ching-chi t'iao-cheng ti hui-ku* (Recalling the readjustment of the economy in the 1960s).

A number of critical economic analyses and previously unavailable speeches have been published in the important Chinese Communist Party journal *Tang-shih yen-chiu* (Research on Party history). Several collections selected from this material have also been published, the most valuable of which is Chu Ch'eng-chia, ed., *Chung-kung tang-shih yen-chiu lun-wen hsuan* (Selected essays on research on the history of the Chinese Communist Party). Chou T'ai-ho, ed., *Tang-tai Chung-kuo ti ching-chi t'i-chih kai-ko* (Reform of the economic system in contemporary China) provides a chronological summary of major reforms and policy initiatives. There is a massive compendium edited by Fang Wei-chung, ed., *Chung-hua jen-min kung-ho-kuo ching-chi ta shih-chi 1949–1980* (A record of major economic events in the People's Republic of China, 1949–1980).

The secondary literature on China's economic development is extensive but uneven. Coverage of the 1950s, for which there were fairly comprehensive reports issued by the state statistical and planning agencies, is generally much more satisfactory than that for the 1960s, for which there was little primary source material until after 1978. The broadest and most satisfactory accounts of the 1950s are those of Choh-ming Li, *Economic development of Communist China*, which focuses on the first plan (1953–57), and Alexander Eckstein, *China's economic revolution*, which covers the era of Mao Tse-tung as a whole but is strongest in its analysis of the 1st FYP and the Great Leap Forward. Roderick MacFarquhar's *Origins of the Cultural Revolution 1: Contradictions among the people 1956–1957* and *Origins of the Cultural Revolution 2: The Great Leap Forward, 1958–1960* provide the most insightful analyses of economic decision making at the highest levels of the Party during the years leading up to the Great Leap Forward and the GLF itself.

The first half of the 1960s have received very little attention from Western scholars. The effectiveness of the statistical blackout maintained by the Chinese in this period is attested by the successful concealment, for two decades, of a massive famine that occurred between 1959 and 1962 and is variously estimated to have caused 16 million to 27 million deaths above those that would have been expected during those years under conditions of normal mortality. While the famine itself is a subject of growing attention, broad studies of economic development during the first half of the 1960s have yet to appear, although some of the monographic studies mentioned below do treat specific topics during this period.

The monographic literature on economic development in the 1950s is extensive. Two landmark studies assess the growth of China's national income: Shigeru Ishikawa's *National income and capital formation in mainland China: An examination of official statistics*, and Ta-chung Liu and Kung-chia Yeh, *The economy of the Chinese mainland: National income and economic development, 1933–1959*. Dwight Perkins, *Market control and planning in Communist China*, traces the expansion of the socialist planning and shrinkage of the market-oriented sectors of the economy during the 1950s. Alexander Eckstein, *Communist China's economic growth and foreign trade*, provides the most comprehensive study of the role of foreign trade in China's growth, particularly the transfer of technology from the Soviet Union in the 1950s. Nicholas R. Lardy, *Economic growth and distribution in China*, analyzes central-provincial fiscal relations to trace the degree of centralization in the allocation of resources in the modern sector of the economy. Audrey Donnithorne, *China's economic system*, provides an exhaustive account of the evolution of the state economic bureaucracy and relates that to patterns of planning and resource allocation.

Major studies of industrial development include Thomas G. Rawski, *China's transition to industrialism*, and Kang Chao, *The rate and pattern of industrial growth in Communist China*. Labor absorption in industry and the urban economy as a whole is treated by John Philip Emerson, *Nonagricultural employment in mainland China, 1949–1958*.

Agricultural development up to the early 1980s is covered by both Nicholas R. Lardy in *Agriculture in China's modern economic development* and Kenneth R. Walker in *Food grain procurement and consumption in China*. The former traces the evolution of the planning system used in agriculture, the latter the development of the state-run system of compulsory farm deliveries.

Earlier agricultural studies that are still quite valuable include Dwight H. Perkins, *Agricultural development in China, 1368–1968*, which places post-1949 developments in long-term historical perspective, and Chao Kang, *Agricultural production in Communist China, 1949–1965*, which traces in detail the economic consequences of the organizational changes in the farm sector up to the Cultural Revolution.

4 AND 9. EDUCATION

The standard primary sources for the years 1949 to 1965 have been cited above, and research on education must rely primarily on them. The official Chinese newspapers, journals, and the occasional compendia of state laws comprise the major source materials. The most easily accessible route to the Chinese originals lies through the clipping file service of the Union Research Institute, which ceased to exist in 1983. This collection is now housed at the Baptist College in Hong Kong, for those who want to avoid the microfilm version. The files on all aspects of education policy and practice, ranging from preschool through university, are voluminous and could provide the basis for many research monographs.

The most useful of the standard translation services for education topics are the U.S. Consulate General, Hong Kong, *Current Background* series (from 1950); and the Consulate's *Selections from China Mainland Magazines* (from 1960; known as *Extracts from China Mainland Magazines* from 1955 to 1960). Other useful translation services are the Consulate's *Survey of the China Mainland Press* (from 1950); *Foreign Broadcast Information Service, Daily Report – Communist China* (U.S. Government; from 1968); *News from Chinese Provincial Radio Stations* (British Regional Information Office, Hong Kong; from 1963); *China Topics* (also BRIO; from 1964); New China News Agency, Hong Kong, *Daily News Release* (from 1948); *Union Research Service* (Union Research Institute, Hong Kong; from 1955); and the various series from the U.S. government's Joint Publications Research Service.

The unofficial Red Guard press from the early years of the Cultural Revolution (1966–68) can also be gleaned with some profit for data on the early 1960s. Caution must be exercised, since the materials were compiled in the heat of rhetorical battle. But they contain information not available elsewhere on the implementation of policy as shown through data provided from individual schools. Once again, the scholar is the unintended beneficiary of social chaos, in this case the Red Guard raids on school offices and filing cabinets. The works of Stanley Rosen and Hong Yung Lee (see Bibliography) are to date the best known of those that have used these materials. The largest compendium of these Red Guard publications is the *Red Guard publications* in twenty volumes, reprinted by the Center for Chinese Research Materials, Association of Research Libraries, Washington, D.C., in 1975, and a multivolume companion supplementary set published in 1980. English translations of similar materials can be found especially in the restricted-circulation *Supplements* to the U.S. Consulate General, Hong

Kong, *Survey of the China Mainland Press* and *Selections from China Mainland Magazines* during the late 1960s.

Academic research is also the beneficiary of the more relaxed policies of the post Mao-era which have, among other things, sought to exonerate the earlier policies Mao's Cultural Revolution denigrated. Thus the years 1968 to 1976 remain largely blank in documentary sources, but much new material began to be published retrospectively during the late 1970s on the much-maligned 17 years from 1949 to 1966. Unfortunately, most of this new material is of the secondary source variety, with the added defect of carrying a clear bias in favor of these 17 years and against the Cultural Revolution. Nevertheless, the current (as of the mid-1980s) publication lists of the People's Education Press (*Jen-min chiao-yü ch'u-pan-she*) offer a good indication of the books being written in China about the earlier years. Much is also being published about the pre-1949 period, with some interesting emphasis on education in the old Communist base areas and on well-known non-Communist educators from the Republican period.

An especially valuable research tool is the 1984 publication, *Chung-kuo chiao-yü nien-chien, 1949–81* (Chinese education yearbook, 1949–81). Among other things, this volume contains 140 pages of reprinted documents and directives on education from 1949 through 1981 – albeit with the inevitable gaps in every category from about 1964 through 1978, the years of Maoist influence. Another useful reference is the 1983 publication *Chung-hua jen-min kung-ho-kuo chiao-yü ta-shih-chi, 1949–1982* (Education chronology of the People's Republic of China, 1949–1982).

Last but not least are the human resources. Interviews treated as oral history, whether conducted in China itself or with Chinese in Hong Kong who have knowledge of the system from past personal experience, remain an important source of information. The books on education that have relied most heavily on interview data are those by Stanley Rosen, Susan Shirk, and Jonathan Unger.

Despite the great wealth of material available, the 1950s in particular have not been well researched by scholars outside China. It was not until the Cultural Revolution decade, 1966–76, that China's "education revolution" put the topic on the list of features worthy of investigation. Hence international attention has focused on that experience and its aftermath. Neither the education specialist nor the social scientist seem to have been overly inspired by the subject in earlier years. And a similar slackening of interest appears to have set in with the collapse of the Cultural Revolution experiment in the late 1970s. There remain a number of unexplored areas from the "17 years."

One of the most important, given its implications for the post-Mao era, is the extent of Soviet influence in the 1950s. Failed or unpopular experiments rarely provide incentive for research. But the "learning from the Soviet Union" phase from 1950 to 1957 is one that merits closer study for what it can tell us about the efficacy of transplanted models and the ongoing influence of institutions established and individuals trained during that period.

Another failed and unexplored experiment is the Great Leap Forward. The education reforms inaugurated at that time were launched in the name of "cultural revolution" and clearly set many precedents for the subsequent 1966–76 Cultural Revolution experiments. Yet the nature of those links has never been documented and definitively drawn – nor has the anatomy of the failure, which must have contained both unintended consequences and unrecorded gains.

Given the state of research on the 1950s, we are blessed with a relative plethora for the early 1960s. But the works of Rosen, Shirk, and Unger, cited above, were based primarily on interview data, and they have left the task of fleshing out the documentary research largely to others. This job, meanwhile, has been only partially filled by the more conventional studies that devote attention to the period, such as those by Theodore Chen, Julia Kwong, Jan-Ingvar Lofstedt, Ronald Price, and Robert Taylor (see footnotes in Chapters 4 and 9, and Bibliography). These have all tended to concentrate more on theory and policy than on the practice and implementation that can be revealed only through interviewing and field research. Now that China has become more accessible to foreign researchers, it will, we hope, become somewhat easier to merge these two aims within individual studies.

5 AND 10. THE PARTY AND THE INTELLECTUALS

There are no basic Chinese-language sources on intellectuals and intellectual trends in the PRC. The main sources of information are scattered in the national newspapers and journals. The Yenan newspaper *Chieh-fang jih-pao* (Liberation daily) is the main source on intellectuals in the guerrilla areas during the Yenan period. It contains discussions of Party policy toward the intellectuals and statements by the intellectuals themselves. Left-wing and Communist intellectuals in Chungking from 1938 to 1946 published in *Hsin-hua jih-pao* (New China daily). After 1949, the major sources of information on Party policy toward intellectuals and Party-intellectual debates are the Party's official newspaper *Jen-min jih-pao* (People's daily) and the intellectuals' newspaper *Kuang-ming jih-pao* (Kuang-ming daily). The journals most concerned with intellectual issues are the Party's theoretical journal *Hsueh-hsi* (Study), which was replaced by *Hung-ch'i* (Red Flag) in the Great Leap Forward. The Communist Youth League's *Chung-kuo ch'ing-nien pao* (China youth news) is another source on intellectual trends. Journals emanating from the major universities also contain intellectual-political debates, but these journals have been difficult to obtain until the post-Mao era.

Other sources of information on intellectuals, particularly the literary intellectuals and the controversies of the 1950s and 1960s, are in *Wen-i pao* (Literary Gazette), *Wen-i hsueh-hsi* (Literary studies), *Jen-min wen-hsueh* (People's literature), and *Shang-hai wen-hsueh* (Shanghai literature). The writings of a number of the leading literary intellectuals of the 1950s such as Chou Yang, Hu Feng, Ting Ling, Feng Hsueh-feng, and Ai Ch'ing can be found in these journals. The works of the controversial intellectuals of the 1960s such as Teng T'o, Wu Han, and Feng Yu-lan can be found in *Li-shih yen-chiu* (Historical research), *Che-hsueh yen-chiu* (Philosophical research), and *Hsueh-hsi yen-chiu* (Academic research).

There are also printed collections of their works: Ma Nan-ts'un (Teng T'o), *Yen-shan yeh-hua* (Evening talks at Yenshan), Wu Nan-hsing (Wu Han, Teng T'o, and Liao Mo-sha), *San-chia ts'un* (Three Family Village), Liao Mo-sha, Hsia Yen, Wu Han, Tang Tao and Meng Chao, *Ch'ang-tuan lu* (The long and the short), Ai Szu-ch'i, *Ai Szu-ch'i wen-chi* (Ai Szu-ch'i's collected works).

Translations of Mao's views on the intellectuals can be found in his *Selected works*, five volumes, in which Mao's Yenan "Talks on literature and art" are the most directly relevant. Later sources for Mao's views on intellectual matters are Mao's *Four essays on philosophy* and Stuart Schram, ed., *Chairman Mao talks to the people: Talks and letters, 1956–1971*. Translations of articles and statements by intellectuals in the Hundred Flowers period are in Roderick MacFarquhar, ed., *The Hundred Flowers*. Translations of literary works and criticisms in the Hundred Flowers are in Nieh Hua-ling, ed., *Literature of the Hundred Flowers*, two volumes.

The most comprehensive discussions of the Party's policy toward the intellectuals and the intellectuals' response are in Merle Goldman's *Literary dissent in Communist China*, for the period of the late 1930s through the Great Leap Forward, and Goldman's *China's intellectuals: Advise and dissent*, for the period from the early 1960s until the post-Mao era. Other works deal with particular aspects of this question. Robert Jay Lifton discusses the effect of thought reform on the intellectuals in *Thought reform and the psychology of totalism: A study of "brainwashing" in China*. Douwe Fokkema in *Literary doctrine in China and Soviet influence 1956–1960* and Rudolf Wagner, "The cog and the scout," in Wolfgang Kubin and Rudolf Wagner, eds., *Essays in modern Chinese literature and literary criticism*, discuss the influence of Soviet intellectual trends on China in the 1950s. Two interesting studies of controversial intellectuals in the early 1960s are James Pusey, *Wu Han: Attacking the present through the past*, and Timothy Cheek, "Deng Tuo: Culture, Leninism and alternative Marxism in the Chinese Communist Party." For studies of the radical intellectuals in the 1960s, see Parris Chang, *Radicals and radical ideology in China's Cultural Revolution*, and Lars Ragvald, *Yao Wen-yuan as a literary critic and theorist: The emergence of Chinese Zhdanovism*.

The main works that look at intellectual developments in a political context are Richard Solomon, *Mao's revolution and the Chinese political culture*, and Roderick MacFarquhar, *The origins of the Cultural Revolution, 1: Contradictions among the people 1956–1957* and *The origins of the Cultural Revolution, 2: The Great Leap Forward, 1958–1960*.

6. FOREIGN RELATIONS: FROM THE KOREAN WAR TO THE BANDUNG LINE

Although there are rich studies on the PRC's foreign relations and domestic politics, few publications are available which focus upon the period from the Korean War to the Bandung Line. Among them, Jacques Guillermaz, *The Chinese Communist Party in power 1949–1976* and Roderick MacFarquhar, *The origins of the Cultural Revolution, 1: Contradictions among the people 1956–1957*, are very reliable surveys of the internal background of China's foreign relations, as well as Franz H. Schurmann, *Ideology and organization in Communist China*. Mineo Nakajima, *Chūgoku: rekishi, shakai, kokusaikankei* (China: History, society, and international relations) is useful for understanding the basic framework of contemporary Chinese affairs.

Outstanding books which give an overview of China's foreign policy are as follows: John King Fairbank, *The United States and China*, 4th ed.; A. Doak Barnett, *Communist China and Asia: Challenge to American policy*; Harold C. Hinton, *China's turbulent quest: An analysis of China's foreign relations since 1945*, rev. ed.; and R. G. Boyd, *Communist China's foreign policy*. One general survey of various aspects of China's foreign relations is Keishirō Iriye and Masashi Andō, eds., *Gendai Chūgoku no kokusaikankei* (International relations of contemporary China). Relatively official views of the Soviet Union are reflected in O. B. Borisov and B. T. Koloskov, *Sino-Soviet relations 1945–1973: A brief history*.

For primary sources, we can use such official Chinese materials as *Mao Tse-tung hsuan chi* (Selected works of Mao Tse-tung) and the series of *Chung-hua jen-min kung-ho-kuo tui-wai kuan-hsi wen-chien chi* (Collected foreign relations documents of the People's Republic of China). For U.S. government documents, see the series of *Foreign Relations of the United States* and the many kinds of National Security Council *NSC Papers*. There are also Mao Tse-tung's unofficially published documents, such as *Mao Tse-tung ssu-hsiang wan-sui!* (Long live Mao Tse-tung Thought); Nikita Khrushchev's memoirs, Strobe Talbott, trans. and ed., *Khrushchev remembers*, with detailed commentary and notes by Edward Crankshaw; and Strobe Talbott, trans. and ed., *Khrushchev remembers: The last testament*.

For the "pro-Soviet" period or the so-called Soviet model in the early 1950s, we can turn first to the following books: on Soviet foreign policy for this period, Max Beloff, *Soviet policy in the Far East 1944–1957*; Henry Wei, *China and Soviet Russia*; J. M. Mackintosh, *Strategy and tactics of*

Soviet foreign policy; and Adam B. Ulam, *Expansion and coexistence: The history of Soviet foreign policy, 1917–67*. These are "classic" studies that provide basic concepts and important analytical frameworks.

Regarding studies on the "hidden" conflicts between the PRC and the Soviet Union, Mineo Nakajima, *Chūso tairitsu to gendai: Sengo Ajia no saikōsatsu* (The Sino-Soviet confrontation and the present age: Reappraisal of postwar Asia) discusses relevant aspects after the Yalta Conference; and Yōnosuke Nagai and Akira Iriye, eds., *The origins of the Cold War in Asia*, is a joint product of American, European, and Japanese scholars.

With respect to Sino-U.S. relations, Tang Tsou, *America's failure in China 1941–50*, is one of the best texts. Dorothy Borg and Waldo Heinrichs, eds., *Uncertain years: Chinese-American relations, 1947–1950*, includes historical essays. See also Nancy B. Tucker, *Patterns in the dust*, and Shigeru Usami "Suchūato taishi no Pekin hōmon keikaku: Ushinawareta rekishi no tenkanten" (Ambassador Stuart's plan to visit Peking: A lost turning point in history), *Kokusai mondai*.

Studies on the Korean War and China are relatively numerous. Ernest R. May, *"Lessons" of the past: The use and misuse of history in American foreign policy*; and Seizaburō Shinobu, *Chōsen Sensō no boppatsu* (The outbreak of the Korean War) include profound historical interpretations of the basic nature of the Korean War as seen from the vantage points of the United States and Japan. As far as China's position is concerned, Allen S. Whiting, *China crosses the Yalu: The decision to enter the Korean War*; Stuart Schram, *Mao Tse-tung*, are fruitful contributions. See also Robert R. Simmons, *The strained alliance: Peking, P'yongyang, Moscow and the politics of the Korean civil war*.

There are fewer studies of China's strategic change toward the Bandung Line, but Edgar Snow, *The other side of the river: Red China today*; Roderick MacFarquhar, *The Hundred Flowers campaign and the Chinese intellectuals*; Mineo Nakajima, *Gendai Chūgoku ron: Ideorogī to seiji no naiteki kōsatsu* (On contemporary China: The internal dynamics of its ideology and politics) are fundamental analyses of the background of the PRC's diplomatic changes.

Donald S. Zagoria, *The Sino-Soviet conflict, 1956–1961* is the best book covering Sino-Soviet ideological disputes. John Gittings, *The role of the Chinese army*, and Peter Van Ness, *Revolution and Chinese foreign policy: Peking's support for wars of national liberation*, are solid studies of the Chinese Army and China's revolutionary diplomacy, respectively.

7. THE GREAT LEAP FORWARD

Although contemporary Chinese sources became less factual and detailed (and, in many cases, less readily available) once the Great Leap Forward ran into trouble, there is nevertheless a rich lode of Chinese-language materials pertinent to it. First, of course, the national periodical and newspaper press (such as *Hung-ch'i, Hsin-Hua pan-yueh k'an, Jen-min jih-pao, Kuang-ming jih-pao*) provides a wealth of data. Many of these are well indexed for the period (both *Jen-min jih-pao* and *Kuang-ming jih-pao* published their own annual indexes). Research guides (such as James Soong's *Red flag, 1958–68: A research guide* and Peter Berton's and Eugene Wu's *Contemporary China: A research guide*) greatly facilitate efficient use of much of the rest. More specialized publications such as ministerial journals are also very helpful (as Lampton makes evident in his study on the politics of medicine). Such journals are available in public health, finance and trade, and other areas.

China has produced several bodies of materials since 1965 that are important for the study of the period from the Great Leap to the Cultural Revolution. The first is the outpouring of Red Guard and other unofficial materials during the Cultural Revolution in the late 1960s. Many of the Red Guard publications are available in the Center for Chinese Research Materials' twenty-volume *Red Guard publications*. China centers both in the United States and abroad have additional batches of Red Guard materials. The two major volumes of Mao's writings entitled *Mao Tse-tung ssu-hsiang wan-sui* unofficially published in 1967 and 1969 and selectively translated by the Joint Publications Research Service in its two-volume *Miscellany of Mao Tse-tung Thought* are major source materials for Mao's unpublished speeches of this period.

Since the Cultural Revolution, three more bodies of materials of particular use to political scientists have appeared. One is a growing outpouring of reminiscences by political leaders and their aids and colleagues, some of which provide insights into the politics of 1958–65. *P'eng Te-huai tzu-shu* (P'eng Te-huai's own account) is an outstanding example. Others, like *Hui-i Wang Chia-hsiang* (Recalling Wang Chia-hsiang), provide occasional nuggets on this period.

A second important source consists of various publications on Party history. A large number of provincial presses have put out Party histories, such as Hupei's *Chung-kuo kung-ch'an-tang li-shih chiang-i* (Teaching materials on the history of the Chinese Communist Party), and there have been general reference publications consisting of questions and answers on Party history and of details on the succession of Party meetings. Finally, statistical compendia fill in many gaps about this period.

Many secondary works on domestic politics are available for the study of 1958–65. One category consists of good histories of national and subnational politics in general that contain detailed sections on this period. Examples include Byung-joon Ahn, *Chinese politics and the Cultural Revolution*; James P. Harrison, *The long march to power*; Maurice Meisner, *Mao's China*; Edward Rice, *Mao's way*; Richard Solomon, *Mao's revolution and the Chinese political culture*; and Ezra Vogel, *Canton under communism*. More specialized longitudinal monographs on specific issues also provide important information. David M. Lampton's *The politics of medicine in China*; Frederick Teiwes' *Politics and purges in China*; and Harry Harding's *Organizing China* are but three examples.

There is also a secondary English-language literature that focuses directly and solely on the years 1958–65. Roderick MacFarquhar's *Origins of the Cultural Revolution*, 2, provides the most detailed political history available. Richard Baum and Frederick Teiwes, *Ssu-ch'ing: The socialist education movement of 1962–1966*; and Baum, *Prelude to revolution*, give good accounts of the socialist education movement in the early 1960s. Ch'en Yun's major economic pronouncements from 1956 to 1962 are covered in Nicholas Lardy and Kenneth Lieberthal, eds., *Chen Yun's strategy for China's development: A non-Maoist alternative*.

The periodical literature on this period is also especially full, including both studies of specific political incidents (such as David Charles, "The Dismissal of Marshal P'eng Teh-huai") and specialized issues (for example, Frederick Teiwes's contribution on provincial budgets to John M. Lindbeck, ed., *China: Management of a revolutionary society*). Several Ph.D. dissertations, such as Nina Halpern's "Economic specialists and the making of Chinese economic policy, 1955–83" (University of Michigan Political Science Department, 1985), also provide important details and insights.

11. THE SINO-SOVIET SPLIT

The relative recentness of this period precludes access to standard U.S. Department of State sources, while the secretiveness of the Soviet Union and the PRC severely limits the value of Soviet and Chinese materials. Exceptions exist in all cases, but largely as notable deviations from official practice. Thus the Freedom of Information Act permitted Jonathan Pollack ("Perception and process in Chinese foreign policy: The Quemoy decision") to illuminate aspects of the 1958 Quemoy crisis, which in turn reflect Soviet and Chinese behavior. Similarly, Khrushchev's memoirs (*Khrushchev remembers*), self-serving as all such efforts must be, are suggestive despite the problem of authenticity. The most revealing sources, of course, are Mao's unpublished speeches and writings (the two principal volumes, issued in 1967 and 1969, were confusingly both entitled *Mao Tse-tung ssu-hsiang wan-sui*). They were issued by an unidentified faction during the Cultural Revolution turmoil and acquired by Taiwan, where the volumes were photocopied and distributed. Less sensational but no less unique was Donald Zagoria's volume, *The Sino-Soviet conflict, 1956–1961*, which originated in the Central Intelligence Agency, where he had worked previously, and which drew on authoritative but highly secret sources, especially for the confrontations at Bucharest and Moscow.

An invaluable supplement to these reliable but unorthodox means of access to otherwise secret activities is the voluminous polemical correspondence exchanged between the Soviet and Chinese Communist Parties and governments during the early 1960s. Superbly reordered and analyzed by John Gittings (in *Survey of the Sino-Soviet dispute*), the attacks and counter-attacks corroborated much of Zagoria's work and in some instances went beyond it. While each side built the best case for itself and the worst for its opponent, much could be gleaned on the range of issues, their timing, and their import, as was ably done at the time by such writers as William E. Griffith (*The Sino-Soviet rift, Sino-Soviet relations 1964–1965, Albania and the Sino-Soviet rift*); Alexander Dallin (*Diversity in international communism*); and G. F. Hudson, Richard Lowenthal, and Roderick MacFarquhar (*The Sino-Soviet dispute*).

Yet remarkable as are such accounts, whether authorized or not, compared with the usual sterile statements issued by the various concerned governments, their accuracy obviously falls short of archival material. For example, M. S. Kapitsa, in private interviews and speeches examined in detail by Pollack, sharply disagrees with Mao on what was the specific position of each side at the Khrushchev-Mao meeting of August 1958 concerning prospective Sino-Soviet military cooperation. Neither Khrushchev nor Mao, nor for that matter the extensive polemical exchanges, revealed the full extent of Soviet nuclear weapons fabrication assistance, as became clear through photographic intelligence in 1963–64.

In addition to the standard Communist constraints on scholarly research and archival publication, the ongoing relationship between Moscow and Peking inhibits their full and frank recounting of past events. Therefore one is forced to surmise and speculate on the basis of admittedly limited and at times tendentious material. Post-Mao memoirs appearing until 1985 did not throw new light on this period, although isolated nuggets pertinent to earlier years emerged in the works of P'eng Te-huai (*P'eng Te-huai tzu-shu*), Wu Hsiu-ch'üan (*Tsai wai-chiao-pu p̄a nien-ti ching-li*), and Wang Ping-nan ("The 9-year Sino-U.S. talks in retrospect").

In sum, the degree to which analysis at this time justifies the rubric of "history" is highly debatable. This caveat applies more strongly to the less salient relationships wherein Peking was often engaged at a clandestine level in addition to the more public one. For the arc of Asia extending around China from Pakistan to Korea, isolated studies such as David Mozingo's *Chinese policy toward Indonesia, 1964–1967*, using intensive interviews with local officials, dot an otherwise barren academic landscape. Even more difficult than laying out the record of interaction is divining the perceptions and decisions that prompted Chinese behavior. The unique capture by, and publication in, the United States of a secret military journal (*Kung-tso t'ung-hsun*) threw a narrow pinpoint of light on the early 1960s as explained to the People's Liberation Army. But to what extent this journal reflected actual thinking at the highest level is uncertain.

This situation stands in marked contrast with domestic political and economic developments that emerged in much clearer perspective through post-Mao publications. Statistical data, personal reminiscences, and documentary collections offer a more fertile field than the relatively thin soil of foreign policy. The absence of a scholarly Chinese history of PRC involvement in world affairs suggests that the limitations are as severe, or perhaps more so, within the country as abroad. One can only hope that Chou En-lai's papers will one day be made available for such a study, so that a more accurate rendition of these critical years can become available for foreign scholars to build upon.

BIBLIOGRAPHY

An inbuilt ambiguity haunts any bibliography of Chinese writings: entries that are immediately intelligible to the reader of English, like *Central Daily News* or *Liberation Daily*, are not directly clued to the Chinese characters in which the originals are written (*Chung-yang jih-pao, Chieh-fang jih-pao*). Yet, on the other hand, an entry like *Chin-tai shih yen-chiu-so*, though more accurate in the esoteric script of romanization, may be translated variously as Modern History Institute or Institute of Modern History. In this situation we have put romanized accuracy ahead of English-translated intelligibility, but with occasional cross-references.

Another problem is that large compilations of documents are usually edited by committees, departments, or other institutional organs, so that listing such works by compiler or editor would confront the reader with many words but little information. In such cases we prefer to list by title. Compilers and editors are then cited in the body of the entry.

Footnote notation systems, like romanization systems, may appeal only to certain people. Yet they are necessary and have to be arbitrary. The sole test is their accuracy and economy. Numbers of issues within volumes of periodicals we unite with a period. (If pages are within a volume only, they are united with its number by a period; e.g., Mao, *SW*, 5.27.) For journals that use the year as the volume number, the year is treated as a volume number; the citation therefore appears as, say, 1981.4, 17–21.

Materials such as speeches, reports, and articles of and about the Chinese leadership are normally cited with reference to their place of origin in the press or published collections, but a certain number of such materials are listed independently in the bibliography.

CHINESE PUBLISHERS

Chung-hua 中華 (major cities)
Commercial Press 商務印書館 (major cities)
Jen-min 人民 (major cities)
She-hui k'o-hsueh ch'u-pan-she 社會科學出版社 (Peking)
Shih-chieh chih-shih ch'u-pan-she 世界知識出版社 (Peking)

WORKS CITED

"Agricultural cooperativization in Communist China." *CB*, 373 (20 January 1956), 1–31.

Ahn, Byung-joon. *Chinese politics and the Cultural Revolution: Dynamics of policy processes*. Seattle, Wash., and London: University of Washington Press, 1976.

Ai Ch'ing 艾青. "Liao-chieh tso-chia, tsun-chung tso-chia" 了解作家, 尊重作家 (Understand writers, respect writers). *CFJP*, 11 March 1942.

Ai Szu-ch'i 艾思奇. *Ai Szu-ch'i wen-chi* 艾思奇文集 (Ai Szu-ch'i collected works). Peking: Jen-min, 1981.

Ambekar, G. V., and Divekar, V. D. *Documents on China's relations with South and South-East Asia 1949–1962*. Bombay: Allied Publishers, 1964.

American Consulate General. *See* U.S. Consulate General.

American Rural Small-Scale Industry Delegation. *Rural small-scale industry in the People's Republic of China*. Berkeley: University of California Press, 1977.

Americans in China, 1971–1980: A guide to the University of Michigan National Archive on Sino-American relations. Ann Arbor: University of Michigan Center for Chinese Studies, 1981.

An Tzu-wen 安子文. "Training the people's civil servants." *People's China*, 1 January 1953.

Andors, Stephen. *China's industrial revolution: Politics, planning, and management, 1949 to the present*. Asia Library Series. New York: Pantheon Books, 1977.

Annales—Economies, Sociétés, Civilisations. Six times a year. Paris: Armand Colin. 1929–

Ansley, Clive. *The heresy of Wu Han*. Toronto: University of Toronto Press, 1971.

Armstrong, J. D. *Revolutionary diplomacy: Chinese foreign policy and the united front doctrine*. Berkeley: University of California Press, 1977.

Association for Asian Studies Newsletter. (Originally *Asian Studies Newsletter*.) Five times a year. Association for Asian Studies, Inc., University of Michigan, Ann Arbor. 1955–   .

Australian Journal of Chinese Affairs. Semi-annual. Canberra: Australian National University, Contemporary China Centre. 1979–   .

Badgley, John H. "Burma and China." In A. M. Halpern, ed., *Policies toward China: Views from six continents*, 303–28.

Balazs, Etienne. *Chinese civilization and bureaucracy*. New Haven: Yale University Press, 1964.

Banister, Judith. "An analysis of recent data on the population of China." *Population and development review*, 10.2 (June 1984), 241–71.

Bao Ruo-wang 包若望 (Jean Pasqualini), and Chelminski, Rudolph. *Prisoner of Mao*. New York: Coward, McCann, 1973.

Barendsen, Robert D. *Half-work half-study schools in Communist China*. Washington, D.C.: U.S. Department of Health, Education, and Welfare, 1964.

Barendsen, Robert D., "The agricultural middle school in Communist China." *CQ*, 8 (October–December 1961) 106–34.

Barnett, A. Doak. *Communist China and Asia: Challenge to American policy*. New York: Harper, 1960.

Barnett, A. Doak. *China on the eve of Communist takeover*. New York: Praeger, 1963.

Barnett, A. Doak. *Communist China: The early years, 1949–55*. New York: Praeger, 1964.

Barnett, A. Doak. *Uncertain passage: China's transition to the post-Mao era*. Washington, D.C.: The Brookings Institution, 1974.

Barnett, A. Doak. *China's economy in global perspective*. Washington, D.C.: The Brookings Institution, 1981.

Barnett, A. Doak. *The making of foreign policy in China*. Boulder, Colo.: Westview Press, 1984.

Barnett, A. Doak, ed. *Chinese Communist politics in action*. Seattle: University of Washington Press, 1969.

Barnett, A. Doak, with Ezra Vogel. *Cadres, bureaucracy and political power in Communist China*. New York: Columbia University Press, 1967.

Bastid-Bruguière, Marianne. "Currents of social change," in *CHOC* 11.535–602.

Baum, Richard. *Prelude to revolution: Mao, the Party, and the peasant question, 1962–66*. New York: Columbia University Press, 1975.

Baum, Richard. "The Cultural Revolution in the countryside: Anatomy of a limited rebellion," in Thomas Robinson, ed., *The Cultural Revolution in China*, 367–476.

Baum, Richard, and Teiwes, Frederick C. *Ssu-ch'ing: The socialist education movement of 1962–1966*. China Research Monographs, No. 2. Berkeley: Center for Chinese Studies, University of California, 1968.

BBC. *See* British Broadcasting Corporation.

BDRC. Biographical dictionary of Republican China.

Becker, C. H., Tawney, R. H., et al. *The reorganization of education in China*. Report of the League of Nations' Mission of Educational Experts, 1932.

Beijing Review. See *Peking Review*.

Beloff, Max. *Soviet policy in the Far East 1944–1957*. London: Oxford University Press, 1953.

Bennett, Gordon. *Huadong: The story of a Chinese people's commune*. Boulder, Colo.: Westview, 1978.

Bennett, Gordon, ed. *China's finance and trade: A policy reader*. White Plains, N.Y.: M. E. Sharpe, 1978.

Benton, Gregor. "The Yan'an 'literary opposition'." *New Left Review*, 92 (1975).

Bereday, George, et al., eds. *The changing Soviet school*. Boston: Houghton Mifflin, 1960.

Bergère, Marie-Claire. "Une crise de subsistence en Chine (1920–1922)." *Annales ESC*, 38.6 (1973), 1361–1402.

Bergère, Marie-Claire. "The Chinese bourgeoisie, 1911–37," in *CHOC*, 12.722–825.

Bernstein, Richard. *From the center of the earth: The search for the truth about China*. Boston: Little, Brown, 1982.

Bernstein, Thomas P. *Up to the mountains and down to the villages: The transfer of youth from urban to rural China*. New Haven, Conn.: Yale University Press, 1977.

Bernstein, Thomas Paul. "Leadership and mobilization in the collectivization of agriculture in China and Russia: A comparison." Columbia University, Ph.D. dissertation, 1970.

Bernstein, Thomas P. "Cadre and peasant behavior under conditions of insecurity and deprivation in the grain supply crisis of the spring of 1955," in A. Doak Barnett, ed., *Chinese Communist politics in action*, 365–99.

Bernstein, Thomas P. "Stalinism, famine, and Chinese peasants: Grain procurements during the Great Leap Forward." *Theory and Society*, 3 (1984), 339–77.

Berton, Peter, and Wu, Eugene. *Contemporary China: A research guide*. Stanford, Calif.: The Hoover Institution, 1967.

Bianco, Lucien. *Origins of the Chinese revolution, 1915–1949*. Trans. from the French by Muriel Bell. Stanford, Calif.: Stanford University Press, 1971.

Bianco, Lucien. "Peasant movements," in *CHOC*, 13.270–328.

Bibliography of Asian Studies. Annual. Ann Arbor, Mich.: Association for Asian Studies, 1956–   .

Bielenstein, Hans. *The bureaucracy of Han times*. New York: Cambridge University Press, 1980.

Black, Cyril Edwin, ed. *The modernization of Japan and Russia: A comparative study*. New York: Free Press, 1975.

Blumenthal, Eileen. "Models in Chinese moral education: Perspectives from children's books." University of Michigan, Ph.D. dissertation, 1976.

Blumenthal, Irene, and Benson, Charles. *Educational reform in the Soviet Union: Implications for developing countries*. World Bank Staff Working Paper, No. 288. Washington, D.C.: World Bank, 1978.

Bodde, Derk. *Peking diary, 1948–1949: A year of revolution*. Greenwich, Conn.: Fawcett Publications, 1967.

Bonavia, David. *The Chinese*. London: Allen Lane, 1981.

Borg, Dorothy, and Heinrichs, Waldo, eds. *Uncertain years: Chinese-*

American relations, 1947–1950. New York: Columbia University Press, 1980.

Borisov, O. B., and Koloskov, B. T. *Sino-Soviet relations 1945–1973: A brief history.* Trans. from the Russian by Yuri Shirokov. Moscow: Progress Publishers, 1975.

Bowie, Robert R., and Fairbank, John K., eds. *Communist China, 1955–1959: Policy documents with analysis.* Center for International Affairs Series. Cambridge, Mass.: Harvard University Press, 1962.

Boyd, R. G. *Communist China's foreign policy.* New York: Praeger, 1962.

Bradbury, William. *Mass behavior in battle and captivity: The Communist soldier in the Korean War.* Chicago: University of Chicago Press, 1968.

Braudel, Fernand. *The perspective of the world.* Vol. 3 of his *Civilization and capitalism: 15th–18th century.* Trans. from the French, ed. *Le temps du monde.* Paris: Colin, 1984; New York: Harper & Row, 1984.

British Broadcasting Corporation. *Summary of world broadcasts. Part 3. The Far East.* London: British Broadcasting Corporation, 1966–69.

Brodsgaard, Kjeld Erik. "Paradigmatic change: Readjustment and reform in the Chinese economy, 1953–1981." *Modern China,* 9.2 (1983), 3–72.

Brugger, William. *Democracy and organisation in the Chinese industrial enterprise (1948–1953).* Cambridge, Eng.: Cambridge University Press, 1976.

Brzezinski, Zbigniew K. *The Soviet bloc: Unity and conflict.* Rev. and enlarged ed. Cambridge, Mass.: Harvard University Press, 1967.

Buck, (John) Lossing. *Land utilization in China.* 3 vols. London: Oxford University Press, 1937; New York: Institute of Pacific Relations, 1937.

Bullard, Monte Ray. "PRC elite studies: A review of the literature," *Asian Survey,* 19:8 (August 1979), 896–910.

Bulletin of the Institute of Modern History, Academia Sinica. See *Chung-yang yen-chiu-yuan chin-tai-shih yen-chiu-so chi-k'an.*

Burns, John. "Chinese peasant interest articulation, 1949–1974." Columbia University, Ph.D. dissertation, 1979.

Butler, Steven. *Conflict and decision making in China's rural administration, 1969–1976.* Ann Arbor: University of Michigan Press, forthcoming.

Butterfield, Fox. *China: Alive in the bitter sea.* New York: Times Books, 1983.

Cambridge History of China, (CHOC). Vol. 3. *Sui and T'ang China, 589–906, Part 1,* ed. Denis Twitchett. (1979). Vol. 10. *Late Ch'ing 1800–1911, Part 1,* ed. John K. Fairbank. (1978). Vol. 11. *Late Ch'ing 1800–1911, Part 2,* ed. John K. Fairbank and Kwang-Ching Liu. (1980). Vol. 12. *Republican China 1912–1949, Part 1,* ed. John K. Fairbank. (1983). Vol. 13. *Republican China 1912–1949, Part 2,* ed. John K. Fairbank and Albert Feuerwerker. (1986). Cambridge, Eng.: Cambridge University Press.

Carrère d'Encausse, Hélène, and Schram, Stuart Reynolds, comps. *Marxism and Asia: An introduction with readings*. London: Allen Lane, Penguin Press, 1969.

CB. See U.S. Consulate General, *Current Background*.

CCP. Chinese Communist Party. *See* Chung-kuo kung-ch'an tang.

CCP. Central Committee. *See* "Resolutions."

Central Intelligence Agency. *The Sino-Soviet dispute and its significance*. Washington, D.C.: CIA, 1 April 1961, TS #142274–b.

CFJP. Chieh-fang jih-pao.

Chan, Anita. *Children of Mao: Personality development and political activism in the Red Guard generation*. Seattle: University of Washington Press, 1985.

Chan, Anita. "Images of China's social structure: The changing perspectives of Canton students." *World Politics*, 34.3 (April 1982), 295–323.

Chan, Anita, Madsen, Richard, and Unger, Jonathan. *Chen village: The recent history of a peasant community in Mao's China*. Berkeley: University of California Press, 1984.

Chan, Anita, Rosen, Stanley, and Unger, Jonathan. "Students and class warfare: The social roots of the Red Guard conflict in Guangzhou." *CQ*, 83 (September 1980), 397–446.

Chang Chien. "More people go to college." *People's China*, 22 (16 November 1954), 23–25.

Chang, Hao. 張灝 *Liang Ch'i-ch'ao and intellectual transition in China, 1890–1907*. Cambridge, Mass.: Harvard University Press, 1971.

Chang, John K. *Industrial development in pre-Communist China, a quantitative analysis*. Chicago: Aldine, 1969.

Chang, K. C. (Kwang-chih) 張光直. *Art, myth and ritual: The path to political authority in ancient China*. Cambridge, Mass.: Harvard University Press, 1983.

Chang Kia-ngau 張嘉璈. *The inflationary spiral: The experience in China, 1939–1950*. Cambridge, Mass.: MIT Press, 1958.

Chang, Parris. *Radicals and radical ideology in China's Cultural Revolution*. New York: Columbia University Press, 1973.

Chang, Parris. *Power and policy in China*. University Park, Pa., and London: The Pennsylvania State University Press, 1975; rev. ed. 1978.

Chang Shou-yung 張壽鏞. *Huang-ch'ao chang-ku hui-pien* 皇朝掌故彙編 (Collected historical records of the Imperial dynasty). 60 chüan. Shanghai: Ch'iu-shih shu-she 求實書社, 1902. Taipei reprint: Wen-hai ch'u-pan-she 文海出版社, 1964.

Chao Chung and Yang I-fan. *Students in mainland China*. Kowloon, Hong Kong: Union Research Institute, 1956; 3rd ed., 1958.

Chao Hsing-han 趙興漢, and Ts'ao Chen-liang 曹振良. "Ch'ien t'an nung-ch'an p'in shou-kou-chung ti i-wu to chia" 淺談農產品收購中的一物多價 (A preliminary discussion of high prices for the procurement of some agricultural commodities). *Chia-ko li-lun yü shih-chien* 價格理論與實踐 (Price theory and practice), 4 (1982), 26–30.

Chao Kang 趙岡. *The rate and pattern of industrial growth in Communist China*. Ann Arbor: University of Michigan Press, 1965.

Chao Kang. *Agricultural production in Communist China, 1949–1965*. Madison: University of Wisconsin Press, 1970.

Chao Kang and Mah Feng-hwa 馬逢華. "A study of the rouble-yuan exchange rate." *CQ*, 17 (January–March 1964), 192–204.

Chao Kuo-chün. *The mass organizations in Communist China*. Cambridge, Mass.: MIT Press, 1953.

Chao Kuo-chün. *Agrarian policies of mainland China: A documentary study, 1949–1956*. Cambridge, Mass.: Harvard University Press, 1957.

Chao Kuo-chün. *Economic planning and organization in mainland China: A documentary study, 1949–1957*. 2 vols. Center for East Asian Studies. Cambridge, Mass.: Harvard University Press, 1959.

Charles, David A. "The dismissal of Marshal P'eng Teh-huai." *CQ*, 8 (October–December 1961), 63–76.

Che-hsueh yen-chiu 哲學研究 (Philosophical research). Peking: 1956–

Cheek, Timothy. "Deng Tuo: Culture, Leninism and alternative Marxism in the Chinese Communist Party." *CQ*, 87 (September 1981), 470–91.

Cheek, Timothy. "The fading of wild lilies: Wang Shiwei and Mao Zedong's 'Yan'an Talks' in the First CPC Rectification Movement." *The Australian Journal of Chinese Affairs*, 11 (January 1984), 25–58.

Chen, Jack. *Inside the Cultural Revolution*. New York: Macmillan, 1975.

Chen Jo-hsi 陳若曦. *The execution of Mayor Yin and other stories from the Great Proletarian Cultural Revolution*. Bloomington, Ind.: Indiana University Press, 1978.

Chen, S. C., and Ridley, Charles P. *The rural people's communes in Lien-chiang*. Stanford, Calif.: The Hoover Institution, 1969.

Chen, Susan Wolf, trans. *Feng Jicai: Chrysanthemums and other stories*. New York: Harcourt Brace Jovanovich, 1985.

Chen, Theodore Hsi-en 陳錫恩. *Thought reform of the Chinese intellectuals*. London: Oxford University Press; Hong Kong: Hong Kong University Press, 1960.

Chen, Theodore Hsi-en. *Chinese education since 1949: Academic and revolutionary models*. New York: Pergamon Press, 1981.

Chen, Wen-hui C. *Wartime "mass" campaigns in Communist China*. Lackland, Tex.: Air Force Personnel and Training Research Center, 1955.

Ch'en Chen-han 陳振漢, Hsu Yü-nan 徐毓枬, Lo Chih-ju 羅志如, Ku Ch'un-fan 谷春帆, Wu Pao-san 巫寶三, and Ning Chia-feng 寧嘉風. "Wo-men tui-yü tang-ch'ien ching-chi k'o-hsueh kung-tso ti i-hsieh i-chien" 我們對於當前經濟科學工作的一些意見 (Some of our views on current work in the science of economics). *Ching-chi yen-chiu* 經濟研究 (Economic research), 5 (1957), appendixes, 123–33.

Ch'en, Jerome 陳志讓. *Mao Tse-tung and the Chinese revolution*. London: Oxford University Press, 1965.

Ch'en, Jerome, ed. *Mao*. Englewood Cliffs, N.J.: Prentice-Hall, 1969.

Ch'en, Jerome, ed. *Mao papers: Anthology and bibliography*. London: Oxford University Press, 1970.

Ch'en Shih-hui 陳詩惠. 'Kuan-yü fan-tui Kao Kang, Jao Shu-shih fan-tang yin-mou huo-tung ti wen-t'i 關於反對高崗, 饒漱行反黨陰謀活動的問題 (Questions concerning opposition to the anti-Party conspiratorial activities of Kao Kang and Jao Shu-shih). In *Chiao-hsueh ts'an-k'ao* 教學參考 (Teaching reference). N.P.: Chung-kung An-hui sheng-wei tang-hsiao t'u-shu tzu-liao shih 中共安徽省委黨校圖書資料室, December 1980.

[Ch'en Yun 陳雲]. *Ch'en Yun t'ung-chih wen-kao hsuan pien (1965–1962)* 陳雲同志文稿選編 (1956–1962) (Selected manuscripts of comrade Ch'en Yun 1956–1962). Peking: Jen-min, 1981.

Ch'en Yun. *Ch'en Yun wen-kao hsuan-pien (1949–1956)* 陳雲文稿選編 (1949–1956) (Selected manuscripts of Ch'en Yun 1949–1956). Peking: Jen-min, 1982.

Ch'en Yun. *Ch'en Yun wen-hsuan (1949–1956)* 陳雲文選 (1949–1956) (Selected works of Ch'en Yun, 1949–1956). Peking: Jen-min, 1984.

Ch'en Yun. *Ch'en Yun wen-hsuan (1956–1985)* 陳雲文選 (Selected works of Ch'en Yun, 1956–1985). Peking: Jen-min, 1986.

Ch'en Yun. "Chia-su fa-chan tan-fei kung-yeh, i-chiu-liu-i nien wu-yueh" 加速發展氮肥工業, 一九六一年五月 (Speed up the development of the chemical fertilizer industry [May 1961]), in *Ch'en Yun t'ung-chih wen-kao hsuan-pien, 1956–1962*, 108–15.

Ch'en Yun. "Ch-ing-p'u nung-ts'un tiao-ch'a, i-chiu-liu-i nien pa-yueh" 青浦農村調查, 一九六一年八月 (An investigation of rural Ch'ing-p'u [August 1961]), in *Ch'en Yun t'ung-chih wen-kao hsuan-pien, 1956–1962*, 130–46.

Ch'en Yun. "Mu-ch'ien ts'ai-cheng ching-chi-ti ch'ing-k'uang ho k'o-fu k'un-nan ti jo-kan pan-fa (i-chiu-liu-erh nien erh-yueh)" 目前財政經濟的情況和克服困難的若干辦法 (1962 年 2 月) (The current financial and economic situation and some methods for overcoming difficulties [February 1962]), in *Ch'en Yun t'ung-chih wen-kao hsuan-pien, 1956–1962*, 157–72.

Ch'en Yun. "Fa-chan nung-yeh shih t'ou-teng ta-shih" 發展農業是頭等大事 (Agricultural development is a matter of major importance), in Ch'en Yun, *Ch'en Yun t'ung-chih wen-kao hsuan-pien, 1949–1956*, 127–30.

Ch'en Yun. "Shih-hsing liang-shih t'ung-kou t'ung-hsiao" 實行糧食統購統銷 (Implementing planned purchase and planned sale of grain), in *Ch'en Yun t'ung-chih wen-kao hsuan-pien 1949–1956*, 189–203.

Cheng Chu-yuan 鄭竹園. *Scientific and engineering manpower in Communist China, 1949–1963*. Washington, D.C.: National Science Foundation, 1965.

Cheng, J. Chester. *The politics of the Chinese Red Army: A translation of the Bulletin of Activities of the People's Liberation Army*. Stanford, Calif.: The Hoover Institution, 1966.

Chiang Kai-shek 蔣介石. *China's destiny*. Introduction by Lin Yutang 林語堂. Trans. Wang Ch'ung-hui 王寵惠. (Chinese edition, 1943). New York: Macmillan, 1947.

Ch'iang Yuan-kan 強遠淦, and Lin Pang-kuang 林邦光. "Shih-lun i-chiu-wu-wu-nien tang-nei kuan-yü nung-yeh ho-tso-hua wen-t'i ti cheng-lun" 試論一九五五年黨內關於農業合作化問題的爭論 (A discussion of the debate within the Party in 1955 concerning the issue of agricultural cooperativization). *Tang-shih yen-chiu* 黨史研究 (Research on party history), 1981.1, 10–17.

Ch'iang Yuan-kan 強遠淦 and Ch'en Hsueh-wei 陳雪薇. "Ch'ung-p'ing i-chiu-wu-liu-nien ti 'fan mao-chin'" 重評一九五六年的'反冒進' (A fresh review of the "anti rash advance" of 1956), *Tang-shih yen-chiu*, 1980. 6, 34–40.

Chieh-fang jih-pao 解放日報 (Liberation daily). Yenan: 1941–45. Cited as *CFJP*.

Ch'ien Mu 錢穆. *Traditional government in Imperial China: A critical analysis*. Trans. Chün-tu Hsueh 薛君度 and George O. Totten, III, with Wallace Johnson et al. Hong Kong: The Chinese University Press; New York: St. Martin's Press, 1982.

Ch'ien Tuan-sheng 錢端升. *The government and politics of China 1912–1949*. Cambridge, Mass.: Harvard University Press, 1950; Stanford, Calif.: Stanford University Press paperback, 1970.

Chin-shih Chung-kuo ching-shih ssu-hsiang yen-t'ao-hui lun-wen-chi 近世中國經世思想研討會論文集 (Proceedings of the Conference of the theory of statecraft of modern China), 25–27 August 1983. Taipei: IMH, Academia Sinica, 1984.

China: Socialist economic development. Annex G. *Education Sector*. World Bank Document (1 June 1981). Washington, D.C.: The World Bank, 1981. *See also* World Bank.

China, socialist economic development. See World Bank.

China Daily. Peking: 1981– .

China News Analysis. Hong Kong, 1953–82; 1984– . Fortnightly. 1953–82 published by Fr. Ladany.

China Quarterly, The. Quarterly. London: Congress for Cultural Freedom (Paris), 1960–68; Contemporary China Institute, School of Oriental and African Studies, 1968– .

China Topics. Irregular. London: n.p., "T. B.," 1961–

China White Paper. See U.S. Department of State.

Chinese Agricultural Yearbook Compilation Commission. See: *Chung-kuo nung-yeh nien-chien 1980*.

Chinese Communist Party Central Committee and the State Council. "Kuan-yü chin-tung ming-ch'un ta-kuei-mo ti k'ai-chan hsing-hsiu nung-t'ien shui-li ho chi-fei yun-tung ti chueh-ting" 關於今冬明春大規模地開展與修農田水利和積肥運動的決定 (Decision concerning the development this winter and next spring of a movement to develop large scale initiation and repair of agriculture water conservancy projects and the collection of manure), in *Jen-min shou-ts'e, 1958* 人民手冊 (1958) (People's handbook, 1958). Peking: Ta-kung-pao ch'u-pan-she, 1958.

Chinese law and government. Quarterly. Armonk, N.Y.: M. E. Sharpe, 1968–

Chinese Statistical Yearbook. See *Chung-kuo t'ung-chi nien-chien*, cited as TCNC.

Chinese studies in philosophy: A journal of translations. Quarterly. Armonk, N.Y.: M. E. Sharpe, 1969–

Chinese studies in history: A journal of translations. (Formerly *Chinese Studies in History and Philosophy*.) Quarterly. Armonk, N.Y.: M. E. Sharpe, 1967–

Ching-chi ts'an-k'ao tzu-liao 經濟參考資料 (Economic reference materials), vol. 1. Peking: Peking University Department of Economics Materials Office, 1979.

Ching-chi yen-chiu 經濟研究 (Economic research). Peking: 1955–

Ch'ing-tai ch'ou-pan i-wu shih-mo 清代籌辦夷務始末·(Complete record of the management of barbarian affairs in the Ch'ing dynasty). 80 *chüan* for the late Tao-kuang period (1836–50); 80 *chüan* for the Hsien-feng period (1851–61); 100 *chüan* for the T'ung-chih period (1862–74). Peiping: Palace Museum photolithograph, 1930.

CHOC. Cambridge History of China.

Chou En-lai 周恩來. "PRC Foreign Minister Chou En-lai's report on the foreign policy at the 33rd Meeting of the Committee of the Central People's Government (19 April 1955)." *Collected foreign relations documents of the People's Republic of China*, 3. Peking: Shih-chieh chih-shih ch'u-pan-she 世界知識出版社, 1958.

Chou En-lai. *Selected works of Zhou Enlai.* Vol. 1. Peking: Foreign Languages Press, 1981.

Chou En-lai. "Report on the proposals for the second five-year plan for development of the national economy," in *Eighth National Congress of the Communist Party of China* vol. 1 *(Documents)*, 277–348.

Chou, Eric. *A man must choose.* New York: Knopf, 1963.

Chou Shun-hsin 周舜莘. *The Chinese inflation, 1937–1949.* New York: Columbia University Press, 1963.

Chou T'ai-ho 周太和, ed. *Tang-tai chung-kuo ti ching-chi t'i-chih kai-ko* 當代中國的經濟體制改革 (Reform of the economic system in contemporary China). Peking: Social Science Publishing House, 1984.

Chow Ching-wen 周鯨文. *Ten years of storm: The true story of the Communist regime in China.* Westport, Conn.: Greenwood Press, 1960.

Chu Ch'eng-chia 朱成甲, ed. *Chung-kung tang-shih yen-chiu lun-wen hsuan* 中共黨史研究論文選 (Selected essays on research on the history of the Chinese Communist Party). 3 vols. Changsha: Hu-nan Jen-min, 1984.

Ch'üan-kuo chu-yao pao-k'an tzu-liao so-yin 全國主要報刊資料索引 (Index to national important periodical materials). Shanghai: Shang-hai-shih pao-k'an t'u-shu-kuan 上海市報刊圖書館，1955–

Ch'üan-kuo hsin shu-mu 全國新書目 (National bibliography of new books). Peking: Wen-hua-pu ch'u-pan-shih-yeh kuan-li-chü t'u-shu-kuan 文化部出版事業管理局圖書館，1955–

Ch'üan-kuo tsung shu-mu 全國總書目 (Cumulative national bibliography). Peking: Chung-hua, 1956–

Chung, Chong-wook. *Maoism and development: The politics of industrial management in China.* Seoul: Seoul National University Press, 1980.

Chung-hua jen-min kung-ho-kuo chiao-yü ta-shih-chi, 1949–1982 中華人民共和國教育大事記. 1949–1982 (Education chronology of the People's Republic of China, 1949–1982). Peking: Chiao-yü k'o-hsueh ch'u-pan-she 教育科學出版社，1983.

Chung-hua jen-min kung-ho-kuo fa-kuei hui-pien 中華人民共和國法規彙編 (Compendium of laws and regulations of the PRC). Peking, 1956–58.

Chung-hua jen-min kung-ho-kuo kuo-chia t'ung-chi chü. 中華人民共和國國家統計局 *Chung-kuo t'ung-chi nien-chien 1981.* 中國統計年鑑 1981 (Chinese statistical yearbook 1981). Peking: Chung-kuo t'ung-chi ch'u-pan-she, 1982. Cited as *TCNC 1981.*

Chung-hua jen-min kung-ho-kuo kuo-chia t'ung-chi chü. *Chung-kuo t'ung-chi nien-chien 1983.* 中國統計年鑑 1983 (Chinese statistical yearbook 1983). Peking: Chung-kuo t'ung-chi ch'u-pan-she, 1983. Cited as *TCNC 1983.*

Chung-hua jen-min kung-ho-kuo kuo-chia t'ung-chi chü. "Chung-kuo ching-chi t'ung-chi tzu-liao hsuan-pien" 中國經濟統計資料選編 (A compilation of Chinese economic statistics), in Hsueh Mu-ch'iao, ed., *Chung-kuo ching-chi nien-chien 1982.*

Chung-hua jen-min kung-ho-kuo tui-wai kuan-hsi wen-chien-chi 中華人民共和國對外關係文件集 (Collected foreign relations documents of the People's Republic of China). 1. Peking: Shih-chieh chih-shih ch'u-pan-she 世界知識出版社，1957–　.

Chung K'an 仲侃. *K'ang Sheng p'ing-chuan* 康生評傳 (Critical biography of K'ang Sheng). Peking: Hung-ch'i ch'u-pan-she 紅旗出版社，1982.

Chung-kuo chiao-yü nien-chien 1949–81 中國教育年鑑 1949–1981 (Chinese education yearbook 1949–81). Peking: Chung-kuo ta-pai-k'o ch'üan-shu ch'u-pan-she 中國大百科全書出版社，1984.

Chung-kuo ching-chi nien-chien 中國經濟年鑑 (Chinese economic yearbook). Peking and Hong Kong: 1984–　. For 1982 ed., see Hsueh Mu-ch'iao. For 1981, 1983 eds, see 5th and 6th items above.

Chung-kuo ch'ing-nien pao 中國青年報 (China youth news). Peking: 21 April 1951 (suspended August 1966, resumed October 1978)–　.

Chung-kuo jen-min kung-ho-kuo kuo-wu-yuan kung-pao 中華人民共和國國務院公報 (*Gazette of the State Council of the People's Republic of China*). Published by the State Council, irregular, 1955–　.

Chung-kuo k'o-hsueh yuan ti-li yen-chiu-so ching-chi ti-li yen-chiu-shih 中國科學院地理研究所經濟地理研究室 (Chinese Academy of Sciences, Geography Research Institute, Economic Geography Research Office). *Chung-kuo nung-yeh ti-li tsung-lun* 中國農業地理總論 (A treatise on China's agricultural geography). Peking: Science Publishing House, 1980.

Chung-kuo kung-ch'an-tang chung-yang wei-yuan-hui 中國共產黨中央委員會 (The Central Committee of the CCP). "Chung-kung chung-yang i-chiu-liu-ssu-nien erh-yueh erh-shih-chiu-jih kei Su-kung chung-yang-ti hsin" 中共中央一九六四年二月二十九日給蘇共中央的信 (Letter of the Central Committee of the CCP to the Central Committee of the CPSU 29 February 1964).

Chung-kuo kung-ch'an-tang li-shih chiang-i 中國共產黨歷史講義 (Teaching materials on the history of the Chinese Communist Party). Wuhan: Hu-pei jen-min. 1984.

Chung-kuo kung-ch'an-tang liu-shih-nien ta-shih chien-chieh 中國共產黨六十年大事簡介 (Brief introduction to major events in the CCP's sixty years). Published by Cheng-chih hsueh-yuan Chung-kung tang-shih chiao-yen shih 政治學院中共黨史教研室 (Political academy, CCP history teaching and research office). Peking: Chieh-fang-chün cheng-chih hsueh-yuan ch'u-pan-she 解放軍政治學院出版社, 1985.

Chung-kuo mei-t'an kung-yeh nien-chien 中國煤炭工業年鑑 (Chinese coal industry yearbook). Peking: Mei-t'an kung-yeh ch'u-pan-she 煤炭工業出版社, 1983– .

Chung-kuo nung-yeh nien-chien 1980 中國農業年鑑 1980 (Chinese agricultural yearbook 1980). Chinese Agricultural Yearbook Compilation Commission. Peking: Agricultural Publishing House, 1981.

Chung-kuo t'ung-chi nien-chien. See: Chung-hua jen-min kung-ho-kuo kuo-chia t'ung-chi chü.

Clark, Grover. *The balance sheet of imperialism: Facts and figures on colonies*. New York: Columbia University Press, 1936.

Clark, Grover. *A place in the sun*. New York: Macmillan, 1936.

Clark, M. Gardner. *The development of China's steel industry and Soviet technical aid*. Ithaca, N.Y.: Committee on the Economy of China of the Social Science Research Council, 1973.

Clubb, O. Edmund. *China and Russia: The great game*. New York: Columbia University Press, 1971.

Coale, Ansley. *Rapid population change in China 1952–1982*. Washington, D.C.: National Academy of Sciences Press, 1984.

Coble, Parks M. *The Shanghai capitalists and the Nationalist Government, 1927–1937*. Cambridge, Mass.: Council on East Asian Studies, Harvard University, 1980.

Cohen, Arthur A. *The communism of Mao Tse-tung*. Chicago: University of Chicago Press, 1964.

Cohen, Arthur A. "How original is 'Maoism?'" *Problems of Communism*, 10.6 (November 1961), 34–42.

Cohen, Jerome Alan, ed. *The criminal process in the People's Republic of China, 1949–1963: An introduction.* Cambridge, Mass.: Harvard University Press, 1968.

Cohen, Paul A. *Between tradition and modernity: Wang T'ao and reform in Late Ch'ing China.* Cambridge, Mass.: Harvard University Press, 1974.

Cohen, Paul A. *Discovering history in China: American historical writing on the recent Chinese past.* New York: Columbia University Press, 1984.

Cohen, Paul A., and Schrecker, John E., eds. *Reform in nineteenth-century China.* Cambridge, Mass.: East Asian Research Center, Harvard University, 1976.

Cohen, Stephen F. *Bukharin and the Bolshevik revolution: A political biography 1888–1938.* New York: Vintage Books, 1975.

Commission Internationale Contre le Regime Concentrationnaire. *White book on forced labour and concentration camps in the People's Republic of China.* Paris: n.p., 1957–58.

Committee on Scholarly Communication with the People's Republic of China (CSCPRC). Various trip reports by academic delegations: *Solid state physics in China* (1975); *Acupuncture anesthesia in the People's Republic of China* (1976); *Solid state physics in the People's Republic of China* (1976); *Insect control in the People's Republic of China* (1977); *Pure and applied mathematics in the People's Republic of China* (1977); *Paleoanthropology in the People's Republic of China* (1977); *Oral contraceptives and steroid chemistry in the People's Republic of China* (1977); *Wheat in the People's Republic of China* (1977); *Astronomy in China* (1979); *Earthquake engineering and hazards reduction in China* (1980); *Oceanography in China* (1980); *Nuclear science in China* (1980); *Animal agriculture in China* (1980); *Report of the CSCPRC Economics Delegation to the People's Republic of China* (1980); *Traditional and contemporary painting in China* (1980); *Engineering education in the People's Republic of China* (1983); *Sociology and anthropology in the People's Republic of China* (1985); *American studies in China* (1985). Washington, D.C.: National Academy of Sciences. See also the overlapping list on p. 563, n. 42.

Communist China 1955–1959; policy documents with analysis. With a foreword by Robert R. Bowie and John K. Fairbank. Cambridge, Mass.: Harvard University Press, 1965.

Comparative Education Review. Quarterly. Comparative and International Education Society. Chicago: University of Chicago Press. 1956– .

"Constitution of the People's Republic of China" (September 20, 1954), in Harold C. Hinton, ed., *The People's Republic of China, 1949–1979: A documentary survey,* 1.99–106.

Contemporary China. Vol. 1. *1955.* Hong Kong: Oxford University Press, 1956. Vol. 2. *1956–1957,* 1958. Vol. 3. *1958–1959,* 1960. Vol. 4. *1959–1960,* 1961. Vol. 5. *1961–1962,* 1963. Vol. 6. *1962–1964,* 1968.

CQ. China Quarterly.

Creel, Herrlee G. *The origins of statecraft in China*. Vol. I, *The Western Chou empire*. Chicago: University of Chicago Press, 1970.

Cressey, George B. *Land of the 500 million: A geography of China*. New York: McGraw Hill, 1955.

CSCPRC. See Committee on Scholarly Communication with the People's Republic of China.

Current Background. See U.S. Consulate General.

Dallin, Alexander, with Harris, Jonathan, and Hodnett, Grey, eds. *Diversity in international communism: A documentary record, 1961–1963*. New York: Columbia University Press, 1963.

Dalrymple, Dana G. "The Soviet famine of 1932–1934." *Soviet Studies*, 15.3 (January 1964), 250–84.

Dardess, John W. *Confucianism and autocracy: Professional elites in the founding of the Ming dynasty*. Berkeley: University of California Press, 1983.

Davis, John Francis. *The Chinese: A general description of the empire of China and its inhabitants*. 2 vols. New York: Harper, 1836.

Davis-Friedmann, Deborah. *Long lives: Chinese elderly and the Communist revolution*. Cambridge, Mass.: Harvard University Press, 1983.

Dawson, Raymond Stanley. *The Chinese chameleon: An analysis of European conceptions of Chinese civilization*. London and New York: Oxford University Press, 1967.

DeBary, William Theodore, and the Conference on Seventeenth Century Chinese Thought. *The unfolding of Neo-Confucianism*. New York: Columbia University Press, 1975.

Deng Xiaoping. See Teng Hsiao-p'ing.

Dennerline, Jerry. "Fiscal reform and local control: The gentry-bureaucratic alliance survives the conquest," in Frederic Wakeman and Carolyn Grant, eds., *Conflict and control in Late Imperial China*, 86–120.

Dernberger, Robert F., ed. *China's developmental experience in comparative perspective*. Cambridge, Mass.: Harvard University Press, 1980.

Dittmer, Lowell. *Liu Shao-ch'i and the Chinese Cultural Revolution: The politics of mass criticism*. Berkeley: University of California Press, 1975.

Donnithorne, Audrey. *China's economic system*. New York: Praeger, 1967.

Donnithorne, Audrey. "China's cellular economy: Some economic trends since the Cultural Revolution," *CQ* 52 (October–December 1972), 605–19.

Donnithorne, Audrey, and Lardy, Nicholas. "Comment: Centralization and decentralization in China's fiscal management," and "Reply," *CQ*, 66 (June 1976), 328–54.

Doolin, Dennis J., trans. *Communist China: The politics of student opposition*. Stanford, Calif.: Hoover Institution, 1964.

Doolin, Dennis J. *Territorial claims in the Sino-Soviet conflict*. Stanford, Calif.: Hoover Institution, 1965.

Doolin, Dennis J., and North, Robert C. *The Chinese People's Republic.* Stanford, Calif.: Hoover Institution, 1966.

Drake, Fred W. *China charts the world: Hsu Chi-yü and his geography of 1848.* Cambridge, Mass.: East Asian Research Center, Harvard University, 1975.

Dreyer, Edward L. *Early Ming China: A political history 1355–1435.* Stanford, Calif.: Stanford University Press, 1982.

Dreyer, June Teufel. *China's forty millions: Minority nationalities and national integration in the People's Republic of China.* Cambridge, Mass.: Harvard University Press, 1976.

Eastman, Lloyd E. *Throne and mandarins: China's search for a policy during the Sino-French controversy, 1880–1885.* Cambridge, Mass.: Harvard University Press, 1967.

Ecklund, George. *Financing the Chinese government budget: Mainland China, 1950–1959.* Chicago: Aldine, 1966.

Eckstein, Alexander. *The national income of Communist China.* Glencoe, Ill.: The Free Press, 1961.

Eckstein, Alexander. *Communist China's economic growth and foreign trade: Implications for U.S. policy.* New York: McGraw-Hill, 1966.

Eckstein, Alexander. *China's economic revolution.* New York: Cambridge University Press, 1977.

Eckstein, Alexander, ed. *Quantitative measures of China's economic output.* Ann Arbor: University of Michigan Press, 1980.

Eckstein, Alexander, Chao Kang, and Chang, John. "The economic development of Manchuria: The rise of a frontier economy." *Journal of economic history*, 34.1 (March 1974), 239–64.

Eckstein, Alexander, Galenson, Walter, and Liu, Ta-chung 劉大中, eds. *Economic trends in Communist China.* Chicago: Aldine, 1968.

ECMM. See U.S. Consulate General, *Extracts from China Mainland Magazines.*

Eighth National Congress of the Communist Party of China. Vol. I: *Documents.* vol. II: *Speeches.* Peking: Foreign Languages Press, 1981.

Eisenstadt, S. N. *Modernization: Growth and diversity.* Bloomington: Indiana University Press, 1963.

Eisenstadt, S. N. *Modernization: Protest and change.* Englewood Cliffs, N.J.: Prentice-Hall, 1966.

Eisenstadt, S. N. *Revolution and the transformation of societies: A comparative study of civilizations.* New York: Free Press, 1978.

Elman, Benjamin A. *From philosophy to philology: Intellectual and social aspects of change in late Imperial China.* Cambridge, Mass.: Council on East Asian Studies, Harvard University, 1984.

Emerson, John Philip. *Nonagricultural employment in mainland China, 1949–1958.* International Population Statistics Reports, Series P-90, No. 21. Washington, D.C.: U.S. Government Printing Office, 1965.

Eoyang, Eugene, ed. *Selected poems of Ai Qing*. Bloomington: University of Indiana Press, 1982.

Evans, Humphrey. *See* Loh, Robert.

Extracts from China Mainland magazines. See U.S. Consulate General.

Fairbank, John K. *China: The people's Middle Kingdom and the U.S.A.* Cambridge, Mass.: Harvard University Press, 1967.

Fairbank, John King, ed. *Chinese thought and institutions*. Chicago: University of Chicago Press, 1957.

Fairbank, John King. *The United States and China*. Cambridge, Mass.: Harvard University Press, 1979. 4th ed., enlarged, 1983.

Fairbank, John K., ed. *The Chinese world order: Traditional China's foreign relations*. Cambridge, Mass.: Harvard University Press, 1968.

Fairbank, J. K., Banno, M. and Yamamoto, S. *Japanese studies of modern China*. Tokyo: Tuttle, 1955; reissued Cambridge, Mass.: Harvard University Press, 1971.

Fairbank, J. K., Bruner, K. F., and Matheson, E. M., eds. *The I. G. in Peking: Letters of Robert Hart, Chinese Maritime Customs, 1868–1907*. 2 vols. Cambridge, Mass.: Harvard University Press, 1975.

Falkenheim, Victor. *Citizens and groups in contemporary China*. Ann Arbor: University of Michigan Press, 1985.

Falkenheim, Victor. "County administration in Fukien," *CQ*, 59 (July–September 1974), 518–43.

Fan, K., ed. *Mao Tse-tung and Lin Piao: Post-revolutionary writings*. Garden City, N.J.: Anchor Books, 1972.

Fang Wei-chung 房維中, ed. *Chung-hua jen-min kung-ho-kuo ching-chi ta-shih-chi 1949–1980* 中華人民共和國經濟大事記 (1949–1980) (A record of major economic events in the People's Republic of China, 1949–1980). Peking: She-hui k'o-hsueh, 1984.

FBIS. Foreign Broadcast Information Service.

Feuerwerker, Albert. *China's early industrialization: Sheng Hsuan-huai (1844–1916) and Mandarin enterprise*. Cambridge, Mass.: Harvard University Press, 1958.

Feuerwerker, Albert. "Economic trends in the late Ch'ing empire, 1870–1911," in *CHOC* 11.1–69.

Feuerwerker, Albert. "The foreign presence in China," in *CHOC* 12.128–207.

Feuerwerker, Albert. "The state and the economy in Late Imperial China." *Theory and Society*, 13 (1984), 297–326.

Feuerwerker, Yi-tse Mei 梅儀慈. *Ding Ling's fiction*. Cambridge, Mass.: Harvard University Press, 1982.

Field, Robert Michael, McGlynn, Kathleen M., and Abnett, William B. "Political conflict and industrial growth in China: 1965–1977," in Joint Economic Committee of the U.S. Congress, *The Chinese economy post-Mao*, 1.239–84.

Fincher, John H. *Chinese democracy: The self-government movement in local, provincial, and national politics 1905–1914.* London: Croom Helm; Canberra: Australian National University Press, 1981.

Fingar, Charles Thomas. "Politics and policy-making in the People's Republic of China, 1954–1955." Stanford University, Ph.D. dissertation, 1977.

First five-year plan for development of the national economy of the People's Republic of China in 1953–1957. Peking: Foreign Languages Press, 1956.

Fletcher, Joseph, F., Jr. "The heyday of the Ch'ing order in Mongolia, Sinkiang and Tibet," in *CHOC* 10.351–408.

Fletcher, Joseph F., Jr., and Li, Gertraude Roth. "The rise of the Manchus," in *CHOC* 9, in press.

Floyd, David, ed. *Mao against Khrushchev,* New York: Praeger, 1963.

Fogel, Joshua A. "A new direction in Japanese sinology." *HJAS*, 44.1 (June 1984), 225–47.

Fokkema, Douwe W. *Literary doctrine in China and Soviet influence 1956–1960.* The Hague: Mouton, 1965.

Foreign Broadcast Information Service. Washington, D.C.: U.S. Department of Commerce. 1958– . Cited as *FBIS.*

Foreign Broadcast Information Service: Communist China. Washington, D.C.: FBIS, 1966–69.

Foreign Relations of the United States, 1866– . Washington, D.C.: U.S. Government Printing Office. Cited as *FRUS.*

Fraser, John. *The Chinese.* New York: Summit Books, 1980.

Fraser, Stewart, ed. *Chinese communist education: Records of the first decade.* Nashville, Tenn.: Vanderbilt University Press, 1965.

Freedman, Maurice. *Lineage organization in southeastern China.* London: Athlone Press, 1958.

Freedman, Maurice. *Chinese lineage and society: Fukien and Kwangtung.* London: Athlone Press, 1966.

Fried, Morton. *The fabric of Chinese society: A study of social life of a Chinese county seat.* New York: Praeger, 1953.

FRUS. Foreign Relations of the United States.

Gaenslen, Frederick. "Culture and decision making: Social influence in China, Japan, Soviet Russia, and the United States." University of Michigan, Ph.D. dissertation, 1984.

Gaimushō chōsa kyoku daiikka 外務省調査局第一課. *Chōsen jihen no keii* 朝戰事變之經緯 (Process of the Korean War). Tokyo: Gaimushō, 1951 (unpublished).

Gale, G. S. *No flies in China.* London: Allen & Unwin, 1955.

Galenson, Walter. *See* Eckstein, Alexander.

Gardner, John. "Educated youth and urban-rural inequalities, 1958–66," in John W. Lewis, ed., *The city in communist China,* 235–86.

Garside, Roger. *Coming alive: China after Mao*. New York: McGraw-Hill, 1981.

Geddes, W. R. *Peasant life in communist China*. Ithaca. N.Y.: Cornell Society for Applied Anthropology, 1963.

Gendai Chūgoku jimmei jiten 現代中國人名辭典 (Modern China biographic dictionary). Tokyo: Gaimushō, 1966.

George, Alexander L. *The Chinese Communist army in action: The Korean War and its aftermath*. New York: Columbia University Press, 1967.

Gernet, Jacques. *A history of Chinese civilization*. New York: Cambridge University Press, 1982. (Trans. J. R. Foster of Gernet, *Le monde Chinois*. Paris: A. Colin, 1972, 1980.)

Gittings, John. *The role of the Chinese army*. New York: Oxford University Press, 1967.

Gittings, John. *Survey of the Sino-Soviet dispute: A commentary and extracts from the recent polemics 1963–1967*. London: Oxford University Press, 1968.

Gittings, John. "The great power triangle and Chinese foreign policy." *CQ*, 39 (July–September 1969), 41–54.

Goldman, Merle. *Literary dissent in Communist China*. Cambridge, Mass.: Harvard University Press. 1967.

Goldman, Merle. *China's intellectuals: Advise and dissent*. Cambridge, Mass.: Harvard University Press, 1981.

Goodman, David S. G. *Beijing street voices*. London: Marion Boyars, 1981.

Goodman, David, ed. *Groups and politics in the People's Republic of China*. New York: M. E. Sharpe, 1984.

Goodrich, L. Carrington, and Fang Chaoying, eds. *Dictionary of Ming biography, 1368–1644*. 2 vols. New York: Columbia University Press, 1976.

Grant, Nigel. *Soviet education*. Middlessex, Eng.: Penguin Books, 4th ed. 1979.

Great trial in Chinese history, A: The trial of the Lin Biao and Jiang Qing counter-revolutionary cliques, Nov. 1980–Jan. 1981. Peking: New World, 1981.

Greenough, Paul R. *Prosperity and misery in modern Bengal: The famine of 1943–1944*. New York: Oxford University Press, 1982.

Gregory, Paul R. and Stuart, Robert C. *Soviet economic structure and performance*. New York: Harper & Row, 1974.

Grieder, Jerome B. *Intellectuals and the state in modern China: A narrative history*. New York: Free Press; London: Collier Macmillan, 1981.

Griffith, William. *Albania and the Sino-Soviet rift*. Cambridge, Mass.: The MIT Press, 1963.

Griffith, William E. *The Sino-Soviet rift*. Cambridge, Mass.: The MIT Press, 1964; London: Allan & Unwin, 1964.

Griffith, William. *Sino-Soviet relations, 1964–1965*. Cambridge, Mass.: The MIT Press, 1967.

Guillain, Robert. *Six hundred million Chinese*. Trans. from French by M. Savill. New York: Criterion books, 1957. Published in England as *The blue ants*. London: Secker & Warburg, 1957.

Guillain, Robert. *When China wakes*. New York: Walker, 1966.

Guillermaz, Jacques. *The Chinese Communist Party in power, 1949–1976*. Trans. Anne Destenay. Boulder, Colo.: Westview Press, 1976.

Gurtov, Melvin. *China and Southeast Asia, the politics of survival: A study of foreign policy interaction*. Lexington, Mass.: D.C. Health (Lexington Books), 1971; Baltimore: Johns Hopkins University Press, 1975.

Halpern, A. M., ed. *Policies toward China: Views from six continents*. New York: McGraw-Hill, 1965.

Halpern, Nina. "Economic specialists and the making of Chinese economic policy, 1955–83." University of Michigan Ph.D. dissertation, 1985.

Hao Meng-pi 郝夢筆 and Tuan Hao-jan 段浩然, eds. *Chung-kuo kung-ch'an-tang liu-shih-nien* 中國共產黨六十年 (Sixty years of the Chinese Communist Party). 2 vols. Peking: Chieh-fang-chün ch'u-pan-she 解放軍出版社, 1984.

Hao Yen-p'ing 郝延平. *The commercial revolution in nineteenth century China: The rise of Sino-Western mercantile capitalism*. Berkeley, Los Angeles, London: University of California Press, 1986.

Harding, Harry. *Organizing China: The problem of bureaucracy, 1949–1976*. Stanford, Calif.: Stanford University Press, 1981.

Harrison, James Pinckney. *The long march to power: A history of the Chinese Communist Party, 1921–72*. New York: Praeger, 1972.

Harvard Journal of Asiatic Studies. Semi-annual from 1977; previously annual. Cambridge, Mass.: Harvard-Yenching Institute, 1936–

Hauser, Ernest O. *Shanghai: City for sale*. New York. Harcourt Brace, 1940.

HC. Hung-ch'i.

Henderson, Gail, and Cohen, Myron. *The Chinese hospital*. New Haven, Conn.: Yale University Press, 1984.

Hevi, Emmanuel John. *An African student in China*. New York: Praeger, 1963.

HHPYK. Hsin-hua pan-yueh k'an.

HHYP. Hsin-hua yueh-pao.

Hinton, Harold C. *Communist China in world politics*. Boston: Houghton Mifflin, 1966.

Hinton, Harold C. *China's turbulent quest: An analysis of China's foreign relations since 1949*. New York: Macmillan, rev. ed. 1972 (1970); paperback, Bloomington: Indiana University Press, 1972.

Hinton, Harold C., ed. *The People's Republic of China, 1949–1979: A documentary survey*. 5 vols. Wilmington, Del.: Scholarly Resources, Inc., 1980.

Hinton, William. *Fanshen*. New York: Monthly Review Press, 1966.

HJAS. Harvard Journal of Asiatic Studies.

Ho Chih 何直 (Ch'in Chao-yang). "Hsien-shih chu-i-kuang – k'uo ti tao-lu" 現實主義 – 廣闊的道路 (Realism – the broad road). *Jen-min wen-hsueh.* 9 (1956), 1–13.

Ho, Ping-ti 何炳棣. *Studies on the population of China 1368–1953.* Cambridge, Mass.: Harvard University Press, 1959.

Ho, Ping-ti. *The ladder of success in imperial China: Aspects of social mobility, 1368–1911.* New York: Columbia University Press, 1962.

Hobbs, Lisa. *I saw Red China.* New York: McGraw-Hill, 1966.

Hollister, W. W. *China's gross national product and social accounts, 1950–1957.* Glencoe, Ill.: Free Press, 1958.

Hou Chi-ming 侯繼明. "Manpower, employment, and unemployment," in Alexander Eckstein, Walter Galenson, and Ta-chung Liu, eds., *Economic trends in Communist China,* 329–96.

Hou Chi-ming and Yu Tzong-shian 于宗先, eds. *Modern Chinese economic history.* Taipei: The Institute of Economics, Academia Sinica, 1979.

Houn, Franklin. *Chinese political traditions.* Washington, D.C.: Public Affairs Press, 1965.

Howe, Christopher. *Employment and economic growth in urban China, 1949–1957.* Cambridge, Eng.: Cambridge University Press, 1971.

Howe, Christopher, ed. *Shanghai: Revolution and development in an Asian metropolis.* Cambridge, Eng.: Cambridge University Press, 1981.

Howe, Christopher. "Industrialization under conditions of long-run population stability: Shanghai's achievement and prospect," in Christopher Howe, ed., *Shanghai: Revolution and development in an Asian metropolis,* 153–87.

Hsiang Ching-ch'üan 項鏡泉. "Liu-shih nien-tai t'iao-cheng shih-ch'i wen-ting wu-chia ching-yen ch'u-t'an" 六十年代調整時期穩定物價經驗初探 (A preliminary assessment of experience in commodity price stabilization in the period of readjustment in the 1960s). *Chia-ko li-lun yü shih-chien* 價格理論與實踐 (Price theory and practice), 2 (1982), 22–25.

Hsiao, Gene, and Witunski, Michael. *Sino-American normalization and its policy implications.* New York: Praeger, 1983

Hsiao, Katherine H. *Money and monetary policy in Communist China.* New York: Columbia University Press, 1971.

Hsiao, Kung-chuan 蕭公權. *Rural China: Imperial control in the nineteenth century.* Seattle: University of Washington Press, 1960.

Hsiao, Kung-chuan. *A history of Chinese political thought.* Trans. F. W. Mote. Vol. 1. *From the beginnings to the sixth century A.D.* Princeton, N.J.: Princeton University Press, 1979.

Hsiao, Theodore E. *The history of modern education in China.* Shanghai: Commercial Press, 1935.

Hsieh, Alice Langley. *Communist China's strategy in the nuclear era.* Englewood Cliffs, N.J.: Prentice-Hall, 1962.

Hsieh, Alice Langley. "China's secret military papers: military doctrine and strategy," *CQ,* 18 (April 1964), 79–99.

Hsieh Tu-yang 謝渡揚. "Hui-ku liu-shih nien-tai ch'u nung-yeh ti t'iao-cheng" 回顧六十年代初農業的調整 (Recalling the readjustment of agriculture at the beginning of the 1960s), in Liu Sui-nien, ed., *Liu-shih nien-tai kuo-min ching-chi t'iao-cheng ti hui-ku*, 50–69.

Hsin-hua hsin-wen-she 新華新聞社 (New China News Agency).

Hsin-hua jih-pao 新華日報 (New China daily). Wuhan, Chungking, et al., 1938–   .

Hsin-hua pan-yueh k'an 新華半月刊 (New China semi-monthly). Peking: 1956–60. See *Hsin-hua yueh-pao*.

Hsin-hua yueh-pao 新華月報 (New China monthly). Monthly. (Title varies: 1956–60 Hsin-hua pan-yueh-k'an). Peking: 1 November 1949–

Hsin-hua yueh-pao wen-chai-pan 新華月報文摘版 (New China monthly digest). Monthly. Peking: 1979–80. From 1981, retitled *Hsin-hua wen-chai* (New China digest).

Hsu Chi-yü 徐繼畬. *Ying-huan chih-lueh* 瀛環志略 (A brief account of the maritime circuit). 10 *chüan*. Foochow, 1850 ed.

Hsu Ti-hua 徐棣華. "Ching-chien chih-kung ho ch'eng chen jen-k'ou" 精簡職工和城鎮人口 (Reducing the number of workers and staff and the urban population), in Liu Sui-nien, ed. *Liu-shih nien-tai kuo-min ching-chi t'iao-cheng ti hui-ku*, 123–37.

Hsueh-hsi 學習 (Study). Peking: September 1949–October 1958.

Hsueh-hsi yü yen-chiu 學習與研究 (Study and research). Peking: 1981–

Hsueh Mu-ch'iao 薛暮橋. *Tang-ch'ien wo-kuo ching-chi jo-kan wen-t'i* 當前我國經濟若干問題 (Some current problems of China's economy). Peking: Jen-min, 1980.

Hsueh Mu-ch'iao, ed. *Chung-kuo ching-chi nien-chien 1982* 中國經濟年鑑 1982 (Chinese economic yearbook 1982). Overseas Chinese Language Edition. Hong Kong: Hong Kong China Economic Yearbook Company, 1983.

Hsueh Mu-ch'iao. "Kuan-yü i-chiu-wu-pa – i-chiu-liu-liu – nien kuo-min ching-chi chien-she ti ch'ing-k'uang ho ching-yen" 關於一九五八～一九六六年國民經濟建設的情況和經驗 (China's experience and situation in economic construction from 1958 to 1966), in *Ching-chi ts'an-k'ao tzu-liao*.

"Hu Feng tui wen-i wen-t'i ti i-chien" 胡風對文藝問題的意見 (Hu Feng's literary opinions). Supplement to *Wen-i pao*, January 1955.

Hu Shi Ming and Seifman, Eli, eds. *Toward a new world outlook: A documentary history of education in the People's Republic of China, 1949–1976*. New York: AMS Press, 1976.

[Huang] Ch'iu-yun 黃秋耘. "Pu yao tsai jen-min ti chi-k'u mien-ch'ien pi-shang yen-ching" 不要在人民的疾苦面前閉上眼睛 (We must not close our eyes to the hardships among the people). *Jen-min wen-hsueh*, 9 (1956), 58–59.

[Huang Ch'iu-yun]. "Tz'u tsai na-li?" 刺在哪裏 (Where is the thorn?). Wen-i hsueh-hsi, 6 (1957), 8–10.

Huang, Joseph. *Heroes and villains in Communist China: The contemporary Chinese novel as reflection of life.* London: C. Hurst, 1973.

Huang Pen-chi 黃本驥. *Li-tai chih-kuan-piao* 歷代職官表 (Tables of official posts in successive dynasties). Shanghai, 1880: Peking: Chung-hua, 1965.

Hucker, Charles O. *China's imperial past, an introduction to Chinese history and culture.* Stanford, Calif.: Stanford University Press, 1975.

Hucker, Charles O. *A dictionary of official titles in imperial China.* Stanford, Calif.: Stanford University Press, 1985.

Hucker, Charles O. "The Tung-lin movement of the Late Ming period," in John K. Fairbank, ed., *Chinese thought and institutions*, 132–62.

Hucker, Charles. "The traditional Chinese Censorate and the new Peking regime," *American Political Science Review*, 45.4 (December 1951), 1041–57.

Hudson, G. F., Lowenthal, Richard, and MacFarquhar, Roderick. *The Sino-Soviet dispute.* New York: Praeger, 1961.

Hui-i Wang Chia-hsiang 回憶王稼祥 (Recalling Wang Chia-hsiang). Peking: Jen-min, 1985.

Hung-ch'i 紅旗 (Red flag). Peking: 1 June 1958–   .

Hunt, Michael H. *The making of a special relationship: The United States and China to 1914.* New York: Columbia University Press, 1983.

Hunter, Edward. *Brain-washing in Red China.* New York: Vanguard Press, 1953.

Hunter, Neale. *Shanghai journal.* New York: Praeger, 1969.

IASP. International Arts and Sciences Press. See: *Chinese Studies in Philosophy* and *Chinese Studies in History*.

Ichiko, Chūzō 市古宙三. "The role of the gentry: An hypothesis," in Mary C. Wright, *China in revolution*, ch. 6, 297–318.

Imahori Seiji 今堀誠二. *Chūgoku gendaishi kenkyū josetsu* 中國現代史研究序説 (An introduction to the study of contemporary Chinese history). Tokyo: Kaisō Shobō, 1976.

IMH. Institute of Modern History, Academia Sinica, Taipei.

Index Foreign Broadcast Information Service Daily Report: China. Monthly plus annual cum. (New Canaan, Conn.: NewsBank, Inc., 1975–   ). From 1975 to 1982, the index was published quarterly, but with Volume 9 in 1983, the publication became a monthly, with an annual cumulative index as well. Beginning in October 1977, FBIS began to compile an index to the Daily Report, as well as the *JPRS* translations. With the fifteenth number in this series covering April–June 1981 (published August 28, 1981), the series acquired the designation "For Official Use Only" and was no longer available to libraries.

Institute of Modern History, Academia Sinica, Taipei. *See* Chung-yang yen-chiu-yuan chin-tai-shih yen-chiu-so.

Irick, Robert L. *Ch'ing policy toward the coolie trade 1847–1878.* San Francisco: Chinese Materials Center, 1982.

Iriye, Akira. *See* Nagai Yōnosuke.

Iriye Keishirō 入江啟四郎, and Andō Masashi 安藤正士, eds. *Gendai Chūgoku no kokusai-kankei* 現代中國之國際關係 (International relations of contemporary China). Tokyo: Nihon Kokusai Mondai Kenkyūjo, 1975.

Ishikawa Shigeru. *National income and capital formation in Mainland China: An examination of official statistics.* Tokyo: Institute of Asian Affairs, 1965.

Israel, John. "Continuities and discontinuities in the ideology of the Great Proletarian Cultural Revolution," in Chalmers Johnson, ed., *Ideology and politics in contemporary China,* 3–46.

Israel, John. "An autonomous academy in a one-party state: The Lienta model." Paper presented at the New England China Seminar Workshop on Chinese intellectuals and the CCP: The search for a new relationship, held at Harvard University, 5 May 1984.

Issues & Studies. Monthly. Institute of International Relations, Taiwan. 1964–

Izumi Hajime 伊豆貝元. "Chōsen sensō o meguru Chū-So tairitsu: Soren no Kokuren Anpoei kesseki no haikei" 朝鮮戦争をめぐる中ソ対立——ソ連の国連安保理欠席の背景 (The Sino-Soviet conflict in the Korean War: Background of the Soviet boycott of the UN Security Council). *Gunji kenkyū,* 10.3 (March 1975).

Jacobs, J. Bruce. "A preliminary model of particularistic ties in Chinese political alliances: Kan-ch'ing and Kuan-hsi in a rural Taiwanese township," *CQ,* 78 (June 1979), 237–73.

JAS. Journal of Asian Studies.

Jen-min jih-pao 人民日報 (People's Daily). Peking: 1949– . Cited as *JMJP.*

Jen-min jih-pao so-yin 人民日報索引 (Index to *People's Daily*). Peking: 1951–

Jen-min shou-ts'e 人民手册 (People's handbook). Shanghai, Tientsin, Peking: 1950–53, 1956–65, 1979.

Jen-min wen-hsueh 人民文學 (People's literature). Peking: 1940–66, 1976–

JMJP. Jen-min jih-pao.

Joffe, Ellis. *Party and army: Professionalism and political control in the Chinese officer corps, 1949–1964.* Cambridge, Mass.: East Asian Research Center, Harvard University, 1965.

Johnson, Chalmers. *Communist policies toward the intellectual class.* Hong Kong: Union Research Institute, 1959.

Johnson, Chalmers, ed. *Ideology and politics in contemporary China.* Seattle: University of Washington Press, 1973.

Johnson, Chalmers, ed. *Change in Communist systems.* Stanford, Calif.: Stanford University Press, 1970.

Joint Economic Committee of the United States Congress. *An economic profile of mainland China*, 2 vols. Washington, D.C.: U.S. Government Printing Office, 1967.

Joint Economic Committee of the United States Congress. *The People's Republic of China: An economic assessment*. Washington, D.C.: U.S. Government Printing Office, 1972.

Joint Economic Committee of the United States Congress. *China: A reassessment of the economy*. Washington, D.C.: U.S. Government Printing Office, 1975.

Joint Economic Committee of the United States Congress. *Chinese economy post-Mao*. Vol. 1. *Policy and performance*. Washington, D.C.: U.S. Government Printing Office, 1978.

Joint Publications Research Service (JPRS). Washington, D.C.: U.S. Government. Various series. See Berton and Wu, *Contemporary China*, 409–11.

Jones, E.L. *The European miracle: Environments, economies and geopolitics in the history of Europe and Asia*. Cambridge, Eng.: Cambridge University Press, 1981.

Jones, Susan Mann, and Kuhn, Philip A. "Dynastic decline and the roots of rebellion," in *CHOC* 10.107–62.

Journal of Economic History. Quarterly. Wilmington, Del.: Economic History Association 1941–   .

Joy, Charles Turner. *How Communists negotiate*. New York: Macmillan, 1955.

JPRS. Joint Publications Research Service.

Kahin, George McTurnin. *The Asian-African Conference, Bandung, Indonesia, April 1955*. Ithaca, N.Y.: Cornell University Press, 1956.

Kahn, Harold L. *Monarchy in the emperor's eyes: Image and reality in the Ch'ien-lung reign*. Cambridge, Mass.: Harvard University Press, 1971.

Kamiya Fuji 神谷不二, ed. "Kim Il-sung's radio speech on the outbreak of the Korean War (26 June 1950)." *Chōsen mondai sengo shiryō* 朝鮮問題戦後資料 (Documents on the postwar Korean problems), I. Tokyo: Nihon Kokusai Mondai Kenkyūjo, 1976.

"Kao-chi chih-shih fen-tzu tso-t'an Ma-Lieh chu-i li-lun hsueh-hsi" 高級知識分子座談馬列主義理論學習 (Higher intellectuals discuss the study of Marxist-Leninist theory). *Hsueh-hsi* (Study), 11 (1957), 2–11.

Karnow, Stanley. *Mao and China: From revolution to revolution*. New York: Viking Press, 1972.

Kau, Michael Y. (Ying-mao) 高英茂, ed. *The Lin Piao affair: Power, politics, and military coup*. White Plains, N.Y.: M. E. Sharpe, 1975.

Kau, Yi-maw (Ying-mao). "Governmental bureaucracy and cadres in urban China under communist rule, 1949–1965." Ph.D. dissertation, Cornell University, 1968.

Kau, Ying-mao, ed., *The People's Liberation Army and China's nation-*

building. White Plains, N.Y.: International Arts and Sciences Press, 1973.

Kau, Ying-mao. *The political work system of the Chinese Communist military*. Providence, R.I.: Brown University, 1971.

Kennedy, Thomas. *Arms of Kiangnan: Modernization of the Chinese ordnance industry 1860–1895*. Boulder, Colo.: Westview Press, 1978.

Khrushchev remembers. Trans. and ed. by Strobe Talbott. Boston: Little, Brown, 1970.

Khrushchev remembers: The last testament. Trans. and ed. Strobe Talbott, with detailed commentary and notes by Edward Crankshaw. Boston: Little, Brown, 1974; New York: Bantam, 1976.

Kinkley, Jeffrey C., ed. *After Mao: Chinese literature and society, 1978–1981*. Cambridge, Mass.: Council on East Asian Studies, Harvard University, 1985.

Klein, Donald W., and Clark, Anne B. *Biographic dictionary of Chinese communism 1921–1965*. 2 vols. Cambridge, Mass.: Harvard University Press, 1971.

Klochko, Mikhail A. *Soviet scientist in Red China*. New York: Praeger, 1964.

KMJP. Kuang-ming jih-pao.

"Ko min-chu tang-p'ai lien-ho hsuan-yen" 各民主黨派聯合宣言 (Joint declaration of the Democratic Parties). *Jen-min jih-pao*, 4 November 1950.

Ko-ming shih ch'ao 革命詩鈔 (A transcript of revolutionary poems). 2 vols. Peking: Pei-ching ti-erh wai-kuo-yü hsueh-yuan Han-yü chiao-yen-shih 北京第二外國語學院漢語教研室, 1977.

Kojima, Reiitsu 小島麗逸. "Grain acquisition and supply in China," *Contemporary China*, 5 (1963), 65–88.

Kuang-ming jih-pao 光明日報 (Enlightenment Daily). Peking: 1949–   . Cited as *KMJP*.

Kuang-ming jih-pao so-yin 光明日報索引 (Index to *Enlightenment Daily*). Peking: 1952–   .

Kubin, Wolfgang, and Wagner, Rudolf, eds. *Essays in modern Chinese literature and literary criticism*. Bochum, West Germany: Studienverlag Brockmeyer, 1982.

Kuhn, Philip A. *Rebellion and its enemies in Late Imperial China: Militarization and social structure, 1796–1864*. Cambridge, Mass.: Harvard University Press, 1970; paperback edition with new preface, 1980.

Kuhn, Philip A. "Local self-government under the Republic: Problems of control, autonomy, and mobilization," in Frederic Wakeman and Carolyn Grant, eds., *Conflict and control in late imperial China*, 257–98.

Kuhn, Philip A., and Jones, Susan Mann. "Introduction," in *Select papers from the Center for Far Eastern Studies*, 3 (1978–79), v–xix.

Kuhn, Philip A. "Local taxation and finance in Republican China," in *Select papers from the Center for Far Eastern Studies*, 3 (1978–79), 100–36.

Kuhn, Philip A. "Late Ch'ing views of the polity," in *Select papers from the Center for Far Eastern Studies*, 4 (1979–80), 1–18.

Kuhn, Philip A. "The Taiping Rebellion," in *CHOC*, 10.264–317.

Kun, Joseph C. "Higher education: Some problems of selection and enrolment." *CQ*, 8 (October–December 1961), 135–48.

Kung-jen jih-pao 工人日報 (Workers' Daily). Peking: 15 July 1949 (suspended 1 April 1967, resumed 6 October 1978)–   .

Kung-tso t'ung-hsun 工作通訊 (Bulletin of activities [of the PLA]). Peking: 1961–   .

Kuo Mo-jo 郭沫若. "Long live the policy – 'Let diverse schools of thought contend!'" *People's China*, 17 (1 September 1956), 7–9.

Kwok, D. W. Y. 郭穎頤. *Scientism in Chinese thought, 1900–1950*. New Haven, Conn.: Yale University Press, 1965.

Kwong, Julia. *Chinese education in transition: Prelude to the Cultural Revolution*. Montreal: McGill-Queen's University Press, 1979.

Kwong, Julia. "The educational experiment of the Great Leap Forward, 1958–59: Its inherent contradictions." *Comparative Education Review*, 3 (October 1979), 443–55.

Kyriak, Theodore, ed. *Bibliography-index to US JPRS research translations*, Vols. 1–8. Annapolis, Md.: Research and Microfilm Publications, Inc., 1962–   .

Labin, Susan. *The anthill: The human condition in Communist China*. New York: Praeger, 1960.

Lach, Donald F. *Asia in the making of Europe*. Vol. I, *The century of discovery*, in 2 books (1965); Vol. II, *A century of wonder*; Book One: *The visual arts* (1970); Book Two: *The literary arts* (1978); Book Three: *The scholarly disciplines* (1978). Chicago: University of Chicago Press.

Lall, Arthur. *How Communist China negotiates*. New York: Columbia University Press, 1968.

Lampton, David M. *The politics of medicine in China: The policy process, 1949–1977*. Boulder, Colo.: Westview Press, 1977.

Lampton, David M. *Policy implementation in post-Mao China*. Berkeley: University of California Press, forthcoming.

Lampton, D. Michael. *Paths to power: Elite mobility in contemporary China*. Ann Arbor: University of Michigan Press, 1985.

Langer, William L. *The diplomacy of imperialism 1892–1902*. 2 vols. 2nd ed. New York: Knopf, 1950.

Lardy, Nicholas R. *Economic growth and distribution in China*. Cambridge, Eng.: Cambridge University Press, 1978.

Lardy, Nicholas R. *Agriculture in China's modern economic development*. Cambridge, Eng.: Cambridge University Press, 1983.

Lardy, Nicholas R. "Regional growth and income distribution in China," in Robert F. Dernberger, ed., *China's development experience in comparative perspective*, 153–90.

Lardy, Nicholas. "Centralization and decentralization in China's fiscal management," *CQ*, 61 (March 1975), 25–60.

Lardy, Nicholas R., and Lieberthal, Kenneth, eds. *Chen Yun's strategy for China's development: A non-Maoist alternative.* Armonk, N.Y.: M. E. Sharpe, 1983.

Latourette, Kenneth Scott. *The Chinese: Their history and culture through 3,000 years of cumulative development and recent radical change.* New York: Macmillan, 1934, 1946, 1962; 4th ed., 2 vols. in one, 1964.

Lattimore, Owen. *Inner Asian frontiers of China.* New York: American Geographical Society, 1940; 2nd ed., 1951.

League of Nations' Mission of Educational Experts. *The reorganization of education in China.* See Becker, C. H., et al.

Lee, Chae-jin. *Communist China's policy toward Laos: A case study, 1954–67.* Lawrence: Center for East Asian Studies, University of Kansas, 1970; paperback, New York: Paragon, 1970.

Lee, Hong Yung. *The politics of the Chinese Cultural Revolution: A case study.* Berkeley: University of California Press, 1978.

Lehmann, David, ed. *Agrarian reform and agrarian reformism: Studies of Peru, Chile, China and India.* London: Faber & Faber, 1974.

Leonard, Jane Kate. *Wei Yuan and China's rediscovery of the maritime world.* Cambridge, Mass.: Council on East Asian Studies, Harvard University, 1984.

Levenson, Joseph R. *Liang Ch'i-ch'ao and the mind of modern China.* Cambridge, Mass.: Harvard University Press, 1953; 2nd rev. ed., 1959; Berkeley: University of California Press, 1959, 1970.

Levenson, Joseph R. *Confucian China and its modern fate.* Vol. 1. *The problem of intellectual continuity* (1958). Vol. 2. *The problem of monarchical decay* (1964). Vol. 3. *The problem of historical significance* (1965). Berkeley: University of California Press.

Levy, Howard S. *Chinese footbinding: The history of a curious erotic custom.* New York: Walton Rawls, 1966.

Lewis, John Wilson. *Leadership in Communist China.* Ithaca, N.Y.: Cornell University Press, 1963.

Lewis, John Wilson. *Chinese Communist Party leadership and the succession to Mao Tse-tung: An appraisal of tensions.* Washington, D.C.: U.S. Department of State Policy Research Study, January 1964.

Lewis, John Wilson, ed. *The city in Communist China.* Stanford, Calif.: Stanford University Press, 1971.

Lewis, John Wilson. *Major doctrines of Communist China.* New York: Norton, 1974.

Lewis, John Wilson. "China's secret military papers: 'continuities' and 'revelations'." *CQ*, 18 (April–June 1964), 68–78.

LHCC. See Lu Hsun. *Lu Hsun ch'üan-chi.*

Li Choh-ming 李卓敏. *Economic development of Communist China: An appraisal of the first five years of industrialization.* Berkeley: University of California Press, 1959.

Li Choh-ming. *The statistical system of Communist China.* Berkeley: University of California Press, 1962.

Li Fu-ch'un 李富春. "Report on the First Five-Year Plan for the development of the national economy of the People's Republic of China (July 5–6, 1955)," in *Communist China 1955–1959: Policy documents with analysis,* 42–91.

Li-shih yen-chiu 歷史研究 (Historical research). Peking: February 1966, December 1974– . Cited as *LSYC.*

Li-tai chih-kuan-piao. See Huang Pen-chi.

Li, Victor. "The Public Security Bureau and political-legal work in Hui-yang, 1952–64," in John Wilson Lewis, ed., *The city in Communist China,* 51–74.

Liang Heng 梁恒, and Shapiro, Judith. *Son of the revolution.* New York: Knopf, 1983.

Liao Kai-lung. "Historical experiences and our road of development (October 25, 1980)," in *Issues & Studies,* 17.10 (October 1981), 65–94; 17.11 (November 1981), 81–110.

Liao Mo-sha 廖沫沙, Hsia Yen 夏衍, Wu Han 吳晗, T'ang T'ao 唐弢, and Meng Ch'ao 孟超. *Ch'ang-tuan lu* 長短錄 (The long and the short). Peking: Jen-min, 1980.

Liao-ning ching-chi t'ung-chi nien-chien 1983. 遼寧經濟統計年鑑 1983 (Liaoning economic statistics yearbook 1983). Shenyang: Jen-min, 1983.

Liao-wang 瞭望 (Outlook). Peking: 1981– .

Lieberthal, Kenneth. *A research guide to central Party and government meetings in China 1949–1975.* White Plains, N.Y.: International Arts and Sciences Press, 1976.

Lieberthal, Kenneth G. *Revolution and tradition in Tientsin, 1949–1952.* Stanford, Calif.: Stanford University Press, 1980.

Lieberthal, Kenneth, et al. *Central documents and Politburo politics in China.* Michigan Papers in Chinese Studies, No. 33. Ann Arbor: University of Michigan, 1978.

Lifton, Robert Jay. *Thought reform and the psychology of totalism: A study of "brainwashing" in China.* New York: Norton, 1961.

Lifton, Robert Jay. *Revolutionary immortality: Mao Tse-tung and the Chinese Cultural Revolution.* New York: Vintage, 1968.

Lindbeck, John M. H. *Understanding China: A report to the Ford Foundation.* New York: Praeger, 1971.

Lindbeck, John M. H., ed. *China: Management of a revolutionary society.* Seattle: University of Washington Press, 1971.

Lindqvist, Sven. *China in crisis.* New York: Crowell, 1963.

Lindsay, Michael. *Notes on educational problems in Communist China,*

1941–47. New York: International Secretariat, Institute of Pacific Relations, 1950.

Lindsay, Michael. *Notes on educational problems in Communist China, 1941–47: With supplements on developments in 1948 and 1949 by Marion Menzies, William Paget, and S. B. Thomas*. Westport, Conn.: Greenwood Press, 1977. Reprint of the 1950 ed.

Link, Perry, ed. *"People or monsters?" and other stories and reportage from China after Mao, by Liu Binyan*. Bloomington: Indiana University Press, 1983.

Link, Perry, ed. *Stubborn weeds*. Bloomington: Indiana University Press, 1983.

Link, Perry, ed. *Roses and thorns*. Berkeley: University of California Press, 1984.

Liu, Alan P. L. *Political culture and group conflict in Communist China*. Santa Barbara, Calif.: Clio Books, 1976.

Liu Binyan. See Link, Perry.

Liu Chih-ming 劉芝明. *Hsiao Chün ssu-hsiang p'i-p'an* 蕭軍思想批判 (Criticism of Hsiao Chün's thought). Dairen: Tung-pei shu-tien 東北書店, 1949.

Liu Chih-ming. "A criticism of the errors of Hsiao Chün and the *Cultural Gazette*," in Hualing Nieh, *Literature of the Hundred Flowers*, 2.294–306.

Liu, James T. C. 劉子健. "The variety of political reforms in Chinese history: A simplified typology," in Paul A. Cohen and John E. Schrecker, *Reform in nineteenth century China*, 9–13.

Liu, Kwang-Ching 劉廣京. "The Ch'ing restoration," in *CHOC*, 10.409–90.

Liu, Kwang-Ching, and Smith, Richard J. "The military challenge: The North-west and the coast," in *CHOC*, 11.202–73.

Liu Shao-ch'i 劉少奇. *Collected works of Liu Shao-ch'i, 1945–1957*. Hong Kong: Union Research Institute, 1969.

Liu Shao-t'ang 劉紹棠, and Ts'ung Wei-hsi 從維熙. "Hsieh chen-shih – she-hui chu-i hsien-shih chu-i ti sheng-ming ho-hsin" 寫真實　社會主義現實主義的生命核心 (Write the truth – the living core of socialist realism). *Wen-i hsueh-hsi*, 1 (1957), 17.

Liu Sui-nien 柳隨年. "'T'iao-cheng kung-ku ch'ung-shih t'i-kao' pa-tzu fang-chen ti t'i-ch'u chi chih-hsing ch'ing-k'uang" "調整、鞏固、充實、提高"八字方針的提出及執行情況 (The proposal and implementation of the eight-character policy of readjustment, consolidation, filling-out, and raising standards). *Tang-shih yen-chiu* 黨史研究 (Research on Party history), 1980.6, 21–33.

Liu Sui-nien, ed. *Liu-shih nien-tai kuo-min ching-chi t'iao-cheng ti hui-ku* 六十年代國民經濟調整的回顧 (Recalling the readjustment of the economy in the 1960s). Peking: Finance and Economics Publishing House, 1982.

Liu Ta-chung 劉大中. See Eckstein, Alexander.

Liu Ta-chung and Yeh Kung-chia 葉孔嘉. *The economy of the Chinese mainland: National income and economic development 1933–1959.* Princeton, N.J.: Princeton University Press, 1965.

Lo Feng. 洛風 "Hai-shih tsa-wen ti shih-tai" 還是雜文的時代 (Still a period of *tsa-wen*). *CFJP*, March 12, 1942.

Lo Hui-min, ed. *The correspondence of G. E. Morrison.* Vol. 1 (1895–1912); vol. 2 (1913–1920). Cambridge, Eng.: Cambridge University Press, 1976.

Lo Keng-mo 駱耕漠. "Kuan-yü wo-kuo chi-hua ching-chi ti hsing-ch'eng chi ch'i fa-chan ti ch'ü-che kuo-ch'eng ti fen-hsi" 關於我國計劃經濟的形成及其發展的曲折過程的分析 (An analysis of the formation of China's planned economy and its course of development). *Ching-chi yen-chiu* 經濟研究 (Economic research), 2 (1981) 37–45.

Lofstedt, Jan-Ingvar. *Chinese educational policy: Changes and contradictions, 1949–79.* Stockholm: Almqvist and Wiksell International, 1980; Atlantic Highlands, N.J.: Humanities Press, 1980.

Loh, Robert, with Humphrey Evans. *Escape from Red China.* New York: Coward-McCann, 1962.

London, Kurt, ed. *Unity and contradiction: Major aspects of Sino-Soviet relations.* New York: Praeger, 1962.

Lowenthal, Richard. "Development vs. Utopia in Communist policy," in Chalmers Johnson, ed., *Change in Communist systems,* 33–116.

LSYC. *Li-shih yen-chiu.*

Lu Hsun 魯迅. *Lu Hsun ch'üan-chi* 魯迅全集 (Complete works of Lu Hsun). 10 vols. Peking: Jen-min wen-hsueh ch'u-pan-she 人民文學出版社, 1956. Cited as *LHCC.*

Lu Hsun. "Ta Hsu Mao-yung kuan-yü k'ang-Jih t'ung-i chan-hsien wen-t'i" 答徐懋庸關於抗日統一戰線問題 (A rejoinder to Hsu Mao-yung concerning the united front against the Japanese). *Lu Hsun ch'üan-chi,* 6.428–41.

Lu K'an-ju 陸侃如. "Hu Shih fan-tung ssu-hsiang kei-yü ku-tien wen-hsueh yen-chiu ti tu-hai" 胡適反動思想給予古典文學研究的毒害 (The poisonous harm of Hu Shih's reactionary thought to the study of classical literature). *Wen-i pao,* 21 (1954), 4–5.

Lu Ting-i 陸定一. "Education and culture in New China." *People's China,* 8 (16 April 1950).

Lubman, Stanley. "Mao and mediation: Politics and dispute resolutions in Communist China," *California Law Review,* 55.5 (November 1967), 1284–1359.

"Lung Yun tai-piao ti fa-yen" 龍雲代表的發言 (Remarks by delegate Lung Yun). *Chung-hua jen-min kung-ho-kuo ti-i-chieh ch'üan-kuo jen-min tai-piao ta-hui ti-ssu-tz'u hui-i hui-k'an* 中華人民共和國第一屆全國人民代表大會第四次會議彙刊 (Minutes of the fourth session of the First National People's Congress of the People's Republic of China). Peking: Jen-min, 1957.

Ma Hung 馬洪, and Sun Shang-ch'ing 孫尚清, eds. *Chung-kuo ching-chi chieh-kou wen-t'i yen-chiu* 中國經濟結構問題研究 (Research on problems in China's economic structure). Peking: Jen-min, 1981.

Ma Nan-ts'un 馬南邨 (Teng T'o 鄧拓). *Yen-shan yeh-hua* 燕山夜話 (Evening talks at Yenshan). Peking: Pei-ching ch'u-pan-she 北京出版社, 1963 and 1979.

Ma Yin-ch'u 馬寅初. *Ma Yin-ch'u ching-chi lun-wen hsuan-chi* 馬寅初經濟論文選集 (Selected economic essays of Ma Yin-ch'u). 2 vols. Peking: Pei-ching ta-hsueh ch'u-pan-she 北京大學出版社, 1981.

Ma Yin-ch'u. "Lien-hsi Chung-kuo shih-chi lai t'an-t'an tsung-ho p'ing-heng li-lun ho an pi-li fa-chan kuei-lü" 聯繫中國實際來談談綜合平衡理論和按比例發展規律 (A discussion of the theory of comprehensive balance and the law of planned proportionate development as it relates to Chinese reality). *Jen-min jih-pao*, 28 and 29 December 1956. Reprinted in *Ma Yin-ch'u ching-chi lun-wen hsuan-chi*, 2.121–44.

Ma Yin-ch'u. "Lien-hsi Chung-kuo shih-chi lai tsai t'an-t'an tsung-ho p'ing-heng li-lun ho an pi-li fa-chan kuei-lü" 聯繫中國實際來再談談綜合平衡理論和按比例發展規律 (A further discussion of the theory of comprehensive balance and the law of planned, proportionate development as it relates to Chinese reality). *Jen-min jih-pao* (11 and 12 May 1957). Reprinted in Ma Yin-ch'u, *Ma Yin-ch'u ching-chi lun-wen hsuan-chi*, 2.145–69.

MacFarquhar, Roderick. *The Hundred Flowers Campaign and the Chinese intellectuals*. New York: Praeger, 1960; Octagon, 1973.

MacFarquhar, Roderick. *Sino-American relations, 1949–1971*. New York: Praeger, 1972.

MacFarquhar, Roderick. *The origins of the Cultural Revolution, 1: Contradictions among the people 1956–1957*. London: Oxford University Press; New York: Columbia University Press, 1974.

MacFarquhar, Roderick. *The origins of the Cultural Revolution, 2: The Great Leap Forward 1958–1960*. London: Oxford University Press; New York: Columbia University Press, 1983.

MacFarquhar, Roderick. "Aspects of the CCP's Eighth Congress (first session)." University Seminar on Modern East Asia: China, Columbia University, February 19, 1969.

Mackerras, Colin. *Amateur theatre in China, 1949–1966*. Canberra: Australian National University Press, 1973.

Mackerras, Colin. "Chinese opera after the Cultural Revolution (1970–1972)," *CQ*, 55 (July–September 1973), 478–510.

Mackintosh, J. M. *Strategy and tactics of Soviet foreign policy*. London: Oxford University Press, 1962.

Mainichi shimbun 每日新聞. Tokyo: 1872–

Mao, *SW*. *Selected works of Mao Tse-tung* (English translation). For Chinese ed., see Mao, *Hsuan-chi*.

Mao Tse-tung 毛澤東. *Selected works of Mao Tse-tung*. Peking: Foreign Languages Press. Vols. 1–3, 1965; 4, 1961; 5, 1977. Cited as Mao, *SW*.

Mao Tse-tung. *Hsuan-chi* 選集 (Selected works). Peking: Jen-min, vols. 1–4, 1960; vol. 5, 1977. Cited as *MTHC*.

Mao Tse-tung. *Socialist upsurge in China's countryside*. Peking: Foreign Languages Press, 1957.

Mao Tse-tung. *Four essays on philosophy*. Peking: Foreign Languages Press, 1966.

Mao Tse-tung ssu-hsiang wan-sui 毛澤東思想萬歲 (Long live Mao Tse-tung Thought). Np.: No pub., 1967. Cited as *Wan-sui* (1967).

Mao Tse-tung ssu-hsiang wan-sui (Long live Mao Tse-tung Thought). Np.: No pub., 1969. Cited as *Wan-sui* (1969).

Mao Tse-tung. *Miscellany of Mao Tse-tung Thought (1949–1968)*. 2 vols. Arlington, Va.: Joint Publications Research Service, Nos. 61269–1 and 2, February 1974.

Mao Tse-tung. "Opening address at the Eighth National Congress of the Communist Party of China" (15 September 1956). *Eighth National Congress of the Communist Party of China. Vol. 1: Documents*, 5–11. Peking: Foreign Languages Press, 1956.

Mao Tse-tung. "Sheng-shih-wei shu-chi hui-i tsung-chieh" 省市委書記會議總結 (Summing up at a meeting of provincial and municipal committee secretaries) (January 1957). *Wan-sui* (1969), 81–90.

Mao Tse-tung. "Tsai Ch'eng-tu hui-i-shang-ti chiang-hua" 在成都會議上的講話 (Talks at the Chengtu Conference) (March 1958). *Wan-sui* (1969), 159–80.

Mao Tse-tung. "Tsai pa-chieh shih-chung ch'uan-hui-shang-ti chiang-hua" 在八屆十中全會上的講話 (Address at the Tenth Plenum of the Eighth Central Committee) (24 September 1962). *Wan-sui* (1969), 430–36.

Mao Tse-tung. "Chien-li kung-ku ti tung-pei ken-chü-ti" 建立鞏固的東北根據地 (Build stable base areas in the Northeast) (28 December 1945). *MTHC*, 4.1177–80.

Mao Tse-tung. "Lun jen-min min-chu chuan-cheng: chi-nien Chung-kuo kung-ch'an-tang erh-shih-pa chou-nien" 論人民民主專政──紀念中國共產黨二十八週年 (On the people's Democratic Dictatorship: In commemoration of the 28th anniversary of the Chinese Communist Party). *MTHC*, 4.1473–86.

Mao Tse-tung. "Tsai Chung-kuo Kung-ch'an-tang ti-ch'i-chieh chung-yang wei-yuan-hui-ti-erh-tz'u ch'üan-t'i hui-i-shang-ti pao-kao" 在中國共產第七屆中央委員會第二次全體會議上的報告 (Report to the Second Plenum of the Seventh Central Committee of the Chinese Communist Party) (5 March 1949). *MTHC*, 4.1425–40.

Mao Tse-tung. "Tsai hsin cheng-chih hsieh-shang-hui-i ch'ou-pei-hui-shang-ti chiang-hua" 在新政治協商會議籌備會上的講話 (Address at the preliminary meeting of the new Political Consultative Conference) (15 June 1949). *MTHC*, 4.1467–71.

Mao Tse-tung. "Tsai Chung-kung chung-yang chao-k'ai ti kuan-yü chih-shih fen-tzu wen-t'i hui-i-shang-ti chiang-hua" 在中共中央召開的關於知識分子問題會議上的講話 (Speech at the Conference on the Question of Intellectuals convened by the CCP Central Committee) (20 January 1956). *Wan-sui* (1969), 28–34.

Mao Tse-tung. "Tsai Shang-hai shih ko-chieh jen-shih hui-i-shang-ti chiang-hua" 在上海市各界人士會議上的講話 (Speech at the Conference of All Circles in Shanghai Municipality) (8 July 1957). *Wan-sui* (1969), 109–21.

Martin, R. Montgomery. *China: Political, commercial and social.* 2 vols. London: James Madden, 1847.

Mathews, Jay and Linda. *One billion: A China chronicle.* New York: Random House, 1983.

May, Ernest R. *"Lessons" of the past: The use and misuse of history in American foreign policy.* New York: Oxford University Press, 1973.

McDougall, Bonnie S. *Popular Chinese literature and performing arts in the People's Republic of China, 1949–1979.* Berkeley: University of California Press, 1984.

McLane, Charles B. *Soviet policy and the Chinese Communists, 1931–1946.* New York: Columbia University Press, 1958.

McMillen, Donald H. *Chinese Communist power and policy in Xinjiang, 1949–1977.* Boulder, Colo.: Westview, 1979.

Meadows, Thomas Taylor. *The Chinese and their rebellions, viewed in connection with their national philosophy, ethics, legislation, and administration.* London: Smith, Elder, 1856; Stanford, Calif.: Academic Reprints, 1953.

Meisner, Maurice. *Mao's China: A history of the People's Republic.* New York: The Free Press, 1977.

Metzger, Thomas A. *The internal organization of Ch'ing bureaucracy: Legal, normative and communication aspects.* Cambridge, Mass.: Harvard University Press, 1973.

Metzger, Thomas A. "Eisenstadt's analysis of the relations between modernization and tradition in China." *Li-shih hsueh-pao,* 12 (June 1984), 344–418.

Michael, Franz. *Mao and the perpetual revolution.* Woodbury, N.Y.: Barron's, 1977.

Ministry of Agriculture Policy Research Office. *Chung-kuo nung-yeh ching-chi kai-yao* 中國農業經濟概要 (An outline of agricultural economics in China). Peking: Nung-yeh ch'u-pan-she 農業出版社, 1982.

Miyazaki Ichisada 宮崎市定. *China's examination hell: The civil service examinations of imperial China.* Trans. Conrad Schirokauer. New York: Weatherhill, 1976; paperback, New Haven, Conn.: Yale University Press, 1981.

Modern China: An international quarterly of history and social science. Quarterly. Beverly Hills, Calif.: Sage Publications, 1975–

Morrison, G. E. *See* Lo Hui-min.

Mosher, Steven. *Broken earth: The rural Chinese.* New York: The Free Press, 1983.

Mote, F. W. *See* Hsiao Kung-chuan.

Mote, Frederick, "Political structure," in Gilbert Rozman, ed., *The modernization of China,* 47–106.

Mozingo, David. *Chinese policy toward Indonesia: 1949–1967.* Ithaca, N.Y.: Cornell University Press, 1976.

MTHC. See *Mao Tse-tung hsuan-chi* (Selected works of Mao Tse-tung).

Murphey, Rhoads. *The outsiders: The Western experience in India and China.* Ann Arbor: University of Michigan Press, 1977.

Nagai Yōnosuke and Iriye Akira 入江昭, eds. *The origins of the cold war in Asia.* Tokyo: University of Tokyo Press; New York: Columbia University Press, 1977.

Nakajima Mineo 中嶋嶺雄. *Gendai Chūgoku ron: ideorogi to seiji no naiteki kōsatsu* 現代中国論——イデオロギーと政治の内的考察 (On contemporary China: the internal dynamics of its ideology and politics). Tokyo: Aoki Shoten 青木書店, 1964, expanded edition, 1971.

Nakajima Mineo. *Chū-So tairitsu to gendai: sengo Ajia no saikōsatsu* 中ソ対立と現代——戦後アジヤの再考察 (The Sino-Soviet confrontation and the present age: Reappraisal of postwar Asia). Tokyo: Chūō kōron sha 中央公論社, 1978.

Nakajima Mineo. *Chūgoku: rekishi, shakai, kokusaikankei* 中國——歷史、社會、國際關係 (China: History, society and international relations). Tokyo: Chūō kōron sha, 1982.

Nakajima, Mineo. "The Kao Kang affair and Sino-Soviet relations." *Review.* Tokyo: Japanese Institute of International Affairs, March 1977.

Nakajima, Mineo. "The Sino-Soviet confrontation: Its roots in the international background of the Korean War." *The Australian Journal of Chinese Affairs,* 1 (January 1979), 19–47.

Nan-fang jih-pao 南方日報 (Southern daily) Canton: 23 October 1949–

Nathan, Andrew J. *Chinese democracy.* New York: Knopf, 1985.

Nathan, Andrew. "A factionalism model for Chinese Communist Party politics," *CQ,* 53 (January–March 1973), 1–33.

Nathan, Andrew, and Winckler, Edwin. "Policy oscillations in the PRC: Critique and reply." *CQ,* 68 (December 1976), 720–50.

National accounts of less-developed countries, 1950–1966. See Organization for Economic Cooperation and Development, Development Center.

National Security Council. *NSC Papers.* Washington, D.C.: U.S. National Archives.

NCNA. *See*: New China News Agency.

Nee, Victor, and Mozingo, David, eds. *State and society in contemporary China.* Ithaca, N.Y.: Cornell University Press, 1983.

Nelsen, Harvey W. *The Chinese military system: An organizational study of the People's Liberation Army*, 2nd ed. Boulder, Colo.: Westview, 1981.

New China Monthly. See *Hsin-hua yueh-pao*.

New China News Agency. *Daily News Release*. Hong Kong: 1948– Cited NCNA.

New China Semi-Monthly. See *Hsin-hua pan-yueh-k'an*.

News from Chinese provincial radio stations. Hong Kong: United Kingdom Regional Information Office, various dates, 1960s.

Nieh, Hualing 聶華苓. *Literature of the Hundred Flowers*. 2 vols. New York: Columbia University Press, 1981.

Nivison, David S. "Communist ethics and Chinese tradition," *JAS*, 16.1 (November 1956), 51–74.

North, Robert C. *See* Doolin, Dennis J.

NSC. *See* National Security Council.

Nunn, G. Raymond, comp. *Chinese periodicals, international holdings, 1949–1960*. 3 vols. Ann Arbor, Mich.: Association for Asian Studies, 1961.

OECD. *See* Organization for Economic Cooperation and Development, *National accounts. . . .*

Oksenberg, Michel C. "Policy formulation in communist China: The case of the mass irrigation campaign, 1957–58." Columbia University, Ph.D. dissertation, 1969.

Oksenberg, Michel C., with Bateman, Nancy, and Anderson, James B., comps. *A bibliography of secondary English-language literature on contemporary Chinese politics*. New York: Columbia University, East Asian Institute, 1969.

Oksenberg, Michel. "Methods of communication within the Chinese bureaucracy," *CQ*, 57 (January–March 1974), 1–39.

Oldham, Geoffrey. "Science in China: A tourist's impression," *Science*, 147.3659 (February 1965), 706–14.

Organization for Economic Cooperation and Development, Development Center. *National accounts of less-developed countries, 1950–1966*. Paris: OECD, 1968.

Orleans, Leo A. *Professional manpower and education in Communist China*. Washington, D.C.: Library of Congress, 1960.

Pannikar, K. M. *In two Chinas*. London: Allen & Unwin, 1955.

Parish, William, ed. *Problems in China's rural development: Evolving issues*. Forthcoming.

Parish, William L., and Whyte, Martin King. *Village and family in contemporary China*. Chicago: University of Chicago Press, 1978.

Pasqualini, Jean. *See* Bao Ruo-wang.

Pauley, Edwin W. *Report on Japanese assets in Manchuria to the President of the United States*. Washington, D.C.: U.S. Government Printing Office, 1946.

Peck, Graham. *Two kinds of time*. Boston: Houghton Mifflin, 1950. Second edition, rev. and abridged, with a new introduction by John K. Fairbank. Boston: Houghton Mifflin (Sentry), 1967.

Pei-ching jih-pao 北京日報 (Peking daily). Peking: 1 October 1952 (suspended 3 September 1966, resumed 20 January 1967)– .

Pei-ching t'u-shu-kuan kuan-ts'ang pao-chih mu-lu 北京圖書館館藏報紙目錄. (Catalogue of newspaper holdings at the Peking Library). Peking: Shu-mu wen-hsien ch'u-pan-she 書目文獻出版社 (Catalogue and Document Press), 1982.

Peking Daily. See *Pei-ching jih-pao*.

Peking Review. Peking: 1958– . (From January 1979, *Beijing Review*.)

[P'eng Te-huai 彭德懷]. *The case of P'eng Te-huai, 1959–1968*. Hong Kong: Union Research Institute, 1968.

P'eng Te-huai. *P'eng Te-huai tzu-shu* 彭德懷自述 (P'eng Te-huai's own account). Peking: Jen-min, 1981. Translated as *Memoirs of a Chinese marshal*. Peking: Foreign Languages Press, 1984.

Pennar, Jaan, et al. *Modernization and diversity in Soviet education*. New York: Praeger, 1971.

People's China. Semi-monthly. Peking: 1950–57. Cited as *PC*.

People's Daily. See *Jen-min jih-pao*.

People's Publishing House. Jen-min ch'u-pan-she.

Pepper, Suzanne. *Civil War in China: The political struggle, 1945–1949*. Berkeley: University of California Press, 1978.

Pepper, Suzanne. *China's universities: Post-Mao enrollment policies and their impact on the structure of secondary education: a research report*. Ann Arbor: Center for Chinese Studies, University of Michigan, 1984.

Pepper, Suzanne. "China's universities: new experiments in Socialist democracy and administrative reform – a research report." *Modern China*, 8:2 (April 1982), 147–204.

Perkins, Dwight. *Market control and planning in Communist China*. Cambridge, Mass.: Harvard University Press, 1966.

Perkins, Dwight H. *Agricultural development in China, 1368–1968*. Chicago: Aldine, 1969.

Perkins, Dwight. "Growth and changing structure of China's twentieth century economy," in *China's modern economy in historical perspective*, 115–65.

Perkins, Dwight H., ed. *China's modern economy in historical perspective*. Stanford, Calif. Stanford University Press, 1975.

Perry, Elizabeth J. "Rural violence in socialist China," *CQ*, 103 (September 1985), 414–40.

Po I-po 薄一波. "Kuan-yü 1958 nien-tu kuo-min ching-chi chi-hua ts'ao-an ti pao-kao" 關於一九五八年度國民經濟計劃草案的報告 (Report on the draft of the 1958 national economic plan), in *Jen-min shou-ts'e, 1959* 人民手冊, 1959 (People's handbook, 1959). Peking: Ta-kung pao, 1959.

Po I-po "Ch'ung-ching ho huai-nien – hsien-kei tang tan-sheng ti liu-shih chou-nien" 崇敬和懷念——獻給黨誕生的六十周年 (Respect and remembrance – marking the sixtieth anniversary of the founding of the Chinese Communist Party). *Hung-ch'i* (Red flag), 13 (1981), 60–67.

Polachek, James. *The inner Opium War*. Forthcoming.

Pollack, Jonathan. "Perception and process in Chinese foreign policy: The Quemoy decision." University of Michigan, Ph.D. dissertation, 1976.

Population and Development Review. Quarterly. New York: Population Council, Center for Policy Studies. 1975– .

Powell, Ralph L. *Politico-military relationships in Communist China*. Washington, D.C.: U.S. Department of State, Bureau of Intelligence and Research, 1963.

PR. See *Peking Review*.

Price, Ronald F. *Education in Communist China*. London: Routledge and Kegan Paul, 1970. 2nd ed. published under the title *Education in modern China*. London: Routledge & Kegan Paul, 1979.

Price, Ronald F. *Marx and education in Russia and China*. London: Croom Helm, 1977.

Proceedings of the conference on the theory of statecraft of Modern China. See *Chin-shih Chung-kuo ching-shih ssu-hsiang yen-t'ao-hui lun-wen chi*.

Pusey, James R. *Wu Han: Attacking the present through the past*. Cambridge, Mass.: East Asian Research Center, Harvard University, 1969.

Pusey, James R. *China and Charles Darwin*. Cambridge, Mass.: Council on East Asian Studies, Harvard University, 1983.

Pye, Lucian. *The spirit of Chinese politics: A psychocultural study of the crisis in political development*. Cambridge, Mass.: The MIT Press, 1968.

Pye, Lucian W. *The dynamics of factions and consensus in Chinese politics: A model and some propositions*. Santa Monica, Calif.: Rand, July 1980.

Pye, Lucian. *The dynamics of Chinese politics*. Cambridge, Mass.: Oelgeschlager, Gunn & Hain, 1981.

Pye, Lucian. "China in context," *Foreign Affairs*, 45.2 (January 1967), 229–45.

Pye, Lucian W., with Pye, Mary W. *Asian power and politics: The cultural dimensions of authority*. Cambridge, Mass.: Belknap Press of Harvard University Press, 1985.

Ragvald, Lars. *Yao Wen-yuan as a literary critic and theorist: The emergence of Chinese Zhdanovism*. Stockholm: University of Stockholm, 1978.

Ragvald, Lars. "The emergence of 'worker-writers' in Shanghai," in Christopher Howe, ed., *Shanghai: Revolution and development in an Asian metropolis*, 301–25.

Rankin, Mary B., Fairbank, John K., and Feuerwerker, Albert. "Introduction: Perspectives on modern China's history," in *CHOC* 13.1–73.

Rawski, Evelyn Sakakida. *Education and popular literacy in Ch'ing China*. Ann Arbor: University of Michigan Press, 1978.

Rawski, Thomas G. *China's transition to industrialism: Producer goods and economic development in the twentieth century*. Ann Arbor: University of Michigan Press, 1980.

Rawski, Thomas G. *China's republican economy: An introduction*. Discussion Paper No. 1. Toronto: University of Toronto, York University, Joint Centre on Modern East Asia, 1978.

Red Guard Publications. 20 vols. Reprinted by Center for Chinese Research Materials, Association of Research Libraries, Washington, D.C., 1975.

Red Guard Publications: Supplement. 8 vols. Reprinted by Center for Chinese Research Materials, Association of Research Libraries, Washington, D.C., 1980.

Remer, C. F. *The foreign trade of China*. Shanghai: The Commercial Press, 1926.

Remer, C. F. *Foreign investment in China*. Honolulu: Institute of Pacific Relations, 1929.

"Resolution on certain questions in the history of our Party since the founding of the People's Republic of China" (27 June 1981). *Beijing Review*, 27 (1981).

"Resolution on the Kao Kang – Jao Shu-shih anti-Party alliance" (March 1955). *CB*, 324 (5 April 1955), 4–6.

Rhoads, Edward J. M. *China's republican revolution: The case of Kwangtung, 1895–1913*. Cambridge, Mass.: Harvard University Press. 1975.

Rhode, Grant F., and Whitlock, Reid E. *Treaties of the People's Republic of China 1949–1978: An annotated compilation*. Boulder, Colo.: Westview Press, 1980.

Rice, Edward E. *Mao's way*. Berkeley: University of California Press, 1972.

Richardson, S. D. *Forestry in Communist China*. Baltimore: Johns Hopkins University Press, 1965.

Richman, Barry. "Capitalists and managers in Communist China," *Harvard Business Review*, 45 (January–February 1967), 57–78.

Rickett, Allyn and Adele. *Prisoners of liberation*. New York: Cameron Associates, 1957.

Ridgway, Matthew. *The Korean War*. Garden City, N.Y.: Doubleday, 1967.

Ridley, Charles, Godwin, Paul, and Doolin, Dennis. *The making of a model citizen in Communist China*. Stanford, Calif.: The Hoover Institution, 1971.

Robinson, Thomas W., ed. *The Cultural Revolution in China*. A Rand Corporation research study. Berkeley, Los Angeles, London: University of California Press, 1971.

Roll, Charles R. "The distribution of rural income in China." Harvard University, Ph.D. dissertation, 1974.

Rosen, Stanley. *The role of sent-down youth in the Chinese Cultural Revolution: The case of Guangzhou*. Berkeley: Center for Chinese Studies, University of California, 1981.

Rosen, Stanley. *Red Guard factionalism and the Cultural Revolution in Guangzhou*. Boulder, Colo.: Westview Press, 1981.

Rostow, W. W., et al. *The prospects for Communist China*. Cambridge, Mass.: The MIT Press and Wiley, 1954.

Rostow, W. W. *The stages of economic growth*. Cambridge, Eng.: Cambridge University Press, 1960; 2nd ed. New York: Norton, 1962.

Rozman, Gilbert, ed. *The modernization of China*. New York: The Free Press; London: Collier-Macmillan, 1981.

Sayeed, Khalid B. "Pakistan and China," in A. M. Halpern, ed., *Policies toward China: Views from six continents*, ch. 8, 229–361.

Scalapino, Robert A., ed. *Elites in the People's Republic of China*. Seattle and London: University of Washington Press, 1972.

Scalapino, R. A., and Yu, George. *Modern China and its revolutionary process: Recurrent challenges to the traditional order 1850–1920*. Berkeley: University of California Press, 1985.

Schein, Edgar H. "The Chinese indoctrination program for prisoners of war." *Psychiatry*, 19.2 (May 1956), 149–72.

Schein, Edgar, with Schneier, Inge, and Barker, Curtis. *Coercive persuasion*. New York: Norton, 1961.

Schiffrin, Harold Z. *Sun Yat-sen: Reluctant revolutionary*. Boston: Little, Brown, 1980.

Schram, Stuart. *Mao Tse-tung*. Harmondsworth, Eng.: Penguin Books, 1967.

Schram, Stuart R. *The political thought of Mao Tse-tung*. New York: Praeger, 1963; rev. and enlarged ed., New York: Praeger, 1969.

Schram, Stuart R., ed. *Authority, participation and cultural change in China*. Cambridge, Eng.: Cambridge University Press, 1973.

Schram, Stuart R. "Introduction: The Cultural Revolution in historical perspective," in Stuart Schram, ed., *Authority, participation and cultural change in China*, 1–108.

Schram, Stuart R., ed. *Mao Tse-tung unrehearsed: Talks and letters, 1956–71*. Middlesex, Eng.: Penguin Books, 1974. Published in the United States as *Chairman Mao talks to the people; talks and letters, 1956–1971*. New York: Pantheon, 1975.

Schram, Stuart R., ed. *The scope of state power in China*. London: The School of Oriental and African Studies, University of London; Hong Kong: The Chinese University Press, The Chinese University of Hong Kong; New York: The Chinese University Press and St. Martin's Press. 1985.

Schram, Stuart. "'Economics in command?' Ideology and policy since the Third Plenum, 1978–84," *CQ*, 99 (September 1984), 417–61.

Schurmann, Franz H. *Ideology and organization in Communist China*. Berkeley and Los Angeles: University of California Press, 1966; 2nd enlarged ed., 1968.

Schurmann, H. F. "Organizational contrasts between Communist China and the Soviet Union," in Kurt London, ed., *Unity and Contradiction*, 65–99.

Schwartz, Benjamin. *Chinese communism and the rise of Mao*. Cambridge, Mass.: Harvard University Press 1951, 1964.

Schwartz, Benjamin I. *In search of wealth and power: Yen Fu and the West*. Cambridge, Mass.: Belknap Press of Harvard University Press, 1964.

Schwartz, Benjamin I. *Communism and China: Ideology in flux*. Cambridge, Mass.: Harvard University Press, 1968.

Schwartz, Benjamin. "On the 'originality' of Mao Tse-tung," *Foreign Affairs*, 34.1 (October 1955), 67–76.

Schwartz, Benjamin. "The legend of the 'Legend of Maoism,'" *CQ*, 2 (April 1960), 35–42.

Schwartz, Benjamin I. "The Chinese perception of world order," in John K. Fairbank, ed., *The Chinese world order*, 276–88.

SCMM. See U.S. Consulate General, *Selections from China Mainland Magazines*.

SCMP. See U.S. Consulate General, *Survey of China Mainland Press*.

Seagrave, Sterling. *The Soong dynasty*. New York: Harper & Row, 1985.

Selden, Mark. *The Yenan way in revolutionary China*. Cambridge, Mass.: Harvard University Press, 1971.

Select papers from the Center for Far Eastern Studies. Vol. 1 (1975–76); Vol. 2 (1977–78); Vol. 3 (1978–79); Vol. 4 (1979–80). Chicago: University of Chicago Press.

Selections from China Mainland magazines. See U.S. Consulate General.

Sen, A. K. *Poverty and famines: An essay on entitlement and deprivation*. Oxford: Oxford University Press, 1981.

Seybolt, Peter J., ed. *Revolutionary education in China: Documents and commentary*. White Plains, N.Y.: International Arts and Sciences Press, 1973.

Seybolt, Peter J. "The Yenan revolution in mass education." *CQ*, 48 (October–December 1971), 641–69.

Seymour, James. *The fifth modernization: China's human rights movement, 1978–1979*. Stanfordville, N.Y.: Human Rights Publishing Group, 1980.

Shang-hai wen-hsueh 上海文學 (Shanghai literature). Monthly. (Superseded *Wen-i yueh-k'an* 文藝月刊). Shanghai: October 1959–December 1963).

Shao Ch'üan-lin 邵荃麟. "Tou-cheng pi-hsu keng shen-ju" 鬥爭必須更深入 (The struggle must penetrate more deeply). *Wen-i pao*, 25 (1957).

Shao Yen-hsiang 邵燕祥. "Ch'ü-ping ho k'u-k'ou" 去病和苦口 (To get rid of the illness and the bitterness of medicine). *Wen-i hsueh-hsi*, 1 (1957), 19–20.

Sheridan, Mary. "The emulation of heroes," *CQ*, 33 (January–March 1968), 47–72.

Shih, Bernadette P. N., and Snyder, Richard L. *Communist Chinese serials*. Cambridge, Mass.: The MIT Libraries, 1963.

Shih Ching-t'ang 史敬棠 et al., eds. Chung-kuo nung-yeh ho-tso-hua yun-tung shih-liao 中國農業合作化運動史料 (Historical materials on

China's cooperatization movement). Peking: San-lien shu-tien 三聯書店, 1957.

Shillinglaw, Geoffrey. "Land reform and peasant mobilization in Southern China 1947–1950," in David Lehmann, ed., *Agrarian reform and agrarian reformism*, 121–55.

Shinobu Seizaburō 信夫清三郎. *Chōsen senso no boppatsu* 朝鮮戰爭の發動 (The outbreak of the Korean War). Tokyo: Fukumura shuppan, 1969.

Shirk, Susan L. *Competitive comrades: Career incentives and student strategies in China*. Berkeley: University of California Press, 1982.

Shirk, Susan. "The 1963 temporary work regulations for full-time middle and primary schools: commentary and translation." *CQ*, 55 (July–September 1973), 511–46.

Shue, Vivienne. *Peasant China in transition: The dynamics of development toward socialism, 1949–1956*. Berkeley: University of California Press, 1980.

Simmons, Robert R. *The strained alliance: Peking, P'yŏngyang, Moscow, and the politics of the Korean Civil War*. New York: The Free Press, 1975; London: Collier-Macmillan, 1975.

Sirr, Henry Charles, M. A. *China and the Chinese: Their religion, character, customs and manufactures; the evils arising from the opium trade; with a glance at our religious, moral, political and commercial intercourse with the country*. 2 vols. London: W. S. Orr, 1849.

Skinner, G. William. "Asian studies and the disciplines." *Asian Studies Newsletter*, 29.4 (April 1984).

Skinner, G. William. "Cities and the hierarchy of local systems," in G. William Skinner, ed., *The city in late imperial China*, 275–351.

Skinner, G. William. "Marketing and social structure in rural China," *JAS*, Part I, 24.1 (November 1964), 3–43; Part II, 24.2 (February 1965), 195–228; Part III, 24.3 (May 1965), 363–99.

Skinner, G. William, ed. *The city in late imperial China*. Stanford, Calif.: Stanford University Press, 1977.

Skinner, G. William, et al., eds. *Modern Chinese society: An analytical bibliography*. 3 vols. Stanford, Calif.: Stanford University Press, 1973.

Smith, Richard J. *China's cultural heritage: The Ch'ing dynasty, 1644–1912*. Boulder, Colo.: Westview Press, 1983.

Snow, Edgar. *Red star over China*. New York: Random House, 1938; 1st rev. and enlarged ed., Grove Press, 1968; Bantam, 1978.

Snow, Edgar. *The other side of the river: Red China today*. New York: Random House, 1961.

Solinger, Dorothy J. *Regional government and political integration in Southwest China, 1949–1954: A case study*. Berkeley: University of California Press, 1977.

Solomon, Richard. *Mao's revolution and the Chinese political culture*. Berkeley: University of California Press, 1971.

Soong, James. *Red Flag, Hung ch'i, 1958–68: A research guide*. Washington, D.C.: Center for Chinese Research Materials, Association of Research Libraries, 1969.

Sorich, Richard, ed. *Contemporary China: A bibliography of reports on China published by the Joint Publications Research Service*. New York: Readex, 1961.

Spence, Jonathan D. *The Gate of Heavenly Peace: The Chinese and their revolution, 1895–1980*. New York: Viking, 1981.

Spence, Jonathan D., and Wills, John E., Jr., eds. *From Ming to Ch'ing: Conquest, region, and continuity in seventeenth-century China*. New Haven, Conn.: Yale University Press, 1979.

Starr, John Bryan. *Continuing the revolution: The political thought of Mao*. Princeton, N.J.: Princeton University Press, 1979.

State Planning Commission. "Ch'u-pu yen-chiu ti kuan-yu ti-erh-ko wu-nien chi-hua ti jo-kan wen-t'i" 初步研究的關於第二個五年計劃的若干問題 (Certain issues in preliminary studies on the second Five-Year Plan). *Chi-hua ching-chi* 計劃經濟 (Economic planning), 4 (1957), 10–12.

State Statistical Bureau. *Ten great years*. Peking: Foreign Languages Press, 1960.

"State Statistical Bureau Communiqué." *People's China*, 20 (16 October 1955), supplement, 8.

State Statistical Bureau. *See* Chung-hua jen-min kung-ho-kuo kuo-chia t'ung-chi chü.

State Statistical Bureau. "Chung-kuo ching-chi t'ung-chi tzu-liao hsuan-pien" 中國經濟統計資料選編 (A compilation of Chinese economic statistics), in Hsueh Mu-ch'iao, ed., *Chung-kuo ching-chi nien-chien 1982*. (Chinese economic yearbook 1982), 8.1–8.137.

Statecraft. See *Proceedings*.

Stavis, Benedict. *People's communes and rural development in China*. Ithaca, N.Y.: Rural Development Committee, Center for International Studies, Cornell University. Rev. ed., 1977.

Stavis, Benedict. *The politics of agricultural mechanization in China*. Ithaca, N.Y.: Cornell University Press, 1978.

Steiner, H. Arthur. "Current 'mass line' tactics in Communist China," *American Political Science Review*, 45.2 (June 1951), 422–36.

Stevenson, William. *The yellow wind*. Boston: Houghton Mifflin, 1959.

Strong, Anna Louise. "Chinese strategy in the Taiwan Strait." *New Times*, 46 (November 1958), 8–11.

Suigo, Carlo. *In the land of Mao Tse-tung*. London: George Allen & Unwin, 1953.

Sun, E-tu Zen 孫任以都. "The rise of the academic community," in *CHOC*, 13.361–420.

Sun Ye-fang 孫冶方. "Chia-ch'iang t'ung-chi kung-tso, kai-ko t'ung-chi t'i-chih" 加強統計工作, 改革統計體制 (Strengthen statistical work, reform the statistical system). *Ching-chi kuan-li* 經濟管理 (Economic management), 1981. 1, 3–5.

Survey of China Mainland Press. See U.S. Consulate General.

Survey of China Mainland Press, Supplements. See U.S. Consulate General.

Suttmeier, Richard P. *Research and revolution: Science policy and societal change in China*. Lexington, Mass., Toronto, London: Lexington Books 1974.

Talbott, Strobe. See *Khrushchev remembers*.

T'an Cheng 譚政. "Speech by Comrade T'an Cheng" (18 September 1956). *Eighth National Congress of the Communist Party of China*, vol. 2: *Speeches*, 259–78.

Tang, Peter S. H. *Communist China today*. 2 vols. Washington, D.C.: Research Institute on the Sino-Soviet Bloc, 1961.

Tang-shih yen-chiu 黨史研究 (Research on Party history). Peking: 1980– . Cited as *TSYC*.

T'ang Ching-kao 唐敬杲, ed. *Ku Yen-wu wen* 顧炎武文 (Selected essays by Ku Yen-wu). Shanghai: Commercial Press (Shang-wu yin-shu-kuan 商務印書館), 1928.

Tanigawa Michio 谷川道雄, ed. *Chūgoku shitaifu kaikyū to chiiki shakai to no kankei ni tsuite no sōgōteki kenkyū* 中国士大夫階級と地域社会との関係についての総合的研究 (Studies on the relationship between the literati class and local society in China). Kyoto: Kyoto University Press, 1983.

Tawney, R. H. *See* Becker.

Taylor, Charles. *Reporter in Red China*. New York: Random House, 1966.

Taylor, Robert. *Education and university enrollment policies in China, 1949–1971*. Canberra: Australian National University Press, 1973.

Taylor, Robert. *China's intellectual dilemma: Politics and university enrollment, 1949–1978*. Vancouver: University of British Columbia Press, 1981.

TCNC. See Chung-hua jen-min kung-ho-kuo kuo-chia t'ung-chi chü, *Ch'ung-kuo t'ung-chi nien-chien*.

Teiwes, Frederick C. *Elite discipline in China: Coercive and persuasive approaches to rectification 1950–1953*. Canberra: Contemporary China Papers, 1978.

Teiwes, Frederick C. *Politics and purges in China: Rectification and the decline of Party norms 1950–1965*. White Plains, N.Y.: M. E. Sharpe, 1979.

Teiwes, Frederick C. 'Provincial politics in China: Themes and variations,' in John M. H. Lindbeck, ed., *China: Management of a revolutionary society*, 116–189.

Ten great years. See State Statistical Bureau.

Teng Hsiao-p'ing wen-hsuan 鄧小平文選 (Selected works of Teng Hsiao-p'ing). Peking: Jen-min, 1983.

Teng Hsiao-p'ing 鄧小平. *Selected works of Deng Xiaoping (1975–1982)*. Beijing: Foreign Languages Press, 1984.

Teng Hsiao-p'ing. "Report on the revision of the constitution of the Communist Party of China" (September 16, 1956). *Eighth National Congress of the Communist Party of China.* Vol. 1: *Documents*, 169–228. Peking: Foreign Languages Press, 1956.

Teng Li-ch'ün 鄧力羣. *Hsiang Ch'en Yun t'ung-chih hsueh-hsi tso ching-chi kung-tso* 向陳雲同志學習做經濟工作 (Study how to do economic work from Comrade Ch'en Yun). Peking: Chung-kung chung-yang tang hsiao ch'u-pan-she 中共中央黨校出版社, 1981.

Teng, Ssu-yü 鄧嗣禹, and Fairbank, John K., et al. *China's response to the West: A documentary survey, 1839–1923.* Cambridge, Mass.: Harvard University Press, 1954; Atheneum paperback, 1963, 1965.

Teng T'o. See Ma Nan-ts'un, Wu Nan-hsing.

Teng Tzu-hui 鄧子恢. "Tsai ch'üan-kuo ti-san-tz'u nung-ts'un kung-tso hui-i-shang ti k'ai-mu tz'u" 在全國第三次農村工作會議上的開幕詞 (Inaugural speech at the third national rural work conference). *Tang-shih yen-chiu* 黨史研究 (Research on party history), 1981. 1, 2–9.

Theory and Society; renewal and critique in social theory. Bi-monthly. Amsterdam: Elsevier Scientific Publishing Co., 1974–   .

Thomas, S. B. *Government and administration in Communist China.* New York: International Secretariat, Institute of Pacific Relations, 1953.

Thornton, Richard C. *China: The struggle for power, 1917–1972.* Bloomington: Indiana University Press, 1973.

Thurston, Anne. "Victims of China's Cultural Revolution: The invisible wounds," *Pacific Affairs*, Part I, 57.4 (Winter 1984–85), 599–620, and Part II, 58.1 (Spring 1985), 5–27.

Thurston, Anne, and Parker, Jason, eds. *Humanistic and social science research in China.* New York: Social Science Research Council, 1980.

Ting Ling 丁玲. *Tao ch'ün-chung-chung ch'ü lo-hu* 到羣衆中去落戶 (Go into the dwellings of the masses). Peking: Tso-chia ch'u-pan-she 作家 出版社, 1954.

Ting Ling. "San-pa-chieh yu-kan" 三八節有感 (Thoughts on March 8). *CFJP*, 9 March 1942.

Ting, William. "Longitudinal study of Chinese military factionalism," *Asian Survey*, 19:8 (August 1979), 789–800.

Tōa Kenkyūjo 東亞研究所, eds. *Iminzoku no Shina tōchi gaisetsu* 異民族之 支那統治概說 (History of the rule of alien peoples over China). Tokyo: Tōa Kenkyūjo, 1943.

Tong, James, ed. "Underground journals in China." *Chinese Law and Government*, Part I, 13.2–3 (Fall–Winter 1980–81), and Part II, 14.3 (Fall 1981).

Townsend, James R. *Political participation in Communist China.* Berkeley: University of California Press, 1967.

Treadgold, Donald, ed. *Soviet and Chinese communism: Similarities and differences.* Seattle: University of Washington Press, 1967.

Tseng Chao-lun 曾昭掄. "Higher education in new China," *People's China*, 12 (16 June 1953), 6–10.

Tsou, Tang 鄒讜. *America's failure in China 1941–50*. Chicago: University of Chicago Press, 1963.

Tsou, Tang. *The Cultural Revolution and post-Mao reform: A historical perspective*. Chicago: University of Chicago Press, 1985.

Tsou, Tang. "Prolegomenon to the study of informal groups in Chinese Communist Party politics," *CQ*, 65 (March 1967), 98–114.

Ts'ui Chieh 崔捷. "Chi-pen chien-she ti t'iao-cheng" 基本建設的調整 (Readjustment of capital construction), in Liu Sui-nien, ed., *Liu-shih nien-tai kuo-min ching-chi t'iao-cheng ti hui-ku*, 70–93.

Tsui-kao jen-min fa-yuan yen-chiu-shih 最高人民法院研究室 (Research Office, Supreme People's Court), ed. *Chung-hua jen-min kung-ho-kuo tsui-kao jen-min fa-yuan t'e-pieh fa-t'ing shen-p'an Lin Piao, Chiang Ch'ing fan-ko-ming chi-t'uan an chu-fan chi-shih* 中華人民共和國最高人民法院特別法庭審判林彪, 江青反革命集團案主犯記事 (Record of the trials of the principal criminals of the Lin Piao and Chiang Ch'ing cliques before the Special Tribunal of the Supreme People's Court of the People's Republic of China). Peking: Fa-lü, 1982.

Tucker, Nancy B. *Patterns in the dust: Chinese-American relations and the recognition controversy, 1949–1950*. New York: Columbia University Press, 1983.

Tung, Chiping, and Evans, Humphrey. *The thought revolution*. New York: Coward McCann, 1966.

Ulam, Adam B. *Expansion and coexistence: The history of Soviet foreign policy, 1917–67*. New York: Praeger, 1968.

Unger, Jonathan. *Education under Mao: Class and competition in Canton schools, 1960–1980*. New York: Columbia University Press, 1982.

Union Research Institute (URI). *CCP documents of the Great Proletarian Cultural Revolution, 1966–1967*. Hong Kong: Union Research Institute, 1968.

Union Research Institute (URI). *Documents of the Chinese Communist Party Central Committee*. Hong Kong: Union Research Institute, 1971.

Union Research Service. Hong Kong: Union Research Institute, 1955– .

U.S. Consulate General. *Current Background*. Hong Kong: U.S. Consulate General, 1950–77. Cited as *CB*.

U.S. Consulate General. *Extracts from China Mainland Magazines*. Hong Kong: U.S. Consulate General, 1955–60. Cited as *ECMM*. Title changed to *Selections from China Mainland Magazines*, 1960–77.

U.S. Consulate General. *Selections from China Mainland Magazines*. Hong Kong: U.S. Consulate General, 1960–77. Cited as *SCMM*.

U.S. Consulate General. *Survey of China Mainland Press*. Hong Kong: U.S. Consulate General, 1950–77. Cited as *SCMP*.

U.S. Consulate General. *Survey of China Mainland Press, Supplements.* Hong Kong: U.S. Consulate General, 1950–77.

U.S. Department of State. *United States relations with China, with special reference to the period 1944–1949.* Washington, D.C., 1949. Reissued with intro. and index by Lyman Van Slyke as *China White Paper*, 2 vols. Stanford, Calif.: Stanford University Press, 1967.

U.S. Department of State. *American foreign policy: basic documents, 1950–55.* 2 vols. Washington, D.C.: U.S. Government Printing Office, 1957; New York: Arno Press, 1971.

U.S. Department of State. "United States policy regarding problems arising from the representation of China in the organs of the United Nations." *Foreign Relations of the United States 1950*, vol. 2. Washington, D.C.: U.S. Government Printing Office, 1976.

U.S. Department of State. "Implications of the Treaty of Alliance and related agreements between the Soviet Union and Communist China: Address by the Secretary of State, March 15, 1950 [excerpt]." *American foreign policy: Basic documents. 1950–55.* New York: Arno Press, 1971.

U.S. Department of State. *Foreign Relations of the US.* See *Foreign Relations....*

U.S. Senate Committee on Foreign Relations. *The United States and Communist China in 1949 and 1950: The question of rapprochement and recognition.* Washington, D.C.: U.S. Government Printing Office, 1973.

URI. Union Research Institute, Hong Kong.

Ūsami Shigeru 宇佐美滋. "Suchuāto taishi no Pekin hōmon keikaku: ushinawareta rekishi no tenkanten" スチュアート大使の北京訪問計画——失われた歴史の轉換点 (Ambassador Stuart's plan to visit Peking: A lost turning point in history). *Kokusai mondai* 國際問題 (International affairs), 198 (September 1976), 45–61.

Van Ness, Peter. *Revolution and Chinese foreign policy: Peking's support for wars of national liberation.* Berkeley: University of California Press, 1970.

Van Slyke, Lyman. "The Chinese Communist movement during the Sino-Japanese War 1937–1945." *CHOC*, 13.609–722.

Van Slyke, Lyman. See U.S. Department of State.

Vogel, Ezra F. *Canton under communism: Programs and policies in a provincial capital, 1949–1968.* Cambridge, Mass.: Harvard University Press, 1969.

Wagner, Rudolf. "The cog and the scout: Functional concepts of literature in socialist political culture," in Wolfgang Kubin and Rudolf Wagner, eds., *Essays in modern Chinese literature and literary criticism*, 334–400.

Wakeman, Frederic, Jr. *The fall of imperial China.* New York: The Free Press, 1975.

Wakeman, Frederic, Jr., and Grant, Carolyn, eds. *Conflict and control in late imperial China.* Berkeley: University of California Press, 1975.

Wakeman, Frederic, Jr., ed. *Ming and Qing historical studies in the People's*

Republic of China. Berkeley: University of California Center for Chinese Studies, 1980.

Wakeman, Frederic, Jr. *The great enterprise: The Manchu reconstruction of the imperial order in seventeenth-century China.* 2 vols. Berkeley: University of California Press, 1986.

Wakeman, Frederic, Jr. "Introduction: The evolution of local control in late imperial China," in Frederic Wakeman and Carolyn Grant, eds., *Conflict and control in late imperial China,* 1–25.

Wakeman, Frederic, Jr. "Localism and loyalism during the Ch'ing conquest of Kiangnan: The tragedy of Chiang-yin," in Frederic Wakeman and Carolyn Grant, eds., *Conflict and control in late imperial China,* 43–85.

Walder, Andrew. "Press accounts and the study of Chinese society," *CQ,* 79 (September 1979), 568–92.

Walker, Kenneth. *Planning in Chinese agriculture: Socialization and the private sector, 1956–1962.* Chicago: Aldine, 1965.

Walker, Kenneth R. *Food grain procurement and consumption in China.* Cambridge, Eng.: Cambridge University Press, 1984.

Walker, Kenneth R. "Collectivisation in retrospect: the 'Socialist high tide' of autumn 1955 – spring 1956." *CQ,* 26 (April–June 1966), 1–43.

Walker, Richard L. *The multi-state system of ancient China.* Hamden, Conn.: Shoe String Press, 1953.

Wan-sui. See *Mao Tse-tung ssu-hsiang wan sui* (Long live Mao Tse-tung Thought).

Wang Chia-chien 王家儉. *Wei Yuan nien-p'u* 魏源年譜 (Chronological biography of Wei Yuan). Taipei: IMH, Academia Sinica, 1967.

Wang Erh-min 王爾敏. "Ching-shih ssu-hsiang chih i-chieh wen-t'i" 經世思想之義界問題 (The problem of defining statecraft thought). *Chin-tai-shih yen-chiu-so chi-k'an* 近代史研究所集刊 (Bulletin of the Institute of Modern History), 13 (June 1984), 27–38.

Wang Hsueh-wen. "The 'Gang of Four' incident: Official exposé by a CCPCC document." *Issues & Studies,* 13.9 (September 1977), 46–58.

Wang Ping-nan 王炳南. *Nine years of Sino-U.S. Talks in Retrospect.* Published simultaneously in *Shijie zhishi* (World knowledge) and *Guangzhou ribao* between Sept. 1984 and Feb. 1985. Trans. in JPRS, *China report: Political, sociological and military affairs,* CPS-85-079, Aug. 7, 1985.

Wang P'ing 王平. "'Ta yueh-chin' ho t'iao-cheng shih-ch'i ti jen-min sheng-huo" "大躍進" 和調整時期的人民生活 (People's living standards during the Great Leap Forward and the period of readjustment), in Liu Sui-nien, ed., *Liu-shih nien-tai kuo-min ching-chi t'iao-cheng ti hui-ku,* 162–78.

Wang Shih-wei 王實味. "Yeh pai-ho-hua" 野百合花 (Wild lily). *CFJP,* 13 March 1942.

Wang, Y. C. 汪一駒. *Chinese intellectuals and the West 1872–1949.* Chapel Hill: University of North Carolina Press, 1966.

Wang Yü-ch'üan 王毓銓. "An outline of the central government of the Former Han dynasty." *HJAS*, 12 (1949), 134–87.

Watson, Burton. *Ssu-ma Ch'ien: Records of the grand historian of China.* 2 vols. New York: Columbia University Press, 1961.

Watson, James L., ed. *Class and social stratification in post-revolution China.* Cambridge, Eng.: Cambridge University Press, 1984.

Weber, Max. *The religion of China: Confucianism and Taoism.* Glencoe, Ill.: The Free Press, 1951. Trans. Hans Gerth. Paperback, Macmillan, 1964, with an introd. by C. K. Yang (Yang Ch'ing-k'un).

Wechsler, Howard J. "The founding of the T'ang Dynasty," *CHOC* 3. 150–87.

Wei, Henry. *China and Soviet Russia.* Princeton, N.J.: D. Van Nostrand, 1956.

Wei, Wen-ch'i. *Courts and policy in Communist China to 1952.* Lackland, Tex.: HRRI Project, 1955.

Wei Yuan 魏源. *Hai-kuo t'u-chih* 海國圖志 (An illustrated treatise on the maritime kingdoms). Several editions: 1844, 50 *chüan*; 1847, 60 *chüan*; 1952, 100 *chüan*.

Wen-i hsueh-hsi 文藝學習 (Literary Studies). Peking: 1954–   .

Wen-i pao 文藝報 (Literary Gazette). Peking: 1949–   .

Whitbeck, Judith. "From *k'ao-cheng* to *ching-shih*: Kung Tzu-chen and the redirection of literati commitment in early nineteenth century China," in *Proceedings of the conference on the theory of statecraft of modern China*, 323–52.

Whitbeck, Judith. "The historical vision of Kung Tzu-chen (1792–1841)." University of California (Berkeley), Ph.D. dissertation, 1980.

White, D. Gordon. "The politics of *Hsia-hsiang* youth." *CQ*, 59 (July–September 1974), 491–517.

White, Lynn T., III. *Careers in Shanghai: The social guidance of personal energies in a developing Chinese city, 1949–1966.* Berkeley: University of California Press, 1978.

White, Theodore, and Jacoby, Annalee. *Thunder out of China.* New York: Sloane, 1946.

White, Tyrene. "Implementing the 'one child per couple' population program in rural China: National goals and local politics," in David M. Lampton, *Policy implementation in post-Mao China.*

Whiting, Allen S. *China crosses the Yalu; the decision to enter the Korean War.* New York: Macmillan, 1960; 2nd ed., Stanford, Calif.: Stanford University Press, 1968.

Whiting, Allen S. *The Chinese calculus of deterrence: India and Indochina.* Ann Arbor: University of Michigan Press, 1975.

Who's who in Communist China. 2 vols. Hong Kong: Union Research Institute, 1969, 1970.

Whyte, Martin King. *Small groups and political rituals in China.* Berkeley: University of California Press, 1974.

Whyte, Martin King. "Educational reform: China in the 1970s and Russia in the 1920s," *Comparative Education Review* 18.1 (February 1974), 112–28.

Wiens, Herold J. *China's march toward the tropics.* Hamden, Conn.: Shoe String Press, 1954.

Wilbur, C. Martin. *The Nationalist Revolution in China, 1923–1928.* Cambridge, Eng.: Cambridge University Press, 1984. Reprinted from *CHOC* 12, 1983.

Williams, S. Wells. *The Middle Kingdom: A survey of the geography, government, education, social life, arts, religion etc. of the Chinese empire and its inhabitants.* 2 vols. New York and London: Wiley and Putnam, 1848. Rev. and enlarged ed., 1883.

Willoughby, W. W. *Foreign rights and interests in China.* Baltimore, Md.: The Johns Hopkins University Press, 1920. 2nd. ed., 1927.

Wills, Maurice. *Turncoat: An American's 12 years in Communist China.* Englewood Cliffs, N.J.: Prentice-Hall, 1968.

Wilson, Richard W. *Learning to be Chinese: The political socialization of children in Taiwan.* Cambridge, Mass.: The MIT Press, 1974.

Winckler, Edwin. *See* Nathan, Andrew.

Witke, Roxane. *Comrade Chiang Ch'ing.* Boston: Little, Brown, 1977.

Wittfogel, Karl A. *Oriental despotism: A comparative study of total power.* New Haven, Conn.: Yale University Press, 1957.

Wittfogel, Karl A. "The legend of 'Maoism,'" *CQ,* 1 and 2 (January and April 1960), 72–86 and 16–31.

Wittfogel, Karl A., and Feng Chia-sheng 馮家昇. *History of Chinese society: Liao (907–1125).* Philadelphia: American Philosophical Society, 1949.

Wolf, Margery. *The house of Lim: A study of a Chinese farm family.* New York: Appleton-Century-Crofts, 1968.

Wolf, Margery. *Revolution postponed: Women in contemporary China.* Stanford, Calif.: Stanford University Press, 1984.

Womack, Brantly. *The foundations of Mao Zedong's political thought 1917–1935.* Honolulu: University Press of Hawaii, 1982.

Wong, John. *Land reform in the People's Repbulic of China: Institutional transformation in agriculture.* New York: Praeger, 1973.

Wong, Paul. *China's higher leadership in the socialist transition.* New York: The Free Press, 1976.

World Bank. *China: Socialist economic development: Vol. 1. The economy, statistical system, and basic data. Vol. 2. The economic sectors: Agriculture, industry, energy and transport and external trade and finance. Vol. 3. The social sectors: Population, health, nutrition and education.* A World Bank country study. Washington, D.C.: The World Bank, 1983.

World Bank. *China: Long-term development issues and options* (A World Bank country economic report). Baltimore, Md., and London: The Johns Hopkins University Press, 1985. Six annex volumes to this book have been published by the World Bank: 1. *China: Issues and prospects in education*. 2. *China: Agriculture to the year 2000*. 3. *China: The energy factor*. 4. *China: Economic model and projections*. 5. *China: Economic structure in international perspective*. 6. *China: The transport sector*. Washington, D.C.: The World Bank, 1985.

Worthy, Edmund Henry, Jr. "The founding of Sung China, 950–1000: Integrative changes in military and political institutions." Princeton University, Ph.D. dissertation, 1975.

Wright, Arthur F. *The Sui dynasty: The unification of China AD 581–617*. New York: Knopf, 1978.

Wright, Arthur F. "Struggle vs. harmony: Symbols of competing values in modern China," *World Politics*, 6.1 (October 1953), 31–44.

Wright, Mary Clabaugh. *The last stand of Chinese conservatism: The T'ung-chih restoration, 1862–1874*. Stanford, Calif.: Stanford University Press, 1957.

Wright, Mary Clabaugh, ed. *China in revolution: The first phase, 1900–1913*. New Haven, Conn.: Yale University Press, 1968.

Wright, Stanley F. *Hart and the Chinese Customs*. Belfast: Mullan, 1950.

Wu, Aitchen K. *China and the Soviet Union*. New York: John Day, 1950.

Wu Ch'ün-kan 吳羣敢. "Kuan-yü 'ta yueh-chin' shih-wu ho t'iao-cheng ti li-shih ching-yen" 關於 "大躍進" 失誤和調整的歷史經驗 (Historical experiences concerning failures in and readjustment of the Great Leap Forward), in Liu Sui-nien, ed., *Liu-shih nien-tai kuo-min ching-chi t'iao-cheng ti hui-ku*, 25–49.

Wu Han. *See* Wu Nan-hsing.

Wu Hsiu-ch'üan (Wu Xiuquan) 伍修權. "Sino-Soviet relations in the early 1950s." *Beijing Review*, 47 (1983), 16–21, 30.

Wu Hsiu-ch'üan. *Tsai Wai-chiao-pu pa nien ti ching-li* 在外交部八年的經歷 (Eight years' experience in the Foreign Ministry). Peking: Shih-chieh chih-shih ch'u-pan-she 世界知識出版社, 1984. (Trans. Wu Xiuquan, *Eight years in the Ministry of Foreign Affairs [January 1950–October 1958] – Memoirs of a diplomat*.) Peking: New World Press, 1985.

Wu Nan-hsing 吳南星 (Wu Han 吳晗, Teng T'o 鄧拓, and Liao Mo-sha 廖沫沙). *San-chia ts'un cha-chi* 三家村札記 (Notes from a three-family village). Peking: Jen-min wen-hsueh ch'u-pan-she 人民文學出版社, 1979.

Wu Yuan-li. *An economic survey of Communist China*. New York: Bookman Associates, 1956.

Xiao Lan, ed. *The Tienanmen poems*. Peking: Foreign Languages Press, 1979.

Yang, C. K. (Ch'ing-k'un) 楊慶堃. *A Chinese village in early Communist transition*. Cambridge, Mass.: The MIT Press, 1959.

Yang, C. K. *The Chinese family in the Communist revolution*. Cambridge, Mass.: The MIT Press, 1959.

Yang, C. K. *Religion in Chinese society*. Berkeley: University of California Press, 1961.

Yang Chien-pai 楊堅白, and Li Hsueh-tseng 李學曾. "Nung, ch'ing, chung chieh-kou" 農輕重結構 (The structure of agriculture, light industry and heavy industry), in Ma Hung and Sun Shang-ch'ing, eds., *Chung-kuo ching-chi chieh-kou wen-t'i yen-chiu* (Research on problems in China's economic structure), 99–136.

Yang, Lien-sheng 楊聯陞. *Studies in Chinese institutional history*. Cambridge, Mass.: Harvard University Press, 1961.

Yang, Lien-sheng. *Excursions in Sinology*. Cambridge, Mass.: Harvard University Press, 1969; French edition, 1964.

Yang, Lien-sheng. "Historical notes on the Chinese world order," in John K. Fairbank, ed., *The Chinese world order*, 20–33.

Yang, Lien-sheng. "Toward a study of dynastic configurations in Chinese history," in Lien-sheng Yang, *Studies in Chinese institutional history*, 1–17. Reprinted from *HJAS*, 17.3–4 (1954).

Yang Yen-nan 楊燕南. *Chung-kung tui Hu Feng ti tou-cheng* 中共對胡風的鬥爭 (The struggle against Hu Feng by the Chinese Communists). Kowloon: Tzu-yu ch'u-pan-she 自由出版社, 1956.

Yao Hsu 姚旭. "K'ang-Mei yuan-Ch'ao ti ying-ming chueh-ts'e-chi-nien Chung-kuo jen-min chih-yuan-chün ch'u-kuo tso-chan san-shih chou-nien" 抗美援朝的英明決策—紀念中國人民志願軍出國作戰三十周年 (A wise decision to resist America, aid Korea: Commemorating the thirtieth anniversary of the Chinese People's Volunteers going abroad to fight). *Tang-shih yen-chiu* (Research on Party history), 5 (1980), 5–14.

Yeh Kung-chia 葉孔嘉. "China's national income, 1931–36," in Chi-ming Hou and Tzong-shian Yu, eds., *Modern Chinese economic history*.

Yen, Maria. *The umbrella garden: A picture of student life in Red China*. New York: Macmillan, 1954.

Young, Arthur N. *China's wartime finance and inflation, 1937–1945*. Cambridge, Mass.: Harvard University Press, 1965.

Young, C. Walter. *The international relations of Manchuria; a digest and analysis of treaties, agreements, and negotiations conerning the three eastern provinces of China, prepared for the 1929 conference of the Institute of Pacific Relations in Kyoto, Japan*. Chicago: University of Chicago Press, 1929.

Yü Ying-shih 余英時, ed., *Early Chinese history in the People's Republic of China, the report of the Han Dynasty studies delegation*. Seattle: School of International Studies, University of Washington, 1981.

Zagoria, Donald S. *The Sino-Soviet conflict, 1956–1961*. Princeton, N.J.: Princeton University Press; London: Oxford University Press, 1962.

Zhou Enlai. *See* Chou En-lai.

APPENDIXES:
MEETINGS AND LEADERS

TABLE 10

Party leadership, 1921–1928[a]

First Congress Shanghai[b] 23–31 July 1921	Second Congress Shanghai 16–23 July 1922	Third Congress Canton 10–20 June 1923
Provisional Central *Bureau*	*Central Executive* *Committee* *Full members*	
Ch'en Tu-hsiu Chang Kuo-t'ao Li Ta	Ch'en Tu-hsiu Li Ta-chao Ts'ai Ho-sen Chang Kuo-t'ao Kao Chün-yü	Ch'en Tu-hsiu Li Ta-chao Ts'ai Ho-sen Mao Tse-tung Wang Ho-po Chu Shao-lien T'an P'ing-shan Hsiang Ying Lo Chang-lung
	Alternate members	
	Teng Chung-hsia Hsiang Ching-yü —[c]	Teng Chung-hsia Hsu Mei-k'un Teng P'ei Li Han-chün Chang Lien-kuang

Fourth Congress Shanghai 11–22 Jan. 1925	Fifth Congress Wuhan 27 April–?? May,[d] 1927	Sixth Congress Moscow 18 June–11 July 1928
Central Executive *Committee*	*Politburo* *Full members*	
Ch'en Tu-hsiu Ch'ü Ch'iu-pai Ts'ai Ho-sen Chang Kuo-t'ao P'eng Shu-chih Li Ta-chao T'an P'ing-shan Li Wei-han Hsiang Ying	Ch'en Tu-hsiu[e] Ts'ai Ho-sen Chou En-lai Li Li-san Li Wei-han[e] Ch'ü Ch'iu-pai T'an P'ing-shan Chang Kuo-t'ao[e] Su Chao-cheng	Hsiang Chung-fa Chou En-lai Su Chao-cheng Ch'ü Ch'iu-pai Ts'ai Ho-sen Hsiang Ying Chang Kuo-t'ao

Table 10 (cont.)

Fourth Congress Shanghai 11–22 Jan. 1925	Fifth Congress Wuhan 27 April–?? May,[d] 1927	Sixth Congress Moscow 18 June–11 July 1928
Central Executive Committee alternate members	*Politburo alternate members*	
Teng P'ei		Li Li-san
Wang Ho-po		Kuan Hsiang-ying
Chang T'ai-lei		Yang Yin
Lo Chang-lung		Hsu Lan-chih
Chu Chin-t'ang		Lu Fu-t'an
		Lo Teng-hsien
		P'eng P'ai

[a] Many major changes took place in the CCP's leadership in the 17 years between the Sixth and Seventh Congresses, most as a result of the emergence of Mao Tse-tung as the dominant figure at the Tsun-yi Conference in January 1935 during the Long March. Only one member of the Politburo chosen in Moscow in 1928 survived the warfare of the subsequent years *and* was reselected in 1945: Chou En-lai.

[b] Fearing arrest, the delegates fled Shanghai, and the last day of the Congress was held on a boat in Chia-hsing South Lake in Chekiang Province.

[c] The name of a third alternate awaits confirmation.

[d] The Congress is said to have lasted about 15 days.

[e] Members of the Politburo Standing Committee.

Source: Chu Ch'eng-chia, ed., *Chung kung tang-shih yen-chiu lun-wen hsuan* (A selection of research papers on the history of the Chinese Communist Party), 3.558–65.

TABLE 11

High-level formal[a] Party meetings, 1945–1965

CCP Seventh National Congress, Yenan	23 Apr.–11 June 1945
1st plenum, 7th CC, Yenan	19 June 1945
2nd plenum, 7th CC, Hsi-pai-p'o (Hopei)	5–13 Mar. 1949
3rd plenum, 7th CC, Peking	6–9 June 1950
4th plenum, 7th CC, Peking	6–10 Feb. 1954
CCP National Conference, Peking	21–31 Mar. 1955
5th plenum, 7th CC, Peking	4 Apr. 1955
6th plenum, 7th CC, Peking	4–11 Oct. 1955
7th plenum, 7th CC, Peking	22 Aug., 8, 13 Sept. 1956
CCP Eighth National Congress, Peking	15–27 Sept. 1956
1st plenum, 8th CC, Peking	28 Sept. 1956
2nd plenum, 8th CC, Peking	10–15 Nov. 1956
3rd plenum, 8th CC, Peking	20 Sept.–9 Oct. 1957
4th plenum, 8th CC, Peking	3 May 1958
CCP Eighth National Congress, Second session, Peking	5–23 May 1958
5th plenum, 8th CC, Peking	25 May 1958
6th plenum, 8th CC, Wuchang	28 Nov.–10 Dec. 1958
7th plenum, 8th CC, Shanghai	2–5 Apr. 1959
8th plenum, 8th CC, Lushan	2–16 Aug. 1959
9th plenum, 8th CC, Peking	14–18 Jan. 1961
10th plenum, 8th CC, Peking	24–27 Sept. 1962

[a] "Formal" is used to distinguish these meetings from other important high-level meetings such as Politburo or central work conferences.

Sources: Chu Ch'eng-chia, ed., *Chung kung tang-shih yen-chiu lun-wen hsuan* (A selection of research papers on the history of the Chinese Communist Party); Hao Meng-pi, Tuan Hao-jan, eds., *Chung-kuo kung-ch'an-tang liu-shih nien* (Sixty years of the Chinese Communist Party).

TABLE 12

Party leadership, 1945–1965

Seventh Congress[a] Yenan 23 Apr.–11 June 1945		Eighth Congress[e] Peking 15–27 Sept. 1956	
		Politburo, *Full members*	
Mao Tse-tung (*Chairman*) ⎤		Mao Tse-tung (*Chairman*) ⎤	
Chu Te		Liu Shao-ch'i	
Liu Shao-ch'i	⎬ *Secretariat*	Chou En-lai	
Chou En-lai		Chu Te	⎬ *Standing*
Jen Pi-shih[b] ⎦		Ch'en Yun	*Committee*
Ch'en Yun		Lin Piao[f]	
K'ang Sheng		Teng Hsiao-p'ing (*General Secretary*) ⎦	
Kao Kang[c]		Lin Po-ch'ü	
P'eng Chen		Tung Pi-wu	
Tung Pi-wu		P'eng Chen	
Lin Po-ch'ü		Lo Jung-huan	
Chang Wen-t'ien		Ch'en I	
P'eng Te-huai		Li Fu-ch'un	
Lin Piao[d]		P'eng Te-huai	
Teng Hsiao-p'ing[d]		Liu Po-ch'eng	
		Ho Lung	
		Li Hsien-nien	
		K'o Ch'ing-shih[g]	
		Li Ching-ch'üan[g]	
		T'an Chen-lin[g]	
		Alternate members	
		Ulanfu	
		Chang Wen-t'ien	
		Lu Ting-i	
		Ch'en Po-ta	
		K'ang Sheng	
		Po I-po	

[a] Chosen at the Seventh CC's 1st plenum after the CCP's Seventh Congress in 1945 and added to at the Seventh CC's 5th plenum after the CCP's National Conference in 1955.
[b] Jen Pi-shih died in 1950.
[c] Kao Kang's purge and suicide were announced at the 1955 National Conference.
[d] Entered the Politburo at the Seventh CC's 5th plenum.
[e] Chosen at the Eighth CC's 1st plenum after the CCP's Eighth Congress in 1956 and added to at the Eighth CC's 5th plenum after the 2nd session of the Eighth Congress in 1958.
[f] Lin Piao was promoted to the Politburo's Standing Committee at the Eighth CC's 5th plenum.
[g] Entered the Politburo at the Eighth CC's 5th plenum.

TABLE 13

State leaders, 1949–1965[a]

	1949 PRC Central People's Government Council	1954 PRC	1959 PRC	1964–5 PRC
Chairman	Mao Tse-tung[b]	Mao Tse-tung[b]	Liu Shao-ch'i[b]	Liu Shao-ch'i[b]
Vice Chairmen	Chu Te[b]	Chu Te[b]	Soong Ching-ling	Soong Ching-ling
	Soong Ching-ling		Tung Pi-wu[b]	Tung Pi-wu[b]
	Chang Lan			
	Liu Shao-ch'i[b]			
	Li Chi-shen			
	Kao Kang[b]			

National People's Congress

		Chairman Liu Shao-ch'i[b]	Chu Te[b]	Chu Te[b]

Government Administration Council

State Council

Premier	Chou En-lai[b]	Chou En-lai[b]	Chou En-lai[b]	Chou En-lai[b]
Vice-premiers	Tung Pi-wu[b]	Ch'en Yun[b]	Ch'en Yun[b]	Lin Piao[b]
	Kuo Mo-jo	Lin Piao	Lin Piao[b]	Ch'en Yun[b]
	Teng Hsiao-p'ing	P'eng Te-huai[b]	P'eng Te-huai[b]	Teng Hsiao-p'ing[b]
	Ch'en Yun[b]	Teng Hsiao-p'ing	Teng Hsiao-p'ing[b]	Ho Lung[b]
	Huang Yen-p'ei	Teng Tzu-hui	Teng Tzu-hui	Ch'en I[b]
		Ho Lung	Ho Lung[b]	K'o Ch'ing-shih[b]
		Ch'en I	Ch'en I[b]	Ulanfu[c]
		Ulanfu	Ulanfu[c]	Li Fu-ch'un[b]
		Li Fu-ch'un	Li Fu-ch'un[b]	Li Hsien-nien[b]
		Li Hsien-nien	Li Hsien-nien[b]	T'an Chen-lin[b]
		Nieh Jung-chen	Nieh Jung-chen	Nieh Jung-chen
		Po I-po	Po I-po[c]	Po I-po[c]
			T'an Chen-lin[b]	Lu Ting-i[c]
			Lu Ting-i[c]	Lo Jui-ch'ing
			Lo Jui-ch'ing	T'ao Chu
			Hsi Chung-hsun	Hsieh Fu-chih

[a] The Central People's Government Council (CPGC) was appointed at the first session of the Chinese People's Political Consultative Conference (CPPCC), which met 21–30 September 1949. The CPPCC appointed Chou En-lai premier of the Government Administration Council on 1 October 1949 and appointed the vice-premiers on 19 October 1949. The 1954, 1959, and 1964–5 appointments were made at the first sessions of the 1st, 2nd, and 3rd National People's Congresses held in those years.
[b] Member of Politburo at time of appointment.
[c] Alternate member of Politburo at time of appointment.

CONVERSION TABLES

Pinyin to Wade-Giles

Pinyin	Wade-Giles	Pinyin	Wade-Giles	Pinyin	Wade-Giles	Pinyin	Wade-Giles
a	a	chu	ch'u	er	erh	hou	hou
ai	ai	chuai	ch'uai			hu	hu
an	an	chuan	ch'uan	fa	fa	hua	hua
ang	ang	chuang	ch'uang	fan	fan	huan	huan
ao	ao	chui	ch'ui	fang	fang	huang	huang
		chun	ch'un	fei	fei	hui	hui
ba	pa	chuo	ch'o	fen	fen	hun	hun
bai	pai	ci	tz'u	feng	feng	huo	huo
ban	pan	cong	ts'ung	fo	fo		
bang	pang	cou	ts'ou	fou	fou	ji	chi
bao	pao	cu	ts'u	fu	fu	jia	chia
bei	pei	cuan	ts'uan			jian	chien
ben	pen	cui	ts'ui	ga	ka	jiang	chiang
beng	peng	cun	ts'un	gai	kai	jiao	chiao
bi	pi	cuo	ts'o	gan	kan	jie	chieh
bian	pien			gang	kang	jin	chin
biao	piao	da	ta	gao	kao	jing	ching
bie	pieh	dai	tai	ge	ke, ko	jiong	chiung
bin	pin	dan	tan	gei	kei	jiu	chiu
bing	ping	dang	tang	gen	ken	ju	chü
bo	po	dao	tao	geng	keng	juan	chüan
bu	pu	de	te	gong	kung	jue	chüeh
		dei	tei	gou	kou	jun	chün
ca	ts'a	deng	teng	gu	ku		
cai	ts'ai	di	ti	gua	kua	ka	k'a
can	ts'an	dian	tien	guai	kuai	kai	k'ai
cang	ts'ang	diao	tiao	guan	kuan	kan	k'an
cao	ts'ao	die	tieh	guang	kuang	kang	k'ang
ce	ts'e	ding	ting	gui	kuei	kao	k'ao
cen	ts'en	diu	tiu	gun	kun	ke	k'o
ceng	ts'eng	dong	tung	guo	kuo	ken	k'en
cha	ch'a	dou	tou			keng	k'eng
chai	ch'ai	du	tu	ha	ha	kong	k'ung
chan	ch'an	duan	tuan	hai	hai	kou	k'ou
chang	ch'ang	dui	tui	han	han	ku	k'u
chao	ch'ao	dun	tun	hang	hang	kua	k'ua
che	ch'e	duo	to	hao	hao	kuai	k'uai
chen	ch'en			he	ho, he	kuan	k'uan
cheng	ch'eng	e	o	hei	hei	kuang	k'uang
chi	ch'ih	ei	ei	hen	hen	kui	k'uei
chong	ch'ung	en	en	heng	heng	kun	k'un
chou	ch'ou	eng	eng	hong	hung	kuo	k'uo

Pinyin	Wade-Giles	Pinyin	Wade-Giles	Pinyin	Wade-Giles	Pinyin	Wade-Giles
la	la	ni	ni	re	je	ti	t'i
lai	lai	nian	nien	ren	jen	tian	t'ien
lan	lan	niang	niang	reng	jeng	tiao	t'iao
lang	lang	niao	niao	ri	jih	tie	t'ieh
lao	lao	nie	nieh	rong	jung	ting	t'ing
le	le	nin	nin	rou	jou	tong	t'ung
lei	lei	ning	ning	ru	ju	tou	t'ou
leng	leng	niu	niu	ruan	juan	tu	t'u
li	li	nong	nung	rui	jui	tuan	t'uan
lia	lia	nou	nou	run	jun	tui	t'ui
lian	lien	nu	nu	ruo	jo	tun	t'un
liang	liang	nü	nü			tuo	t'o
liao	liao	nuan	nuan	sa	sa		
lie	lieh	nüe	nueh	sai	sai	wa	wa
lin	lin	nuo	no	san	san	wai	wai
ling	ling			sang	sang	wan	wan
liu	liu	o	o	sao	sao	wang	wang
lo	lo	ou	ou	se	se	wei	wei
long	lung			sen	sen	wen	wen
lou	lou	pa	p'a	seng	seng	weng	weng
lu	lu	pai	p'ai	sha	sha	wo	wo
luan	luan	pan	p'an	shai	shai	wu	wu
lun	lun	pang	p'ang	shan	shan		
luo	lo	pao	p'ao	shang	shang	xi	hsi
lü	lü	pei	p'ei	shao	shao	xia	hsia
lüe	lueh	pen	p'en	she	she	xian	hsien
		peng	p'eng	shei	shei	xiang	hsiang
ma	ma	pi	p'i	shen	shen	xiao	hsiao
mai	mai	pian	p'ien	sheng	sheng	xie	hsieh
man	man	piao	p'iao	shi	shih	xin	hsin
mang	mang	pie	p'ieh	shou	shou	xing	hsing
mao	mao	pin	p'in	shu	shu	xiong	hsiung
mei	mei	ping	p'ing	shua	shua	xiu	hsiu
men	men	po	p'o	shuai	shuai	xu	hsu
meng	meng	pou	p'ou	shuan	shuan	xuan	hsuan
mi	mi	pu	p'u	shuang	shuang	xue	hsueh
mian	mien			shui	shui	xun	hsun
miao	miao	qi	ch'i	shun	shun		
mie	mieh	qia	ch'ia	shuo	shuo	ya	ya
min	min	qian	ch'ien	si	szu, ssu	yan	yen
ming	ming	qiang	ch'iang	song	sung	yang	yang
miu	miu	qiao	ch'iao	sou	sou	yao	yao
mo	mo	qie	ch'ieh	su	su	ye	yeh
mou	mou	qin	ch'in	suan	suan	yi	i
mu	mu	qing	ch'ing	sui	sui	yin	yin
		qiong	ch'iung	sun	sun	ying	ying
na	na	qiu	ch'iu	suo	so	yong	yung
nai	nai	qu	ch'ü			you	yu
nan	nan	quan	ch'üan	ta	t'a	yu	yü
nang	nang	que	ch'üeh	tai	t'ai	yuan	yuan
nao	nao	qun	ch'ün	tan	t'an	yue	yueh
ne	ne			tang	t'ang	yun	yun
nei	nei	ran	jan	tao	t'ao		
nen	nen	rang	jang	te	t'e	za	tsa
neng	neng	rao	jao	teng	t'eng	zai	tsai

Pinyin	Wade-Giles	Pinyin	Wade-Giles	Pinyin	Wade-Giles	Pinyin	Wade-Giles
zan	tsan	zhan	chan	zhou	chou	zi	tzu
zang	tsang	zhang	chang	zhu	chu	zong	tsung
zao	tsao	zhao	chao	zhua	chua	zou	tsou
ze	tse	zhe	che	zhuai	chuai	zu	tsu
zei	tsei	zhei	chei	zhuan	chuan	zuan	tsuan
zen	tsen	zhen	chen	zhuang	chuang	zui	tsui
zeng	tseng	zheng	cheng	zhui	chui	zun	tsun
zha	cha	zhi	chih	zhun	chun	zuo	tso
zhai	chai	zhong	chung	zhuo	cho		

Wade-Giles to Pinyin

Wade-Giles	Pinyin	Wade-Giles	Pinyin	Wade-Giles	Pinyin	Wade-Giles	Pinyin
a	a	ch'ü	qu	hsiu	xiu	ku	gu
ai	ai	chua	zhua	hsiung	xiong	k'u	ku
an	an	chuai	zhuai	hsü	xu	kua	gua
ang	ang	ch'uai	chuai	hsüan	xuan	k'ua	kua
ao	ao	chuan	zhuan	hsüeh	xue	kuai	guai
		ch'uan	chuan	hsün	xun	k'uai	kuai
cha	zha	chüan	juan	hu	hu	kuan	guan
ch'a	cha	ch'üan	quan	hua	hua	k'uan	kuan
chai	zhai	chuang	zhuang	huai	huai	kuang	guang
ch'ai	chai	ch'uang	chuang	huan	huan	k'uang	kuang
chan	zhan	chüeh	jue	huang	huang	kuei	gui
ch'an	chan	ch'üeh	que	hui	hui	k'uei	kui
chang	zhang	chui	zhui	hun	hun	kun	gun
ch'ang	chang	ch'ui	chui	hung	hong	k'un	kun
chao	zhao	chun	zhun	huo	huo	kung	gong
ch'ao	chao	ch'un	chun			k'ung	kong
che	zhe	chün	jun	i	yi	kuo	guo
ch'e	che	ch'ün	qun			k'uo	kuo
chei	zhei	chung	zhong	jan	ran		
chen	zhen	ch'ung	chong	jang	rang	la	la
ch'en	chen			jao	rao	lai	lai
cheng	zheng	e	e, o	je	re	lan	lan
ch'eng	cheng	en	en	jên	ren	lang	lang
chi	ji	eng	eng	jeng	reng	lao	lao
ch'i	qi	erh	er	jih	ri	le	le
chia	jia			jo	ruo	lei	lei
ch'ia	qia	fa	fa	jou	rou	leng	leng
chiang	jiang	fan	fan	ju	ru	li	li
ch'iang	qiang	fang	fang	jua	rua	lia	lia
chiao	jiao	fei	fei	juan	ruan	liang	liang
ch'iao	qiao	fen	fen	jui	rui	liao	liao
chieh	jie	feng	feng	jun	run	lieh	lie
ch'ieh	qie	fo	fo	jung	rong	lien	lian
chien	jian	fou	fou			lin	lin
ch'ien	qian	fu	fu	ka	ga	ling	ling
chih	zhi			k'a	ka	liu	liu
ch'ih	chi	ha	ha	kai	gai	lo	luo, lo
chin	jin	hai	hai	k'ai	kai	lou	lou
ch'in	qin	han	han	kan	gan	lu	lu
ching	jing	hang	hang	k'an	kan	luan	luan
ch'ing	qing	hao	hao	kang	gang	lun	lun
chio	jue	hen	hen	k'ang	kang	lung	long
ch'io	que	heng	heng	kao	gao	lü	lü
chiu	jiu	ho	he	k'ao	kao	lüeh	lüe
ch'iu	qiu	hou	hou	kei	gei		
chiung	jiong	hsi	xi	k'ei	kei	ma	ma
ch'iung	qiong	hsia	xia	ken	gen	mai	mai
cho	zhuo	hsiang	xiang	k'en	ken	man	man
ch'o	chuo	hsiao	xiao	keng	geng	mang	mang
chou	zhou	hsieh	xie	k'eng	keng	mao	mao
ch'ou	chou	hsien	xian	ko	ge	mei	mei
chu	zhu	hsin	xin	k'o	ke	men	men
ch'u	chu	hsing	xing	kou	gou	meng	meng
chü	ju	hsio	xue	k'ou	kou	mi	mi

Wade-Giles	Pinyin	Wade-Giles	Pinyin	Wade-Giles	Pinyin	Wade-Giles	Pinyin
miao	miao	peng	beng	suan	suan	ts'eng	ceng
mieh	mie	p'eng	peng	sui	sui	tso	zuo
mien	mian	pi	bi	sun	sun	ts'o	cuo
min	min	p'i	pi	sung	song	tsou	zou
ming	ming	piao	biao			ts'ou	cou
miu	miu	p'iao	piao	ta	da	tsu	zu
mo	mo	pieh	bie	t'a	ta	ts'u	cu
mou	mou	p'ieh	pie	tai	dai	tsuan	zuan
mu	mu	pien	bian	t'ai	tai	ts'uan	cuan
		p'ien	pian	tan	dan	tsui	zui
na	na	pin	bin	t'an	tan	ts'ui	cui
nai	nai	p'in	pin	tang	dang	tsun	zun
nan	nan	ping	bing	t'ang	tang	ts'un	cun
nang	nang	p'ing	ping	tao	dao	tsung	zong
nao	nao	po	bo	t'ao	tao	ts'ung	cong
nei	nei	p'o	po	te	de	tu	du
nen	nen	p'ou	pou	t'e	te	t'u	tu
neng	neng	pu	bu	tei	dei	tuan	duan
ni	ni	p'u	pu	ten	den	t'uan	tuan
niang	niang			teng	deng	tui	dui
niao	niao	sa	sa	t'eng	teng	t'ui	tui
nieh	nie	sai	sai	ti	di	tun	dun
nien	nian	san	san	t'i	ti	t'un	tun
nin	nin	sang	sang	tiao	diao	tung	dong
ning	ning	sao	sao	t'iao	tiao	t'ung	tong
niu	niu	se	se	tieh	die	tzu	zi
no	nuo	sen	sen	t'ieh	tie	tz'u	ci
nou	nou	seng	seng,	tien	dian		
nu	nu		sheng	t'ien	tian	wa	wa
nü	nu	sha	sha	ting	ding	wai	wai
nuan	nuan	shai	shai	t'ing	ting	wan	wan
nüeh	nüe	shan	shan	tiu	diu	wang	wang
nung	nong	shang	shang	to	duo	wei	wei
		shao	shao	t'o	tuo	wen	wen
o	e, o	she	she	tou	dou	wo	wo
ong	weng	shei	shei	t'ou	tou	wu	wu
ou	ou	shen	shen	tsa	za		
		sheng	sheng	ts'a	ca		
pa	ba	shih	shi	tsai	zai	ya	ya
p'a	pa	shou	shou	ts'ai	cai	yang	yang
pai	bai	shu	shu	tsan	zan	yao	yao
p'ai	pai	shua	shua	ts'an	can	yeh	ye
pan	ban	shuai	shuai	tsang	zang	yen	yan
p'an	pan	shuan	shuan	ts'ang	cang	yin	yin
pang	bang	shuang	shuang	tsao	zao	ying	ying
p'ang	pang	shui	shui	ts'ao	cao	yo	yue, yo
pao	bao	shun	shun	tse	ze	yu	you
p'ao	pao	shuo	shuo	ts'e	ce	yü	yu
pei	bei	so	suo	tsei	zei	yüan	yuan
p'ei	pei	sou	sou	tsen	zen	yüeh	yue
pen	ben	ssu	si	ts'en	cen	yün	yun
p'en	pen	su	su	tseng	zeng	yung	yong

GLOSSARY-INDEX

Acheson, Dean, 263, 264, 270; on Asian concerns of U.S., 271

Administration, bureaucratic: basic to unity, 21–22; Manchu experience in, 30–31

Administration, PRC: regional, 79, 81–83, 95; military, 79; Military Control Commissions, 79; Military Administrative Committees, 79; people's governments, 79, 81–82, 95; Party versus specialists, 107–108, 303; civil service grades in, 303

Afghanistan, 507

Afro-Asia, Chinese relations with, 283–284, 480, 526, 531–536, 538

Afro-Asian People's Solidarity Organization (AAPSO), 533

Agrarian system: primary, in China, 18–19; stability fostered by, 20; politically inert rural population of, 22; reform in, 69–70, 83

Agricultural Producers' Cooperative (APC), 111, 114, 157, 365; stages of, 111, 113, 117, 169; speed of setting up, 114–117, 119, 167–170, 212, 362; and mechanization, 127; peasant withdrawals from, 140; coercion to join, 166; and procurement of cereal, 166; allotment of credit to, 171; and 2nd FYP, 183; and rural education, 212, 401; slowed growth under, 361–366; mergers of into communes, 364, 404

Agriculture: and study of farm economy, 5; primary role of in China, 18, 145; Mao's push for cooperativization, 60, 66, 110–111, 114, 168–169, 335; change to collective ownership, 92, 157; cooperativization of, 110–119; mechanization of, 113, 114, 127; draft program for development of, 121; investment in, 126, 157–158, 390, 396; effects of lag in production, 141; lack of mechanical technology, 145, 182; transformation of, 160–174; rates of growth, 160–162, 172; linkages with industry, 161–162, 174–175; APCs and disruption, 169; price planning in, 170; consumption gains in, 172; and 2nd FYP, 182, 361–362; specialized education in, 199; under 1st FYP, 299–300, 360–362; and GLF, 305, 309–310, 318, 322, 329, 331, 369–370, 382; decollectivization advocated, 329, 330, 331, 333, 334, 382–383; export to Soviets, 361; Ch'en Yun on reforms needed, 384–385; CCP policy after GLF, 388–391; restoration of private plots, 389; specialization program, 390, 391, 392; recovery after GLF, 391–392; translations of documents on, 558

Ahn, Byung-joon, 322

Ai Ch'ing 艾青, 224, 225, 229, 244,

newspaper" (Liu Pin-yen), 247, 255

International Supervisory Control Commission (ICC) in Indochina, 502, 503, 504, 525

Interviews, as source material: with former PRC residents, 418, 543, 544–545, 567–571; with Chinese sojourners abroad, 543, 569; with foreign residents on business or diplomatic assignment, 543, 569; monographs based on, 544, 571; availability of transcripts of, 570–571; of Chinese officials, 572; and the totalitarian image, 578

Investment: agricultural, 157, 158, 390, 396; industrial, 158, 175, 396–397; under the GLF, 380, 384; scale and pattern of, 386–388

Iraq, 489

Irrigation: disruption of by war, 149; mass mobilization for, 363; under the GLF, 364; effects of faulty projects, 370; increases in, 392

Ishibashi administration, 287, 288

Italy, unification of, 13

Jakarta, 507, 508, 509, 535

Jao Shu-shih 饒漱石, 56, 58; expulsion of, 97

Japan, 518, 550, 573; invasion by (1931–45), 5, 44; study of Chinese resources by, 5; model of political reform from, 10; second united front against (1937–45), 33; influence on Chinese education, 35; agriculture in, 145, 147; and Manchuria, 147, 148; Sino-Soviet treaty against, 267–268; relations with, 287–289, 526, 532; interviews with émigrés by, 569. *See also* Sino-Japanese War

jen 仁 (benevolence), 452

Jen-min wen-hsueh 人民文學. See *People's Literature*

Jen Pi-shih 任弼時, see Appendix

Johnson, Lyndon B., 529

Joint Publications Research Service (JPRS), U.S. translation series, 557–558, 559

Joint stock companies with Soviets, 179–180, 268; Mao's reaction to, 269; terminated, 180, 281

Jordan, 489

Journals: and criticism, 244–245; editors of, 245; content of, 245–247; in Anti-Rightist Campaign, 255; discontinuities in, 545

Joy, C. Turner, 563

Kabul, 507

Kaganovich, Lazar, 99; purged, 286

Kamchatka, 528

kan-ch'ing 感情 (feeling of intimacy) 574

K'ang-hsi 康熙 Emperor, 31, 247

K'ang Sheng 康生, 131, 230, 296, 298, 351, 355, 357, 358, 455; on machine tractor stations, 127; as adviser to Mao on Soviet affairs, 319–320, 343–344; ambitions of, 332; and Chiang Ch'ing, 343–345, 355, 460, 461, 466; on counterrevolutionaries, 343; at Tenth Plenum, 344; links to education, 344; on class struggle in literature, 344–346; in Five-Man Group, 346, 466; ruthlessness of, 347; and the nine polemics, 352–353; on public security, 343, 358; and radical intellectuals, 457

K'ang Yu-wei 康有為, 9

Kansu 甘肅: railroads to, 176;

311–316, 336, 346, 411, 584;
attack on P'eng Te-huai at,
311–316; P'eng's criticism of
GLF, 312, 380, 515; consequences
of, 316–322; Chiang Ch'ing at,
343. *See also* Eighth Plenum of the
Eighth Central Committee
Luta 旅大 (Lü-shun 旅順, Ta-lien
大連 – Port Arthur, Dairen), 83
Lysenkoism, 244

Ma Feng 馬峰, 469
Ma Hsu-lun 馬敍倫, 198, 206–207
Ma Yin-ch'u 馬寅初, 182
Macao, 527
Macartney mission (1793), 1
MacFarquhar, Roderick, 312
Mach, Ernst, 445
Machine tractor station (MTS),
Soviet, 127
Machinery, 367; production of
under 1st FYP, 175; agricultural,
under 2nd FYP, 182, 361; imports
for GLF, 380; cuts in production
of, 387
Madsen, Richard, 571
Magnitogorsk, 318
Malaysia, 508, 535, 536
Malenkov, Georgi, 99; purge of, 286
Mali, 533
Malinovsky, Rodion, 490
Malraux, André, 356
Manchuria: economic growth in,
147, 148; Japan in, 148; Soviet
removal of industrial stock from,
149; Hsiao Chün in, 231–232;
Soviet rights in, 264–265
Manchus, 13; as Chinese rulers,
30–31
Manichaeans (Ming-chiao 明教), 31
Manufacturing: enterprises closed
after GLF, 387. *See also* Heavy
industry; Light industry
Mao Tse-tung 毛澤東, 13, 584,

589; use of peasantry by, 26;
and model of Chu Yuan-
chang, 31; as a unifier, 32; and
establishment of PRC, 51, 259;
initial accomplishments of, 56;
early role of, 59–63; nationalism
of, 64, 68; on agrarian reform, 69,
83–84, 86; on urban phase of
revolution, 73; on united front,
76–78; on distinction between
civil and military, 81; on
counterrevolutionaries, 89–90; on
socialist transformation, 93; on
participation in organizations, 94;
on Soviet model, 96–97; and
Kao–Jao affair, 98, 100, 102–103;
on power of Party, 107, 109; on
cooperatives, 110, 114, 115–117,
168, 261; on commerce and
industry, 120–122; on adjusting
new socialist system, 122–125;
on changes in Soviet model,
125–126; and the Eighth Party
Congress, 130; succession to, 130,
314–315; on rectification, 134–
135; and Hundred Flowers, 135–
137, 472; and Anti-Rightist
Campaign, 138–142, 168; basic
review by, 141–142; and Soviet
aid, 179–180, 183; and the 2nd
FYP, 180; on education, 193, 212,
399, 402, 406, 408, 412–413, 417,
421, 425, 429; on speed of APCs,
212, 293, 360, 362; and the
intellectuals, 219, 224, 228, 435,
436, 437; on literature, 228, 245,
434; and Hsiao Chün, 231–232;
and Hu Feng, 241; thoughts of,
questioned, 252; and relations
with Soviets, 259, 262, 284–287,
308–309, 351–352; and Stalin,
262–270, 279; and United States,
262–263, 498; on entering Korean
War, 271–272, 274–275; on

Socialist transformation (*cont.*)
class struggle, 122–123; new
problems created by, 124; success
of, considered premature, 141
Solzhenitsyn, Alexander, 245, 566
Somalia, 533
Soong Ching-ling 宋慶齡, 83. *See
also* Appendix
Soong, T. V. (Sung Tzu-wen
宋子文), 266
Sources of research on China, 543,
545–547; limitations of, 543; and
secrecy of government, 543–544;
gaps in, 544, 545, 546–547;
Chinese press, 547; strategies for
using, 552–554; translations from
press, 555–559; memoirs and
travelogues, 560–564; creative
arts, 564–566; interviews with
former PRC residents, 567–571;
field research, 572–576; English-
language secondary literature,
576–590
South Korea: in Korean War, 272;
38th parallel crossed by troops of,
274
South Manchurian Railway, 159,
265
South Vietnam, 503, 526, 529, 537
Southeast Asia Treaty Organization
(SEATO), 505, 534; maneuvers
of, 503; and Indonesia, 507; and
Laos, 525
Southwest Associated University
(Lien-ta: 聯大 in Kunming), 36
Southwest China: run by Military
Administrative Committee, 79;
backward area, 82; APCs in, 167;
"third line" in, 341
Souvanna Phouma, 502, 504, 507,
525
Soviet-Chinese Friendship
Association, 286
Soviet Union: as foreign model, 10,

32, 482, 492, 533, 573, 579;
military aid from, 34; conflicts
within Communist Party, 56;
model in building socialism, 57,
63–67, 78; pursuit of power in,
61; nature of model, 66–67;
Chinese divergences from, 78–79;
influence in Northeast China,
83; public security work in,
90; economic aid from, 92, 96,
294; and planned economic
construction, 96; Kao Kang's ties
to, 100; model for Constitution of
PRC, 104–107, 108; model of
agricultural reform in, 110, 111–
117, 157; and intellectuals, 123,
234–235, 244–245; model
adapted by CCP, 125–129, 141,
157–158; on decentralization,
127; on military modernization,
149; and Manchuria, 149; 1st FYP
of, 155, 158, 298; role in China's
industrial development, 157–158,
159, 177–180, 299; growing
Chinese independence from, 180,
183–184; educational heritage
from, 197–203, 205, 208–209,
398, 403, 408–409, 413, 414–415;
rectification methods of, 227, 237;
criticized by Hsiao Chün, 232–
233; influence on Chinese writers,
245, 247, 252; overview of PRC
relations with, 259–262; and
the Korean War, 277–278,
539; relations with China after
Stalin's death, 280–282, 319;
development of Sino-Soviet
tensions, 284–287, 294–296, 309,
478; termination of aid from, 319,
322, 326, 435, 478, 501, 517, 519;
and Vietnam, 340; Mao on
degeneration of, 334, 352–353;
withdrawal of advisers, 352, 393,
394, 434, 484, 517; exports to,